SELECTIONS FOR CONTRACTS

RESTATEMENT, SECOND, OF CONTRACTS
RESTATEMENT, THIRD, OF SURETYSHIP AND
GUARANTY (EXCERPT)
RESTATEMENT, THIRD, OF RESTITUTION AND
UNJUST ENRICHMENT (SELECTED SECTIONS)
RESTATEMENT OF EMPLOYMENT LAW (SELECTED SECTIONS)
UCC ARTICLES 1 AND 2
UCC ARTICLES 3 AND 9 (SELECTED SECTIONS)
REPRESENTATIVE STATUTES OF FRAUDS
FEDERAL ARBITRATION ACT (EXCERPT)
PRINCIPLES OF SOFTWARE CONTRACTS (SELECTED SECTIONS)
RESTATEMENT OF THE LAW, CONSUMER CONTRACTS,
TENTATIVE DRAFT (2019)
ALI-ELI PRINCIPLES FOR A DATA ECONOMY—DATA TRANSACTIONS
AND DATA RIGHTS (SELECTED SECTIONS)
UNIFORM ELECTRONIC TRANSACTIONS ACT
ELECTRONIC SIGNATURES IN GLOBAL AND
NATIONAL COMMERCE ACT (SELECTED SECTIONS)
CONVENTION ON CONTRACTS FOR
THE INTERNATIONAL SALE OF GOODS
UNIDROIT PRINCIPLES
SELECTED CONTRACTS

2021 Edition

Compiled by

E. ALLAN FARNSWORTH
Late Alfred McCormack Professor of Law
Columbia University

CAROL SANGER
Barbara Aronstein Black Professor of Law
Columbia University

NEIL B. COHEN
Jeffrey D. Forchelli Professor of Law
Brooklyn Law School

RICHARD R.W. BROOKS
Emilie M. Bullowa Professor of Law
New York University School of Law

LARRY T. GARVIN
Lawrence D. Stanley Professor of Law
The Ohio State University

FOUNDATION
PRESS

© 1980, 1988, 1992, 1998, 2001, 2003 FOUNDATION PRESS
© 2007, 2008, 2010, 2011 THOMSON REUTERS/FOUNDATION PRESS
© 2013 by LEG, Inc. d/b/a West Academic Publishing
© 2015, 2016, 2018, 2019 LEG, Inc. d/b/a West Academic
© 2021 LEG, Inc. d/b/a West Academic
    444 Cedar Street, Suite 700
    St. Paul, MN 55101
    1-877-888-1330

Printed in the United States of America

ISBN: 978-1-63659-381-4

TABLE OF CONTENTS

TABLE OF CONTENTS

SELECTIONS FOR CONTRACTS

RESTATEMENT, SECOND, OF CONTRACTS
RESTATEMENT, THIRD, OF SURETYSHIP AND
GUARANTY (EXCERPT)
RESTATEMENT, THIRD, OF RESTITUTION AND
UNJUST ENRICHMENT (SELECTED SECTIONS)
RESTATEMENT OF EMPLOYMENT LAW (SELECTED SECTIONS)
UCC ARTICLES 1 AND 2
UCC ARTICLES 3 AND 9 (SELECTED SECTIONS)
REPRESENTATIVE STATUTES OF FRAUDS
FEDERAL ARBITRATION ACT (EXCERPT)
PRINCIPLES OF SOFTWARE CONTRACTS (SELECTED SECTIONS)
RESTATEMENT OF THE LAW, CONSUMER CONTRACTS,
TENTATIVE DRAFT (2019)
ALI-ELI PRINCIPLES FOR A DATA ECONOMY—DATA TRANSACTIONS
AND DATA RIGHTS (SELECTED SECTIONS)
UNIFORM ELECTRONIC TRANSACTIONS ACT
ELECTRONIC SIGNATURES IN GLOBAL AND
NATIONAL COMMERCE ACT (SELECTED SECTIONS)
CONVENTION ON CONTRACTS FOR
THE INTERNATIONAL SALE OF GOODS
UNIDROIT PRINCIPLES
SELECTED CONTRACTS

2021 Edition

RESTATEMENT OF THE LAW, SECOND, CONTRACTS

COMPILERS' NOTE

The American Law Institute was formed in 1923 as the outgrowth of a "Committee on the Establishment of a Permanent Organization for the Improvement of the Law." Its members were to be 400 practitioners, judges and law professors; there are now about 4,000. The idea of the Institute, and of "restating" the law, was broached by Professor William Draper Lewis and fostered by Elihu Root and others. The Carnegie Corporation supported work on the original Restatement, comprising nine subjects, which was completed by 1944.

Contracts was one of the first three subjects upon which the Institute began work, and the Restatement of Contracts was completed in 1932. Professor Samuel Williston acted as Reporter, with responsibility for preparing drafts. (Professor Arthur L. Corbin served as Reporter for the Chapter on Remedies.) Other experts in the subject were formed into a Committee of Advisers who conferred with the Reporter over the whole period in producing drafts for submission to the Council of the Institute. The plan was "that the drafts of the different chapters submitted to the Council shall be the product of the committee composed of the Reporter and his advisers; that these drafts after discussion and amendment by the Council and before revision shall be submitted as tentative drafts for criticism and suggestion with a view to their improvement to the annual meetings of the Institute and to bar associations and the profession generally." Restatement of Contracts, Introduction, p. x. Final promulgation depended on approval of the text by both the Council and the full meeting of Institute members. The same procedure was followed in making revisions and in preparing the Restatement, Second.

In 1962 the Institute initiated the preparation of the Restatement, Second, of Contracts, parts of which are reproduced here. Professor Robert Braucher served as Reporter until his appointment to the Supreme Judicial Court of Massachusetts in 1971; he was succeeded by Professor E. Allan Farnsworth. The work was completed in 1980.

As originally conceived, the first Restatement was to be accompanied by treatises citing and discussing case authority, but experience proved that group production of such volumes was not feasible. As they stand, the Restatements consist of sections stating rules or principles (the so-called black letter), each followed by one or more comments with illustrations, and in the Restatement, Second, also by Reporter's Notes in which supporting authorities are collected. (Reproduced here are the black let-

1

ter of selected sections and in a few instances their comments and illustrations.)

Assaults on the Restatement, along with sympathetic appraisals, have
produced a rich literature. An eminent critic of the Restatement of Contracts immediately objected that the American Law Institute "seems constantly to be seeking the force of a statute without statutory enactment."
Clark, The Restatement of the Law of Contracts, 42 Yale L.J. 643, 654
(1933).[1] To what measure of authority is the Restatement entitled, then,
in the courts?

This general question can have only a general answer. The Supreme
Court of Oregon has emphasized the difference between statutory and
Restatement texts:[2]

> Although this court frequently quotes sections of the Restatements
> of the American Law Institute, it does not literally "adopt" them in
> the manner of a legislature enacting, for instance, a draft prepared
> by the Commissioners on Uniform State Laws, such as the Residen-
> tial Landlord and Tenant Act. In the nature of common law, such
> quotations in opinions are no more than shorthand expressions of
> the court's view that the analysis summarized in the Restatement
> corresponds to Oregon law applicable to the facts of the case before
> the court. They do not enact the exact phrasing of the Restatement
> rule, complete with comments, illustrations, and caveats. Such
> quotations should not be relied on in briefs as if they committed
> his court or lower courts to track every detail of the Restatement
> analysis in other cases. The Restatements themselves purport to be
> just that, "restatements" of law found in other sources, although at
> times they candidly report that the law is in flux and offer a formula
> preferred on policy grounds.

There is agreement among those who applaud the Restatement and
those who deprecate it about the persuasiveness of an ideal restatement
of the law. "A restatement, then, can have no other authority than as the
product of men learned in the subject who have studied and deliberated
over it. It needs no other, and what could be higher?" Clark, op. cit. supra,
p. 655. Judge Herbert Goodrich, for many years Director of the Institute,
explained:

> If an advocate thinks the Restatement was wrong as applied to
> his case, he can urge the court not to follow it, but to apply some
> other rule. If the court agrees, it will do so, but it will so do with

---

[1] On occasion a legislature has given
statutory backing to the Restatement.
The Virgin Islands Code (Title 1, § 4)
provides: "The rules of the common law, as
expressed in the restatements of the law
approved by the American Law Institute
. . . , shall be the rules of decision . . . in
cases to which they apply, in the absence of
local laws to the contrary." Note, however,
that this provision has been held to have
been implicitly repealed by subsequent
legislation. See Government of the Virgin
Islands v. Conner, 60 V.I. 597 (2014).

[2] Brewer v. Erwin, 600 P.2d 398, 410 n.
12 (Or.1979).

the knowledge that the rule which it rejects has been written by the people who by training and reputation are supposed to be eminently learned in the particular subject and that the specialist's conclusions have been discussed and defended before a body of very able critics. The presumption is in favor of the Restatement. . . . Yet it can be overthrown and that fact leaves Restatement acceptance to persuasion. It is common law "persuasive authority" with a high degree of persuasion.

Restatement and Codification, David D. Field Centenary Essays 241, 244–45 (1949).

The Restatement Second. To a substantial extent the Restatement Second reflects the thought of two men in particular: Professor Arthur Corbin and Professor Karl Llewellyn, who shared an attitude toward law sometimes described as "legal realism."[3] Professor Corbin prepared a critical review of the original Restatement, which "has been the basis for much of the work on the revision."[4] He served also as consultant for the Restatement, Second, in its early stages. Professor Llewellyn's efforts affected the revision less directly, largely through the impact of his contributions to the Uniform Commercial Code.

In restating the law of contracts for the second half of the twentieth century, an obvious difficulty arose from the fact that large tracts of the subject had recently been occupied by legislation such as the Code and, to a lesser extent, consumer-protection statutes. Indeed, the worth of the enterprise was questioned on the ground of an apparently diminishing importance of common law doctrine. In response, Professor Braucher made this claim:

> The effort to restate the law of contracts in modern terms highlights the reliance of private autonomy in an era of expanding government activity. . . . Freedom of contract, refined and redefined in response to social change, has power as it always had.[5]

A continuing theme of controversy about the Restatements is the wisdom or unwisdom of departing from rules derived from existing precedents, in the interest of a more just and more convenient regime of law. Professor Herbert Wechsler, when Director of the Institute, proposed "a working formula" that received the unanimous approval of the Council: "we should feel obliged in our deliberations to give weight to all of the considerations that the courts, under a proper view of the judicial function, deem it right to weigh in theirs."[6] An example of creative restating

---

[3] For symposia devoted to the Restatement, Second, see 81 Colum.L.Rev. 1 (1981) and 67 Cornell L.Rev. 631 (1982).

[4] Braucher, Formation of Contract and the Second Restatement, 78 Yale L.J. 598 (1969). See also Perillo, Twelve Letters from Arthur L. Corbin to Robert Braucher Annotated, 50 Wash. & Lee L. Rev. 755 (1993).

[5] Id. at 615–16. For another comment by Professor Braucher, see Offer and Acceptance in the Second Restatement, 74 Yale L.J. 302 (1964).

[6] Wechsler, The Course of the Restatements, 55 A.B.A.J. 147, 150 (1969).

from the first Restatement of Contracts was the formulation of the doctrine of promissory estoppel, in section 90.[7]

---

[7] The Oregon opinion quoted above refers to a section of the Torts Restatement as a "bold sally." Notwithstanding that, the section has gained widespread adherence.

RESTATEMENT (SECOND) OF CONTRACTS[1]

Table of Contents

CHAPTER 1.   MEANING OF TERMS

CHAPTER 2.   FORMATION OF CONTRACTS—
PARTIES AND CAPACITY

CHAPTER 3.   FORMATION OF CONTRACTS—
MUTUAL ASSENT

TOPIC 1.   IN GENERAL

TOPIC 2.   MANIFESTATION OF ASSENT IN GENERAL

TOPIC 3. MAKING OF OFFERS

TOPIC 4. DURATION OF THE OFFEREE'S POWER OF ACCEPTANCE

TOPIC 5. ACCEPTANCE OF OFFERS

CHAPTER 6. MISTAKE

CHAPTER 7. MISREPRESENTATION, DURESS AND UNDUE INFLUENCE

TOPIC 1. MISREPRESENTATION

TOPIC 2. DURESS AND UNDUE INFLUENCE

CHAPTER 8.   UNENFORCEABILITY ON GROUNDS OF PUBLIC POLICY

CHAPTER 9.   THE SCOPE OF CONTRACTUAL OBLIGATIONS

CHAPTER 12.   DISCHARGE BY ASSENT OR ALTERATION

CHAPTER 13.   JOINT AND SEVERAL PROMISORS AND PROMISEES

CHAPTER 14. CONTRACT BENEFICIARIES

CHAPTER 15. ASSIGNMENT AND DELEGATION

TOPIC 1. WHAT CAN BE ASSIGNED OR DELEGATED

TOPIC 2. MODE OF ASSIGNMENT OR DELEGATION

TOPIC 3. EFFECT BETWEEN ASSIGNOR AND ASSIGNEE

TOPIC 4. EFFECT ON THE OBLIGOR'S DUTY

CHAPTER 1. MEANING OF TERMS

§ 1.   Contract Defined

A contract is a promise or a set of promises for the breach of which the law gives a remedy, or the performance of which the law in some way recognizes as a duty.

§ 2.   Promise; Promisor; Promisee; Beneficiary

(1)   A promise is a manifestation of intention to act or refrain from acting in a specified way, so made as to justify a promisee in understanding that a commitment has been made.

(2)   The person manifesting the intention is the promisor.

(3)   The person to whom the manifestation is addressed is the promisee.

(4)   Where performance will benefit a person other than the promisee, that person is a beneficiary.

§ 3.   Agreement Defined; Bargain Defined

An agreement is a manifestation of mutual assent on the part of two or more persons. A bargain is an agreement to exchange promises or to exchange a promise for a performance or to exchange performances.

§ 4.   How a Promise May Be Made

A promise may be stated in words either oral or written, or may be inferred wholly or partly from conduct.

§ 5.   Terms of Promise, Agreement, or Contract

(1)   A term of a promise or agreement is that portion of the intention or assent manifested which relates to a particular matter.

(2)   A term of a contract is that portion of the legal relations resulting from the promise or set of promises which relates to a particular matter, whether or not the parties manifest an intention to create those relations.

§ 6.   Formal Contracts

The following types of contracts are subject in some respects to special rules that depend on their formal characteristics and differ from those governing contracts in general:

(a)   Contracts under seal,

(b)   Recognizances,

(c)   Negotiable instruments and documents,

(d)   Letters of credit.

§ 7. Voidable Contracts

A voidable contract is one where one or more parties have the power, by a manifestation of election to do so, to avoid the legal relations created by the contract, or by ratification of the contract to extinguish the power of avoidance.

§ 8. Unenforceable Contracts

An unenforceable contract is one for the breach of which neither the remedy of damages nor the remedy of specific performance is available, but which is recognized in some other way as creating a duty of performance, though there has been no ratification.

CHAPTER 2. FORMATION OF CONTRACTS—PARTIES AND CAPACITY

§ 9. Parties Required

There must be at least two parties to a contract, a promisor and a promisee, but there may be any greater number.

§ 10. Multiple Promisors and Promisees of the Same Performance

(1) Where there are more promisors than one in a contract, some or all of them may promise the same performance, whether or not there are also promises of separate performances.

(2) Where there are more promisees than one in a contract, a promise may be made to some or all of them as a unit, whether or not the same or another performance is separately promised to one or more of them.

§ 11. When a Person May Be Both Promisor and Promisee

A contract may be formed between two or more persons acting as a unit and one or more but fewer than all of these persons, acting either singly or with other persons.

§ 12. Capacity to Contract

(1) No one can be bound by contract who has not legal capacity to incur at least voidable contractual duties. Capacity to contract may be partial and its existence in respect of a particular transaction may depend upon the nature of the transaction or upon other circumstances.

(2) A natural person who manifests assent to a transaction has full legal capacity to incur contractual duties thereby unless he is

    (a) under guardianship, or

    (b) an infant, or

(c)   mentally ill or defective, or

(d)   intoxicated.

§ 13.   Persons Affected by Guardianship

A person has no capacity to incur contractual duties if his property is under guardianship by reason of an adjudication of mental illness or defect.

§ 14.   Infants

Unless a statute provides otherwise, a natural person has the capacity to incur only voidable contractual duties until the beginning of the day before the person's eighteenth birthday.

§ 15.   Mental Illness or Defect

(1)   A person incurs only voidable contractual duties by entering into a transaction if by reason of mental illness or defect

(a)   he is unable to understand in a reasonable manner the nature and consequences of the transaction, or

(b)   he is unable to act in a reasonable manner in relation to the transaction and the other party has reason to know of his condition.

(2)   Where the contract is made on fair terms and the other party is without knowledge of the mental illness or defect, the power of avoidance under Subsection (1) terminates to the extent that the contract has been so performed in whole or in part or the circumstances have so changed that avoidance would be unjust. In such a case a court may grant relief on such equitable terms as justice requires.

§ 16.   Intoxicated Persons

A person incurs only voidable contractual duties by entering into a transaction if the other party has reason to know that by reason of intoxication

(a)   he is unable to understand in a reasonable manner the nature and consequences of the transaction, or

(b)   he is unable to act in a reasonable manner in relation to the transaction.

CHAPTER 3.   FORMATION OF CONTRACTS—MUTUAL ASSENT

TOPIC 1.   IN GENERAL

§ 17.   Requirement of a Bargain

(1)   Except as stated in Subsection (2), the formation of a contract requires a bargain in which there is a manifestation of mutual assent to the exchange and a consideration.

(2)   Whether or not there is a bargain a contract may be formed under special rules applicable to formal contracts or under the rules stated in §§ 82–94.

TOPIC 2.   MANIFESTATION OF ASSENT IN GENERAL

§ 18.   Manifestation of Mutual Assent

Manifestation of mutual assent to an exchange requires that each party either make a promise or begin or render a performance.

§ 19.   Conduct as Manifestation of Assent

(1)   The manifestation of assent may be made wholly or partly by written or spoken words or by other acts or by failure to act.

(2)   The conduct of a party is not effective as a manifestation of his assent unless he intends to engage in the conduct and knows or has reason to know that the other party may infer from his conduct that he assents.

(3)   The conduct of a party may manifest assent even though he does not in fact assent. In such cases a resulting contract may be voidable because of fraud, duress, mistake, or other invalidating cause.

§ 20.   Effect of Misunderstanding

(1)   There is no manifestation of mutual assent to an exchange if the parties attach materially different meanings to their manifestations and

(a)   neither party knows or has reason to know the meaning attached by the other; or

(b)   each party knows or each party has reason to know the meaning attached by the other.

(2)   The manifestations of the parties are operative in accordance with the meaning attached to them by one of the parties if

(a)   that party does not know of any different meaning attached by the other, and the other knows the meaning attached by the first party; or

(b) that party has no reason to know of any different meaning attached by the other, and the other has reason to know the meaning attached by the first party.

Comment:

... *b.* *The need for interpretation.* The meaning given to words or other conduct depends to a varying extent on the context and on the prior experience of the parties. Almost never are all the connotations of a bargain exactly identical for both parties; it is enough that there is a core of common meaning sufficient to determine their performances with reasonable certainty or to give a reasonably certain basis for an appropriate legal remedy. See § 33. But material differences of meaning are a standard cause of contract disputes, and the decision of such disputes necessarily requires interpretation of the language and other conduct of the parties in the light of the circumstances.

c. *Interpretation and agreement.* There is a problem of interpretation in determining whether a contract has been made as well as in determining what obligations a contract imposes. Where one party makes a precise and detailed offer and the other accepts it, or where both parties sign the same written agreement, there may be an "integrated" agreement (see § 209) and the problem is then one of interpreting the offer or written agreement. In other cases agreement may be found in a jumble of letters, telegrams, acts and spoken words. In either type of case, the parties may have different understandings, intentions and meanings. Even though the parties manifest mutual assent to the same words of agreement, there may be no contract because of a material difference of understanding as to the terms of the exchange. Where there is no integration, the parties may also differ as to whether there was an offer of any kind, or whether there was an acceptance. Rules of interpretation governing various situations are stated in Chapter 9 on the scope of contractual obligations; those rules are applicable in the determination of what each party "knows or has reason to know."

§ 21. Intention to Be Legally Bound

Neither real nor apparent intention that a promise be legally binding is essential to the formation of a contract, but a manifestation of intention that a promise shall not affect legal relations may prevent the formation of a contract.

Comment:

... *c.* *Social engagements and domestic arrangements.* In some situations the normal understanding is that no legal obligation arises, and some unusual manifestation of intention is necessary to create a contract. Traditional examples are social engagements and agreements within a family group. See §§ 189–91. Where the family relation is not close, valuable services rendered in the home may make binding an express or implied promise to pay for the services; but even in such cases it would often be understood that there is no legal obligation while the agreement is entirely executory on both sides. See Comment a to § 19, Comment b to § 32.

§ 22.   Mode of Assent: Offer and Acceptance

(1)   The manifestation of mutual assent to an exchange ordinarily takes the form of an offer or proposal by one party followed by an acceptance by the other party or parties.

(2)   A manifestation of mutual assent may be made even though neither offer nor acceptance can be identified and even though the moment of formation cannot be determined.

§ 23.   Necessity That Manifestations Have Reference to Each Other

It is essential to a bargain that each party manifest assent with reference to the manifestation of the other.

TOPIC 3.   MAKING OF OFFERS

§ 24.   Offer Defined

An offer is the manifestation of willingness to enter into a bargain, so made as to justify another person in understanding that his assent to that bargain is invited and will conclude it.

Comment:

a.   Offer as promise. An offer may propose an executed sale or barter rather than a contract, or it may propose the exchange of a promise for a performance or an exchange of promises, or it may propose two or more such transactions in combination or in the alternative. In the normal case of an offer of an exchange of promises, or in the case of an offer of a promise for an act, the offer itself is a promise, revocable until accepted. There may also be an offer of a performance, to be exchanged either for a return promise (§ 55) or for a return performance; in such cases the offer is not necessarily a promise, but there are often warranties or other incidental promises.

§ 25.   Option Contracts

An option contract is a promise which meets the requirements for the formation of a contract and limits the promisor's power to revoke an offer.

§ 26.   Preliminary Negotiations

A manifestation of willingness to enter into a bargain is not an offer if the person to whom it is addressed knows or has reason to know that the person making it does not intend to conclude a bargain until he has made a further manifestation of assent.

§ 27.   Existence of Contract Where Written Memorial Is Contemplated

Manifestations of assent that are in themselves sufficient to conclude a contract will not be prevented from so operating by the fact that the parties also manifest an intention to prepare and adopt a written memorial thereof; but the circumstances may show that the agreements are preliminary negotiations.

§ 28.   Auctions

(1)   At an auction, unless a contrary intention is manifested,

(a)   the auctioneer invites offers from successive bidders which he may accept or reject;

(b)   when goods are put up without reserve, the auctioneer makes an offer to sell at any price bid by the highest bidder, and after the auctioneer calls for bids the goods cannot be withdrawn unless no bid is made within a reasonable time;

(c)   whether or not the auction is without reserve, a bidder may withdraw his bid until the auctioneer's announcement of completion of the sale, but a bidder's retraction does not revive any previous bid.

(2)   Unless a contrary intention is manifested, bids at an auction embody terms made known by advertisement, posting or other publication of which bidders are or should be aware, as modified by any announcement made by the auctioneer when the goods are put up.

§ 29.   To Whom an Offer Is Addressed

(1)   The manifested intention of the offeror determines the person or persons in whom is created a power of acceptance.

(2)   An offer may create a power of acceptance in a specified person or in one or more of a specified group or class of persons, acting separately or together, or in anyone or everyone who makes a specified promise or renders a specified performance.

§ 30.   Form of Acceptance Invited

(1)   An offer may invite or require acceptance to be made by an affirmative answer in words, or by performing or refraining from performing a specified act, or may empower the offeree to make a selection of terms in his acceptance.

(2)   Unless otherwise indicated by the language or the circumstances, an offer invites acceptance in any manner and by any medium reasonable in the circumstances.

§ 31.   Offer Proposing a Single Contract or a Number of Contracts

An offer may propose the formation of a single contract by a single acceptance or the formation of a number of contracts by successive acceptances from time to time.

§ 32.   Invitation of Promise or Performance

In case of doubt an offer is interpreted as inviting the offeree to accept either by promising to perform what the offer requests or by rendering the performance, as the offeree chooses.

§ 33.   Certainty

(1)   Even though a manifestation of intention is intended to be understood as an offer, it cannot be accepted so as to form a contract unless the terms of the contract are reasonably certain.

(2)   The terms of a contract are reasonably certain if they provide a basis for determining the existence of a breach and for giving an appropriate remedy.

(3)   The fact that one or more terms of a proposed bargain are left open or uncertain may show that a manifestation of intention is not intended to be understood as an offer or as an acceptance.

§ 34.   Certainty and Choice of Terms; Effect of Performance or Reliance

(1)   The terms of a contract may be reasonably certain even though it empowers one or both parties to make a selection of terms in the course of performance.

(2)   Part performance under an agreement may remove uncertainty and establish that a contract enforceable as a bargain has been formed.

(3)   Action in reliance on an agreement may make a contractual remedy appropriate even though uncertainty is not removed.

TOPIC 4.   DURATION OF THE OFFEREE'S POWER OF ACCEPTANCE

§ 35.   The Offeree's Power of Acceptance

(1)   An offer gives to the offeree a continuing power to complete the manifestation of mutual assent by acceptance of the offer.

(2)   A contract cannot be created by acceptance of an offer after the power of acceptance has been terminated in one of the ways listed in § 36.

§ 36.   Methods of Termination of the Power of Acceptance

(1)   An offeree's power of acceptance may be terminated by

    (a)   rejection or counter-offer by the offeree, or

    (b)   lapse of time, or

    (c)   revocation by the offeror, or

    (d)   death or incapacity of the offeror or offeree.

(2) In addition, an offeree's power of acceptance is terminated by the non-occurrence of any condition of acceptance under the terms of the offer.

§ 37. Termination of Power of Acceptance Under Option Contract

Notwithstanding §§ 38–49, the power of acceptance under an option contract is not terminated by rejection or counter-offer, by revocation, or by death or incapacity of the offeror, unless the requirements are met for the discharge of a contractual duty.

§ 38. Rejection

(1) An offeree's power of acceptance is terminated by his rejection of the offer, unless the offeror has manifested a contrary intention.

(2) A manifestation of intention not to accept an offer is a rejection unless the offeree manifests an intention to take it under further advisement.

§ 39. Counter-Offers

(1) A counter-offer is an offer made by an offeree to his offeror relating to the same matter as the original offer and proposing a substituted bargain differing from that proposed by the original offer.

(2) An offeree's power of acceptance is terminated by his making of a counter-offer, unless the offeror has manifested a contrary intention or unless the counter-offer manifests a contrary intention of the offeree.

§ 40. Time When Rejection or Counter-Offer Terminates the Power of Acceptance

Rejection or counter-offer by mail or telegram does not terminate the power of acceptance until received by the offeror, but limits the power so that a letter or telegram of acceptance started after the sending of an otherwise effective rejection or counter-offer is only a counter-offer unless the acceptance is received by the offeror before he receives the rejection or counter-offer.

§ 41. Lapse of Time

(1) An offeree's power of acceptance is terminated at the time specified in the offer, or, if no time is specified, at the end of a reasonable time.

(2) What is a reasonable time is a question of fact, depending on all the circumstances existing when the offer and attempted acceptance are made.

(3) Unless otherwise indicated by the language or the circumstances, and subject to the rule stated in § 49, an offer sent by mail is seasonably

accepted if an acceptance is mailed at any time before midnight on the day on which the offer is received.

§ 42.   Revocation by Communication From Offeror Received by Offeree

An offeree's power of acceptance is terminated when the offeree receives from the offeror a manifestation of an intention not to enter into the proposed contract.

§ 43.   Indirect Communication of Revocation

An offeree's power of acceptance is terminated when the offeror takes definite action inconsistent with an intention to enter into the proposed contract and the offeree acquires reliable information to that effect.

§ 44.   Effect of Deposit on Revocability of Offer

An offeror's power of revocation is not limited by the deposit of money or other property to be forfeited in the event of revocation, but the deposit may be forfeited to the extent that it is not a penalty.

§ 45.   Option Contract Created by Part Performance or Tender

(1)   Where an offer invites an offeree to accept by rendering a performance and does not invite a promissory acceptance, an option contract is created when the offeree tenders or begins the invited performance or tenders a beginning of it.

(2)   The offeror's duty of performance under any option contract so created is conditional on completion or tender of the invited performance in accordance with the terms of the offer.

Comment:

a.   Offer limited to acceptance by performance only. This Section is limited to cases where the offer does not invite a promissory acceptance. Such an offer has often been referred to as an "offer for a unilateral contract." Typical illustrations are found in offers of rewards or prizes and in non-commercial arrangements among relatives and friends. See Comment b to § 32. As to analogous cases arising under offers which give the offeree power to accept either by performing or by promising to perform, as he chooses, see §§ 32, 62.

b.   Manifestation of contrary intention. The rule of this Section is designed to protect the offeree in justifiable reliance on the offeror's promise, and the rule yields to a manifestation of intention which makes reliance unjustified. A reservation of power to revoke after performance has begun means that as yet there is no promise and no offer. See §§ 2, 24. In particular, if the performance is one which requires the cooperation of both parties, such as the payment of money or the manual delivery of goods, a person who reserves the right to refuse to receive the performance has not made an offer. See § 26.

Illustrations:

1.   B owes A $5000 payable in installments over a five-year period. A proposes that B discharge the debt by paying $4,500 cash within one month, but reserves the right

26

to refuse any such payment. A has not made an offer. A tender by B in accordance with the proposal is an offer by B.

2.   A, an insurance company, issues a bulletin to its agents, entitled "Extra Earnings Agreement," providing for annual bonus payments to the agents varying according to "monthly premiums in force" and "lapse ratio," but reserving the right to change or discontinue the bonus, individually or collectively, with or without notice, at any time before payment. There is no offer or promise.

c.   *Tender of performance.* A proposal to receive a payment of money or a delivery of goods is an offer only if acceptance can be completed without further cooperation by the offeror. If there is an offer, it follows that acceptance must be complete at the latest when performance is tendered. A tender of performance, so bargained for and given in exchange for the offer, ordinarily furnishes consideration and creates a contract. See §§ 17, 71, 72.

This is so whether or not the tender carries with it any incidental promises. See §§ 54, 62. If no commitment is made by the offeree, the contract is an option contract. See § 25.

Illustration:

3.   A promises B to sell him a specified chattel for $5, stating that B is not to be bound until he pays the money. B tenders $5 within a reasonable time, but A refuses to accept the tender. There is a breach of contract.

d.   *Beginning to perform.* If the invited performance takes time, the invitation to perform necessarily includes an invitation to begin performance. In most such cases the beginning of performance carries with it an express or implied promise to complete performance. See § 62. In the less common case where the offer does not contemplate or invite a promise by the offeree, the beginning of performance nevertheless completes the manifestation of mutual assent and furnishes consideration for an option contract. See § 25. If the beginning of performance requires the cooperation of the offeror, tender of part performance has the same effect. Part performance or tender may also create an option contract in a situation where the offeree is invited to take up the option by making a promise, if the offer invites a preliminary performance before the time for the offeree's final commitment.

Illustrations:

4.   A offers a reward for the return of lost property. In response to the offer, B searches for the property and finds it. A then notifies B that the offer is revoked. B makes a tender of the property to A conditional on payment of the reward, and A refuses. There is a breach of contract by A.

5.   A, a magazine, offers prizes in a subscription contest. At a time when B has submitted the largest number of subscriptions, A cancels the contest. A has broken its contract with B.

6.   A writes to her daughter B, living in another state, an offer to leave A's farm to B if B gives up her home and cares for A during A's life, B remaining free to terminate the arrangement at any time. B gives up her home, moves to A's farm, and begins caring for A. A is bound by an option contract.

7.   A offers to sell a piece of land to B, and promises that if B incurs expense in employing experts to appraise the property the offer will be irrevocable for 30 days. B hires experts and pays for their transportation to the land. A is bound by an option contract.

8. In January A, an employer, publishes a notice to his employees, promising a stated Christmas bonus to any employee who is continuously in A's employ from January to Christmas. B, an employee hired by the week, reads the notice and continues at work beyond the expiration of the current week. A is bound by an option contract, and if B is continuously in A's employ until Christmas a notice of revocation of the bonus is ineffective.

e.   Completion of performance. Where part performance or tender by the offeree creates an option contract, the offeree is not bound to complete performance. The offeror alone is bound, but his duty of performance is conditional on completion of the offeree's performance. If the offeree abandons performance, the offeror's duty to perform never arises. See § 224, defining "condition," and Illustration 4 to that Section. But the condition may be excused, for example, if the offeror prevents performance, waives it, or repudiates. See Comment b to § 225 and §§ 239, 278.

f.   Preparations for performance. What is begun or tendered must be part of the actual performance invited in order to preclude revocation under this Section. Beginning preparations, though they may be essential to carrying out the contract or to accepting the offer, is not enough. Preparations to perform may, however, constitute justifiable reliance sufficient to make the offeror's promise binding under § 87(2).

In many cases what is invited depends on what is a reasonable mode of acceptance. See § 30. The distinction between preparing for performance and beginning performance in such cases may turn on many factors: the extent to which the offeree's conduct is clearly referable to the offer, the definite and substantial character of that conduct, and the extent to which it is of actual or prospective benefit to the offeror rather than the offeree, as well as the terms of the communications between the parties, their prior course of dealing, and any relevant usages of trade.

Illustration:

9. A makes a written promise to pay $5000 to B, a hospital, "to aid B in its humanitarian work." Relying upon this and other like promises, B proceeds in its humanitarian work, expending large sums of money and incurring large liabilities. Performance by B has begun, and A's offer is irrevocable.

g.   Agency contracts. This Section frequently applies to agency arrangements, particularly offers made to real estate brokers. Sometimes there is a return promise by the agent, particularly if there is an agreement for exclusive dealing, since such an agreement normally imposes an obligation on the agent to use best efforts. See Uniform Commercial Code § 2–306(2); compare Restatement, Second, Agency § 378. In other cases the agent does not promise to act, but the principal must compensate him if he does act. The rules governing the principal's duty of compensation are stated in detail in Chapter 14 of the Restatement, Second, Agency, particularly §§ 443–57.

§ 46.   Revocation of General Offer

Where an offer is made by advertisement in a newspaper or other general notification to the public or to a number of persons whose identity is unknown to the offeror, the offeree's power of acceptance is terminated when a notice of termination is given publicity by advertisement or other general notification equal to that given to the offer and no better means of notification is reasonably available.

§ 47. Revocation of Divisible Offer

An offer contemplating a series of independent contracts by separate acceptances may be effectively revoked so as to terminate the power to create future contracts, though one or more of the proposed contracts have already been formed by the offeree's acceptance.

§ 48. Death or Incapacity of Offeror or Offeree

An offeree's power of acceptance is terminated when the offeree or offeror dies or is deprived of legal capacity to enter into the proposed contract.

§ 49. Effect of Delay in Communication of Offer

If communication of an offer to the offeree is delayed, the period within which a contract can be created by acceptance is not thereby extended if the offeree knows or has reason to know of the delay, though it is due to the fault of the offeror; but if the delay is due to the fault of the offeror or to the means of transmission adopted by him, and the offeree neither knows nor has reason to know that there has been delay, a contract can be created by acceptance within the period which would have been permissible if the offer had been dispatched at the time that its arrival seems to indicate.

TOPIC 5. ACCEPTANCE OF OFFERS

§ 50. Acceptance of Offer Defined; Acceptance by Performance; Acceptance by Promise

(1) Acceptance of an offer is a manifestation of assent to the terms thereof made by the offeree in a manner invited or required by the offer.

(2) Acceptance by performance requires that at least part of what the offer requests be performed or tendered and includes acceptance by a performance which operates as a return promise.

(3) Acceptance by a promise requires that the offeree complete every act essential to the making of the promise.

§ 51. Effect of Part Performance Without Knowledge of Offer

Unless the offeror manifests a contrary intention, an offeree who learns of an offer after he has rendered part of the performance requested by the offer may accept by completing the requested performance.

§ 52. Who May Accept an Offer

An offer can be accepted only by a person whom it invites to furnish the consideration.

§ 53. Acceptance by Performance; Manifestation of Intention Not to Accept

(1)   An offer can be accepted by the rendering of a performance only if the offer invites such an acceptance.

(2)   Except as stated in § 69, the rendering of a performance does not constitute an acceptance if within a reasonable time the offeree exercises reasonable diligence to notify the offeror of non-acceptance.

(3)   Where an offer of a promise invites acceptance by performance and does not invite a promissory acceptance, the rendering of the invited performance does not constitute an acceptance if before the offeror performs his promise the offeree manifests an intention not to accept.

§ 54. Acceptance by Performance; Necessity of Notification to Offeror

(1)   Where an offer invites an offeree to accept by rendering a performance, no notification is necessary to make such an acceptance effective unless the offer requests such a notification.

(2)   If an offeree who accepts by rendering a performance has reason to know that the offeror has no adequate means of learning of the performance with reasonable promptness and certainty, the contractual duty of the offeror is discharged unless

(a)   the offeree exercises reasonable diligence to notify the offeror of acceptance, or

(b)   the offeror learns of the performance within a reasonable time, or

(c)   the offer indicates that notification of acceptance is not required.

§ 55. Acceptance of Non-Promissory Offers

Acceptance by promise may create a contract in which the offeror's performance is completed when the offeree's promise is made.

§ 56. Acceptance by Promise; Necessity of Notification to Offeror

Except as stated in § 69 or where the offer manifests a contrary intention, it is essential to an acceptance by promise either that the offeree exercise reasonable diligence to notify the offeror of acceptance or that the offeror receive the acceptance seasonably.

§ 57. Effect of Equivocal Acceptance

Where notification is essential to acceptance by promise, the offeror is not bound by an acceptance in equivocal terms unless he reasonably understands it as an acceptance.

§ 58. Necessity of Acceptance Complying With Terms of Offer

An acceptance must comply with the requirements of the offer as to the promise to be made or the performance to be rendered.

§ 59. Purported Acceptance Which Adds Qualifications

A reply to an offer which purports to accept it but is conditional on the offeror's assent to terms additional to or different from those offered is not an acceptance but is a counter-offer.

§ 60. Acceptance of Offer Which States Place, Time or Manner of Acceptance

If an offer prescribes the place, time or manner of acceptance its terms in this respect must be complied with in order to create a contract. If an offer merely suggests a permitted place, time or manner of acceptance, another method of acceptance is not precluded.

§ 61. Acceptance Which Requests Change of Terms

An acceptance which requests a change or addition to the terms of the offer is not thereby invalidated unless the acceptance is made to depend on an assent to the changed or added terms.

§ 62. Effect of Performance by Offeree Where Offer Invites Either Performance or Promise

(1) Where an offer invites an offeree to choose between acceptance by promise and acceptance by performance, the tender or beginning of the invited performance or a tender of a beginning of it is an acceptance by performance.

(2) Such an acceptance operates as a promise to render complete performance.

§ 63. Time When Acceptance Takes Effect

Unless the offer provides otherwise,

(a) an acceptance made in a manner and by a medium invited by an offer is operative and completes the manifestation of mutual assent as soon as put out of the offeree's possession, without regard to whether it ever reaches the offeror; but

(b) an acceptance under an option contract is not operative until received by the offeror.

Comment:

a. Rationale. It is often said that an offeror who makes an offer by mail makes the post office his agent to receive the acceptance, or that the mailing of a letter of acceptance puts it irrevocably out of the offeree's control. Under United States postal regulations, however, the sender of a letter has long had the power to stop delivery and reclaim the letter. A better explanation of the rule that the acceptance takes effect on dispatch is that the offeree needs a dependable basis for his decision whether to accept. In many legal systems such a basis is provided by a general rule that an offer is irrevocable unless it provides otherwise. The common law provides such a basis through the rule that a revocation of an offer is ineffective if received after an acceptance has been properly dispatched. See Comment c to § 42. Acceptance by telegram is governed in this respect by the same considerations as acceptance by mail. . . .

c. Revocation of acceptance. The fact that the offeree has power to reclaim his acceptance from the post office or telegraph company does not prevent the acceptance from taking effect on dispatch. Nor, in the absence of additional circumstances, does the actual recapture of the acceptance deprive it of legal effect, though as a practical matter the offeror cannot assert his rights unless he learns of them. An attempt to revoke the acceptance by an overtaking communication is similarly ineffective, even though the revocation is received before the acceptance is received. After mailing an acceptance of a revocable offer, the offeree is not permitted to speculate at the offeror's expense during the time required for the letter to arrive.

A purported revocation of acceptance may, however, affect the rights of the parties. It may amount to an offer to rescind the contract or to a repudiation of it, or it may bar the offeree by estoppel from enforcing it. In some cases it may be justified as an exercise of a right of stoppage in transit or a demand for assurance of performance. Compare Uniform Commercial Code

§§ 2–609, 2–702, 2–705. Or the contract may be voidable for mistake or misrepresentation, §§ 151–54, 164. See particularly the provisions of § 153 on unilateral mistake.

Illustrations:

. . .7.   A mails an offer to B to appoint B A's exclusive distributor in a specified area. B duly mails an acceptance. Thereafter B mails a letter which is received by A before the acceptance is received and which rejects the offer and makes a counter-offer. On receiving the rejection and before receiving the acceptance, A executes a contract appointing C as exclusive distributor instead of B. B is estopped to enforce the contract. Compare § 40.

f. Option contracts. An option contract provides a dependable basis for decision whether to exercise the option, and removes the primary reason for the rule of Subsection (1). Moreover, there is no objection to speculation at the expense of a party who has irrevocably assumed that risk. Option contracts are commonly subject to a definite time limit, and the usual understanding is that the notification that the option has been exercised must be received by the offeror before that time. Whether or not there is such a time limit, in the absence of a contrary provision in the option contract, the offeree takes the risk of loss or delay in the transmission of the acceptance and remains free to revoke the acceptance until it arrives. Similarly, if there is such a mistake on the part of the offeror as justifies the rescission of his unilateral obligation, the right to rescind is not lost merely because a letter of acceptance is posted. See §§ 151–54.

§ 64.   Acceptance By Telephone or Teletype

Acceptance given by telephone or other medium of substantially instantaneous two-way communication is governed by the principles applicable to acceptances where the parties are in the presence of each other.

§ 65. Reasonableness of Medium of Acceptance

Unless circumstances known to the offeree indicate otherwise, a medium of acceptance is reasonable if it is the one used by the offeror or one customary in similar transactions at the time and place the offer is received.

§ 66. Acceptance Must Be Properly Dispatched

An acceptance sent by mail or otherwise from a distance is not operative when dispatched, unless it is properly addressed and such other precautions taken as are ordinarily observed to insure safe transmission of similar messages.

§ 67. Effect of Receipt of Acceptance Improperly Dispatched

Where an acceptance is seasonably dispatched but the offeree uses means of transmission not invited by the offer or fails to exercise reasonable diligence to insure safe transmission, it is treated as operative upon dispatch if received within the time in which a properly dispatched acceptance would normally have arrived.

§ 68. What Constitutes Receipt of Revocation, Rejection, or Acceptance

A written revocation, rejection, or acceptance is received when the writing comes into the possession of the person addressed, or of some person authorized by him to receive it for him, or when it is deposited in some place which he has authorized as the place for this or similar communications to be deposited for him.

§ 69. Acceptance by Silence or Exercise of Dominion

(1) Where an offeree fails to reply to an offer, his silence and inaction operate as an acceptance in the following cases only:

(a) Where an offeree takes the benefit of offered services with reasonable opportunity to reject them and reason to know that they were offered with the expectation of compensation.

(b) Where the offeror has stated or given the offeree reason to understand that assent may be manifested by silence or inaction, and the offeree in remaining silent and inactive intends to accept the offer.

(c) Where because of previous dealings or otherwise, it is reasonable that the offeree should notify the offeror if he does not intend to accept.

(2) An offeree who does any act inconsistent with the offeror's ownership of offered property is bound in accordance with the offered terms unless they are manifestly unreasonable. But if the act is wrongful as against the offeror it is an acceptance only if ratified by him.

§ 70.   Effect of Receipt By Offeror of a Late or Otherwise Defective Acceptance

A late or otherwise defective acceptance may be effective as an offer to the original offeror, but his silence operates as an acceptance in such a case only as stated in § 69.

CHAPTER 4.   FORMATION OF CONTRACTS—CONSIDERATION

TOPIC 1.   THE REQUIREMENT OF CONSIDERATION

§ 71.   Requirement of Exchange; Types of Exchange

(1)   To constitute consideration, a performance or a return promise must be bargained for.

(2)   A performance or return promise is bargained for if it is sought by the promisor in exchange for his promise and is given by the promisee in exchange for that promise.

(3)   The performance may consist of

(a)   an act other than a promise, or

(b)   a forbearance, or

(c)   the creation, modification, or destruction of a legal relation.

(4)   The performance or return promise may be given to the promisor or to some other person. It may be given by the promisee or by some other person.

Comment:

a.   Other meanings of "consideration." The word "consideration" has often been used with meanings different from that given here. It is often used merely to express the legal conclusion that a promise is enforceable. Historically, its primary meaning may have been that the conditions were met under which an action of assumpsit would lie. It was also used as the equivalent of the quid pro quo required in an action of debt. A seal, it has been said, "imports a consideration," although the law was clear that no element of bargain was necessary to enforcement of a promise under seal. On the other hand, consideration has sometimes been used to refer to almost any reason asserted for enforcing a promise, even though the reason was insufficient. In this sense we find references to promises "in consideration of love and affection," to "illegal consideration," to "past consideration," and to consideration furnished by reliance on a gratuitous promise.

Consideration has also been used to refer to the element of exchange without regard to legal consequences. Consistent with that usage has been the use of the phrase "sufficient consideration" to express the legal conclusion that one requirement for an enforceable bargain is met. Here § 17 states the element of exchange required for a contract enforceable as a bargain as "a consideration." Thus "consideration" refers to an element of exchange which is sufficient to satisfy the legal requirement; the word "sufficient" would be redundant and is not used.

b. "Bargained for." In the typical bargain, the consideration and the promise bear a reciprocal relation of motive or inducement: the consideration induces the making of the promise and the promise induces the furnishing of the consideration. Here, as in the matter of mutual assent, the law is concerned with the external manifestation rather than the undisclosed mental state: it is enough that one party manifests an intention to induce the other's response and to be induced by it and that the other responds in accordance with the inducement. See § 81; compare §§ 19, 20. But it is not enough that the promise induces the conduct of the promisee or that the conduct of the promisee induces the making of the promise; both elements must be present, or there is no bargain. Moreover, a mere pretense of bargain does not suffice, as where there is a false recital of consideration or where the purported consideration is merely nominal. In such cases there is no consideration and the promise is enforced, if at all, as a promise binding without consideration under §§ 82–94. See Comments b and c to § 87.

Illustrations:

1. A offers to buy a book owned by B and to pay B $10 in exchange therefor. B accepts the offer and delivers the book to A. The transfer and delivery of the book constitute a performance and are consideration for A's promise. See Uniform Commercial Code §§ 2–106, 2–301. This is so even though A at the time he makes the offer secretly intends to pay B $10 whether or not he gets the book, or even though B at the time he ac-

cepts secretly intends not to collect the $10.

2. A receives a gift from B of a book worth $10. Subsequently A promises to pay B the value of the book. There is no consideration for A's promise. This is so even though B at the time he makes the gift secretly hopes that A will pay him for it. As to the enforcement of such promises, see § 86.

3. A promises to make a gift of $10 to B. In reliance on the promise B buys a book from C and promises to pay C $10 for it. There is no consideration for A's promise. As to the enforcement of such promises, see § 90.

4. A desires to make a binding promise to give $1000 to his son B. Being advised that a gratuitous promise is not binding, A writes out and signs a false recital that B has sold him a car for $1000 and a promise to pay that amount. There is no consideration for A's promise.

5. A desires to make a binding promise to give $1000 to his son B. Being advised that a gratuitous promise is not binding, A offers to buy from B for $1000 a book worth less than $1. B accepts the offer knowing that the purchase of the book is a mere pretense. There is no consideration for A's promise to pay $1000.

c. Mixture of bargain and gift. In most commercial bargains there is a rough equivalence between the value promised and the value received as consideration. But the social functions of bargains include the provision of opportunity for free individual action and exercise of judgment and the fixing of values by private action, either generally or for purposes of the particular transaction. Those functions would be impaired by judicial review of the values so fixed. Ordinarily, therefore, courts do not inquire into the adequacy of consideration, particularly where one or both of the values exchanged are difficult to measure. See § 79. Even where both parties know that a transaction is in part a bargain and in part a gift, the element of bargain may nevertheless furnish consideration for the entire transaction.

On the other hand, a gift is not ordinarily treated as a bargain, and a promise to make a gift is not made a bargain by the promise of the prospective donee to accept the gift, or by his acceptance of part of it. This may be true even though the terms of gift impose a burden on the donee as well as the donor. See Illustration 2 to § 24. In such cases the distinction between bargain and gift may be a fine one, depending on the motives manifested by the parties. In some cases there may be no bargain so long as the agreement is entirely executory, but performance may furnish consideration or the agreement may become fully or partly enforceable by virtue of the reliance of one party or the unjust enrichment of the other. Compare § 90.

Illustrations:

6. A offers to buy a book owned by B and to pay B $10 in exchange therefor. B's transfer and delivery of the book are consideration for A's promise even though both parties know that such books regularly sell for $5 and that part of A's motive in making the offer is to make a gift to B. See §§ 79, 81.

7. A owns land worth $10,000 which is subject to a mortgage to secure a debt of $5,000. A promises to make a gift of the land to his son B and to pay off the mortgage, and later gives B a deed subject to the mortgage. B's acceptance of the deed is not consideration for A's promise to pay the mortgage debt.

8. A and B agree that A will advance $1000 to B as a gratuitous

loan. B's promise to accept the loan is not consideration for A's promise to make it. But the loan when made is consideration for B's promise to repay.

d. *Types of consideration.* Consideration may consist of a performance or of a return promise. Consideration by way of performance may be a specified act of forbearance, or any one of several specified acts or forbearances of which the offeree is given the choice, or such conduct as will produce a specified result. Or either the offeror or the offeree may request as consideration the creation, modification or destruction of a purely intangible legal relation. Not infrequently the consideration bargained for is an act with the added requirement that a certain legal result shall be produced. Consideration by way of return promise requires a promise as defined in § 2. Consideration may consist partly of promise and partly of other acts or forbearances, and the consideration invited may be a performance or a return promise in the alternative. Though a promise is itself an act, it is treated separately from other acts. See § 75.

Illustrations:

9. A promises B, his nephew aged 16, that A will pay B $1000 when B becomes 21 if B does not smoke before then. B's forbearance to smoke is a performance and if bargained for is consideration for A's promise.

10. A says to B, the owner of a garage, "I will pay you $100 if you will make my car run properly." The production of this result is consideration for A's promise.

11. A has B's horse in his possession. B writes to A, "If you will promise me $100 for the horse, he is yours." A promptly replies making the requested promise. The property in the horse at once passes to

A. The change in ownership is consideration for A's promise.

12.   A promises to pay B $1,000 if B will make an offer to C to sell C certain land for $25,000 and will leave the offer open for 24 hours. B makes the requested offer and forbears to revoke it for 24 hours, but C does not accept. The creation of a power of acceptance in C is consideration for A's promise.

13.   A mails a written order to B, offering to buy specified machinery on specified terms. The order provides "Ship at once." B's prompt shipment or promise to ship is consideration for A's promise to pay the price. See § 32; Uniform Commercial Code § 2–206(1)(b).

  e.   *Consideration moving from or to a third person.* It matters not from whom the consideration moves or to whom it goes. If it is bargained for and given in exchange for the promise, the promise is not gratuitous.

Illustrations:

14.   A promises B to guarantee payment of a bill of goods if B sells the goods to C. Selling the goods to C is consideration for A's promise.

15.   A makes a promissory note payable to B in return for a payment by B to C. The payment is consideration for the note.

16.   A, at C's request and in exchange for $1 paid by C, promises B to give him a book. The payment is consideration for A's promise.

17.   A promises B to pay B $1, in exchange for C's promise to A to give A a book. The promises are consideration for one another.

18.   A promises to pay $1,000 to B, a bank, in exchange for the delivery of a car by C to A's son D. The delivery of the car is consideration for A's promise.

§ 72.   Exchange of Promise for Performance

Except as stated in §§ 73 and 74, any performance which is bargained for is consideration.

§ 73.   Performance of Legal Duty

Performance of a legal duty owed to a promisor which is neither doubtful nor the subject of honest dispute is not consideration; but a similar performance is consideration if it differs from what was required by the duty in a way which reflects more than a pretense of bargain.

§ 74.   Settlement of Claims

(1)   Forbearance to assert or the surrender of a claim or defense which proves to be invalid is not consideration unless

  (a)   the claim or defense is in fact doubtful because of uncertainty as to the facts or the law, or

  (b)   the forbearing or surrendering party believes that the claim or defense may be fairly determined to be valid.

(2)   The execution of a written instrument surrendering a claim or defense by one who is under no duty to execute it is consideration if the execution of the written instrument is bargained for even though he is not

asserting the claim or defense and believes that no valid claim or defense exists.

§ 75.   Exchange of Promise for Promise

Except as stated in §§ 76 and 77, a promise which is bargained for is consideration if, but only if, the promised performance would be consideration.

Comment:

a.   The executory exchange. In modern times the enforcement of bargains is not limited to those partly completed, but is extended to the wholly executory exchange in which promise is exchanged for promise. In such a case the element of unjust enrichment is not present; the element of reliance, if present at all, is less tangible and direct than in the case of the half-completed exchange. The promise is enforced by virtue of the fact of bargain, without more. Since the principle that bargains are binding is widely understood and is reinforced in many situations by custom and convention, the fact of bargain also tends to satisfy the cautionary and channeling functions of form. Compare Comments b and c to § 72. Evidentiary safeguards, however, are largely left to the Statute of Frauds rather than to the requirement of consideration. See Chapter 5.

b.   Promise and performance. The principle of this Section is that, in determining whether there is consideration, one's word is as good as one's deed but no better. More detailed rules are stated in §§ 76–78 for cases in which the application of this principle has produced problems. Certain cases which have sometimes been thought to be exceptions to the principle are commented upon below.

c.   Performance of legal duty and settlement of claims. A promise to perform a legal duty is not consideration for a return promise unless performance would be. Similarly, a promise to surrender a claim or defense or to forbear from asserting it is consider-

ation only if performance would be. Thus a promise of such performance may raise the same questions as the performance would: Is the duty owed to the maker of the return promise? Is the claim or defense known to be invalid? See §§ 73, 74.

Illustrations:

1.   A promises to pay a debt to B, or to perform an existing contractual duty to B, or to perform his duty as a public official. The legal duty is neither doubtful nor the subject of honest dispute, but A would not have fulfilled the duty but for B's return promise. A's promise is not consideration for B's return promise. Compare § 73.

2.   A promises B to surrender or to forbear suit upon a claim either against B or against C. A knows the claim is invalid. A's promise is not consideration for a return promise by B. Compare § 74.

d.   "Void" promises. The value of a promise does not necessarily depend upon the availability of a legal remedy for breach, and bargains are often made in consideration of promises which are voidable or unenforceable. Such a promise may be consideration for a return promise. See § 78. But it is sometimes suggested that a promise is not consideration if it is not binding, or if it is "void." The examples used commonly involve total lack of capacity to contract (see §§ 12, 13), indefinite promises (see §§ 33–34), promises lacking consideration, or promises unenforceable as against public policy (see Chapter 8). Such cases are not exceptions to the rule stated in this Section. In some of them there is no promise within the definition in § 2, in others the return promise would not be binding whether the consideration consisted of a promise or of performance, in some the invalidity of the return promise rests on other policies than those embodied in the requirement of consideration.

Illustrations:

3.   While A's property is under guardianship by reason of an adjudication of mental illness, A makes an agreement with B in which B makes a promise. B's promise is not a contract, whether the consideration consists of a promise by A or performance by A. Compare § 13; Restatement of Restitution § 139.

4.   A promises to forbear suit against B in exchange for B's promise to pay a liquidated and undisputed debt to A. A's promise is not binding because B's promise is not consideration under § 73, but A's promise is nevertheless consider-

ation for B's. Moreover, B's promise would be enforceable without consideration under § 82. On either basis, B's promise is conditional on A's forbearance and can be enforced only if the condition is met.

5.   A, a married man, and B, an unmarried woman, make mutual promises to marry. B neither knows nor has reason to know that A is married. B's promise is consideration and B may recover damages from A for breach of his promise though B would have a defense to a similar action by A. See § 180.

6.   A promises B $100 in return for B's promise to cut timber on land upon which A is a trespasser. B neither knows nor has reason to know that A is not privileged to cut the timber. B's promise is consideration and B may recover damages from A for breach of his promise though B would have a defense to a similar action by A. See Illustration 2 to § 180.

§ 76. Conditional Promise

(1)   A conditional promise is not consideration if the promisor knows at the time of making the promise that the condition cannot occur.

(2)   A promise conditional on a performance by the promisor is a promise of alternative performances within § 77 unless occurrence of the condition is also promised.

§ 77. Illusory and Alternative Promises

A promise or apparent promise is not consideration if by its terms the promisor or purported promisor reserves a choice of alternative performances unless

(a)   each of the alternative performances would have been consideration if it alone had been bargained for; or

(b)   one of the alternative performances would have been consideration and there is or appears to the parties to be a substantial possibility that before the promisor exercises his choice events may eliminate the alternatives which would not have been consideration.

39

§ 78. Voidable and Unenforceable Promises

The fact that a rule of law renders a promise voidable or unenforceable does not prevent it from being consideration.

§ 79. Adequacy of Consideration; Mutuality of Obligation

If the requirement of consideration is met, there is no additional requirement of

(a)   a gain, advantage, or benefit to the promisor or a loss, disadvantage, or detriment to the promisee; or

(b)   equivalence in the values exchanged; or

(c)   "mutuality of obligation."

Comment:

. . . b.   Benefit   and   detriment. Historically, the common law action of debt was said to require a quid pro quo, and that requirement may have led to statements that consideration must be a benefit to the promisor. But contracts were enforced in the common-law action of assumpsit without any such requirement; in actions of assumpsit the emphasis was rather on the harm to the promisee, and detrimental reliance on a promise may still be the basis of contractual relief. See § 90. But reliance is not essential to the formation of a bargain, and remedies for breach have long been given in cases of exchange of promise for promise where neither party has begun to perform. Today when it is said that consideration must involve a detriment to the promisee, the supposed requirement is often qualified by a statement that a "legal detriment" is sufficient even though there is no economic detriment or other actual loss. It is more realistic to say simply that there is no requirement of detriment.

c.   Exchange of unequal values. To the extent that the apportionment of productive energy and product in the economy are left to private action, the parties to transactions are free to fix their own valuations. The resolution of disputes often requires a determination of value in the more general sense

of market value, and such values are commonly fixed as an approximation based on a multitude of private valuations. But in many situations there is no reliable external standard of value, or the general standard is inappropriate to the precise circumstances of the parties. Valuation is left to private action in part because the parties are thought to be better able than others to evaluate the circumstances of particular transactions. In any event, they are not ordinarily bound to follow the valuations of others.

Ordinarily, therefore, courts do not inquire into the adequacy of consideration. This is particularly so when one or both of the values exchanged are uncertain or difficult to measure. But it is also applied even when it is clear that the transaction is a mixture of bargain and gift. See Comment c to § 71. Gross inadequacy of consideration may be relevant to issues of capacity, fraud and the like, but the requirement of consideration is not a safeguard against imprudent and improvident contracts except in cases where it appears that there is no bargain in fact. . . .

e.   Effects of gross inadequacy. Although the requirement of consideration may be met despite a great difference in the values exchanged, gross inadequacy of consideration may be relevant in the application of other rules. Inadequacy "such as shocks the conscience" is often said to be a "badge of fraud," justifying a denial of specific performance. See § 364(1)(c). Inadequacy may also help to justify rescission or cancellation on the ground of lack of capacity (see §§ 15, 16), mistake, misrepresentation, duress or undue influence (see Chapters 6 and 7). Unequal bargains are also limited by the statutory law of usury, by regulation of the rates of public utilities and some other enterprises, and by special rules developed for the sale of an expectation of inheritance, for contractual penalties and forfeitures (see §§ 229, 356), and for agreements between secured lender and borrower (see Restatement of Security § 55, Uniform Commercial Code § 9–501).

f.   Mutuality. The word "mutuality," though often used in connection with the law of Contracts, has no defi-

nite meaning. "Mutual assent" as one element of a bargain is the subject of Topic 2 of this Chapter. "Mutuality of remedy" is dealt with in Comment c to § 363. Clause (c) of this Section negates any supposed requirement of "mutuality of obligation." Such a requirement has sometimes been asserted in the form, "Both parties must be bound or neither is bound." That statement is obviously erroneous as applied to an exchange of promise for performance; it is equally inapplicable to contracts governed by §§ 82–94 and to contracts enforceable by virtue of their formal characteristics under § 6. Even in the ordinary case of the exchange of promise for promise, § 78 makes it clear that voidable and unenforceable promises may be consideration. The only requirement of "mutuality of obligation" even in cases of mutual promises is that stated in §§ 76–77.

§ 80.   Multiple Exchanges

(1)   There is consideration for a set of promises if what is bargained for and given in exchange would have been consideration for each promise in the set if exchanged for that promise alone.

(2)   The fact that part of what is bargained for would not have been consideration if that part alone had been bargained for does not prevent the whole from being consideration.

§ 81.   Consideration as Motive or Inducing Cause

(1)   The fact that what is bargained for does not of itself induce the making of a promise does not prevent it from being consideration for the promise.

(2)   The fact that a promise does not of itself induce a performance or return promise does not prevent the performance or return promise from being consideration for the promise.

TOPIC 2.   CONTRACTS WITHOUT CONSIDERATION

§ 82.   Promise to Pay Indebtedness; Effect on the Statute of Limitations

(1)   A promise to pay all or part of an antecedent contractual or quasi-contractual indebtedness owed by the promisor is binding if the indebt-

edness is still enforceable or would be except for the effect of a statute of limitations.

(2)   The following facts operate as such a promise unless other facts indicate a different intention:

(a)   A voluntary acknowledgment to the obligee, admitting the present existence of the antecedent indebtedness; or

(b)   A voluntary transfer of money, a negotiable instrument, or other thing by the obligor to the obligee, made as interest on or part payment of or collateral security for the antecedent indebtedness; or

(c)   A statement to the obligee that the statute of limitations will not be pleaded as a defense.

§ 83.   Promise to Pay Indebtedness Discharged in Bankruptcy

An express promise to pay all or part of an indebtedness of the promisor, discharged or dischargeable in bankruptcy proceedings begun before the promise is made, is binding.

§ 84.   Promise to Perform a Duty in Spite of Non-Occurrence of a Condition

(1)   Except as stated in Subsection (2), a promise to perform all or part of a conditional duty under an antecedent contract in spite of the non-occurrence of the condition is binding, whether the promise is made before or after the time for the condition to occur, unless

(a)   occurrence of the condition was a material part of the agreed exchange for the performance of the duty and the promisee was under no duty that it occur; or

(b)   uncertainty of the occurrence of the condition was an element of the risk assumed by the promisor.

(2)   If such a promise is made before the time for the occurrence of the condition has expired and the condition is within the control of the promisee or a beneficiary, the promisor can make his duty again subject to the condition by notifying the promisee or beneficiary of his intention to do so if

(a)   the notification is received while there is still a reasonable time to cause the condition to occur under the antecedent terms or an extension given by the promisor; and

(b)   reinstatement of the requirement of the condition is not unjust because of a material change of position by the promisee or beneficiary; and

(c)   the promise is not binding apart from the rule stated in Subsection (1).

§ 85.   Promise to Perform a Voidable Duty

Except as stated in § 93, a promise to perform all or part of an anteced-ent contract of the promisor, previously voidable by him, but not avoided prior to the making of the promise, is binding.

§ 86.   Promise for Benefit Received

(1)   A promise made in recognition of a benefit previously received by the promisor from the promisee is binding to the extent necessary to prevent injustice.

(2)   A promise is not binding under Subsection (1)

(a)   if the promisee conferred the benefit as a gift or for other rea-sons the promisor has not been unjustly enriched; or

(b)   to the extent that its value is disproportionate to the benefit.

Comment:

a.   "Past consideration"; "moral obligation." Enforcement of promises to pay for benefit received has some-times been said to rest on "past consid-eration" or on the "moral obligation" of the promisor, and there are statutes in such terms in a few states. Those terms are not used here: "past consideration" is inconsistent with the meaning of consideration stated in § 71, and there seems to be no consensus as to what constitutes a "moral obligation." The mere fact of promise has been thought to create a moral obligation, but it is clear that not all promises are enforced. Nor are moral obligations based solely on gratitude or sentiment sufficient of themselves to support a subsequent promise.

Illustrations:

1.   A gives emergency care to B's adult son while the son is sick and without funds far from home. B subsequently promises to reimburse A for his expenses. The promise is not binding under this Section.

2.   A lends money to B, who later dies. B's widow promises to pay the debt. The promise is not binding under this Section.

3.   A has immoral relations with B, a woman not his wife, to her injury. A's subsequent promise to reimburse B for her loss is not bind-ing under this Section.

b.   Rationale. Although in gen-eral a person who has been unjustly enriched at the expense of another is required to make restitution, restitu-tion is denied in many cases in order to protect persons who have had benefits thrust upon them. See Restatement of Restitution §§ 1, 2, 112. In other cases restitution is denied by virtue of rules designed to guard against false claims, stale claims, claims already litigated, and the like. In many such cases a subsequent promise to make restitu-tion removes the reason for the denial of relief, and the policy against unjust enrichment then prevails. Compare Restatement, Second, Agency § 462 on ratification of the acts of a person who officiously purports to act as an agent. Enforcement of the subsequent prom-ise sometimes makes it unnecessary to decide a difficult question as to the lim-its on quasi-contractual relief.

Many of the cases governed by the rules stated in §§ 82–85 are within the broader principle stated in this Sec-tion. But the broader principle is not so firmly established as those rules, and it may not be applied if there is doubt whether the objections to restitution are fully met by the subsequent promise. Facts such as the definite and substantial character of the benefit received, formality in the making of the promise, part performance of the promise, reliance on the promise or the probability of such reliance may be relevant to show that no imposition results from enforcement.

c.   *Promise to correct a mistake.* One who makes a mistake in the conferring of a benefit is commonly entitled to restitution regardless of any promise. But restitution is often denied to avoid prejudice to the recipient of the benefit. Thus restitution of the value of services or of improvements to land or chattels may require a payment which the recipient cannot afford. See Restatement of Restitution §§ 41, 42. Where a subsequent promise shows that the usual protection is not needed in the particular case, restitution is granted to the extent promised.

Illustrations:

4.   A is employed by B to repair a vacant house. By mistake A repairs the house next door, which belongs to C. A subsequent promise by C to pay A the value of the repairs is binding.

5.   A pays B a debt and gets a signed receipt. Later B obtains a default judgment against A for the amount of the debt, and A pays again. B's subsequent promise to refund the second payment if A has a receipt is binding.

d.   *Emergency services and necessaries.* The law of restitution in the absence of promise severely limits recovery for necessaries furnished to a person under disability and for emergency services. See Restatement of Restitution §§ 113–17, 139. A subsequent promise in such a case may remove doubt as to the reality of the benefit and as to its value, and may negate

any danger of imposition or false claim. A positive showing that payment was expected is not then required; an intention to make a gift must be shown to defeat restitution.

Illustrations:

6.   A finds B's escaped bull and feeds and cares for it. B's subsequent promise to pay reasonable compensation to A is binding.

7.   A saves B's life in an emergency and is totally and permanently disabled in so doing. One month later B promises to pay A $15 every two weeks for the rest of A's life, and B makes the payments for 8 years until he dies. The promise is binding.

e.   *Benefit conferred as a gift.* In the absence of mistake or the like, there is no element of unjust enrichment in the receipt of a gift, and the rule of this Section has no application to a promise to pay for a past gift. Similarly, when a debt is discharged by a binding agreement, the transaction is closed even though full payment is not made. But marginal cases arise in which both parties understand that what is in form a gift is intended to be reimbursed indirectly, or in which a subsequent promise to pay is expressly contemplated. See Illustration 3 to § 83. Enforcement of the subsequent promise is proper in some such cases.

Illustrations:

8.   A submits to B at B's request a plan for advertising products manufactured by B, expecting payment only if the plan is adopted. Because of a change in B's selling arrangements, B rejects the plan without giving it fair consideration. B's subsequent promise to reimburse A's expenses in preparing the plan is binding.

9.   A contributes capital to B, an insurance company, on the un-

derstanding that B is not liable to reimburse A but that A will be reimbursed through salary and commissions. Later A withdraws from the company and B promises to pay him ten percent of premiums received until he is reimbursed. The promise is binding.

f.   Benefit conferred pursuant to contract. By virtue of the policy of enforcing bargains, the enrichment of one party as a result of an unequal exchange is not regarded as unjust, and this Section has no application to a promise to pay or perform more or to accept less than is called for by a pre-existing bargain between the same parties. Compare §§ 79, 89. Similarly, if a third person receives a benefit as a result of the performance of a bargain, this Section does not make binding the subsequent promise of the third person to pay extra compensation to the performing party. But a promise to pay in substitution for the return performance called for by the bargain may be binding under this Section.

Illustration:

10.   A digs a well on B's land in performance of a bargain with B's tenant C. C is unable to pay as agreed, and B promises to pay A the reasonable value of the well. The promise is binding.

g.   Obligation unenforceable under the Statute of Frauds. A promise to pay a debt unenforceable under the Statute of Frauds is very similar to the promises governed by §§ 82–85. But the problem seldom arises. Part performance often renders the Statute inapplicable; if it does not, the contract can be made enforceable by a subsequent memorandum. See § 136. In any event, the Statute does not ordinarily foreclose the remedy of restitution. See § 375. Where the question does arise, the new promise is binding if the policy of the Statute is satisfied.

Illustration:

11.   By statute an agreement authorizing a real estate broker to sell land for compensation is void unless the agreement or a memorandum thereof is in writing. A, a real estate broker, procures a purchaser for B's land without any written agreement. In the written sale agreement, signed by B, B promises to pay A $200, the usual commission, "for services rendered." The promise is binding.

h.   Obligation unenforceable because usurious. If a promise is unenforceable because it is usurious, an agreement in renewal or substitution for it that provides for a payment including the usurious interest is also unenforceable, even though the interest from the date of renewal or substitution is not usurious. However, a promise to pay the original debt with interest that is not usurious in substitution for the usurious interest is enforceable.

i.   Partial enforcement. The rules stated in §§ 82–85 refer to promises to perform all or part of an antecedent duty, and do not make enforceable a promise to do more. Similarly, where a benefit received is a liquidated sum of money, a promise is not enforceable under this Section beyond the amount of the benefit. Where the value of the benefit is uncertain, a promise to pay the value is binding and a promise to pay a liquidated sum may serve to fix the amount due if in all the circumstances it is not disproportionate to the benefit. See Illustration 7. A promise which is excessive may sometimes be enforced to the extent of the value of the benefit, and the remedy may be thought of as quasi-contractual rather than contractual. In other cases a promise of disproportionate value may tend to show unfair pressure or other conduct by the promisee such that justice does not require any enforcement of the promise. Compare Comment c to § 72.

Illustrations:

12.   A, a married woman of sixty, has rendered household services without compensation over a period of years for B, a man of eighty living alone and having no close relatives. B has a net worth of three million dollars and has often assured A that she will be well paid for her services, whose reasonable value is not in excess of $6,000. B executes and delivers to A a written promise to pay A $25,000 "to be taken from my estate." The promise is binding.

13.   The facts being otherwise as stated in Illustration 12, B's promise is made orally and is to leave A his entire estate. A cannot recover more than the reasonable value of her services.

§ 87.   Option Contract

(1)   An offer is binding as an option contract if it

(a)   is in writing and signed by the offeror, recites a purported consideration for the making of the offer, and proposes an exchange on fair terms within a reasonable time; or

(b)   is made irrevocable by statute.

(2)   An offer which the offeror should reasonably expect to induce action or forbearance of a substantial character on the part of the offeree before acceptance and which does induce such action or forbearance is binding as an option contract to the extent necessary to avoid injustice.

Comment:

a.   Consideration and form. The traditional common-law devices for making a firm offer or option contract are the giving of consideration and the affixing of a seal. See §§ 25, 95. But the firm offer serves a useful purpose even though no preliminary bargain is made: it is often a necessary step in the making of the main bargain proposed, and it partakes of the natural formalities inherent in business transactions. The erosion of the formality of the seal has made it less and less satisfactory as a universal formality. As literacy has spread, the personal signature has become the natural formality and the seal has become more and more anachronistic. The rules stated in this section reflect the judicial and legislative response to this situation.

b.   Nominal consideration. Offers made in consideration of one dollar paid or promised are often irrevocable under Subsection (1)(a). The irrevocability of an offer may be worth much or little to the offeree, and the courts do not ordinarily inquire into the adequacy of the consideration bargained for. See § 79. Hence a comparatively small payment may furnish consideration for the irrevocability of an offer proposing a transaction involving much larger sums. But gross disproportion between the payment and the value of the option commonly indicates that the payment was not in fact bargained for but was a mere formality or pretense. In such a case there is no consideration as that term is defined in § 71.

Nevertheless, such a nominal consideration is regularly held sufficient to support a short-time option proposing an exchange on fair terms. The fact that the option is an appropriate preliminary step in the conclusion of a socially useful transaction provides a sufficient substantive basis for enforcement, and a signed writing taking a form appropriate to a bargain satisfies the desiderata of form. In the absence of statute, however, the bargaining form is essential: a payment of one dollar by each party to the other is so obviously not a bargaining transaction that it does not provide even the form of an exchange. . . .

c. *False recital of nominal consideration.* A recital in a written agreement that a stated consideration has been given is evidence of that fact as against a party to the agreement, but such a recital may ordinarily be contradicted by evidence that no such consideration was given or expected. See § 218. In cases within Subsection (1)(a), however, the giving and recital of nominal consideration performs a formal function only. The signed writing has vital significance as a formality, while the ceremonial manual delivery of a dollar or a peppercorn is an inconsequential formality. In view of the dangers of permitting a solemn written agreement to be invalidated by oral testimony which is easily fabricated, therefore, the option agreement is not invalidated by proof that the recited consideration was not in fact given. A fictitious rationalization has sometimes been used for this rule: accep-

tance of delivery of the written instrument conclusively imports a promise to make good the recital, it is said, and that promise furnishes consideration. Compare § 218. But the sound basis for the rule is that stated above. . . .

e. *Reliance.* Subsection (2) states the application of § 90 to reliance on an unaccepted offer, with qualifications which would not be appropriate in some other types of cases covered by § 90. It is important chiefly in cases of reliance that is not part performance. If the beginning of performance is a reasonable mode of acceptance, it makes the offer fully enforceable under § 45 or § 62; if not, the offeror commonly has no reason to expect part performance before acceptance. But circumstances may be such that the offeree must undergo substantial expense, or undertake substantial commitments, or forego alternatives, in order to put himself in a position to accept by either promise or performance. The offer may be made expressly irrevocable in contemplation of reliance by the offeree. If reliance follows in such cases, justice may require a remedy. Compare Restatement, Second, Torts § 325; Restatement, Second, Agency § 378. But the reliance must be substantial as well as foreseeable. . . .

§ 88. Guaranty

A promise to be surety for the performance of a contractual obligation, made to the obligee, is binding if

    (a) the promise is in writing and signed by the promisor and recites a purported consideration; or

    (b) the promise is made binding by statute; or

    (c) the promisor should reasonably expect the promise to induce action or forbearance of a substantial character on the part of the promisee or a third person, and the promise does induce such action or forbearance.

§ 89. Modification of Executory Contract

A promise modifying a duty under a contract not fully performed on either side is binding

(a)   if the modification is fair and equitable in view of circumstances not anticipated by the parties when the contract was made; or

(b)   to the extent provided by statute; or

(c)   to the extent that justice requires enforcement in view of material change of position in reliance on the promise.

Comment:

a.   Rationale. This Section relates primarily to adjustments in on-going transactions. Like offers and guaranties, such adjustments are ancillary to exchanges and have some of the same presumptive utility. See §§ 72, 87, 88. Indeed, paragraph (a) deals with bargains which are without consideration only because of the rule that performance of a legal duty to the promisor is not consideration. See § 73. This Section is also related to § 84 on waiver of conditions: it may apply to cases in which § 84 is inapplicable because a condition is material to the exchange or risk. As in cases governed by § 84, relation to a bargain tends to satisfy the cautionary and channeling functions of legal formalities. See Comment c to § 72. The Statute of Frauds may prevent enforcement in the absence of reliance. See §§ 149–50. Otherwise formal requirements are at a minimum.

b.   Performance of legal duty. The rule of § 73 finds its modern justification in cases of promises made by mistake or induced by unfair pressure. Its application to cases where those elements are absent has been much criticized and is avoided if paragraph (a) of this Section is applicable. The limitation to a modification which is "fair and equitable" goes beyond absence of coercion and requires an objectively demonstrable reason for seeking a modification. Compare Uniform Commercial Code § 2–209 Comment. The reason for modification must rest in circumstances not "anticipated" as part of the context in which the contract was made, but a frustrating event may be unanticipated for this purpose if it was not adequately covered, even though it was foreseen as a remote possibility. When such a reason is present, the relative financial strength of the parties, the formality with which the modification is made, the extent to which it is performed or relied on and other circumstances may be relevant to show or negate imposition or unfair surprise.

The same result called for by paragraph (a) is sometimes reached on the ground that the original contract was "rescinded" by mutual agreement and that new promises were then made which furnished consideration for each other. That theory is rejected here because it is fictitious when the "rescission" and new agreement are simultaneous, and because if logically carried out it might uphold unfair and inequitable modifications.

Illustrations:

1.   By a written contract A agrees to excavate a cellar for B for a stated price. Solid rock is unexpectedly encountered and A so notifies B. A and B then orally agree that A will remove the rock at a unit price which is reasonable but nine times that used in computing the original price, and A completes the job. B is bound to pay the increased amount.

2.   A contracts with B to supply for $300 a laundry chute for a building B has contracted to build for the Government for $150,000. Later A discovers that he made an error as to the type of material to be used and should have bid $1,200. A offers to supply the chute for $1000, eliminating overhead and profit. After ascertaining that other sup-

pliers would charge more, B agrees. The new agreement is binding.

3.   A is employed by B as a designer of coats at $90 a week for a year beginning November 1 under a written contract executed September 1. A is offered $115 a week by another employer and so informs B. A and B then agree that A will be paid $100 a week and in October execute a new written contract to that effect, simultaneously tearing up the prior contract. The new contract is binding.

4.   A contracts to manufacture and sell to B 2,000 steel roofs for corn cribs at $60. Before A begins manufacture a threat of a nationwide steel strike raises the cost of steel about $10 per roof, and A and B agree orally to increase the price to $70 per roof. A thereafter manufactures and delivers 1700 of the roofs, and B pays for 1,500 of them at the increased price without protest, increasing the selling price of the corn cribs by $10. The new agreement is binding.

5.   A contracts to manufacture and sell to B 100,000 castings for lawn mowers at 50 cents each. After partial delivery and after B has contracted to sell a substantial number of lawn mowers at a fixed price, A notifies B that increased metal costs require that the price be increased to 75 cents. Substitute castings are available at 55 cents, but only after several months delay. B protests but is forced to agree to the new price to keep its plant in operation. The modification is not binding.

c.   *Statutes.* Uniform Commercial Code § 2–209 dispenses with the requirement of consideration for an agreement modifying a contract for the sale of goods. Under that section the original contract can provide against oral modification, and the require-

ments of the Statute of Frauds must be met if the contract as modified is within its provisions; but an ineffective modification can operate as a waiver. The Comment indicates that extortion of a modification without legitimate commercial reason is ineffective as a violation of the duty of good faith imposed by the Code. A similar limitation may be applicable under statutes which give effect to a signed writing as a substitute for the seal, or under statutes which give effect to acceptance by the promisee of the modified performance. In some States statutes or constitutional provisions flatly forbid the payment of extra compensation to Government contractors.

d.   *Reliance.* Paragraph (c) states the application of § 90 to modification of an executory contract in language adapted from Uniform Commercial Code § 2–209. Even though the promise is not binding when made, it may become binding in whole or in part by reason of action or forbearance by the promisee or third persons in reliance on it. In some cases the result can be viewed as based either on estoppel to contradict a representation of fact or on reliance on a promise. Ordinarily reliance by the promisee is reasonably foreseeable and makes the modification binding with respect to performance by the promisee under it and any return performance owed by the promisor. But as under § 84 the original terms can be reinstated for the future by reasonable notification received by the promisee unless reinstatement would be unjust in view of a change of position on his part. Compare Uniform Commercial Code § 2–209(5).

Illustrations:

6.   A defaults in payment of a premium on a life insurance policy issued by B, an insurance company. Pursuant to the terms of the policy, B notifies A of the lapse of the policy and undertakes to continue the

insurance until a specified future date, but by mistake specifies a date two months later than the insured would be entitled to under the policy. On inquiry by A two years later, B repeats the mistake, offering A an option to take a cash payment. A fails to do so, and dies one month before the specified date. B is bound to pay the insurance.

7.   A is the lessee of an apartment house under a 99-year lease from B at a rent of $10,000 per year. Because of war conditions many of the apartments become vacant, and in order to enable A to stay in business B agrees to reduce the rent to $5,000. The reduced rent is paid for five years. The war being over, the apartments are then fully rented,

and B notifies A that the full rent called for by the lease must be paid. A is bound to pay the full rent only from a reasonable time after the receipt of the notification.

8.   A contracts with B to carry a shipment of fish under refrigeration. During the short first leg of the voyage the refrigeration equipment on the ship breaks down, and A offers either to continue under ventilation or to hold the cargo at the first port for later shipment. B agrees to shipment under ventilation but later changes his mind. A receives notification of the change before he has changed his position. A is bound to ship under refrigeration.

§ 90.   Promise Reasonably Inducing Action or Forbearance

(1)   A promise which the promisor should reasonably expect to induce action or forbearance on the part of the promisee or a third person and which does induce such action or forbearance is binding if injustice can be avoided only by enforcement of the promise. The remedy granted for breach may be limited as justice requires.

(2)   A charitable subscription or a marriage settlement is binding under Subsection (1) without proof that the promise induced action or forbearance.

Comment:

a.   Relation to other rules. Obligations and remedies based on reliance are not peculiar to the law of contracts. This Section is often referred to in terms of "promissory estoppel," a phrase suggesting an extension of the doctrine of estoppel. Estoppel prevents a person from showing the truth contrary to a representation of fact made by him after another has relied on the representation. See Restatement, Second, Agency § 8B; Restatement, Second, Torts §§ 872, 894. Reliance is also a significant feature of numerous rules in the law of negligence, deceit and restitution. See, e.g., Restatement, Second, Agency §§ 354, 378; Restatement,

Second, Torts §§ 323, 537; Restatement of Restitution § 55. In some cases those rules and this Section overlap; in others they provide analogies useful in determining the extent to which enforcement is necessary to avoid injustice.

It is fairly arguable that the enforcement of informal contracts in the action of assumpsit rested historically on justifiable reliance on a promise. Certainly reliance is one of the main bases for enforcement of the half-completed exchange, and the probability of reliance lends support to the enforcement of the executory exchange. See Comments to §§ 72, 75. This Section thus states a basic principle which often renders inquiry unnecessary as to the precise scope of the policy of enforcing bargains. Sections 87–89 state particular applications of the same principle to promises ancillary to bargains, and it also applies in a wide variety of noncommercial situations. See, e.g., § 94.

Illustration:

1. A, knowing that B is going to college, promises B that A will give him $5,000 on completion of his course. B goes to college, and borrows and spends more than $5,000 for college expenses. When he has nearly completed his course, A notifies him of an intention to revoke the promise. A's promise is binding and B is entitled to payment on completion of the course without regard to whether his performance was "bargained for" under § 71.

b. Character of reliance protected. The principle of this Section is flexible. The promisor is affected only by reliance which he does or should foresee, and enforcement must be necessary to avoid injustice. Satisfaction of the latter requirement may depend on the reasonableness of the promisee's reliance, on its definite and substantial character in relation to the remedy sought, on the formality with which the promise is made, on the extent to which the evidentiary, cautionary, deterrent and channeling functions of form are met by the commercial setting or otherwise, and on the extent to which such other policies as the enforcement of bargains and the prevention of unjust enrichment are relevant. Compare Comment to § 72. The force of particular factors varies in different types of cases: thus reliance need not be of substantial character in charitable subscription cases, but must in cases of firm offers and guaranties. Compare Subsection (2) with §§ 87, 88.

Illustrations:

2. A promises B not to foreclose, for a specified time, a mortgage which A holds on B's land. B thereafter makes improvements on the land. A's promise is binding and may be enforced by denial of foreclosure before the time has elapsed.

3. A sues B in a municipal court for damages for personal injuries caused by B's negligence. After the one year statute of limitations has run, B requests A to discontinue the action and start again in the superior court where the action can be consolidated with other actions against B arising out of the same accident. A does so. B's implied promise that no harm to A will result bars B from asserting the statute of limitations as a defense.

4. A has been employed by B for 40 years. B promises to pay A a pension of $200 per month when A retires. A retires and forbears to work elsewhere for several years while B pays the pension. B's promise is binding.

c. Reliance by third persons. If a promise is made to one party for the benefit of another, it is often foreseeable that the beneficiary will rely on the promise. Enforcement of the promise in such cases rests on the same basis and depends on the same factors as in cases of reliance by the promisee. Justifiable reliance by third persons who are not beneficiaries is less likely, but may sometimes reinforce the claim of the promisee or beneficiary.

Illustrations:

5. A holds a mortgage on B's land. To enable B to obtain a loan, A promises B in writing to release part of the land from the mortgage upon payment of a stated sum. As A contemplated, C lends money to B on a second mortgage, relying on A's promise. The promise is binding and may be enforced by C.

6. A executes and delivers a promissory note to B, a bank, to

give B a false appearance of assets, deceive the banking authorities, and enable the bank to continue to operate. After several years B fails and is taken over by C, a representative of B's creditors. A's note is enforceable by C.

7.   A and B, husband and wife, are tenants by the entirety of a tract of land. They make an oral promise to B's niece C to give her the tract. B, C and C's husband expend money in building a house on the tract and C and her husband take possession and live there for several years until B dies. The expenditures by B and by C's husband are treated like those by C in determining whether justice requires enforcement of the promise against A.

d.   Partial enforcement. A promise binding under this section is a contract, and full-scale enforcement by normal remedies is often appropriate. But the same factors which bear on whether any relief should be granted also bear on the character and extent of the remedy. In particular, relief may sometimes be limited to restitution or to damages or specific relief measured by the extent of the promisee's reliance rather than by the terms of the promise. See §§ 84, 89; compare Restatement, Second, Torts § 549 on damages for fraud. Unless there is unjust enrichment of the promisor, damages should not put the promisee in a better position than performance of the promise would have put him. See §§ 344, 349. In the case of a promise to make a gift it would rarely be proper to award consequential damages which would place a greater burden on the promisor than performance would have imposed.

Illustrations:

8.   A applies to B, a distributor of radios manufactured by C, for a "dealer franchise" to sell C's products. Such franchises are revocable at will. B erroneously informs A that C has accepted the application and will soon award the franchise, that A can proceed to employ salesmen and solicit orders, and that A will receive an initial delivery of at least 30 radios. A expends $1,150 in preparing to do business, but does not receive the franchise or any radios. B is liable to A for the $1,150 but not for the lost profit on 30 radios. Compare Restatement, Second, Agency § 329.

9.   The facts being otherwise as stated in Illustration 8, B gives A the erroneous information deliberately and with C's approval and requires A to buy the assets of a deceased former dealer and thus discharge C's "moral obligation" to the widow. C is liable to A not only for A's expenses but also for the lost profit on 30 radios.

10.   A, who owns and operates a bakery, desires to go into the grocery business. He approaches B, a franchisor of supermarkets. B states to A that for $18,000 B will establish A in a store. B also advises A to move to another town and buy a small grocery to gain experience. A does so. Later B advises A to sell the grocery, which A does, taking a capital loss and foregoing expected profits from the summer tourist trade. B also advises A to sell his bakery to raise capital for the supermarket franchise, saying "Everything is ready to go. Get your money together and we are set." A sells the bakery taking a capital loss on this sale as well. Still later, B tells A that considerably more than an $18,000 investment will be needed, and the negotiations between the parties collapse. At the point of collapse many details of the proposed agreement between the parties are unresolved. The assurances from B to A are promises on which B reasonably should have expected A to rely, and A is entitled to

his actual losses on the sales of the bakery and grocery and for his moving and temporary living expenses. Since the proposed agreement was never made, however, A is not entitled to lost profits from the sale of the grocery or to his expectation interest in the proposed franchise from B.

11. A is about to buy a house on a hill. Before buying he obtains a promise from B, who owns adjoining land, that B will not build on a particular portion of his lot, where a building would obstruct the view from the house. A then buys the house in reliance on the promise. B's promise is binding, but will be specifically enforced only so long as A and his successors do not permanently terminate the use of the view.

12. A promises to make a gift of a tract of land to B, his son-in-law. B takes possession and lives on the land for 17 years, making valuable improvements. A then dispossesses B, and specific performance is denied because the proof of the terms of the promise is not sufficiently clear and definite. B is entitled to a lien on the land for the value of the improvements, not exceeding their cost.

e. Gratuitous promises to procure insurance. This Section is to be applied with caution to promises to procure insurance. The appropriate remedy for breach of such a promise makes the promisor an insurer, and thus may result in a liability which is very large in relation to the value of the promised service. Often the promise is properly to be construed merely as a promise to use reasonable efforts to procure the insurance, and reliance by the promisee may be unjustified or may be justified only for a short time. Or it may be doubtful whether he did in fact rely. Such difficulties may be removed if the proof of the promise and the reliance are clear, or if the promise is made with some formality, or if part performance or a commercial setting or a potential benefit to the promisor provide a substitute for formality.

Illustrations:

13. A, a bank, lends money to B on the security of a mortgage on B's new home. The mortgage requires B to insure the property. At the closing of the transaction A promises to arrange for the required insurance, and in reliance on the promise B fails to insure. Six months later the property, still uninsured, is destroyed by fire. The promise is binding.

14. A sells an airplane to B, retaining title to secure payment of the price. After the closing A promises to keep the airplane covered by insurance until B can obtain insurance. B could obtain insurance in three days but makes no effort to do so, and the airplane is destroyed after six days. A is not subject to liability by virtue of the promise.

f. Charitable subscriptions, marriage settlements, and other gifts. One of the functions of the doctrine of consideration is to deny enforcement to a promise to make a gift. Such a promise is ordinarily enforced by virtue of the promisee's reliance only if his conduct is foreseeable and reasonable and involves a definite and substantial change of position which would not have occurred if the promise had not been made. In some cases, however, other policies reinforce the promisee's claim. Thus the promisor might be unjustly enriched if he could reclaim the subject of the promised gift after the promisee has improved it.

Subsection (2) identifies two other classes of cases in which the promisee's claim is similarly reinforced. American courts have traditionally favored charitable subscriptions and marriage settlements, and have found consideration in many cases where the element of exchange was doubtful or nonexistent. Where recovery is rested on reliance in such cases, a probability of reliance is enough, and no effort is made to sort out mixed motives or to consider whether partial enforcement would be appropriate.

Illustrations:

15. A promises B $5,000, knowing that B desires that sum for the purchase of a parcel of land. Induced thereby, B secures without any payment an option to buy the parcel. A then tells B that he withdraws his promise. A's promise is not binding.

16. A orally promises to give her son B a tract of land to live on. As A intended, B gives up a homestead elsewhere, takes possession of the land, lives there for a year and makes substantial improvements. A's promise is binding.

17. A orally promises to pay B, a university, $100,000 in five annual installments for the purposes of its fund-raising campaign then in progress. The promise is confirmed in writing by A's agent, and two annual installments are paid before A dies. The continuance of the fund-raising campaign by B is sufficient reliance to make the promise binding on A and his estate.

18. A and B are engaged to be married. In anticipation of the marriage A and his father C enter into a formal written agreement by which C promises to leave certain property to A by will. A's subsequent marriage to B is sufficient reliance to make the promise binding on C and his estate.

§ 91. Effect of Promises Enumerated in §§ 82–90 When Conditional

If a promise within the terms of §§ 82–90 is in terms conditional or performable at a future time the promisor is bound thereby, but performance becomes due only upon the occurrence of the condition or upon the arrival of the specified time.

§ 92. To Whom Promises Enumerated in §§ 82–85 Must Be Made

The new promise referred to in §§ 82–85 is not binding unless it is made to a person who is then an obligee of the antecedent duty.

§ 93. Promises Enumerated in §§ 82–85 Made in Ignorance of Facts

A promise within the terms of §§ 82–85 is not binding unless the promisor knew or had reason to know the essential facts of the previous transaction to which the promise relates, but his knowledge of the legal effect of the facts is immaterial.

§ 94. Stipulations

A promise or agreement with reference to a pending judicial proceeding, made by a party to the proceeding or his attorney, is binding without consideration. By statute or rule of court such an agreement is generally binding only

(a)   if it is in writing and signed by the party or attorney, or

(b)   if it is made or admitted in the presence of the court, or

(c)   to the extent that justice requires enforcement in view of material change of position in reliance on the promise or agreement.

TOPIC 3.   CONTRACTS UNDER SEAL; WRITING AS A STATUTORY SUBSTITUTE FOR THE SEAL

§ 95.   Requirements for Sealed Contract or Written Contract or Instrument

(1)   In the absence of statute a promise is binding without consideration if

(a)   it is in writing and sealed; and

(b)   the document containing the promise is delivered; and

(c)   the promisor and promisee are named in the document or so described as to be capable of identification when it is delivered.

(2)   When a statute provides in effect that a written contract or instrument is binding without consideration or that lack of consideration is an affirmative defense to an action on a written contract or instrument, in order to be subject to the statute a promise must either

(a)   be expressed in a document signed or otherwise assented to by the promisor and delivered; or

(b)   be expressed in a writing or writings to which both promisor and promisee manifest assent.

§ 96.   What Constitutes a Seal

(1)   A seal is a manifestation in tangible and conventional form of an intention that a document be sealed.

(2)   A seal may take the form of a piece of wax, a wafer or other substance affixed to the document or of an impression made on the document.

(3)   By statute or decision in most States in which the seal retains significance a seal may take the form of a written or printed seal, word, scrawl or other sign.

§ 97.   When a Promise Is Sealed

A written promise is sealed if the promisor affixes or impresses a seal on the document or adopts a seal already thereon.

§ 98. Adoption of a Seal by Delivery

Unless extrinsic circumstances manifest a contrary intention, the delivery of a written promise by the promisor amounts to the adoption of any seal then on the document which has apparent reference to his signature or to the signature of another party to the document.

§ 99. Adoption of the Same Seal by Several Parties

Any number of parties to the same instrument may adopt one seal.

§ 100. Recital of Sealing or Delivery

A recital of the sealing or of the delivery of a written promise is not essential to its validity as a contract under seal and is not conclusive of the fact of sealing or delivery unless a statute makes a recital of sealing the equivalent of a seal.

§ 101. Delivery

A written promise, sealed or unsealed, may be delivered by the promisor in escrow, conditionally to the promisee, or unconditionally.

§ 102. Unconditional Delivery

A written promise is delivered unconditionally when the promisor puts it out of his possession and manifests an intention that it is to take effect at once according to its terms.

§ 103. Delivery in Escrow; Conditional Delivery to the Promisee

(1) A written promise is delivered in escrow by the promisor when he puts it into the possession of a person other than the promisee without reserving a power of revocation and manifests an intention that the document is to take effect according to its terms upon the occurrence of a stated condition but not otherwise.

(2) A written promise is delivered conditionally to the promisee when the promisor puts it into the possession of the promisee without reserving a power of revocation and manifests an intention that the document is to take effect according to its terms upon the occurrence of a stated condition but not otherwise.

(3) Delivery of a written promise in escrow or its conditional delivery to the promisee has the same effect as unconditional delivery would have if the requirement of the condition were expressed in the writing.

(4) In the absence of a statute modifying the significance of a seal, delivery of a sealed promise in escrow or its conditional delivery to the promisee is irrevocable for the time specified by the promisor for the occurrence of the condition, or, if no time is specified, for a reasonable time.

§ 104. Acceptance or Disclaimer by the Promisee

(1) Neither acceptance by the promisee nor knowledge by him of the existence of a promise is essential to the formation of a contract by the delivery of a written promise which is binding without consideration.

(2) A promisee who has not manifested assent to a written promise may, within a reasonable time after learning of its existence and terms, render it inoperative by disclaimer.

(3) Acceptance or disclaimer is irrevocable.

§ 105. Acceptance Where Return Promise Is Contemplated

Where a conveyance or a document containing a promise also purports to contain a return promise by the grantee or promisee, acceptance by the grantee or promisee is essential to create any contractual obligation other than an option contract binding on the grantor or promisor.

§ 106. What Amounts to Acceptance of Instrument

Acceptance of a conveyance or of a document containing a promise is a manifestation of assent to the terms thereof made, either before or after delivery, in accordance with any requirements imposed by the grantor or promisor. If the acceptance occurs before delivery and is not binding as an option contract, it is revocable until the moment of delivery.

§ 107. Creation of Unsealed Contract by Acceptance by Promisee

Where a grantee or promisee accepts a sealed document which purports to contain a return promise by him, he makes the return promise. But if he does not sign or seal the document his promise is not under seal, and whether it is binding depends on the rules governing unsealed contracts.

§ 108. Requirement of Naming or Describing Promisor and Promisee

A promise under seal is not binding without consideration unless both the promisor and the promisee are named in the document or so described as to be capable of identification when it is delivered.

§ 109. Enforcement of a Sealed Contract by Promisee Who Does Not Sign or Seal It

The promisee of a promise under seal is not precluded from enforcing it as a sealed contract because he has not signed or sealed the document, unless his doing so was a condition of the delivery, whether or not the document contains a promise by him.

CHAPTER 5. THE STATUTE OF FRAUDS

§ 110. Classes of Contracts Covered

(1) The following classes of contracts are subject to a statute, commonly called the Statute of Frauds, forbidding enforcement unless there is a written memorandum or an applicable exception:

(a) a contract of an executor or administrator to answer for a duty of his decedent (the executor-administrator provision);

(b) a contract to answer for the duty of another (the suretyship provision);

(c) a contract made upon consideration of marriage (the marriage provision);

(d) a contract for the sale of an interest in land (the land contract provision);

(e) a contract that is not to be performed within one year from the making thereof (the one-year provision).

(2) The following classes of contracts, which were traditionally subject to the Statute of Frauds, are now governed by Statute of Frauds provisions of the Uniform Commercial Code:

(a) a contract for the sale of goods for the price of $500 or more (Uniform Commercial Code § 2–201);

(b) a contract for the sale of securities (Uniform Commercial Code § 8–319);

(c) a contract for the sale of personal property not otherwise covered, to the extent of enforcement by way of action or defense beyond $5,000 in amount or value of remedy (Uniform Commercial Code § 1–206).

(3) In addition the Uniform Commercial Code requires a writing signed by the debtor for an agreement which creates or provides for a security interest in personal property or fixtures not in the possession of the secured party.

(4) Statutes in most states provide that no acknowledgment or promise is sufficient evidence of a new or continuing contract to take a case out of the operation of a statute of limitations unless made in some writing signed by the party to be charged, but that the statute does not alter the effect of any payment of principal or interest.

(5) In many states other classes of contracts are subject to a requirement of a writing.

TOPIC 1. THE EXECUTOR-ADMINISTRATOR PROVISION

§ 111. Contract of Executor or Administrator

A contract of an executor or administrator to answer personally for a duty of his decedent is within the Statute of Frauds if a similar contract to answer for the duty of a living person would be within the Statute as a contract to answer for the duty of another.

TOPIC 2. THE SURETYSHIP PROVISION

§ 112. Requirement of Suretyship

A contract is not within the Statute of Frauds as a contract to answer for the duty of another unless the promisee is an obligee of the other's duty, the promisor is a surety for the other, and the promisee knows or has reason to know of the suretyship relation.

§ 113. Promises of the Same Performance for the Same Consideration

Where promises of the same performance are made by two persons for a consideration which inures to the benefit of only one of them, the promise of the other is within the Statute of Frauds as a contract to answer for the duty of another, whether or not the promise is in terms conditional on default by the one to whose benefit the consideration inures, unless

    (a)   the other is not a surety for the one to whose benefit the consideration inures; or

    (b)   the promises are in terms joint and do not create several duties or joint and several duties; or

    (c)   the promisee neither knows nor has reason to know that the consideration does not inure to the benefit of both promisors.

§ 114. Independent Duty of Promisor

A contract to perform or otherwise to satisfy all or part of a duty of a third person to the promisee is not within the Statute of Frauds as a contract to answer for the duty of another if, by the terms of the promise when it is made, performance thereof can involve no more than

    (a)   the application of funds or property held by the promisor for the purpose, or

    (b)   performance of any other duty owing, irrespective of his promise, by the promisor to the promisee, or

    (c)   performance of a duty which is either owing, irrespective of his promise, by the promisor to the third person, or which the promisee reasonably believes to be so owing.

§ 115. Novation

A contract that is itself accepted in satisfaction of a previously existing duty of a third person to the promisee is not within the Statute of Frauds as a contract to answer for the duty of another.

§ 116. Main Purpose; Advantage to Surety

A contract that all or part of a duty of a third person to the promisee shall be satisfied is not within the Statute of Frauds as a promise to answer for the duty of another if the consideration for the promise is in fact or apparently desired by the promisor mainly for his own economic advantage, rather than in order to benefit the third person. If, however, the consideration is merely a premium for insurance, the contract is within the Statute.

Comment:

a.   Rationale. This Section states what is often called the "main purpose" or "leading object" rule. Where the surety-promisor's main purpose is his own pecuniary or business advantage, the gratuitous or sentimental element often present in suretyship is eliminated, the likelihood of disproportion in the values exchanged between promisor and promisee is reduced, and the commercial context commonly provides evidentiary safeguards. Thus there is less need for cautionary or evidentiary formality than in other cases of suretyship. The situation is comparable to a sale or purchase of a third person's obligation, which is also outside the purposes of the suretyship provision of the Statute of Frauds. See §§ 121, 122. Historically, the rule could be reconciled with the words of the Statute on the ground that a promisor who received a bargained-for benefit could be sued in debt or indebitatus assumpsit; hence he promised to pay his own debt rather than the debt "of another," and the promise was not "special" in the sense that special assumpsit was the only appropriate remedy. In modern times, however, the rule is applied in terms of its reason rather than to accord with abandoned procedural categories.

b.   Factors affecting application of the rule. The fact that there is consideration for the surety's promise is insufficient to bring the rule into play. Slight and indirect possible advantage to the promisor is similarly insufficient. The expected advantage must be such as to justify the conclusion that his main purpose in making the promise is to advance his own interests. Facts such as the following tend to indicate such a main purpose when there is an expected pecuniary or business advantage: prior default, inability or repudiation of the principal obligor; forbearance of the creditor to enforce a lien on property in which the promisor has an interest or which he intends to use; equivalence between the value of the benefit and the amount promised; lack of participation by the principal obligor in the making of the surety's promise; a larger transaction to which the suretyship is incidental. The benefit may be supplied to the promisor by the promisee, by the principal obligor, or by some other person; if it is substantial and meets the main purpose test it may come indirectly through benefit to the principal obligor.

Illustrations:

1.   D owes C $1,000. C is about to levy an attachment on D's factory. S, who is a friend of D's desiring to prevent his friend's financial ruin, orally promises C that if

C will forbear to take legal proceedings against D for three months S will pay D's debt if D fails to do so. S has no purpose to benefit himself and C has no reason to suppose so. S's promise is not enforceable.

2. D owes C $1,000. C is about to levy an attachment on D's factory. S, who is also a creditor of D's, fearing that the attachment will ruin D's business and thereby destroy his own chance of collecting his claim, orally promises C that if C will forbear to take legal proceedings against D for three months, S will pay D's debt if D fails to do so. S's promise is enforceable.

3. D contracts with S to build a house for S. C contracts with D to furnish materials for the purpose. D, in violation of his contract with C, fails to pay C for some of the materials furnished. C justifiably refuses to furnish further materials. S orally promises C, that if C will continue to furnish D with materials that C had previously agreed to furnish, S will pay the price not only for the materials already furnished but also for the remaining materials if D fails to do so. S's promise is enforceable.

4. C, a bank, discounts negotiable promissory notes of D, a corporation. D becomes financially involved. An official bank examiner threatens to close the bank on account of the impairment of its assets because of the loans to D. S, a substantial shareholder of the bank, in consideration of forbearance by the examiner, orally promises the bank that if D fails to pay the note, he will do so. The promise of S is enforceable.

c. *Insurance premiums.* The rule of this Section excludes from the main purpose rule contracts of guaranty insurance whether making such contracts is or is not the promisor's regular business. Promises of commercial surety companies are practically always in writing. See Restatement of Security § 82 Comment i, defining "compensated surety." An isolated oral guaranty by an individual is within the reason of the Statute if a small fee is paid for guaranty of a much larger debt.

Illustration:

5. In consideration of a premium of $100, S guarantees C in an unsigned writing the fidelity of D, C's employee, during D's term of employment. The guaranty is not enforceable.

§ 117. Promise to Sign a Written Contract of Suretyship

A promise to sign a written contract as a surety for the performance of a duty owed to the promisee or to sign a negotiable instrument for the accommodation of a person other than the promisee is within the Statute of Frauds.

§ 118. Promise to Indemnify a Surety

A promise to indemnify against liability or loss made to induce the promisee to become a surety is not within the Statute of Frauds as a contract to answer for the duty of another.

§ 119. Assumption of Duty by Another

A contract not within the Statute of Frauds as a contract to answer for the duty of another when made is not brought within it by a subsequent promise of another person to assume performance of the duty as principal obligor.

§ 120. Obligations on Negotiable Instruments

(1) An obligation on a negotiable instrument or a guaranty written on the instrument is not within the Statute of Frauds.

(2) A promise to pay a negotiable instrument, made by a party to it who has been or may be discharged by the holder's failure or delay in making presentment or giving notice of dishonor or in making protest, is not within the Statute of Frauds.

§ 121. Contract of Assignor or Factor

(1) A contract by the assignor of a right that the obligor of the assigned right will perform his duty is not within the Statute of Frauds as a contract to answer for the duty of another.

(2) A contract by an agent with his principal that a purchaser of the principal's goods through the agent will pay their price to the principal is not within the Statute of Frauds as a contract to answer for the duty of another.

§ 122. Contract to Buy a Right From the Obligee

A contract to purchase a right which the promisee has or may acquire against a third person is not within the Statute of Frauds as a contract to answer for the duty of another.

§ 123. Contract to Discharge the Promisee's Duty

A contract to discharge a duty owed by the promisee to a third person is not within the Statute of Frauds as a contract to answer for the duty of another.

TOPIC 3. THE MARRIAGE PROVISION

§ 124. Contract Made Upon Consideration of Marriage

A promise for which all or part of the consideration is either marriage or a promise to marry is within the Statute of Frauds, except in the case of an agreement which consists only of mutual promises of two persons to marry each other.

TOPIC 4. THE LAND CONTRACT PROVISION

§ 125. Contract to Transfer, Buy, or Pay for an Interest in Land

(1) A promise to transfer to any person any interest in land is within the Statute of Frauds.

(2) A promise to buy any interest in land is within the Statute of Frauds, irrespective of the person to whom the transfer is to be made.

(3) When a transfer of an interest in land has been made, a promise to pay the price, if originally within the Statute of Frauds, ceases to be within it unless the promised price is itself in whole or in part an interest in land.

(4) Statutes in most states except from the land contract and one-year provisions of the Statute of Frauds short-term leases and contracts to lease, usually for a term not longer than one year.

§ 126. Contract to Procure Transfer or to Act as Agent

(1) A contract to procure the transfer of an interest in land by a person other than the promisor is within the Statute of Frauds.

(2) A contract to act as agent for another in endeavoring to procure the transfer of any interest in land by someone other than the promisor is not within the Statute of Frauds as a contract for the sale of an interest in land.

§ 127. Interest in Land

An interest in land within the meaning of the Statute is any right, privilege, power or immunity, or combination thereof, which is an interest in land under the law of property and is not "goods" within the Uniform Commercial Code.

§ 128. Boundary and Partition Agreements

(1) A contract between owners of adjoining tracts of land fixing a dividing boundary is within the Statute of Frauds but if the location of the boundary was honestly disputed the contract becomes enforceable notwithstanding the Statute when the agreed boundary has been marked or has been recognized in the subsequent use of the tracts.

(2) A contract by joint tenants or tenants in common to partition land into separate tracts for each tenant is within the Statute of Frauds but becomes enforceable notwithstanding the Statute as to each tract when possession of it is taken in severalty in accordance with the agreement.

§ 129. Action in Reliance; Specific Performance

A contract for the transfer of an interest in land may be specifically enforced notwithstanding failure to comply with the Statute of Frauds if it is established that the party seeking enforcement, in reasonable reliance on the contract and on the continuing assent of the party against whom enforcement is sought, has so changed his position that injustice can be avoided only by specific enforcement.

Comment:

a.   Historical note and modern justifications. This Section restates what is widely known as the "part performance doctrine." Part performance is not an accurate designation of such acts as taking possession and making improvements when the contract does not provide for such acts, but such acts regularly bring the doctrine into play. The doctrine is contrary to the words of the Statute of Frauds, but it was established by English courts of equity soon after the enactment of the Statute. Payment of purchase-money, without more, was once thought sufficient to justify specific enforcement, but a contrary view now prevails, since in such cases restitution is an adequate remedy. English decisions treated a transfer of possession of the land as sufficient, if unequivocally referable to the oral agreement, apparently on the ground that the promise to transfer had been executed by a common-law conveyance. Such decisions are not generally followed in the United States. Enforcement has instead been justified on the ground that repudiation after "part performance" amounts to a "virtual fraud." A more accurate statement is that courts with equitable powers are vested by tradition with what in substance is a dispensing power based on the promisee's reliance, a discretion to be exercised with caution in the light of all the circumstances. Compare § 90.

b.   Rationale. Two distinct elements enter into the application of the rule of this Section: first, the extent to which the evidentiary function of the statutory formalities is fulfilled by the conduct of the parties; second, the reliance of the promisee, providing a compelling substantive basis for relief in addition to the expectations created by the promise. The evidentiary element can be satisfied by painstaking examination of the evidence and realistic appraisal of the probabilities on the part of the trier of fact; this is commonly summarized in a standard that calls upon the trier of the facts to be satisfied by "clear and convincing evidence." The substantive element requires consideration of the adequacy of the remedy of restitution. . . .

d.   Transfer of possession and reasonable reliance. Where specific enforcement is rested on a transfer of possession plus either part payment of the price or the making of improvements, it is commonly said that the action taken by the purchaser must be unequivocally referable to the oral agreement. But this requirement is not insisted on if the making of the promise is admitted or is clearly proved. The promisee must act in reasonable reliance on the promise, before the promisor has repudiated it, and the action must be such that the remedy of restitution is inadequate. If these requirements are met, neither taking of possession nor payment of money nor the making of improvements is essential. Thus, the rendering of peculiar services not readily compensable in money may justify specific performance, particularly if the promisee has also taken other action in reliance on the promise.

TOPIC 5.   THE ONE-YEAR PROVISION

§ 130.   Contract Not to Be Performed Within a Year

(1)   Where any promise in a contract cannot be fully performed within a year from the time the contract is made, all promises in the contract are within the Statute of Frauds until one party to the contract completes his performance.

(2)   When one party to a contract has completed his performance, the one-year provision of the Statute does not prevent enforcement of the promises of other parties.

Comment:

a.   Possibility   of   performance within one year. The English Statute of Frauds applied to an action "upon any agreement that is not to be performed within the space of one year from the making thereof." The design was said to be not to trust to the memory of witnesses for a longer time than one year, but the statutory language was not appropriate to carry out that purpose. The result has been a tendency to construction narrowing the application of the statute. Under the prevailing interpretation, the enforceability of a contract under the one-year provision does not turn on the actual course of subsequent events, nor on the expectations of the parties as to the probabilities. Contracts of uncertain duration are simply excluded; the provision covers only those contracts whose performance cannot possibly be completed within a year.

Illustrations:

   ... 3.   A   and   B,   a   railway, agree that A will provide grading and ties and B will construct a switch and maintain it as long as A needs it for shipping purposes. A plans to use it for shipping lumber from adjoining land which contains enough lumber to run a mill for 30 years, and uses the switch for 15 years. The contract is not within the one-year provision of the Statute.

   4.   A   orally   promises   B   to sell him five crops of potatoes to be grown on a specified farm in Minnesota, and B promises to pay a stated price on delivery. The contract is within the Statute of Frauds. It is impossible in Minnesota for five crops of potatoes to mature in one year.

b.   Discharge within a year. Any contract may be discharged by a subsequent agreement of the parties, and performance of many contracts may be excused by supervening events or by the exercise of a power to cancel granted by the contract. The possibility that such a discharge or excuse may occur within a year is not a possibility that the contract will be "performed" within a year. This is so even though the excuse is articulated in the agreement. This distinction between performance and excuse for nonperformance is sometimes tenuous; it depends on the terms and the circumstances, particularly on whether the essential purposes of the parties will be attained. Discharge by death of the promisor may be the equivalent of performance in case of a promise to forbear, such as a contract not to compete.

TOPIC 6.   SATISFACTION OF THE STATUTE BY A MEMORANDUM

§ 131.   General Requisites of a Memorandum

Unless additional requirements are prescribed by the particular statute, a contract within the Statute of Frauds is enforceable if it is evidenced by any writing, signed by or on behalf of the party to be charged, which

   (a)   reasonably identifies the subject matter of the contract,

(b)   is sufficient to indicate that a contract with respect thereto has been made between the parties or offered by the signer to the other party, and

(c)   states with reasonable certainty the essential terms of the unperformed promises in the contract.

Comment:

. . . *c.*   *Rationale.* The primary purpose of the Statute is evidentiary, to require reliable evidence of the existence and terms of the contract and to prevent enforcement through fraud or perjury of contracts never in fact made. The contents of the writing must be such as to make successful fraud unlikely, but the possibility need not be excluded that some other subject matter or person than those intended will also fall within the words of the writing. Where only an evidentiary purpose is served, the requirement of a memorandum is read in the light of the dispute which arises and the admissions of the party to be charged; there is no need for evidence on points not in dispute.

The suretyship and marriage provisions of the Statute perform a cautionary as well as an evidentiary function. See §§ 112, 124. The land contract provision performs a channeling function. See Statutory Note preceding § 110. Even where these provisions are involved, however, there is no evidence of a statutory purpose to facilitate repudiation of firm oral agreements fairly made, to protect a promisor from temptation to perjure himself by false denial of the promise, or to reward a candid contract-breaker by denying enforcement.

d.   *Types of documents.* The statutory memorandum may be a written contract, but under the traditional statutory language any writing, formal or informal, may be sufficient, including a will, a notation on a check, a receipt, a pleading, or an informal letter. Neither delivery nor communication is essential. See § 133. Writing for this purpose includes any intentional reduction to tangible form. See Uniform Commercial Code § 1–201. . . .

e.   *Subject matter.* A memorandum, like a contract, must be read in its context and need not be comprehensible to persons not familiar with the particular type of transaction. Without reference to executory oral promises, the memorandum in context must indicate with reasonable certainty the nature of the transaction and must provide a basis for identifying the land, goods or other subject matter. . . .

f.   *Contract between the parties.* A memorandum must be sufficient to indicate that a contract has been made between the parties with respect to an identified subject matter or that the signer has offered such a contract to the other party. The parties must be reasonably identified; the identification may consist of a name or initials, even though there may be others with the same name or initials, or of any other reasonably accurate mode of description. Identification of the agent of a party in the memorandum sufficiently refers to the party, whether or not the agent is himself a party. See Restatement, Second, Agency § 153. Where there is no dispute as to the parties, a party may be sufficiently identified by possession of a memorandum signed by the other party. A signed written offer to the public may be sufficient even though the offeree is not identified. . . .

g.   *Terms; accuracy.* The degree of particularity with which the terms of the contract must be set out cannot be reduced to a formula. The writing must be the agreement or a memorandum "thereof"; a memorandum of a different agreement will not suffice. The "essential" terms of unperformed promises must be stated; "details or particulars" need not. What is essential depends on the agreement and its context and also on the subsequent conduct of the parties, including the dispute which arises and the remedy sought. Omission or erroneous statement of an agreed term makes no difference if the same term is supplied by implication or by rule of law. Erroneous statement of a term can sometimes be corrected by reformation. See § 155. Otherwise omission or misstatement of an essential term means that the memorandum is insufficient. Uniform Commercial Code § 2–201, however, states a different rule for sale of goods.

§ 132. Several Writings

The memorandum may consist of several writings if one of the writings is signed and the writings in the circumstances clearly indicate that they relate to the same transaction.

§ 133. Memorandum Not Made as Such

Except in the case of a writing evidencing a contract upon consideration of marriage, the Statute may be satisfied by a signed writing not made as a memorandum of a contract.

§ 134. Signature

The signature to a memorandum may be any symbol made or adopted with an intention, actual or apparent, to authenticate the writing as that of the signer.

§ 135. Who Must Sign

Where a memorandum of a contract within the Statute is signed by fewer than all parties to the contract and the Statute is not otherwise satisfied, the contract is enforceable against the signers but not against the others.

§ 136. Time of Memorandum

A memorandum sufficient to satisfy the Statute may be made or signed at any time before or after the formation of the contract.

§ 137. Loss or Destruction of a Memorandum

The loss or destruction of a memorandum does not deprive it of effect under the Statute.

§ 138. Unenforceability

Where a contract within the Statute of Frauds is not enforceable against the party to be charged by an action against him, it is not enforceable by a set-off or counterclaim in an action brought by him, or as a defense to a claim by him.

TOPIC 7.　CONSEQUENCES OF NON-COMPLIANCE

§ 139.　Enforcement by Virtue of Action in Reliance

(1)　A promise which the promisor should reasonably expect to induce action or forbearance on the part of the promisee or a third person and which does induce the action or forbearance is enforceable <u>notwithstanding the Statute of Frauds</u> if injustice can be avoided only by enforcement of the promise. The remedy granted for breach is to be limited as justice requires.

(2)　In determining whether injustice can be avoided only by enforcement of the promise, the following circumstances are significant:

(a)　the availability and adequacy of other remedies, particularly cancellation and restitution;

(b)　the definite and substantial character of the action or forbearance in relation to the remedy sought;

(c)　the extent to which the action or forbearance corroborates evidence of the making and terms of the promise, or the making and terms are otherwise established by clear and convincing evidence;

(d)　the reasonableness of the action or forbearance;

(e)　the extent to which the action or forbearance was foreseeable by the promisor.

Comment:

a.　Relation to other rules. This Section is complementary to § 90, which dispenses with the requirement of consideration if the same conditions are met, but it also applies to promises supported by consideration. Like § 90, this Section overlaps in some cases with rules based on estoppel or fraud; it states a basic principle which sometimes renders inquiry unnecessary as to the precise scope of other policies. Sections 128 and 129 state particular applications of the same principle to land contracts; §§ 125(3) and 130(2) also rest on it in part. See also Uniform Commercial Code §§ 2–201(3), 8–319(b). Where a promise is made without intention to perform, remedies under this Section may be alternative to remedies for fraud. See Comment b to § 313; Restatement, Second, Torts § 530.

b.　Avoidance of injustice. Like § 90 this Section states a flexible principle, but the requirement of consideration is more easily displaced than the requirement of a writing. The reliance must be foreseeable by the promisor, and enforcement must be necessary to avoid injustice. Subsection (2) lists some of the relevant factors in applying the latter requirement. Each factor relates either to the extent to which reliance furnishes a compelling substantive basis for relief in addition to the expectations created by the promise or to the extent to which the circumstances satisfy the evidentiary purpose of the Statute and fulfill any cautionary, deterrent and channeling functions it may serve.

Illustrations:

1.　A is lessee of a building for five years at $75 per month and has

68

sublet it for three years at $100 per month. A seeks to induce B to purchase the building, and to that end orally promises to assign to B the lease and sublease and to execute a written assignment as soon as B obtains a deed. B purchases the building in reliance on the promise. B is entitled to the rentals from the sublease.

2. A is a pilot with an established airline having rights to continued employment, and could take up to six months leave without prejudice to those rights. He takes such leave to become general manager of B, a small airline which hopes to expand if a certificate to operate over an important route is granted. When his six months leave is about to expire, A demands definite employment because of that fact, and B orally agrees to employ A for two years and on the granting of the certificate to give A an increase in salary and a written contract. In reliance on this agreement A lets his right to return to his prior employer expire. The certificate is soon granted, but A is discharged in breach of the agreement. The Statute of Frauds does not prevent recovery of damages by A.

c.   Particular factors. The force of the factors listed varies in different types of cases, and additional factors may affect particular types of contracts. Thus reliance of the kinds usual in suretyship transactions is not sufficient to justify enforcement of an oral guaranty, where the evidentiary and cautionary functions performed by the statutory formalities are not fulfilled. See Comment a to § 112. In the case of a contract between prospective spouses made upon consideration of marriage, the policy of the Statute is reinforced by a policy against legal interference in the marriage relation, and reliance incident to the marriage relation does not make the contract enforceable. See

Comment d to § 124. Where restitution is an unavailable remedy because to grant it would nullify the statutory purpose, a remedy based on reliance will ordinarily also be denied. See Comment a to § 375.

Illustration:

3. A orally promises to pay B a commission for services in negotiating the sale of a business opportunity, and B finds a purchaser to whom A sells the business opportunity. A statute extends the Statute of Frauds to such promises, and is interpreted to preclude recovery of the reasonable value of such services. The promise is not made enforceable by B's reliance on it.

d.   Partial enforcement; particular remedies. The same factors which bear on whether any relief should be granted also bear on the character and extent of the remedy. In particular, the remedy of restitution is not ordinarily affected by the Statute of Frauds (see § 375); where restitution is an adequate remedy, other remedies are not made available by the rule stated in this Section. Again, when specific enforcement is available under the rule stated in § 129, an ordinary action for damages is commonly less satisfactory, and justice then does not require enforcement in such an action. See Comment c to § 129. In some cases it may be appropriate to measure relief by the extent of the promisee's reliance rather than by the terms of the promise. See § 90 Comment e and Illustrations.

Illustration:

4. A renders services to B under an oral contract within the Statute by which B promises to pay for the services. On discharge without cause in breach of the contract, A is entitled to the reasonable value of the services, but in the absence of additional circumstances is not en-

titled to damages for wrongful discharge.

§ 140.   Defense of Failure to Perform

The Statute of Frauds does not invalidate defenses based on the plaintiff's failure to perform a condition of his claim or defenses based on his present or prospective breach of the contract he seeks to enforce.

§ 141.   Action for Value of Performance Under Unenforceable Contract

(1)   In an action for the value of performance under a contract, except as stated in Subsection (2), the Statute of Frauds does not invalidate any defense which would be available of the contract were enforceable against both parties.

(2)   Where a party to a contract which is unenforceable against him refuses either to perform the contract or to sign a sufficient memorandum, the other party is justified in suspending any performance for which he has not already received the agreed return, and such a suspension is not a defense in an action for the value of performance rendered before the suspension.

§ 142.   Tort Liability for Acts Under Unenforceable Contract

Where because of the existence of a contract conduct would not be tortious, unenforceability of the contract under the Statute of Frauds does not make the conduct tortious if it occurs without notice of repudiation of the contract.

§ 143.   Unenforceable Contract as Evidence

The Statute of Frauds does not make an unenforceable contract inadmissible in evidence for any purpose other than its enforcement in violation of the Statute.

§ 144.   Effect of Unenforceable Contract as to Third Parties

Only a party to a contract or a transferee or successor of a party to the contract can assert that the contract is unenforceable under the Statute of Frauds.

§ 145.   Effect of Full Performance

Where the promises in a contract have been fully performed by all parties, the Statute of Frauds does not affect the legal relations of the parties.

§ 146.   Rights of Competing Transferees of Property

(1)   Where a contract to transfer property or a transfer was unenforceable against the transferor under the Statute of Frauds but subsequently becomes enforceable, the contract or transfer has whatever priority it

would have had aside from the Statute of Frauds over an intervening contract by the transferor to transfer the same property to a third person.

(2)   If the third person obtains title to the property by an enforceable transaction before the prior contract becomes enforceable, the prior contract is unenforceable against him and does not affect his title.

§ 147.   Contract Containing Multiple Promises

(1)   Where performance of the promises in a contract which subject it to the Statute of Frauds is exclusively beneficial to one party, that party by agreeing to forego the performance may render the remainder of the contract enforceable, but this rule does not apply to a contract to transfer property on the promisor's death.

(2)   Where the promises in a contract which subject it to the Statute have become enforceable or where the duty to perform them has been discharged by performance or otherwise, the Statute does not prevent enforcement of the remaining promises.

(3)   Except as stated in this Section, where some of the unperformed promises in a contract are unenforceable against a party under the Statute of Frauds, all the promises in the contract are unenforceable against him.

§ 148.   Rescission by Oral Agreement

Notwithstanding the Statute of Frauds, all unperformed duties under an enforceable contract may be discharged by an oral agreement of rescission. The Statute may, however, apply to a contract to rescind a transfer of property.

§ 149.   Oral Modification

(1)   For the purpose of determining whether the Statute of Frauds applies to a contract modifying but not rescinding a prior contract, the second contract is treated as containing the originally agreed terms as modified. The Statute may, however, apply independently of the original terms to a contract to modify a transfer of property.

(2)   Where the second contract is unenforceable by virtue of the Statute of Frauds and there has been no material change of position in reliance on it, the prior contract is not modified.

§ 150.   Reliance on Oral Modification

Where the parties to an enforceable contract subsequently agree that all or part of a duty need not be performed or of a condition need not occur, the Statute of Frauds does not prevent enforcement of the subsequent agreement if reinstatement of the original terms would be unjust in view of a material change of position in reliance on the subsequent agreement.

CHAPTER 6. MISTAKE

§ 151. Mistake Defined

A mistake is a belief that is not in accord with the facts.

Comment:

a. Belief as to facts. In this Restatement the word "mistake" is used to refer to an erroneous belief. A party's erroneous belief is therefore said to be a "mistake" of that party. The belief need not be an articulated one, and a party may have a belief as to a fact when he merely makes an assumption with respect to it, without being aware of alternatives. The word "mistake" is not used here, as it is sometimes used in common speech, to refer to an improvident act, including the making of a contract, that is the result of such an erroneous belief. This usage is avoided here for the sake of clarity and consistency. Furthermore, the erroneous belief must relate to the facts as they exist at the time of the making of the contract. A party's prediction or judgment as to events to occur in the future, even if erroneous, is not a "mistake" as that word is defined here. An erroneous belief as to the contents or effect of a writing that expresses the agreement is, however, a mistake. Mistake alone, in the sense in which the word is used here, has no legal consequences. The legal consequences of mistake in connection with the creation of contractual liability are determined by the rules stated in the rest of this Chapter.

Illustrations:

1. A contracts with B to raise and float B's boat which has run aground on a reef. At the time of making the contract, A believes that the sea will remain calm until the work is completed. Several days later, during a sudden storm, the boat slips into deep water and fills with mud, making it more difficult for A to raise it. Although A may have shown poor judgment in making the contract, there was no mistake of either A or B, and the rules stated in this Chapter do not apply. Whether A is discharged by supervening impracticability is governed by the rules stated in Chapter 11. See Illustration 5 to § 261. If, however, the boat had already slipped into deep water at the time the contract was made, although they both believed that it was still on the reef, there would have been a mistake of both A and B. Its legal consequences, if any, would be governed by the rule stated in § 152.

2. A contracts to sell and B to buy stock amounting to a controlling interest in C Corporation. At the time of making the contract, both A and B believe that C Corporation will have earnings of $1,000,000 during the following fiscal year. Because of a subsequent economic recession, C Corporation earns less than $500,000 during that year. Although B may have shown poor judgment in making the contract, there was no mistake of either A or B, and the rules stated in this Chapter do not apply. See Uniform Commercial Code § 8–306(2).

b. Facts include law. The rules stated in this Chapter do not draw the distinction that is sometimes made between "fact" and "law." They treat the law in existence at the time of the making of the contract as part of the total state of facts at that time. A party's erroneous belief with respect to the law, as found in statute, regulation, judicial decision, or elsewhere, or with respect to the legal consequences of his acts, may, therefore, come within these rules.

Illustration:

3.   A contracts to sell a tract of land to B. Both parties understand that B plans to erect an office building on the land and believe that he can lawfully do so. Unknown to them, two days earlier a municipal ordinance was enacted requiring a permit for lawful erection of such a building. There is a mistake of both A and B. Its legal consequences, if any, are governed by the rule stated in § 152. See Illustration 7 to § 152.

§ 152.   When Mistake of Both Parties Makes a Contract Voidable

(1)   Where a mistake of both parties at the time a contract was made as to a basic assumption on which the contract was made has a material effect on the agreed exchange of performances, the contract is voidable by the adversely affected party unless he bears the risk of the mistake under the rule stated in § 154.

(2)   In determining whether the mistake has a material effect on the agreed exchange of performances, account is taken of any relief by way of reformation, restitution, or otherwise.

Comment:

a.   Rationale. Before making a contract, a party ordinarily evaluates the proposed exchange of performances on the basis of a variety of assumptions with respect to existing facts. Many of these assumptions are shared by the other party, in the sense that the other party is aware that they are made. The mere fact that both parties are mistaken with respect to such an assumption does not, of itself, afford a reason for avoidance of the contract by the adversely affected party. Relief is only appropriate in situations where a mistake of both parties has such a material effect on the agreed exchange of performances as to upset the very basis for the contract.

This Section applies to such situations. Under it, the contract is voidable by the adversely affected party if three conditions are met. First, the mistake must relate to a "basic assumption on which the contract was made." Second, the party seeking avoidance must show that the mistake has a material effect on the agreed exchange of performances. Third, the mistake must not be one as to which the party seeking relief bears the risk. The parol evidence rule does not preclude the use of prior or contemporaneous agreements or negotiations to establish that the parties were mistaken. See § 214(d). However, since mistakes are the exception rather than the rule, the trier of the facts should examine the evidence with particular care when a party attempts to avoid liability by proving mistake. See Comment c to § 155. The rule stated in this Section is subject to that in § 157 on fault of the party seeking relief. It is also subject to the rules on exercise of the power of avoidance stated in §§ 378–85.

b.   Basic assumption. A mistake of both parties does not make the contract voidable unless it is one as to a basic assumption on which both parties made the contract. The term "basic assumption" has the same meaning here as it does in Chapter 11 in connection with impracticability (§§ 261, 266(1)) and frustration (§§ 265, 266(2)). See Uniform Commercial Code § 2–615(a). For example, market conditions and the financial situation of the parties are ordinarily not such assumptions, and, generally, just as shifts in market conditions or financial ability do not effect discharge under the rules governing impracticability, mistakes as to market conditions or financial ability do not justify avoidance under the rules governing mistake. See Comment b to § 261. The parties may have had such a "basic assumption," even though they were not conscious of alternatives. See Introductory Note to Chapter 11. Where, for example, a party purchases an annuity on the life of another person, it can be said that it was a basic assumption that the other person was alive at the time, even though the parties never consciously addressed themselves to the possibility that he was dead. See Illustration 6.

Illustrations:

1.   A contracts to sell and B to buy a tract of land, the value of which has depended mainly on the timber on it. Both A and B believe that the timber is still there, but in fact it has been destroyed by fire. The contract is voidable by B.

2.   A contracts to sell and B to buy a tract of land, on the basis of the report of a surveyor whom A has employed to determine the acreage. The price is, however, a lump sum not calculated from the acreage. Because of an error in computation by the surveyor, the tract contains ten per cent more acreage than he reports. The contract is voidable by A. Compare Illustrations 8 and 11 to this Section and Illustration 2 to § 158.

3.   A contracts to sell and B to buy a tract of land. B agrees to pay A $100,000 in cash and to assume a mortgage that C holds on the tract. Both A and B believe that the amount of the mortgage is $50,000, but in fact it is only $10,000. The contract is voidable by A, unless the court supplies a term under which B is entitled to enforce the contract if he agrees to pay an appropriate

additional sum, and B does so. See Illustration 2 to § 158.

4.   A contracts to sell and B to buy a debt owed by C to A, and secured by a mortgage. Both A and B believe that there is a building on the mortgaged land so that the value of the mortgaged property exceeds that of the debt, but in fact there is none so that its value is less than half that of the debt. The contract is voidable by B. See § 333.

5.   A contracts to assign to B for $100 a $10,000 debt owed to A by C, who is insolvent. Both A and B believe that the debt is unsecured and is therefore, virtually worthless, but in fact it is secured by stock worth approximately $5,000. The contract is voidable by A.

6.   A pays B, an insurance company, $100,000 for an annuity contract under which B agrees to make quarterly payments to C, who is 50 years old, in a fixed amount for the rest of C's life. A and B believe that C is in good health and has a normal life expectancy, but in fact C is dead. The contract is voidable by A.

c.   Material effect on agreed exchange. A party cannot avoid a contract merely because both parties were mistaken as to a basic assumption on which it was made. He must, in addition, show that the mistake has a material effect on the agreed exchange of performances. It is not enough for him to prove that he would not have made the contract had it not been for the mistake. He must show that the resulting imbalance in the agreed exchange is so severe that he can not fairly be required to carry it out. Ordinarily he will be able to do this by showing that the exchange is not only less desirable to him but is also more advantageous to the other party. Sometimes this is so because the adversely affected party will give, and the other party will receive, something more than they supposed. Sometimes it is so because the other party will give, and the adversely affected party will receive, something less than they supposed. In such cases the materiality of the effect on the agreed exchange will be determined by the overall impact on both parties. In exceptional cases the adversely affected party may be able to show that the effect on the agreed exchange has been material simply on the ground that the exchange has become less desirable for him, even though there has been no effect on the other party. Cases of hardship that result in no advantage to the other party are, however, ordinarily appropriately left to the rules on impracticability and frustration. See Illustration 9 and § 266. The standard of materiality here, as elsewhere in this Restatement (e.g., § 237), is a flexible one to be applied in the light of all the circumstances.

Illustrations:

7.   The facts being as stated in Illustration 3 to § 151, in determining whether the effect on the agreed exchange is material, and the contract therefore voidable by B, the court will consider not only the decrease in its desirability to B but also any advantage to A through his receiving a higher price than the land would have brought on the market had the facts been known. See Illustration 3 to § 151.

8.   A contracts to sell and B to buy a tract of land, which they believe contains 100 acres, at a price of $1,000 an acre. In fact the tract contains 110 acres. The contract is not voidable by either A or B, unless additional facts show that the effect on the agreed exchange of performances is material.

9.   A contracts to sell and B to buy a dredge which B tells A he intends to use for a special and unusual purpose, but B does not rely

on A's skill and judgment. A and B believe that the dredge is fit for B's purpose, but in fact it is not, although it is merchantable. The contract is not voidable by B because the effect on the agreed exchange of performances is not material. If B's purpose is substantially frustrated, he may have relief under § 266(2). See also Uniform Commercial Code §§ 2–314, 2–315.

d.   Significance of other relief. Under the rule stated in Subsection (2), before determining the effect on the agreed exchange, the court will first take account of any relief that may be available to him or granted to the other party under the rules stated in §§ 155 (see Illustration 10) and 158 (see Illustration 11). A party may choose to seek relief by means of reformation even though it makes his own performance more onerous when, absent reformation, the contract would be voidable by the other party. See Introductory Note and Comment e to § 155.

Illustrations:

10.   A and B agree that A will sell and B will buy a tract of land for $100,000, payable by $50,000 in cash and the assumption of an existing mortgage of $50,000. In reducing the agreement to writing, B's lawyer erroneously omits the provision for assumption of the mortgage, and neither A nor B notices the omission. Under the rule stated in § 155, at the request of either party, the court will decree that the writing be reformed to add the provision for assumption of the mortgage. The contract is, therefore, not voidable by A because, when account is taken of the availability to him of reformation, the effect on the agreed exchange of performances is not material. See Illustration 1 to § 155.

11.   A contracts to sell and B to buy a tract of land, described in the

contract as containing 100 acres, at a price of $100,000, calculated from the acreage at $1,000 an acre. In fact the tract contains only 90 acres. If B is entitled to a reduction in price of $10,000, under the rule stated in § 158(2), the contract is not voidable by B because when account is taken of the availability to him of a reduction in price, the effect on the agreed exchange of performances is not material. See Illustration 1 to § 158. As to the possibility of an argument based on frustration, see § 266(2).

e.   Allocation of risk. A party may be considered to have undertaken to perform in spite of a mistake that has a material effect on the agreed exchange of performances. He then bears the risk of the mistake. Because of the significance of the allocation of risk in the law of mistake, the scope of this exception is spelled out in detail in § 154. (It is assumed in the illustrations to the present Section that the adversely affected party does not bear the risk of the mistake under the rule stated in § 154. See, e.g., Illustration 14.)

f.   Releases. Releases of claims have afforded particularly fertile ground for the invocation of the rule stated in this Section. It is, of course, a traditional policy of the law to favor compromises as a means of settling claims without resort to litigation. See Comment a to § 74. Nevertheless, a claimant who has executed such a release may later wish to attack it. The situation may arise with respect to any claim, but a particularly common example involves claims for personal injury, where the claimant may have executed the release without full knowledge of the extent or, perhaps, even of the nature of his injuries. Such a claimant has a variety of possible grounds for attacking the release on discovering that his injuries are more serious than he had initially supposed. He may seek to have the release interpreted against the draftsman so as to be inapplicable to the newly discovered injuries (§ 206). He may seek to have the release reformed on the ground that it does not correctly express the prior agreement of the parties (§ 155). He may seek to avoid the release on the ground that it was unfairly obtained through misrepresentation, duress or undue influence (Chapter 7). He may seek to have the release, or at least that part purporting to cover the newly discovered injuries, held unenforceable as unconscionable (§ 208). Or he may seek to avoid the release on the ground that both he and the other party were mistaken as to the nature or extent of his injuries. Assuming that the release is properly interpreted to cover unknown injuries and that it was not unfairly obtained or unconscionable, his case will turn on the application of the rule stated in this Section to his claim of mistake. In dealing with such attacks on releases, a court should be particularly sensitive to obscure or misleading language and especially alert to the possibility of unfairness or unconscionability. However, the same rules relating to mistake apply to such releases as apply to other contracts, and if the results sometimes seem at variance with those rules, the variance can usually be attributed to the presence of one of the alternative grounds listed above.

A claimant's attempt at avoidance based on mistake of both parties, therefore, will frequently turn on a determination, in the light of all the circumstances, of the basic assumptions of the parties at the time of the release. These circumstances may include the fair amount that would be required to compensate the claimant for his known injuries, the probability that the other party would be held liable on that claim, the amount received by the claimant in settlement of his claim, and the relationship between the known injuries and the newly discovered injuries. If, for example, the amount received by the claimant is reasonable in comparison with the fair amount required to compensate him for his known injuries and the probability of the other party being held liable on that claim, this suggests that the parties assumed that his injuries were only those known. Furthermore, even if the parties do not assume that his injuries are only those known, they may assume that any unknown injuries are of the same general nature as the known ones, while differing in extent. Although the parties may fix the assumptions on which the contract is based by an express provision, fairly bargained for, the common recital that the release covers all injuries, known or unknown and of whatever nature or extent, may be disregarded as unconscionable if, in view of the circumstances of the parties, their legal representation, and the setting of the negotiations, it flies in the face of what would otherwise be regarded as a basic assumption of the parties. What has been said here with respect to releases of claims for personal injury is generally true for releases executed in other contexts.

Illustrations:

12.   A has a claim against B for B's admitted negligence, which appears to have caused damage to A's automobile in an amount fairly valued at $600. In consideration of B's payment of $600, A executes a release of "all claims for injury to person or property" that he may have against B. Both A and B believe that A has suffered damage to property only, but A later discovers that he has also suffered personal injuries in the extent of $20,000. The release is voidable by A.

13.   A has a claim against B for B's admitted negligence, which appears to have caused personal injuries to A's back in an amount fairly valued at $10,000, although the parties are aware that A may re-quire further treatment. In consideration of B's payment of $15,000, A executes a release of "all claims for injury to person or property" that he may have against B. A later incurs additional expenses of $20,000 in connection with his back, which was injured more seriously than he had believed. The release is not voidable by A.

g.   *Relation to breach of warranty.* The rule stated in this Section has a close relationship to the rules governing warranties sale by a seller of goods or of other kinds of property. A buyer usually finds it more advantageous to rely on the law of warranty than on the law of mistake. Because of the broad scope of a seller's warranties, a buyer is more often entitled to relief based on a claim of breach of warranty than on a claim based on mistake. Furthermore, because relief for breach of warranty is generally based on the value that the property would have had if it had been as warranted (see Uniform Commercial Code § 2–714(2)), it is ordinarily more extensive than that afforded if he merely seeks to avoid the contract on the ground of mistake. Nevertheless, the warranties are not necessarily exclusive and, even absent a warranty, a buyer may be able to avoid on the ground of mistake if he brings himself within the rule stated in this Section. The effect, on a buyer's claim of mistake, of language purporting to disclaim the seller's responsibility for the goods is governed by the rules on interpretation stated in Chapter 9.

Illustration:

14.   A, a violinist, contracts to sell and B, another violinist, to buy a violin. Both A and B believe that the violin is a Stradivarius, but in fact it is a clever imitation. A makes no express warranty and, because he is not a merchant with respect to violins, makes no implied warranty of merchantability under Uniform

Commercial Code § 2–314. The contract is voidable by B.

h.   Mistakes as to different assumptions. The rule stated in this Section applies only where both parties are mistaken as to the same basic assumption. Their mistakes need not be, and often they will not be, identical. If, however, the parties are mistaken as to different assumptions, the rule stated in § 153, rather than that stated in this Section, applies.

§ 153.   When Mistake of One Party Makes a Contract Voidable

Where a mistake of one party at the time a contract was made as to a basic assumption on which he made the contract has a material effect on the agreed exchange of performances that is adverse to him, the contract is voidable by him if he does not bear the risk of the mistake under the rule stated in § 154, and

(a)   the effect of the mistake is such that enforcement of the contract would be unconscionable, or

(b)   the other party had reason to know of the mistake or his fault caused the mistake.

Comment:

. . . b.   Similarity to rule where both are mistaken. In order for a party to have the power to avoid a contract for a mistake that he alone made, he must at least meet the same requirements that he would have had to meet had both parties been mistaken (§ 152). The mistake must be one as to a basic assumption on which the contract was made; it must have a material effect on the agreed exchange of performances; and the mistaken party must not bear the risk of the mistake. The most common sorts of such mistakes occur in bids on construction contracts and result from clerical errors in the computation of the price or in the omission of component items. . . . Where only one party is mistaken, however, he must meet either the additional requirement stated in Subparagraph (a) or one of the additional requirements stated in Subparagraph (b).

c.   Additional requirement of unconscionability. Under Subparagraph (a), the mistaken party must in addition show that enforcement of the contract would be unconscionable. The reason for this additional requirement is that, if only one party was mistaken, avoidance of the contract will more clearly disappoint the expectations of the other party than if he too was mistaken. . . . The mistaken party bears the substantial burden of establishing unconscionability and must ordinarily show not only the position he would have been in had the facts been as he believed them to be but also the position in which he finds himself as a result of his mistake. For example, in the typical case of a mistake as to the price in a bid, the builder must show the profit or loss that will result if he is required to perform, as well as the profit that he would have made had there been no mistake. . . .

f.   Allocation of risk. Here, as under § 152, a party may undertake to perform in spite of a mistake that would otherwise allow him to avoid the contract. It is, of course, unusual for a party to bear the risk of a mistake that the other party had reason to know of or that was caused by his fault within Subparagraph (b). Because of the significance of allocation of risk in the law of mistake, the scope of this exception is spelled out in detail in § 154. . . .

§ 154. When a Party Bears the Risk of a Mistake

A party bears the risk of a mistake when

(a)   the risk is allocated to him by agreement of the parties, or

(b)   he is aware, at the time the contract is made, that he has only limited knowledge with respect to the facts to which the mistake relates but treats his limited knowledge as sufficient, or

(c)   the risk is allocated to him by the court on the ground that it is reasonable in the circumstances to do so.

Comment:

a.   Rationale. Absent provision to the contrary, a contracting party takes the risk of most supervening changes in circumstances, even though they upset basic assumptions and unexpectedly affect the agreed exchange of performances, unless there is such extreme hardship as will justify relief on the ground of impracticability of performance or frustration of purpose. A party also bears the risk of many mistakes as to existing circumstances even though they upset basic assumptions and unexpectedly affect the agreed exchange of performances. For example, it is commonly understood that the seller of farm land generally cannot avoid the contract of sale upon later discovery by both parties that the land contains valuable mineral deposits, even though the price was negotiated on the basic assumption that the land was suitable only for farming and the effect on the agreed exchange of performances is material. In such a case a court will ordinarily allocate the risk of the mistake to the seller, so that he is under a duty to perform regardless of the mistake. The rule stated in this Section determines whether a party bears the risk of a mistake for the purposes of both §§ 152 and 153. Stating these rules in terms of the allocation of risk avoids such artificial and specious distinctions as are sometimes drawn between "intrinsic" and "extrinsic" mistakes or between mistakes that go to the "identity" or "existence" of the subject matter and those that go merely to its "attributes," "quality" or "value." Even though a mistaken party does not bear the risk of a mistake, he may be barred from avoidance if the mistake was the result of his failure to act in good faith and in accordance with reasonable standards of fair dealing. See § 157.

b.   Allocation by agreement. The most obvious case of allocation of the risk of a mistake is one in which the parties themselves provide for it by their agreement. Just as a party may agree to perform in spite of impracticability or frustration that would otherwise justify his non-performance, he may also agree, by appropriate language or other manifestations, to perform in spite of mistake that would otherwise justify his avoidance. An insurer, for example, may expressly undertake the risk of loss of property covered as of a date already past. Whether the agreement places the risk on the mistaken party is a question to be answered under the rules generally applicable to the scope of contractual obligations, including those on interpretation, usage and unconscionability. See Chapter 9.

Illustration:

1.   A contracts to sell and B to buy a tract of land. A and B both believe that A has good title, but neither has made a title search. The contract provides that A will convey only such title as he has, and A makes no representation with respect to title. In fact, A's title is

defective. The contract is not voidable by B, because the risk of the mistake is allocated to B by agreement of the parties.

c.   Conscious ignorance. Even though the mistaken party did not agree to bear the risk, he may have been aware when he made the contract that his knowledge with respect to the facts to which the mistake relates was limited. If he was not only so aware that his knowledge was limited but undertook to perform in the face of that awareness, he bears the risk of the mistake. It is sometimes said in such a situation that, in a sense, there was not mistake but "conscious ignorance."

Illustration:

2.   The facts being otherwise as stated in Illustration 2 to § 152, A proposes to B during the negotiations the inclusion of a provision under which the adversely affected party can cancel the contract in the event of a material error in the surveyor's report, but B refuses to agree to such a provision. The contract is not voidable by A, because A bears the risk of the mistake.

d.   Risk allocated by the court. In some instances it is reasonably clear that a party should bear the risk of a mistake for reasons other than those stated in Subparagraphs (a) and (b). In such instances, under the rule stated in Subparagraph (c), the court will allocate the risk to that party on the ground that it is reasonable to do so. A court will generally do this, for example, where the seller of farm land seeks to avoid the contract of sale on the ground that valuable mineral rights have newly been found. See Comment a. In dealing with such issues, the court will consider the purposes of the parties and will have recourse to its own general knowledge of human behavior in bargain transactions, as it will in the analogous situation in which it is asked to supply a term under the rule stated

in § 204. The rule stated in Subsection (c) is subject to contrary agreement and to usage (§ 221).

Illustrations:

3.   The facts being otherwise as stated in Illustration 6 to § 152, C is not dead but is afflicted with an incurable fatal disease and cannot live more than a year. The contract is not voidable by A, because the court will allocate to A the risk of the mistake.

4.   A, an owner of land, and B, a builder, make a contract under which B is to take from A's land, at a stated rate per cubic yard, all the gravel and earth necessary for the construction of a bridge, an amount estimated to be 114,000 cubic yards. A and B believe that all of the gravel and earth is above water level and can be removed by ordinary means, but in fact about one quarter of it is below water level, so that removal will require special equipment at an additional cost of about twenty percent. The contract is not voidable by B, because the court will allocate to B the risk of the mistake. Compare Illustration 5 to § 266.

5.   A contracts with B to build a house on B's land. A and B believe that subsoil conditions are normal, but in fact some of the land must be drained at an expense that will leave A no profit under the contract. The contract is not voidable by A, because the court will allocate to A the risk of the mistake. Compare Illustration 8 to § 266.

6.   The facts being otherwise as stated in Illustration 1 to § 153, the $50,000 error in A's bid is the result of A's mistaken estimate as to the amount of labor required to do the work. A cannot avoid the contract, because the court will allocate to A the risk of the mistake.

§ 155. When Mistake of Both Parties as to Written Expression Justifies Reformation

Where a writing that evidences or embodies an agreement in whole or in part fails to express the agreement because of a mistake of both parties as to the contents or effect of the writing, the court may at the request of a party reform the writing to express the agreement, except to the extent that rights of third parties such as good faith purchasers for value will be unfairly affected.

§ 156. Mistake as to Contract Within the Statute of Frauds

If reformation of a writing is otherwise appropriate, it is not precluded by the fact that the contract is within the Statute of Frauds.

§ 157. Effect of Fault of Party Seeking Relief

A mistaken party's fault in failing to know or discover the facts before making the contract does not bar him from avoidance or reformation under the rules stated in this Chapter, unless his fault amounts to a failure to act in good faith and in accordance with reasonable standards of fair dealing.

§ 158. Relief Including Restitution

(1) In any case governed by the rules stated in this Chapter, either party may have a claim for relief including restitution under the rules stated in §§ 240 and 376.

(2) In any case governed by the rules stated in this Chapter, if those rules together with the rules stated in Chapter 16 will not avoid injustice, the court may grant relief on such terms as justice requires including protection of the parties' reliance interest.

CHAPTER 7. MISREPRESENTATION, DURESS AND UNDUE INFLUENCE

TOPIC 1. MISREPRESENTATION

§ 159. Misrepresentation Defined

A misrepresentation is an assertion that is not in accord with the facts.

§ 160. When Action is Equivalent to an Assertion (Concealment)

Action intended or known to be likely to prevent another from learning a fact is equivalent to an assertion that the fact does not exist.

§ 161.   When Non-Disclosure Is Equivalent to an Assertion

A person's non-disclosure of a fact known to him is equivalent to an assertion that the fact does not exist in the following cases only:

    (a)   where he knows that disclosure of the fact is necessary to prevent some previous assertion from being a misrepresentation or from being fraudulent or material.

    (b)   where he knows that disclosure of the fact would correct a mistake of the other party as to a basic assumption on which that party is making the contract and if non-disclosure of the fact amounts to a failure to act in good faith and in accordance with reasonable standards of fair dealing.

    (c)   where he knows that disclosure of the fact would correct a mistake of the other party as to the contents or effect of a writing, evidencing or embodying an agreement in whole or in part.

    (d)   where the other person is entitled to know the fact because of a relation of trust and confidence between them.

Comment:

. . . d.   Known mistake as to a basic assumption. In many situations, if one party knows that the other is mistaken as to a basic assumption, he is expected to disclose the fact that would correct the mistake. A seller of real or personal property is, for example, ordinarily expected to disclose a known latent defect of quality or title that is of such a character as would probably prevent the buyer from buying at the contract price. An owner is ordinarily expected to disclose a known error in a bid that he has received from a contractor. See Comment e to § 153. The mistake must be as to a basic assumption, as is also required by the rules on mistake stated in § 152 (see Illustrations 4, 5 and 6) and § 153 (see Illustrations 8 and 9). The rule stated in Clause (b), is, however, broader than these rules for mistake because it does not require a showing of a material effect on the agreed exchange and is not affected by the fact that the party seeking relief bears the risk of the mistake (§ 154). Nevertheless, a party need not correct all mistakes of the other and is expected only to act in good faith and in accordance with reasonable standards of fair dealing, as reflected in prevailing business ethics. A party may, therefore, reasonably expect the other to take normal steps to inform himself and to draw his own conclusions. If the other is indolent, inexperienced or ignorant, or if his judgment is bad or he lacks access to adequate information, his adversary is not generally expected to compensate for these deficiencies. A buyer of property, for example, is not ordinarily expected to disclose circumstances that make the property more valuable than the seller supposes. Compare Illustrations 10 and 11. In contrast to the rules stated in Clauses (a) and (d), that stated in Clause (b) is limited to non-disclosure by a party to the transaction. Actual knowledge is required for the application of the rule stated in Clause (b). The case of a party who does not know but has reason to know of a mistake is governed by the rule stated in § 153(b). As to knowledge in the case of an organization, see the analogous rule in Uniform Commercial Code § 1–201(27).

Illustrations:

5. A, seeking to induce B to make a contract to buy A's house, knows that B does not know that the house is riddled with termites but does not disclose this to B. B makes the contract. A's non-disclosure is equivalent to an assertion that the house is not riddled with termites, and this assertion is a misrepresentation. Whether the contract is voidable by B is determined by the rule stated in § 164. . . .

7. A, seeking to induce B to make a contract to sell land, knows that B does not know that the land has appreciably increased in value because of a proposed shopping center but does not disclose this to B. B makes the contract. Since B's mistake is not one as to a basic assumption . . ., A's non-disclosure is not equivalent to an assertion that the value of the land has not appreciably increased, and this assertion is not a misrepresentation. The contract is not voidable by B. . . .

10. A, seeking to induce B to make a contract to sell A land, learns from government surveys that the land contains valuable mineral deposits and knows that B does not know this, but does not disclose this to B. B makes the contract. A's non-disclosure does not amount to a failure to act in good faith and in accordance with reasonable standards of fair dealing and is therefore not equivalent to an assertion that the land does not contain valuable mineral deposits. The contract is not voidable by B.

11. The facts being otherwise as stated in Illustration 10, A learns of the valuable mineral deposits from trespassing on B's land and not from government surveys. A's non-disclosure is equivalent to an assertion that the land does not contain valuable mineral deposits, and this assertion is a misrepresentation. Whether the contract is voidable by B is determined by the rule stated in § 164.

§ 162. When a Misrepresentation Is Fraudulent or Material

(1) A misrepresentation is fraudulent if the maker intends his assertion to induce a party to manifest his assent and the maker

    (a) knows or believes that the assertion is not in accord with the facts, or

    (b) does not have the confidence that he states or implies in the truth of the assertion, or

    (c) knows that he does not have the basis that he states or implies for the assertion.

(2) A misrepresentation is material if it would be likely to induce a reasonable person to manifest his assent, or if the maker knows that it would be likely to induce the recipient to do so.

§ 163. When a Misrepresentation Prevents Formation of a Contract

If a misrepresentation as to the character or essential terms of a proposed contract induces conduct that appears to be a manifestation of assent by one who neither knows nor has reasonable opportunity to know of the character or essential terms of the proposed contract, his conduct is not effective as a manifestation of assent.

§ 164.   When a Misrepresentation Makes a Contract Voidable

(1)   If a party's manifestation of assent is induced by either a fraudulent or a material misrepresentation by the other party upon which the recipient is justified in relying, the contract is voidable by the recipient.

(2)   If a party's manifestation of assent is induced by either a fraudulent or a material misrepresentation by one who is not a party to the transaction upon which the recipient is justified in relying, the contract is voidable by the recipient, unless the other party to the transaction in good faith and without reason to know of the misrepresentation either gives value or relies materially on the transaction.

§ 165.   Cure by Change of Circumstances

If a contract is voidable because of a misrepresentation and, before notice of an intention to avoid the contract, the facts come into accord with the assertion, the contract is no longer voidable unless the recipient has been harmed by relying on the misrepresentation.

§ 166.   When a Misrepresentation as to a Writing Justifies Reformation

If a party's manifestation of assent is induced by the other party's fraudulent misrepresentation as to the contents or effect of a writing evidencing or embodying in whole or in part an agreement, the court at the request of the recipient may reform the writing to express the terms of the agreement as asserted,

(a)   if the recipient was justified in relying on the misrepresentation, and

(b)   except to the extent that rights of third parties such as good faith purchasers for value will be unfairly affected.

§ 167.   When a Misrepresentation Is an Inducing Cause

A misrepresentation induces a party's manifestation of assent if it substantially contributes to his decision to manifest his assent.

§ 168.   Reliance on Assertions of Opinion

(1)   An assertion is one of opinion if it expresses only a belief, without certainty, as to the existence of a fact or expresses only a judgment as to quality, value, authenticity, or similar matters.

(2)   If it is reasonable to do so, the recipient of an assertion of a person's opinion as to facts not disclosed and not otherwise known to the recipient may properly interpret it as an assertion

(a)   that the facts known to that person are not incompatible with his opinion, or

(b)   that he knows facts sufficient to justify him in forming it.

§ 169.   When Reliance on an Assertion of Opinion Is Not Justified

To the extent that an assertion is one of opinion only, the recipient is not justified in relying on it unless the recipient

(a)   stands in such a relation of trust and confidence to the person whose opinion is asserted that the recipient is reasonable in relying on it, or

(b)   reasonably believes that, as compared with himself, the person whose opinion is asserted has special skill, judgment or objectivity with respect to the subject matter, or

(c)   is for some other special reason particularly susceptible to a misrepresentation of the type involved.

§ 170.   Reliance on Assertions as to Matters of Law

If an assertion is one as to a matter of law, the same rules that apply in the case of other assertions determine whether the recipient is justified in relying on it.

§ 171.   When Reliance on an Assertion of Intention Is Not Justified

(1)   To the extent that an assertion is one of intention only, the recipient is not justified in relying on it if in the circumstances a misrepresentation of intention is consistent with reasonable standards of dealing.

(2)   If it is reasonable to do so, the promisee may properly interpret a promise as an assertion that the promisor intends to perform the promise.

§ 172.   When Fault Makes Reliance Unjustified

A recipient's fault in not knowing or discovering the facts before making the contract does not make his reliance unjustified unless it amounts to a failure to act in good faith and in accordance with reasonable standards of fair dealing.

§ 173.   When Abuse of a Fiduciary Relation Makes a Contract Voidable

If a fiduciary makes a contract with his beneficiary relating to matters within the scope of the fiduciary relation, the contract is voidable by the beneficiary, unless

(a)   it is on fair terms, and

(b)   all parties beneficially interested manifest assent with full understanding of their legal rights and of all relevant facts that the fiduciary knows or should know.

TOPIC 2.   DURESS AND UNDUE INFLUENCE

§ 174.   When Duress by Physical Compulsion Prevents Formation of a Contract

If conduct that appears to be a manifestation of assent by a party who does not intend to engage in that conduct is physically compelled by duress, the conduct is not effective as a manifestation of assent.

§ 175.   When Duress by Threat Makes a Contract Voidable

(1)   If a party's manifestation of assent is induced by an improper threat by the other party that leaves the victim no reasonable alternative, the contract is voidable by the victim.

(2)   If a party's manifestation of assent is induced by one who is not a party to the transaction, the contract is voidable by the victim unless the other party to the transaction in good faith and without reason to know of the duress either gives value or relies materially on the transaction.

Comment:

. . . *c.   Subjective test of induce-ment.* In order to constitute duress, the improper threat must induce the making of the contract. The rule for causation in cases of misrepresentation stated in § 167 is also applied to analogous cases of duress. No special rule for causation in cases of duress is stated here because of the infrequency with which the problem arises. A party's manifestation of assent is induced by duress if the duress substantially contributes to his decision to manifest his assent. Compare § 167. The test is subjective and the question is, did the threat actually induce assent on the part of the person claiming to be the victim of duress. Threats that would suffice to induce assent by one person may not suffice to induce assent by another. All attendant circumstances must be considered, including such matters as the age, background and relationship of the parties. Persons of a weak or cowardly nature are the very ones that need protection; the courageous can usually protect themselves. Timid and inexperienced persons are particularly subject to threats, and it does not lie in the mouths of the unscrupulous to excuse their imposition on such persons on the ground of their victims' infirmities. However, here as under § 167 circumstantial evidence may be useful in determining whether a threat did in fact induce assent. For example, although it is not essential that a reasonable person would have believed that the maker of the threat had the ability to execute it, this may be relevant in determining whether the threat actually induced assent. Similarly, such factors as the availability of disinterested advice and the length of time that elapses between the making of the threat and the assent may also be relevant in determining whether the threat actually induced the assent.

Illustrations:

8.   A, seeking to induce B to make a contract to sell land to A, threatens to poison B unless B makes the contract. The threat would not be taken seriously by a reasonable person, but B is easily frightened and attaches importance to the threat in deciding to make the contract. The contract is voidable by B.

9.   A seeks to induce B, A's wife, who has a history of severe emotional disturbances, to sign a

separation agreement on unfavorable terms. B has no lawyer, while A does. A tells B that if she does not sign the agreement he will charge her with desertion, she will never see her children again and she will get back none of her personal property, which is in A's possession. B signs the separation agreement. The agreement is voidable by B.

§ 176. When a Threat Is Improper

(1)   A threat is improper if

(a)   what is threatened is a crime or a tort, or the threat itself would be a crime or a tort if it resulted in obtaining property,

(b)   what is threatened is a criminal prosecution,

(c)   what is threatened is the use of civil process and the threat is made in bad faith, or

(d)   the threat is a breach of the duty of good faith and fair dealing under a contract with the recipient.

(2)   A threat is improper if the resulting exchange is not on fair terms, and

(a)   the threatened act would harm the recipient and would not significantly benefit the party making the threat,

(b)   the effectiveness of the threat in inducing the manifestation of assent is significantly increased by prior unfair dealing by the party making the threat, or

(c)   what is threatened is otherwise a use of power for illegitimate ends.

§ 177. When Undue Influence Makes a Contract Voidable

(1)   Undue influence is unfair persuasion of a party who is under the domination of the person exercising the persuasion or who by virtue of the relation between them is justified in assuming that that person will not act in a manner inconsistent with his welfare.

(2)   If a party's manifestation of assent is induced by undue influence by the other party, the contract is voidable by the victim.

(3)   If a party's manifestation of assent is induced by one who is not a party to the transaction, the contract is voidable by the victim unless the other party to the transaction in good faith and without reason to know of the undue influence either gives value or relies materially on the transaction.

CHAPTER 8. UNENFORCEABILITY ON GROUNDS OF PUBLIC POLICY

TOPIC 1. UNENFORCEABILITY IN GENERAL

§ 178. When a Term Is Unenforceable on Grounds of Public Policy

(1) A promise or other term of an agreement is unenforceable on grounds of public policy if legislation provides that it is unenforceable or the interest in its enforcement is clearly outweighed in the circumstances by a public policy against the enforcement of such terms.

(2) In weighing the interest in the enforcement of a term, account is taken of

(a) the parties' justified expectations,

(b) any forfeiture that would result if enforcement were denied, and

(c) any special public interest in the enforcement of the particular term.

(3) In weighing a public policy against enforcement of a term, account is taken of

(a) the strength of that policy as manifested by legislation or judicial decisions,

(b) the likelihood that a refusal to enforce the term will further that policy,

(c) the seriousness of any misconduct involved and the extent to which it was deliberate, and

(d) the directness of the connection between that misconduct and the term.

Comment:

... *b. Balancing of interests.* Only infrequently does legislation, on grounds of public policy, provide that a term is unenforceable. When a court reaches that conclusion, it usually does so on the basis of a public policy derived either from its own perception of the need to protect some aspect of the public welfare or from legislation that is relevant to that policy although it says nothing explicitly about unenforceability. See § 179. In some cases the contravention of public policy is so grave, as when an agreement involves a serious crime or tort, that unenforceability is plain. In other cases the contravention is so trivial as that it plainly does not preclude enforcement. In doubtful cases, however, a decision as to enforceability is reached only after a careful balancing, in the light of all the circumstances, of the interest in the enforcement of the particular promise against the policy against the enforcement of such terms. The most common factors in the balancing process are set out in Subsections (2) and (3). Enforcement will be denied only if the factors that argue against enforcement clearly outweigh the law's traditional interest in protecting the expectations of the parties, its abhorrence of any unjust enrichment, and any public interest in the enforcement of the particular term. . . .

d. Connection with term. The extent to which a refusal to enforce a promise or other term on grounds of public policy will further that policy depends not only on the strength of the policy but also on the relation of the term to that policy and to any misconduct involved. In most cases there is a promise that involves conduct offensive to the policy. The promise may be one to engage in such conduct. See Illustration 6. Or it may be one that tends to induce the other party to engage in such conduct. This tendency may result from the fact that the promise is made in return for the promisee's engaging in the conduct (see Illustration 7) or in return for the promisee's return promise to engage in the conduct (see Illustration 8). Or it may result from the fact that the duty to perform the promise is conditional on the promisee's engaging in the conduct (see Illustration 9). In such cases, it is the tendency itself that makes the promise unenforceable, even though the promise does not actually induce the conduct. There are other situations in which the conduct is not itself against public policy, but it is against public policy to promise to engage in such conduct or to attempt to induce it. It is sometimes objectionable to make a commitment to engage in conduct that is not in itself objectionable. This is the case, for example, for a promise to vote in a particular way. See Illustration 10. It is sometimes objectionable to attempt to induce conduct that is not in itself objectionable. This is the case, for example, for a promise made in consideration of the promisee's voting in a particular way. See Illustration 11. This list does not exhaust all of the possible relations between the conduct and the promise that may justify a decision that the promise is unenforceable. But as the relation between the conduct and the promise becomes tenuous, it becomes difficult to justify unenforceability unless serious misconduct is involved. A party will not be barred from enforcing a promise because of misconduct that is so remote or collateral that refusal to enforce the promise will not deter such conduct and enforcement will not amount to an inappropriate use of the judicial process. See Illustrations 15 and 16. However, a new promise to perform an earlier promise that was unenforceable on grounds of public policy is also unenforceable on those grounds unless the circumstances that made the first promise unenforceable no longer exist. The rules stated in §§ 183 and 184 involve special applications of these general principles concerning the relation between the conduct and the promise.

Illustrations:

. . . 12. A induces B to make an agreement to buy goods on credit from A by bribing B's purchasing agent. A delivers the goods to B. A's bribe tends to induce the agent to violate his fiduciary duty. B's promise to pay the price is unenforceable on grounds of public policy. See § 193.

13. A, who wants to induce B to buy goods from him, promises to pay C $1,000 if he will bribe B's purchasing agent to arrange the sale. C does so. C's bribe tends to induce the agent to violate his fiduciary duty. A's promise is unenforceable on grounds of public policy. See § 193.

14. A, who wants to induce B to buy goods from him, promises to pay C $1,000 if he arranges the sale. C arranges the sale by bribing B's purchasing agent. C's bribe tends to induce the agent to violate his fiduciary duty. A's promise is

unenforceable on grounds of public policy. See § 193. . . .

e. Other factors. A court will be reluctant to frustrate a party's legitimate expectations unless there is a corresponding benefit to be gained in deterring misconduct or avoiding an inappropriate use of the judicial process. The promisee's ignorance or inadvertence, even if it does not bring him within the rule stated in § 180, is one factor in determining the weight to be attached to his expectations. To the extent, however, that he engaged in misconduct that was serious or deliberate, his claim to protection of his expectations fails. The interest in favor of enforcement becomes much stronger after the promisee has relied substantially on those expectations as by preparation or performance. The court will then take into account any enrichment of the promisor and any forfeiture by the promisee if he should lose his right to the agreed exchange after he has relied substantially on those expectations. See Comment b to § 227. The possibility of restitution may be significant in this connection. In addition to the interest of the promisee, the court will also weigh any interest that the public or third parties may have in the enforcement of the term in question. Such an interest may be particularly evident where the policy involved is designed to protect third parties. . . .

f. Effect on rest of agreement. The rules stated in this Section determine only whether a particular promise or other term is unenforceable. The question of the effect of such a determination on the rest of the agreement is sometimes a complex one. If there is only one promise in the transaction and it is unenforceable, then the question will not arise. (As to the divisibility of such a promise, however, see §§ 184, 185). This is the case for offers that have been accepted by a performance rather than by a promise (§ 53), for promises enforceable because of reliance by the promisee (§ 90), and for promises under seal (§ 95). Furthermore, even when there is another promise, it too is often unenforceable under the rules stated in this Section. This is the case, for example, where one party's promise is unenforceable because the promised conduct offends public policy and the other party's return promise is unenforceable because it tends to induce that conduct. See Illustration 8. There are, however, situations in which only one party's promise is unenforceable while the other party's return promise is enforceable, as is the case where the promisee of the return promise belongs to the class sought to be protected by the policy in question. (That an unenforceable promise may be consideration for a return promise, see § 78.) Finally, there are circumstances in which the unenforceability of one part of an agreement does not entail the unenforceability of the rest of the agreement, and these are dealt with in §§ 183 and 184. As to the effect of public policy on conditions, see § 185.

§ 179. Bases of Public Policies Against Enforcement

A public policy against the enforcement of promises or other terms may be derived by the court from

    (a)   legislation relevant to such a policy, or

    (b)   the need to protect some aspect of the public welfare, as is the case for the judicial policies against, for example,

        (i)   restraint of trade (§§ 186–188),

        (ii)   impairment of family relations (§§ 189–191), and

(iii) interference with other protected interests (§§ 192–196, 356).

§ 180.   Effect of Excusable Ignorance

If a promisee is excusably ignorant of facts or of legislation of a minor character, of which the promisor is not excusably ignorant and in the absence of which the promise would be enforceable, the promisee has a claim for damages for its breach but cannot recover damages for anything that he has done after he learns of the facts or legislation.

§ 181.   Effect of Failure to Comply With Licensing or Similar Requirement

If a party is prohibited from doing an act because of his failure to comply with a licensing, registration or similar requirement, a promise in consideration of his doing that act or of his promise to do it is unenforceable on grounds of public policy if

(a)   the requirement has a regulatory purpose, and

(b)   the interest in the enforcement of the promise is clearly outweighed by the public policy behind the requirement.

§ 182.   Effect of Performance if Intended Use Is Improper

If the promisee has substantially performed, enforcement of a promise is not precluded on grounds of public policy because of some improper use that the promisor intends to make of what he obtains unless the promisee

(a)   acted for the purpose of furthering the improper use, or

(b)   knew of the use and the use involves grave social harm.

§ 183.   When Agreement Is Enforceable as to Agreed Equivalents

If the parties' performances can be apportioned into corresponding pairs of part performances so that the parts of each pair are properly regarded as agreed equivalents and one pair is not offensive to public policy, that portion of the agreement is enforceable by a party who did not engage in serious misconduct.

§ 184.   When Rest of Agreement Is Enforceable

(1)   If less than all of an agreement is unenforceable under the rule stated in § 178, a court may nevertheless enforce the rest of the agreement in favor of a party who did not engage in serious misconduct if the performance as to which the agreement is unenforceable is not an essential part of the agreed exchange.

(2)   A court may treat only part of a term an unenforceable under the rule stated in Subsection (1) if the party who seeks to enforce the term obtained it in good faith and in accordance with reasonable standards of fair dealing.

§ 185. Excuse of a Condition on Grounds of Public Policy

To the extent that a term requiring the occurrence of a condition is unenforceable under the rule stated in § 178, a court may excuse the non-occurrence of the condition unless its occurrence was an essential part of the agreed exchange.

TOPIC 2.   RESTRAINT OF TRADE

§ 186. Promise in Restraint of Trade

(1) A promise is unenforceable on grounds of public policy if it is unreasonably in restraint of trade.

(2) A promise is in restraint of trade if its performance would limit competition in any business or restrict the promisor in the exercise of a gainful occupation.

§ 187. Non-Ancillary Restraints on Competition

A promise to refrain from competition that imposes a restraint that is not ancillary to an otherwise valid transaction or relationship is unreasonably in restraint of trade.

§ 188. Ancillary Restraints on Competition

(1) A promise to refrain from competition that imposes a restraint that is ancillary to an otherwise valid transaction or relationship is unreasonably in restraint of trade if

    (a) the restraint is greater than is needed to protect the promisee's legitimate interest, or

    (b) the promisee's need is outweighed by the hardship to the promisor and the likely injury to the public.

(2) Promises imposing restraints that are ancillary to a valid transaction or relationship include the following:

    (a) a promise by the seller of a business not to compete with the buyer in such a way as to injure the value of the business sold;

    (b) a promise by an employee or other agent not to compete with his employer or other principal;

    (c) a promise by a partner not to compete with the partnership.

Comment:

    a.   *Rule of reason.* The rules stated in this Section apply to promises not to compete that, because they impose ancillary restraints, are not necessarily invalid. Subsection (1) restates in more detail the general rule of reason of § 186 as it applies to such promises. Under this formulation the restraint may be unreasonable in either of two situations. The first occurs when the restraint is greater than necessary to protect the legitimate interests of the promisee. The second occurs when, even though the restraint is not greater

92

than necessary to protect those interests, the promisee's need for protection is outweighed by the hardship to the promisor and the likely injury to the public. In the second situation the court may be faced with a particularly difficult task of balancing competing interests. No mathematical formula can be offered for this process.

b.   Need of the promisee. If a restraint is not ancillary to some transaction or relationship that gives rise to an interest worthy of protection, the promise is necessarily unreasonable under the rule stated in the preceding Section. In some instances, however, a promise to refrain from competition is a natural and reasonable means of protecting a legitimate interest of the promisee arising out of the transaction to which the restraint is ancillary. In those instances the same reasons argue for its enforceability as in the case of any other promise. For example, competitors who are combining their efforts in a partnership may promise as part of the transaction not to compete with the partnership. Assuming that the combination is not monopolistic, such promises, reasonable in scope, will be upheld in view of the interest of each party as promisee. See Subsection (2)(c) and Comment h. (It is assumed in the Illustrations to this Section that the arrangements are not objectionable on grounds other than those that come within its scope.) The extent to which the restraint is needed to protect the promisee's interests will vary with the nature of the transaction. Where a sale of good will is involved, for example, the buyer's interest in what he has acquired cannot be effectively realized unless the seller engages not to act so as unreasonably to diminish the value of what he has sold. The same is true of any other property interest of which exclusive use is part of the value. See Subsection (2)(a) and Comment f. In the case of a post-employment restraint, however, the promisee's interest is less

clear. Such a restraint, in contrast to one accompanying a sale of good will, is not necessary in order for the employer to get the full value of what he has acquired. Instead, it must usually be justified on the ground that the employer has a legitimate interest in restraining the employee from appropriating valuable trade information and customer relationships to which he has had access in the course of his employment. Arguably the employer does not get the full value of the employment contract if he cannot confidently give the employee access to confidential information needed for most efficient performance of his job. But it is often difficult to distinguish between such information and normal skills of the trade, and preventing use of one may well prevent or inhibit use of the other. See Subsection (2)(b) and Comment g. Because of this difference in the interest of the promisee, courts have generally been more willing to uphold promises to refrain from competition made in connection with sales of good will than those made in connection with contracts of employment.

c.   Harm to the promisor and injury to the public. Even if the restraint is no greater than is needed to protect the promisee's interest, the promisee's need may be outweighed by the harm to the promisor and the likely injury to the public. In the case of a sale of a business, the harm caused to the seller may be excessive if the restraint necessitates his complete withdrawal from business; the likely injury to the public may be too great if it has the effect of removing a former competitor from competition. See Comment f. In the case of a post-employment restraint, the harm caused to the employee may be excessive if the restraint inhibits his personal freedom by preventing him from earning his livelihood if he quits; the likely injury to the public may be too great if it is seriously harmed by the impairment of his economic mobility or by the unavailability of the skills developed in his employment. See Comment g. Not every restraint causes injury to the public, however, and even a post-employment restraint may increase efficiency by encouraging the employer to entrust confidential information to the employee.

d.   *Extent of the restraint.* The extent of the restraint is a critical factor in determining its reasonableness. The extent may be limited in three ways: by type of activity, by geographical area, and by time. If the promise proscribes types of activity more extensive than necessary to protect those engaged in by the promisee, it goes beyond what is necessary to protect his legitimate interests and is unreasonable. If it covers a geographical area more extensive than necessary to protect his interests, it is also unreasonable. And if the restraint is to last longer than is required in light of those interests, taking account of such factors as the permanent or transitory nature of technology and information, it is unreasonable. Since, in any of these cases, the restraint is too broad to be justified by the promisee's need, a court may hold it to be unreasonable without the necessity of weighing the countervailing interests of the promisor and the public. What limits as to activity, geographical area, and time are appropriate in a particular case depends on all the circumstances. As to the possibility of divisibility, see § 183.

e.   *Examples of ancillary restraints.* The rule stated in Subsection (1) has its most significant applications with respect to the three types of promises set out in Subsection (2). In each of these situations the promisee may have need for protection sufficient to sustain a promise to refrain from competition as long as it is reasonable in extent. They involve promises by the seller of a business, by an employee or agent, and by a partner. The list is not an exclusive one and there may be other situations in which a valid transaction or relationship gives the promisee a legitimate interest sufficient to sustain a promise not to compete.

f.   *Promise by seller of a business.* A promise to refrain from competition made in connection with a sale of a business may be reasonable in the light of the buyer's need to protect the value of the good will that he has acquired. In effect, the seller promises not to act so as to diminish the value of what he has sold. An analogous situation arises when the value of a corporation's business depends largely on the good will of one or more of the officers or shareholders. In that situation, officers or shareholders, either on the sale of their shares or on the sale of the corporation's business, may make an enforceable promise not to compete with the corporation or with the purchaser of its business, just as the corporation itself could on sale of its business make an enforceable promise to refrain from competition.

Illustrations:

1.   A sells his grocery business to B and as part of the agreement promises not to engage in a business of the same kind within a hundred miles for three years. The business of both A and B extends to a radius of a hundred miles, so that competition anywhere within that radius would harm B's business. The restraint is not more extensive than is necessary for B's protection. A's promise is not unreasonably in restraint of trade and enforcement is not precluded on grounds of public policy.

2.   The facts being otherwise as stated in Illustration 1, neither A's nor B's business extends to a radius of a hundred miles. The area fixed is more extensive than is necessary for B's protection. A's promise is unreasonably in restraint of trade and is unenforceable on grounds of

public policy. As to the possibility of refusal to enforce limited to part of the promise, see § 184(2).

3.   A sells his grocery business to B and as part of the agreement promises not to engage in business of any kind within the city for three years. The activity proscribed is more extensive than is necessary for B's protection. A's promise is unreasonably is restraint of trade and is unenforceable on grounds of public policy. As to the possibility of refusal to enforce only part of promise, see § 184(2).

4.   A sells his grocery business to B and as part of the agreement promises not to engage in a business of the same kind within the city for twenty-five years, although B has ample opportunity to make A's former good will his own in a much shorter period of time. The time fixed is longer than is necessary for A's protection. A's promise is unreasonably in restraint of trade and is unenforceable on grounds of public policy. As to the possibility of refusal to enforce only part of the promise, see § 184(2).

5.   A, a corporation, sells its business to B. As part of the agreement, C and D, officers and large shareholders of A, promise not to compete with B within the territory in which A did business for three years. Their promises are not unreasonably in restraint of trade and enforcement is not precluded on grounds of public policy.

g.   *Promise by employee or agent.* The employer's interest in exacting from his employee a promise not to compete after termination of the employment is usually explained on the ground that the employee has acquired either confidential trade information relating to some process or method or the means to attract customers away from the employer. Whether the risk that the employee may do injury to the employer is sufficient to justify a promise to refrain from competition after the termination of the employment will depend on the facts of the particular case. Post-employment restraints are scrutinized with particular care because they are often the product of unequal bargaining power and because the employee is likely to give scant attention to the hardship he may later suffer through loss of his livelihood. This is especially so where the restraint is imposed by the employer's standardized printed form. Cf. § 208. A line must be drawn between the general skills and knowledge of the trade and information that is peculiar to the employer's business. If the employer seeks to justify the restraint on the ground of the employee's knowledge of a process or method, the confidentiality of that process or method and its technological life may be critical. The public interest in workable employer-employee relationships with an efficient use of employees must be balanced against the interest in individual economic freedom. The court will take account of any diminution in competition likely to result from slowing down the dissemination of ideas and of any impairment of the function of the market in shifting manpower to areas of greatest productivity. If the employer seeks to justify the restraint on the ground of the employee's ability to attract customers, the nature, extent and locale of the employee's contacts with customers are relevant. A restraint is easier to justify if it is limited to one field of activity among many that are available to the employee. The same is true if the restraint is limited to the taking of his former employer's customers as contrasted with competition in general. A restraint may be ancillary to a relationship although, as in the case of an employment at will, no contract of employment is involved. Analogous rules apply to restraints imposed on agents by their principals. As to the duty of an agent not to compete with his principal during the agency relationship, see Restatement, Second, Agency §§ 393, 394.

Illustrations:

6. A employs B as a fitter of contact lenses under a one-year employment contract. As part of the employment agreement, B promises not to work as a fitter of contact lenses in the same town for three years after the termination of his employment. B works for A for five years, during which time he has close relationships with A's customers, who come to rely upon him. B's contacts with A's customers are such as to attract them away from A. B's promise is not unreasonably in restraint of trade and enforcement is not precluded on grounds of public policy.

7. A employs B as advertising manager of his retail clothing store. As part of the employment agreement, B promises not to work in the retail clothing business in the same town for three years after the termination of his employment. B works for A for five years but does not deal with customers and acquires no confidential trade information in his work. B's promise is unreasonably in restraint of trade and is unenforceable on grounds of public policy. Compare Illustration 1 to § 185.

8. A employs B as an instructor in his dance studio. As part of the employment agreement, B promises not to work as a dance instructor in the same town for three years after the termination of his employment. B works for five years and deals directly with customers but does not work with any customer for a substantial period of time and acquires no confidential information in his work. B's promise is unreasonably in restraint of trade

and is unenforceable on grounds of public policy.

9. A employs B as a research chemist in his nationwide pharmaceutical business. As part of the employment agreement, B promises not to work in the pharmaceutical industry at any place in the country for three years after the termination of his employment. B works for five years and acquires valuable confidential information that would be useful to A's competitors and would unreasonably harm A's business. B can find employment as a research chemist outside of the pharmaceutical industry. B's promise is not unreasonably in restraint of trade and enforcement is not precluded on grounds of public policy.

10. A employs B to work with rapidly changing technology, some parts of which entail valuable confidential information. As part of the agreement B promises not to work for any competitor of A for ten years after the termination of the employment. The confidential information made available to A will probably remain valuable for only a much shorter period. The time fixed is longer than is necessary for A's protection. B's promise is unreasonably in restraint of trade and is unenforceable on grounds of public policy. As to the possibility of refusal to enforce only part of the promise, see § 184(2).

h. Promise by partner. A rule similar to that applicable to an employee or agent applies to a partner who makes a promise not to compete that is ancillary to the partnership agreement or to an agreement by which he disposes of his partnership interest. The same is true of joint adventurers, who are treated as partners in this respect.

Illustrations:

11. A, B and C form a partnership to practice veterinary medicine in a town for ten years. In the partnership agreement, each promises that if, on the termination of the partnership, the practice is continued by the other two members, he will not practice veterinary medicine in the same town during its continuance up to a maximum of three years. The restraint is not more extensive than is necessary for the protection of each partner's interest in the partnership. Their promises are not unreasonably in restraint of trade and enforcement is not precluded on grounds of public policy.

12. A, an experienced dentist and oral surgeon, takes into partnership B, a younger dentist and oral surgeon. In the partnership agreement, B promises that, if he withdraws from the partnership, he will not practice dentistry or oral surgery in the city for three years. Their practice is limited to oral surgery, and does not include dentistry. The activity proscribed is more extensive than is necessary for A's protection. B's promise is unreasonably in restraint of trade and is unenforceable on grounds of public policy. As to the possibility of refusal to enforce only part of the promise, see § 184(2).

13. A works for five years as a partner in a nationwide firm of accountants. In the partnership agreement, A promises not to engage in accounting in any city where the firm has an office for three years after his withdrawal from the partnership. The firm has offices in the twenty largest cities in the United States. A's promise imposes great hardship on him because this area includes almost all that in which he could engage in a comparable accounting practice. The promise is unreasonably in restraint of trade and is unenforceable on grounds of public policy. As to the possibility of refusal to enforce only part of the promise, see § 184(2).

14. A, a doctor who has a general practice in a remote area, takes into partnership B, a younger doctor. In the partnership agreement, B promises that, if he withdraws from the partnership, he will not engage in the practice of medicine within the area for three years. If B's unavailability in the area will be likely to cause injury to the public because of the shortage of doctors there, the court may determine that B's promise is unreasonably in restraint of trade and is unenforceable on grounds of public policy.

15. A and B attend an art auction and each plans to bid on a valuable painting. They decide to acquire it as a joint venture and each promises the other to bid for its purchase jointly and, if successful, to deal with it jointly. Their promises are not unreasonably in restraint of trade and are not unenforceable on grounds of public policy. Compare Illustrations 3 and 4 to § 187.

TOPIC 3. IMPAIRMENT OF FAMILY RELATIONS

§ 189. Promise in Restraint of Marriage

A promise is unenforceable on grounds of public policy if it is unreasonably in restraint of marriage.

§ 190.   Promise Detrimental to Marital Relationship

(1)   A promise by a person contemplating marriage or by a married person, other than as part of an enforceable separation agreement, is unenforceable on grounds of public policy if it would change some essential incident of the marital relationship in a way detrimental to the public interest in the marriage relationship. A separation agreement is unenforceable on grounds of public policy unless it is made after separation or in contemplation of an immediate separation and is fair in the circumstances.

(2)   A promise that tends unreasonably to encourage divorce or separation is unenforceable on grounds of public policy.

§ 191.   Promise Affecting Custody

A promise affecting the right of custody of a minor child is unenforceable on grounds of public policy unless the disposition as to custody is consistent with the best interest of the child.

TOPIC 4.   INTERFERENCE WITH OTHER PROTECTED INTERESTS

§ 192.   Promise Involving Commission of a Tort

A promise to commit a tort or to induce the commission of a tort is unenforceable on grounds of public policy.

§ 193.   Promise Inducing Violation of Fiduciary Duty

A promise by a fiduciary to violate his fiduciary duty or a promise that tends to induce such a violation is unenforceable on grounds of public policy.

§ 194.   Promise Interfering with Contract with Another

A promise that tortiously interferes with performance of a contract with a third person or a tortiously induced promise to commit a breach of contract is unenforceable on grounds of public policy.

§ 195.   Term Exempting From Liability for Harm Caused Intentionally, Recklessly or Negligently

(1)   A term exempting a party from tort liability for harm caused intentionally or recklessly is unenforceable on grounds of public policy.

(2)   A term exempting a party from tort liability for harm caused negligently is unenforceable on grounds of public policy if

(a)   the term exempts an employer from liability to an employee for injury in the course of his employment;

(b)   the term exempts one charged with a duty of public service from liability to one to whom that duty is owed for compensation for breach of that duty, or

(c)   the other party is similarly a member of a class protected against the class to which the first party belongs.

(3)   A term exempting a seller of a product from his special tort liability for physical harm to a user or consumer is unenforceable on grounds of public policy unless the term is fairly bargained for and is consistent with the policy underlying that liability.

§ 196.   Term Exempting From Consequences of Misrepresentation

A term unreasonably exempting a party from the legal consequences of a misrepresentation is unenforceable on grounds of public policy.

TOPIC 5.   RESTITUTION

§ 197.   Restitution Generally Unavailable

Except as stated in §§ 198 and 199, a party has no claim in restitution for performance that he has rendered under or in return for a promise that is unenforceable on grounds of public policy unless denial of restitution would cause disproportionate forfeiture.

Comment:

a.   Rationale. In general, if a court will not, on grounds of public policy, aid a promisee by enforcing the promise, it will not aid him by granting him restitution for performance that he has rendered in return for the unenforceable promise. Neither will it aid the promisor by allowing a claim in restitution for performance that he has rendered under the unenforceable promise. It will simply leave both parties as it finds them, even though this may result in one of them retaining a benefit that he has received as a result of the transaction.

Illustrations:

1.   A, the owner of a newspaper, promises B that he will publish a statement about C known to A and B to be false and defamatory, if B pays him $10,000. B pays A $10,000. Since A's promise is unenforceable on grounds of public policy (§ 192), B has no claim in restitution against A. See Illustration 6 to § 178.

2.   A induces B to make an agreement to buy goods on credit from A by bribing B's purchasing agent. A's bribe tends to induce the agent to violate his fiduciary duty. A delivers the goods to B. Since B's promise to pay the price is unenforceable on grounds of public policy, A has no claim in restitution against B. See § 193 and Illustration 14 to § 178.

b.   Exceptions. Exceptions to the rule denying restitution are made in favor of a party who is excusably ignorant or is not equally in the wrong (§ 198) and in favor of a party who has withdrawn or where the situation is contrary to public policy (§ 199). These exceptions are dealt with in the two sections that follow. In addition, the rule is subject to the exception stated in this Section that allows restitution in favor of a party who would otherwise suffer a forfeiture that is disproportionate in relation to the contravention of public policy involved. Account will be taken of such factors as the extent of the party's deliberate involvement in any misconduct, the gravity of that misconduct, and the strength of the public policy. See § 178(3). The exception is especially appropriate in the case of technical rules or regulations that are drawn so that their strict application would result in such forfeiture if restitution were not allowed. Here, as elsewhere in this Restatement, the term "forfeiture" is used to refer to the denial of compensation that results when the obligee loses his right to the agreed exchange after he has relied substantially, as by preparation or performance, on the expectation of that exchange. See Comment b to § 227 and Comment b to § 229. Whether the forfeiture is "disproportionate" for the purposes of this Section will depend on the extent of that denial of compensation as compared with the gravity of the public interest involved and the extent of the contravention. If the claimant has threatened grave social harm, no forfeiture will be disproportionate. Restitution under this Section is subject to the rules of §§ 370–77.

Illustrations:

3.   A makes an agreement with B to sell to B for $10,000 a painting that A, as B knows, has already contracted to sell to C. B pays A $5,000 in advance of delivery. Al-though B's promise to pay the price is unenforceable on grounds of public policy (§ 194), denial of restitution would cause B disproportionate forfeiture. B has a claim in restitution against A for $5,000.

4.   A, a foreign corporation, makes an agreement with B to sell B goods for $1,000. A delivers the goods but does not comply with a state statute that prohibits a foreign corporation from doing business in the state without appointing an agent for service of process and provides that contracts made in violation of the statute are unenforceable. Although B's promise to pay the price is unenforceable on grounds of public policy, denial of restitution would cause A disproportionate forfeiture. A has a claim in restitution against B for the goods or their value to B.

5.   A, a city, makes an agreement with B under which B is to install traffic signals for $50,000. In making the agreement, A fails to comply with a state statute that prescribes procedures for making municipal contracts, so that A's promise is unenforceable on grounds of public policy. Although B knows this, he installs the signals. In determining whether B has a claim in restitution against A for the value of the signals to A, the court will consider the extent of the forfeiture that would result from the denial of such a claim in relation to the gravity of the public policy involved and the extent of the contravention.

§ 198.   Restitution in Favor of Party Who Is Excusably Ignorant or Is Not Equally in the Wrong

A party has a claim in restitution for performance that he has rendered under or in return for a promise that is unenforceable on grounds of public policy if

(a) he was excusably ignorant of the facts or of legislation of a minor character, in the absence of which the promise would be enforceable, or

(b) he was not equally in the wrong with the promisor.

§ 199. Restitution Where Party Withdraws or Situation Is Contrary to Public Interest

A party has a claim in restitution for performance that he has rendered under or in return for a promise that is unenforceable on grounds of public policy if he did not engage in serious misconduct and

(a) he withdraws from the transaction before the improper purpose has been achieved, or

(b) allowance of the claim would put an end to a continuing situation that is contrary to the public interest.

CHAPTER 9.   THE SCOPE OF CONTRACTUAL OBLIGATIONS

TOPIC 1.   THE MEANING OF AGREEMENTS

§ 200. Interpretation of Promise or Agreement

Interpretation of a promise or agreement or a term thereof is the ascertainment of its meaning.

§ 201. Whose Meaning Prevails

(1) Where the parties have attached the same meaning to a promise or agreement or a term thereof, it is interpreted in accordance with that meaning.

(2) Where the parties have attached different meanings to a promise or agreement or a term thereof, it is interpreted in accordance with the meaning attached by one of them if at the time the agreement was made

(a) that party did not know of any different meaning attached by the other, and the other knew the meaning attached by the first party; or

(b) that party had no reason to know of any different meaning attached by the other, and the other had reason to know the meaning attached by the first party.

(3) Except as stated in this Section, neither party is bound by the meaning attached by the other, even though the result may be a failure of mutual assent.

Comment:

. . . *d.   Misunderstanding.* Subsection (2) follows the terminology of § 20, referring to the understanding of each party as the meaning "attached" by him to a term of a promise or agreement. Where the rules stated in Subsections (1) and (2) do not apply, neither party is bound by the understanding of the other. The result may be an entire failure of agreement or a failure to agree as to a term. There may be a binding contract despite failure to agree as to a term, if the term is not essential or if it can be supplied. See § 204. In some cases a party can waive the misunderstanding and enforce the contract in accordance with the understanding of the other party.

§ 202.   Rules in Aid of Interpretation

(1)   Words and other conduct are interpreted in the light of all the circumstances, and if the principal purpose of the parties is ascertainable it is given great weight.

(2)   A writing is interpreted as a whole, and all writings that are part of the same transaction are interpreted together.

(3)   Unless a different intention is manifested,

(a)   where language has a generally prevailing meaning, it is interpreted in accordance with that meaning;

(b)   technical terms and words of art are given their technical meaning when used in a transaction within their technical field.

(4)   Where an agreement involves repeated occasions for performance by either party with knowledge of the nature of the performance and opportunity for objection to it by the other, any course of performance accepted or acquiesced in without objection is given great weight in the interpretation of the agreement.

(5)   Wherever reasonable, the manifestations of intention of the parties to a promise or agreement are interpreted as consistent with each other and with any relevant course of performance, course of dealing, or usage of trade.

§ 203.   Standards of Preference in Interpretation

In the interpretation of a promise or agreement or a term thereof, the following standards of preference are generally applicable:

(a)   an interpretation which gives a reasonable, lawful, and effective meaning to all the terms is preferred to an interpretation which leaves a part unreasonable, unlawful, or of no effect;

(b)   express terms are given greater weight than course of performance, course of dealing, and usage of trade, course of performance is given greater weight than course of dealing or usage of trade, and course of dealing is given greater weight than usage of trade;

(c)   specific terms and exact terms are given greater weight than general language;

(d)   separately negotiated or added terms are given greater weight than standardized terms or other terms not separately negotiated.

§ 204.   Supplying an Omitted Essential Term

When the parties to a bargain sufficiently defined to be a contract have not agreed with respect to a term which is essential to a determination of their rights and duties, a term which is reasonable in the circumstances is supplied by the court.

TOPIC 2.   CONSIDERATIONS OF FAIRNESS AND THE PUBLIC INTEREST

§ 205.   Duty of Good Faith and Fair Dealing

Every contract imposes upon each party a duty of good faith and fair dealing in its performance and its enforcement.

§ 206.   Interpretation Against the Draftsman

In choosing among the reasonable meanings of a promise or agreement or a term thereof, that meaning is generally preferred which operates against the party who supplies the words or from whom a writing otherwise proceeds.

§ 207.   Interpretation Favoring the Public

In choosing among the reasonable meanings of a promise or agreement or a term thereof, a meaning that serves the public interest is generally preferred.

§ 208.   Unconscionable Contract or Term

If a contract or term thereof is unconscionable at the time the contract is made a court may refuse to enforce the contract, or may enforce the remainder of the contract without the unconscionable term, or may so limit the application of any unconscionable term as to avoid any unconscionable result.

Comment:

a.   Scope. Like the obligation of good faith and fair dealing (§ 205), the policy against unconscionable contracts or terms applies to a wide variety of types of conduct. The determination that a contract or term is or is not unconscionable is made in the light of its setting, purpose and effect. Relevant factors include weaknesses in the contracting process like those involved in more specific rules as to contractual capacity, fraud, and other invalidating causes; the policy also overlaps with rules which render particular bargains or terms unenforceable on grounds of public policy. Policing against unconscionable contracts or terms has sometimes been accomplished "by adverse construction of language, by manipulation of the rules of offer and acceptance or by determinations that the clause is contrary to public policy or to the dominant purpose of the contract." Uniform Commercial Code § 2–302 Comment 1. Particularly in the case of standardized agreements, the rule of this Section permits the court to pass directly on the unconscionability of the contract or clause rather than to avoid unconscionable results by interpretation. Compare § 211.

b. Historic standards. Traditionally, a bargain was said to be unconscionable in an action at law if it was "such as no man in his senses and not under delusion would make on the one hand, and as no honest and fair man would accept on the other;" damages were then limited to those to which the aggrieved party was "equitably" entitled. Hume v. United States, 132 U.S. 406 (1889), quoting Earl of Chesterfield v. Janssen, 2 Ves.Sen. 125, 155, 28 Eng.Rep. 82, 100 (Ch.1750). Even though a contract was fully enforceable in an action for damages, equitable remedies such as specific performance were refused where "the sum total of its provisions drives too hard a bargain for a court of conscience to assist." Campbell Soup Co. v. Wentz, 172 F.2d 80, 84 (3d Cir.1948). Modern procedural reforms have blurred the distinction between remedies at law and in equity. For contracts for the sale of goods, Uniform Commercial Code § 2–302 states the rule of this Section without distinction between law and equity. Comment 1 to that section adds, "The principle is one of the prevention of oppression and unfair surprise (Cf. Campbell Soup Co. v. Wentz,) and not of disturbance of allocation of risks because of superior bargaining power."

c. Overall imbalance. Inadequacy of consideration does not of itself invalidate a bargain, but gross disparity in the values exchanged may be an important factor in a determination that a contract is unconscionable and may be sufficient ground, without more, for denying specific performance. See §§ 79, 364. Such a disparity may also corroborate indications of defects in the bargaining process, or may affect the remedy to be granted when there is a violation of a more specific rule. Theoretically it is possible for a contract to be oppressive taken as a whole, even though there is no weakness in the bargaining process and no single term which is in itself unconscionable. Ordinarily, however, an unconscionable contract involves other factors as well as overall imbalance.

Illustrations:

1. A, an individual, contracts in June to sell at a fixed price per ton to B, a large soup manufacturer, the carrots to be grown on A's farm. The contract, written on B's standard printed form, is obviously drawn to protect B's interests and not A's; it contains numerous provisions to protect B against various contingencies and none giving analogous protection to A. Each of the clauses can be read restrictively so that it is not unconscionable, but several can be read literally to give unrestricted discretion to B. In January, when the market price has risen above the contract price, A repudiates the contract, and B seeks specific performance. In the absence of justification by evidence of commercial setting, purpose, or effect, the court may determine that the contract as a whole was unconscionable when made, and may then deny specific performance.

2. A, a homeowner, executes a standard printed form used by B, a merchant, agreeing to pay $1,700 for specified home improvements. A also executes a credit application asking for payment in 60 monthly installments but specifying no rate. Four days later A is informed that the credit application has been ap-

proved and is given a payment schedule calling for finance and insurance charges amounting to $800 in addition to the $1,700. Before B does any of the work, A repudiates the agreement, and B sues A for $800 damages, claiming that a commission of $800 was paid to B's salesman in reliance on the agreement. The court may determine that the agreement was unconscionable when made, and may then dismiss the claim.

d. Weakness in the bargaining process. A bargain is not unconscionable merely because the parties to it are unequal in bargaining position, nor even because the inequality results in an allocation of risks to the weaker party. But gross inequality of bargaining power, together with terms unreasonably favorable to the stronger party, may confirm indications that the transaction involved elements of deception or compulsion, or may show that the weaker party had no meaningful choice, no real alternative, or did not in fact assent or appear to assent to the unfair terms. Factors which may contribute to a finding of unconscionability in the bargaining process include the following: belief by the stronger party that there is no reasonable probability that the weaker party will fully perform the contract; knowledge of the stronger party that the weaker party will be unable to receive substantial benefits from the contract; knowledge of the stronger party that the weaker party is unable reasonably to protect his interests by reason of physical or mental infirmities, ignorance, illiteracy or inability to understand the language of the agreement, or similar factors. See Uniform Consumer Credit Code § 6.111.

Illustration:

3. A, literate only in Spanish, is visited in his home by a salesman of refrigerator-freezers for B. They negotiate in Spanish; A tells the salesman he cannot afford to buy the appliance because his job will end in one week, and the salesman tells A that A will be paid numerous $25 commissions on sales to his friends. A signs a complex installment contract printed in English. The contract provides for a cash price of $900 plus a finance charge of $250. A defaults after paying $32, and B sues for the balance plus late charges and a 20% attorney's fee authorized by the contract. The appliance cost B $350. The court may determine that the contract was unconscionable when made, and may then limit B's recovery to a reasonable sum.

e. Unconscionable terms. Particular terms may be unconscionable whether or not the contract as a whole is unconscionable. Some types of terms are not enforced, regardless of context; examples are provisions for unreasonably large liquidated damages, or limitations on a debtor's right to redeem collateral. See Uniform Commercial Code §§ 2–718, 9–501(3). Other terms may be unconscionable in some contexts but not in others. Overall imbalance and weaknesses in the bargaining process are then important.

Illustrations:

4. A, a packer, sells and ships 300 cases of canned catsup to B, a wholesale grocer. The contract provides, "All claims other than swells must be made within ten days from receipt of goods." Six months later a government inspector, upon microscopic examination of samples, finds excessive mold in the cans and obtains a court order for destruction of the 270 remaining cases in B's warehouse. In the absence of justifying evidence, the court may determine that the quoted clause is unconscionable as applied to latent defects and does not bar a claim for

damages for breach of warranty by B against A.

5. A, a retail furniture store, sells furniture on installment credit to B, retaining a security interest. As A knows, B is a woman of limited education, separated from her husband, maintaining herself and seven children by means of $218 per month public assistance. After 13 purchases over a period of five years for a total of $1,200, B owes A $164. B then buys a stereo set for $514. Each contract contains a paragraph of some 800 words in extremely fine print, in the middle of which are the words "all payments shall be credited pro rata on all outstanding accounts." The effect of this language is to keep a balance due on each item until all are paid for. On B's default, A sues for possession of all the items sold. It may be determined that either the quoted clause or the contract as a whole was unconscionable when made.

6. A, a corporation with its principal office in State X, contracts with B, a resident of State X, to make improvements on B's home in State X. The contract is made on A's standard printed form, which contains a clause by which the parties submit to the jurisdiction of a court in State Y, 200 miles away. No reason for the clause appears except to make litigation inconvenient and expensive for B. The clause is unconscionable.

f. Law and fact. A determination that a contract or term is unconscionable is made by the court in the light of all the material facts. Under Uniform Commercial Code § 2–302, the determination is made "as a matter of law," but the parties are to be afforded an opportunity to present evidence as to commercial setting, purpose and effect to aid the court in its determination. Incidental findings of fact are made

by the court rather than by a jury, but are accorded the usual weight given to such findings of fact in appellate review. An appellate court will also consider whether proper standards were applied.

Illustration:

7. A, a finance company, lends money to B, a manufacturing company, on the security of an assignment by B of its accounts receivable. The agreement provides for loans of 75% of the value of assigned accounts acceptable to A, and forbids B to dispose of or hypothecate any assets without A's written consent. The agreed interest rate of 18% would be usurious but for a statute precluding a corporation from raising the defense of usury. Substantial advances are made, and the balance owed is $14,000 when B becomes bankrupt, three months after the first advance. A determination that the agreement is unconscionable on its face, without regard to context, is error. The agreement is unconscionable only if it is not a reasonable commercial device in the light of all the circumstances when it was made.

g. Remedies. Perhaps the simplest application of the policy against unconscionable agreements is the denial of specific performance where the contract as a whole was unconscionable when made. If such a contract is entirely executory, denial of money damages may also be appropriate. But the policy is not penal: unless the parties can be restored to their pre-contract positions, the offending party will ordinarily be awarded at least the reasonable value of performance rendered by him. Where a term rather than the entire contract is unconscionable, the appropriate remedy is ordinarily to deny effect to the unconscionable term. In such cases as that of an exculpatory term, the effect may be to enlarge the liability of the offending party.

TOPIC 3. EFFECT OF ADOPTION OF A WRITING

§ 209. Integrated Agreements

(1) An integrated agreement is a writing or writings constituting a final expression of one or more terms of an agreement.

(2) Whether there is an integrated agreement is to be determined by the court as a question preliminary to determination of a question of interpretation or to application of the parol evidence rule.

(3) Where the parties reduce an agreement to a writing which in view of its completeness and specificity reasonably appears to be a complete agreement, it is taken to be an integrated agreement unless it is established by other evidence that the writing did not constitute a final expression.

§ 210. Completely and Partially Integrated Agreements

(1) A completely integrated agreement is an integrated agreement adopted by the parties as a complete and exclusive statement of the terms of the agreement.

(2) A partially integrated agreement is an integrated agreement other than a completely integrated agreement.

(3) Whether an agreement is completely or partially integrated is to be determined by the court as a question preliminary to determination of a question of interpretation or to application of the parol evidence rule.

Comment:

a. Complete integration. The definition in Subsection (1) is to be read with the definition of integrated agreement in § 209, to reject the assumption sometimes made that because a writing has been worked out which is final on some matters, it is to be taken as including all the matters agreed upon. Even though there is an integrated agreement, consistent additional terms not reduced to writing may be shown, unless the court finds that the writing was assented to by both parties as a complete and exclusive statement of all the terms. Upon such a finding, however, evidence of the alleged making of consistent additional terms must be kept from the trier of fact. See § 216; Uniform Commercial Code § 2–202 Comment 3.

b. Proof of complete integration. That a writing was or was not adopted as a completely integrated agreement may be proved by any relevant evidence. A document in the form of a written contract, signed by both parties and apparently complete on its face, may be decisive of the issue in the absence of credible contrary evidence. But a writing cannot of itself prove its own completeness, and wide latitude must be allowed for inquiry into circumstances bearing on the intention of the parties.

Illustration:

1. A, a college, owns premises which have no toilet or plumbing facilities or heating equipment. In negotiating a lease to B for use of the premises as a radio station, A orally agrees to permit the use of facilities in an adjacent building and to provide heat. The parties subsequently execute a written lease agreement which makes no mention of facilities or heat. The question whether the written lease was adopted as a completely integrated agreement is to be decided on the basis of all relevant evidence of the prior and contemporaneous conduct and language of the parties.

c.   Partial integration. It is often clear from the face of a writing that it is incomplete and cannot be more than a partially integrated agreement. Incompleteness may also be shown by other writings, which may or may not become part of a completely or partially integrated agreement. Or it may be shown by any relevant evidence, oral or written, that an apparently complete writing never became fully effective, or that it was modified after initial adoption.

Illustration:

2. A writes to B a letter offer containing four provisions. B replies by letter that three of the provisions are satisfactory, but makes a counter proposal as to the fourth. After further discussion of the fourth provision, the parties come to oral agreement on a revision of it, but make no further statements as to the other three terms. A's letter is a partially integrated agreement with respect to the first three provisions.

§ 211.   Standardized Agreements

(1)   Except as stated in Subsection (3), where a party to an agreement signs or otherwise manifests assent to a writing and has reason to believe that like writings are regularly used to embody terms of agreements of the same type, he adopts the writing as an integrated agreement with respect to the terms included in the writing.

(2)   Such a writing is interpreted wherever reasonable as treating alike all those similarly situated, without regard to their knowledge or understanding of the standard terms of the writing.

(3)   Where the other party has reason to believe that the party manifesting such assent would not do so if he knew that the writing contained a particular term, the term is not part of the agreement.

Comment:

a.   Utility of standardization. Standardization of agreements serves many of the same functions as standardization of goods and services; both are essential to a system of mass production and distribution. Scarce and costly time and skill can be devoted to a class of transactions rather than to details of individual transactions. Legal rules which would apply in the absence of agreement can be shaped to fit the particular type of transaction, and extra copies of the form can be used for purposes such as record-keeping, coordination and supervision. Forms can be tailored to office routines, the training of personnel, and the requirements of mechanical equipment. Sales personnel and customers are freed from attention to numberless variations and can focus on meaningful choice among a limited number of significant features:

transaction-type, style, quantity, price, or the like. Operations are simplified and costs reduced, to the advantage of all concerned.

b.   Assent to unknown terms. A party who makes regular use of a standardized form of agreement does not ordinarily expect his customers to understand or even to read the standard terms. One of the purposes of standardization is to eliminate bargaining over details of individual transactions, and that purpose would not be served if a substantial number of customers retained counsel and reviewed the standard terms. Employees regularly using a form often have only a limited understanding of its terms and limited authority to vary them. Customers do not in fact ordinarily understand or even read the standard terms. They trust to the good faith of the party using the form and to the tacit representation that like terms are being accepted regularly by others similarly situated. But they understand that they are assenting to the terms not read or not understood, subject to such limitations as the law may impose.

c.   Review of unfair terms. Standardized agreements are commonly prepared by one party. The customer assents to a few terms, typically inserted in blanks on the printed form, and gives blanket assent to the type of transaction embodied in the standard form. He is commonly not represented in the drafting, and the draftsman may be tempted to overdraw in the interest of his employer. The obvious danger of overreaching has resulted in government regulation of insurance policies, bills of lading, retail installment sales, small loans, and other particular types of contracts. Regulation sometimes includes administrative review of standard terms, or even prescription of terms. Apart from such regulation, standard terms imposed by one party are enforced. But standard terms may be superseded by separately negotiated or added terms (§ 203), they are construed against the draftsman (§ 206), and they are subject to the overriding obligation of good faith (§ 205) and to the power of the court to refuse to enforce an unconscionable contract or term (§ 208). Moreover, various contracts and terms are against public policy and unenforceable.

d.   Non-contractual documents. The same document may serve both contractual and other purposes, and a party may assent to it for other purposes without understanding that it embodies contract terms. He may nevertheless be bound if he has reason to know that it is used to embody contract terms. Insurance policies, steamship tickets, bills of lading, and warehouse receipts are commonly so obviously contractual in form as to give the customer reason to know their character. But baggage checks or automobile parking lot tickets may appear to be mere identification tokens, and a party without knowledge or reason to know that the token purports to be a contract is then not bound by terms printed on the token. Documents such as invoices, instructions for use, and the like, delivered after a contract is made, may raise similar problems.

e.   Equality of treatment. One who assents to standard contract terms normally assumes that others are doing likewise and that all who do so are on an equal footing. In the case of a public utility, that assumption is fortified by statutory and common law limitations on discrimination among customers; a term prescribed by statute or regulation in the case of an insurance policy also carries an assurance of equal treatment. Apart from government regulation, courts in construing and applying a standardized contract seek to effectuate the reasonable expectations of the average member of the public who accepts it. The result may be to give the advantage of a restrictive reading to some sophisticated customers who contracted with knowledge of an ambiguity or dispute.

f.   Terms excluded. Subsection (3) applies to standardized agreements the general principles stated in §§ 20 and 201. Although customers typically adhere to standardized agreements and are bound by them without even appearing to know the standard terms in detail, they are not bound to unknown terms which are beyond the range of reasonable expectation. A debtor who delivers a check to his creditor with the amount blank does not authorize the insertion of an infinite figure. Similarly, a party who adheres to the other party's standard terms does not assent to a term if the other party has reason to believe that the adhering party would not have accepted the agreement if he had known that the agreement contained the particular term. Such a belief or assumption may be shown by the prior negotiations or inferred from the circumstances. Reason to believe may be inferred from the fact that the term is bizarre or oppressive, from the fact that it eviscerates the non-standard terms explicitly agreed to, or from the fact that it eliminates the dominant purpose of the transaction. The inference is reinforced if the adhering party never had an opportunity to read the term, or if it is illegible or otherwise hidden from view. This rule is closely related to the policy against unconscionable terms and the rule of interpretation against the draftsman. See §§ 206 and 208.

§ 212.   Interpretation of Integrated Agreement

(1)   The interpretation of an integrated agreement is directed to the meaning of the terms of the writing or writings in the light of the circumstances, in accordance with the rules stated in this Chapter.

(2)   A question of interpretation of an integrated agreement is to be determined by the trier of fact if it depends on the credibility of extrinsic evidence or on a choice among reasonable inferences to be drawn from extrinsic evidence. Otherwise a question of interpretation of an integrated agreement is to be determined as a question of law.

§ 213.   Effect of Integrated Agreement on Prior Agreements (Parol Evidence Rule)

(1)   A binding integrated agreement discharges prior agreements to the extent that it is inconsistent with them.

(2)   A binding completely integrated agreement discharges prior agreements to the extent that they are within its scope.

(3)   An integrated agreement that is not binding or that is voidable and avoided does not discharge a prior agreement. But an integrated agreement, even though not binding, may be effective to render inoperative a term which would have been part of the agreement if it had not been integrated.

§ 214.   Evidence of Prior or Contemporaneous Agreements and Negotiations

Agreements and negotiations prior to or contemporaneous with the adoption of a writing are admissible in evidence to establish

(a) that the writing is or is not an integrated agreement;

(b) that the integrated agreement, if any, is completely or partially integrated;

(c) the meaning of the writing, whether or not integrated;

(d) illegality, fraud, duress, mistake, lack of consideration, or other invalidating cause;

(e) ground for granting or denying rescission, reformation, specific performance, or other remedy.

§ 215. Contradiction of Integrated Terms

Except as stated in the preceding Section, where there is a binding agreement, either completely or partially integrated, evidence of prior or contemporaneous agreements or negotiations is not admissible in evidence to contradict a term of the writing.

§ 216. Consistent Additional Terms

(1) Evidence of a consistent additional term is admissible to supplement an integrated agreement unless the court finds that the agreement was completely integrated.

(2) An agreement is not completely integrated if the writing omits a consistent additional agreed term which is

(a) agreed to for separate consideration, or

(b) such a term as in the circumstances might naturally be omitted from the writing.

§ 217. Integrated Agreement Subject to Oral Requirement of a Condition

Where the parties to a written agreement agree orally that performance of the agreement is subject to the occurrence of a stated condition, the agreement is not integrated with respect to the oral condition.

§ 218. Untrue Recitals; Evidence of Consideration

(1) A recital of a fact in an integrated agreement may be shown to be untrue.

(2) Evidence is admissible to prove whether or not there is consideration for a promise, even though the parties have reduced their agreement to a writing which appears to be a completely integrated agreement.

TOPIC 4. SCOPE AS AFFECTED BY USAGE

§ 219. Usage

Usage is habitual or customary practice.

§ 220. Usage Relevant to Interpretation

(1) An agreement is interpreted in accordance with a relevant usage if each party knew or had reason to know of the usage and neither party knew or had reason to know that the meaning attached by the other was inconsistent with the usage.

(2) When the meaning attached by one party accorded with a relevant usage and the other knew or had reason to know of the usage, the other is treated as having known or had reason to know the meaning attached by the first party.

§ 221. Usage Supplementing an Agreement

An agreement is supplemented or qualified by a reasonable usage with respect to agreements of the same type if each party knows or has reason to know of the usage and neither party knows or has reason to know that the other party has an intention inconsistent with the usage.

§ 222. Usage of Trade

(1) A usage of trade is a usage having such regularity of observance in a place, vocation, or trade as to justify an expectation that it will be observed with respect to a particular agreement. It may include a system of rules regularly observed even though particular rules are changed from time to time.

(2) The existence and scope of a usage of trade are to be determined as questions of fact. If a usage is embodied in a written trade code or similar writing the interpretation of the writing is to be determined by the court as a question of law.

(3) Unless otherwise agreed, a usage of trade in the vocation or trade in which the parties are engaged or a usage of trade of which they know or have reason to know gives meaning to or supplements or qualifies their agreement.

§ 223. Course of Dealing

(1) A course of dealing is a sequence of previous conduct between the parties to an agreement which is fairly to be regarded as establishing a common basis of understanding for interpreting their expressions and other conduct.

(2) Unless otherwise agreed, a course of dealing between the parties gives meaning to or supplements or qualifies their agreement.

TOPIC 5. CONDITIONS AND SIMILAR EVENTS

§ 224. Condition Defined

A condition is an event, not certain to occur, which must occur, unless its non-occurrence is excused, before performance under a contract becomes due.

Comment:

a. "Condition" limited to event. "Condition" is used in this Restatement to denote an event which qualifies a duty under a contract. See the Introductory Note to this Topic. It is recognized that "condition" is used with a wide variety of other meanings in legal discourse. Sometimes it is used to denote an event that limits or qualifies a transfer of property. In the law of trusts, for example, it is used to denote an event such as the death of the settlor that qualifies his disposition of property in trust. See Restatement, Second, Trusts § 360. See also the rules on "conditional" delivery (§ 103) and "conditional" assignment (§§ 103, 331). Sometimes it is used to refer to a term (§ 5) in an agreement that makes an event a condition, or more broadly to refer to any term in an agreement (e.g., "standard conditions of sale"). For the sake of precision, "condition" is not used here in these other senses.

Illustration:

1. A contracts to sell and B to buy goods pursuant to a writing which provides, under the heading "Conditions of Sale," that "the obligations of the parties are conditional on B obtaining from X Bank by June 30 a letter of credit" on stated terms. The quoted language is a term of the agreement (§ 5), not a condition. The event referred to by the term, obtaining the letter of credit by June 30, is a condition.

b. Uncertainty of event. Whether the reason for making an event a condition is to shift to the obligee the risk of its non-occurrence, or whether it is to induce the obligee to cause the event to occur (see Introductory Note to this Topic), there is inherent in the concept of condition some degree of uncertainty as to the occurrence of the event. Therefore, the mere passage of time, as to which there is no uncertainty, is not a condition and a duty is unconditional if nothing but the passage of time is necessary to give rise to a duty of performance. Moreover, an event is not a condition, even though its occurrence is uncertain, if it is referred to merely to measure the passage of time after which an obligor is to perform. See Comment b to § 227. Performance under a contract becomes due when all necessary events, including any conditions and the passage of any required time, have occurred so that a failure of performance will be a breach. See §§ 231–43.

The event need not, in order to be a condition, be one that is to occur after the making of the contract, although that is commonly the case. It may relate to the present or even to the past, as is the case where a marine policy insures against a loss that may already have occurred. Furthermore, a duty may be conditioned upon the failure of something to happen rather than upon its happening, and in that case its failure to happen is the event that is the condition.

Illustrations:

2. A tells B, "If you will paint my house, I will pay you $1,000 on condition that 30 days have passed after you have finished." B paints A's house. Although A is not under a duty to pay B $1,000 until 30 days

have passed, the passage of that time is not a condition of A's duty to pay B $1,000.

3.   A contracts to sell and B to buy goods to be shipped "C.I.F.," payment to be "on arrival of goods." Risk of loss of the goods passes from A to B when A, having otherwise complied with the C.I.F. term of the contract, puts the goods in the possession of the carrier (Uniform Commercial Code § 2–320(2)). If the goods are lost in transit, B is under a duty to pay the price when the goods should have arrived (Uniform Commercial Code §§ 2–709(1)(a), 2–321(3)). The arrival of the goods is not a condition of B's duty to pay for the goods.

c.   *Necessity of a contract.* In order for an event to be a condition, it must qualify a duty under an existing contract. Events which are part of the process of formation of a contract, such as offer and acceptance, are therefore excluded under the definition in this section. It is not customary to call such events conditions. But cf. § 36(2) ("condition of acceptance"). For the most part, they are required by law and may not be dispensed with by the parties, while conditions are the result of, or at least subject to, agreement. Where, however, an offer has become an option contract, e.g., by the payment of a dollar (§ 87), the acceptance is a condition under the definition in this section.

Illustration:

4.   A tells B, "I promise to pay you $1,000 if you paint my house." B begins to paint A's house. Since B's beginning of the invited performance gives rise to an option contract, B's completion of performance is a condition of A's duty under that contract to pay B $1,000. See § 45.

d.   *Relationship of conditions.* A duty may be subject to any number of conditions, which may be related to each other in various ways. They may be cumulative so that performance will not become due unless all of them occur. They may be alternative so that performance may become due if any one of them occurs. Or some may be cumulative and some alternative. Furthermore, a condition may qualify the duties of both parties. Cf. § 217.

Illustrations:

5.   A, as the result of financial reverses, sells B a valuable painting for $1,000,000, but reserves a right to repurchase it by tendering the same price on or before August 18 if he again finds himself in such a financial condition that he can keep it for his personal enjoyment. A's tender of $1,000,000 by August 18 and his being in such financial condition that he can keep the painting for his personal enjoyment are cumulative conditions and redelivery of the painting does not become due unless both of them occur.

6.   A purchases land from Mrs. B, who is unable to get Mr. B to join her in signing the deed because they are engaged in divorce proceedings. A takes possession under a deed signed by Mrs. B, pays Mrs. B $10,000 and promises to pay an additional $5,000 "if, within one year, (1) Mr. and Mrs. B execute a quitclaim deed to A, or (2) Mrs. B furnishes A with a certificate of the death of Mr. B with Mrs. B surviving him, or (3) Mrs. B as a single person executes a quitclaim deed to A after having been awarded the land following the entry of a final decree of divorce from Mr. B." The three enumerated events are alternative conditions and A's payment of $5,000 to Mrs. B becomes due if any of them occurs.

7.   A and B contract to merge their corporate holdings into a single new company. It is agreed that the project is not to be operative un-

less the parties raise $600,000 additional capital. The raising of the additional capital is a condition of the duties of both A and B. If it is not raised, neither A's nor B's performance becomes due.

e.   Occurrence of event as discharge. Parties sometimes provide that the occurrence of an event, such as the failure of one of them to commence an action within a prescribed time, will extinguish a duty after performance has become due, along with any claim for breach. Such an event has often been called a "condition subsequent," while an event of the kind defined in this section has been called a "condition precedent." This terminology is not followed here. Since a "condition subsequent," so-called, is subject to the rules on discharge in § 230, and not to the following rules on conditions, it is not called a "condition" in this Restatement. Occasionally, although the language of an agreement says that if an event does not occur a duty is "extinguished," "discharged," or "terminated," it can be seen from the circumstances that the event must ordinarily occur before performance of the duty can be expected. When a court concludes that, for this reason, performance is not to become due unless the event occurs, the event is, in spite of the language, a condition of the duty. See § 227(3). See also Comment a to § 230.

Illustrations:

8.   A insures B's property against theft. The policy provides that B's failure to notify A within 30 days after loss shall "terminate" A's duty to pay and that suit must be brought within one year after loss. Since it can be seen from the circumstances that notice must ordinarily be given before payment by A can be expected, B's notification of A within 30 days after loss is a condition of A's duty. B's bringing suit against A within a year after loss is not a condition of A's duty. B's failure to bring suit within that time will discharge A's duty after payment has become due, along with any claim for breach.

9.   A and B make a contract under which A promises to pay B $10,000 in annual installments of $1,000 each, beginning the following January 1, with a provision that "no installments whether or not overdue and unpaid shall be payable in case of A's death within the 10 years." A's being alive is a condition of his duty to pay any installment. A's death within ten years will discharge his duty to pay any installment after payment has become due, along with any claim for breach.

f.   Sealed contracts. The rules governing conditions stated in the Restatement of this Subject are applicable to sealed as well as unsealed contracts. The same rules have traditionally been applied to both types of contract with technical exceptions that are no longer of significance.

§ 225.   Effects of the Non-Occurrence of a Condition

(1)   Performance of a duty subject to a condition cannot become due unless the condition occurs or its non-occurrence is excused.

(2)   Unless it has been excused, the non-occurrence of a condition discharges the duty when the condition can no longer occur.

(3)   Non-occurrence of a condition is not a breach by a party unless he is under a duty that the condition occur.

§ 226. How an Event May Be Made a Condition

An event may be made a condition either by the agreement of the parties or by a term supplied by the court.

§ 227. Standards of Preference With Regard to Conditions

(1)   In resolving doubts as to whether an event is made a condition of an obligor's duty, and as to the nature of such an event, an interpretation is preferred that will reduce the obligee's risk of forfeiture, unless the event is within the obligee's control or the circumstances indicate that he has assumed the risk.

(2)   Unless the contract is of a type under which only one party generally undertakes duties, when it is doubtful whether

(a)   a duty is imposed on an obligee that an event occur, or

(b)   the event is made a condition of the obligor's duty, or

(c)   the event is made a condition of the obligor's duty and a duty is imposed on the obligee that the event occur,

the first interpretation is preferred if the event is within the obligee's control.

(3)   In case of doubt, an interpretation under which an event is a condition of an obligor's duty is preferred over an interpretation under which the non-occurrence of the event is a ground for discharge of that duty after it has become a duty to perform.

Comment:

a.   Scope. The present Section states three standards of preference used in the process of interpretation with regard to conditions. They supplement the standards of preference in § 203, as well as the other rules set out in Topics 1 through 4 of this Chapter.

b.   Condition or not. The non-occurrence of a condition of an obligor's duty may cause the obligee to lose his right to the agreed exchange after he has relied substantially on the expectation of that exchange, as by preparation or performance. The word "forfeiture" is used in this Restatement to refer to the denial of compensation that results in such a case. The policy favoring freedom of contract requires that, within broad limits (see § 229), the agreement of the parties should be honored even though forfeiture results. When, how-ever, it is doubtful whether or not the agreement makes an event a condition of an obligor's duty, an interpretation is preferred that will reduce the risk of forfeiture. For example, under a provision that a duty is to be performed "when" an event occurs, it may be doubtful whether it is to be performed only if that event occurs, in which case the event is a condition, or at such time as it would ordinarily occur, in which case the event is referred to merely to measure the passage of time. In the latter case, if the event does not occur some alternative means will be found to measure the passage of time, and the non-occurrence of the event will not prevent the obligor's duty from becoming one of performance. If the event is a condition, however, the obligee takes the risk that its non-occurrence will discharge the obligor's duty. See § 225(2). When the nature of the condition is such that the uncertainty as to the event will be resolved before either party has relied on its anticipated occurrence, both parties can be entirely relieved of their duties, and the obligee risks only the loss of his expectations. When, however, the nature of the condition is such that the uncertainty is not likely to be resolved until after the obligee has relied by preparing to perform or by performing at least in part, he risks forfeiture. If the event is within his control, he will often assume this risk. If it is not within his control, it is sufficiently unusual for him to assume the risk that, in case of doubt, an interpretation is preferred under which the event is not a condition. The rule is, of course, subject to a showing of a contrary intention, and even without clear language, circumstances may show that he assumed the risk of its non-occurrence.

Although the rule is consistent with a policy of avoiding forfeiture and unjust enrichment, it is not directed at the avoidance of actual forfeiture and unjust enrichment. Since the intentions of the parties must be taken as of the time the contract was made, the test is whether a particular interpretation would have avoided the risk of forfeiture viewed as of that time, not whether it will avoid actual forfeiture in the resolution of a dispute that has arisen later. Excuse of the non-occurrence of a condition because of actual forfeiture is dealt with in § 229, and rules for the avoidance of unjust enrichment as such are dealt with in the Restatement of Restitution and in Chapter 16 of this Restatement, particularly §§ 370–77.

Illustrations:

1.   A, a general contractor, contracts with B, a sub-contractor, for the plumbing work on a construction project. B is to receive $100,000, "no part of which shall be due until five days after Owner shall have paid Contractor there-for." B does the plumbing work, but the owner becomes insolvent and fails to pay A. A is under a duty to pay B after a reasonable time.

2.   A, a mining company, hires B, an engineer, to help reopen one of its mines for "$10,000 to be payable as soon as the mine is in successful operation." $10,000 is a reasonable compensation for B's service. B performs the required services, but the attempt to reopen the mine is unsuccessful and A abandons it. A is under a duty to pay B $10,000 after the passage of a reasonable time.

3.   A, a mining company, contracts with B, the owner of an untested experimental patented process, to help reopen one of its mines for $5,000 paid in advance and an additional "$15,000 to be payable as soon as the mine is in successful operation." $10,000 is a reasonable compensation for B's services. B performs the required services, but because the process proves to be unsuccessful, A abandons the attempt to reopen the mine. A is under no duty to pay B any additional amount. In all the circumstances the risk of failure of the process was, to that extent, assumed by B.

4.   A contracts to sell and B to buy land for $100,000. At the same time, A contracts to pay C, a real estate broker, as his commission, $5,000 "on the closing of title." B refuses to consummate the sale. Absent a showing of a contrary intention, a court may conclude that C assumed this risk, and that A's duty is conditional on the sale being consummated. A is then under no duty to pay C.

c.   Nature of event. In determining the nature of the event that is made a condition by the agreement, as in determining whether the agreement makes an event a condition in the first place (see Comment b), it will not ordinarily be supposed that a party has assumed the risk of forfeiture. Where the language is doubtful, an interpretation is generally preferred that will avoid this risk. This standard of preference finds an important application in the case of promises to pay for work done if some independent third party, such as an architect, surveyor or engineer, is satisfied with it, where the risk of forfeiture in the case of a judgment that is dishonest or based on a gross mistake as to the facts is substantial. The standard does not, however, help a party if the condition is within his control or if the circumstances otherwise indicate that he assumed that risk.

Illustrations:

5. A contracts with B to repair B's building for $20,000, payment to be made "on the satisfaction of C, B's architect, and the issuance of his certificate." A makes the repairs, but C refuses to issue his certificate, and explains why he is not satisfied. Other experts in the field consider A's performance to be satisfactory and disagree with C's explanation. A has no claim against B. The quoted language is sufficiently clear that Subsection (1) does not apply. If C is honestly not satisfied, B is under no duty to pay A, and it makes no difference if his dissatisfaction was not reasonable.

6. The facts being otherwise as stated in Illustration 5, C refuses to issue his certificate although he admits that he is satisfied. A has a claim against B for $20,000. The quoted language will be interpreted so that the requirement of the certificate is merely evidentiary and the condition occurs when there is, as here, adequate evidence that C is honestly satisfied.

7. The facts being otherwise as stated in Illustration 5, C does not make a proper inspection of the work and gives no reasons for his dissatisfaction. A has a claim against B for $20,000. In using the quoted language, A and B assumed that C would exercise an honest judgment and by failing to make a proper inspection, C did not exercise such a judgment. Since the parties have omitted an essential term to cover this situation, the court will supply a term (see § 204) requiring A to pay B if C ought reasonably to have been satisfied.

8. The facts being otherwise as stated in Illustration 5, C makes a gross mistake with reference to the facts on which his refusal to give a certificate is based. A has a claim against B for $20,000. In using the quoted language, A and B assumed that C would exercise his judgment without a gross mistake as to the facts. Since the parties have omitted an essential term to cover this situation, the court will supply a term (see § 204) requiring A to pay B if C ought reasonably to have been satisfied.

d. *Condition or duty.* When an obligor wants the obligee to do an act, the obligor may make his own duty conditional on the obligee doing it and may also have the obligee promise to do it. Or he may merely make his own duty conditional on the obligee doing it. Or he may merely have the obligee promise to do it. (See Introductory Note to this Topic and Comment d to § 225). It may not be clear, however, which he has done. The rule in Subsection (2) states a preference for an interpretation that merely imposes a duty on the obligee to do the act and does not make the doing of the act a condition of the obligor's duty. The preferred interpretation avoids the harsh results that might otherwise result from the non-occurrence of a condition and still gives adequate protection to the obligor under the rules of Chapter 10 relating to performances to be exchanged under an exchange of promises. Under those rules, particularly §§ 237–41, the obligee's failure to perform his duty has, if it is material, the effect of the non-occurrence of a condition of the obligor's duty. Unless the agreement makes it clear that the event is required as a condition, it is fairer to apply these more flexible rules. The obligor will, in any case, have a remedy for breach. In many instances the rule in Subsection (1) will also apply and will reinforce the preference stated in Subsection (2).

This standard of preference applies only where the event is within the obligee's control. Where it is within the obligor's control (e.g., his honest satisfaction with the obligee's performance), within a third party's control (e.g., an architect's satisfaction with performance), or within no one's control (e.g., the accidental destruction of the subject matter), the preferential rule does not apply since it is not usual for the obligee to undertake a duty that such an event will occur. Although the obligee can, by appropriate language, undertake a duty that an event that is not within his control will occur, such an undertaking must be derived from the agreement of the parties under the general rules of interpretation stated earlier in the present Chapter without resort to this standard of preference.

Furthermore, this standard of preference does not apply when the contract is of a type under which only the obligor generally undertakes duties. It therefore does not apply to the typical insurance contract under which only the insurer generally undertakes duties, and a term requiring an act to be done by the insured is not subject to this standard of preference. In view of the general understanding that only the insurer undertakes duties, the term will be interpreted as making that event a condition of the insurer's duty rather than as imposing a duty on the insured.

Illustrations:

9. On August 1, A contracts to sell and B to buy goods, "selection to be made by buyer before September 1." B merely has a duty to make his selection by September 1, and his making it by that date is not a condition of A's duty. A failure by B to make a selection by September 1 is a breach, and if material it operates as the non-occurrence of a condition of A's duty. See §§ 237, 241.

10. A, B, and C make a contract under which A agrees to buy the inventory of B's grocery business, C agrees to finance A's down payment, and B agrees to subordinate A's obligation to him to pay the balance to A's obligation to C to repay the amount of the down payment. The contract provides that "C shall maintain the books of account for A, and shall inventory A's stock of merchandise every two months, rendering statements to B." C merely has a duty to do these acts and doing them is not a condition of B's duty. A failure by C to do them is a breach, and if material it operates as the non-occurrence of a condition of B's duty. See §§ 237, 241.

11. A insures B's house against fire for $50,000 under a policy providing, "other insurance is prohibited." Because the insured has undertaken no other duties under the contract, Subsection (2) does not apply. Because a policy of fire insurance is a type of contract under which only the insurer generally undertakes duties, the absence of other insurance is merely a condition of A's duty, and B is not under a duty not to procure other insurance.

e. Condition or discharge. Circumstances may show that the parties intended to make an event a condition of an obligor's duty even though their language appears to make the non-occurrence of the event a ground for discharge of his duty after performance has become due. See Comment e to § 224. An example is the traditional form of bond, which states that the obligor is under a duty to perform, but that the duty will be discharged if something happens. The language, in spite of its form, is interpreted so that the failure of that thing to happen is a condition of the obligor's duty. Unless that condition occurs, no performance is due. Although this form of expression persists in legal documents, only rarely do the parties intend that one of them shall be under a duty to perform which is to cease on the occurrence of something that is still uncertain. The clearest language is therefore necessary to justify such an interpretation, and if the language is doubtful a contrary interpretation is preferred.

Illustrations:

12. In return for a fee paid by X, A signs and delivers to B a bond which reads: "I acknowledge myself to be indebted to B in the sum of $50,000. The condition of this obligation is such that if X shall faithfully perform his duties as executor of the will of Y, this obligation shall be void, but otherwise of full effect." X's failure faithfully to perform his duties is a condition of A's duty under the bond.

13. A promises to pay B $10,000 for a quantity of oil, and promises to pay B an additional $5,000 "but if a greater quantity of oil arrives in vessels during the first quarter of the year than arrived during the same quarter last year, then this obligation to be void." A's payment of the additional $5,000 is not due until the end of the first quarter, and the failure of a greater quantity of oil to arrive by that time is a condition of A's duty to pay the additional $5,000.

§ 228. Satisfaction of the Obligor as a Condition

When it is a condition of an obligor's duty that he be satisfied with respect to the obligee's performance or with respect to something else, and it is practicable to determine whether a reasonable person in the position of the obligor would be satisfied, an interpretation is preferred under which the condition occurs if such a reasonable person in the position of the obligor would be satisfied.

§ 229. Excuse of a Condition to Avoid Forfeiture

To the extent that the non-occurrence of a condition would cause disproportionate forfeiture, a court may excuse the non-occurrence of that condition unless its occurrence was a material part of the agreed exchange.

§ 230. Event That Terminates a Duty

(1) Except as stated in Subsection (2), if under the terms of the contract the occurrence of an event is to terminate an obligor's duty of immediate performance or one to pay damages for breach, that duty is discharged if the event occurs.

(2) The obligor's duty is not discharged if occurrence of the event

(a) is the result of a breach by the obligor of his duty of good faith and fair dealing, or

(b) could not have been prevented because of impracticability and continuance of the duty does not subject the obligor to a materially increased burden.

(3) The obligor's duty is not discharged if, before the event occurs, the obligor promises to perform the duty even if the event occurs and does not revoke his promise before the obligee materially changes his position in reliance on it.

CHAPTER 10. PERFORMANCE AND NON-PERFORMANCE

TOPIC 1. PERFORMANCES TO BE EXCHANGED UNDER AN EXCHANGE OF PROMISES

§ 231. Criterion for Determining When Performances Are to Be Exchanged Under an Exchange of Promises

Performances are to be exchanged under an exchange of promises if each promise is at least part of the consideration for the other and the performance of each promise is to be exchanged at least in part for the performance of the other.

§ 232. When it is Presumed That Performances Are to Be Exchanged Under an Exchange of Promises

Where the consideration given by each party to a contract consists in whole or in part of promises, all the performances to be rendered by each party taken collectively are treated as performances to be exchanged under an exchange of promises, unless a contrary intention is clearly manifested.

Comment:

a. Reason for presumption. The rules applicable to performances to be exchanged under an exchange of promises are designed to give the parties maximum protection, consistent with freedom of contract, against disappointment of their expectation of a subsequent exchange of those performances. When the parties have exchanged promises, there is ordinarily every reason to suppose that they contracted on the basis of such an expectation since the exchange of promises would otherwise have little purpose. Even absent a showing of their actual inten- tions, fairness dictates that such an expectation be assumed. This Section therefore states a presumption in favor of the conclusion that, in such a case, the performances are to be exchanged under the exchange of promises. For one of the parties to show that the expectation was otherwise, the contrary intention must be clearly manifested. The presumption applies regardless of whether the promises are written or oral or both, and even where a nego- tiable instrument is involved. See Uni- form Commercial Code § 3–408. It also applies even though the consideration given by a party consists partly of some performance and only partly of a promise (see Comment c to § 231), although it is possible that in such a case the promise may be so minor and incidental that its non-performance would not be a material failure of performance. See Comment b to § 241.

Illustrations:

1.   A, a wholesaler, promises to sell and B, a retailer, promises to buy goods together with related advertising material, payment to be made within 30 days of delivery. A also promises not to sell similar advertising material to any other retailer in B's city. A sells similar advertising material to another retailer in B's city, and B thereupon refuses to take or pay for the goods. A's selling B goods together with advertising material and not selling others similar advertising material, taken collectively, and B's payment are to be exchanged under the exchange of promises. Therefore, under the rule stated in § 237, if A's failure of performance is material, A has no claim against B.

2.   A promises to sell to B a lot in a subdivision for $8,000. B promises to pay in four annual installments of $2,000 each, beginning one year after execution of the contract. A promises to begin to make improvements and pave the streets within 60 days and to complete work within a reasonable time and promises to deliver a deed at the time of the final payment. A fails to pave the streets, and B thereupon refuses to pay any installments. A's making improvements, paving streets, and delivering a deed, taken collectively, and B's paying installments are to be exchanged under the exchange of promises. Therefore, under the rule stated in § 237, if A's failure of performance is material, A has no claim against B.

3.   A employs B under a five-year employment contract, which contains a valid covenant under which B promises not to engage in the same business in a designated area for two years after the termination of the employment. It expressly provides that "this covenant is independent of any other provision in this agreement." After B has begun work, A unjustifiably discharges him, and B thereupon engages in business in violation of the covenant. A's employing B and B's working for A are to be exchanged under the exchange of promises. The quoted words indicate an intention that A's employing B is not to be exchanged for B's refraining from engaging in the same business. If the court concludes that this intention is clearly manifested, A has a claim against B for damages for breach of his promise not to compete.

4.   A contracts to sell and B to buy a machine, to be delivered immediately, for $10,000. As part of the same bargain, B gives A his negotiable promissory note for $10,000 to A's order, payable in 90 days, but the note makes no reference to the transaction out of which it arises. A fails to deliver the machine. A's delivering the machine and B's paying the note are to be exchanged under the exchange of promises. Therefore, under the rule stated in § 237, A has no claim on the note or the contract against B. See Uniform Commercial Code §§ 3–306, 3–408, and 3–307(3).

b.   Promises taken collectively. When the rule stated in this Section applies, all of the performances to be rendered by each party taken collectively are to be exchanged under the exchange of promises. A court need not determine whether separate performances on either side are the subject of a single promise or of separate promises. Nor need a court concern itself with the relationship among separate promises viewed as of the time of their making. Instead the court is to focus on the relative importance of the failure of performance in the light of the situation of the parties at the time of that failure. See §§ 237, 238, 241.

c. Performances need not be treated as equivalent. When an exchange consists exclusively of promises, the values of the performances to be subsequently exchanged are usually regarded by the parties as equivalent. This is not always so since a party may make what is often called an "aleatory" promise, under which his duty to perform is conditional on the occurrence of a fortuitous event. Or it may be understood that the value of one party's performance will be affected by chance, as where he promises to deliver his output or to pay during another's lifetime. Even when one or both of the parties makes such a promise, however, they contemplate a subsequent exchange of performances, subject of course to the occurrence of the required conditions. Such cases are therefore subject to the rules stated in this Chapter (see § 239), along with some special rules relating to the election of remedies which are stated in §§ 378–80.

Illustration:

5.   A, an insurance company, issues to B a group health insurance policy covering B's employees for one year beginning January 1 in return for B's promise to pay the premium on February 1. During the month of January A unjustifiably rejects proper claims filed by B's employees under the policy. B refuses to pay the premium on February 1. A's paying proper claims of B's employees and B's paying the premium are to be exchanged under the exchange of promises. Therefore, under the rule stated in § 237, if A's breach is material, A has no claim against B.

§ 233.   Performance at One Time or in Installments

(1)   Where performances are to be exchanged under an exchange of promises, and the whole of one party's performance can be rendered at one time, it is due at one time, unless the language or the circumstances indicate the contrary.

(2)   Where only a part of one party's performance is due at one time under Subsection (1), if the other party's performance can be so apportioned that there is a comparable part that can also be rendered at that time, it is due at that time, unless the language or the circumstances indicate the contrary.

§ 234.   Order of Performances

(1)   Where all or part of the performances to be exchanged under an exchange of promises can be rendered simultaneously, they are to that extent due simultaneously, unless the language or the circumstances indicate the contrary.

(2)   Except to the extent stated in Subsection (1), where the performance of only one party under such an exchange requires a period of time, his performance is due at an earlier time than that of the other party, unless the language or the circumstances indicate the contrary.

Comment:

a.   Advantages of simultaneous performance. A requirement that the parties perform simultaneously where their performances are to be exchanged under an exchange of promises is fair for two reasons. First, it offers both parties maximum security against disappointment of their expectations of a subsequent exchange of performances by allowing each party to defer his own performance until he has been assured that the other will perform. This advantage is implemented by the rule stated in § 238, which deals with offers to perform. Second, it avoids placing on either party the burden of financing the other before the latter has performed. Subsection (1) therefore imposes a requirement of simultaneous performance whenever this is feasible under the contract, in the absence of language or circumstances indicating a contrary intention. A notable example of such a requirement is that laid down for contracts for the sale of goods by Uniform Commercial Code §§ 2–507 and 2–511. The requirement is subject to the agreement of the parties, as by an express provision extending credit to the buyer, or one requiring him to pay against documents or to furnish a letter of credit. Even absent an express provision, a contrary intention may be shown by circumstances including usage of trade and course of dealing (§§ 221, 223; Uniform Commercial Code § 1–205).

b.   When simultaneous performance possible under agreement. In the absence of language or circumstances showing a contrary intention, the requirement of simultaneous performance stated in Subsection (1) applies whenever such performance is possible, consistent with the terms of the contract. A major instance where simultaneous performance is not possible occurs when one party's performance is continuous over some substantial period of time, a situation that is dealt with in Subsection (2). However, as is the case for the requirement of the preceding section that the whole performance be possible at one time, the requirement of simultaneous performance is not to be applied so literally as to exclude instances in which the objectives of the requirement can be fulfilled although performance cannot be instantaneous. See Comment a to § 233. A less important instance where simultaneous performance is not possible occurs when distance and lack of adequate communications make it impossible to assure the parties that performance is taking place at the same time, so that although the performance of each party can be instantaneous, the two performances cannot be simultaneous within the meaning of Subsection (1). Cases in which simultaneous performance is possible under the terms of the contract can be grouped into five categories: (1) where the same time is fixed for the performance of each party; (2) where a time is fixed for the performance of one of the parties and no time is fixed for the other; (3) where no time is fixed for the performance of either party; (4) where the same period is fixed within which each party is to perform; (5) where different periods are fixed within which each party is to perform. The requirement of simultaneous performance applies to the first four categories. The requirement does not apply to the fifth category, even if simultaneous performance is possible, because in fixing different periods for performance the parties must have contemplated the possibility of performance at different times under their agreement. Therefore in cases in the fifth category the circumstances show an intention contrary to the rule stated in Subsection (1).

Illustrations:

1.   A promises to sell land to B, delivery of the deed to be on July 1. B promises to pay A $50,000, pay-

ment to be made on July 1. Delivery of the deed and payment of the price are due simultaneously.

2.   A promises to sell land to B, the deed to be delivered on July 1. B promises to pay A $50,000, no provision being made for the time of payment. Delivery of the deed and payment of the price are due simultaneously.

3.   A promises to sell land to B and B promises to pay A $50,000, no provision being made for the time either of delivery of the deed or of payment. Delivery of the deed and payment of the price are due simultaneously.

4.   A promises to sell land to B, delivery of the deed to be on or before July 1. B promises to pay A $50,000, payment to be on or before July 1. Delivery of the deed and payment of the price are due simultaneously.

5.   A promises to sell land to B, delivery of the deed to be on or before July 1. B promises to pay A $50,000, payment to be on or before August 1. Delivery of the deed and payment of the prices are not due simultaneously.

c.   When simultaneous performance possible in part. The requirement of simultaneous performance stated in Subsection (1) also applies where only part rather than all of the performance of one party can be performed simultaneously with either part or all of the performance of the other party. It therefore applies to the situations discussed in Comment b to § 233 and exemplified by Illustration 3 to that section. But it is broader than this and also applies, for example, to instances where some part performance of one party can be rendered simultaneously with the entire performance of the other party. See Comment f and Illustration 12.

Illustrations:

6.   A promises to sell land to B, delivery of the deed to be four years from the following July 1. B promises to pay A $50,000 in installments of $10,000 on each July 1 for five years. Delivery of the deed and payment of the last installment are due simultaneously.

7.   A promises to sell land to B, delivery of the deed to be one year from July 1. B promises to pay A $50,000 in installments of $10,000 on each July 1 for five years. Delivery of the deed and payment of the second installment are due simultaneously.

d.   When simultaneous performance later becomes possible. Although different times or periods were originally fixed for the performance of each party, performance by the party who is to perform first may sometimes be delayed until the time for performance by the other party has arrived. If the latter party is entitled to and does assert that his remaining duties of performance are discharged because of the delay, under the rule stated in § 237, no question of the order of performance remains. Unless the delay is justified, he will also have a claim for damages for total breach based on all of his remaining rights to performance. (§§ 236(1), 243(1)). If, however, he is not entitled to assert that his remaining duties of performance are discharged, or if he does not assert this even though he is entitled to do so, a question of the order of performances remains. Unless the delay is justified he will, of course, have a claim for damages for partial breach because of the delay. Whether or not the delay is justified, he can at least insist on simultaneous performance. (As to judicial supervision of the requirement of simultaneous performance where the injured party has brought an action before the time when his own performance is due and that time then arrives before he has obtained and enforced a judgment, see Comment c and Illustration 5 to § 238.) There may be circumstances, however, in which it is appropriate for him to require the other party to perform first, as where the parties to a sale of goods contemplate that the buyer will need the time specified between delivery and payment to resell the goods in order to pay the price. In such a case the right of the party in delay to receive payment may be subject to postponement.

Illustration:

8.   The facts being otherwise as stated in Illustration 6, B duly pays the first three installments, but unjustifiably does not pay the fourth until the fifth is due. If B's failure to pay the fourth installment discharges A's remaining duties of performance under the rule stated in § 237, A has a claim for damages for total breach (§ 243(1)), and no further performance is due from either party. Otherwise B's failure to pay the fourth installment gives rise to only a claim for damages for partial breach because of the delay, and, unless circumstances make it appropriate for A to require B to pay the fourth installment first, delivery of the deed and payment of the fourth and fifth installments are then due simultaneously.

e.   Where performance requires a period of time. Where the performance of one party requires a period of time and the performance of the other party does not, their performance can not be simultaneous. Since one of the parties must perform first, he must forego the security that a requirement of simultaneous performance affords against disappointment of his expectation of an exchange of performances, and he must bear the burden of financing the other party before the latter has performed. See Comment a. Of course the parties can by express provision mitigate the harshness of a rule that requires that one completely perform before the other perform at all. They often do this, for example, in construction contracts by stating a formula under which payment is to be made at stated intervals as work progresses. But it is not feasible for courts to devise such formulas for the wide variety of such cases that come before them in which the parties have made no provision. Centuries ago, the principle became settled that where work is to be done by one party and payment is to be made by the other, the performance of the work must precede payment, in the absence of a showing of a contrary intention. It is sometimes supposed, that this principle grew out of employment contracts, and reflects a conviction that employers as a class are more likely to be responsible than are workmen paid in advance. Whether or not the explanation is correct, most parties today contract with reference to the principle, and unless they have evidenced a contrary intention it is at least as fair as the opposite rule would be.

f.   Applicability of rule. The rule stated in Subsection (2) usually finds its application to contracts involving services, such as construction and employment contracts. The common practice of making express provision for progress payments has diminished its importance with regard to the former, and the widespread enactment of state wage statutes giving the employee a right to the frequent periodic payment of wages has lessened its significance with regard to the latter. Nevertheless, it is a helpful rule for residual cases not otherwise provided for. It applies not only to contracts under which the performance of one party is more or less continuous, but also to contracts where performance consists of a series of acts with an interval of time between them. See Comment c. Under a contract of the latter type, simultaneity may be possible in part and, to the extent that it is possible, the rule stated in Subsection (2) is subject to that stated in Subsection (1). See Illustrations 6 and 12.

Illustrations:

9. A contracts to do the concrete work on a building being constructed by B for $10 a cubic yard. In the absence of language or circumstances indicating the contrary, payment by B is not due until A has finished the concrete work.

10. The facts being otherwise as stated in Illustration 9, B promises to furnish a bond to secure his payment. No provision is made as to the time for furnishing the bond. No performance by A is due until B has furnished the bond. Although the doing of the concrete work by A requires a period of time and the furnishing of the bond by B does not, the circumstance that the bond is required to secure payment by B indicates that B must furnish the bond first.

11. A contracts to make alterations in B's home for $5,000. $500 is to be paid on the signing of the contract, $1,500 on the starting of work, $2,000 on the completion of rough carpentry and rough plumbing, and $1,000 on the completion of the job. Payment by B is due as the work progresses according to the terms of the contract.

12. A promises to sell land to B, in return for which B promises to pay A $10,000 a year for five years on July 1 of each year. No provision is made as to the time for delivery of a deed. Delivery of a deed is not due until July 1 of the fifth year, at which time delivery of the deed and payment of the last installment are due simultaneously. See Illustration 6.

TOPIC 2. EFFECT OF PERFORMANCE AND NON-PERFORMANCE

§ 235. Effect of Performance as Discharge and of Non-Performance as Breach

(1) Full performance of a duty under a contract discharges the duty.

(2) When performance of a duty under a contract is due any non-performance is a breach.

§ 236. Claims for Damages for Total and for Partial Breach

(1) A claim for damages for total breach is one for damages based on all of the injured party's remaining rights to performance.

(2) A claim for damages for partial breach is one for damages based on only part of the injured party's remaining rights to performance.

§ 237. Effect on Other Party's Duties of a Failure to Render Performance

Except as stated in § 240, it is a condition of each party's remaining duties to render performances to be exchanged under an exchange of promises that there be no uncured material failure by the other party to render any such performance due at an earlier time.

Comment:

a.   Effect of non-occurrence of condition. Under the rule stated in this Section, a material failure of performance, including defective performance as well as an absence of performance, operates as the non-occurrence of a condition. Under § 225, the non-occurrence of a condition has two possible effects on the duty subject to that condition. See Comment a to § 225. The first is that of preventing performance of the duty from becoming due, at least temporarily (§ 225(1)). The second is that of discharging the duty when the condition can no longer occur (§ 225(2)). A material failure of performance has, under this Section, these effects on the other party's remaining duties of performance with respect to the exchange. It prevents performance of those duties from becoming due, at least temporarily, and it discharges those duties if it has not been cured during the time in which performance can occur. The occurrence of conditions of the type dealt with in this Section is required out of a sense of fairness rather than as a result of the agreement of the parties. Such conditions are therefore sometimes referred to as "constructive conditions of exchange." Cf. § 204. What is sometimes referred to as "failure of consideration" by courts and statutes (e.g., Uniform Commercial Code § 3–408) is referred to in this Restatement as "failure of performance" to avoid confusion with the absence of consideration. Circumstances significant in determining whether a failure is material are set out in § 241. Circumstances significant in determining the period of time after which remaining duties are discharged, if a material failure has not been cured, are set out in § 242. The rules stated in this Section and the one following apply without regard to whether or not the failure of performance is a breach. They apply, for example, even though the failure is justified on the ground of impracticability of performance (Chap-

ter 11). Illustrations of the operation of these rules in situations in which the failure is justified are given in other chapters under the sections that deal with the particular justification, such as impracticability. See, e.g., §§ 267, 268. The illustrations in this Chapter concern, for the most part, their operation in situations where the failure is a breach. But see, e.g., Illustration 3. The rules of this Section and the one following apply even when the promise of the party in default is unenforceable under the Statute of Frauds, while the promise of the other party is enforceable. See § 140. They are, of course, subject to variation by agreement of the parties.

Illustrations:

1.   A contracts to build a house for B for $50,000, progress payments to be made monthly in an amount equal to 85% of the price of the work performed during the preceding month, the balance to be paid on the architect's certificate of satisfactory completion of the house. Without justification B fails to make a $5,000 progress payment. A thereupon stops work on the house and a week goes by. A's failure to continue the work is not a breach and B has no claim against A. B's failure to make the progress payment is an uncured material failure of performance which operates as the non-occurrence of a condition of A's remaining duties of performance under the exchange. If B offers to make the delayed payment and in all the circumstances it is not too late to cure the material breach, A's duties to continue the work are not discharged. A has a claim against B for damages for partial breach because of the delay.

2.   The facts being otherwise as stated in Illustration 1, B fails to make the progress payment or to give any explanation or assur-

ances for one month. If, in all the circumstances, it is now too late for B to cure his material failure of performance by making the delayed payment, A's duties to continue the work are discharged. Because B's failure to make the progress payment was a breach, A also has a claim against B for total breach of contract (§ 243).

3. A, a theater manager, contracts with B, an actress, for performance by her for a period of six months in a play that A is about to present. B dies during the first week of the performance. A's remaining duties with respect to the exchange of performances are discharged by B's uncured material failure of performance. Because B's failure is justified on the ground of impossibility (§ 262), A has no claim against B's estate.

b. First material failure of performance. In many disputes over failure of performance, both parties fail to finish performance, and the question is whether one of them is justified in so doing by the other party's failure. (Compare Comment d.) This Section states the fundamental rule under which that question is to be answered. (The liability of the other party for damages for total breach is governed by the rule stated in § 243.) The rule is based on the principle that where performances are to be exchanged under an exchange of promises, each party is entitled to the assurance that he will not be called upon to perform his remaining duties of performance with respect to the expected exchange if there has already been an uncured material failure of performance by the other party. The central problem is in determining which party is chargeable with the first uncured material failure of performance. In determining the relative times when performance is due, the terms of the agreement and the supplementary rules on time for performance

should be considered (§§ 233, 234). In determining whether there has been a failure of performance, the terms of the agreement and the supplementary rules such as those on omitted essential terms (§ 204) and the duty of good faith and fair dealing (§ 205) should be considered. In determining whether a failure of performance is material, the circumstances listed in § 241 should be considered. Even if the failure is material, it may still be possible to cure it by subsequent performance without a material failure. In the event of cure the injured party may still have a claim for any remaining non-performance as well as for any delay. In determining when it is too late to cure a failure of performance, the circumstances listed in § 242 should be considered. In making all of these determinations the situation of the parties is to be viewed as of the time for performance and in terms of the actual failure. If, for example, under the terms of the agreement the order of performance depends on an event subsequent to the time of the making of the contract, that event is to be taken into account.

Illustrations:

4. A contracts to sell and B to buy at a stated price four parcels of land which A does not own but which the parties expect A to acquire by purchase at a foreclosure sale. A bids on the four parcels at the foreclosure sale, but each time B bids against him and acquires all four for less than the contract price. A does not convey the four parcels to B. B has no claim against A. B's bidding at the sale was a material breach of his duty of good faith and fair dealing (§ 205), which operated as the non-occurrence of a condition of A's duties and discharged them.

5. A, a contractor, and B, a subcontractor, make a contract under which B promises to install sewer pipe in a trench which A is to dig

and maintain during installation. A unjustifiably so fails to maintain the trench that it fills with water, severely hindering installation. B thereupon stops work and refuses to continue unless the breach is cured. A does not cure his breach. If A's breach is material (§ 241), it operates as the non-occurrence of a condition of B's duty to build the sewer, discharging it, and A has no claim against B. If A's breach is not material, B's duties are not discharged, and B's stopping work and refusing to continue is a breach.

6.   A contracts to sell and B to buy on 30 days credit 3,000 tons of iron rails at a stated price. B purchases iron rails heavily from various sources for use in his business, and in consequences A has difficulty in securing 3,000 tons and the market price is substantially increased. A fails to deliver the rails. B has a claim against A for breach of contract. B's purchase of iron rails from other sources for use in his business is not a failure of performance because B is under no duty to refrain from purchasing for that purpose. A's failure to deliver the rails is therefore a breach.

7.   The facts being otherwise as stated in Illustration 6, B maliciously buys iron rails heavily from various sources in order to prevent A from performing his contract with B. B has no claim against A. B's malicious purchase of iron rails from other sources is material breach of his duty of good faith and fair dealing (§ 204), which operates as the non-occurrence of a condition of A's duty to deliver the rails, discharging it.

c.   Ignorance immaterial. The non-occurrence of a condition of a party's duty has the effects stated in § 225 even though that party does not know of its non-occurrence. See Comment e

to § 225. It follows that one party's material failure of performance has the effect of the non-occurrence of a condition of the other party's remaining duties, under the rule stated in this Section, even though that other party does not know of the failure. If the other party is discharged as the result of an unjustified material failure of which he is ignorant, he has a claim for damages for total breach (§ 245). But any loss that he has suffered as a result of his own actions taken in ignorance of the breach cannot be recovered since his actions were not caused by the other's breach. See Illustrations 8 and 9.

A party's ignorance may, however, cause him to lose rights under rules other than the one stated in this section. He may, for example, be precluded from relying on a condition where, through ignorance, he fails to make timely objection. So, under Uniform Commercial Code § 2–608, a buyer of goods who accepts them in ignorance of their defects loses his right to insist upon strict performance as a condition of his duty to pay the price. Other rules may preclude a party from relying on a failure of performance as the non-occurrence of a condition where, because of unreasonable ignorance, he has accepted the other party's performance or has given no reasons or the wrong reasons for its rejection. See, e.g., §§ 246 and 248; Uniform Commercial Code §§ 2–605, 2–607.

Illustrations:

8.   A and B make an employment contract. After the service has begun, A, the employee, commits a material breach of his duty to give efficient service that would justify B in discharging him. B is not aware of this but discharges A for an inadequate reason. A has no claim against B for discharging him. B has a claim against A for damages for total breach (§ 243) based on B's loss due to A's failure to give effi-

cient service up to the time of discharge, but not for damages based on the loss of A's services after that time, because that loss was caused by B's discharge of A and not by A's failure to give efficient service.

9. A contracts to sell and B to buy goods on 30 days credit. A delivers defective goods, which B rejects in ignorance of their defects. A has no claim against B. B has a claim against A for total breach (§ 243), but can recover nominal damages only since the unavailability of the goods to B was caused by B's rejection and not by their defects.

10. The facts being otherwise as stated in Illustration 9, when B rejects the goods he states an insufficient reason, which induces a failure by A to cure the defects in the goods. B is precluded from relying on the defects to justify his rejection, not because of his ignorance itself, but because his giving of an insufficient reason for rejection excused the non-occurrence of the condition of his duty to take and pay for the goods (§ 248; Uniform Commercial Code § 2–605).

d. Substantial performance. In an important category of disputes over failure of performance, one party asserts the right to payment on the ground that he has completed his performance, while the other party refuses to pay on the ground that there is an uncured material failure of performance. (Compare Comment b.) A typical example is that of the building contractor who claims from the owner payment of the unpaid balance under a construction contract. In such cases it is common to state the issue, not in terms of whether there has been an uncured material failure by the contractor, but in terms of whether there has been substantial performance by him. This manner of stating the issue does not change its substance, however, and the rule stated in this Section also applies to such cases. If there has been substantial although not full performance, the building contractor has a claim for the unpaid balance and the owner has a claim only for damages. If there has not been substantial performance, the building contractor has no claim for the unpaid balance, although he may have a claim in restitution (§ 374). The considerations in determining whether performance is substantial are those listed in § 241 for determining whether a failure is material. See Comment b to § 241. If, however, the parties have made an event a condition of their agreement, there is no mitigating standard of materiality or substantiality applicable to the non-occurrence of that event. If, therefore, the agreement makes full performance a condition, substantial performance is not sufficient and if relief is to be had under the contract, it must be through excuse of the non-occurrence of the condition to avoid forfeiture. See § 229 and Illustration 1 to that section.

Illustration:

11. A contracts to build a house for B, for which B promises to pay $50,000 in monthly progress payments equal to 85% of the value of the work with the balance to be paid on completion. When A completes construction, B refuses to pay the $7,500 balance claiming that there are defects that amount to an uncured material breach. If the breach is material, A's performance is not substantial and he has no claim under the contract against B, although he may have a claim in restitution (§ 374). If the breach is not material, A's performance is said to be substantial, he has a claim under the contract against B for $7,500, and B has a claim against A for damages because of the defects.

e. Duties affected. Under the rule stated in this Section, only duties with respect to the performances to be exchanged under the particular exchange of promises are affected by a failure of one of those performances. A duty under a separate contract is not affected (see Comment d to § 231 and Illustration 5 to that section), nor is a duty under the same contract affected if it was not one to render a performance to be exchanged under an exchange of promises (see Illustrations 3 and 4 to § 232). Furthermore, only duties to render performance are affected. A claim for damages that has already arisen as a result of a claim for partial breach is not discharged under the rule stated in this Section.

Illustration:

12. A contracts to build a building for B. B delays making the site available to A, giving A a claim against B for damages for partial breach. A then commits a material breach and B properly cancels the contract. B has a claim against A for damages for total breach, but A still has a claim against B for damages for partial breach.

§ 238. Effect on Other Party's Duties of a Failure to Offer Performance

Where all or part of the performances to be exchanged under an exchange of promises are due simultaneously, it is a condition of each party's duties to render such performance that the other party either render or, with manifested present ability to do so, offer performance of his part of the simultaneous exchange.

Comment:

a.   Effect of offer to perform. Where the performances are to be exchanged simultaneously under an exchange of promises, each party is entitled to refuse to proceed with that simultaneous exchange until he is reasonably assured that the other party will perform at the same time. If a party actually performs, his performance both discharges his own duty (§ 235(1)) and amounts to the occurrence of a condition of the other party's duty (§ 237). But it is not necessary that he actually perform in order to produce this latter effect. It is enough that he make an appropriate offer to perform, since it is a condition of each party's duties of performance with respect to the exchange that there be no uncured material failure by the other party at least to offer performance. Circumstances significant in determining whether a failure is material are set out in § 241. Such an offer of performance by a party amounts to the occurrence of a condition of the other party's duty to render performance, although it does not amount to performance by the former. Until a party has at least made such an offer, however, the other party is under no duty to perform, and if both parties fail to make such an offer, neither party's failure is a breach. (If one of the parties is already in breach, as where he has repudiated or has failed to go to the place appointed for the simultaneous exchange, the other party's duty to render performance may already have been discharged under §§ 253(2) or 237, giving him a claim for damages for total breach under §§ 253(1) or 243(1).) When it is too late for either to make such an offer, both parties are discharged by the non-occurrence of a condition. A failure to offer performance can be cured, if an appropriate offer is made in time (§ 242). Cf. Comment b to § 237. The fact that a party is ignorant of a defect in the other party's offer is immaterial. See Comment c to § 237.

Illustrations:

1. A contracts to sell and B to buy a machine for $10,000, delivery of the machine and payment of the price to be made at a stated place on July 1. On July 1 both parties are present at that place, but A neither delivers nor offers to deliver the machine and B neither pays nor offers to pay the price. A has no claim against B, and B has no claim against A. See Uniform Commercial Code §§ 2–507(1) and 2–511(1). If, however, B had committed a material breach by failing to go to the stated place, A would have had a claim against B for damages for total breach. See §§ 237, 243.

2. The facts being otherwise as stated in Illustration 1, on July 2, B, with manifested present ability to do so, offers to pay the price if A simultaneously delivers the machine, but A refuses to deliver the machine. If the delay of one day does not exceed the time after which A is discharged (§ 242), A's refusal is a breach. If it exceeds that time, B has no claim against A.

b.   What amounts to an offer to perform. An offer of performance meets the requirement stated in this Section even though it is conditional on simultaneous performance by the other party. The offer must be accompanied with manifested present ability to make it good, but the offeror need not go so far as actually to hold out that which he is to deliver. (On the meaning of the term "manifested," see Comment b to § 2.) Thus the Uniform Commercial Code § 2–503(1) requires only "that the seller put and hold conforming goods at the buyer's disposition and give the buyer any notice reasonably necessary to enable him to take delivery." In this respect the requirement of this Section is less exacting than that of tender under, for example, § 45 or § 62. Any conduct, including tender, that goes beyond an offer of performance will, of course, also satisfy the requirement. The requirement of an offer of performance is to be applied in the light of what is reasonably to be expected by the parties in view of the practical difficulties of absolute simultaneity (see Comment b to § 234) and is subject to the agreement of the parties, as supplemented or qualified by usage (§§ 221, 222) and course of dealing (§ 223).

Illustration:

3. A contracts to sell and B to buy land for $50,000. The land is to be conveyed free of liens and encumbrances, but B knows that it is subject to a $30,000 mortgage held by C which A expects to satisfy out of the $50,000 purchase price. A, in the presence of B and C, makes a conditional offer of a deed of the property subject to the mortgage, and both A and C present documents that are legally sufficient to satisfy the mortgage debt to be delivered immediately on payment of the price by B. B thereupon refuses to pay the price. In view of the circumstances at the time the contract was made, A's offer is sufficient, and A has a claim against B for damages for total breach of contract.

c.   Judicial supervision. In an action for specific performance or for the price, a court may ensure that the party seeking relief makes an offer of performance that meets the requirements of this Section by granting relief conditional on such an offer. Uniform Commercial Code § 2–709(2), for example, provides that "where the seller sues for the price, he must hold for the buyer any goods which have been identified to the contract and are still in his control" See Illustration 4. See also Comment a to § 358 with respect to specific performance. If performances, although not originally due simultaneously, have become due simultaneously after the commencement of the action because the earlier performance has been delayed, the granting of such relief is equally appropriate. Even though the performances do not become due simultaneously until after judgment, the court may exercise its power on either the defendant's request or on its own motion. See Illustration 5.

Illustrations:

4.   The facts being otherwise as stated in Illustration 1, on July 1, A puts the machine at B's disposition and requests that he pay for it. B refuses to pay and A, after attempting unsuccessfully to resell the machine, brings an action for the price under Uniform Commercial Code § 2–709. A court will award judgment for the full price only if A holds the machine for the buyer during the action. See Uniform Commercial Code § 2–709(2).

5.   A promises to sell real estate to B, delivery of the deed to be four years from July 1. B promises to pay $50,000 in installments of $10,000 on each July 1 for five years. B duly pays the first three installments but does not pay the fourth, and A brings an action to recover it. A has judgment but the judgment is not collected until after the July 1 when the payment of the fifth installment and the delivery are due. The court will restrain collection of the judgment until A makes an offer to transfer the real estate conditional on being paid the amount of the judgment and also the fifth installment of the price. See Illustration 8 to § 234 and Illustration 2 to § 358.

§ 239.   Effect on Other Party's Duties of a Failure Justified By Non-Occurrence of a Condition

(1)   A party's failure to render or to offer performance may, except as stated in Subsection (2), affect the other party's duties under the rules stated in §§ 237 and 238 even though failure is justified by the non-occurrence of a condition.

(2)   The rule stated in Subsection (1) does not apply if the other party assumed the risk that he would have to perform in spite of such a failure.

§ 240.   Part Performances as Agreed Equivalents

If the performances to be exchanged under an exchange of promises can be apportioned into corresponding pairs of part performances so that the parts of each pair are properly regarded as agreed equivalents, a party's performance of his part of such a pair has the same effect on the other's duties to render performance of the agreed equivalent as it would have if only that pair of performances had been promised.

§ 241.   Circumstances Significant in Determining Whether a Failure Is Material

In determining whether a failure to render or to offer performance is material, the following circumstances are significant:

(a)   the extent to which the injured party will be deprived of the benefit which he reasonably expected;

(b)   the extent to which the injured party can be adequately compensated for the part of that benefit of which he will be deprived;

(c)   the extent to which the party failing to perform or to offer to perform will suffer forfeiture;

(d)   the likelihood that the party failing to perform or to offer to perform will cure his failure, taking account of all the circumstances including any reasonable assurances;

(e)   the extent to which the behavior of the party failing to perform or to offer to perform comports with standards of good faith and fair dealing.

Comment:

a.   Nature of significant circumstances. The application of the rules stated in §§ 237 and 238 turns on a standard of materiality that is necessarily imprecise and flexible. (Contrast the situation where the parties have, by their agreement, made an event a condition. See § 226 and Comments a and c thereto and § 229.) The standard of materiality applies to contracts of all types and without regard to whether the whole performance of either party is to be rendered at one time or part performances are to be rendered at different times. See Uniform Commercial Code § 2–612. It also applies to pairs of agreed equivalents under § 240. See Illustration 2. It is to be applied in the light of the facts of each case in such a way as to further the purpose of securing for each party his expectation of an exchange of performances. This Section therefore states circumstances, not rules, which are to be considered in determining whether a particular failure is material. A determination that a failure is not material means only that it does not have the effect of the non-occurrence of a condition under §§ 237 and 238. Even if not material, the failure may be a breach and give rise to a claim for damages for partial breach (§§ 236, 243).

Illustrations:

1.   A, a subcontractor, contracts to do excavation and earth moving on a housing subdivision project for B, the owner and general contractor, and to do all work "in a workmanlike manner." B is to make monthly progress payments for the work performed during the preceding month less a retainer of ten percent. A negligently damages a building with his bulldozer causing serious damage and denies any liability for B's loss. When B refuses to make further progress payments until A repairs the damage or admits liability, A notifies B that he cancels the contract. If the court determines that A's breach is material, A has no claim against B. B has a claim against A for damages for breach of contract.

2.   The facts being otherwise as stated in Illustration 6 to § 240, A completes the part concerned with the excavation and grading of lots and streets but fails in a minor respect to comply with the specifications. If a court determines that the failure is not material, A has a claim against B for $75,000 under the contract for the excavation and grading. B has a claim for damages against A for his failure fully to perform as to excavation and grading and also for his unjustified refusal to make street improvements.

b.   Loss of benefit to injured party. Since the purpose of the rules stated in §§ 237 and 238 is to secure the parties' expectation of an exchange of performances, an important circumstance in determining whether a failure is material is the extent to which the injured party will be deprived of the benefit which he reasonably expected from the exchange (Subsection (a)). If the consideration given by either party consists partly of some performance and only partly of a promise (see Comment a to § 232), regard must be had to the entire exchange, including that performance, in applying this criterion. Although the relationship between the monetary loss to the injured party as a result of the failure and the contract price may be significant, no simple rule based on the ratio of the one to the other can be laid down, and here, as elsewhere under this Section, all relevant circumstances must be considered. In construction contracts, for example, defects affecting structural soundness are ordinarily regarded as particularly significant. In the sale of goods a particularly exacting standard has evolved. There it has long been established that, in the absence of a showing of a contrary intention, a buyer is entitled to expect strict performance of the contract, and Uniform Commercial Code § 2–601 carries forward this expectation by allowing the buyer to reject "if the goods or the tender of delivery fail in any respect to conform to the contract." The Code, however, compensates to some extent for the severity of this standard by extending the seller's right to cure beyond the point when the time for performance has expired in some instances (§ 2–508(2)), by allowing revocation of acceptance only if a nonconformity "substantially impairs" the value of the goods to the buyer (§ 2–608(1)), and by allowing the injured party to treat a nonconformity or default as to one installment under an installment contract as a breach of the whole only if it "substantially impairs" the value of the whole (§ 2–612(3)).

c.   Adequacy of compensation for loss. The second circumstance, the extent to which the injured party can be adequately compensated for his loss of benefit (Subsection (b)), is a corollary of the first. Difficulty that he may have in proving with sufficient certainty the

amount of that loss will affect the adequacy of compensation. If the failure is a breach, the injured party always has a claim for damages, and the question becomes one of the adequacy of that claim to compensate him for the lost benefit. Where the failure is not a breach, the question becomes one of the adequacy of any claim, such as one in restitution, to which the injured party may be entitled. This is a particularly important circumstance when the party in breach seeks specific performance. Such relief may be granted if damages can adequately compensate the injured party for the defect in performance. See Comment c to § 242.

d.   Forfeiture by party who fails. Because a material failure acts as the non-occurrence of a condition, the same risk of forfeiture obtains as in the case of conditions generally if the party who fails to perform or tender has relied substantially on the expectation of the exchange, as through preparation or performance. Therefore a third circumstance is the extent to which the party failing to perform or to make an offer to perform will suffer forfeiture if the failure is treated as material. For this reason a failure is less likely to be regarded as material if it occurs late, after substantial preparation or performance, and more likely to be regarded as material if it occurs early, before such reliance. For the same reason the failure is more likely to be regarded as material if such preparation or performance as has taken place can be returned to and salvaged by the party failing to perform or tender, and less likely to be regarded as material if it cannot. These factors argue against a finding of material failure and in favor of one of substantial performance where a builder has completed performance under a construction contract and, because the building is on the owner's land, can salvage nothing if he is denied recovery of the balance of the price. Even in such a case, however, the potential forfeiture may be mitigated if the builder has a claim in restitution (§§ 370–77, especially § 374) or if he has already received progress payments under a provision of the contract. The same factors argue for a finding of material failure where a seller tenders goods and can salvage them by resale to others if they are rejected and he is denied recovery of the price. This helps to explain the severity of the rule as applied to the sale of goods. See Comment b. Even in such a case, however, the potential forfeiture may be aggravated if the seller has manufactured the goods specially for the buyer or has spent substantial sums in shipment.

Illustrations:

3. A contracts to sell and B to buy 300 crates of Australian onions, shipment to be from Australia in March. A has 300 crates ready for shipment in March, but government requisitions prevent him from loading more than 240 crates on the only ship available in March. B refuses to accept or pay for the onions when they are tendered. Under the circumstances stated in Subsections (a) and (c), A's failure is material and A has no claim against B. If A's failure is unjustified, B has a claim against A for damages for partial breach because of the delay even if A cures his failure, and has a claim against A for damages for total breach if A does not cure his failure (§ 243).

4. The facts being otherwise as stated in Illustration 2 to § 232, B can have the part of the street in front of his own lot paved for $500, but this will not give him the expected access to his lot because the rest of the street is not paved. Under the circumstances stated in Subsections (a), (b), and (c), the failure of performance is material and A has no claim against B. If A's failure is unjustified, B has a claim against A

for damages for partial breach because of the delay even if A cures his failure, and has a claim against A for damages for total breach if A does not cure his failure (§ 243).

e. *Uncertainty.* A material failure by one party gives the other party the right to withhold further performance as a means of securing his expectation of an exchange of performances. To the extent that that expectation is already reasonably secure, in spite of the failure, there is less reason to conclude that the failure is material. The likelihood that the failure will be cured is therefore a significant circumstance in determining whether it is material (Subsection (d)). The fact that the injured party already has some security for the other party's performance argues against a determination that the failure is material. So do reasonable assurances of performance given by the other party after his failure. So does a shift in the market that makes performance of the contract more favorable to the other party. On the other hand, defaults by the other party under other contracts or as to other installments under the same contract argue for a determination of materiality. So does such financial weakness of the other party as suggests an inability to cure. This circumstance differs from the notion of reasonable grounds for insecurity (§ 251), in that the former can become relevant only after there has been an actual failure to perform or to tender. On discharge by repudiation, see § 253(2).

Illustration:

5. A contracts to sell and B to buy land for $25,000. B is to make a $5,000 down payment and pay the balance in four annual installments of $5,000 each. A is to proceed immediately to have abstracts of title prepared showing a marketable title and to deliver them prior to the time for payment of the first annual

installment. Without explanation, A fails to have abstracts prepared for delivery prior to the time for payment of the first annual installment. B refuses to pay that installment. Under the circumstances stated in Subsections (a)–(d), the failure of performance is material and A has no claim against B. B has a claim against A for damages for partial breach based on the delay if A cures his failure and a claim for damages for total breach if he does not (§ 243).

f.   Absence of good faith or fair dealing. A party's adherence to standards of good faith and fair dealing (§ 205) will not prevent his failure to perform a duty from amounting to a breach (§ 236(2)). Nor will his adherence to such standards necessarily prevent his failure from having the effect of the non-occurrence of a condition (§ 237; cf. § 238). The extent to which the behavior of the party failing to perform or to offer to perform comports with standards of good faith and fair dealing is, however, a significant circumstance in determining whether the failure is material (Subsection (e)). In giving weight to this factor courts have often used such less precise terms as "wilful." Adherence to the standards stated in Subsection (e) is not conclusive, since other circumstances may cause a failure to be material in spite of such adherence. Nor is non-adherence conclusive, and other circumstances may cause a failure not to be material in spite of such non-adherence.

Illustrations:

6.   A contracts to build a house for B, using pipe of Reading manufacture. In return, B agrees to pay $75,000, with provision for progress payments. Without B's knowledge, a subcontractor mistakenly uses pipe of Cohoes manufacture which is identical in quality and is distinguishable only by the name of the manufacturer which is stamped on it. The substitution is not discovered until the house is completed, when replacement of the pipe will require destruction of substantial parts of the house. B refuses to pay the unpaid balance of $10,000. Under the circumstances stated in Subsections (a), (c), and (e), the failure of performance is not material and A has a claim against B for the unpaid balance of $10,000, subject to a claim by B against A for damages for A's breach of his duty to use Reading pipe. See Illustration 1 to § 229.

7.   A contracts to build a supermarket for B. In return B agrees to pay $250,000, with provision for progress payments. A completes performance except that, angered by a dispute over an unrelated transaction, he refuses to build a cover over a compressor. B can have the cover built by another builder for $300. B refuses to pay the unpaid balance of $40,000. In spite of the circumstances stated in Subsection (e), under the circumstances stated in Subsections (a), (b), and (c), the failure of performance is not material and A has a claim against B for the unpaid balance of $40,000, subject to a claim by B against A for damages for A's breach of his duty to build a cover over the compressor.

§ 242.   Circumstances Significant in Determining When Remaining Duties Are Discharged

In determining the time after which a party's uncured material failure to render or to offer performance discharges the other party's remaining duties to render performance under the rules stated in §§ 237 and 238, the following circumstances are significant:

(a)   those stated in § 241;

(b)   the extent to which it reasonably appears to the injured party that delay may prevent or hinder him in making reasonable substitute arrangements;

(c)   the extent to which the agreement provides for performance without delay, but a material failure to perform or to offer to perform on a stated day does not of itself discharge the other party's remaining duties unless the circumstances, including the language of the agreement, indicate that performance or an offer to perform by that day is important.

Comment:

a.   Cure. Under §§ 237 and 238, a party's uncured material failure to perform or to offer to perform not only has the effect of suspending the other party's duties (§ 225(1)) but, when it is too late for the performance or the offer to perform to occur, the failure also has the effect of discharging those duties (§ 225(2)). Ordinarily there is some period of time between suspension and discharge, and during this period a party may cure his failure. Even then, since any breach gives rise to a claim, a party who has cured a material breach has still committed a breach, by his delay, for which he is liable in damages. Furthermore, in some instances timely performance is so essential that any delay immediately results in discharge and there is no period of time during which the injured party's duties are merely suspended and the other party can cure his failure.

b.   Significant circumstances. This Section states circumstances which are to be considered in determining whether there is still time to cure a particular failure, or whether the period of time for discharge has expired. They are similar to the circumstances stated in the preceding section. The importance of delay to the injured party will depend on the extent to which it will deprive him of the benefit which he reasonably expected (§ 241(a)) and on

the extent to which he can be adequately compensated (§ 241(b)). The extent of the forfeiture by the party failing to perform or to offer to perform (§ 241(c)) is also significant in determining the importance of delay. The likelihood that the injured party's withholding of performance will induce the other party to cure his failure is particularly important (§ 241(d)), because the very reason for suspending rather than immediately discharging the injured party's duties is that this will induce cure. The reasonableness of the injured party's conduct in communicating his grievances and in seeking satisfaction is a factor to be considered in this connection. Where performance is to extend over a period of time, as where delivery of goods is to be in installments, so that a continuing relationship between the parties is contemplated, the injured party may be expected to give more opportunity for cure than in the case of an isolated exchange. On discharge by repudiation, see § 253(2). Finally, the nature of the behavior of the party failing to perform or to offer to perform may be considered here as under the preceding section (§ 241(e)).

Illustration:

1.   The facts being otherwise as stated in Illustration 1 to § 237, B tenders the progress payment after a two-day delay along with

damages for the delay. A refuses to accept the payment and resume work and notifies B that he cancels the contract. B's tender cured his breach before A's remaining duties to render performance were discharged, and B has a claim against A for total breach of contract, subject to a claim by A against B for damages for partial breach because of the delay.

c.   *Substitute arrangements.* It is often said that in commercial transactions, notably those for the sale of goods, prompt performance by a party is essential if he is to be allowed to require the other to perform or, as it is sometimes put, "time is of the essence." The importance of prompt delivery by a seller of goods generally derives from the circumstance that goods, as contrasted for example with land, are particularly likely to be subject to rapid fluctuations in market price. Therefore, even a relatively short delay in a rising market may adversely affect the buyer by causing a sharp increase in the cost of "cover." See Uniform Commercial Code §§ 2–712, 2–713. A less rigid standard applies to contracts for the sale of goods to be delivered in installments or to be specially manufactured for the buyer. On the other hand, considerable delay does not preclude enforcement of a contract for the sale of land if damages are adequate to compensate for the delay and there are no special circumstances indicating that prompt performance was essential and no express provision requiring such performance. But these are all merely particular applications of a more general principle. Subsection (b) states that principle. Under any contract, the extent to which it reasonably appears to the injured party that delay may prevent or hinder him from making reasonable substitute arrangements is a consideration in determining the effect of delay. Cf. § 241(a), (b). As in the case of § 241 (see Comment c), a party in breach who seeks specific performance may be granted relief with compensation for the delay, in circumstances where he would have no claim for damages.

Illustrations:

2.   A, a theater manager, contracts with B, an actress, for her performance for six months in a play that A is about to present. B becomes ill during the second month of the performance, and A immediately engages another actress to fill B's place during the remainder of the six months. B recovers at the end of ten days and offers to perform the remainder of the contract, but A refuses. Whether B's failure to render performance due to illness immediately discharges A's remaining duties of performance, instead of merely suspending them, depends on the circumstances stated in Subsection (b) and in § 241(b) and (d), and in particular on the possibility as it reasonably appears to A when B becomes ill of the illness being only temporary and of A's obtaining an adequate temporary substitute.

3.   A contracts to sell and B to buy 1,000 shares of stock traded on a national securities exchange, delivery and payment to be on February 1. B offers to pay the price on February 1, but A unjustifiably and without explanation fails to offer to deliver the stock until February 2. B then refuses to accept the stock or pay the price. Under the circumstances stated in Subsection (b) and in § 241(a) and (c), the period of time has passed after which B's remaining duties to render performance are discharged because of A's material breach and A therefore has no claim against B. B has a claim against A for breach.

4.   A contracts to sell and B to buy land, the transfer to be on February 1. B tenders the price on

February 1, but A does not tender a deed until February 2. B then refuses to accept the deed or pay the price. Under the circumstances stated in Subsections (b) and (c) and in § 241(a), in the absence of special circumstances, the period of time has not passed after which B's remaining duties to render performance are discharged. Although A's breach is material, it has been cured. A has a claim against B for damages for total breach of contract, subject to a claim by B against A for damages for partial breach because of the delay.

5.   A agrees to sell and B to buy land, the transfer to be on February 1. A tenders a sufficient deed on February 1, but B explains that although he wants to carry out the contract he would like to have a few weeks more to raise the amount of the price. A replies that unless B tenders the price immediately he will not deliver the deed. On February 15, B sues for specific performance, offering in his pleading to pay the agreed price with interest to compensate A for the delay. In the circumstances stated in Subsection (b) and in § 241(a), (b), and (d), the period of time has not passed after which A's remaining duties to render performance are discharged. Although B's breach is material, the court may decree specific performance subject to B's tender of the price and payment by B of damages for partial breach to compensate A for the delay.

6.   A contracts to sell and B to buy 5,000 tons of iron at a stated price, delivery to be in five monthly installments of 1,000 tons each on the first of each month and payment for each installment to be made on the tenth of that month. A makes the first three deliveries on the first of the month but, although the market price for iron is falling,

he delays twelve days in making the fourth delivery, explaining to B that temporary labor troubles have caused the delay. B notifies A that he refuses to take or pay for the fourth delivery and that he cancels the contract. Whether the period of time has passed after which B's remaining duties to render performance are discharged, so that B's notification is not a repudiation, depends on the circumstances stated in Subsection (b) and in § 241(a), (b), (d), and (e). See Uniform Commercial Code § 2–612.

7.   A contracts to sell and B to buy 5,000 tons of iron at a stated price, delivery to be in five monthly installments of 1,000 tons each on the first of each month and payment for each installment to be made on the tenth of that month. A makes the first four deliveries on the first of the month, and B makes the first three payments by the tenth but does not make the fourth payment. The market price for iron is falling and B gives no assurances or explanation for the delay. On the twentieth of the month A notifies B that he will make no further deliveries and that he cancels the contract. Whether the period of time has passed after which A's remaining duties to render performance are discharged, so that A's notification is not a repudiation, depends on the circumstances stated in Subsection (b) and in § 241(a), (b), (d), and (e). See Uniform Commercial Code § 2–612.

d.   Effect of agreement. The agreement of the parties often contains a provision for the time of performance or tender. It may simply provide for performance on a stated date. In that event, a material breach on that date entitles the injured party to withhold his performance and gives him a claim for damages for delay, but it does not of itself discharge the other party's remaining duties. Only if the circumstances, viewed as of the time of the breach, indicate that performance or tender on that day is of genuine importance are the injured party's remaining duties discharged immediately, with no period of time during which they are merely suspended. It is, of course, open to the parties to make performance or tender by a stated date a condition by their agreement, in which event, absent excuse (see Comment b to § 225 and Comment c to § 229), delay beyond that date results in discharge (§ 225(2)). Such stock phrases as "time is of the essence" do not necessarily have this effect, although under Subsection (c) they are to be considered along with other circumstances in determining the effect of delay.

Illustrations:

8. A contracts to charter a vessel belonging to B and to pay stipulated freight "on condition that the vessel arrive in New York ready for loading by March 1." B promises that the vessel will arrive by that date and carry A's cargo. B unjustifiably fails to have the vessel in New York to be loaded until March 2. A refuses to load the vessel. Whether or not the period of time has passed after which B's uncured material failure would discharge A's remaining duties to render performance, A's duties are discharged under § 225(2) by the non-occurrence of an event that is made a condition by the agreement of the parties. B has no claim against A. A has a claim against B for damages for total breach.

9. The facts being otherwise as stated in Illustration 4, the parties use a printed form contract that provides that "time is of the essence." Absent other circumstances indicating that performance by February 1 is of genuine importance, A has a claim against B for damages for total breach of contract.

10. The facts being otherwise as stated in Illustration 4, the contract provides that A's rights are "conditional on his tendering a deed on or before February 1." A has no claim against B. But cf. Illustration 4 to § 229.

e. Excuse and reinstatement. Just as a party may under § 84 promise to perform in spite of the complete non-occurrence of a condition, he may under that section promise to perform in spite of a delay in its occurrence. If he places no limit on the delay, his power to impose a time limit by later notification of the other party is subject to the rules on reinstatement stated in § 84(2).

§ 243. Effect of a Breach by Non-Performance as Giving Rise to a Claim for Damages for Total Breach

(1) With respect to performances to be exchanged under an exchange of promises, a breach by non-performance gives rise to a claim for damages for total breach only if it discharges the injured party's remaining duties to render such performance, other than a duty to render an agreed equivalent under § 240.

(2) Except as stated in Subsection (3), a breach by nonperformance accompanied or followed by a repudiation gives rise to a claim for damages for total breach.

(3) Where at the time of the breach the only remaining duties of performance are those of the party in breach and are for the payment

of money in installments not related to one another, his breach by non-performance as to less than the whole, whether or not accompanied or followed by a repudiation, does not give rise to a claim for damages for total breach.

(4) In any case other than those stated in the preceding subsections, a breach by non-performance gives rise to a claim for total breach only if it so substantially impairs the value of the contract to the injured party at the time of the breach that it is just in the circumstances to allow him to recover damages based on all his remaining rights to performance.

§ 244. Effect of Subsequent Events on Duty to Pay Damages

A party's duty to pay damages for total breach by non-performance is discharged if it appears after the breach that there would have been a total failure by the injured party to perform his return promise.

§ 245. Effect of a Breach by Non-Performance as Excusing the Non-Occurrence of a Condition

Where a party's breach by non-performance contributes materially to the non-occurrence of a condition of one of his duties, the non-occurrence is excused.

Comment:

a. Excuse of non-occurrence of condition. Where a duty of one party is subject to the occurrence of a condition, the additional duty of good faith and fair dealing imposed on him under § 205 may require some cooperation on his part, either by refraining from conduct that will prevent or hinder the occurrence of that condition or by taking affirmative steps to cause its occurrence. Under § 235(2), non-performance of that duty when performance is due is a breach. See Illustration 3 to § 235. Under this Section it has the further effect of excusing the non-occurrence of the condition itself, so that performance of the duty that was originally subject to its occurrence can become due in spite of its non-occurrence. See Comments b and c to § 225. The rule stated in this Section only applies, however, where the lack of cooperation constitutes a breach, either of a duty imposed by the terms of the agreement itself or of a duty imposed by a term supplied by the court. There is no breach if the risk of such a lack of cooperation was assumed by the other party or if the lack of cooperation is justifiable.

Illustrations:

1. A contracts with B to repair B's building for $20,000, payment to be made "on the satisfaction of C, B's architect, and the issuance of his certificate." A fully performs his duty to make the repairs, but B induces C to refuse to issue his certificate. A has a claim against B for $20,000. B's breach of his duty of good faith and fair dealing contributed materially to the non-occurrence of the condition, the issuance of the certificate, excusing it. Cf. Illustrations 5, 6, 7, and 8 to § 227.

2. A contracts to sell and B to buy land for $100,000. At the same time A contracts to pay C, a real estate broker, as his commission, $5,000 "on the closing of title." A unjustifiably refuses to consummate the sale. C has a claim against A

for $5,000, less any expenses that C saved because the sale was not consummated. A's breach of his duty of good faith and fair dealing contributed materially to the non-occurrence of the condition, the closing of title, excusing it. See Illustration 4 to § 227.

3. A contracts to sell and B to buy a house for $50,000, with the provision, "This contract is conditional on approval by X Bank of B's pending mortgage application." B fails to make reasonable efforts to obtain approval and, when the X Bank disapproves the application, refuses to perform when A tenders a deed. A has a claim against B for total breach of contract. B's breach of his duty of good faith and fair dealing contributed materially to the non-occurrence of the condition, approval of the application, excusing it. Cf. Illustration 8 to § 225.

4. A contracts to sell and B to buy A's rights as one of three lessees under a mining lease in Indian lands. The contract states that it is "subject only to approval by the Secretary of the Interior," which is required by statute. B files a request for approval but A fails to support B's request by giving necessary cooperation. Approval is denied and A cannot convey his rights. B has a claim against A for total breach of contract. A's breach of his duty of good faith and fair dealing contributed materially to the non-occurrence of the condition, approval by the Secretary of the Interior, excusing it.

b. Contribute materially. Although it is implicit in the rule that the condition has not occurred, it is not necessary to show that it would have occurred but for the lack of cooperation. It is only required that the breach have contributed materially to the non-occurrence. Nevertheless, if it can

be shown that the condition would not have occurred regardless of the lack of cooperation, the failure of performance did not contribute materially to its non-occurrence and the rule does not apply. The burden of showing this is properly thrown on the party in breach.

Illustrations:

5. A and B, about to become man and wife, make an ante-nuptial contract under which A is to pay B $100,000 if B survives A. Four years after their marriage, A shoots both B and himself. B dies instantly and A dies the following day. B's estate has a claim against A's estate for $100,000. A's breach of his duty of good faith and fair dealing contributed materially to the non-occurrence of the condition, B's surviving A, excusing it. The fact that B's estate cannot show that B would otherwise have survived A does not prevent it from recovering the $100,000. Compare the rule on certainty in § 352.

6. A, the owner of a manufacturing plant, contracts to transfer the plant to B. B is to pay A $500,000 plus a bonus of $100,000 if the profits from the plant exceed a stated amount during the first year of its operation. Six months after the transfer B sells the plant to C, who dismantles it. B refuses to pay the bonus. Whether A has a claim against B depends on whether B's failure to operate the plant for a year is a breach of his duty of good faith and fair dealing which contributed materially to the non-occurrence of the condition, the profits exceeding the stated amount during the first year, excusing it. The fact that A cannot show that the profits would otherwise have exceeded the stated amount does not prevent him from recovering. If, however, B shows that they would not have exceeded that amount, A cannot

recover. Compare the rule on certainty in § 352.

7.   The facts being otherwise as stated in Illustration 4, A shows that even if he had given his cooperation, the Secretary of the Interior would have withheld approval on other grounds. B has no claim against A for breach of contract. A's breach of his duty of good faith and fair dealing did not contribute materially to the non-occurrence of the condition, and its non-occurrence is not excused.

c.   Exceptions. Under §§ 237 and 238, it may be required as a condition of one party's duty that the other party perform or offer to perform his duty. A breach by the first party of his duty of good faith and fair dealing will, if material and not cured in time, discharge that duty of the other party (§ 237), eliminating the requirement that the other party perform or offer to perform it. The discharge of the duty has the additional effect of excusing the non-occurrence of the condition. But non-occurrence of the condition is excused only if the duty is discharged. The rule stated in this Section is, therefore, not applicable to such situations. See Illustrations 4, 5, and 7 to § 237.

§ 246.   Effect of Acceptance as Excusing the Non-Occurrence of a Condition

(1)   Except as stated in Subsection (2), an obligor's acceptance or his retention for an unreasonable time of the obligee's performance, with knowledge of or reason to know of the non-occurrence of a condition of the obligor's duty, operates as a promise to perform in spite of that non-occurrence, under the rules stated in § 84.

(2)   If at the time of its acceptance or retention the obligee's performance involves such attachment to the obligor's property that removal would cause material loss, the obligor's acceptance or retention of that performance operates as a promise to perform in spite of the non-occurrence of the condition, under the rules stated in § 84, only if the obligor with knowledge of or reason to know of the defects manifests assent to the performance.

§ 247.   Effect of Acceptance of Part Performance as Excusing the Subsequent Non-Occurrence of a Condition

An obligor's acceptance of part of the obligee's performance, with knowledge or reason to know of the non-occurrence of a condition of the obligor's duty, operates as a promise to perform in spite of a subsequent non-occurrence of the condition under the rules stated in § 84 to the extent that it justifies the obligee in believing that subsequent performances will be accepted in spite of that non-occurrence.

§ 248.   Effect of Insufficient Reason for Rejection as Excusing the Non-Occurrence of a Condition

Where a party rejecting a defective performance or offer of performance gives an insufficient reason for rejection, the non-occurrence of a condition of his duty is excused only if he knew or had reason to know of that non-occurrence and then only to the extent that the giving of an insufficient reason substantially contributes to a failure by the other party to cure.

§ 249.   When Payment Other Than by Legal Tender Is Sufficient

Where the payment or offer of payment of money is made a condition of an obligor's duty, payment or offer of payment in any manner current in the ordinary course of business satisfies the requirement unless the obligee demands payment in legal tender and gives any extension of time reasonably necessary to procure it.

TOPIC 3. EFFECT OF PROSPECTIVE NON-PERFORMANCE

§ 250.   When a Statement or an Act Is a Repudiation

A repudiation is

(a)   a statement by the obligor to the obligee indicating that the obligor will commit a breach that would of itself give the obligee a claim for damages for total breach under § 243, or

(b)   a voluntary affirmative act which renders the obligor unable or apparently unable to perform without such a breach.

Comment:

a.   Consequences of repudiation. A statement by a party to the other that he will not or cannot perform without a breach, or a voluntary affirmative act that renders him unable or apparently unable to perform without a breach may impair the value of the contract to the other party. It may have several consequences under this Restatement. If it accompanies a breach by non-performance that would otherwise give rise to only a claim for damages for partial breach, it may give rise to a claim for damages for total breach instead (§ 243). Even if it occurs before any breach by non-performance, it may give rise to a claim for damages for total breach (§ 253(1)), discharge the other party's duties (§ 253(2)), or excuse the non-occurrence of a condition (§ 255).

b.   Nature of statement. In order to constitute a repudiation, a party's language must be sufficiently positive to be reasonably interpreted to mean that the party will not or cannot perform. Mere expression of doubt as to his willingness or ability to perform is not enough to constitute a repudiation, although such an expression may give an obligee reasonable grounds to believe that the obligor will commit a serious breach and may ultimately result in a repudiation under the rule stated in § 251. However, language that under a fair reading "amounts to a statement of intention not to perform except on conditions which go beyond the contract" constitutes a repudiation. Comment 2 to Uniform Commercial Code § 2–610. Language that is accompanied by a breach by non-performance may amount to a repudiation even though, standing alone, it would not be sufficiently positive. See § 243(2). The statement must be made to an obligee under the contract, including a third party beneficiary or an assignee.

Illustrations:

1.   On April 1, A contracts to sell and B to buy land, delivery of

the deed and payment of the price to be on July 30. On May 1, A tells B that he will not perform. A's statement is a repudiation.

2. A contracts to build a house for B for $50,000, progress payments to be made monthly in an amount equal to 85% of the price of the work performed during the preceding month, the balance to be paid on the architect's certificate of satisfactory completion of the house. Without justification B fails to make a $5,000 progress payment and tells A that because of financial difficulties he will be unable to pay him anything for at least another month. If, after a month, it would be too late for B to cure his material failure of performance by making the delayed payment, B's statement is a repudiation. See Illustration 2 to § 237.

3. The facts being otherwise as stated in Illustration 1, A does not tell B that he will not perform but says, "I am not sure that I can perform, and I do not intend to do so unless I am legally bound to." A's statement is not a repudiation.

4. The facts being otherwise as in Illustration 1, A tells C, a third person having no right under the contract, and not B, that he will not perform. C informs B of this conversation, although not requested by A to do so. A's statement is not a repudiation. But see Comments b and c to § 251.

c. Nature of act. In order to constitute a repudiation, a party's act must be both voluntary and affirmative, and must make it actually or apparently impossible for him to perform. An act that falls short of these requirements may, however, give reasonable grounds to believe that the obligor will commit a serious breach for the purposes of the rule stated in § 251. The effect of bankruptcy is governed in large part

by federal law. In liquidation cases, for example, Bankruptcy Reform Act § 365(a), (d) and (e) gives the trustee the power to assume or reject an executory contract within a statutory period, and the obligee must give him the time to exercise this power. A contract not assumed during this period is deemed to be rejected. Under Bankruptcy Reform Act § 365(g)(1), notwithstanding state law, the trustee's rejection of a contract "constitutes a breach of such contract immediately before the date of the filing of the petition" The rules stated in this Restatement apply to the extent that they are consistent with federal bankruptcy law.

Illustrations:

5. The facts being otherwise as stated in Illustration 1, A says nothing to B on May 1, but on that date he contracts to sell the land to C. A's making of the contract with C is a repudiation.

6. The facts being otherwise as stated in Illustration 1, A says nothing to B on May 1, but on that date he mortgages the land to C as security for a $40,000 loan which is not payable until one year later. A's mortgaging the land is a repudiation. Compare Illustration 4 to § 251.

7. A contracts to employ B, and B to work for A, the employment to last a year beginning in ten days. Three days after making the contract B embarks on a ship for a voyage around the world. B's embarking for the voyage is a repudiation.

d. Gravity of threatened breach. In order for a statement or an act to be a repudiation, the threatened breach must be of sufficient gravity that, if the breach actually occurred, it would of itself give the obligee a claim for damages for total breach under § 243(1). Generally, a party acts at his peril if, insisting on what he mistakenly believes to be his rights, he refuses to perform his duty. His statement is a repudiation if the threatened breach would, without more, have given the injured party a claim for damages for total breach. Modern procedural devices, such as the declaratory judgment, may be used to mitigate the harsh results that might otherwise result from this rule. Furthermore, if the threatened breach would not itself have given the injured party a claim for damages for total breach, the statement or voluntary act that threatens it is not a repudiation. But where a party wrongfully states that he will not perform at all unless the other party consents to a modification of his contract rights, the statement is a repudiation even though the concession that he seeks is a minor one, because the breach that he threatens in order to exact it is a complete refusal of performance.

Illustrations:

8.   On April 1, A contracts to sell and B to buy land for $50,000, delivery of the deed and payment of the price to be on August 1. On May 1, the parties make an enforceable modification under which delivery of the deed and payment of the price are to be on July 30 instead of August 1. On June 1, A tells B that he will not deliver a deed until August 1. A's statement is not a repudiation unless the one-day delay would, in the absence of a repudiation, have given B a claim for damages for total breach. See Illustration 4 to § 242.

9.   The facts being otherwise as stated in Illustration 8, A tells B that he will not deliver a deed at all unless B agrees to accept it on August 1. A's statement is a repudiation. The result is the same even though A acts in the erroneous belief that the modification has no legal effect.

§ 251.   When a Failure to Give Assurance May Be Treated as a Repudiation

(1)   Where reasonable grounds arise to believe that the obligor will commit a breach by non-performance that would of itself give the obligee a claim for damages for total breach under § 243, the obligee may demand adequate assurance of due performance and may, if reasonable, suspend any performance for which he has not already received the agreed exchange until he receives such assurance.

(2)   The obligee may treat as a repudiation the obligor's failure to provide within a reasonable time such assurance of due performance as is adequate in the circumstances of the particular case.

Comment:

a.   Rationale. Ordinarily an obligee has no right to demand reassurance by the obligor that the latter will perform when his performance is due. However, a contract "imposes an obligation on each party that the other's expectation of receiving due performance will not be impaired." Uniform Commercial Code § 2–609(1). When,

therefore, an obligee reasonably believes that the obligor will commit a breach by non-performance that would of itself give him a claim for damages for total breach (§ 243), he may, under the rule stated in this Section, be entitled to demand assurance of performance. The rule is a generalization, applicable without regard to the subject matter of the contract, from that of Uniform Commercial Code § 2–609. The latter applies only to contracts for the sale of goods and gives a party a right to adequate assurance of performance where "reasonable grounds for insecurity arise with respect to the performance" of the other party. Both rules rest on the principle that the parties to a contract look to actual performance "and that a continuing sense of reliance and security that the promised performance will be forthcoming when due, is an important feature of the bargain." Comment 1 to Uniform Commercial Code § 2–609. This principle is closely related to the duty of good faith and fair dealing in the performance of the contract (§ 205). See also Comment b to § 141. The rule stated in this Section may be modified by agreement of the parties. . .

b.   *Relation to other rules.* An obligee who believes, for whatever reason, that the obligor will not or cannot perform without a breach, is always free to act on that belief. If he is not himself under a duty to perform before the obligor, he may simply await the obligor's performance and, if his belief is confirmed, he will have a claim for damages for breach by non-performance. If he can prove that his belief would have been confirmed, he is at least shielded from liability even if he has failed to give a performance that is due before that of the obligor or has, by making alternative arrangements, done an act that amounts to a repudiation. For example, under § 254, the obligee's duty to pay damages for total breach by repudiation is discharged if the obligor himself would not or could not have performed when his performance was due. If, however, the obligee's belief is incorrect, his own failure to perform or his making of alternate arrangements may subject him to a claim for damages for total breach. This Section affords him an opportunity, in appropriate cases, to demand assurance of due performance and thereby avoid the uncer-

tainties that would otherwise inhere in acting on his belief. . . .

c.   *Reasonable grounds for belief.* Whether "reasonable grounds" have arisen for an obligee's belief that there will be a breach must be determined in the light of all the circumstances of the particular case. The grounds for his belief must have arisen after the time when the contract was made and cannot be based on facts known to him at that time. Nor, since the grounds must be reasonable, can they be based on events that occurred after that time but as to which he took the risk when he made the contract. But minor breaches may give reasonable grounds for a belief that there will be more serious breaches, and the mere failure of the obligee to press a claim for damages for those minor breaches will not preclude him from basing a demand for assurances on them. Compare § 241(d), Comment e to that section, and Comment b to § 242. Even circumstances that do not relate to the particular contract, such as defaults under other contracts, may give reasonable grounds for such a belief. See Comment a to § 252. Conduct by a party that indicates his doubt as to his willingness or ability to perform but that is not sufficiently positive to amount to a repudiation (see Comment b to § 250), may give reasonable grounds for such a belief. And events that indicate a party's apparent inability, but do not amount to a repudiation because they are not voluntary acts, may also give reasonable grounds for such a belief. . . . [I]n order for this Section to apply, the breach that the obligee believes the obligor will commit must be a breach by non-performance that would so substantially impair the value of the contract to the obligee that it would of itself, unaccompanied by a repudiation, give him a claim for damages for total breach under § 243. . . .

e.   *Nature and time of assurance.* Whether an assurance of due performance is "adequate" depends on what it is reasonable to require in a particular case taking account of the circumstances of that case. The relationship between the parties, any prior dealings that they have had, the reputation of the party whose performance has been called into question, the nature of the grounds for insecurity, and the time within which the assurance must be furnished are all relevant factors. (If the obligor's insolvency constitutes the grounds for the obligee's insecurity, the special rule stated in § 252 empowers him to suspend performance until he receives assurance in the form of actual performance, an offer of performance, or reasonable security.) What is a "reasonable time" within which to give assurance under Subsection (2) will also depend on the particular circumstances. Like the demand, the assurance is subject to the general requirement of good faith and fair dealing in the enforcement of the contract (§ 205; see Comment d).

§ 252.   Effect of Insolvency

(1)   Where the obligor's insolvency gives the obligee reasonable grounds to believe that the obligor will commit a breach under the rule stated in § 251, the obligee may suspend any performance for which he has not already received the agreed exchange until he receives assurance in the form of performance itself, an offer of performance, or adequate security.

(2)   A person is insolvent who either has ceased to pay his debts in the ordinary course of business or cannot pay his debts as they become due or is insolvent within the meaning of the federal bankruptcy law.

§ 253.   Effect of a Repudiation as a Breach and on Other Party's Duties

(1)   Where an obligor repudiates a duty before he has committed a breach by non-performance and before he has received all of the agreed exchange for it, his repudiation alone gives rise to a claim for damages for total breach.

(2)   Where performances are to be exchanged under an exchange of promises, one party's repudiation of a duty to render performance discharges the other party's remaining duties to render performance.

Comment:

a.   *Breach.* An obligee under a contract is ordinarily entitled to the protection of his expectation that the obligor will perform. For this reason, a repudiation by the obligor under § 250 or § 251 generally gives rise to a claim for damages for total breach even though it is not accompanied or preceded by a breach by non-performance. Such a repudiation is sometimes elliptically called an "anticipatory breach," meaning a breach by anticipatory repudiation, because it occurs before there is any breach by non-performance. If there is a breach by non-performance, in addition to the repudiation under § 250 or § 251 the breach is not one by repudiation alone and the rules stated in § 243 rather than those stated in Subsection (1) apply. If, under § 251, it was a breach by non-performance that gave the obligee grounds to believe that the obligor would commit a more serious breach, the obligor's failure to give assurances cannot give rise to a breach by repudiation alone. The measure of damages in the case of a claim under this Section is governed by the rules stated in Topic 2 of Chapter 16.

Illustrations:

1. On April 1, A and B make a contract under which B is to work for A for three months beginning on June 1. On May 1, A repudiates by telling B he will not employ him. On May 15, B commences an action against A. B's duty to work for A is discharged and he has a claim against A for damages for total breach.

2. On July 1, A contracts to sell and B to buy a quantity of barrel staves, delivery and payment to be on December 1. On August 1, A repudiates by writing B that he will be unable to deliver staves at the contract price. On September 1, B commences an action against A. B's duty to pay for the staves is discharged and he has a claim against A for damages for total breach. See Uniform Commercial Code § 2–610.

b. Discharge. Under Subsection (1) a breach by repudiation alone can only give rise to a claim for total breach, although a breach by non-performance, even if coupled with a repudiation, can generally give rise to either a claim for partial breach or to one for total breach (§§ 236, 237). Of course, in appropriate circumstances, the injured party can, after a breach by repudiation alone, pursue alternative relief by seeking, for example, a decree of specific performance or an injunction. See Topic 3 of Chapter 16. Nevertheless, the rule stated in Subsection (1) is one of those rules that are peculiar to breach by repudiation alone and differ from those applicable to a breach by non-performance. (Another such rule is that a breach by repudiation alone can be totally nullified by the party in breach (§ 257), while a breach by non-performance, whether coupled

with a repudiation or not, cannot be.) Subsection (2) states a corollary of this rule that a breach by repudiation always gives rise to a claim for damages for total breach: where performances are to be exchanged under an exchange of promises, one party's repudiation discharges any remaining duties of performance of the other party with respect to the expected exchange.

c. Scope. If an obligor repudiates under § 250 or § 251 before he has received all of the agreed exchange for his promise, the repudiation alone gives rise to a claim for damages for total breach under Subsection (1). The most important example of such a case occurs when performances are to be exchanged under an exchange of promises and one party repudiates a duty with respect to the expected exchange before the other party has fully performed that exchange. See Illustrations 1 and 2. (A repudiation of a duty whose performance is not part of the expected exchange, and for which there is therefore no agreed exchange, does not come within the rule stated in Subsection (1). See, e.g., Illustration 3 to § 232.) Another example occurs when one party repudiates a duty under an option contract before the other party has exercised the option by giving the agreed exchange. See Illustration 3. However, it is one of the established limits on the doctrine of "anticipatory breach" that an obligor's repudiation alone, whether under § 250 or § 251, gives rise to no claim for damages at all if he has already received all of the agreed exchange for it. The rule stated in Subsection (1) does not, therefore, allow a claim for damages for total breach in such a case.

Illustrations:

3. On February 1, A and B make an option contract under which, in consideration for B's payment of $100, A promises to convey to B a parcel of land on May 1 for

$50,000, if B tenders that sum by that date. On March 1, A repudiates by selling the parcel to C. On April 1, B commences an action against A. Since A has not received the $50,000, the agreed exchange for his duty to sell the parcel to B, B has a claim against A for damages for total breach.

4.   On February 1, A and B make a contract under which, as consideration for B's immediate payment of $50,000, A promises to convey to B a parcel of land on May 1. On March 1, A repudiates by selling the parcel to C. On April 1, B commences an action against A. Since A has received the $50,000, the agreed exchange for his duty to sell the parcel to B, B has no claim against A for damages for breach of contract until performance is due on May 1.

5.   On February 1, A and B make a contract under which, as consideration for A's conveying a parcel of land to B, B promises to make annual payments of $10,000 for five years. B makes the payments for the first two years and on March 1 of the third year repudiates by telling A that he will not make any further payments. A commences an action against B. Since B has received the land, the agreed exchange for his duty to pay the remaining installments, A has no claim against B for damages for breach of contract until performance is due on the following February 1.

6.   On January 15, A and B make a contract under which A promises to convey to B a parcel of land on February 1, and B prom-ises to pay A $10,000 at that time and the balance of $40,000 in four annual installments. A conveys the parcel to B and B pays A $10,000. On March 1, B repudiates by telling A that he will not make any further payments. A commences an action against B. Since B has received the land, the agreed exchange for his duty to make the remaining payments, A has no claim against B for damages for breach of contract, until performance is due on the following February 1.

d.   Avoiding harsh results of limitation. The limitation described in Comment c sometimes avoids difficult problems of forecasting damages and is supported by the clear weight of authority. It has, however, been subjected to considerable criticism, and instances of its actual application are infrequent. Compare, for example, Illustration 3 with Illustration 4. A court can often avoid harsh results by making available other types of relief, such as a declaratory judgment or restitution. See §§ 345, 373 and Comment a to § 373. Insurance contracts are subject to special considerations which may make it appropriate to grant equitable relief in, for example, a suit for reinstatement. The degree to which the limitation might yield on a showing of manifest injustice, as where the refusal to pay is not in good faith, is unclear. Compare Comment d to § 243. Furthermore, if the repudiation is coupled with a breach by non-performance that would otherwise give rise to a claim for damages for only partial breach, it may give rise instead to a claim for damages for total breach, but whether it does so is governed by § 243 and not by this Section.

§ 254.   Effect of Subsequent Events on Duty to Pay Damages

(1)   A party's duty to pay damages for total breach by repudiation is discharged if it appears after the breach that there would have been a total failure by the injured party to perform his return promise.

(2) A party's duty to pay damages for total breach by repudiation is discharged if it appears after the breach that the duty that he repudiated would have been discharged by impracticability or frustration before any breach by non-performance.

Comment:

a. Non-performance by injured party after repudiation. If the parties are to exchange performances under an exchange of promises, each party's duties to render performance are generally regarded as conditional on the other party's performance, or at least on his readiness to perform (§§ 237, 238, 251, 253). This principle applies even though one party is already in breach by repudiation. His duty to pay damages is discharged if it subsequently appears that there would have been a total failure of performance by the injured party. A failure is total in this context if it would have been sufficient to have discharged any remaining duties of the party in breach to render his performance. See § 242. The result follows even if it appears that the failure would have been justified and not a breach. Cf. § 244.

Illustration:

1. On April 1, A and B make a personal service contract under which A promises to employ B for six months beginning July 1 and B promises to work for A during that period. On May 1, A repudiates the contract. On June 1, B falls ill and is unable to perform during the en-tire period. A's duty to pay B damages for total breach by repudiation is discharged.

b. Impracticability or frustration after repudiation. Under the rule stated in § 253(1), a party's breach by anticipatory repudiation immediately gives rise to a claim for damages for total breach. If it subsequently appears that the duty that he repudiated would have been discharged by supervening impracticability (§ 261) or frustration (§ 265) before any breach by non-performance, his duty to pay damages is discharged. Impracticability or frustration that would have occurred after breach by non-performance may affect the measure of damages but does not discharge the duty to pay damages; cf. §§ 344, 347, 352.

Illustration:

2. On April 1, A and B make a personal service contract under which A promises to employ B for 6 months beginning July 1 and B promises to work for A during that period. On May 1, B repudiates the contract. On June 1, B falls ill and is unable to perform during the entire period. B's duty to pay damages to A for his anticipatory repudiation is discharged.

§ 255. Effect of a Repudiation as Excusing the Non-Occurrence of a Condition

Where a party's repudiation contributes materially to the non-occurrence of a condition of one of his duties, the non-occurrence is excused.

§ 256. Nullification of Repudiation or Basis for Repudiation

(1) The effect of a statement as constituting a repudiation under § 250 or the basis for a repudiation under § 251 is nullified by a retraction of the statement if notification of the retraction comes to the attention of the injured party before he materially changes his position in reliance

on the repudiation or indicates to the other party that he considers the repudiation to be final.

(2)   The effect of events other than a statement as constituting a repudiation under § 250 or the basis for a repudiation under § 251 is nullified if, to the knowledge of the injured party, those events have ceased to exist before he materially changes his position in reliance on the repudiation or indicates to the other party that he considers the repudiation to be final.

Comment:

a.   Effect of nullification. A repudiation may have three consequences: it may give rise to a claim for damages for total breach (§ 253(1)(1)), discharge duties (§ 253(2)(2)), and excuse the non-occurrence of a condition (§ 255). A party's manifestation of doubt or apparent inability may entitle the other party to demand adequate assurance of due performance and to treat a failure to give such assurance as a repudiation under the rule stated in § 251. If, however, the effect of the statement or other events constituting the repudiation under § 250 or the basis for the repudiation under § 251 is nullified as provided in this Section, none of these consequences follows. Such a nullification does not, of course, alter the consequences of any breach by non-performance that may have taken place. If, for example, a repudiation accompanies a breach by non-performance, nullification of the repudiation leaves the injured party a claim for damages for the breach, although the claim may no longer be one for damages for total breach (see Comment b to § 243). If the repudiation is wholly anticipatory, nullification leaves the injured party with no claim at all. Compare the effect of events subsequent to a total breach by repudiation (§ 254). . . .

b.   Manner of retraction. It is not necessary for the repudiator to use words in order to retract his statement. Conduct, such as an offer of performance, may be adequate to convey the idea of retraction to the injured party.

c.   Time for nullification. Once the injured party has materially changed his position in reliance on the repudiation, nullification would clearly be unjust. In the interest of certainty, however, it is undesirable to make the injured party's rights turn exclusively on such a vague criterion, and he may therefore prevent subsequent nullification by indicating to the other party that he considers the repudiation final. It is, for example, enough under Uniform Commercial Code § 2–612 that "the aggrieved party has since the repudiation cancelled or materially changed his position or otherwise indicated that he considers the repudiation final." Cancellation of the contract or the commencement of an action claiming damages for total breach would be sufficient. (See Comment 1 to Uniform Commercial Code § 2–611.). . .

§ 257.   Effect of Urging Performance in Spite of Repudiation

The injured party does not change the effect of a repudiation by urging the repudiator to perform in spite of his repudiation or to retract his repudiation.

TOPIC 4. APPLICATION OF PERFORMANCES

§ 258. Obligor's Direction of Application

(1)   Except as stated in Subsection (2), as between two or more contractual duties owed by an obligor to the same obligee, a performance is applied according to a direction made by the obligor to the obligee at or before the time of performance.

(2)   If the obligor is under a duty to a third person to devote a performance to the discharge of a particular duty that the obligor owes to the obligee and the obligee knows or has reason to know this, the obligor's performance is applied to that duty.

§ 259. Creditor's Application

(1)   Except as stated in Subsections (2) and (3), if the debtor has not directed application of a payment as between two or more matured debts, the payment is applied according to a manifestation of intention made within a reasonable time by the creditor to the debtor.

(2)   A creditor cannot apply such a payment to a debt if

(a)   the debtor could not have directed its application to that debt, or

(b)   a forfeiture would result from a failure to apply it to another debt and the creditor knows or has reason to know this, or

(c)   the debt is disputed or is unenforceable on grounds of public policy.

(3)   If a creditor is owed one such debt in his own right and another in a fiduciary capacity, he cannot, unless empowered to do so by the beneficiary, effectively apply to the debt in his own right a greater proportion of a payment than that borne by the unsecured portion of that debt to the unsecured portions of both claims.

§ 260. Application of Payments Where Neither Party Exercises His Power

(1)   If neither the debtor nor the creditor has exercised his power with respect to the application of a payment as between two or more matured debts, the payment is applied to debts to which the creditor could have applied it with just regard to the interests of third persons, the debtor and the creditor.

(2)   In applying payments under the rule stated in Subsection (1), a payment is applied to the earliest matured debt and ratably among debts of the same maturity, except that preference is given

(a)   to a debt that the debtor is under a duty to a third person to pay immediately, and

(b)   if he is not under such a duty,

   (i)   to overdue interest rather than principal, and

   (ii)   to an unsecured or precarious debt rather than one that is secured or certain of payment.

CHAPTER 11. IMPRACTICABILITY OF PERFORMANCE AND FRUSTRATION OF PURPOSE

§ 261.   Discharge by Supervening Impracticability

Where, after a contract is made, a party's performance is made impracticable without his fault by the occurrence of an event the non-occurrence of which was a basic assumption on which the contract was made, his duty to render that performance is discharged, unless the language or the circumstances indicate the contrary.

Comment:

a.   *Scope.* Even though a party, in assuming a duty, has not qualified the language of his undertaking, a court may relieve him of that duty if performance has unexpectedly become impracticable as a result of a supervening event (see Introductory Note to this Chapter). This Section states the general principle under which a party's duty may be so discharged. The following three sections deal with the three categories of cases where this general principle has traditionally been applied: supervening death or incapacity of a person necessary for performance (§ 262), supervening destruction of a specific thing necessary for performance (§ 263), and supervening prohibition or prevention by law (§ 264). But, like Uniform Commercial Code § 2–615(a), this Section states a principle broadly applicable to all types of impracticability and it "deliberately refrains from any effort at an exhaustive expression of contingencies" (Comment 2 to Uniform Commercial Code § 2–615). The principle, like others in this Chapter, yields to a contrary agreement by which a party may assume a greater as well as a lesser obligation. By such an agreement, for example, a party may undertake to achieve a result irrespective of supervening events that may render its achievement impossible, and if he does so his non-performance is a breach even if it is caused by such an event. See Comment c. The rule stated in this Section applies only to discharge a duty to render a performance and does not affect a claim for breach that has already arisen. The effect of events subsequent to a breach on the amount of damages recoverable is governed by the rules on remedies stated in Chapter 16. See Comment e to § 347. Their effect on a claim for breach by anticipatory repudiation is governed by the rules on discharge stated in Chapter 12. Cases of existing, as opposed to supervening, impracticability are governed by § 266 rather than this Section.

b.   *Basic assumption.* In order for a supervening event to discharge a duty under this Section, the non-occurrence of that event must have been a "basic assumption" on which both parties made the contract (see Introductory Note to this Chapter). This is the criterion used by Uniform Commercial Code § 2–615(a). Its application is simple enough in the cases of the death of a person or destruction of a specific thing necessary for performance. The continued existence of the person or thing (the non-occurrence of the death of destruction) is ordinarily a basic assumption on which the contract was made, so that death or destruction effects a discharge. Its application is also simple enough in the cases of market shifts or the financial inability of one of the parties. The continuation of existing market conditions and of the financial situation of the parties are ordinarily not such assumptions, so that mere market shifts or financial inability do not usually effect discharge under the rule stated in this Section. In borderline cases this criterion is sufficiently flexible to take account of factors that bear on a just allocation of risk. The fact that the event was foreseeable, or even foreseen, does not necessarily compel a conclusion that its non-occurrence was not a basic assumption. See Comment c to this Section and Comment a to § 265.

Illustrations:

1.   On June 1, A agrees to sell and B to buy goods to be delivered in October at a designated port. The port is subsequently closed by quarantine regulations during the entire month of October, no commercially reasonable substitute performance is available (see Uniform Commercial Code § 2–614(1)), and A fails to deliver the goods. A's duty to deliver the goods is discharged, and A is not liable to B for breach of contract.

2.   A contracts to produce a movie for B. As B knows, A's only source of funds is a $100,000 deposit in C bank. C bank fails, and A does not produce the movie. A's duty to produce the movie is not discharged, and A is liable to B for breach of contract.

3.   A and B make a contract under which B is to work for A for two years at a salary of $50,000 a year. At the end of one year, A discontinues his business because governmental regulations have made it unprofitable and fires B. A's duty to employ B is not discharged, and A is liable to B for breach of contract.

4.   A contracts to sell and B to buy a specific machine owned by A to be delivered on July 30. On July 29, as a result of a creditor's suit against A, a receiver is appointed and takes charge of all of A's assets, and A does not deliver the goods on July 30. A's duty to deliver the goods is not discharged, and A is liable to B for breach of contract.

c.   Contrary indication. A party may, by appropriate language, agree to perform in spite of impracticability that would otherwise justify his non-performance under the rule stated in this Section. He can then be held liable for damages although he cannot perform. Even absent an express agreement, a court may decide, after considering all the circumstances, that a party impliedly assumed such a greater obligation. In this respect the rule stated in this Section parallels that of Uniform Commercial Code § 2–615, which applies "Except so far as a seller may have assumed a greater obligation. . . ." Circumstances relevant in deciding whether a party has assumed a greater obligation include his ability to have inserted a provision in the contract expressly shifting the risk of impracticability to the other party. This will depend on the extent to which the agreement was standardized (cf. § 211), the degree to which the other party supplied the terms (cf. § 206), and, in the case of a particular trade or other group, the frequency with which language so allocating the risk is used in that trade or group (cf. § 219). The fact that a supplier has not taken advantage of his opportunity expressly to shift the risk of a shortage in his supply by means of contract language may be regarded as more significant where he is middleman, with a variety of sources of supply and an opportunity to spread the risk among many customers on many transactions by slight adjustment of his prices, than where he is a producer with a limited source of supply, few outlets, and no comparable opportunity. A commercial practice under which a party might be expected to insure or otherwise secure himself against a risk also militates against shifting it to the other party. If the supervening event was not reasonably foreseeable when the contract was made, the party claiming discharge can hardly be expected to have provided against its occurrence. However, if it was reasonably foreseeable, or even foreseen, the opposite conclusion does not necessarily follow. Factors such as the practical difficulty of reaching agreement on the myriad of conceivable terms of a complex agreement may excuse a failure to deal with improbable contingencies. See Comment b to this Section and Comment a to § 265.

Illustration:

> 5. A, who has had many years of experience in the field of salvage, contracts to raise and float B's boat, which has run aground. The contract, prepared by A, contains no clause limiting A's duty in the case of unfavorable weather, unforeseen circumstances, or otherwise. The boat then slips into deep water and fills with mud, making it impracticable for A to raise it. If the court concludes, on the basis of such circumstances as A's experience and the absence of any limitation in the contract that A prepared, that A assumed an absolute duty, it will decide that A's duty to raise and float the boat is not discharged and that A is liable to B for breach of contract.

d. Impracticability. Events that come within the rule stated in this Section are generally due either to "acts of God" or to acts of third parties. If the event that prevents the obligor's performance is caused by the obligee, it will ordinarily amount to a breach by the latter and the situation will be governed by the rules stated in Chapter 10, without regard to this Section. See Illustrations 4–7 to § 237. If the event is due to the fault of the obligor himself, this Section does not apply. As used here "fault" may include not only "willful" wrongs, but such other types of conduct as that amounting to breach of contract or to negligence. See Comment 1 to Uniform Commercial Code § 2–613. Although the rule stated in this Section is sometimes phrased in terms of "impossibility," it has long been recognized that it may operate to discharge a party's duty even though the event has not made performance absolutely impossible. This Section, therefore, uses "impracticable," the term employed by Uniform Commercial Code § 2–615(a), to describe the required extent of the impediment to performance. Performance may be impracticable because extreme and unreasonable difficulty, expense, injury, or loss to one of the parties will be involved. A severe shortage of raw materials or of supplies due to war, embargo, local crop failure, unforeseen shutdown of major sources of supply, or the like, which either causes a marked increase in cost or prevents performance altogether may bring the case within the rule stated in this Section. Performance may also be impracticable because it will involve a risk of injury to person or to property, of one of the parties or of others, that is disproportionate to the ends to be attained by performance. However, "impracticability" means more than "impracticality." A mere change in the degree of difficulty or expense due to such causes as increased wages, prices of raw materials, or costs of construction, unless well beyond the normal range, does not amount to impracticability since it is this sort of risk that a fixed-price contract is intended to cover. Furthermore, a party is expected to use reasonable efforts to surmount obstacles to performance (see § 205), and a performance is impracticable only if it is so in spite of such efforts.

Illustrations:

6.　A contracts to repair B's grain elevator. While A is engaged in making repairs, a fire destroys the elevator without A's fault, and A does not finish the repairs. A's duty to repair the elevator is discharged, and A is not liable to B for breach of contract. See Illustration 3 to § 263.

7.　A contracts with B to carry B's goods on his ship to a designated foreign port. A civil war then unexpectedly breaks out in that country and the rebels announce that they will try to sink all vessels bound for that port. A refuses to perform. Although A did not contract to sail on the vessel, the risk of injury to others is sufficient to make A's performance impracticable. A's duty to carry the goods to the designated port is discharged, and A is not liable to B for breach of contract. Compare Illustration 5 to § 262.

8.　The facts being otherwise as stated in Illustration 7, the rebels announce merely that they will confiscate all vessels found in the designated port. The goods can be bought and sold on markets throughout the world. A refuses to perform. Although there is no risk of injury to persons, the court may conclude that the risk of injury to property is disproportionate to the ends to be attained. A's duty to carry the goods to the designated port is then discharged, and A is not liable to B for breach of contract. If, however, B is a health organization and the goods are scarce medical supplies vital to the health of the population of the designated port, the court may conclude that the risk is not disproportionate to the ends to be attained and may reach a contrary decision.

9.　Several months after the nationalization of the Suez Canal, during the international crisis resulting from its seizure, A contracts to carry a cargo of B's wheat on A's ship from Galveston, Texas to Bandar Shapur, Iran for a flat rate. The contract does not specify the route, but the voyage would normally be through the Straits of Gibraltar and the Suez Canal, a distance of 10,000 miles. A month later, and several days after the ship has left Galveston, the Suez Canal is closed by an outbreak of hostilities, so that the only route to Bandar Shapur is the longer 13,000 mile voyage around the Cape of Good Hope. A refuses to complete the voyage unless B pays additional compensation. A's duty to carry B's cargo is not discharged, and A is liable to B for breach of contract.

10.　The facts being otherwise as in Illustration 9, the Suez Canal is closed while A's ship is in the Canal, preventing the completion of the voyage. A's duty to carry B's cargo is discharged, and A is not liable to B for breach of contract.

11.　A contracts to construct and lease to B a gasoline service station. A valid zoning ordinance is subsequently enacted forbidding the construction of such a station but permitting variances in appropriate cases. A, in breach of his duty of good faith and fair dealing (§ 205), makes no effort to obtain a variance, although variances have been granted in similar cases, and fails to construct the station. A's performance has not been made impracticable. A's duty to construct is not discharged, and A is liable to B for breach of contract.

e.　"Subjective" and "objective" impracticability. It is sometimes said that the rule stated in this Section applies only when the performance itself is made impracticable, without regard to the particular party who is to perform. The difference has been described as that between "the thing cannot be done" and "I cannot do it," and the former has been characterized as "objective" and the latter as "subjective." This Section recognizes that if the performance remains practicable and it is merely beyond the party's capacity to render it, he is ordinarily not discharged, but it does not use the terms "objective" and "subjective" to express this. Instead, the rationale is that a party generally assumes the risk of his own inability to perform his duty. Even if a party contracts to render a performance that depends on some act by a third party, he is not ordinarily discharged because of a failure by that party because this is also a risk that is commonly understood to be on the obligor. See Comment c. But see Comment a to § 262.

Illustrations:

12. A, a milkman, and B, a dairy farmer, make a contract under which B is to sell and A to buy all of A's requirements of milk, but not less than 200 quarts a day, for one year. B may deliver milk from any source but expects to deliver milk from his own herd. B's herd is destroyed because of hoof and mouth disease and he fails to deliver any milk. B's duty to deliver milk is not discharged, and B is liable to A for breach of contract. See Illustration 1 to § 263; compare Illustration 7 to § 263.

13. A contracts to sell and B to buy on credit 1,500,000 gallons of molasses "of the usual run from the C sugar refinery." C delivers molasses to others but fails to deliver any to A, and A fails to deliver any to B. A's duty to deliver molasses is not discharged, and A is liable to B for breach of contract. If A has a con-

tract with C, C may be liable to A for breach of contract.

14. A, a general contractor, is bidding on a construction contract with B which gives B the right to disapprove the choice of subcontractors. A makes a contract with C, a subcontractor, under which, if B awards A the contract, A will obtain B's approval of C and C will do the excavation for A. A is awarded the contract by B, but B disapproves A's choice of C, and A has the excavation work done by another subcontractor. A's duty to have C do the excavation is not discharged, and A is liable to C for breach of contract.

f.   Alternative performances. A contract may permit a party to choose to perform in one of several different ways, any of which will discharge his duty. Where the duty is to render such an alternative performance, the fact that one or more of the alternatives has become impracticable will not discharge the party's duty to perform if at least one of them remains practicable. The form of the promise is not controlling, however, and not every promise that is expressed in alternative form gives rise to a duty to render an alternative performance. For example, a surety's undertaking that either the principal will perform or the surety will compensate the creditor does not ordinarily impose such a duty. See Restatement of Security § 117. Nor does a promise either to render a performance or pay liquidated damages impose such a duty. Furthermore, a duty that is originally one to render alternative performances ceases to be such a duty if all but one means of performance have been foreclosed, as by the lapse of time or the occurrence of a condition including election by the obligor, or on the grounds of public policy (Chapter 8) or unconscionability (§ 208).

Illustrations:

15.   On June 1, A contracts to sell and B to buy whichever of three specified machines A chooses to deliver on October 1. Two of the machines are destroyed by fire on July 1, and A fails to deliver the third on October 1. A's duty to deliver a machine is not discharged, and A is liable to B for breach of contract. If all three machines had been destroyed, A's duty to deliver a machine would have been discharged, and A would not have been liable to B for breach of contract. See Uniform Commercial Code § 2–613.

16.   A contracts to repair B's building. The contract contains a valid provision requiring A to pay liquidated damages if he fails to make any of the repairs. S is surety for A's performance. Before A is able to begin, B's building is destroyed by fire. Neither A's nor S's duty is one to render an alternative performance. A's duty to repair the building is discharged, and A is not liable to B for liquidated damages or otherwise for breach of contract. S's duty as surety for A is also discharged, and S is not liable to B for breach of contract.

§ 262.   Death or Incapacity of Person Necessary for Performance

If the existence of a particular person is necessary for the performance of a duty, his death or such incapacity as makes performance impracticable is an event the non-occurrence of which was a basic assumption on which the contract was made.

§ 263.   Destruction, Deterioration or Failure to Come Into Existence of Thing Necessary for Performance

If the existence of a specific thing is necessary for the performance of a duty, its failure to come into existence, destruction, or such deterioration as makes performance impracticable is an event the non-occurrence of which was a basic assumption on which the contract was made.

§ 264.   Prevention by Governmental Regulation or Order

If the performance of a duty is made impracticable by having to comply with a domestic or foreign governmental regulation or order, that regulation or order is an event the non-occurrence of which was a basic assumption on which the contract was made.

§ 265.   Discharge by Supervening Frustration

Where, after a contract is made, a party's principal purpose is substantially frustrated without his fault by the occurrence of an event the non-occurrence of which was a basic assumption on which the contract was made, his remaining duties to render performance are discharged, unless the language or the circumstances indicate the contrary.

Comment:

a.   *Rationale.* This Section deals with the problem that arises when a change in circumstances makes one party's performance virtually worthless to the other, frustrating his purpose in making the contract. It is distinct from

161

the problem of impracticability dealt with in the four preceding sections because there is no impediment to performance by either party. Although there has been no true failure of performance in the sense required for the application of the rule stated in § 237, the impact on the party adversely affected will be similar. The rule stated in this Section sets out the requirements for the discharge of that party's duty. First, the purpose that is frustrated must have been a principal purpose of that party in making the contract. It is not enough that he had in mind some specific object without which he would not have made the contract. The object must be so completely the basis of the contract that, as both parties understand, without it the transaction would make little sense. Second, the frustration must be substantial. It is not enough that the transaction has become less profitable for the affected party or even that he will sustain a loss. The frustration must be so severe that it is not fairly to be regarded as within the risks that he assumed under the contract. Third, the non-occurrence of the frustrating event must have been a basic assumption on which the contract was made. This involves essentially the same sorts of determinations that are involved under the general rule on impracticability. See Comments b and c to § 261. The foreseeability of the event is here, as it is there, a factor in that determination, but the mere fact that the event was foreseeable does not compel the conclusion that its non-occurrence was not such a basic assumption.

Illustrations:

1. A and B make a contract under which B is to pay A $1,000 and is to have the use of A's window on January 10 to view a parade that has been scheduled for that day. Because of the illness of an important official, the parade is cancelled. B refuses to use the window or pay the $1,000. B's duty to pay $1,000 is discharged, and B is not liable to A for breach of contract.

2. A contracts with B to print an advertisement in a souvenir program of an international yacht race, which has been scheduled by a yacht club, for a price of $10,000. The yacht club cancels the race because of the outbreak of war. A has already printed the programs, but B refuses to pay the $10,000. B's duty to pay $10,000 is discharged, and B is not liable to A for breach of contract. A may have a claim under the rule stated in § 272(1).

3. A, who owns a hotel, and B, who owns a country club, make a contract under which A is to pay $1,000 a month and B is to make the club's membership privileges available to the guests in A's hotel free of charge to them. A's building is destroyed by fire without his fault, and A is unable to remain in the hotel business. A refuses to make further monthly payments. A's duty to make monthly payments is discharged, and A is not liable to B for breach of contract.

4. A leases neon sign installations to B for three years to advertise and illuminate B's place of business. After one year, a government regulation prohibits the lighting of such signs. B refuses to make further payments of rent. B's duty to pay rent is discharged, and B is not liable to A for breach of contract. See Illustration 7.

5. A contracts to sell and B to buy a machine, to be delivered to B in the United States. B, as A knows, intends to export the machine to a particular country for resale. Before delivery to B, a government regulation prohibits export of the machine to that country. B refuses to take or pay for the machine. If B can reasonably make other disposi-

tion of the machine, even though at some loss, his principal purpose of putting the machine to commercial use is not substantially frustrated. B's duty to take and pay for the machine is not discharged, and B is liable to A for breach of contract.

6.   A leases a gasoline station to B. A change in traffic regulations so reduces B's business that he is unable to operate the station except at a substantial loss. B refuses to make further payments of rent. If B can still operate the station, even though at such a loss, his principal purpose of operating a gasoline station is not substantially frustrated. B's duty to pay rent is not discharged, and B is liable to A for breach of contract. The result would be the same if substantial loss were caused instead by a government regulation rationing gasoline or a termination of the franchise under which B obtained gasoline.

b.   Limitations on scope. The rule stated in this Section is subject to limitations similar to those stated in § 261 with respect to impracticability. It applies only when the frustration is without the fault of the party who seeks to take advantage of the rule, and it does not apply if the language or circumstances indicate the contrary. Frustration by circumstances existing at the time of the making of the contract rather than by supervening circumstances is governed by the similar rule stated in § 266(2).

Illustration:

7.   The facts being otherwise as in Illustration 4, the government regulation provides for a procedure under which B can apply for an exemption, but B, in breach of his duty of good faith and fair dealing (§ 205), fails to make such an application. Unless it is found that such an application would have been unsuccessful, B's duty to pay rent is not discharged, and B is liable to A for breach of contract. Cf. Illustration 11 to § 261; Illustration 3 to § 264.

§ 266.   Existing Impracticability or Frustration

(1)   Where, at the time a contract is made, a party's performance under it is impracticable without his fault because of a fact of which he has no reason to know and the non-existence of which is a basic assumption on which the contract is made, no duty to render that performance arises, unless the language or circumstances indicate the contrary.

(2)   Where, at the time a contract is made, a party's principal purpose is substantially frustrated without his fault by a fact of which he has no reason to know and the non-existence of which is a basic assumption on which the contract is made, no duty of that party to render performance arises, unless the language or circumstances indicate the contrary.

§ 267.   Effect on Other Party's Duties of a Failure Justified by Impracticability or Frustration

(1)   A party's failure to render or to offer performance may, except as stated in Subsection (2), affect the other party's duties under the rules stated in §§ 237 and 238 even though the failure is justified under the rules stated in this Chapter.

(2)   The rule stated in Subsection (1) does not apply if the other party assumed the risk that he would have to perform despite such a failure.

§ 268.   Effect on Other Party's Duties of a Prospective Failure Justified by Impracticability or Frustration

(1)   A party's prospective failure of performance may, except as stated in Subsection (2), discharge the other party's duties or allow him to suspend performance under the rules stated in §§ 251(1) and 253(2) even though the failure would be justified under the rules stated in this Chapter.

(2)   The rule stated in Subsection (1) does not apply if the other party assumed the risk that he would have to perform in spite of such a failure.

§ 269.   Temporary Impracticability or Frustration

Impracticability of performance or frustration of purpose that is only temporary suspends the obligor's duty to perform while the impracticability or frustration exists but does not discharge his duty or prevent it from arising unless his performance after the cessation of the impracticability or frustration would be materially more burdensome than had there been no impracticability or frustration.

§ 270.   Partial Impracticability

Where only part of an obligor's performance is impracticable, his duty to render the remaining part is unaffected if

(a)   it is still practicable for him to render performance that is substantial, taking account of any reasonable substitute performance that he is under a duty to render; or

(b)   the obligee, within a reasonable time, agrees to render any remaining performance in full and to allow the obligor to retain any performance that has already been rendered.

§ 271.   Impracticability as Excuse for Non-Occurrence of a Condition

Impracticability excuses the non-occurrence of a condition if the occurrence of the condition is not a material part of the agreed exchange and forfeiture would otherwise result.

§ 272.   Relief Including Restitution

(1)   In any case governed by the rules stated in this Chapter, either party may have a claim for relief including restitution under the rules stated in §§ 240 and 377.

(2)   In any case governed by the rules stated in this Chapter, if those rules together with the rules stated in Chapter 16 will not avoid injustice,

the court may grant relief on such terms as justice requires including protection of the parties' reliance interests.

CHAPTER 12. DISCHARGE BY ASSENT OR ALTERATION

TOPIC 1. THE REQUIREMENT OF CONSIDERATION

§ 273. Requirement of Consideration or a Substitute

Except as stated in §§ 274–77, an obligee's manifestation of assent to a discharge is not effective unless

    (a) it is made for consideration,

    (b) it is made in circumstances in which a promise would be enforceable without consideration, or

    (c) it has induced such action or forbearance as would make a promise enforceable.

§ 274. Cancellation, Destruction or Surrender of a Writing

An obligee's cancellation, destruction or surrender to the obligor of a writing of a type customarily accepted as a symbol or as evidence of his right discharges without consideration the obligor's duty if it is done with the manifested intention to discharge it.

§ 275. Assent to Discharge Duty of Return Performance

If a party, before he has fully performed his duty under a contract, manifests to the other party his assent to discharge the other party's duty to render part or all of the agreed exchange, the duty is to that extent discharged without consideration.

§ 276. Assent to Discharge Duty to Transfer Property

A duty of an obligor in possession of identified personal property to transfer an interest in that property is discharged without consideration if the obligee manifests to the obligor his assent to the discharge of that duty.

§ 277. Renunciation

    (1) A written renunciation signed and delivered by the obligee discharges without consideration a duty arising out of a breach of contract.

    (2) A renunciation by the obligee on his acceptance from the obligor of some performance under a contract discharges without consideration a duty to pay damages for a breach that gives rise only to a claim for damages for partial breach of contract.

TOPIC 2.   SUBSTITUTED PERFORMANCE, SUBSTITUTED CONTRACT, ACCORD AND ACCOUNT STATED

§ 278.   Substituted Performance

(1)   If an obligee accepts in satisfaction of the obligor's duty a performance offered by the obligor that differs from what is due, the duty is discharged.

(2)   If an obligee accepts in satisfaction of the obligor's duty a performance offered by a third person, the duty is discharged, but an obligor who has not previously assented to the performance for his benefit may in a reasonable time after learning of it render the discharge inoperative from the beginning by disclaimer.

§ 279.   Substituted Contract

(1)   A substituted contract is a contract that is itself accepted by the obligee in satisfaction of the obligor's existing duty.

(2)   The substituted contract discharges the original duty and breach of the substituted contract by the obligor does not give the obligee a right to enforce the original duty.

§ 280.   Novation

A novation is a substituted contract that includes as a party one who was neither the obligor nor the obligee of the original duty.

§ 281.   Accord and Satisfaction

(1)   An accord is a contract under which an obligee promises to accept a stated performance in satisfaction of the obligor's existing duty. Performance of the accord discharges the original duty.

(2)   Until performance of the accord, the original duty is suspended unless there is such a breach of the accord by the obligor as discharges the new duty of the obligee to accept the performance in satisfaction. If there is such a breach, the obligee may enforce either the original duty or any duty under the accord.

(3)   Breach of the accord by the obligee does not discharge the original duty, but the obligor may maintain a suit for specific performance of the accord, in addition to any claim for damages for partial breach.

§ 282.   Account Stated

(1)   An account stated is a manifestation of assent by debtor and creditor to a stated sum as an accurate computation of an amount due the creditor. A party's retention without objection for an unreasonably long time of a statement of account rendered by the other party is a manifestation of assent.

(2)   The account stated does not itself discharge any duty but is an admission by each party of the facts asserted and a promise by the debtor to pay according to its terms.

TOPIC 3.   AGREEMENT OF RESCISSION, RELEASE AND CONTRACT NOT TO SUE

§ 283.   Agreement of Rescission

(1)   An agreement of rescission is an agreement under which each party agrees to discharge all of the other party's remaining duties of performance under an existing contract.

(2)   An agreement of rescission discharges all remaining duties of performance of both parties. It is a question of interpretation whether the parties also agree to make restitution with respect to performance that has been rendered.

§ 284.   Release

(1)   A release is a writing providing that a duty owed to the maker of the release is discharged immediately or on the occurrence of a condition.

(2)   The release takes effect on delivery as stated in §§ 101–03 and, subject to the occurrence of any condition, discharges the duty.

§ 285.   Contract Not to Sue

(1)   A contract not to sue is a contract under which the obligee of a duty promises never to sue the obligor or a third person to enforce the duty or not to do so for a limited time.

(2)   Except as stated in Subsection (3), a contract never to sue discharges the duty and a contract not to sue for a limited time bars an action to enforce the duty during that time.

(3)   A contract not to sue one co-obligor bars levy of execution on the property of the promisee during the agreed time but does not bar an action or the recovery of judgment against any co-obligor.

TOPIC 4.   ALTERATION

§ 286.   Alteration of Writing

(1)   If one to whom a duty is owed under a contract alters a writing that is an integrated agreement or that satisfies the Statute of Frauds with respect to that contract, the duty is discharged if the alteration is fraudulent and material.

(2)   An alteration is material if it would, if effective, vary any party's legal relations with the maker of the alteration or adversely affect that

party's legal relations with a third person. The unauthorized insertion in a blank space in a writing is an alteration.

§ 287. Assent to or Forgiveness of Alteration

(1) If a party, knowing of an alteration that discharges his duty, manifests assent to the altered terms, his manifestation is equivalent to an acceptance of an offer to substitute those terms.

(2) If a party, knowing of an alteration that discharges his duty, asserts a right under the original contract or otherwise manifests a willingness to remain subject to the original contract or to forgive the alteration, the original contract is revived.

CHAPTER 13. JOINT AND SEVERAL PROMISORS AND PROMISEES

TOPIC 1. JOINT AND SEVERAL PROMISORS

§ 288. Promises of the Same Performance

(1) Where two or more parties to a contract make a promise or promises to the same promisee, the manifested intention of the parties determines whether they promise that the same performance or separate performances shall be given.

(2) Unless a contrary intention is manifested, a promise by two or more promisors is a promise that the same performance shall be given.

§ 289. Joint, Several, and Joint and Several Promisors of the Same Performance

(1) Where two or more parties to a contract promise the same performance to the same promisee, each is bound for the whole performance thereof, whether his duty is joint, several, or joint and several.

(2) Where two or more parties to a contract promise the same performance to the same promisee, they incur only a joint duty unless an intention is manifested to create several duties or joint and several duties.

(3) By statute in most states some or all promises which would otherwise create only joint duties create joint and several duties.

§ 290. Compulsory Joinder of Joint Promisors

(1) By statute in most states where the distinction between joint duties and joint and several duties retains significance, an action can be maintained against one or more promisors who incur only a joint duty, even though other promisors subject to the same duty are not served with process.

(2)   In the absence of statute, an action can be maintained against promisors who incur only a joint duty without joinder of those beyond the jurisdiction of the court, the representatives of deceased promisors, or those against whom the duty is not enforceable at the time of suit.

§ 291.   Judgment in an Action Against Co-Promisors

In an action against promisors of the same performance, whether their duties are joint, several, or joint and several, judgment can properly be entered for or against one even though no judgment or a different judgment is entered with respect to another, except that judgment for one and against another is improper where there has been a determination on the merits and the liability of one cannot exist without the liability of the other.

§ 292.   Effect of Judgment for or Against Co-Promisors

(1)   A judgment against one or more promisors does not discharge other promisors of the same performance unless joinder of the other promisors is required by the rule stated in § 290. By statute in most states judgment against one promisor does not discharge co-promisors even where such joinder is required.

(2)   The effect of judgment for one or more promisors of the same performance is determined by the rules of res judicata relating to suretyship or vicarious liability.

§ 293.   Effect of Performance or Satisfaction on Co-Promisors

Full or partial performance or other satisfaction of the contractual duty of a promisor discharges the duty to the obligee of each other promisor of the same performance to the extent of the amount or value applied to the discharge of the duty of the promisor who renders it.

§ 294.   Effect of Discharge on Co-Promisors

(1)   Except as stated in § 295, where the obligee of promises of the same performance discharges one promisor by release, rescission or accord and satisfaction,

   (a)   co-promisors who are bound only by a joint duty are discharged unless the discharged promisor is a surety for the co-promisor;

   (b)   co-promisors who are bound by joint and several duties or by several duties are not discharged except to the extent required by the law of suretyship.

(2)   By statute in many states a discharge of one promisor does not discharge other promisors of the same performance except to the extent required by the law of suretyship.

(3)   Any consideration received by the obligee for discharge of one promisor discharges the duty of each other promisor of the same perfor-

mance to the extent of the amount or value received. An agreement to the contrary is not effective unless it is made with a surety and expressly preserves the duty of his principal.

§ 295.   Effect of Contract Not to Sue; Reservation of Rights

(1)   Where the obligee of promises of the same performance contracts not to sue one promisor, the other promisors are not discharged except to the extent required by the law of suretyship.

(2)   Words which purport to release or discharge a promisor and also to reserve rights against other promisors of the same performance have the effect of a contract not to sue rather than a release or discharge.

(3)   Any consideration received by the obligee for a contract not to sue one promisor discharges the duty of each other promisor of the same performance to the extent of the amount or value received. An agreement to the contrary is not effective unless it is made with a surety and expressly preserves the duty of his principal.

§ 296.   Survivorship of Joint Duties

On the death of one of two or more promisors of the same performance in a contract, the estate of the deceased promisor is bound by the contract, whether the duty was joint, several, or joint and several.

TOPIC 2.   JOINT AND SEVERAL PROMISEES

§ 297.   Obligees of the Same Promised Performance

(1)   Where a party to a contract makes a promise to two or more promisees or for the benefit of two or more beneficiaries, the manifested intention of the parties determines whether he promises the same performance to all, a separate performance to each, or some combination.

(2)   Except to the extent that a different intention is manifested or that the interests of the obligees in the performance or in the remedies for breach are distinct, the rights of obligees of the same performance are joint.

§ 298.   Compulsory Joinder of Joint Obligees

(1)   In an action based on a joint right created by a promise, the promisor by making appropriate objection can prevent recovery of judgment against him unless there are joined either as plaintiffs or as defendants all the surviving joint obligees.

(2)   Except in actions on negotiable instruments and except as stated in § 300, any joint obligee unless limited by agreement may sue in the name of all the joint obligees for the enforcement of the promise by a money judgment.

§ 299. Discharge by or Tender to One Joint Obligee

Except where the promise is made in a negotiable instrument and except as stated in § 300, any joint obligee, unless limited by agreement, has power to discharge the promisor by receipt of the promised performance or by release or otherwise, and tender to one joint obligee is equivalent to a tender to all.

§ 300. Effect of Violation of Duty to a Co-Obligee

(1) If an obligee attempts or threatens to discharge the promisor in violation of his duty to a co-obligee of the same performance, the co-obligee may obtain an injunction forbidding the discharge.

(2) A discharge of the promisor by an obligee in violation of his duty to a co-obligee of the same performance is voidable to the extent necessary to protect the co-obligee's interest in the performance, except to the extent that the promisor has given value or otherwise changed his position in good faith and without knowledge or reason to know of the violation.

§ 301. Survivorship of Joint Rights

On the death of a joint obligee, unless a contrary intention was manifested, the surviving obligees are solely entitled as against the promisor to receive performance, to discharge the promisor, or to sue for the enforcement of the promise by a money judgment. On the death of the last surviving obligee, only his estate is so entitled.

CHAPTER 14. CONTRACT BENEFICIARIES

§ 302. Intended and Incidental Beneficiaries

(1) Unless otherwise agreed between promisor and promisee, a beneficiary of a promise is an intended beneficiary if recognition of a right to performance in the beneficiary is appropriate to effectuate the intention of the parties and either

(a) the performance of the promise will satisfy an obligation of the promisee to pay money to the beneficiary; or

(b) the circumstances indicate that the promisee intends to give the beneficiary the benefit of the promised performance.

(2) An incidental beneficiary is a beneficiary who is not an intended beneficiary.

Comment:

a. Promisee and beneficiary. This Section distinguishes an "intended" beneficiary, who acquires a right by virtue of a promise, from an "inciden-tal" beneficiary, who does not. See §§ 304, 315. Section 2 defines "promisee" as the person to whom a promise is addressed, and "beneficiary" as a person other than the promisee who will be benefitted by performance of the promise. Both terms are neutral with respect to rights and duties: either or both or neither may have a legal right to performance. Either promisee or beneficiary may but need not be connected with the transaction in other ways: neither promisee nor beneficiary is necessarily the person to whom performance is to be rendered, the person who will receive economic benefit, or the person who furnished the consideration.

b.   *Promise to pay the promisee's debt.* The type of beneficiary covered by Subsection (1)(a) is often referred to as a "creditor beneficiary." In such cases the promisee is surety for the promisor, the promise is an asset of the promisee, and a direct action by beneficiary against promisor is normally appropriate to carry out the intention of promisor and promisee, even though no intention is manifested to give the beneficiary the benefit of the promised performance. Promise of a performance other than the payment of money may be governed by the same principle if the promisee's obligation is regarded as easily convertible into money, as in cases of obligations to deliver commodities or securities which are actively traded in organized markets. Less liquid obligations are left to Subsection (1)(b).

A suretyship relation may exist even though the duty of the promisee is voidable or is unenforceable by reason of the statute of limitations, the Statute of Frauds, or a discharge in bankruptcy, and Subsection (1)(a) covers such cases. The term "creditor beneficiary" has also sometimes been used with reference to promises to satisfy a supposed or asserted duty of the promisee, but there is no suretyship if the promisee has never been under any duty to the beneficiary. Hence such cases are not covered by Subsection (1)(a). The beneficiary of a promise to discharge a lien on the promisee's property, or of a promise to satisfy a duty of a third

person, is similarly excluded from Subsection (1)(a). Such beneficiaries may, however, be "intended beneficiaries" under Subsection (1)(b).

Illustrations:

1.   A owes C a debt of $100. The debt is barred by the statute of limitations or by a discharge in bankruptcy, or is unenforceable because of the Statute of Frauds. B promises A to pay the barred or unenforceable debt. C is an intended beneficiary under Subsection (1)(a).

2.   B promises A to furnish support for A's minor child C, whom A is bound by law to support. C is an intended beneficiary under Subsection (1)(a).

3.   B promises A to pay whatever debts A may incur in a certain undertaking. A incurs in the undertaking debts to C, D and E. If the promise is interpreted as a promise that B will pay C, D and E, they are intended beneficiaries under Subsection (1)(a); if the money is to be paid to A in order that he may be provided with money to pay C, D and E, they are at most incidental beneficiaries.

c.   *Gift promise.* Where the promised performance is not paid for by the recipient, discharges no right that he has against anyone, and is apparently designed to benefit him, the promise is often referred to as a "gift promise." The beneficiary of such a promise is often referred to as a "donee beneficiary"; he is an intended beneficiary under Subsection (1)(b). The contract need not provide that performance is to be rendered directly to the beneficiary: a gift may be made to the beneficiary, for example, by payment of his debt. Nor is any contact or communication with the beneficiary essential.

Illustrations:

4. A, an insurance company, promises B in a policy of insurance to pay $10,000 on B's death to C, B's wife. C is an intended beneficiary under Subsection (1)(b).

5. C is a troublesome person who is annoying A. A dislikes him but, believing the best way to obtain freedom from annoyance is to make a present, secures from B a promise to give C a box of cigars. C is an intended beneficiary under Subsection (1)(b).

6. A's son C is indebted to D. With the purpose of assisting C, A secures from B a promise to pay the debt to D. Both C and D are intended beneficiaries under Subsection (1)(b).

7. A owes C $100 for money lent. B promises A to pay C $200, both as a discharge of the debt and as an indication of A's gratitude to C for making the loan. C is an intended beneficiary under Subsection (1)(a) as to the amount of the debt and under Subsection (1)(b) as to the excess.

8. A conveys land to B in consideration of B's promise to pay $15,000 as follows: $5,000 to C, A's wife, on whom A wishes to make a settlement, $5,000 to D to whom A is indebted in that amount, and $5,000 to E, a life insurance company, to purchase an annuity payable to A during his life. C is an intended beneficiary under Subsection (1)(b); D is an intended beneficiary under Subsection (1)(a); E is an incidental beneficiary.

9. A owes C $100. Not knowing of any such debt, B promises A to pay $100 to C. C is an intended beneficiary under Subsection (1)(a) if A manifests an intention that the payment is to satisfy the debt, an intended beneficiary under Subsection (1)(b) if A manifests an intention to make a gift of $100, leaving outstanding the original debt.

d. Other intended beneficiaries. Either a promise to pay the promisee's debt to a beneficiary or a gift promise involves a manifestation of intention by the promisee and promisor sufficient, in a contractual setting, to make reliance by the beneficiary both reasonable and probable. Other cases may be quite similar in this respect. Examples are a promise to perform a supposed or asserted duty of the promisee, a promise to discharge a lien on the promisee's property, or a promise to satisfy the duty of a third person. In such cases, if the beneficiary would be reasonable in relying on the promise as manifesting an intention to confer a right on him, he is an intended beneficiary. Where there is doubt whether such reliance would be reasonable, considerations of procedural convenience and other factors not strictly dependent on the manifested intention of the parties may affect the question whether under Subsection (1) recognition of a right in the beneficiary is appropriate. In some cases an overriding policy, which may be embodied in a statute, requires recognition of such a right without regard to the intention of the parties.

Illustrations:

10. A, the operator of a chicken processing and fertilizer plant, contracts with B, a municipality, to use B's sewage system. With the purpose of preventing harm to landowners downstream from its system, B obtains from A a promise to remove specified types of waste from its deposits into the system. C, a downstream landowner, is an intended beneficiary under Subsection (1)(b).

11. A, a corporation, contracts with B, an insurance company, that B shall pay to any future buyer of a car from A the loss he may suf-

fer by the burning or theft of the car within one year after sale. Later A sells a car to C, telling C about the insurance. C is an intended beneficiary.

12. B contracts to build a house for A. Pursuant to the contract, B and his surety S execute a payment bond to A by which they promise A that all of B's debts for labor and materials on the house will be paid. B later employs C as a carpenter and buys lumber from D. C and D are intended beneficiaries of S's promise to A, whether or not they have power to create liens on the house.

13. C asserts that A owes him $100. A does not owe this money, or think that he owes it, but rather than engage in litigation and in order to obtain peace of mind A secures a promise from B to pay C $100. C is an intended beneficiary.

14. A, a labor union, enters into a collective bargaining agreement with B, an employer, in which B promises not to discriminate against any employee because of his membership in A. All B's employees who are members of A are intended beneficiaries of the promise.

15. A buys food from B, a grocer, for household use, relying on B's express warranty. C, A's minor child, is injured in person by breach of the warranty. Under Uniform Commercial Code § 2–318, without regard to the intention of A or B, the warranty extends to C.

e.   Incidental beneficiaries. Performance of a contract will often benefit a third person. But unless the third person is an intended beneficiary as here defined, no duty to him is created. See § 315.

Illustrations:

16. B contracts with A to erect an expensive building on A's land. C's adjoining land would be enhanced in value by the performance of the contract. C is an incidental beneficiary.

17. B contracts with A to buy a new car manufactured by C. C is an incidental beneficiary, even though the promise can only be performed if money is paid to C.

18. A, a labor union, promises B, a trade association, not to strike against any member of B during a certain period. One of the members of B charters a ship from C on terms under which such a strike would cause financial loss to C. C is an incidental beneficiary of A's promise.

19. A contracts to erect a building for C. B then contracts with A to supply lumber needed for the building. C is an incidental beneficiary of B's promise, and B is an incidental beneficiary of C's promise to pay A for the building.

f.   Trust and agency. Where money or property is transferred from one person to another with an intention to benefit a third person, the manifested intention of the parties determines whether the transferee is an agent for the transferor or the third person or a trustee for the third person or whether the third person is the beneficiary of a promise made by the transferee. See Restatement, Second, Agency §§ 14B, 14L; Restatement, Second, Trusts §§ 8, 14. Similarly, an agreement between two parties may constitute one the agent of the other to confer a benefit on a third person, or the promise of one may be made to the other as trustee for a third person, or a third person may be the beneficiary of a promise of either or both; the manifested intention of the parties determines which of these possible relations is created for the particular purpose involved. There is a fiduciary relation between agent and principal or between trustee and beneficiary, but not between promisor or promisee and beneficiary of a contract. Agency requires the consent of the principal and the agent; a trust or a contract for the benefit of a third person does not require the consent of the beneficiary. Either the promisee or the beneficiary of a promise may be made a trustee of rights arising by virtue of the promise; although the beneficiary of such a trust is a beneficiary of the promise under this Section, his rights must be enforced in accordance with the law of Trusts. See Restatement, Second, Trusts §§ 26, 177, 199.

Illustration:

20. A, an insurance company, promises B in a policy of insurance to pay $10,000 on B's death to C as trustee for B's wife D. C is an intended beneficiary and may enforce his rights as trustee; D's rights as beneficiary of the trust and the contract are enforceable only in the manner in which rights of other trust beneficiaries are enforced.

§ 303. Conditional Promises; Promises Under Seal

The statements in this Chapter are applicable to both conditional and unconditional promises and to sealed and unsealed promises.

§ 304. Creation of Duty to Beneficiary

A promise in a contract creates a duty in the promisor to any intended beneficiary to perform the promise, and the intended beneficiary may enforce the duty.

§ 305. Overlapping Duties to Beneficiary and Promisee

(1) A promise in a contract creates a duty in the promisor to the promisee to perform the promise even though he also has a similar duty to an intended beneficiary.

(2) Whole or partial satisfaction of the promisor's duty to the beneficiary satisfies to that extent the promisor's duty to the promisee.

§ 306. Disclaimer by a Beneficiary

A beneficiary who has not previously assented to the promise for his benefit may in a reasonable time after learning of its existence and terms render any duty to himself inoperative from the beginning by disclaimer.

§ 307. Remedy of Specific Performance

Where specific performance is otherwise an appropriate remedy, either the promisee or the beneficiary may maintain a suit for specific enforcement of a duty owed to an intended beneficiary.

Comment:

a. Suit by beneficiary. Whether specific performance is an appropriate remedy is determined by the rules stated in §§ 357–69. Where a contract creates a duty to a beneficiary under the rule stated in § 304, the beneficiary is a proper party plaintiff either in an action for damages or in a suit for specific performance. He is the real party in interest within the meaning of any statute requiring suit to be brought by such a party. There is no general requirement that the promisee be made a party, but the promisee is ordinarily a proper party and the circumstances may be such that a final decree should await joinder of the promisee. As to grant of an injunction instead of specific performance, see § 357(2).

b. *Suit by promisee.* Even though a contract creates a duty to a beneficiary, the promisee has a right to performance. See § 305. The promisee cannot recover damages suffered by the beneficiary, but the promisee is a proper party to sue for specific performance if that remedy is otherwise appropriate under the rules stated in §§ 357–69. Where a statute requires suit to be prosecuted in the name of the real party in interest, the promisee is commonly permitted to sue either as the "trustee of an express trust" or by an express provision for "a party with whom or in whose name a contract has been made for the benefit of another." See Federal Rules of Civil Procedure Rule 17. There is no general requirement that the beneficiary be joined in such a suit; whether he should or must be made a party depends on the circumstances.

c. *Promise to pay the promisee's debt.* Where the promised performance will satisfy an obligation of the promisee to pay money to the beneficiary, the promisee may suffer substantial damages as a result of breach. He is entitled to recover such damages so long as there is no conflict with rights of the beneficiary or the promisor. But the promisee as surety for the promisor is not permitted to compete with the beneficiary for the assets of the promisor, and the promisor is ordinarily entitled to protection against enforced

double liability. See §§ 305, 310. These difficulties can be avoided by specific performance of the surety's right to exoneration. See Restatement of Security § 112.

Illustration:

1. A, a stockholder of X, a corporation, guarantees payment of a debt owed by X to C. A sells his stock to B, who agrees to assume and pay A's obligation on the guaranty. B fails to pay, and C sues A on the guaranty. A may obtain a decree directing B to pay the debt to C.

d. *Gift promise.* Where the promisee intends to make a gift of the promised performance to the beneficiary, the beneficiary ordinarily has an economic interest in the performance but the promisee does not. Thus the promisee may suffer no damages as the result of breach by the promisor. In such cases the promisee's remedy in damages is not an adequate remedy within the rules stated in §§ 359 and 360, and specific performance may be appropriate. See Illustration 1 to § 305. The court may of course so fashion its decree as to protect the interests of the promisee and beneficiary without unnecessary injury to the promisor or innocent third persons. See § 358.

Illustration:

2. As part of a separation agreement B promises his wife A not to change the provision in B's will for C, their son. A dies and B changes his will to C's detriment, adding also a provision that C will forfeit any bequest if he questions the change before any tribunal. A's personal representative may sue for specific performance of B's promise.

§ 308.   Identification of Beneficiaries

It is not essential to the creation of a right in an intended beneficiary that he be identified when a contract containing the promise is made.

§ 309. Defenses Against the Beneficiary

(1) A promise creates no duty to a beneficiary unless a contract is formed between the promisor and the promisee; and if a contract is voidable or unenforceable at the time of its formation the right of any beneficiary is subject to the infirmity.

(2) If a contract ceases to be binding in whole or in part because of impracticability, public policy, non-occurrence of a condition, or present or prospective failure of performance, the right of any beneficiary is to that extent discharged or modified.

(3) Except as stated in Subsections (1) and (2) and in § 311 or as provided by the contract, the right of any beneficiary against the promisor is not subject to the promisor's claims or defenses against the promisee or to the promisee's claims or defenses against the beneficiary.

(4) A beneficiary's right against the promisor is subject to any claim or defense arising from his own conduct or agreement.

§ 310. Remedies of the Beneficiary of a Promise to Pay the Promisee's Debt; Reimbursement of Promisee

(1) Where an intended beneficiary has an enforceable claim against the promisee, he can obtain a judgment or judgments against either the promisee or the promisor or both based on their respective duties to him. Satisfaction in whole or in part of either of these duties, or of a judgment thereon, satisfies to that extent the other duty or judgment, subject to the promisee's right of subrogation.

(2) To the extent that the claim of an intended beneficiary is satisfied from assets of the promisee, the promisee has a right of reimbursement from the promisor, which may be enforced directly and also, if the beneficiary's claim is fully satisfied, by subrogation to the claim of the beneficiary against the promisor, and to any judgment thereon and to any security therefor.

§ 311. Variation of a Duty to a Beneficiary

(1) Discharge or modification of a duty to an intended beneficiary by conduct of the promisee or by a subsequent agreement between promisor and promisee is ineffective if a term of the promise creating the duty so provides.

(2) In the absence of such a term, the promisor and promisee retain power to discharge or modify the duty by subsequent agreement.

(3) Such a power terminates when the beneficiary, before he receives notification of the discharge or modification, materially changes his position in justifiable reliance on the promise or brings suit on it or manifests assent to it at the request of the promisor or promisee.

(4)   If the promisee receives consideration for an attempted discharge or modification of the promisor's duty which is ineffective against the beneficiary, the beneficiary can assert a right to the consideration so received. The promisor's duty is discharged to the extent of the amount received by the beneficiary.

§ 312.   Mistake as to Duty to Beneficiary

The effect of an erroneous belief of the promisor or promisee as to the existence or extent of a duty owed to an intended beneficiary is determined by the rules making contracts voidable for mistake.

§ 313.   Government Contracts

(1)   The rules stated in this Chapter apply to contracts with a government or governmental agency except to the extent that application would contravene the policy of the law authorizing the contract or prescribing remedies for its breach.

(2)   In particular, a promisor who contracts with a government or governmental agency to do an act for or render a service to the public is not subject to contractual liability to a member of the public for consequential damages resulting from performance or failure to perform unless

(a)   the terms of the promise provide for such liability; or

(b)   the promisee is subject to liability to the member of the public for the damages and a direct action against the promisor is consistent with the terms of the contract and with the policy of the law authorizing the contract and prescribing remedies for its breach.

§ 314.   Suretyship Defenses

An intended beneficiary who has an enforceable claim against the promisee is affected by the incidents of the suretyship of the promisee from the time he has knowledge of it.

§ 315.   Effect of a Promise of Incidental Benefit

An incidental beneficiary acquires by virtue of the promise no right against the promisor or the promisee.

CHAPTER 15.   ASSIGNMENT AND DELEGATION

§ 316.   Scope of This Chapter

(1)   In this Chapter, references to assignment of a right or delegation of a duty or condition, to the obligee or obligor of an assigned right or delegated duty, or to an assignor or assignee, are limited to rights, duties, and conditions arising under a contract or for breach of a contract.

(2) The statements in this Chapter are qualified in some respects by statutory and other rules governing negotiable instruments and documents, relating to interests in land, and affecting other classes of contracts.

TOPIC 1. WHAT CAN BE ASSIGNED OR DELEGATED

§ 317. Assignment of a Right

(1) An assignment of a right is a manifestation of the assignor's intention to transfer it by virtue of which the assignor's right to performance by the obligor is extinguished in whole or in part and the assignee acquires a right to such performance.

(2) A contractual right can be assigned unless

(a) the substitution of a right of the assignee for the right of the assignor would materially change the duty of the obligor, or materially increase the burden or risk imposed on him by his contract, or materially impair his chance of obtaining return performance, or materially reduce its value to him, or

(b) the assignment is forbidden by statute or is otherwise inoperative on grounds of public policy, or

(c) assignment is validly precluded by contract.

§ 318. Delegation of Performance of Duty

(1) An obligor can properly delegate the performance of his duty to another unless the delegation is contrary to public policy or the terms of his promise.

(2) Unless otherwise agreed, a promise requires performance by a particular person only to the extent that the obligee has a substantial interest in having that person perform or control the acts promised.

(3) Unless the obligee agrees otherwise, neither delegation of performance nor a contract to assume the duty made with the obligor by the person delegated discharges any duty or liability of the delegating obligor.

§ 319. Delegation of Performance of Condition

(1) Where a performance by a person is made a condition of a duty, performance by a person delegated by his satisfies that requirement unless the delegation is contrary to public policy or the terms of the agreement.

(2) Unless otherwise agreed, an agreement requires performance of a condition by a particular person only to the extent that the obligor has

a substantial interest in having that person perform or control the acts required.

§ 320. Assignment of Conditional Rights

The fact that a right is created by an option contract or is conditional on the performance of a return promise or is otherwise conditional does not prevent its assignment before the condition occurs.

§ 321. Assignment of Future Rights

(1) Except as otherwise provided by statute, an assignment of a right to payment expected to arise out of an existing employment or other continuing business relationship is effective in the same way as an assignment of an existing right.

(2) Except as otherwise provided by statute and as stated in Subsection (1), a purported assignment of a right expected to arise under a contract not in existence operates only as a promise to assign the right when it arises and as a power to enforce it.

§ 322. Contractual Prohibition of Assignment

(1) Unless the circumstances indicate the contrary, a contract term prohibiting assignment of "the contract" bars only the delegation to an assignee of the performance by the assignor of a duty or condition.

(2) A contract term prohibiting assignment of rights under the contract, unless a different intention is manifested,

(a) does not forbid assignment of a right to damages for breach of the whole contract or a right arising out of the assignor's due performance of his entire obligation;

(b) gives the obligor a right to damages for breach of the terms forbidding assignment but does not render the assignment ineffective;

(c) is for the benefit of the obligor, and does not prevent the assignee from acquiring rights against the assignor or the obligor from discharging his duty as if there were no such prohibition.

§ 323. Obligor's Assent to Assignment or Delegation

(1) A term of a contract manifesting an obligor's assent to the future assignment of a right or an obligee's assent to the future delegation of the performance of a duty or condition is effective despite any subsequent objection.

(2) A manifestation of such assent after the formation of a contract is similarly effective if made for consideration or in circumstances in which a promise would be binding without consideration, or if a material change of position takes place in reliance on the manifestation.

TOPIC 2. MODE OF ASSIGNMENT OR DELEGATION

§ 324. Mode of Assignment in General

It is essential to an assignment of a right that the obligee manifest an intention to transfer the right to another person without further action or manifestation of intention by the obligee. The manifestation may be made to the other or to a third person on his behalf and, except as provided by statute or by contract, may be made either orally or by a writing.

§ 325. Order as Assignment

(1) A written order drawn upon an obligor and signed and delivered to another person by the obligee is an assignment if it is conditional on the existence of a duty of the drawee to the drawer to comply with the order and the drawer manifests an intention that a person other than the drawer is to retain the performance.

(2) An order which directs the drawee to render a performance without reference to any duty of the drawee is not of itself an assignment, even though the drawee is under a duty to the drawer to comply with the order and even though the order indicates a particular account to be debited or any other fund or source from which reimbursement is expected.

§ 326. Partial Assignment

(1) Except as stated in Subsection (2), an assignment of a part of a right, whether the part is specified as a fraction, as an amount, or otherwise, is operative as to that part to the same extent and in the same manner as if the part had been a separate right.

(2) If the obligor has not contracted to perform separately the assigned part of a right, no legal proceeding can be maintained by the assignor or assignee against the obligor over his objection, unless all the persons entitled to the promised performance are joined in the proceeding, or unless joinder is not feasible and it is equitable to proceed without joinder.

§ 327. Acceptance or Disclaimer by the Assignee

(1) A manifestation of assent by an assignee to the assignment is essential to make it effective unless

    (a) a third person gives consideration for the assignment, or

    (b) the assignment is irrevocable by virtue of the delivery of a writing to a third person.

(2) An assignee who has not manifested assent to an assignment may, within a reasonable time after learning of its existence and terms, render it inoperative from the beginning by disclaimer.

§ 328. Interpretation of Words of Assignment; Effect of Acceptance of Assignment

(1) Unless the language or the circumstances indicate the contrary, as in an assignment for security, an assignment of "the contract" or of "all my rights under the contract" or an assignment in similar general terms is an assignment of the assignor's rights and a delegation of his unperformed duties under the contract.

(2) Unless the language or the circumstances indicate the contrary, the acceptance by an assignee of such an assignment operates as a promise to the assignor to perform the assignor's unperformed duties, and the obligor of the assigned rights is an intended beneficiary of the promise.

Caveat: The Institute expresses no opinion as to whether the rule stated in Subsection (2) applies to an assignment by a purchaser of his rights under a contract for the sale of land.

§ 329. Repudiation by Assignor and Novation With Assignee

(1) The legal effect of a repudiation by an assignor of his duty to the obligor of the assigned right is not limited by the fact that the assignee is a competent person and has promised to perform the duty.

(2) If the obligor, with knowledge of such a repudiation, accepts any performance from the assignee without reserving his rights against the assignor, a novation arises by which the duty of the assignor is discharged and a similar duty of the assignee is substituted.

Comment:

a.   Repudiation and its effects. In some cases a repudiation by one party to a contract discharges the duty of the other party; in some cases it requires the other to treat as total a breach which might otherwise be partial, or it may itself be a total breach. See § 253; Uniform Commercial Code § 2–610. For these purposes repudiation includes a positive statement by an assignor that he will not or cannot substantially perform his duties, or any voluntary affirmative action which renders substantial performance apparently impossible. In some circumstances a statement that he doubts whether he will substantially perform, or that he takes no responsibility for performance, or even a failure to give adequate assurance of performance may have a similar effect. See §§ 250–51.

b.   Scope of obligor's assent. The assignment of a contractual right and delegation to the assignee of the assignor's duty is often a matter of course. The obligor of the assigned right may then have a right to withhold performance until he receives adequate assurance of performance by the assignee. Section 251. Failure to demand such assurance and acceptance of performance by the assignee manifest the obligor's assent to the assignment and delegation (see § 323), but not to the discharge of the assignor's duty. However, when the obligor knows that the delegating assignor has repudiated his duty he has reason to know that the performance of the assignee is offered by way of novation, and his silent acceptance of the performance operates as acceptance of the offer of novation. Compare § 69.

Illustrations:

1. A is under a contract with B to build a house for $10,000. A assigns his rights under the contract to C, who agrees to assume A's duty to build the house. B is informed of the assignment and assumption, and makes no objection as C partly performs. A remains bound to B as surety for C's performance.

2. In Illustration 1, A withdraws from the construction business and informs B that he takes no further responsibility for C's performance. B makes no objection and C proceeds with the work. A is discharged.

c. Reservation of rights. The obligor of an assigned right cannot be forced to assent to a repudiation by the assignor or to an offer of a substituted contract with the assignee. To avoid the implication that his silence gives assent, he must manifest either to the assignor or to the assignee his intention to retain unimpaired his rights against the assignor, but no particular form is required. See Uniform Commercial Code §§ 1–207, 3–606; § 281. If the terms of the assignment so provide, the delegation or assumption of duty may be defeated in such a case, and the repudiation may be retracted before it has been acted on. See Uniform Commercial Code § 2–611. Where the assignee continues performance, the reservation of rights by the obligor means that the assignor, if compelled to pay for the assignee's default, will have a right over against the assignee.

Illustration:

3. In Illustration 2, on being informed of A's repudiation, B notifies A or C that further performance is "without prejudice." A is not discharged.

§ 330. Contracts to Assign in the Future, or to Transfer Proceeds to Be Received

(1) A contract to make a future assignment of a right, or to transfer proceeds to be received in the future by the promisor, is not an assignment.

(2) Except as provided by statute, the effect of such a contract on the rights and duties of the obligor and third persons is determined by the rules relating to specific performance of contracts.

TOPIC 3. EFFECT BETWEEN ASSIGNOR AND ASSIGNEE

§ 331. Partially Effective Assignments

An assignment may be conditional, revocable, or voidable by the assignor, or unenforceable by virtue of a Statute of Frauds.

§ 332. Revocability Of Gratuitous Assignments

(1) Unless a contrary intention is manifested, a gratuitous assignment is irrevocable if

(a) the assignment is in a writing either signed or under seal that is delivered by the assignor; or

(b)   the assignment is accompanied by delivery of a writing of a type customarily accepted as a symbol or as evidence of the right assigned.

(2)   Except as stated in this Section, a gratuitous assignment is revocable and the right of the assignee is terminated by the assignor's death or incapacity, by a subsequent assignment by the assignor, or by notification from the assignor received by the assignee or by the obligor.

(3)   A gratuitous assignment ceases to be revocable to the extent that before the assignee's right is terminated he obtains

   (a)   payment or satisfaction of the obligation, or

   (b)   judgment against the obligor, or

   (c)   a new contract of the obligor by novation.

(4)   A gratuitous assignment is irrevocable to the extent necessary to avoid injustice where the assignor should reasonably expect the assignment to induce action or forbearance by the assignee or a subassignee and the assignment does induce such action or forbearance.

(5)   An assignment is gratuitous unless it is given or taken

   (a)   in exchange for a performance or return promise that would be consideration for a promise; or

   (b)   as security for or in total or partial satisfaction of a pre-existing debt or other obligation.

§ 333.   Warranties of an Assignor

(1)   Unless a contrary intention is manifested, one who assigns or purports to assign a right by assignment under seal or for value warrants to the assignee

   (a)   that he will do nothing to defeat or impair the value of the assignment and has no knowledge of any fact which would do so;

   (b)   that the right, as assigned, actually exists and is subject to no limitations or defenses good against the assignor other than those stated or apparent at the time of the assignment;

   (c)   that any writing evidencing the right which is delivered to the assignee or exhibited to him to induce him to accept the assignment is genuine and what it purports to be.

(2)   An assignment does not of itself operate as a warranty that the obligor is solvent or that he will perform his obligation.

(3)   An assignor is bound by affirmations and promises to the assignee with reference to the right assigned in the same way and to the same extent that one who transfers goods is bound in like circumstances.

(4)   An assignment of a right to a sub-assignee does not operate as an assignment of the assignee's rights under his assignor's warranties unless an intention is manifested to assign the rights under the warranties.

TOPIC 4. EFFECT ON THE OBLIGOR'S DUTY

§ 334. Variation of Obligor's Duty by Assignment

(1)   If the obligor's duty is conditional on the personal cooperation of the original obligee or another person, an assignee's right is subject to the same condition.

(2)   If the obligor's duty is conditional on cooperation which the obligee could properly delegate to an agent, the condition may occur if there is similar cooperation by an assignee.

Comment:

...*b.   Terms   of   assignment.* Whether there is a material change in the obligor's duty depends not only on the terms of the contract creating the duty and on the circumstances, but also on the terms of the assignment. Commonly an assignment manifests an intention that the obligor render performance to the assignee rather than to the assignor. Such a change is immaterial in the usual case of a duty to pay money, but material where personal cooperation is made a condition of the duty. Even in the latter case, however, it is at least theoretically possible to assign the right without departing from the requirement.

Illustrations:

3.   B contracts with A to furnish A's family with all the oil it shall need for the ensuing year at a fixed price. A assigns his rights under the contract to C. C can acquire no right against B that C's family shall be supplied with oil, but may acquire a right that A's family shall be supplied, if such is the intention of the parties.

4.   B contracts with A to serve A as a valet. A, for value, assigns his rights under the contract to C. C acquires no right to have B act as valet to C. If the assignment manifests an intent to give C a right to have B act as valet to A, C acquires such a right. . . .

§ 335. Assignment by a Joint Obligee

A joint obligee may effectively assign his right, but the assignee can enforce it only in the same manner and to the same extent as the assignor could have enforced it.

§ 336. Defenses Against an Assignee

(1)   By an assignment the assignee acquires a right against the obligor only to the extent that the obligor is under a duty to the assignor; and if the right of the assignor would be voidable by the obligor or unenforceable against him if no assignment had been made, the right of the assignee is subject to the infirmity.

(2)   The right of an assignee is subject to any defense or claim of the obligor which accrues before the obligor receives notification of the assignment, but not to defenses or claims which accrue thereafter except as stated in this Section or as provided by statute.

(3)   Where the right of an assignor is subject to discharge or modification in whole or in part by impossibility, illegality, non-occurrence of a condition, or present or prospective failure of performance by an obligee, the right of the assignee is to that extent subject to discharge or modification even after the obligor receives notification of the assignment.

(4)   An assignee's right against the obligor is subject to any defense or claim arising from his conduct or to which he was subject as a party or a prior assignee because he had notice.

Comment:

... *b. Accrued defenses.* Unlike the negotiation of a negotiable instrument, the assignment of a non-negotiable contractual right ordinarily transfers what the assignor has but only what he has. The assignee's right depends on the validity and enforceability of the contract creating the right, and is subject to limitations imposed by the terms of that contract and to defenses which would have been available against the obligee had there been no assignment. Until the obligor receives notification of an assignment, he is entitled to treat the obligee as owner of the right, and the assignee's right is subject to defenses and claims arising from dealings between assignor and obligor in relation to the contract before notification. See § 338. ...

g. Estoppel. Even though an obligor's agreement not to assert a defense or claim is not binding or is voidable or unenforceable, he may be estopped to assert the claim or defense against an assignee. Where he makes a representation of fact with the intention of inducing an assignee or prospective assignee to act in reliance on the representation, and an assignee does so act, the doctrine of estoppel bars the obligor from contradicting the representation in litigation against the assignee if contradiction would be inequitable. Compare § 90. Application of the doctrine depends on all the circumstances. The representation may be express or it may be implied from conduct, in unusual cases even from failure to act. In some circumstances estoppel may rest on the obligor's reason to know that the assignee may rely, even though there is no intention to induce reliance.

h. Conduct of the assignee. The conduct of the assignee or his agents may, like that of any obligee, give rise to defenses and claims which may be asserted against him by the obligor. An obligee who is subject to such a defense or claim cannot improve his position by assigning the right to an assignee who is not subject to the defense or claim and then taking a reassignment.

§ 337.   Elimination of Defenses by Subsequent Events

Where the right of an assignor is limited or voidable or unenforceable or subject to discharge or modification, subsequent events which would eliminate the limitation or defense have the same effect on the right of the assignee.

§ 338. Discharge of an Obligor After Assignment

(1)   Except as stated in this Section, notwithstanding an assignment, the assignor retains his power to discharge or modify the duty of the obligor to the extent that the obligor performs or otherwise gives value until but not after the obligor receives notification that the right has been assigned and that performance is to be rendered to the assignee.

(2)   So far as an assigned right is conditional on the performance of a return promise, and notwithstanding notification of the assignment, any modification of or substitution for the contract made by the assignor and obligor in good faith and in accordance with reasonable commercial standards is effective against the assignee. The assignee acquires corresponding rights under the modified or substituted contract.

(3)   Notwithstanding a defect in the right of an assignee, he has the same power his assignor had to discharge or modify the duty of the obligor to the extent that the obligor gives value or otherwise changes his position in good faith and without knowledge or reason to know of the defect.

(4)   Where there is a writing of a type customarily accepted as a symbol or as evidence of the right assigned, a discharge or modification is not effective

(a)   against the owner or an assignor having a power of avoidance, unless given by him or by a person in possession of the writing with his consent and any necessary indorsement or assignment;

(b)   against a subsequent assignee who takes possession of the writing and gives value in good faith and without knowledge or reason to know of the discharge or modification.

§ 339. Protection of Obligor in Cases of Adverse Claims

Where a claim adverse to that of an assignee subjects the obligor to a substantial risk beyond that imposed on him by his contract, the obligor will be granted such relief as is equitable in the circumstances.

TOPIC 5.   PRIORITIES BETWEEN ASSIGNEE AND ADVERSE CLAIMANTS

§ 340. Effect of Assignment on Priority and Security

(1)   An assignee is entitled to priority of payment from the obligor's insolvent estate to the extent that the assignor would have been so entitled in the absence of assignment.

(2)   Where an assignor holds collateral as security for the assigned right and does not effectively transfer the collateral to the assignee, the assignor is a constructive trustee of the collateral for the assignee in ac-

cordance with the rules stated for pledges in §§ 29–34 of the Restatement of Security.

§ 341.   Creditors of an Assignor

(1)   Except as provided by statute, the right of an assignee is superior to a judicial lien subsequently obtained against the property of the assignor, unless the assignment is ineffective or revocable or is voidable by the assignor or by the person obtaining the lien or is in fraud of creditors.

(2)   Notwithstanding the superiority of the right of an assignee, an obligor who does not receive notification of the assignment until after he has lost his opportunity to assert the assignment as a defense in the proceeding in which the judicial lien was obtained is discharged from his duty to the assignee to the extent of his satisfaction of the lien.

Comment:

a.   Priority of assignee. An effective assignment extinguishes the assignor's right without any notification of the obligor. Any proceeds of the assigned right received by the assignor thereafter are held in constructive trust for the assignee. See Restatement of Restitution § 165. A creditor of the assignor who claims the assigned right by garnishment, levy of execution or like process is not a bona fide purchaser, even though he has no notice of the assignment. Unless protected by statute or by estoppel or like doctrine, he is subject to the assignee's right. Compare § 342; see Restatement of Restitution § 173. "Judicial lien," as used in this Section, has the same meaning as it does in the Bankruptcy Reform Act of 1978.

b.   Defective assignment. An assignor's trustee in bankruptcy can in general reach all of the assignor's legal or equitable interest in any of his property, including powers that he might have exercised for his own benefit and property transferred by him in fraud of creditors. See Bankruptcy Reform Act of 1978, 11 U.S.C. §§ 541(a), (b), 548 (1978). In addition, a person against whom a transfer is voidable can reach the property transferred. In such cases, therefore, the assignee's right is not superior to that of the lien obtained by garnishment or like process. A revocable gratuitous assignment, for example, does not limit the power of the assignor's creditors to levy on the assigned claim. See § 332.

c.   Protection of obligor. An obligor garnished by a creditor of the assignor cannot safely pay even in response to a judgment if he has received notification of the assignment, but he is entitled to protection against double liability by interpleader or like remedy. See § 339. If the garnished obligor has not received notification, the assignee's right against him is discharged to the same extent as the assignor's right would have been in the absence of assignment. See §§ 336, 338.

Such a discharge of the obligor does not necessarily terminate the assignee's rights against the assignor and the garnishing creditor. The assignee is entitled to restitution from the assignor to the extent that the assignor has been unjustly enriched by the discharge of his debt. See Restatement of Restitution § 118. The garnishing creditor takes free of the assignee's right to the extent that he becomes a bona fide purchaser or that the assignee is barred by estoppel, laches, res judicata, or other defense. See Restatement of Restitution §§ 131, 173, 179.

Illustration:

1. A has a right against B and assigns it to C for value. X, a creditor of A, serves garnishment process on B in an action against A, and obtains judgment against B before B receives notification of the assignment. A month later, before any payment or satisfaction or issue of execution and within the time specified in local procedural rules, B and C move to reopen the judgment. The motion should be granted, and C is entitled to judgment against B to the exclusion of X.

d. *Filing statutes.* Creditors are commonly among the beneficiaries of statutes requiring public filing of notices of certain types of transactions. The Uniform Commercial Code makes a general requirement of filing to "perfect" a nonpossessory "security inter-est" in personal property, including "any sale of accounts or chattel paper." See §§ 9–102, 9–302. An unperfected security interest is subordinate to the rights of "a person who becomes a lien creditor before the security interest is perfected." See § 9–301. Transfers of wage claims, rights under insurance policies or deposit accounts, and various other transactions are excluded from coverage. See § 9–104. With respect to certain international open accounts receivable, § 9–103(3)(c) provides alternatives of the application of the filing law of the American jurisdiction in which the debtor has its executive offices or perfection "by notification to the account debtor." Wage assignment statutes also often provide for public filing or for notification of the obligor or both. See Statutory Note preceding § 316.

§ 342. Successive Assignees From the Same Assignor

Except as otherwise provided by statute, the right of an assignee is superior to that of a subsequent assignee of the same right from the same assignor, unless

(a) the first assignment is ineffective or revocable or is voidable by the assignor or by the subsequent assignee; or

(b) the subsequent assignee in good faith and without knowledge or reason to know of the prior assignment gives value and obtains

(i) payment or satisfaction of the obligation,

(ii) judgment against the obligor,

(iii) a new contract with the obligor by novation, or

(iv) possession of a writing of a type customarily accepted as a symbol or as evidence of the right assigned.

Comment:

. . . c. *Filing statutes.* . . . The current formulation [of this rule] is found in Bankruptcy Reform Act of 1978, 11 U.S.C. § 547(e)(1)(B) (1978): a transfer of a fixture or property other than real property is perfected when a creditor on a simple contract cannot acquire a judicial lien that is superior to the interest of the transferee.

The subject is now largely governed by the Uniform Commercial Code, except in cases of wage claims, some rights under insurance policies, deposit accounts, and certain other excluded types of transactions. See § 9–104.[1]

Under the Code, filing or the taking of possession is generally required to "perfect" a "security interest," which includes the interest of a buyer of accounts or chattel paper. Sections 1–201(37), 9–302 [Now §§ 1–203, 9–310]. An unperfected security interest is subordinate to the rights of a person who is not a secured party to the extent that he gives value for accounts or general intangibles without knowledge of the security interest and before it is perfected. Section 9–301 [Now § 9–317]. As between secured parties,

priority is determined by the order of filing or perfection, or if neither security interest is filed or perfected, by the order of attachment. Sections 9–312(5) and (6) [Now § 9–322].

d.   Defective assignment. If the prior assignment is revocable or voidable by the assignor a subsequent assignment is an effective manifestation of an intent to revoke or avoid. The subsequent assignment therefore has priority. A subsequent assignment may be similarly used to effectuate a power of avoidance of the subsequent assignee.

§ 343.   Latent Equities

If an assignor's right against the obligor is held in trust or constructive trust for or subject to a right of avoidance or equitable lien of another than the obligor, an assignee does not so hold it if he gives value and becomes an assignee in good faith and without notice of the right of the other.

CHAPTER 16.   REMEDIES

TOPIC 1.   IN GENERAL

§ 344.   Purposes of Remedies

Judicial remedies under the rules stated in this Restatement serve to protect one or more of the following interests of a promisee:

(a)   his "expectation interest," which is his interest in having the benefit of his bargain by being put in as good a position as he would have been in had the contract been performed,

(b)   his "reliance interest," which is his interest in being reimbursed for loss caused by reliance on the contract by being put in as good a position as he would have been in had the contract not been made, or

(c)   his "restitution interest," which is his interest in having restored to him any benefit that he has conferred on the other party.

---

[1] Now § 9–109. Under the current version of Article 9, it is possible to take a security interest in a deposit account, except for consumer transactions, and many insurance claims.

§ 345. Judicial Remedies Available

The judicial remedies available for the protection of the interests stated in § 344 include a judgment or order

(a)   awarding a sum of money due under the contract or as damages,

(b)   requiring specific performance of a contract or enjoining its non-performance,

(c)   requiring restoration of a specific thing to prevent unjust enrichment,

(d)   awarding a sum of money to prevent unjust enrichment,

(e)   declaring the rights of the parties, and

(f)   enforcing an arbitration award.

TOPIC 2.   ENFORCEMENT BY AWARD OF DAMAGES

§ 346. Availability of Damages

(1)   The injured party has a right to damages for any breach by a party against whom the contract is enforceable unless the claim for damages has been suspended or discharged.

(2)   If the breach caused no loss or if the amount of the loss is not proved under the rules stated in this Chapter, a small sum fixed without regard to the amount of loss will be awarded as nominal damages.

Comment:

a.   Right to damages. Every breach of contract gives the injured party a right to damages against the party in breach, unless the contract is not enforceable against that party, as where he is not bound because of the Statute of Frauds. The resulting claim may be one for damages for total breach of one for damages for only partial breach. See § 236. Although a judgment awarding a sum of money as damages is the most common judicial remedy for breach of contract, other remedies, including equitable relief in the form of specific performance or an injunction, may be also available, depending on the circumstances. See Topic 3. In the exceptional situation of a contract for transfer of an interest in land that is unenforceable under the Statute of Frauds, action in reliance makes the contract enforceable by specific performance even though it gives rise to no claim for damages for breach. See Comment c to § 129. A duty to pay damages may be suspended or discharged by agreement or otherwise, and if it is discharged the claim for damages is extinguished. See Introductory Note to Chapter 12. When this happens, the right to enforcement by other means such as specific performance or an injunction is also extinguished. If the duty of performance, as distinguished from the duty to pay damages, has been suspended or discharged, as by impracticability of performance or frustration of purpose, there is then no breach and this Section is not applicable.

The parties can by agreement vary the rules stated in this Section, as long as the agreement is not invalid for unconscionability (§ 208) or on other grounds. The agreement may provide for a remedy such as repair or replacement in substitution for damages. See Uniform Commercial Code § 2–719.

b. Nominal damages. Although a breach of contract by a party against whom it is enforceable always gives rise to a claim for damages, there are instances in which the breach causes no loss. See Illustration 1. There are also instances in which loss is caused but recovery for that loss is precluded because it cannot be proved with reasonable certainty or because of one of the other limitations stated in this Chapter. See §§ 350–53. In all these instances the injured party will nevertheless get judgment for nominal damages, a small sum usually fixed by judicial practice in the jurisdiction in which the action is brought. Such a judgment may, in the discretion of the court, carry with it an award of court costs. Costs are generally awarded if a significant right was involved or the claimant made a good faith effort to prove damages, but not if the maintenance of the action was frivolous or in bad faith. Unless a significant right is involved, a court will not reverse and remand a case for a new trial if only nominal damages could result.

Illustration:

    1. A contracts to sell to B 1,000 shares of stock in X Corporation for $10 a share to be delivered on June 1, but breaks the contract by refusing on that date to deliver the stock. B sues A for damages, but at trial it is proved that B could have purchased 1,000 shares of stock in X Corporation on the market on June 1 for $10 a share and therefore has suffered no loss. In an action by B against A, B will be awarded nominal damages.

c. Beneficiaries of gift promises. If a promisee makes a contract, intending to give a third party the benefit of the promised performance, the third party may be an intended beneficiary who is entitled to enforce the contract. See § 302(1)(b). Such a gift promise creates overlapping duties, one to the beneficiary and the other to the promisee. If the performance is not forthcoming, both the beneficiary and the promisee have claims for damages for breach. If the promisee seeks damages, however, he will usually be limited to nominal damages: although the loss to the beneficiary may be substantial, the promisee cannot recover for that loss and he will ordinarily have suffered no loss himself. In such a case the remedy of specific performance will often be an appropriate one for the promisee. See § 307.

Illustration:

    2. As part of a separation agreement B promises his wife A not to change the provision in B's will for C, their son. A dies and B changes his will to C's detriment, adding also a provision that C will forfeit any bequest if he questions the change before any tribunal. In an action by A's personal representative against B, the representative can get a judgment for nominal damages. As to the representative's right to specific performance, see Illustration 2 to § 307.

§ 347. Measure of Damages in General

Subject to the limitations stated in §§ 350–53, the injured party has a right to damages based on his expectation interest as measured by

(a)   the loss in the value to him of the other party's performance caused by its failure or deficiency, plus

(b)   any other loss, including incidental or consequential loss, caused by the breach, less

(c)   any cost or other loss that he has avoided by not having to perform.

Comment:

a.   Expectation interest. Contract damages are ordinarily based on the injured party's expectation interest and are intended to give him the benefit of his bargain by awarding him a sum of money that will, to the extent possible, put him in as good a position as he would have been in had the contract been performed. See § 344(1)(a). In some situations the sum awarded will do this adequately as, for example, where the injured party has simply had to pay an additional amount to arrange a substitute transaction and can be adequately compensated by damages based on that amount. In other situations the sum awarded cannot adequately compensate the injured party for his disappointed expectation as, for example, where a delay in performance has caused him to miss an invaluable opportunity. The measure of damages stated in this Section is subject to the agreement of the parties, as where they provide for liquidated damages (§ 356) or exclude liability for consequential damages.

b.   Loss in value. The first element that must be estimated in attempting to fix a sum that will fairly represent the expectation interest is the loss in the value to the injured party of the other party's performance that is caused by the failure of, or deficiency in, that performance. If no performance is rendered, the loss in value caused by the breach is equal to the value that the performance would have had to the injured party. If defective or partial performance is rendered, the loss in value caused by the breach is equal to the difference between the value that the performance would have had if there had been no breach and the value of such performance as was actually rendered. In principle, this requires a determination of the values of those performances to the injured party himself and not their values to some hypothetical reasonable person or on some market. They therefore depend on his own particular circumstances or those of his enterprise, unless consideration of these circumstances is precluded by the limitation of foreseeability (§ 351). Where the injured party's expected advantage consists largely or exclusively of the realization of profit, it may be possible to express this loss in value in terms of money with some assurance. In other situations, however, this is not possible and compensation for lost value may be precluded by the limitation of certainty. See § 352. In order to facilitate the estimation of loss with sufficient certainty to award damages, the injured party is sometimes given a choice between alternative bases of calculating his loss in value. The most important of these are stated in § 348. See also §§ 349 and 373.

c.   Other loss. Subject to the limitations stated in §§ 350–53, the injured party is entitled to recover for all loss actually suffered. Items of loss other than loss in value of the other party's performance are often characterized as incidental or consequential. Incidental losses include costs incurred in a reasonable effort, whether successful or not, to avoid loss, as where a party pays brokerage fees in arranging or attempting to arrange a substitute transaction. Consequential losses include such items as injury to person or property resulting from defective performance. The terms used to describe the type of loss are not, however, controlling, and the general principle is that all losses, however described, are recoverable.

d.   Cost or other loss avoided. Sometimes the breach itself results in a saving of some cost that the injured party would have incurred if he had had to perform. See Illustration 5. Furthermore, the injured party is expected to take reasonable steps to avoid further loss. See § 350. Where he does this by discontinuing his own performance, he avoids incurring additional costs of performance. See Illustration 6. This cost avoided is subtracted from the loss in value caused by the breach in calculating his damages. If the injured party avoids further loss by making substitute arrangements for the use of his resources that are no longer needed to perform the contract, the net profit from such arrangements is also subtracted. The value to him of any salvageable materials that he has acquired for performance is also subtracted. See Illustration 7. Loss avoided is subtracted only if the saving results from the injured party not having to perform rather than from some unrelated event. If no cost or other loss has been avoided, however, the injured party's damages include the full amount of the loss in value with no subtraction, subject to the limitations stated in §§ 350–53. The intended "donee" beneficiary of a gift promise usually suffers loss to the full extent of the value of the promised performance, since he is ordinarily not required to do anything, and so avoids no cost on breach. See § 302(1)(b).

Illustrations:

> . . . 5.   A contracts to build a hotel for B for $500,000 and to have it ready for occupancy by May 1. B's occupancy of the hotel is delayed for a month because of a breach by A. The cost avoided by B as a result of not having to operate the hotel during May is subtracted from the May rent lost in determining B's damages.

> 6.   A contracts to build a house for B for $100,000. When it is partly built, B repudiates the contract and A stops work. A would have to spend $60,000 more to finish the house. The $60,000 cost avoided by A as a result of not having to finish the house is subtracted from the $100,000 price lost in determining A's damages. A has a right to $40,000 in damages from B, less any progress payments that he has already received.

> 7.   The facts being otherwise as stated in Illustration 6, A has bought materials that are left over and that he can use for other purposes, saving him $5,000. The $5,000 cost avoided is subtracted in determining A's damages, resulting in damages of only $35,000 rather than $40,000. . . .

e.   Actual loss caused by breach. The injured party is limited to damages based on his actual loss caused by the breach. If he makes an especially favorable substitute transaction, so that he sustains a smaller loss than might have been expected, his damages are reduced by the loss avoided as a result of that transaction. If he arranges a substitute transaction that he would not have been expected to do under the rules on avoidability (§ 350), his damages are similarly limited by the loss so avoided. Recovery can be had only for loss that would not have occurred but for the breach. See § 346. If, after the breach, an event occurs that would have discharged the party in breach on grounds of impracticability of performance or frustration of purpose, damages are limited to the loss sustained prior to that event. Compare § 254(2). The principle that a party's liability is not reduced by payments or other benefits received by the injured party from collateral sources is less compelling in the case of a breach of contract than in the case of a tort. The effect of the receipt of unemployment benefits by a discharged employee will turn on the court's perception of legislative policy rather than on the rule stated in this Section.

f. Lost volume. Whether a subsequent transaction is a substitute for the broken contract sometimes raises difficult questions of fact. If the injured party could and would have entered into the subsequent contract, even if the contract had not been broken, and could have had the benefit of both, he can be said to have "lost volume" and the subsequent transaction is not a substitute for the broken contract. The injured party's damages are then based on the net profit that he has lost as a result of the broken contract. Since entrepreneurs try to operate at optimum capacity, however, it is possible that an additional transaction would not have been profitable and that the injured party would not have chosen to expand his business by undertaking it had there been no breach. It is sometimes assumed that he would have done so, but the question is one of fact to be resolved according to the circumstances of each case. See Uniform Commercial Code § 2–708(2).

§ 348. Alternatives to Loss in Value of Performance

(1) If a breach delays the use of property and the loss in value to the injured party is not proved with reasonable certainty, he may recover damages based on the rental value of the property or on interest on the value of the property.

(2) If a breach results in defective or unfinished construction and the loss in value to the injured party is not proved with sufficient certainty, he may recover damages based on

(a) the diminution in the market price of the property caused by the breach, or

(b) the reasonable cost of completing performance or of remedying the defects if that cost is not clearly disproportionate to the probable loss in value to him.

(3) If a breach is of a promise conditioned on a fortuitous event and it is uncertain whether the event would have occurred had there been no breach, the injured party may recover damages based on the value of the conditional right at the time of breach.

Comment:

a. Reason for alternative bases. Although in principle the injured party is entitled to recover based on the loss in value to him caused by the breach, in practice he may be precluded from recovery on this basis because he cannot show the loss in value to him with sufficient certainty. See § 352. In such a case, if there is a reasonable alternative to loss in value, he may claim damages based on that alternative. This Section states the rules that have been developed for three such cases.

b. Breach that delays the use of property. If the breach is one that prevents for a period of time the use of property from which profits would have been made, the loss in value to the injured party is based on the profits that he would have made during that period. If those profits cannot be proved

195

with reasonable certainty (§ 352), two other bases for recovery are possible. One is the fair rental value of the property during the period of delay. Damages based on fair rental value include an element of profit since the fair rental value of property depends on what it would command on the market and this turns on the profit that would be derived from its use. For this reason, uncertainty as to profits may result in uncertainty in fair rental value. Another possible basis for recovery, as a last resort, is the interest on the value of the property that has been made unproductive by the breach, if that value can be shown with reasonable certainty. Although these two other bases will ordinarily give a smaller recovery than loss in value, it is always open to the party in breach to show that this is not so and to hold the injured party to a smaller recovery based on loss in value to him.

Illustration:

    1.   A contracts with B to construct an outdoor drive-in theatre, to be completed by June 1. A does not complete the work until September 1. If B cannot prove his lost profits with reasonable certainty, he can recover damages based on the rental value of the theatre property or based on the interest on the value of the theatre property itself if he can prove either of these values with reasonable certainty. See Illustration 2 to § 352.

c.   Incomplete or defective performance. If the contract is one for construction, including repair or similar performance affecting the condition of property, and the work is not finished, the injured party will usually find it easier to prove what it would cost to have the work completed by another contractor than to prove the difference between the values to him of the finished and the unfinished performance. Since the cost to complete is usually

less than the loss in value to him, he is limited by the rule on avoidability to damages based on cost to complete. See § 350(1). If he has actually had the work completed, damages will be based on his expenditures if he comes within the rule stated in § 350(2).

Sometimes, especially if the performance is defective as distinguished from incomplete, it may not be possible to prove the loss in value to the injured party with reasonable certainty. In that case he can usually recover damages based on the cost to remedy the defects. Even if this gives him a recovery somewhat in excess of the loss in value to him, it is better that he receive a small windfall than that he be undercompensated by being limited to the resulting diminution in the market price of his property.

Sometimes, however, such a large part of the cost to remedy the defects consists of the cost to undo what has been improperly done that the cost to remedy the defects will be clearly disproportionate to the probable loss in value to the injured party. Damages based on the cost to remedy the defects would then give the injured party a recovery greatly in excess of the loss in value to him and result in a substantial windfall. Such an award will not be made. It is sometimes said that the award would involve "economic waste," but this is a misleading expression since an injured party will not, even if awarded an excessive amount of damages, usually pay to have the defects remedied if to do so will cost him more than the resulting increase in value to him. If an award based on the cost to remedy the defects would clearly be excessive and the injured party does not prove the actual loss in value to him, damages will be based instead on the difference between the market price that the property would have had without the defects and the market price of the property with the defects. This diminution in market price is the least possible loss in value to the injured party, since he could always sell the property on the market even if it had no special value to him.

Illustrations:

2. A contracts to build a house for B for $100,000 but repudiates the contract after doing part of the work and having been paid $40,000. Other builders will charge B $80,000 to finish the house. B's damages include the $80,000 cost to complete the work less the $60,000 cost avoided or $20,000, together with damages for any loss caused by delay. See Illustration 12 to § 347.

3. A contracts to build a house for B for $100,000. When it is completed, the foundations crack, leaving part of the building in a dangerous condition. To make it safe would require tearing down some of the walls and strengthening the foundation at a cost of $30,000 and would increase the market value of the house by $20,000. B's damages include the $30,000 cost to remedy the defects.

4. A contracts to build a house for B for $100,000 according to specifications that include the use of Reading pipe. After completion, B discovers that A has used Cohoes pipe, an equally good brand. To replace the Cohoes pipe with Reading pipe would require tearing down part of the walls at a cost of over $20,000 and would not affect the market price of the house. In an action by B against A, A gives no proof of any special value that Reading pipe would have to him. B's damages do not include the $20,000 cost to remedy the defects because that cost is clearly disproportionate to the loss in value to B. B can recover only nominal damages.

d. *Fortuitous event as condition.* In the case of a promise conditioned on a fortuitous event (see Comment a to § 379), a breach that occurs before the happening of the fortuitous event may make it impossible to determine whether the event would have occurred had there been no breach. It would be unfair to the party in breach to award damages on the assumption that the event would have occurred, but equally unfair to the injured party to deny recovery of damages on the ground of uncertainty. The injured party has, in any case, the remedy of restitution (see § 373). Under the rule stated in Subsection (3) he also has the alternative remedy of damages based on the value of his conditional contract right at the time of breach, or what may be described as the value of his "chance of winning." The value of that right must itself be proved with reasonable certainty, as it may be if there is a market for such rights or if there is a suitable basis for determining the probability of the occurrence of the event.

The rule stated in this Subsection is limited to aleatory promises and does not apply if the promise is conditioned on some event, such as return performance by the injured party, that is not fortuitous. If, for example, an owner repudiates a contract to pay for repairs to be done by a contractor and then maintains that the contractor could not or would not have done the work had he not repudiated, the contractor must prove that he could and would have performed. If he fails to do this, he has no remedy in damages. He is not entitled to claim damages under the rule stated in Subsection (3).

Illustration:

5. A offers a $100,000 prize to the owner whose horse wins a race at A's track. B accepts by entering his horse and paying the registration fee. When the race is run, A wrongfully prevents B's horse from taking part. Although B cannot prove that his horse would have

won the race, he can prove that it was considered to have one chance in four of winning because one fourth of the money bet on the race was bet on his horse. B has a right to damages of $25,000 based on the value of the conditional right to the prize.

§ 349. Damages Based on Reliance Interest

As an alternative to the measure of damages stated in § 347, the injured party has a right to damages based on his reliance interest, including expenditures made in preparation for performance or in performance, less any loss that the party in breach can prove with reasonable certainty the injured party would have suffered had the contract been performed.

§ 350. Avoidability as a Limitation on Damages

(1) Except as stated in Subsection (2), damages are not recoverable for loss that the injured party could have avoided without undue risk, burden or humiliation.

(2) The injured party is not precluded from recovery by the rule stated in Subsection (1) to the extent that he has made reasonable but unsuccessful efforts to avoid loss.

§ 351. Unforeseeability and Related Limitations on Damages

(1) Damages are not recoverable for loss that the party in breach did not have reason to foresee as a probable result of the breach when the contract was made.

(2) Loss may be foreseeable as a probable result of a breach because it follows from the breach

(a) in the ordinary course of events, or

(b) as a result of special circumstances beyond the ordinary course of events, that the party in breach had reason to know.

(3) A court may limit damages for foreseeable loss by excluding recovery for loss of profits, by allowing recovery only for loss incurred in reliance, or otherwise if it concludes that in the circumstances justice so requires in order to avoid disproportionate compensation.

Comment:

a. Requirement of foreseeability. A contracting party is generally expected to take account of those risks that are foreseeable at the time he makes the contract. He is not, however, liable in the event of breach for loss that he did not at the time of contracting have reason to foresee as a probable result of such a breach. The mere circumstance that some loss was foreseeable, or even that some loss of the same general kind was foreseeable, will not suffice if the loss that actually occurred was not foreseeable. It is enough, however, that the loss was foreseeable as a probable, as distinguished from a necessary, result of his breach. Furthermore, the party in breach need not have made a "tacit agreement" to be liable for the loss. Nor must he have had the loss in mind when making the contract, for the test is an objective one based on what he had reason to foresee. There is no requirement of foreseeability with respect to the injured party. In spite of these qualifications, the requirement of foreseeability is a more severe limitation of liability than is the requirement of substantial or "proximate" cause in the case of an action in tort or for breach of warranty. Compare Restatement, Second, Torts § 431; Uniform Commercial Code § 2–715(2)(b). Although the recovery that is precluded by the limitation of foreseeability is usually based on the expectation interest and takes the form of lost profits (see Illustration 1), the limitation may also preclude recovery based on the reliance interest (see Illustration 2).

Illustrations:

1. A, a carrier, contracts with B, a miller, to carry B's broken crankshaft to its manufacturer for repair. B tells A when they make the contract that the crankshaft is part of B's milling machine and that it must be sent at once, but not that the mill is stopped because B has no replacement. Because A delays in carrying the crankshaft, B loses profit during an additional period while the mill is stopped because of the delay. A is not liable for B's loss of profit. That loss was not foreseeable by A as a probable result of the breach at the time the contract was made because A did not know that the broken crankshaft was necessary for the operation of the mill.

2. A contracts to sell land to B and to give B possession on a stated date. Because A delays a short time in giving B possession, B incurs unusual expenses in providing for cattle that he had already purchased to stock the land as a ranch. A had no reason to know when they made the contract that B had planned to purchase cattle for this purpose. A is not liable for B's expenses in providing for the cattle because that loss was not foreseeable by A as a probable result of the breach at the time the contract was made.

b. *"General" and "special" damages.* Loss that results from a breach in the ordinary course of events is foreseeable as the probable result of the breach. See Uniform Commercial Code § 2–714(1). Such loss is sometimes said to be the "natural" result of the breach, in the sense that its occurrence accords with the common experience of ordinary persons. For example, a seller of a commodity to a wholesaler usually has reason to foresee that his failure to deliver the commodity as agreed will probably cause the wholesaler to lose a reasonable profit on it. See Illustrations 3 and 4. Similarly, a seller of a machine to a manufacturer usually has reason to foresee that his delay in delivering the machine as agreed will probably cause the manufacturer to lose a reasonable profit from its use, although courts have been somewhat more cautious in allowing the manufacturer recovery for loss of such profits than in allowing a middleman recovery for loss of profits on an intended resale. See Illustration 5. The damages recoverable for such loss that results in the ordinary course of events are sometimes called "general" damages.

If loss results other than in the ordinary course of events, there can be no recovery for it unless it was foreseeable by the party in breach because of special circumstances that he had reason to know when he made the contract. See Uniform Commercial Code § 2–715(2)(a). For example, a seller who fails to deliver a commodity to a wholesaler is not liable for the wholesaler's loss of profit to the extent that it is extraordinary nor for his loss due to unusual terms in his resale contracts unless the seller had reason to know of these special circumstances. See Illustration 6. Similarly, a seller who delays in delivering a machine to a manufacturer is not liable for the manufacturer's loss of profit to the extent that it results from an intended use that was abnormal unless the seller had reason to know of this special circumstance. See Illustration 7. In the case of a written agreement, foreseeability is sometimes established by the use of recitals in the agreement itself. The parol evidence rule (§ 213) does not, however, preclude the use of negotiations prior to the making of the contract to show for this purpose circumstances that were then known to a party. The damages recoverable for loss that results other than in the ordinary course of events are sometimes called "special" or "consequential" damages. These terms are often misleading, however, and it is not necessary to distinguish between "general" and "special" or "consequential" damages for the purpose of the rule stated in this Section.

Illustrations:

3.   A and B make a written contract under which A is to recondition by a stated date a used machine owned by B so that it will be suitable for sale by B to C. A knows when they make the contract that B has contracted to sell the machine to C but knows nothing of the terms of B's contract with C. Because A delays in returning the machine to B, B is unable to sell it to C and loses the profit that he would have made on that sale. B's loss of reasonable profit was foreseeable by A as a probable result of the breach at the time the contract was made.

4.   A, a manufacturer of machines, contracts to make B his exclusive selling agent in a specified area for the period of a year. Because A fails to deliver any machines, B loses the profit on contracts that he would have made for their resale. B's loss of reasonable profit was foreseeable by A as a probable result of the breach at the time the contract was made.

5.   A and B make a contract under which A is to recondition by a stated date a used machine owned by B so that it will be suitable for use in B's canning factory. A knows that the machine must be reconditioned by that date if B's factory is to operate at full capacity during the canning season, but nothing is said of this in the written contract. Because A delays in returning the machine to B, B loses its use for the entire canning season and loses the profit that he would have made had his factory operated at full capacity. B's loss of reasonable profit was foreseeable by A as a probable result of the breach at the time the contract was made.

6.   The facts being otherwise as stated in Illustration 3, the profit that B would have made under his contract with A was extraordinarily large because C promised to pay an exceptionally high price as a result of a special need for the machine of which A was unaware. A is not liable for B's loss of profit to the extent that it exceeds what would ordinarily result from such a contract. To that extent the loss was not foreseeable by A as a probable result of the breach at the time the contract was made.

7.   The facts being otherwise as stated in Illustration 5, the profit that B would have made from the use of the machine was unusually large because of an abnormal use to which he planned to put it of which A was unaware. A is not liable for B's loss of profit to the extent that it exceeds what would ordinarily result from the use of such a machine. To that extent the loss was not foreseeable by A at the time the contract was made as a probable result of the breach.

c.   *Litigation or settlement caused by breach.* Sometimes a breach of contract results in claims by third persons against the injured party. The party in breach is liable for the amount of any judgment against the injured party together with his reasonable expenditures in the litigation, if the party in breach had reason to foresee such expenditures as the probable result of his breach at the time he made the contract. See Illustrations 8, 10, 11 and 12. This is so even if the judgment in the litigation is based on a liquidated damage clause in the injured party's contract with the third party. See Illustration 8. A failure to notify the party in breach in advance of the litigation may prevent the result of the litigation from being conclusive as to him. But to the extent that the injured party's loss resulting from litigation is reasonable, the fact that the party in breach was not notified does not prevent the inclusion of that loss in the damages assessed against him. In furtherance of the policy favoring private settlement of disputes, the injured party is also allowed to recover the reasonable amount of any settlement made to avoid litigation, together with the costs of settlement. See Illustration 9.

Illustrations:

8. The facts being otherwise as stated in Illustration 3, B not only loses the profit that he would have made on sale of the machine to C, but is held liable for damages in an action brought by C for breach of contract. The damages paid to C and B's reasonable expenses in defending the action were also foreseeable by A as a probable result of the breach at the time he made the contract with B. The result is the same even though they were based on a liquidated damage clause in the contract between B and C if A knew of the clause or if the use of such a clause in the contract between B and C was foreseeable by A at the time he made the contract with B.

9. The facts being otherwise as stated in Illustration 3, B not only loses the profit that he would have made on sale of the machine to C, but settles with C by paying C a reasonable sum of money to avoid litigation. The amount of the settlement paid to C and B's reasonable expenses in settling were also foreseeable by A at the time he made the contract with B as a probable result of the breach.

10. A contracts to supply B with machinery for unloading cargo. A, in breach of contract, furnishes defective machinery, and C, an employee of B, is injured. C sues B and gets a judgment, which B pays. The amount of the judgment and B's reasonable expenditures in defending the action were foreseeable by A at the time the contract was made as a probable result of the breach.

11. A contracts to procure a right of way for B, for a railroad. Because A, in breach of contract, fails to do this, B has to acquire the right of way by condemnation proceedings. B's reasonable expenditures in those proceedings were foreseeable by A at the time the contract was made as a probable result of the breach.

12. A leases land to B with a covenant for quiet enjoyment. C brings an action of ejectment against B and gets judgment. B's reasonable expenditures in defending the action were foreseeable by A as the probable result of the breach at the time the contract was made.

d. *Unavailability of substitute.* If several circumstances have contributed to cause a loss, the party in breach is not liable for it unless he had reason to foresee all of them. Sometimes a loss would not have occurred if the injured party had been able to make substitute arrangements after breach, as, for example, by "cover" through purchase of substitute goods in the case of a buyer of goods (see Uniform Commercial Code § 2–712). If the inability of the injured party to make such arrangements was foreseeable by the party in breach at the time he made the contract, the resulting loss was foreseeable. See Illustration 13. On the impact of this principle on contracts to lend money, see Comment e.

Illustration:

13.   A contracts with B, a farmer, to lease B a machine to be used harvesting B's crop, delivery to be made on July 30. A knows when he makes the contract that B's crop will be ready on that date and that B cannot obtain another machine elsewhere. Because A delays delivery until August 10, B's crop is damaged and he loses profit. B's loss of profit was foreseeable by A at the time the contract was made as a probable result of the breach.

e.   *Breach of contract to lend money.* The limitation of foreseeability is often applied in actions for damages for breach of contracts to lend money. Because credit is so widely available, a lender often has no reason to foresee at the time the contract is made that the borrower will be unable to make substitute arrangements in the event of breach. See Comment d. In most cases, then, the lender's liability will be limited to the relatively small additional amount that it would ordinarily cost to get a similar loan from another lender. However, in the less common situation in which the lender has reason to foresee that the borrower will be unable to borrow elsewhere or will be delayed in borrowing elsewhere, the lender may be liable for much heavier damages based on the borrower's inability to take advantage of a specific opportunity (see Illustration 14), his having to postpone or abandon a profitable project (see Illustration 15), or his for-

feiture of security for failure to make prompt payment (see Illustration 16).

Illustrations:

14.   A contracts to lend B $100,000 for one year at eight percent interest for the stated purpose of buying a specific lot of goods for resale. B can resell the goods at a $20,000 profit. A delays in making the loan, and although B can borrow money on the market at ten percent interest, he is unable to do so in time and loses the opportunity to buy the goods. Unless A had reason to foresee at the time that he made the contract that such a delay in making the loan would probably cause B to lose the opportunity, B can only recover damages based on two percent of the amount of the loan.

15.   A contracts to lend $1,000,000 to B for the stated purpose of enabling B to build a building and takes property of B as security. After construction is begun, A refuses to make the loan or release the security. Because B lacks further security, he is unable to complete the building, which becomes a total loss. B's loss incurred in partial construction of the building was foreseeable by A at the time of the contract as a probable result of the breach.

16.   A, who holds B's land as security for a loan, contracts to lend B a sum of money sufficient to pay off other liens on the land at the current rate of interest. A repudiates and informs B in time to obtain money elsewhere on the market, but B is unable to do so. The liens are foreclosed and the land sold at a loss. Unless A knew when he made the contract that B would probably be unable to borrow the money elsewhere, B's loss on the foreclosure sale was not foreseeable as a probable result of A's breach.

f. Other limitations on damages. It is not always in the interest of justice to require the party in breach to pay damages for all of the foreseeable loss that he has caused. There are unusual instances in which it appears from the circumstances either that the parties assumed that one of them would not bear the risk of a particular loss or that, although there was no such assumption, it would be unjust to put the risk on that party. One such circumstance is an extreme disproportion between the loss and the price charged by the party whose liability for that loss is in question. The fact that the price is relatively small suggests that it was not intended to cover the risk of such liability. Another such circumstance is an informality of dealing, including the absence of a detailed written contract, which indicates that there was no careful attempt to allocate all of the risks. The fact that the parties did not attempt to delineate with precision all of the risks justifies a court in attempting to allocate them fairly. The limitations dealt with in this Section are more likely to be imposed in connection with contracts that do not arise in a commercial setting. Typical examples of limitations imposed on damages under this discretionary power involve the denial of recovery for loss of profits and the restriction of damages to loss incurred in reliance on the contract. Sometimes these limits are covertly imposed, by means of an especially demanding requirement of foreseeability or of certainty. The rule stated in this Section recognizes that what is done in such cases is the imposition of a limitation in the interests of justice.

Illustrations:

17. A, a private trucker, contracts with B to deliver to B's factory a machine that has just been repaired and without which B's factory, as A knows, cannot reopen. Delivery is delayed because A's truck breaks down. In an action by B against A for breach of contract the court may, after taking into consideration such factors as the absence of an elaborate written contract and the extreme disproportion between B's loss of profits during the delay and the price of the trucker's services, exclude recovery for loss of profits.

18. A, a retail hardware dealer, contracts to sell B an inexpensive lighting attachment, which, as A knows, B needs in order to use his tractor at night on his farm. A is delayed in obtaining the attachment and, since no substitute is available, B is unable to use the tractor at night during the delay. In an action by B against A for breach of contract, the court may, after taking into consideration such factors as the absence of an elaborate written contract and the extreme disproportion between B's loss of profits during the delay and the price of the attachment, exclude recovery for loss of profits.

19. A, a plastic surgeon, makes a contract with B, a professional entertainer, to perform plastic surgery on her face in order to improve her appearance. The result of the surgery is, however, to disfigure her face and to require a second operation. In an action by B against A for breach of contract, the court may limit damages by allowing recovery only for loss incurred by B in reliance on the contract, including the fees paid by B and expenses for hospitalization, nursing care and medicine for both operations, together with any damages for the worsening of B's appearance if these can be proved with reasonable certainty, but not including any loss resulting from the failure to improve her appearance.

§ 352. Uncertainty as a Limitation on Damages

Damages are not recoverable for loss beyond an amount that the evidence permits to be established with reasonable certainty.

Comment:

a.   Requirement   of   certainty. A party cannot recover damages for breach of a contract for loss beyond the amount that the evidence permits to be established with reasonable certainty. See Illustration 1. Courts have traditionally required greater certainty in the proof of damages for breach of a contract than in the proof of damages for a tort. The requirement does not mean, however, that the injured party is barred from recovery unless he establishes the total amount of his loss. It merely excludes those elements of loss that cannot be proved with reasonable certainty. The main impact of the requirement of certainty comes in connection with recovery for lost profits. Although the requirement of certainty is distinct from that of foreseeability (§ 351), its impact is similar in this respect. Although the requirement applies to damages based on the reliance as well as the expectation interest, there is usually little difficulty in proving the amount that the injured party has actually spent in reliance on the contract, even if it is impossible to prove the amount of profit that he would have made. In such a case, he can recover his loss based on his reliance interest instead of on his expectation interest. See § 349 and Illustrations 1, 2 and 3.

Doubts are generally resolved against the party in breach. A party who has, by his breach, forced the injured party to seek compensation in damages should not be allowed to profit from his breach where it is established that a significant loss has occurred. A court may take into account all the circumstances of the breach, including willfulness, in deciding whether to require a lesser degree of certainty, giving greater discretion to the trier of the facts. Damages need not be calculable with mathematical accuracy and are often at best approximate. See Comment 1 to Uniform Commercial Code § 1–106. This is especially true for items such as loss of good will as to which great precision cannot be expected. See Illustration 4. Furthermore, increasing receptiveness on the part of courts to proof by sophisticated economic and financial data and by expert opinion has made it easier to meet the requirement of certainty.

Illustrations:

1.   A contracts to publish a novel that B has written. A repudiates the contract and B is unable to get his novel published elsewhere. If the evidence does not permit B's loss of royalties and of reputation to be estimated with reasonable certainty, he cannot recover damages for that loss, although he can recover nominal damages. See Illustration 1 to § 347.

2.   A contracts to sell B a tract of land on which B plans to build an outdoor drive-in theatre. A breaks the contract by selling the land to C, and B is unable to build the theatre. If, because of the speculative nature of the new enterprise the evidence does not permit B's loss of profits to be estimated with reasonable certainty, his recovery will be limited to expenses incurred in reliance or, if none can be proved with reasonable certainty, to nominal damages.

3.   A and B make a contract under which A is to construct a building of radical new design for B for $5,000,000. After A has spent $3,000,000 in reliance, B repudiates the contract and orders A off the

site. If the evidence does not permit A's lost profits to be estimated with reasonable certainty, he can recover the $3,000,000 that he has spent in reliance. He must, however, then prove that amount with reasonable certainty.

4. A, a manufacturer, makes a contract with B, a wholesaler, to sell B a quantity of plastic. B resells the plastic to dealers. The plastic is discovered to be defective and B has many complaints from dealers, some of which refuse to place further orders with him. B can recover the loss of good will if his loss can be estimated with reasonable certainty by such evidence as his business records before and after the transaction and the testimony of his salespersons and that of dealers.

b. Proof of profits. The difficulty of proving lost profits varies greatly with the nature of the transaction. If, for example, it is the seller who claims lost profit on the ground that the buyer's breach has caused him to lose a sale, proof of lost profit will ordinarily not be difficult. If, however, it is the buyer who claims lost profit on the ground that the seller's breach has caused him loss in other transactions, the task of proof is harder. Furthermore, if the transaction is more complex and extends into the future, as where the seller agrees to furnish all of the buyer's requirements over a period of years, proof of the loss of profits caused by the seller's breach is more difficult. If the breach prevents the injured party from carrying on a well-established business, the resulting loss of profits can often be proved with sufficient certainty. Evidence of past performance will form the basis for a reasonable prediction as to the future. See Illustration 5. However, if the business is a new one or if it is a speculative one that is subject to great fluctuations in volume, costs or prices, proof will be more difficult. Nevertheless, damages

may be established with reasonable certainty with the aid of expert testimony, economic and financial data, market surveys and analyses, business records of similar enterprises, and the like. See Illustration 6. Under a contract of exclusive agency for the sale of goods on commission, the agent can often prove with sufficient certainty the profits that he would have made had he not been discharged. Proof of the sales made by the agent in the agreed territory before the breach, or of the sales made there by the principal after the breach, may permit a reasonably accurate estimate of the agent's loss of commissions. However, if the agency is not an exclusive one, so that the agent's ability to withstand competition is in question, such a showing will be more difficult, although the agent's past record may give a sufficient basis for judging this. See Illustration 7.

Illustrations:

5. A contracts with B to remodel B's existing outdoor drive-in theatre, work to be completed on June 1. A does not complete the work until September 1. B can use records of the theatre's prior and subsequent operation, along with other evidence, to prove his lost profits with reasonable certainty.

6. A contracts with B to construct a new outdoor drive-in theatre, to be completed on June 1. A does not complete the theatre until September 1. Even though the business is a new rather than an established one, B may be able to prove his lost profits with reasonable certainty. B can use records of the theatre's subsequent operation and of the operation of similar theatres in the same locality, along with other evidence including market surveys and expert testimony, in attempting to do this.

7. A contracts with B to make B his exclusive agent for the sale of

machine tools in a specified territory and to supply him with machine tools at stated prices. After B has begun to act as A's agent, A repudiates the agreement and replaces him with C. B can use evidence as to sales and profits made by him before the repudiation and made by C after the repudiation in attempting to prove his lost profits with reasonable certainty. It would be more difficult, although not necessarily impossible, for B to succeed in this attempt if his agency were not exclusive.

c.   Alternative   remedies. The necessity of proving damages can be avoided if another remedy, such as a decree of specific performance or an injunction, is granted instead of damages. Although the availability of such a remedy does not preclude an award of damages as an alternative, it may justify a court in requiring greater certainty of proof if damages are to be awarded. See Illustration 8.

Illustration:

8.   A, a steel manufacturer, and B, a dealer in scrap steel, contract for the sale by A to B of all of A's output of scrap steel for five years at a price fixed in terms of the market price. B's profit will depend largely on the amount of A's output and the cost of transporting the scrap to B's purchasers. A repudiates the contract at the end of one year. Whether B can recover damages based on lost profits over the remaining four years will depend on whether he can prove A's output and the transportation costs with reasonable certainty. If he can do so for part of the remaining four years, he can recover damages based on lost profits for that period. The availability of the remedy of specific performance is a factor that will influence a court in requiring greater certainty.

§ 353.   Loss Due to Emotional Disturbance

Recovery for emotional disturbance will be excluded unless the breach also caused bodily harm or the contract or the breach is of such a kind that serious emotional disturbance was a particularly likely result.

§ 354.   Interest as Damages

(1)   If the breach consists of a failure to pay a definite sum in money or to render a performance with fixed or ascertainable monetary value, interest is recoverable from the time for performance on the amount due less all deductions to which the party in breach is entitled.

(2)   In any other case, such interest may be allowed as justice requires on the amount that would have been just compensation had it been paid when performance was due.

§ 355.   Punitive Damages

Punitive damages are not recoverable for a breach of contract unless the conduct constituting the breach is also a tort for which punitive damages are recoverable.

§ 356. Liquidated Damages and Penalties

(1) Damages for breach by either party may be liquidated in the agreement but only at an amount that is reasonable in the light of the anticipated or actual loss caused by the breach and the difficulties of proof of loss. A term fixing unreasonably large liquidated damages is unenforceable on grounds of public policy.

(2) A term in a bond providing for an amount of money as a penalty for non-occurrence of the condition of the bond is unenforceable on grounds of public policy to the extent that the amount exceeds the loss caused by such non-occurrence.

Comment:

a. Liquidated damages or penalty. The parties to a contract may effectively provide in advance the damages that are to be payable in the event of breach as long as the provision does not disregard the principle of compensation. The enforcement of such provisions for liquidated damages saves the time of courts, juries, parties and witnesses and reduces the expense of litigation. This is especially important if the amount in controversy is small. However, the parties to a contract are not free to provide a penalty for its breach. The central objective behind the system of contract remedies is compensatory, not punitive. Punishment of a promisor for having broken his promise has no justification on either economic or other grounds and a term providing such a penalty is unenforceable on grounds of public policy. See Chapter 8. The rest of the agreement remains enforceable, however, under the rule stated in § 184(1), and the remedies for breach are determined by the rules stated in this Chapter. See Illustration 1. A term that fixes an unreasonably small amount as damages may be unenforceable as unconscionable. See § 208. As to the liquidation of damages and modification or limitation of remedies in contracts of sale, see Uniform Commercial Code §§ 2–718, 2–719.

b. Test of penalty. Under the test stated in Subsection (1), two factors combine in determining whether an amount of money fixed as damages is so unreasonably large as to be a penalty. The first factor is the anticipated or actual loss caused by the breach. The amount fixed is reasonable to the extent that it approximates the actual loss that has resulted from the particular breach, even though it may not approximate the loss that might have been anticipated under other possible breaches. See Illustration 2. Furthermore, the amount fixed is reasonable to the extent that it approximates the loss anticipated at the time of the making of the contract, even though it may not approximate the actual loss. See Illustration 3. The second factor is the difficulty of proof of loss. The greater the difficulty either of proving that loss has occurred or of establishing its amount with the requisite certainty (see § 351), the easier it is to show that the amount fixed is reasonable. To the extent that there is uncertainty as to the harm, the estimate of the court or jury may not accord with the principle of compensation any more than does the advance estimate of the parties. A determination whether the amount fixed is a penalty turns on a combination of these two factors. If the difficulty of proof of loss is great, considerable latitude is allowed in the approximation of anticipated or actual harm. If, on the other hand, the difficulty of proof of loss is slight, less latitude is allowed in that approximation. If, to take an extreme case, it is clear that no loss at all has occurred, a provision fixing a substantial sum as damages is unenforceable. See Illustration 4.

Illustrations:

1. A and B sign a written contract under which A is to act in a play produced by B for a ten week season for $4,000. A term provides that "if either party shall fail to perform as agreed in any respect he will pay $10,000 as liquidated damages and not as a penalty." A leaves the play before the last week to take another job. The play is sold out for that week and A is replaced by a suitable understudy. The amount fixed is unreasonable in the light of both the anticipated and the actual loss and, in spite of the use of the words "liquidated damages," the term provides for a penalty and is unenforceable on grounds of public policy. The rest of the agreement is enforceable (§ 184(1)), and B's remedies for A's breach are governed by the rules stated in this Chapter.

2. A, B and C form a partnership to practice veterinary medicine in a town for ten years. In the partnership agreement, each promises that if, on the termination of the partnership, the practice is continued by the other two members, he will not practice veterinary medicine in the same town during its continuance up to a maximum of three years. A term provides that for breach of this duty "he shall forfeit $50,000 to be collected by the others as damages. "A leaves the partnership, and the practice is continued by B and C. A immediately begins to practice veterinary medicine in the same town. The loss actually caused to B and C is difficult of proof and $50,000 is not an unreasonable estimate of it. Even though $50,000 may be unreasonable in relation to the loss that might have resulted in other circumstances, it is not unreasonable in relation to the actual loss. Therefore, the term does not provide for a penalty and its enforcement is not precluded on grounds of public policy. See Illustration 14 to § 188.

3. A contracts to build a grandstand for B's race track for $1,000,000 by a specified date and to pay $1,000 a day for every day's delay in completing it. A delays completion for ten days. If $1,000 is not unreasonable in the light of the anticipated loss and the actual loss to B is difficult to prove, A's promise is not a term providing for a penalty and its enforcement is not precluded on grounds of public policy.

4. The facts being otherwise as stated in Illustration 3, B is delayed for a month in obtaining permission to operate his race track so that it is certain that A's delay of ten days caused him no loss at all. Since the actual loss to B is not difficult to prove, A's promise is a term providing for a penalty and is unenforceable on grounds of public policy.

c. Disguised penalties. Under the rule stated in this Section, the validity of a term providing for damages depends on the effect of that term as interpreted according to the rules stated in Chapter 9. Neither the parties' actual intention as to its validity nor their characterization of the term as one for liquidated damages or a penalty is significant in determining whether the term is valid. Sometimes parties attempt to disguise a provision for a penalty by using language that purports to make payment of the amount an alternative performance under the contract, that purports to offer a discount for prompt performance, or that purports to place a valuation on property to be delivered. Although the parties may in good faith contract for alternative performances and fix discounts or valuations, a court will look to the substance of the agreement to determine whether this is the case or whether the parties have attempted to disguise a provision for a penalty that is unenforceable under this Section. In determining whether a contract is one for alternative performances, the relative value of the alternatives may be decisive.

Illustration:

5. A contracts to build a house for B for $50,000 by a specified date or in the alternative to pay B $1,000 a week during any period of delay. A delays completion for ten days. If $1,000 a week is unreasonable in the light of both the anticipated and actual loss, A's promise to pay $1,000 a week is, in spite of its form, a term providing for a penalty and is unenforceable on grounds of public policy.

d. Related types of provisions. This Section does not purport to cover the wide variety of provisions used by parties to control the remedies available to them for breach of contract. A term that fixes as damages an amount that is unreasonably small does not come within the rule stated in this Section, but a court may refuse to enforce it as unconscionable under the rule stated in § 208. A mere recital of the harm that may occur as a result of a breach of contract does not come with-

in the rule stated in this Section, but may increase damages by making that harm foreseeable under the rule stated § 351. As to the effect of a contract provision on the right to equitable relief, see Comment a to § 359. As to the effect of a term requiring the occurrence of a condition where forfeiture would result, see § 229. Although attorneys' fees are not generally awarded to the winning party, if the parties provide for the award of such fees the court will award a sum that it considers to be reasonable. If, however, the parties specify the amount of such fees, the provision is subject to the test stated in this Section.

e. Penalties in bonds. Bonds often fix a flat sum as a penalty for non-occurrence of the condition of the bond. A term providing for a penalty is not unenforceable in its entirety but only to the extent that it exceeds the loss caused by the non-occurrence of the condition.

Illustration:

6. A executes a bond obligating himself to pay B $10,000, on condition that the bond shall be void, however, if C, who is B's cashier, shall properly account for all money entrusted to him. C defaults to the extent of $500. A's promise is unenforceable on grounds of public policy to the extent that it exceeds the actual loss, $500.

TOPIC 3. ENFORCEMENT BY SPECIFIC PERFORMANCE AND INJUNCTION

§ 357. Availability of Specific Performance and Injunction

(1) Subject to the rules stated in §§ 359–69, specific performance of a contract duty will be granted in the discretion of the court against a party who has committed or is threatening to commit a breach of the duty.

(2) Subject to the rules stated in §§ 359–69, an injunction against breach of a contract duty will be granted in the discretion of the court against a party who has committed or is threatening to commit a breach of the duty if

(a)   the duty is one of forbearance, or

(b)   the duty is one to act and specific performance would be denied only for reasons that are inapplicable to an injunction.

§ 358.   Form of Order and Other Relief

(1)   An order of specific performance or an injunction will be so drawn as best to effectuate the purposes for which the contract was made and on such terms as justice requires. It need not be absolute in form and the performance that it requires need not be identical with that due under the contract.

(2)   If specific performance or an injunction is denied as to part of the performance that is due, it may nevertheless be granted as to the remainder.

(3)   In addition to specific performance or an injunction, damages and other relief may be awarded in the same proceeding and an indemnity against future harm may be required.

§ 359.   Effect of Adequacy of Damages

(1)   Specific performance or an injunction will not be ordered if damages would be adequate to protect the expectation interest of the injured party.

(2)   The adequacy of the damage remedy for failure to render one part of the performance due does not preclude specific performance or injunction as to the contract as a whole.

(3)   Specific performance or an injunction will not be refused merely because there is a remedy for breach other than damages, but such a remedy may be considered in exercising discretion under the rule stated in § 357.

§ 360.   Factors Affecting Adequacy of Damages

In determining whether the remedy in damages would be adequate, the following circumstances are significant:

(a)   the difficulty of proving damages with reasonable certainty,

(b)   the difficulty of procuring a suitable substitute performance by means of money awarded as damages, and

(c)   the likelihood that an award of damages could not be collected.

§ 361.   Effect of Provision for Liquidated Damages

Specific performance or an injunction may be granted to enforce a duty even though there is a provision for liquidated damages for breach of that duty.

§ 362. Effect of Uncertainty of Terms

Specific performance or an injunction will not be granted unless the terms of the contract are sufficiently certain to provide a basis for an appropriate order.

Comment:

. . . b. Degree of certainty required. If specific performance or an injunction is to be granted, it is important that the terms of the contract are sufficiently certain to enable the order to be drafted with precision because of the availability of the contempt power for disobedience. Before concluding that the required certainty is lacking, however, a court will avail itself of all of the usual aids in determining the scope of the agreement. Apparent difficulties of enforcement due to uncertainty may disappear in the light of courageous common sense. Expressions that at first appear incomplete may not appear so after resort to usage (§ 221) or the addition of a term supplied by law (§ 204). A contract is not too uncertain merely because a promisor is given a choice of performing in several ways, whether expressed as alternative performances or otherwise. He may be ordered to make the choice and to perform accordingly, and, if he fails to make the choice, the court may choose for him and order specific performance. Even though subsidiary terms have been left to determination by future agreement, if performance has begun by mutual consent, equitable relief may be appropriate with the court supplying the missing terms so as to assure the promisor all advantages that he reasonably expected.

§ 363. Effect of Insecurity as to the Agreed Exchange

Specific performance or an injunction may be refused if a substantial part of the agreed exchange for the performance to be compelled is unperformed and its performance is not secured to the satisfaction of the court.

§ 364. Effect of Unfairness

(1)   Specific performance or an injunction will be refused if such relief would be unfair because

(a)   the contract was induced by mistake or by unfair practices,

(b)   the relief would cause unreasonable hardship or loss to the party in breach or to third persons, or

(c)   the exchange is grossly inadequate or the terms of the contract are otherwise unfair.

(2)   Specific performance or an injunction will be granted in spite of a term of the agreement if denial of such relief would be unfair because it would cause unreasonable hardship or loss to the party seeking relief or to third persons.

§ 365. Effect of Public Policy

Specific performance or an injunction will not be granted if the act or forbearance that would be compelled or the use of compulsion is contrary to public policy.

§ 366. Effect of Difficulty in Enforcement or Supervision

A promise will not be specifically enforced if the character and magnitude of the performance would impose on the court burdens in enforcement or supervision that are disproportionate to the advantages to be gained from enforcement and to the harm to be suffered from its denial.

§ 367. Contracts for Personal Service or Supervision

(1) A promise to render personal service will not be specifically enforced.

(2) A promise to render personal service exclusively for one employer will not be enforced by an injunction against serving another if its probable result will be to compel a performance involving personal relations the enforced continuance of which is undesirable or will be to leave the employee without other reasonable means of making a living.

§ 368. Effect of Power of Termination

(1) Specific performance or an injunction will not be granted against a party who can substantially nullify the effect of the order by exercising a power of termination or avoidance.

(2) Specific performance or an injunction will not be denied merely because the party seeking relief has a power to terminate or avoid his duty unless the power could be used, in spite of the order, to deprive the other party of reasonable security for the agreed exchange for his performance.

§ 369. Effect of Breach by Party Seeking Relief

Specific performance or an injunction may be granted in spite of a breach by the party seeking relief, unless the breach is serious enough to discharge the other party's remaining duties of performance.

TOPIC 4.   RESTITUTION

§ 370. Requirement That Benefit Be Conferred

A party is entitled to restitution under the rules stated in this Restatement only to the extent that he has conferred a benefit on the other party by way of part performance or reliance.

§ 371. Measure of Restitution Interest

If a sum of money is awarded to protect a party's restitution interest, it may as justice requires be measured by either

(a) the reasonable value to the other party of what he received in terms of what it would have cost him to obtain it from a person in the claimant's position, or

(b)   the extent to which the other party's property has been increased in value or his other interests advanced.

§ 372.   Specific Restitution

(1)   Specific restitution will be granted to a party who is entitled to restitution, except that:

(a)   specific restitution based on a breach by the other party under the rule stated in § 373 may be refused in the discretion of the court if it would unduly interfere with the certainty of title to land or otherwise cause injustice, and

(b)   specific restitution in favor of the party in breach under the rule stated in § 374 will not be granted.

(2)   A decree of specific restitution may be made conditional on return of or compensation for anything that the party claiming restitution has received.

(3)   If specific restitution, with or without a sum of money, will be substantially as effective as restitution in money in putting the party claiming restitution in the position he was in before rendering any performance, the other party can discharge his duty by tendering such restitution before suit is brought and keeping his tender good.

§ 373.   Restitution When Other Party Is in Breach

(1)   Subject to the rule stated in Subsection (2), on a breach by nonperformance that gives rise to a claim for damages for total breach or on a repudiation, the injured party is entitled to restitution for any benefit that he has conferred on the other party by way of part performance or reliance.

(2)   The injured party has no right to restitution if he has performed all of his duties under the contract and no performance by the other party remains due other than payment of a definite sum of money for that performance.

§ 374.   Restitution in Favor of Party in Breach

(1)   Subject to the rule stated in Subsection (2), if a party justifiably refuses to perform on the ground that his remaining duties of performance have been discharged by the other party's breach, the party in breach is entitled to restitution for any benefit that he has conferred by way of part performance or reliance in excess of the loss that he has caused by his own breach.

(2)   To the extent that, under the manifested assent of the parties, a party's performance is to be retained in the case of breach, that party is not entitled to restitution if the value of the performance as liquidated damages is reasonable in the light of the anticipated or actual loss caused by the breach and the difficulties of proof of loss.

§ 375. Restitution When Contract Is Within Statute of Frauds

A party who would otherwise have a claim in restitution under a contract is not barred from restitution for the reason that the contract is unenforceable by him because of the Statute of Frauds unless the Statute provides otherwise or its purpose would be frustrated by allowing restitution.

§ 376. Restitution When Contract Is Voidable

A party who has avoided a contract on the ground of lack of capacity, mistake, misrepresentation, duress, undue influence or abuse of a fiduciary relation is entitled to restitution for any benefit that he has conferred on the other party by way of part performance or reliance.

Comment:

a. Recovery of benefit on avoidance. A party who exercises his power of avoidance is entitled to recover in restitution for any benefit that he has conferred on the other party through part performance of or reliance on the contract. The benefit from his part performance includes that resulting from the use by the other party of whatever he has received up to the time that it is returned on avoidance. Furthermore, under the rule stated in § 384, a party seeking restitution must generally return any benefit that he has himself received. If he has received and must return land, for example, he may have made improvements on the land in reliance on the contract and he is entitled, on avoidance and return of the land, to recover the reasonable value of those improvements (§ 371(b)). The rule stated in this Section applies to avoidance on any ground, including lack of capacity (§§ 14–16), mistake (§§ 152, 153), misrepresentation (§ 164), duress (§ 175), undue influence (§ 177) or abuse of a fiduciary relation (§ 173). Uncertainties in measuring the benefit, however, are more likely to be resolved in favor of the party seeking restitution if the other party engaged in misconduct, as in cases of fraudulent misrepresentation, duress or undue influence. In cases of mental incompetency the rule stated in this Section is supplemented by that stated in § 15(2) and in cases of mistake it is supplemented by that stated in § 158.

Illustrations:

1. A contracts to sell an automobile to B, an infant, for $2,000. After A has delivered the automobile and B has paid the $2,000, B disaffirms the contract on the ground of infancy (§ 14), tenders the automobile back to A, and sues A for $2,000. B can recover the $2,000 from A in restitution.

2. A contracts to sell and B to buy for $100,000 a tract of land, the value of which has depended mainly on the timber on it. Both A and B believe that the timber is still there, but in fact it has been destroyed by fire. After A has conveyed the land to B and B has paid the $100,000, B discovers the mistake. B disaffirms the contract for mistake (§ 152), tenders a deed to the land to A, and sues A for $100,000. B can recover $100,000 from A in restitution. See Illustration 1 to § 152.

3. A submits a $150,000 offer in response to B's invitation for bids on the construction of a building. A believes that this is the total of a column of figures, but he has made an error by inadvertently omitting $50,000, and in fact the total is $200,000. Because B had estimat-

ed the expected cost as $180,000 and the 10 other bids were all in the range between $180,000 and $200,000, B had reason to know of A's mistake. A discovers the mistake after he has done part of the work, disaffirms the contract on the ground of mistake (§ 153), and sues B in restitution for the benefit conferred on B as measured by the reasonable value of A's performance. A can recover the reasonable value of his performance in restitution and if the cost of the work done can be determined under the next lowest bid, that cost is evidence of its reasonable value. See Illustration 9 to § 153.

4.   A fraudulently induces B to make a contract to buy a tract of land for $100,000. After A has conveyed the land and B has paid the price, B makes improvements on the land with a reasonable val-

ue of $20,000. B then discovers the fraud, disaffirms the contract for misrepresentation (§ 164), tenders a deed to the land to A, and sues A for $100,000 plus $20,000, the reasonable value of the improvements, less $5,000, the value to B of the use of the land. B can recover $115,000 in restitution from A. See Illustration 1 to § 164.

5.   A fraudulently induces B to make a contract to sell a tract of land for $100,000. After B has conveyed the land and A has paid the price, A farms the land at a net profit of $10,000. B then discovers the fraud, disaffirms the contract for misrepresentation, tenders back the $100,000, and sues A for specific restitution plus the $10,000 profit that A made by farming the land. B can recover the land and $10,000 in restitution from A.

§ 377.   Restitution in Cases of Impracticability, Frustration, Non-Occurrence of Condition or Disclaimer by Beneficiary

A party whose duty of performance does not arise or is discharged as a result of impracticability of performance, frustration of purpose, non-occurrence of a condition or disclaimer by a beneficiary is entitled to restitution for any benefit that he has conferred on the other party by way of part performance or reliance.

TOPIC 5.   PRECLUSION BY ELECTION AND AFFIRMANCE

§ 378.   Election Among Remedies

If a party has more than one remedy under the rules stated in this Chapter, his manifestation of a choice of one of them by bringing suit or otherwise is not a bar to another remedy unless the remedies are inconsistent and the other party materially changes his position in reliance on the manifestation.

§ 379.   Election to Treat Duties of Performance Under Aleatory Contract as Discharged

If a right or duty of the injured party is conditional on an event that is fortuitous or is supposed by the parties to be fortuitous, he cannot treat his remaining duties to render performance as discharged on the ground of the other party's breach by non-performance if he does not manifest to the other party his intention to do so before any adverse change in the situation of the injured party resulting from the occurrence of that event or a material change in the probability of its occurrence.

§ 380.   Loss of Power of Avoidance by Affirmance

(1)   The power of a party to avoid a contract for incapacity, duress, undue influence or abuse of a fiduciary relation is lost if, after the circumstances that made the contract voidable have ceased to exist, he manifests to the other party his intention to affirm it or acts with respect to anything that he has received in a manner inconsistent with disaffirmance.

(2)   The power of a party to avoid a contract for mistake or misrepresentation is lost if after he knows or has reason to know of the mistake or of the misrepresentation if it is non-fraudulent or knows of the misrepresentation if it is fraudulent, he manifests to the other party his intention to affirm it or acts with respect to anything that he has received in a manner inconsistent with disaffirmance.

(3)   If the other party rejects an offer by the party seeking avoidance to return what he has received, the party seeking avoidance if entitled to restitution can, after the lapse of a reasonable time, enforce a lien on what he has received by selling it and crediting the proceeds toward his claim in restitution.

§ 381.   Loss of Power of Avoidance by Delay

(1)   The power of a party to avoid a contract for incapacity, duress, undue influence or abuse of a fiduciary relation is lost if, after the circumstances that made it voidable have ceased to exist, he does not within a reasonable time manifest to the other party his intention to avoid it.

(2)   The power of a party to avoid a contract for misrepresentation or mistake is lost if after he knows of a fraudulent misrepresentation or knows or has reason to know of a non-fraudulent misrepresentation or mistake he does not within a reasonable time manifest to the other party his intention to avoid it. The power of a party to avoid a contract for non-fraudulent misrepresentation or mistake is also lost if the contract has been so far performed or the circumstances have otherwise so changed that avoidance would be inequitable and if damages will be adequate compensation.

(3)   In determining what is a reasonable time, the following circumstances are significant:

(a)   the extent to which the delay enabled or might have enabled the party with the power of avoidance to speculate at the other party's risk;

(b)   the extent to which the delay resulted or might have resulted in justifiable reliance by the other party or by third persons;

(c)   the extent to which the ground for avoidance was the result of any fault by either party; and

(d)   the extent to which the other party's conduct contributed to the delay.

(4)   If a right or duty of the party who has the power of avoidance for non-fraudulent misrepresentation or mistake is conditional on an event that is fortuitous or is supposed by the parties to be fortuitous, a manifestation of intention under Subsection (1) or (2) is not effective unless it is made before any adverse change in his situation resulting from the occurrence of that event or a material change in the probability of its occurrence.

§ 382.   Loss of Power to Affirm by Prior Avoidance

(1)   If a party has effectively exercised his power of avoidance, a subsequent manifestation of intent to affirm is inoperative unless the other party manifests his assent to affirmance by refusal to accept a return of his performance or otherwise.

(2)   A party has not exercised his power of avoidance under the rule stated in Subsection (1) until

(a)   he has regained all or a substantial part of what he would be entitled to by way of restitution on avoidance,

(b)   he has obtained a final judgment of or based on avoidance, or

(c)   the other party has materially relied on or manifested his assent to a statement of disaffirmance.

§ 383.   Avoidance in Part

A contract cannot be avoided in part except that where one or more corresponding pairs of part performances have been fully performed by one or both parties the rest of the contract can be avoided.

§ 384.   Requirement That Party Seeking Restitution Return Benefit

(1)   Except as stated in Subsection (2), a party will not be granted restitution unless

(a)   he returns or offers to return, conditional on restitution, any interest in property that he has received in exchange in substantially as good condition as when it was received by him, or

(b)   the court can assure such return in connection with the relief granted.

(2)   The requirement stated in Subsection (1) does not apply to property

   (a)   that was worthless when received or that has been destroyed or lost by the other party or as a result of its own defects,

   (b)   that either could not from the time of receipt have been returned or has been used or disposed of without knowledge of the grounds for restitution if justice requires that compensation be accepted in its place and the payment of such compensation can be assured, or

   (c)   as to which the contract apportions the price if that part of the price is not included in the claim for restitution.

§ 385.   Effect of Power of Avoidance on Duty of Performance or on Duty Arising Out of Breach

(1)   Unless an offer to restore performance received is a condition of avoidance, a party has no duty of performance while his power of avoidance exists.

(2)   If an offer to restore performance received is a condition of avoidance, a duty to pay damages is terminated by such an offer made before the power of avoidance is lost.

RESTATEMENT (THIRD) OF SURETYSHIP AND GUARANTY

CHAPTER 2. FORMATION, ENFORCEMENT, AND INTERPRETATION OF THE SECONDARY OBLIGATION

TOPIC 2. ENFORCEMENT OF THE SECONDARY OBLIGATION

§ 11. Statute of Frauds

(1) Pursuant to the Statute of Frauds, a contract creating a secondary obligation is unenforceable as a contract to answer for the duty of another unless there is a written memorandum satisfying the Statute of Frauds or an exception applies.

(2) Without limiting the generality of subsection (1):

(a) When promises of the same performance are made by both the principal obligor and the secondary obligor for a consideration that benefits only the principal obligor, the promise of the secondary obligor is within the Statute of Frauds as a contract to answer for the duty of another, whether or not the promise is in terms conditional on default by the principal obligor, unless:

(i) the promises are in terms joint and do not create several duties or joint and several duties; or

(ii) the obligee neither knows nor has reason to know that the consideration does not inure to the benefit of the secondary obligor.

(b) A promise to enter into a written contract as secondary obligor for the performance of a duty owed to the obligee is within the Statute of Frauds.

(c) A contract by a person to purchase a right that the obligee has or may acquire against an obligor is within the Statute of Frauds as a contract to answer for the duty of another if the circumstances indicate that the purpose of the contract is to protect the obligee against loss arising from potential non-performance by the obligor by giving the obligee recourse against the purchaser as secondary obligor.

(3) Notwithstanding subsection (1):

(a) A contract creating a secondary obligation is not a contract to answer for the duty of another within the Statute of Frauds unless the obligee is a party to the contract and the obligee knows or has reason to know that the secondary obligor has suretyship status.

(b)   A contract to perform or otherwise satisfy all or part of a duty of the principal obligor to the obligee is not within the Statute of Frauds as a contract to answer for the duty of another if, by the terms of the promise when it is made, performance thereof can involve no more than:

(i)   the application of funds or property held by the secondary obligor for the purpose; or

(ii)   performance of any other duty owing, irrespective of the contract, by the secondary obligor to the obligee; or

(iii)   performance of a duty that is either owing, irrespective of the contract, by the secondary obligor to the principal obligor, or that the obligee reasonably believes to be so owing.

(c)   A contract that all or part of the duty of the principal obligor to the obligee shall be satisfied by the secondary obligor is not within the Statute of Frauds as a promise to answer for the duty of another if the consideration for the promise is in fact or apparently desired by the secondary obligor mainly for its own economic benefit, rather than the benefit of the principal obligor. If, however, the consideration is merely a fee for incurring the secondary obligation, the contract is within the Statute of Frauds.

(d)   A promise to indemnify against liability or loss made by the principal obligor or any other person to induce the secondary obligor to enter into the secondary obligation is not within the Statute of Frauds as a contract to answer for the duty of another.

(e)   A contract not within the Statute of Frauds as a contract to answer for the duty of another at the time the contract was made is not brought within the Statute by a subsequent promise of another person to assume performance of the duty as principal obligor.

(f)   A contract pursuant to which the assignor of a right promises that the obligor of the assigned right will perform its obligation is not within the Statute of Frauds as a contract to answer for the duty of another.

(g)   A promise by an obligee's agent that a purchaser of the obligee's goods or services through the agent will pay the price of the goods to the obligee is not within the Statute of Frauds as a contract to answer for the duty of another.

(h)   A secondary obligor's promise to the principal obligor to discharge a duty owed by the principal obligor to the obligee is not within the Statute of Frauds as a contract to answer for the duty of another.

Comment:

a. The Statute of Frauds. The so-called "suretyship provision" of the Statute of Frauds was included in different language in § 4 of the English Statute of Frauds, enacted in 1677. The English Statute was repealed in 1954 except for the suretyship and land contract provisions.

Section 4 of the English statute was generally copied in the United States, and the American statutes remain in force. In Maryland and New Mexico the English statute is in force by judicial decision. All the other states but Louisiana have statutes similar to the English statute, with some provisions omitted in a few states:

Alabama	Code § 8–9–2 (1993)
Alaska	Stat. § 09.25.010 (3) (1994)
Arizona	Rev. Stat. Ann. § 44–101 (1994)
Arkansas	Stat. § 4–59–101 (Michie 1987)
California	Civ. Code §§ 1624 (West 1985) (Supp.1996), 2793 (West 1993); but see § 2794 (West 1993)
Colorado	Rev. Stat. § 38–10–112 (1)(b) (1982) (Supp.1995)
Connecticut	Gen. Stat. § 52–550 (a)(2) (1991) (Supp.1995)
Delaware	Code tit. 6, § 2714; but see § 2712 (1993)
Dist. of Col.	Code § 28–3502 (1991)
Florida	Stat. § 725.01 (West 1988)
Georgia	Off. Code Ann. § 13–5–30 (1982) (Supp.1995); but see § 10–7–4 (1994)
Hawaii	Rev. Stat. § 656–1 (2) (1993)
Idaho	Code § 9–505 (1990) (Supp.1995)
Illinois	740 ILCS 80/1 (1995)
Indiana	Code Ann. § 32–2–1–1 (Burns 1995)
Iowa	Code § 622.32 (1950)
Kansas	Stat. Ann. § 33–106 (1993)
Kentucky	Rev. Stat. §§ 371.010 (4), 371.065 (Baldwin 1987) (Supp.1994)
Maine	Rev. Stat. tit. 33, § 51 (West 1988)
Massachusetts	Gen. Laws ch. 259, § 1 (1992)
Michigan	Comp. Laws § 566.132 (1993)
Minnesota	Stat. § 513.01 (1990)
Mississippi	Code § 15–3–1 (a) (1995)
Missouri	Rev. Stat. § 432.010 (1992)
Montana	Code § 28–2–903 (1)(b), but see § 28–11–105 (1995)
Nebraska	Rev. Stat. § 36–202 (1993)
Nevada	Rev. Stat. Ann. § 111.220 (Michie 1986)
New Hampshire	Rev. Stat. § 506:2 (1983)

New Jersey	Rev. Stat. § 25:1–5
New York	Gen. Oblig. Law § 5–701 (1989) (Supp.1996)
North Carolina	Gen. Stat. § 22–1 (1965)
North Dakota	Cent. Code § 9–06–04 (1987) (Supp.1995), but see § 22–01–05 (1991)
Ohio	Rev. Code § 1335.05 (Anderson 1993)
Oklahoma	Stat. tit. 15, § 136 (1983)
Oregon	Rev. Stat. § 41.580 (1)(b) (1993)
Pennsylvania	Con. Stat. tit. 33 § 3; but see § 4 (1967)
Rhode Island	Gen. Laws § 9–1–4 (4) (1985)
South Carolina	Code § 32–3–10 (2) (Law. Co-op. 1991)
South Dakota	Laws § 56–1–4; but see §§ 56–1–5 through 56–1–9 (1988)
Tennessee	Code § 29–2–101 (2) (1980)
Texas	Bus. & Com. Code § 26.01 (b)(2) (West 1987)
Utah	Code § 25–5–4 (1989)
Vermont	Stat. Ann. tit. 12, § 181 (1973) (Supp.1994)
Virginia	Code § 11–2 (1993)
Washington	Rev. Code § 19.36.010 (1989)
West Virginia	Code § 55–1–1 (d) (1994)
Wisconsin	Stat. § 241.02 (b) (1994)
Wyoming	Stat. Ann. § 1–23–105 (ii) (1988)

This section addresses the applicability of the Statute of Frauds to contracts creating secondary obligations. Satisfaction of the Statute is the subject of Restatement, Contracts, Topic 6, §§ 131–137. The consequences of noncompliance are the subject of Restatement, Second, Contracts, Topic 7, §§ 138–147.

b.   *The statutory purpose.* In general, the primary purpose of the Statute of Frauds is assumed to be evidentiary. In the case of secondary obligations, however, the Statute also serves the cautionary function of guarding the promisor against ill-considered action. The suretyship provision of the Statute is not limited to important or complex contracts, but applies to secondary obligations created by promises made to an obligee of the underlying obligation. Such promises serve a useful purpose, and the requirement of consideration is commonly met by the same promise or performance that is consideration for the principal obligation. However, other considerations militate in favor of requiring a writing: the motivation of the secondary obligor is often essentially gratuitous; its obligation depends on a contingency that may seem remote at the time of contracting; and natural formalities that often attend an extension of credit are unlikely to provide reliable evidence of the existence and terms of the secondary obligor's undertaking. Reliance of the kinds usual in such situations—extension of credit or forbearance to pursue the principal obligor—does not render the requirement inapplicable. It should be noted that the determination of what constitutes a writing or a signature in an environment of electronic data transmission must continue to evolve.

Illustrations:

1. D commits a tort against C. S orally promises C to pay C the damages that C suffered from the tort if D fails to do so. S's promise is within the Statute of Frauds because D is under a direct duty to C and S's promise is to perform D's duty if D fails to do so.

2. S orally promises C to guarantee the performance of any duty that D may incur to C within the ensuing year. Relying on this promise, C enters into a contract with D, by which D undertakes within the year to select materials for a house and to act as supervising architect during its construction. D, without excuse, fails to perform his contract. S's promise is within the Statute of Frauds.

3. D, an infant, obtains goods on credit from C, who is induced to part with them by S's oral guaranty that D will pay the price as agreed. The goods are not necessaries but D is subject to a duty to pay for them, though the duty is voidable. S's promise is within the Statute of Frauds.

4. D, a mentally impaired person under guardianship, obtains goods on credit from C, who is induced to part with them by S's oral guaranty that D will keep his promise to pay the price. D's promise is void. S's promise is not within the Statute of Frauds because there is no underlying obligation.

Comment to Subsection (2)(a):

c. Rationale. Unless a contrary intention is manifested, the fact that promises of the same performance are made by two persons for a consideration that inures to the benefit of only one of them sufficiently shows that the other is a secondary obligor. In addition, because an obligee who has reason to know that the consideration inures to the benefit of only one has reason to know of the suretyship status, the exception set forth in subsection (3)(a) does not apply.

d. Joint obligations. Historically, joint promisors were treated for many purposes as a unit. Hence, as against one joint promisor the obligation of his co-promisor was not treated as that "of another" within the Statute of Frauds, even though a suretyship relation in fact existed between them. In modern times the historic rules governing joint obligations have been greatly modified by statute or decision in most states. See Restatement, Second, Contracts, Chapter 13. But where the distinction between joint duties and joint and several duties retains significance, the suretyship provision of the Statute of Frauds does not apply to the suretyship status between joint promisors.

Illustrations:

5. D and S jointly and orally promise C to pay C for goods that C knows are to be delivered for the exclusive benefit of D. If S is under no several duty, his promise is not within the Statute of Frauds.

6. The facts being otherwise as stated in Illustration 5, the promise is joint and several. S's promise is within the Statute of Frauds.

7. The facts being otherwise as stated in Illustration 6, C has no reason to know that the goods are not for the benefit of both parties. S's promise is not within the Statute of Frauds.

Comment to Subsection (2)(b):

e. Scope. The promises covered by this subsection are not in terms promises to answer for a duty of another. They are promises to execute written instruments by which the promisor will on signing undertake to answer for such a duty. In substance, however, such promises, if binding, subject the promisor to an action if the performance due from the principal obligor is not rendered. This subsection is applicable whether the promise relates to an existing duty or to one expected to arise in the future.

Illustrations:

> 8.   In consideration of a loan by C to D, S orally promises C to execute a written instrument guaranteeing the debt. S's promise is within the Statute of Frauds.

> 9.   D owes C $1,000. In consideration of C's forbearance to sue D, S orally promises C that S will sign as acceptor for the accommodation of D a draft for $1,000 to be drawn by D. S's promise is within the Statute of Frauds.

Comment to Subsection (2)(c):

f.   Secondary obligation in the form of contract to purchase. Ordinarily a promise to buy a right and a promise to pay the debt of another are quite different transactions. Thus, a promise to buy does not generally result in the promisor having suretyship status and the promise is not within the suretyship provision of the Statute of Frauds. The promise may nevertheless be within other Statute of Fraud provisions, particularly Uniform Commercial Code §§ 1–206, 9–203 (1995). See Restatement, Second, Contracts § 110. Where, however, a promise to buy a debt is conditional on the debtor's actual or potential default and the amount to be paid is essentially the same as if the debt had been guaranteed, the promisor is a secondary obligor with suretyship status and the promise is within the suretyship provision of the Statute of Frauds. The distinction between a contract to buy in which the promisor has suretyship status and one in which the promisor does not have that status

does not lie in any formal difference in the words used but in the reality of the transaction. For the purposes of the Statute of Frauds, the test is whether in all the circumstances the essential purpose of the promise is to protect the promisee against the actual or potential nonperformance of the debtor by giving the promisee recourse against the promisor. Compare § 1, Comment h and Illustrations 13–14.

Illustration:

> 10.   D corporation owes C $1,000, which is due. S orally promises C that if C will grant D an extension of 60 days, S will purchase the debt at that time if it is not then paid. The circumstances indicate that S is really guaranteeing the account, and the promise is unenforceable.

Comment to Subsection (3)(a):

g.   Promisee must be obligee; "reason to know." The suretyship provision does not apply to a promise unless the promisee is the obligee. Moreover, the obligee-promisee must know or have reason to know of the secondary obligor's suretyship status, either from the terms of its contract with the principal obligor or the secondary obligor or from extrinsic facts.

Illustrations:

> 11.   S, for consideration, orally promises E to pay a debt of E's child D to C, if D fails to pay it at maturity. S's promise is not within the Statute of Frauds because it was made to E, not to the obligee C.

> 12.   In an unsigned writing, D and S severally and unconditionally promise C, for consideration inuring to the benefit of both D and S, that C shall be paid the sum of $100 a month for the next six months. D has induced S to make this promise by promising to hold S harmless, making S a secondary obligor. If C

knows or has reason to know of this contract between D and S when S makes the promise to C, S's promise is unenforceable. Otherwise S's promise is not within the Statute of Frauds.

Comment to Subsection (3)(b):

h.   Rationale. Where the secondary obligor, if it performs the secondary obligation, will be doing no more than it is bound to do by reason of a duty other than that imposed by the secondary obligation, the promise is not within the Statute of Frauds. In such a case, even though the secondary obligor has suretyship status, the secondary obligor promises to answer for its own obligation as well as that of another and is not within the reason of the Statute. The terms of the secondary obligation will commonly refer to the independent duty, but need not do so. The independent duty may exist when the secondary obligation is created or may arise subsequently.

i.   Application of funds. Paragraph (3)(b)(i) deals primarily with cases where the secondary obligor is a trustee and the obligee a beneficiary of the trust, although the trust relationship is not essential. In such cases, the secondary obligation usually shows by its terms the independent duty and the limitation of the secondary obligation. To the extent that the secondary obligation goes beyond the duty, the case is not within paragraph (3)(b)(i).

Illustrations:

13.   D owes C $100 and pays that sum to S in trust to pay it to C. Then or thereafter S orally promises C to pay D's debt. Whether or not C knows of the trust, C acquires an enforceable right against S.

14.   D pays $100 to S in trust to apply it to whatever judgment C may recover against D in an action then pending. S orally promises C to pay the judgment in full. C recovers judgment for $125. C has an enforceable right against S for only $100.

j.   Other independent duties. Where the secondary obligor merely promises to perform an independent duty owed to the obligee or to the principal obligor, the secondary obligation is not within the Statute. In such cases the terms of the secondary obligation often do not disclose the independent duty. Where the obligee in good faith believes, at the time that the secondary obligation is created, that an independent duty is owed by the secondary obligor to his co-obligor, the same rule is applied even though the duty does not in fact exist.

Illustrations:

15.   S is a member of a partnership. After S retires but before the debts of the partnership are paid, S orally promises C, a partnership creditor whose claim relates to a transaction predating S's retirement, to pay the amount due C. The promise is not within the Statute of Frauds.

16.   S, at D's request, orally promises C to guarantee the payment by D to C of the price of any goods sold by C to D, to the extent of the indebtedness S may owe D at the time that C notifies S that D has defaulted. C thereupon sells goods to D. S's promise is not within the Statute of Frauds.

17.   S and D severally promise C to pay for goods to be delivered to D. The goods are actually for S and D is the actual secondary obligor, but S and D lead C to suppose that S is the secondary obligor. S's promise is not within the Statute of Frauds; under subsection (2)(a)(ii) neither is D's.

Comment to Subsection (3)(c):

k.   Rationale. This subsection states what is often called the "main purpose" or "leading object" rule. Where the secondary obligors's main purpose is its own pecuniary or business advantage, the gratuitous or sentimental element often present in suretyship is eliminated, the likelihood of disproportion in the values exchanged between secondary obligor and obligee is reduced, and the commercial context commonly provides evidentiary safeguards. Thus, there is less need for cautionary or evidentiary formality than in other secondary obligations. Historically, the rule could be reconciled with the terms of the Statute on the ground that a secondary obligor who received a bargained-for benefit could be sued in debt or indebitatus assumpsit; hence, it promised to pay its debt rather than the debt "of another," and the promise was not "special" in the sense that special assumpsit was the only appropriate remedy. In modern times, however, the rule is applied in terms of its reason rather than to accord with abandoned procedural categories.

l.   Factors affecting application of the rule. The fact that there is consideration for the secondary obligation is insufficient to bring the rule of subsection (3)(c) into play. Slight and indirect possible advantage to the secondary obligor is similarly insufficient. The expected advantage must be such as to justify the conclusion that the main purpose of the secondary obligor in making the promise is to advance its own interests. The following factors tend to indicate such a main purpose when there is an expected pecuniary or business advantage: prior default; inability or repudiation of the principal obligor; forbearance of the obligee to enforce a lien on property in which the secondary obligor has an interest or which it intends to use; equivalence between the value of the benefit and the amount promised; and lack of par-ticipation by the principal obligor in the making of the secondary obligor's promise. The benefit may be supplied to the secondary obligor by the obligee, by the principal obligor, or by some other person; if it is substantial and meets the main purpose test it may come indirectly through benefit to the principal obligor.

Illustrations:

18.   D owes C $1,000. C is about to levy an attachment on D's factory. S, who is a friend of D desiring to prevent D's financial ruin, orally promises C that if C will forbear to take legal proceedings against D for three months, S will pay D's debt if D fails to do so. S has no purpose to benefit herself and C has no reason to suppose so. S's promise is not enforceable.

19.   D owes C $1,000. C is about to levy an attachment on D's factory. S, also a creditor of D, fearing that the attachment will ruin D's business and thereby destroy S's chance of collecting S's own claim, orally promises C that if C will forbear to take legal proceedings against D for three months, S will pay D's debt if D fails to do so. S's promise is enforceable.

20.   D contracts with S to build a house for S. C contracts with D to furnish materials for the purpose. D fails to pay C for some of the materials furnished. C justifiably refuses to furnish further materials. S orally promises C that, if C will continue to furnish D with materials that C had previously agreed to furnish, S will pay the price not only for the materials already furnished but also for the remaining materials if D fails to do so. S's promise is enforceable.

m.   Premiums. Excluded from the main purpose rule are contracts of guaranty insurance, whether or not making such contracts is the secondary obligor's regular business. Promises of commercial surety companies are practically always in writing. An isolated oral guaranty by an individual is within the reason of the Statute if a small fee is paid for guaranty of a much larger debt.

Illustration:

21. In consideration of a premium of $100, S guarantees C in an unsigned writing the fidelity of D, C's employee, during D's term of employment. The guaranty is not enforceable.

Comment to Subsection (3)(d):

n. Principal obligor as indemnitor. Where the indemnitor is the principal obligor, the promise to indemnify is not within the Statute of Frauds because it is not a promise to answer for the debt of another.

Illustrations:

22. I promises to indemnify S if S will guarantee I's obligation to C. I's promise is not within the Statute of Frauds. S's promise is.

23. I promises to indemnify S if S will sign an accommodation note to C for I's benefit. I's promise is not within the Statute of Frauds.

o. Third party indemnitor. The principal obligor owes several duties to the secondary obligor. See §§ 18, 21–22. A promise by a third party to indemnify the secondary obligor against breach of these duties is, strictly speaking, a promise to answer for the default of the principal obligor in the event of the breach of its duties to the secondary obligor. Such treatment is appropriate when it accords with the understanding of the parties. Commonly, however, the parties treat the promise to indemnify as a promise to a prospective debtor rather than as a promise to a prospective creditor. So viewed, the promise is not within the Statute. See subsection (3)(h). Many such cases are also with the main purpose rule. See subsection (3)(c). In any event, they do not ordinarily present the need for cautionary and evidentiary formalities that the Statute is designed to meet.

Illustrations:

24. I requests S to indorse notes made by I's child D, in order to enable D to obtain credit for use in D's business, and orally promises to indemnify S for any resulting loss. S indorses the notes as requested. I's promise is not within the Statute of Frauds.

25. To induce C, a commercial surety company, to file a bond in an action against D Corporation, S gives C a written guaranty against loss. After judgment against D corporation, I, a shareholder of D Corporation, orally promises S to indemnify S against loss. Unless I's promise is within the main purpose rule, it is within the Statute of Frauds because it was not made to induce C to enter into its contract.

Comment to Subsection (3)(e):

p. Scope. An obligor of a duty may become a secondary obligor by agreement with another who subsequently assumes the duty, thereby becoming the principal obligor, but this will not make the original promise subject to the Statute of Frauds. The rule stated in this subsection applies, for example, where a partner retires from a partnership and the remaining partners agree to assume all of the partnership obligations. If the obligation on which the retiring partner was originally bound was oral, it does not becomes unenforceable merely because, as between the retiring partner and the others, the retiring partner becomes a secondary obligor.

Comment to Subsections (3)(f) and (3)(g):

q.   *Rationale.* The promisors referred to in these subsections become secondary obligors for the debts of others, but the promises are commonly made in contexts that provide evidence of the promises and eliminate the need of cautionary formality. The assignor's promise that the obligor of an assigned right will perform its obligation is ordinarily made to provide recourse against the assignor as part of the sale of that right and, thus, is for a consideration wholly for the assignor's own benefit. See subsection (3)(c). The selling agent who guarantees customers' accounts is commonly called a "del credere factor"; an important inducement for the promise is the agent's desire to advance his or her own interest. In addition, the guaranty is likely to be part of a course of business rather than an isolated transaction.

Illustrations:

26.   S, who is owed $1,000 by D, sells that claim against D to C, orally guaranteeing that D will pay the debt. As a result of this sale, C becomes the obligee and S becomes a secondary obligor with suretyship status. However, S's promise is not within the Statute.

27.   S is engaged in selling goods for others on commission. To induce C to employ S, S orally guarantees payment by those to whom S sells C's goods. Later, S sells goods for C on credit to D. S's promise is not within the Statute.

Comment to Subsection (3)(h):

r.   Rationale. In most cases, the promise described in this subsection will give the obligee as beneficiary a direct right against the secondary obligor without destroying its right against the principal obligor. The promise is not within the Statute of Frauds, however, because the Statute is designed to require written evidence only in the case where the promise is made to the obligee. In contrast to the language of the Statute, the contract considered in subsection (3)(h) is one to answer for the default of the promisee, not for the default "of another."

Illustration:

28.   D owes C $100. S orally promises D that S will discharge the debt, or promises to lend D money with which to pay it. In either case, S's promise is not within the Statute of Frauds.

RESTATEMENT (THIRD) OF RESTITUTION AND UNJUST ENRICHMENT

(SELECTED SECTIONS)

§ 1. Restitution and Unjust Enrichment

A person who is unjustly enriched at the expense of another is subject to liability in restitution.

Comment:

... *b. Unjust enrichment.* The law of restitution is predominantly the law of unjust enrichment, but "unjust enrichment" is a term of art. The substantive part of the law of restitution is concerned with identifying those forms of enrichment that the law treats as "unjust" for purposes of imposing liability. . . .

In reality, the law of restitution is very far from imposing liability for every instance of what might plausibly be called unjust enrichment. The law's potential for intervention in transactions that might be challenged as inequitable is narrower, more predictable, and more objectively determined than the unconstrained implications of the words "unjust enrichment." Equity and good conscience might see an unjust enrichment in the performance of a valid but unequal bargain, or in the legally protected refusal to perform an equal one (as where the statute of limitations bars enforcement of a valid debt). Beyond these merely legal instances, moreover, "unjust enrichment" (in the natural and nontechnical sense of the words) might seem to be a pervasive fact of human experience—given any prior standard (such as equality or merit) by which people's relative entitlements might be measured.

The concern of restitution is not, in fact, with unjust enrichment in any such broad sense, but with a narrower set of circumstances giving rise to what might more appropriately be called unjustified enrichment. Compared to the open-ended implications of the term "unjust enrichment," instances of unjustified enrichment are both predictable and objectively determined, because the justification in question is not moral but legal. Unjustified enrichment is enrichment that lacks an adequate legal basis; it results from a transaction that the law treats as ineffective to work a conclusive alteration in ownership rights. Broadly speaking, an ineffective transaction for these purposes is one that is nonconsensual. . . .

c. Restitution and restoration. Employed to denote liability based on unjust enrichment, the word "restitution" is a term of art that has frequently proved confusing. . . . On the one hand, there are significant instances of liability based on unjust enrichment that do not involve the restoration of anything the claimant previously possessed. The most notable examples are cases involving the disgorgement of profits, or other benefits wrongfully obtained, in excess of the plaintiff's loss. . . . On the other hand, there are numerous situations in which a claimant's undoubted right to the restitution (or restoration) of something does not depend on the unjust enrichment of the defendant. Thus if a transfer has been induced by misrepresentation, the transferor is entitled to rescission and restitution even if the transferee—having paid market value—cannot plausibly be said to have been enriched. . . .

229

e. Liability and remedy. The fact that the word "restitution" is used to designate both liabilities and remedies in unjust enrichment leads to a series of common misunderstandings:. . .

Finally and most generally, the choice of the word "restitution" as the name for the subject has led to a common misconception about what "the law of restitution" involves. This is the idea that restitution is essentially a remedy, and that the remedy of restitution is a device available in appropriate circumstances—as an alternative to damages—to enforce obligations derived from torts, contracts, and other topics of substantive law. . . . A liability in unjust enrichment (restitution) is enforced by restitution's characteristic remedies, some (but not all) of which involve a literal restitution or giving back; and a claim in unjust enrichment (restitution) is subject to characteristic defenses. . . .

Particular contexts invite further qualification. There are remedies for breach of contract that have frequently been called "restitution" and have sometimes been explained in terms of unjust enrichment. This Restatement describes them as a part of contract law, not restitution, and it rejects the supposed connection with principles of unjust enrichment. . . .

§ 2.   Limiting Principles

(1)   The fact that a recipient has obtained a benefit without paying for it does not of itself establish that the recipient has been unjustly enriched.

(2)   A valid contract defines the obligations of the parties as to matters within its scope, displacing to that extent any inquiry into unjust enrichment.

(3)   There is no liability in restitution for an unrequested benefit voluntarily conferred, unless the circumstances of the transaction justify the claimant's intervention in the absence of contract.

(4)   Liability in restitution may not subject an innocent recipient to a forced exchange: in other words, an obligation to pay for a benefit that the recipient should have been free to refuse.

Comment:

. . . *c. Restitution subordinate to contract.* Judicial statements to the effect that "there can be no unjust enrichment in contract cases" can be misleading if taken casually. Restitution claims of great practical significance arise in a contractual context, but they occur at the margins, when a valuable performance has been rendered under a contract that is invalid, or subject to avoidance, or otherwise ineffective to regulate the parties' obligations. Applied to any such circumstance, the statement that there can be no unjust enrichment in contract cases is plainly erroneous. . . .

Properly interpreted, however, the same statement acknowledges an important limit to liability in unjust enrichment. Contract is superior to restitution as a means of regulating voluntary transfers because it eliminates, or minimizes, the fundamental difficulty of valuation. Considerations of both justice and efficiency require that private transfers be made pursuant to contract whenever reasonably possible, and that the parties' own definition of their respective obligations—assuming the validity of their agreement by all pertinent tests—take precedence over the obligations that the law would impose in the absence of agreement.

Restitution is accordingly subordinate to contract as an organizing principle of private relationships, and the terms of an enforceable agreement normally displace any claim of unjust enrichment within their reach. . . .

d. *Benefits voluntarily conferred.* Instead of proposing a bargain, the restitution claimant first confers a benefit, then seeks payment for its value. When this manner of proceeding is unacceptable—as it usually is, if the claimant neglects an opportunity to contract—a claim based on unjust enrichment will be denied.

The limitation of § 2(3) is traditionally expressed by denying restitution to a claimant characterized as "officious," an "intermeddler," or a "volunteer."

This section states the same rule, substituting a functional explanation for the familiar epithets. Because contract is strongly preferred over restitution as a basis for private obligations (see Comment c), restitution is not usually available to a claimant who has neglected a suitable opportunity to make a contract beforehand.

There are cases in which a claimant may indeed recover compensation for unrequested benefits intentionally conferred—because the claimant's intervention was justified under the circumstances, and because a liability in restitution will not prejudice the recipient. . . . Some are cases of emergency intervention, where the claimant intervenes to protect the interests of the recipient or of third persons. . . .

§ 3. Wrongful Gain

A person is not permitted to profit by his own wrong.

Comment:

a. *General principles and scope; relation to other sections.* The present section marks one of the cornerstones of the law of restitution and unjust enrichment. The general principle it identifies is the one underlying the "disgorgement" remedies in restitution, whereby a claimant potentially recovers more than a provable loss so that the defendant may be stripped of a wrongful gain. . . .

Breach of an enforceable contract is not a source of unjust enrichment or wrongful gain, except in the special case of profitable and opportunistic breach (§ 39). . . .

c. *Recovery exceeding the claimant's loss.* When the defendant has acted in conscious disregard of the claimant's rights, the whole of the resulting gain is treated as unjust enrichment, even though the defendant's gain may exceed both (i) the measurable injury to the claimant, and (ii) the reasonable

value of a license authorizing the defendant's conduct. . . .

Restitution requires full disgorgement of profit by a conscious wrongdoer, not just because of the moral judgment implicit in the rule of this section, but because any lesser liability would provide an inadequate incentive to lawful behavior. If A anticipates (accurately) that unauthorized interference with B's entitlement may yield profits exceeding any damages B could prove, A has a dangerous incentive to take without asking—since the nonconsensual transaction promises to be more profitable than the forgone negotiation with B. The objective of that part of the law of restitution summarized by the rule of § 3 is to frustrate any such calculation.

It follows that "inadequacy of a remedy at law" is not a requirement of a claim in restitution to disgorgement of wrongful gain. See § 4(2). With the sole exception of § 39—where inadequacy of contract damages is one of the conditions of the restitution claim—it may be assumed in disgorgement cases that the injury to the claimant could be calculated with precision, and that damages would yield what is ordinarily regarded as full compensation for the harm. Yet a remedy limited to compensation does not vindicate the claimant's right to insist that the transaction at issue—typically, some use by the defendant of the claimant's property—take place by agreement with the claimant or not at all. If a conscious wrongdoer were able to make profitable, unauthorized use of the claimant's property, then pay only the objective value of the assets taken or the harm inflicted, the anomalous result would be to legitimate a kind of private eminent domain (in favor of a wrongdoer) and to subject the claimant to a forced exchange. The law of restitution responds to this anomaly by making the wrongdoer liable to disgorge profits wrongfully obtained, whenever such profits exceed recoverable damages. . . .

§ 4. Restitution May Be Legal or Equitable or Both

(1) Liabilities and remedies within the law of restitution and unjust enrichment may have originated in law, in equity, or in a combination of the two.

(2) A claimant otherwise entitled to a remedy for unjust enrichment, including a remedy originating in equity, need not demonstrate the inadequacy of available remedies at law.

Comment:

a. *General principles and scope.* The status of restitution as belonging to law or to equity has been ambiguous from the outset. The answer is that restitution may be either or both. . . . The chameleon-like qualities of the term "restitution" permit its invocation in a variety of circumstances where the legal or equitable nature of a given remedy may not be apparent. . . .

c. *Persistent errors.* . . . The most widespread error is the assertion that a claim in restitution or unjust enrichment is by its nature equitable rather than legal. From this false premise a court may conclude, depending on the problem at hand, (i) that there is no right to jury trial of a particular issue; (ii) that the remedy in question is available where it might otherwise not be, because the relevant statute authorizes "equitable relief"; or (iii) that the claim in question may be dismissed because the plaintiff has an adequate remedy at law. The first two conclusions may be justifiable for other reasons, but courts frequently reach them by mischaracterizing the law of restitution and unjust enrichment. . . . The third conclusion is simply wrong. See Comment *e.* . . .

e. *Adequacy of remedies at law.* Courts too often recite that one of the requirements of a claim based on unjust enrichment is the absence of an adequate legal remedy. This spurious proposition rests on an obvious fallacy, and it obscures what courts are actually doing when they invoke it. See § 4(2).

The quickest demonstration of the fallacy involved in any such statement lies in the fact that a modern claim in restitution or unjust enrichment is so often the equivalent of a cause of action that was available at law. See Comments *b* and *c*. Whenever the claim in unjust enrichment might be so characterized, the suggestion that the claimant must show the absence of a remedy at law is a palpable error. Courts that dismiss a claim of unjust enrichment based on a supposed "inadequacy" requirement are usually motivated by different concerns. . . .

The rule of § 39, allowing disgorgement of profits realized by an opportunistic breach of contract, inquires whether "the available damage remedy affords inadequate protection to the promisee's contractual entitlement." The particular concerns about adequacy of damages that explain this reference in the context of § 39 recur nowhere else in this Restatement. Section 4(2) is stated in broad terms, without reference to § 39, in order to convey as clearly as possible a general truth about the modern law of restitution and unjust enrichment; but § 4(2) may be qualified by reference to § 39(1), to the extent of any perceived inconsistency.

§ 5. Invalidating Mistake

(1) A transfer induced by invalidating mistake is subject to rescission and restitution. The transferee is liable in restitution as necessary to avoid unjust enrichment. . . .

(2) An invalidating mistake may be a misapprehension of either fact or law. There is invalidating mistake only when

   (a)   but for the mistake the transaction in question would not have taken place; and

   (b)   the claimant does not bear the risk of the mistake.

(3) A claimant bears the risk of a mistake when

   (a)   the risk is allocated to the claimant by agreement of the parties;

   (b)   the claimant has consciously assumed the risk by deciding to act in the face of a recognized uncertainty; or

   (c)   allocation to the claimant of the risk in question accords with the common understanding of the transaction concerned.

(4) A claimant does not bear the risk of a mistake merely because the mistake results from the claimant's negligence.

Comment:

. . . *d.   Mutual and unilateral mistake.* The distinction drawn in the law of contracts between mutual and unilateral mistake has no direct application to the law of restitution. When a plaintiff seeks restitution on account of mistake, the basis of liability is that the plaintiff has conferred an unintended benefit on the defendant; the unintentional character of the plaintiff's act is independent of the defendant's state of mind. In many restitution scenarios, moreover, the usual distinction between unilateral and mutual mistake has no meaningful application. If an insurance company pays a beneficiary more than is due on a policy, and the beneficiary assumes that the payment received reflects the amount due, there is a sense in which the company has committed a unilateral mistake; there is another sense in which both parties share a common mistake as to their contractual position. In such a situation, the attempted distinction between mutual and unilateral mistake is simply beside the point. . . .

g.   Mistake of fact and mistake of law. The present section rejects any distinction between mistake of fact and mistake of law, adopting a conclusion reached long ago by the better-reasoned American decisions. The old distinction between mistake of fact and mistake of law is repudiated because it has always been theoretically unsound; because the two types of mistake are frequently impossible to distinguish as a practical matter; and because the distinction, even when it is possible, has no relevance to the real analysis by which restitution is either granted or withheld. If a benefit is conferred by mistake, in circumstances that would otherwise support a claim in restitution, neither the unjustified enrichment of the recipient nor the unintentional dispossession of the transferor is affected by a determination that the mistake was one of fact, one of law, or an amalgam of the two.

§ 10. Mistaken Improvements

A person who improves the real or personal property of another, acting by mistake, has a claim in restitution as necessary to prevent unjust enrichment. A remedy for mistaken improvement that subjects the owner to a forced exchange will be qualified or limited to avoid undue prejudice to the owner.

§ 12. Mistake in Expression

If an instrument is intended to transfer an interest in property or to embody an obligation pursuant to a valid agreement, and

(a) by a mistake as to its contents or legal effect, the instrument fails to reflect the terms of the agreement; and

(b) performance or enforcement on the terms of the instrument has resulted or would result in the unjust enrichment of one party at the expense of another;

then the person disadvantaged by the mistake has a claim in restitution as necessary to prevent the unjust enrichment of the other.

Comment:

. . . *b. Relation to contract law.* The rule stated in this section overlaps with the doctrine of reformation in the law of contracts. A claim to reformation of an executory contract might be brought within the terms of this section or of Restatement Second, Contracts § 155. A uniform legal response is susceptible of consistent alternative explanations. The rationale in contract is that reformation gives effect to the real agreement of the parties; the rationale in restitution is that reformation avoids the unjust enrichment of one party at the expense of the other.

Cases in which a contracting party seeks reformation of an executory contract, or of an instrument intended to embody the contractual obligation, might be explained equally well by either rationale. . . . Where property has already been transferred, the intuitive applicability of restitution and contract principles may diverge. Supposing that Blackacre has been conveyed under a mistaken deed description, the error might result in the conveyance of either more or less land than the parties intended.. . . Either way, the party adversely affected might seek to reform the deed to conform to the agreement. In the case of underperformance, the immediate explanation of the grantee's claim is in terms of contract; while in the case of overperformance, it is natural for the mistaken grantor to focus on the grantee's unjust enrichment. As in the case of mistaken payments, the focus of restitution for mistake in expression is accordingly on overperformance rather than underperformance of a contractual obligation. . . .

e. Mutual mistake. A mistake in expression justifying relief under this section need not be "mutual," nor does restitution depend on attributing the mistake to one person rather than another. The distinction between mutual and unilateral mistake is relevant to the contract problem of mistake in basic assumptions: it may accordingly be relevant to determining whether the parties (as the claimant necessarily alleges) formed a valid agreement with which the instrument in question is inconsistent. See Restatement Second, Contracts §§ 152–154. But the distinction is not helpful in analyzing the problem of mistake in expression, which can only arise against the background of an otherwise valid agreement.

The relevant mistake in such cases consists in the assumption that an instrument correctly reflects the terms of the transaction as agreed, when in fact it does not. The circumstance that potentially justifies a claim in restitution is the fact of a divergence between the terms of the instrument and the terms of the agreement, not the degree to which the parties may have turned their minds to the correctness of an instrument that they may or may not have prepared.

§ 13. Fraud and Misrepresentation

(1) A transfer induced by fraud or material misrepresentation is subject to rescission and restitution. The transferee is liable in restitution as necessary to avoid unjust enrichment.

(2) A transfer induced by fraud is void if the transferor had neither knowledge of, nor reasonable opportunity to learn, the character of the resulting transfer or its essential terms. Otherwise the transferee obtains voidable title.

Comment:

. . . *b. Relation to contract law.* Because most transfers are made pursuant to contract, rules that determine when such a transfer is subject to rescission for fraudulent inducement necessarily coincide with rules that determine when the agreement itself is subject to avoidance. In the case of a contractual transfer, therefore, the consequences of fraudulent inducement may be simultaneously a part of contract law and of the law of restitution. The rules here stated are intended to be fully consistent with the rules stated in Restatement Second, Contracts §§ 163–164, 372, and 376.

Where contract is concerned with the effectiveness of an agreement, the focus of restitution is on the effectiveness of any resulting transfer. Although many issues of fraudulent inducement are simultaneously a question of contract and of restitution, the overlap between the subjects at this point is not complete. Avoidance of a wholly executory contract, whether the reason is fraud or something else, presents no issue of restitution. Reversal of a completed exchange—whatever the basis of invalidity—is squarely within the province of restitution, while it is explained only awkwardly as a liability in contract. . . .

§ 14. Duress

(1) Duress is coercion that is wrongful as a matter of law.

(2) A transfer induced by duress is subject to rescission and restitution. The transferee is liable in restitution as necessary to avoid unjust enrichment.

(3) If the effect of duress is tantamount to physical compulsion, a transfer induced by duress is void. If not, a transfer induced by duress conveys voidable title.

Comment:

...b. *The problem of definition.* Duress is frequently defined as a threat that overcomes a person's free will or destroys a person's "apparent consent." Such a definition underscores the element that duress has in common with the other transactional defects addressed in this Topic, all of which make a transfer subject to rescission on grounds related to the validity of the transferor's consent to the transaction. As a standard for identifying the circumstances that constitute duress, however, a definition that relies on such measures as "overcoming the plaintiff's will" or "leaving the plaintiff no reasonable alternative" is unsatisfactory for several reasons.

As a purely descriptive matter, such formulas imply that the coercive pressure that constitutes duress must be overwhelming in degree, foreclosing any realistic choice between courses of action. Yet there are numerous circumstances in which this is plainly not the case. Where coercion is independently tortious or illegal, the party seeking rescission need only establish that the coercion induced the transfer. The same standard is likely to apply when one party exerts pressure on another in bad faith, to extract a payment to which the first party has no colorable claim. In other cases, the conclusion that particular acts constitute duress is facilitated by analyzing the transaction in reverse. If unjust enrichment is easy to demonstrate and easy to measure (as where the claimant, in response to pressure, has overpaid a subsisting obligation), relatively modest pressure may be found to constitute duress if there is no other basis on which to order restitution. . . .

A definition of duress that refers to overcoming the will or destroying the free agency of the victim necessarily implies either that there is a protected realm of uncoerced transactions, or that there is a threshold of resistance to pressure beyond which the victim, initially a free agent, no longer acts voluntarily. Neither implication is satisfactory, in view of the constraints to which every human choice is evidently subject; in particular, the significant coercion that may be lawfully exercised, in many circumstances, by a simple refusal to deal except on a party's own terms. The conclusion of every bargain transaction might be said to involve overcoming the other party's will, but few bargains will be condemned as involuntary. The fact that one party to a bargain has been obliged to choose between undesirable courses of action—even if it might be commonly said that he had "no reasonable alternative"—does not of itself make the bargain involuntary, so long as the other party's threat or refusal is not regarded as wrongful.

Ultimately the idea of duress turns on a distinction, not between voluntary and coerced transactions, but between permissible and impermissible forms of coercion. A decision about what constitutes wrongful coercion performs the whole work of the definition. . . .

§ 16. Incapacity of Transferor

(1) A transfer by a person lacking requisite legal capacity is subject to rescission and restitution unless ratified. The transferee is liable in restitution as necessary to avoid unjust enrichment.

(2) Except as otherwise provided by statute:

(a) A transfer by a minor confers voidable title.

(b) When a transfer is challenged on the ground of mental capacity:

(i) if at the time of the transfer the transferor's incapacity has been adjudicated and is continuing, the transfer is void;

(ii) if the transferor's incapacity is only adjudicated thereafter, the transfer confers voidable title. . . .

(3) If the transferee has dealt with the transferor in good faith on reasonable terms, then notwithstanding the transferor's incapacity

(a) rescission and restitution leaves the transferor liable in restitution for benefits received in the transaction . . . ; and

(b) the court may qualify or deny the right to rescission to avoid an inequitable result. . . .

Comment:

a. General principles and scope; relation to other sections. . . . When a transfer occurs as part of an exchange transaction, the rules of this section overlap substantially with the corresponding rules of contract law. See Restatement Second, Contracts §§ 12–16. Both the test of incapacity, and the rules relating to such collateral matters as disaffirmance and ratification, will be the same whether the case arises in restitution or in contract. But the characteristic applications of the two bodies of law are to different stages of the exchange transaction. Where lack of capacity is interposed as a defense to a party's obligation under a wholly executory contract, the case presents no issue of restitution. Conversely, where a party seeks to rescind an executed conveyance on the ground of incapacity, the enforceability of a purported contractual obligation is no longer directly relevant. . . .

e. Unjust enrichment as a result of rescission; good faith of transferee; notice of incapacity. Like the other voidable transfers described in this Chapter, a transfer by a person who lacks legal capacity is not the product of the transferor's unimpeded and legally effective consent. But the problem of incapacity differs significantly from other transactional defects that share this common feature. Unlike fraud, duress, or undue influence, a finding of incapacity does not establish that the transferor has been the victim of a wrong. Unlike most transfers induced by mistake, a transfer by an incapacitated person does not necessarily result in the unjust enrichment of the transferee. A transfer by an incapacitated person that is only voidable, not void, is not necessarily one that the law endeavors to suppress. Unlike most transfers subject to rescission, a transfer by an incapacitated person may be part of a transaction that is fair, reasonable, and ultimately beneficial to the transferor. In some circumstances, moreover, the effect of unwinding a transaction on the ground of incapacity would be to create unjust enrichment, rather than to reverse it. . . .

American law has traditionally shown greater indulgence toward minority than toward other forms of incapacity. In some jurisdictions it may still be the law that a minor may avoid an executed purchase and recover the price paid, without any obligation of counter-restitution beyond restoration of that part of the purchased property (if any) remaining in the minor's possession. If by contrast an adult transferor lacks mental capacity—and such incapacity has not previously been adjudicated—the same transaction may not even be subject to rescission if the court finds that it was made on reasonable terms. The position of this Restatement is that the remedy of rescission and restitution for incapacity (with the corollary obligation of counter-restitution by the claimant) is in principle the same, whatever the nature of the incapacity; that avoidance for incapacity is justified only to the extent that it serves a legitimate protective function; and that rescission must not result in unjust enrichment of the incapacitated claimant, at the expense of a person who has dealt with the claimant in good faith on reasonable terms. . . .

§ 20.   Protection of Another's Life or Health

(1)   A person who performs, supplies, or obtains professional services required for the protection of another's life or health is entitled to restitution from the other as necessary to prevent unjust enrichment, if the circumstances justify the decision to intervene without request.

(2)   Unjust enrichment under this section is measured by a reasonable charge for the services in question.

Comment:

a.   General principles and scope; relation to other sections. The claim for emergency medical services rendered in the absence of contract is one of restitution's paradigms. Its significance lies not in its practical utility—a litigated claim under this section being a rarity—but in the clarity with which it reflects the general principles that justify a claim to compensation for nonbargained benefits voluntarily conferred. An emergency that threatens life or health offers the ultimate justification for conferring a benefit in the absence of contract, if need be, asserting a claim for payment only after services have been rendered. . . .

b.   Professional services. Emergency assistance rendered by a nonprofessional, however valuable, does not give rise to a claim in restitution under existing law. The result is that professional providers of medical assistance are routinely given an enforceable claim to compensation; while the nonprofessional rescuer or good Samaritan enjoys only such rewards as others may choose to bestow. See Illustration 7. The claim by a rescuer to recover for injuries suffered in the course of the rescue is a particularly compelling one, but such a recovery reflects compensation and insurance principles, not principles of unjust enrichment.

Practical concerns are often advanced to account for this difference in treatment. It is one thing to encourage professional intervention in emergencies, another to create financial incentives for would-be rescuers who might better remain on the sidelines. The problem of valuation is even more of an obstacle. Services of physicians, hospitals, and ambulance drivers are readily valued, while emergency rescue by a bystander is literally priceless. The fact that it is impossible to assign a value to the rescue of human life explains why the rule of § 20 is limited to professional services while the rule of § 21 (protection of another's property) is not. Unsolicited intervention to protect a person's stray livestock or unmoored sailboat can be valued with relative ease, because it usually takes the form of services (by stables and dockyards) for which there is a market. The same difficulty explains the traditional refusal in admiralty to make any award in respect of "pure life salvage," in circumstances where salvage of property would be readily compensated.

The most important objection, in terms of its implications for broader restitution doctrine, is an even more basic one. The law does not require that every benefit be paid for. See § 2(1). A heroic rescue may confer a benefit of inestimable value, but it is likely to be purely altruistic in origin. The imposition of restitutionary liability in such circumstances—a principle that would become visible only when the claim was resisted—transforms an act of self-sacrifice into a contentious exchange of values. The law avoids these unedifying consequences by presuming that an emergency rescue is a gratuitous act. The heroic bystander receives nothing; the heroic professional receives a "reasonable and customary charge" for professional services, but nothing extra for heroism. See Illustration 2.

Illustrations:

1.   Doctor is summoned by Bystander to attend accident Victim, who is lying unconscious. Doctor performs emergency surgery. Doctor's reasonable and customary charge for the services rendered is $1000, which Victim refuses to pay. Doctor has a claim in restitution for $1000 against Victim.

2.   Same facts as Illustration 1, except that the circumstances of the accident are such that both Bystander and Doctor act courageously and at great personal risk in coming to the aid of Victim. Their heroic intervention is not, in itself, a source of unjust enrichment. Bystander has no claim in restitution under this section, while Doctor's entitlement to restitution is limited (as in Illustration 1) to his reasonable and customary charge of $1000 for professional services rendered. . . .

7.   A acts in an emergency to save the lives of B and C, sustaining crippling injuries as a result. In gratitude for A's assistance, B promises to pay him a weekly pension of $100. B's promise is unsupported by consideration, but it may nevertheless be enforceable as a matter of contract law. (If such a promise is enforceable, B's recognition of the fact and value of the benefit conferred by A is a significant part of the rationale. See Restatement Second, Contracts § 86, Comment d, Illustration 7.) Unlike B, C makes no promise of compensation and later rejects A's suggestion that he is entitled to a reward. A is possibly entitled to enforce B's promise, but A has no claim in restitution against either B or C.

c.   *Measure of benefit.* Because the ultimate benefits of medical treatment are both contingent and difficult to value, marginal cases within the rule of § 20 may pose problems in measuring enrichment. The practical answer to what is largely a classroom paradox is that services that are medically necessary are presumed to be beneficial, without regard to their ultimate outcome; moreover, that it is appropriate to value such services as if the recipient had requested them. The result, as in most cases of quantum meruit, is a liability measured by market value (§ 50(2)(b)).

d.   Refusal. There can be no claim under this section for services that a recipient having full legal capacity has attempted to refuse; or for which such a recipient has communicated to the provider, before the services were rendered, an unwillingness to pay. Capacity to consent is capacity to refuse. Conversely, the circumstances in which emergency medical care must be provided will sometimes justify a court in concluding that the recipient's apparent refusal either to accept services or to pay for them is without legal effect. See Illustration 9.

Illustration:

9.   Patient is involuntarily detained in Hospital's psychiatric unit, pursuant to emergency hospitalization procedures required by statute. Patient refuses to pay for treatment, signing documents relating to financial responsibility only under compulsion. Following Patient's release, Hospital seeks payment for services to Patient on a theory of restitution. The court determines that the services rendered by Hospital, in the face of Patient's refusal to accept or pay for them, were necessary, appropriate, and beneficial to Patient; and that Patient's mental impairment at the time of hospitalization deprived Patient's refusal of legal effect. Hospital has a claim in restitution for the amount of its reasonable and customary charge.

§ 21.   Protection of Another's Property

(1)   A person who takes effective action to protect another's property from threatened harm is entitled to restitution from the other as necessary to prevent unjust enrichment, if the circumstances justify the decision to intervene without request. Unrequested intervention is justified only when it is reasonable to assume the owner would wish the action performed.

(2)   Unjust enrichment under this section is measured by the loss avoided or by a reasonable charge for the services provided, whichever is less.

Comment:

. . . b.   Unrequested intervention. The requirement that "the circumstances justify the decision to intervene without request" is one that is common to all claims within §§ 20–22. . . . As with claims based on the preservation of life and health under § 20, the essence of the emergency that will justify a claimant's unrequested intervention under § 21 is the threat of imminent harm in circumstances where bargaining between the parties is impracticable. But whereas the obstacle to negotiation in § 20 is the incapacity of the person benefited, in cases under § 21 the usual difficulty is merely the inability to identify and communicate with the owner before steps must be taken to preserve the property in question. A strong case for relief under § 21 is one in which it is safe to assume what the outcome of the forgone negotiation would have been. . . .

§ 25.   Uncompensated Performance under Contract with Third Person

(1)   If the claimant renders to a third person a contractual performance for which the claimant does not receive the promised compensa-

tion, and the effect of the claimant's uncompensated performance is to confer a benefit on the defendant, the claimant is entitled to restitution from the defendant as necessary to prevent unjust enrichment.

(2)   There is unjust enrichment for purposes of subsection (1) only if the following three conditions are met:

(a)   Liability in restitution may not subject the defendant to a forced exchange (§ 2(4)). This condition is likely to be satisfied if the benefit realized by the defendant

(i)   is one for which the defendant has expressed a willingness to pay,

(ii)   saves the defendant an otherwise necessary expense, or

(iii)   is realized by the defendant in money.

(b)   Absent liability in restitution, the claimant will not be compensated for the performance in question, and the defendant will retain the benefit of the claimant's performance free of any liability to pay for it.

(c)   Liability in restitution will not subject the defendant to an obligation from which it was understood by the parties that the defendant would be free. . . .

Comment:

a.   *General principles and scope.* Most transactions for which restitution may be available by the rule of this section fall within one of two common (though nonexclusive) patterns. In a first set of cases, A is a subcontractor, B is a property owner, and C (now unavailable) is the general contractor with whom both parties have dealt. In a second, A has performed work benefiting B's property under a contract with C, who is typically a tenant or a family member of B; C had an interest in seeing the work performed but no authority to bind B to pay for it. In either setting, the exit or insolvency of C leaves A without compensation for work that was performed as requested. If a further consequence of the interrupted transaction is that B stands to obtain a valuable benefit without paying for it, the outcome may be one that the law will characterize as unjust enrichment. . . .

b.   *Threshold limits to the claim.* . . . Restitution under this section is initially limited, in other words, to circumstances in which the imposition of a new, noncontractual liability. . .will not contradict or undermine preexisting contractual dispositions regulating the three-cornered transaction that brings the parties together. But frequently it will not. A transaction in which A renders services to B without receiving the compensation promised by C is by definition one that has not gone as anticipated; the turn of events by which B stands to benefit at A's expense often lies outside the range of contingencies that the parties have regulated by agreement. So long as contract is not a bar, the availability of restitution in this context depends above all on whether a remedy may be granted to A without subjecting B to a forced exchange. . . .

d.   *Measure of recovery.* Cases governed by § 25 often present a disparity between a recovery in restitution and the compensation to which the claimant would have been entitled under the defaulted contract. A successful claimant under this section recovers the amount of the benefit conferred on the defendant or the claimant's cost of performance, whichever is less. Because the claimant's recovery is based on the defendant's enrichment, and not on the claimant's contract with an absent third person, the claimant necessarily bears the risk that fluctuations in value, whatever their origin, will cause the value placed in the hands of the defendant to be less than the cost of performance. . . .

§ 31.   Unenforceability

(1)   A person who renders performance under an agreement that cannot be enforced against the recipient by reason of

(a)   indefiniteness, or

(b)   the failure to satisfy an extrinsic requirement of enforceability such as the Statute of Frauds,

has a claim in restitution against the recipient as necessary to prevent unjust enrichment. There is no unjust enrichment if the claimant receives the counterperformance specified by the parties' unenforceable agreement.

(2)   There is no claim under this section if enforcement of the agreement is barred by the applicable statute of limitations, nor in any other case in which the allowance of restitution would defeat the policy of the law that makes the agreement unenforceable. Restitution is appropriate except to the extent that forfeiture is an intended or acceptable consequence of unenforceability.

Comment:

a.   General principles and scope; unenforceable agreements; relation to other sections. . . . Section 31 describes a claim in restitution to recover benefits directly conferred as the performance required or invited by an unenforceable agreement. For example, given an oral or indefinite contract for the sale of realty that the vendor subsequently repudiates, the purchaser's claim to restitution of the price already paid is within the rule of this section. See Illustration 8. The related claim in respect of benefits indirectly conferred in the course of the interrupted transaction—to employ the same example, the purchaser's claim for the value of improvements made to the property before the vendor's repudiation—is described by § 27.

b.   The effect of performance. Performance of a contract that is unenforceable for the reasons identified in subsection (1) does not ordinarily result in forfeiture. Under many circumstances, full or even partial performance of an agreement that would have been unenforceable under the Statute of Frauds so long as it remained executory will render the agreement enforceable by the performing party according to its terms. The scope of this "performance exception" is determined by the contract law of each jurisdiction, but it is a rule to which principles of unjust enrichment visibly contribute. Where the contract remains unenforceable notwithstanding the claimant's performance, relief (if any) takes the form of the restitution claim described in this section.

Assuming that straightforward enforcement of the contract is for some reason unavailable, the question arises whether the allowance of even partial relief on another theory will tend to undermine or stultify the rule by which enforcement is denied. The answer depends on the reasons for denying enforcement of the contract. Recognition of an alternative liability in restitution presents no conflict with competing legal objectives if the reason for unenforceability of the underlying agreement is its indefiniteness. See Comment d. Where by contrast a statute bars enforcement of the agreement, courts will often inquire whether a recovery in restitution too closely resembles what the claimant would have obtained by enforcing the contract—thereby defeating the policy of the statute in question. Statutes of limitations present the most obvious example. See subsection (2).

At the opposite extreme, if enforcement is barred by one of the common provisions of the Statute of Frauds—those derived more or less directly from the English act of 1677—it is universally accepted that relief via restitution is outside the bar of the statute. See Comment f. . . . The more difficult choices arise under modern regulatory statutes that require a writing as a condition of enforcing particular agreements, such as contracts for real estate brokerage, home improvements, or contingent fees for legal services. In such cases a court may be obliged to determine whether the policy of a statute mandates forfeiture (with concomitant unjust enrichment) as a consequence of unenforceability.

c.   *Restitution and reliance.* This section describes a liability based on the unjust enrichment of the recipient of the claimant's contractual performance. The language of restitution is sometimes employed to veil what could be more candidly described as enforcement based on reliance. These are cases awarding compensation for losses incurred in performing (or preparing to perform) an unenforceable contract, notwithstanding the absence of benefit to the defendant as a result of the plaintiff's expenditure. A straightforward account of such outcomes describes them in terms of promissory liability (circumventing unacceptable consequences of the Statute of Frauds), not as restitution based on unjust enrichment.

d.   *Indefiniteness.* If a contract cannot be enforced because the terms specified by the parties fail to yield "a reasonably certain basis for giving an appropriate remedy" via damages or specific performance (U.C.C. § 2–204(3)), a performing party is entitled to restitution of a prepaid price, or to the value of a contractual performance for which the performer has not received the promised equivalent.

A transaction resulting in an indefinite contract must not be confused with a failed negotiation producing no contract at all. There is no claim under this section for a performance for which the defendant did not—at least implicitly—agree to pay, or for the value of performance exceeding the price the defendant promised to pay for it.

Illustrations:

. . . 3.   Husband and Wife agree that Wife will pay Husband's law school tuition from her own earnings in exchange for Husband's promise to bear the cost of Wife's future education. Wife pays a total of $48,000 pursuant to this agreement. After Husband obtains a law degree, the parties agree to defer Wife's further studies until Husband's income is higher. The marriage is dissolved a few months thereafter. There is no marital property to be divided, and spousal support is not sought by either party; but Wife demands that Husband be required to bear her educational expenses. The court determines that the parties' agreement was binding and that their contractual obligations were independent of the continuation of the marriage. Husband's obligation to Wife is nevertheless unenforceable by reason of indefiniteness, because the parties reached no agreement about the nature, extent, or timing of Wife's future education. Wife has a claim against Husband under the rule of this section to recover $48,000. . . .

e. Quantum meruit. . . . In modern practice, a claim styled "quantum meruit" typically seeks compensation for services rendered in the expectation of payment, but in the absence of explicit agreement as to amount. Based on the circumstances of the transaction, it may be appropriate to find an implied promise by the defendant to compensate the plaintiff—usually at the customary wage or "going rate" for the work done. If so, the measure of the plaintiff's contractual expectation is described by the words "quantum meruit" (or "as much as he is entitled to"), but the defendant's obligation is fully explained as a matter of contract. In such a case it would be erroneous to associate "quantum meruit" with a liability in unjust enrichment, or to view the plaintiff's action as one for restitution rather than contract damages. See Illustration 6. Changing the facts only slightly yields a case in which it may be much harder to conclude that the defendant promised to pay a reasonable price for services received, although the law imposes the same obligation in the absence of agreement. See Illustration 7. Whether "quantum meruit" in the latter case should be explained in terms of implied contract or unjust enrichment (or both) may be difficult to say, but it is also unnecessary to decide: the justifications overlap, and they yield the same recovery in any event. . . .

i. Measure of recovery. Restitution based on performance of an unenforceable contract is likely to yield a smaller recovery than damages for breach. For reasons applicable to contract remedies generally, a recovery measured by benefit conferred is often less than the contractual expectation (which would give the claimant the full benefit of the bargain); it will often be less than damages measured by the claimant's expenditures in reliance (which would reimburse expenditures not resulting in measurable benefit). See Restatement Second, Contracts § 344, Comment a. Restitution by the rule of this section is measured by the value of the claimant's performance to the recipient, not by what was promised in exchange, nor by what the claimant's performance cost the claimant. See Illustration 20.

Nevertheless, the terms of the unenforceable contract will influence and may even determine the measure of recovery in restitution. The critical fact in this context is that the claimant's performance was requested. (The fact that the parties' contract is unenforceable for reasons addressed by § 31—unlike a contract vitiated by fraud or duress—carries no implication that the recipient did not validly assent to the price term.) The value to the recipient of a requested performance—if performed as requested—is normally market value when no price has been specified; otherwise, the lesser of market value and a price the recipient has expressed a willingness to pay. . . . Where there is a disparity between contract and market prices, restitution will be for the lesser amount. . .

If the parties have specified a price for a performance that has no definitive market value—as in most cases of personal services—the value to the recipient of claimant's performance may properly be determined, for restitution purposes, by what the recipient has offered to pay. The effect of restitution in such a case may be indistinguishable from a partial enforcement, since it awards the contract price so far as the claimant has performed. Restitution remains easily distinguishable from contract damages, even if the price term is accepted as the measure of enrichment, because it affords no remedy in respect of the executory portion of the contract.

In the rare case in which the claimant might prove that a requested performance had a market value in excess of the promised compensation, recovery in restitution will be limited by the contract price. § 50(2)(b). Had the contractual exchange been substantially performed on both sides—notwithstanding its unenforceability for one of the reasons stated in this section—there would have been no unjust enrichment of the defendant, because an agreed-upon exchange of values (unaffected by such defects as fraud and mistake) does not result in unjust enrichment. See § 31(1). It follows that a liability in restitution under this section cannot exceed what would have been the defendant's liability in contract, had the contract been enforceable.

§ 32. Illegality

A person who renders performance under an agreement that is illegal or otherwise unenforceable for reasons of public policy may obtain restitution from the recipient in accordance with the following rules:

(1) Restitution will be allowed, whether or not necessary to prevent unjust enrichment, if restitution is required by the policy of the underlying prohibition.

(2) Restitution will also be allowed, as necessary to prevent unjust enrichment, if the allowance of restitution will not defeat or frustrate the policy of the underlying prohibition. There is no unjust enrichment if the claimant receives the counterperformance specified by the parties' unenforceable agreement.

(3) Restitution will be denied, notwithstanding the enrichment of the defendant at the claimant's expense, if a claim under subsection (2) is foreclosed by the claimant's inequitable conduct.

§ 33. Incapacity of Recipient

(1) A person who renders performance under an agreement that is unenforceable by reason of the other party's legal incapacity has a claim in restitution against the recipient as necessary to prevent unjust enrichment. There is no unjust enrichment if the claimant receives the counterperformance specified by the parties' unenforceable agreement.

(2) Restitution under this section is available only to a person who has dealt with the recipient in good faith on reasonable terms.

(3) Notwithstanding the unjust enrichment of the recipient, restitution may be limited or denied if it would be inconsistent with the protection that the doctrine of incapacity is intended to afford in the circumstances of the case.

Comment:

... c. *Incapacity and unjust enrichment.* The rule stated in this section reflects two essential premises. The first is that the doctrine of incapacity, in all of its applications, serves primarily a protective function. Infants, the mentally incompetent, and (in the case of municipal corporations) taxpayers are protected by the rules of incapacity against certain risks that persons of full legal capacity are free to assume. The protection so afforded is potentially costly. Legal incapacity is legal disability, and a person who lacks the capacity to undertake a legally binding obligation is foreclosed from participating in transactions that may be advantageous or even vitally necessary. Significant costs are imposed on the other party to the transaction, whenever a person who has dealt in good faith with an incapacitated counterparty is required to forfeit an otherwise valid legal entitlement. It follows that the contours of legal responsibility in these cases are determined, not by measuring "capacity to contract" against some a priori standard, but by weighing at each point the value of the protection secured against the cost of securing it.

The second premise underlying the rule of this section is that the dictates of equity and good conscience are independent of the capacity to contract. Neither the restitution claim asserted by a given plaintiff, nor the wider legal interest in avoiding unjust enrichment, is in any way diminished because the benefit in question was conferred on a person, natural or artificial, lacking full legal capacity. The consequence, as expressed by the former Restatement of this subject, is that "Incapacity to enter into a contract or to incur liability in tort is not in itself a defense in an action for restitution." Restatement of Restitution § 139 (1937). ...

d. Liability in contract distinguished from liability in restitution; measure of benefit. Liability to honor a promise, on the one hand, and liability to restore or pay for a benefit received, on the other, are distinct grounds of legal responsibility that sometimes yield congruent results. Because the incapacitated person's contractual undertaking is ex hypothesi invalid, such a party can be under no liability to accept or pay for a contractual performance that remains executory; nor will a liability in respect of benefits already received be imposed (or measured) by the terms of an invalid contract. ... On the other hand, where the contract price of the benefit conferred is the same as the value of the benefit as determined by the court, the recipient's liability in restitution—while distinguishable in concept—may be identical in extent to a liability on the invalid contract. ...

Because the value of a contractual performance is not definitively established by a contract that is unenforceable by reason of incapacity, the principal obstacle to a restitution claim under this section is the familiar problem of measuring benefit to the recipient. See §§ 49–50. ... Where the recipient retains undiminished the whole of the benefit conferred, there is usually no hardship in requiring the recipient to restore it—even if liability in restitution is indistinguishable in effect from a liability on the unenforceable contract. Where the extent of the recipient's enrichment is debatable, or where the benefit conferred has been dissipated in whole or part, the protective policy embodied in the recipient's incapacity to contract may justify a narrower measure of benefit than would be appropriate in the case of a recipient who lacked the same claim to special protection. ...

Liability under this section does not require that a benefit conferred on an incapacitated recipient consist of "necessaries." The familiar notion that an infant's contract is enforceable if for necessaries—like the proposition of the older common law, that an infant's contract was enforceable if and only if the contract was beneficial to the infant—expresses a restitution idea, imperfectly assimilated to the language of contract: namely, that the liability of the infant in such cases is not really in contract (on the promise) but rather in unjust enrichment (for benefits received). There is liability for necessar-

ies, in other words, because necessaries are presumptively beneficial. Accepting the premise, however, that liability in such cases is based not on contract but on unjust enrichment—so that there is no liability in excess of benefit received—the classification of certain benefits as "necessaries" is rendered superfluous, because it is subsumed within the basic inquiry into measure of enrichment.

§ 34. Mistake or Supervening Change of Circumstances

(1)   A person who renders performance under a contract that is subject to avoidance by reason of mistake or supervening change of circumstances has a claim in restitution to recover the performance or its value, as necessary to prevent unjust enrichment. If the case is one in which the requirements of § 54 can be met, the remedy of rescission and restitution permits the reversal of the transaction without the need to demonstrate unjust enrichment.

(2)   For purposes of subsection (1):

(a)   the value of a nonreturnable contractual performance is measured by reference to the recipient's contractual expectations; and

(b)   the recipient's liability in restitution may be reduced to allow for loss incurred in reliance on the contract.

Comment:

a.   *General principles and scope; relation to Restatement Second, Contracts.* Contract law—applying the related tests of mistake, impossibility, impracticability, and frustration—permits the avoidance of an obligation on which the parties ostensibly agreed but for which (as a result of their failure to apprehend or anticipate relevant circumstances) they did not actually bargain. To the extent the obligation in question remains executory, the issue between the parties is limited to the enforceability of the challenged agreement. Such a question is purely a matter of contract law. If the obligation has been partially or wholly performed, the same challenge to the transaction presents what is simultaneously a question

of contract and a question of restitution.

Claims within the rule of this section take two principal forms. In the case of a partially completed exchange, the party disadvantaged by the sequence of performance stands in the same position as one who has rendered performance under an agreement that is subsequently revealed to be unenforceable for some other reason. Compare §§ 31–33. The claimant has conferred a benefit at the request of the defendant, without obtaining the promised exchange; enforcement of the contract is unavailable, in this case because the parties' agreement has been set aside on the ground of mistake. The claimant's recourse is a claim in restitution measured by the defendant's net enrichment. . . . The second type of restitution claim seeks to unwind a completed transaction. Although the contract has been fully performed according to its terms, the disadvantaged party asserts that the resulting exchange, in its actual realization, finds no adequate basis in contract because it is not what the parties had in mind. See Comments e and f. . . .

b. *Extent of performance.* Confronted with a disparity between anticipation and realization that interrupts a contractual performance—or that leads one party to argue that a completed performance should be unwound—a court will ordinarily ask whether the risks associated with the disparity in question have been allocated by the parties, expressly or by implication; and whether the contractual exchange of values (executory, completed, or somewhere in between) is fairly comprehended within the parties' agreement.

The relevant aspect of contract doctrine (frequently called "mistake in basic assumptions") and the associated analytical method (usually explained in terms of risk allocation) are accordingly the same, whether they are deployed defensively (to resist enforcement of the contract) or affirmatively (to unwind a completed transaction). Yet the contract defense and the affirmative restitution claim are not available on equal terms. Given an equivalent disparity between anticipation and realization, in every setting where the facts permit the comparison, a court will more readily deny enforcement to an executory agreement than order restitution of the same values once they have been exchanged. To put the matter another way: across a broad range of cases involving "mistake in basic assumptions," the predictable outcome is the denial of relief to the moving party. See Illustrations 1–2.

Illustrations:

1. Rose 2d of Aberlone, a purebred cow belonging to Farmer, fails to breed in season; on examination by a veterinarian she is determined to be barren. Farmer sells Rose to Breeder for $300, a price based on her value as beef. Before the day fixed for delivery and payment, Rose is discovered to be with calf; her value as a breeding animal is not less than $3000. Farmer repudiates the sale, and Breeder sues for specific performance or damages. Breeder's claim is in contract, not restitution; Farmer's defense asserts a theory of mistake as the ground for avoidance. Breeder's claim will predictably be denied.

2. Same facts as Illustration 1, except that Rose's fertility is discovered after Rose has been delivered and paid for. Farmer brings suit to rescind the completed exchange. The plaintiff's claim is now in restitution, not contract, though it alleges the identical mistake as the ground for avoidance. Farmer's claim will predictably be denied.

The paradoxical conclusion—that the legal validity of a contractual exchange may depend on the extent to which it has been performed—is partly explained by reference to the extra costs of unwinding any completed transaction. And yet courts will indeed unwind completed transactions in other circumstances, where the alternative to intervention is an exchange that a court views as extracontractual—meaning that the transaction, as revealed in performance, is outside the scope of the parties' agreement. . . . Evidently courts will intervene to allocate or reassign some unanticipated risks more readily than others. The task of drawing the necessary distinctions is a notoriously difficult problem of contract law that is outside the scope of this Restatement. . . .

e.   Unwinding a completed transaction. Rescission and restitution, even of a fully completed exchange, is a basic remedial response if the underlying contract has been induced by fraud. Courts are much less likely to unwind an executed contract as a remedy for mistake. The question, simply put, is whether the exchange that has taken place is sufficiently grounded in the parties' bargain to be confirmed as legally effective. In addressing this question, many risks of variation that were not the subject of explicit negotiation will be found to have been allocated by implication, or will be assigned as a matter of law, to the disadvantaged party. See § 5, Comment b.

So long as an agreement has been freely negotiated. . . contract law generally assumes that buyers bear the risk of having paid too much, while sellers bear the risk of having accepted too little. Barriers to relief become nearly insuperable once the exchange has been fully performed. Compare Illustrations 1 and 2. . . .

Cases that do allow rescission and restitution on grounds of mistake most often involve a claimant who has paid for something that (unknown to the parties) never existed, no longer exists, or does not belong to the seller. . . . An occasional case presents the converse situation, in which the claimant has surrendered something that proves to be significantly more valuable than the parties supposed. . . . Either version yields a contract case that is ostensibly concerned with "mutual mistake in formation," but that closely resembles a restitution case of "mistake in performance"—yielding a relatively straight-forward claim based on mistaken payment or mistake in conferring benefits other than money.

The suggested hypothesis is thus that a court will occasionally order rescission and restitution as a remedy for mistake as to value, but only in those cases where the effect of the remedy closely resembles restitution of a mistaken performance—typically an overpayment, or a payment where no payment was actually due. Where by contrast the effect of rescission and restitution would be the repricing or reallocation of risks over which the parties have explicitly or implicitly bargained—however mistakenly—the remedy will be denied. . . .

Restitution in this context does not depend on whether the mistake in question is "mutual" or "unilateral." An exchange that corresponds to the understanding of one party but not the other can claim no more than a tenuous basis in the parties' agreement. The distinction is of practical significance, however, because a party who is not himself mistaken, and who is unaware that the other is acting under a mistake, will be protected in his reliance on the other's expressions of assent. The consequence is that restitution for unilateral mistake in basic assumptions will be available only when the defendant had reason to know of the claimant's mistake or when the defendant has taken no action in reliance on the parties' apparent bargain. Conversely, knowledge by one party of the other's mistake as to value is not grounds for avoidance when the mistaken party bears the risk of the mistake in question. . . .

§ 35.   Performance of Disputed Obligation

(1)   If one party to a contract demands from the other a performance that is not in fact due by the terms of their agreement, under circumstances making it reasonable to accede to the demand rather than to insist on an immediate test of the disputed obligation, the party on whom the demand is made may render such performance under protest or with

reservation of rights, preserving a claim in restitution to recover the value of the benefit conferred in excess of the recipient's contractual entitlement.

(2) The claim described in subsection (1) is available only to a party acting in good faith and in the reasonable protection of its own interests. It is not available where there has been an accord and satisfaction, or where a performance with reservation of rights is inadequate to discharge the claimant's obligation to the recipient.

§ 36. Restitution to a Party in Default

(1) A performing party whose material breach prevents a recovery on the contract has a claim in restitution against the recipient of performance, as necessary to prevent unjust enrichment.

(2) Enrichment from receipt of an incomplete or defective contractual performance is measured by comparison to the recipient's position had the contract been fully performed. The claimant has the burden of establishing the fact and amount of any net benefit conferred.

(3) A claim under this section may be displaced by a valid agreement of the parties establishing their rights and remedies in the event of default.

(4) If the claimant's default involves fraud or other inequitable conduct, restitution may on that account be denied.

Comment:

a.   General principles and scope; relation to contract law. . . . [T]his section applies to cases in which (i) the performing party has no enforceable rights under the contract, whether by a rule of substantial performance, of severability, or otherwise; and (ii) the claim based on unjust enrichment is not displaced by a valid contractual provision imposing forfeiture or liquidated damages. Where a remedy to the party in default is neither conferred nor foreclosed by valid terms of the agreement, restitution authorizes a claim as necessary to avoid unjust enrichment. The principal task confronting the restitution claimant is to establish that an incomplete or defective performance has in fact conferred a net benefit on the recipient, taking into account the various costs to which the defendant has been subjected in the wake of the claimant's default. . . .

b.   Willful or deliberate default. Courts in many jurisdictions continue to state that restitution is unavailable to a party whose contractual default is willful or deliberate. The quality of the breach in a particular case manifestly determines the claimant's equitable posture in seeking restitution. The claimant's conduct may be culpable or excusable; it may reflect opportunism or merely inadequate resources; it may manifest a conscious disregard of the defendant's legal entitlement, on the one hand, or simple inadvertence, on the other. The court's sense of the claimant's relative equitable position will in many instances determine the success or failure of the claim.

It is potentially misleading, however, to describe willful or deliberate default as an absolute bar to the claim under this section. In the large and significant class of cases where the claimant's defaulted obligation is to pay money, the breach of contract—the failure to pay a debt when due—is most often the result of a conscious election. Even a debtor who faces financial hardship normally has a choice to pay one creditor rather than another. It can be difficult to explain why breach in such instances should not be qualified as "willful" or "deliberate"; yet the same instances include some of the foremost illustrations of cases in which modern American law authorizes restitution to the party in default. See Comment d.

Although restitution is undeniably available in some cases of deliberate default, there remain many circumstances in which the quality of the claimant's breach will effectively bar the claim. The significance of "deliberateness" in this context lies in the extraordinary costs that will frequently be imposed by an election to discontinue a contractual performance already under way. Assuming a simple choice between performance and breach, the election to perform yields a straightforward claim to the price specified by contract, securing contractual expectations on both sides; while the election to default, and then to pursue a claim in restitution, draws the litigants and the court into a complex, extracontractual evaluation of both benefit conferred and injury inflicted. The remedial inefficiency of the latter course is obvious, as is the risk that the innocent party will incur substantial uncompensated costs in consequence of the claimant's election to breach. Judicial awareness of these factors accounts for the traditional rule that denies restitution whenever default is "willful or deliberate." The omission of this condition from § 36 must not be taken to imply that such factors have somehow become irrelevant. . . .

c.   Amount of recovery; burden of proof. There is a claim in restitution in respect of defaulted contractual performance only if and to the extent the claimant can prove that the benefit

thereby conferred, net of losses attributable to claimant's default, results in the enrichment of the defendant. . . .

Net enrichment is measured by reference to the defendant's contractual expectation. . . . The uniform test is to compare the defendant's actual position with the position the defendant would have occupied in the absence of breach. Given the difficulty in many circumstances of quantifying the injury to the defendant from the claimant's breach, the appropriate reduction may be liberally estimated. The object is to insure that the nonbreaching defendant will under no circumstance be left with a net loss from the transaction . . .

When the claimant seeks restitution of the value of a nonreturnable performance, it may be necessary to choose between alternative measures of the benefit conferred. To the extent the claimant's breach of contract includes an element of fault, the equities of the claim under § 36 will tend to favor the application of the most restrictive test among those proposed by § 49(3). This will ordinarily mean either (i) a ratable portion of the contract price, (ii) the market value of the benefit conferred, or (iii) the resulting addition to the defendant's wealth, whichever is least. . . .

e.   Benefit conferred in goods or services. . . . A party in default under a contract to render personal services is ordinarily entitled to restitution by the rule of this section unless the nature of the default indicates fraud or inequitable conduct. Even if the claimant has been guilty of conscious wrongdoing, the tendency of more recent decisions—where the facts permit—is to distinguish periods of faithful and disloyal service, awarding the value of services performed during the former but not the latter. . . .

Claims in respect of legal services make up an important subcategory of cases within this section. . . . Within the terms of the present section, the question is whether the lawyer's breach of duty involves fraud or inequitable conduct: professional and fiduciary obligations to the client increase the likelihood that a lawyer's default may be of this character. Absent such a bar, even

a lawyer discharged for cause may recover for the value of services rendered, provided that those services have conferred a net benefit on the client. By contrast, restitution will uniformly be denied to a lawyer who abandons a representation without justification. . . .

§ 37. Rescission for Material Breach

(1)   Except as provided in subsection (2), a plaintiff who is entitled to a remedy for the defendant's material breach or repudiation may choose rescission as an alternative to enforcement if the further requirements of § 54 can be met.

(2)   Rescission as a remedy for breach of contract is not available against a defendant whose defaulted obligation is exclusively an obligation to pay money.

Comment:

a.   General principles and scope; relation to other sections. This section describes an alternative remedy for breach of contract that is sometimes called "restitution" but is more easily recognized under the name "rescission.". . .

Rescission is one of the principal asset-based remedies in restitution, and breach of contract is only one of the problems to which it is a possible response. (In addition to its role as a remedy for material breach, rescission may be an obvious choice when there has been performance under a contract that is subject to avoidance for fraud, mistake, or similar grounds of invalidity.) Section 54 presents a general account of the remedy called "rescission and restitution," setting forth the objectives, requirements, and operation of the remedy in the various settings where it may be employed. . . .

b.   Rescission in practice. In theory, and sometimes in practice, rescission pursuant to § 37 permits a plaintiff who has paid in advance for a defaulted performance to recover an amount exceeding compensatory damages. Such outcomes are rare, because a prepaid seller will almost never forfeit a profit

that might be earned, at the seller's option, by performing the contract or simply by releasing the buyer. . . . The simple rule is that a plaintiff who seeks only the return of a prepaid price will not (for reasons of both fairness and economy) be put to the burden of proving damages from the defendant's breach. There is no comparable windfall to the plaintiff if the sequence of performance is reversed, because rescission is not available as a remedy for payment default. . . .

Ordinarily, the reason to elect rescission is the relative certainty of the remedy compared with the difficulty (and expense) of proving damages or obtaining specific performance. Plaintiffs in these cases forgo the benefit of a (presumably advantageous) bargain because the anticipated recovery from rescission, net of the cost of obtaining it, is higher. . . .

c.   The quality of defendant's breach. Any breach of contract that results in quantifiable injury gives the plaintiff a remedy in damages, but the remedy of rescission is available only in cases of significant default. Short of a repudiation, the defendant's breach must be "material," "substantial," "essential," or "vital"; it must "go to the root" of the defendant's obligation, or be "tantamount to a repudiation." To replace this familiar catalogue of adjectives, both Restatements of Contracts employ the expression "total breach." See Restatement of Contracts § 313(1) (1932); Restatement Second, Contracts §§ 236(1), 243, 253, & 373. The reformed terminology is not entirely successful, because the expression "total breach" is easily misconstrued. In particular, it is not a requirement of "total breach" by the Restatement definition that the defendant have failed to render any part of the promised contractual performance. The present Restatement employs the term "material breach" to designate what both Restatements of Contracts call "total breach," only because its meaning is more readily understood.

Of course the real test is not verbal but functional. The effect of rescission, at a minimum, is to deprive the defendant of the benefit of the bargain. To the extent of the defendant's expense in the course of partial performance, rescission imposes on the defendant an additional loss. If the defendant repudiates the contract, or commits a breach by nonperformance of equivalent gravity, these consequences are presumably justifiable. On the other hand, if the defendant's breach is relatively minor in the context of the overall undertaking, and if the injury to the plaintiff is appropriately remedied by an award of damages, the same consequences of rescission might impose an unacceptable and punitive forfeiture. If the plaintiff (having suffered a loss of $5) could threaten to impose a loss of $100 on the defendant by seeking rescission instead of $5 damages, the availability of rescission would become a source of costly opportunism. The requirement of repudiation or material breach is a safeguard against this misuse of a remedy that is intended as a shield and not a sword. . . .

§ 38. Performance-Based Damages

(1) As an alternative to damages based on the expectation interest (Restatement Second, Contracts § 347), a plaintiff who is entitled to a remedy for material breach or repudiation may recover damages measured by the cost or value of the plaintiff's performance.

(2) Performance-based damages are measured by

(a) uncompensated expenditures made in reasonable reliance on the contract, including expenditures made in preparation for performance or in performance, less any loss the defendant can prove with reasonable certainty the plaintiff would have suffered had the contract been performed (Restatement Second, Contracts § 349); or

(b) the market value of the plaintiff's uncompensated contractual performance, not exceeding the price of such performance as determined by reference to the parties' agreement.

(3) A plaintiff whose damages are measured by the rules of subsection (2) may also recover for any other loss, including incidental or consequential loss, caused by the breach.

Comment:

a. *General principles and scope; relation to Restatement Second, Con-* tracts. The remedy described in the present section is one of the two principal devices sometimes referred to as "restitution for breach of contract," the other being rescission (§ 37). Though called "restitution" it is simply an award of damages. It is distinguished from ordinary contract damages, measured by the plaintiff's expectation interest, because it permits a plaintiff who cannot prove expectation to recover damages calculated on an alternative basis.

Damages of this kind have traditionally been associated with the idea of "restitution" because they tend to "restore": they restore the plaintiff to the precontractual position, or they restore to the plaintiff either the cost or the value of the plaintiff's uncompensated performance. Cost of performance is the measure more frequently employed: the plaintiff recovers damages measured by unreimbursed expenditure in reliance on the contract, subject to provable expectation as a cap. Less often, the basis of the performance-based damage calculation is the value of the plaintiff's uncompensated performance, not exceeding the price of such performance at the contract rate. Damages measured by expenditure are commonly called "reliance damages." Damages measured by the value of performance go by various names, including both "restitution" and "reliance" as well as "quantum meruit." Conceptual and terminological confusion has obscured the fact that the measures of cost and value are—for the most part—parallel versions of a single alternative damage remedy. See Comment b.

Either approach to damages under this section yields a second-best, "fallback" alternative to damages measured by expectancy. A plaintiff who can prove expectation damages will seek to recover them, because they yield the benefit of a favorable bargain and the highest recovery. The rule of the present section offers a remedial alternative in cases where the plaintiff cannot establish expectation damages—either because of difficulties of proof, or because contractual expectancy is prov-

able but negative. Performance-based damages yield a partial recovery in such cases, though they do not permit a complete escape from an unfavorable bargain: a plaintiff who was obligated to perform at a loss may not characterize losses from performance as damages from breach. (A plaintiff whose performance of a losing contract is interrupted by the defendant's breach does avoid the further losses that the plaintiff would have incurred in completing performance. See Comment d.) By contrast, a plaintiff who is entitled to rescission as a remedy for material breach will sometimes escape entirely the consequences of an unfavorable bargain.

The usual application of the rule of § 38, therefore, is either to a case in which the plaintiff's contractual expectation cannot be established at all, or to a case in which—although the plaintiff's expectancy cannot be known with certainty—it can be shown to lie somewhere within an upper limit. In either case, an alternative damage calculation by the rule of § 38 protects the plaintiff's expectancy so far as the evidence permits, based on a rebuttable presumption that the plaintiff was neither performing at a loss nor selling at less than market value. More specifically, the presumption is that the plaintiff's earnings from performance would have been at least sufficient to defray the plaintiff's reliance expenditures; alternatively, that the plaintiff's unknown expectancy would have been at least equal to the market value of the plaintiff's performance. Either presumption may be rebutted by the defendant, on proof that the plaintiff's contractual expectancy was something less than the damages sought by this alternative measure.

Frequently—most obviously, where the remedy for the defendant's breach is the recovery of money paid to the defendant—there is no meaningful distinction between the cost and value of the plaintiff's performance. In other cases, the plaintiff's choice between cost and value as the basis of the alternative damage calculation (that is, between subsections (2)(a) and (2)(b)) is determined by which yields the larger recovery—or merely by which is the more easily measured. See Comment b.

This account of performance-based damages differs substantially from the description of the same remedies in the first and second Restatements of Contracts, but the present revision—outside one narrow field—will not alter the results of cases. Its purpose is rather to provide a simplified and rationalized explanation of some straightforward contract remedies that have become needlessly difficult to describe. Because this Restatement recognizes the terms of the contract as a limit on any damage recovery, it modifies the prior treatment of those few cases—prominent in theory, but rare in practice—in which a plaintiff seeks "restitution" to escape the consequences of an unfavorable bargain. See Comment c. Apart from its treatment of "losing contracts," however, the simpler rule of the present section yields the same outcomes as Restatement Second, Contracts §§ 349 and 373.

As the Illustrations to this section will make clear, damages by the alternative measures here described are available when the effect of the defendant's breach or repudiation is to discharge the plaintiff's remaining duties of performance—making the award of damages a full reckoning of the parties' contractual obligations. Plaintiff's entitlement in such circumstances is to "damages for total breach" (Restatement Second, Contracts §§ 236(1), 243, 253), as opposed to compensation for some limited respect in which the defendant's performance has been deficient. Because the expression "total breach" is frequently misunderstood, this Restatement refers instead to "damages for material breach or repudiation."

See § 37, Comment c. But there is no intention to disturb the distinction between total and partial breach drawn by the prior Restatement.

b.   Cost or value; "reliance damages"; special damages. A plaintiff who cannot prove expectation damages—because a benefit of the bargain cannot be established with sufficient certainty—may prove and recover, as an alternative measure of damages, either the cost or the value of the plaintiff's uncompensated performance. See Comment a. Damages so measured are a second-best remedy. They omit any element of profit: a plaintiff who could show lost profit from performance would prove and recover ordinary expectation damages. A recovery based on cost will be reduced (or eliminated altogether) if the defendant can prove that the plaintiff would have suffered a loss had the contract been performed. A recovery based on value will be limited to the contract rate for the performance in question—when such a rate may be determined—even if this is insufficient to allow the plaintiff to recoup the cost of performance. . . .

A plaintiff with a choice will ordinarily base the alternative damage claim on reliance expenditures, rather than on the value of performance. This is because expenditures are generally easier to prove, and because expenditure in the course of partial performance (often involving preparations for performance, or the costs of "incidental reliance") typically exceeds the value of the performance actually rendered. The distinction between cost and value is ignored in many cases, where the two characterizations of the alternative damage claim are effectively interchangeable. . . .

Less familiar than cases of "reliance damages," only because they are far less numerous, are cases in which it is easier to establish the market value of a contractual performance than to measure the plaintiff's expenditures in performance. Section 38(2)(b) allows a plaintiff to recover damages equal to that market value, so long as the parties' agreement does not establish a lower price for the performance in question. . . .

c.   *Contract terms respected.* Performance-based damages by the rule of this section are a substitute for damages based on expectancy, and they are limited by expectancy at most points where expectancy can be established. Breach of contract does not make the defendant a guarantor of the profitability of the plaintiff's bargain; damages compensate loss attributable to the breach, not loss attributable to an unfavorable exchange. Performance-based damages, like expectation damages, respect the price terms and the risk allocations established by the parties' agreement.

Damages measured by the cost of the plaintiff's performance are reduced to the extent the defendant can prove that the plaintiff would have suffered a loss had the contract been performed. In this regard the rule of § 38(2)(a) is identical to Restatement Second, Contracts § 349. The fact that "reliance damages" are reduced by anticipated losses, while a recovery based on rescission is not, may determine the plaintiff's choice between the two. . . .

When performance-based damages are measured by the value of a performance rather than its cost, the damage calculation is also limited by the price term of the contract, but the limit is imposed differently. In determining damages by the rule of § 38(2)(b), the value of a plaintiff's performance may not exceed the contract rate (if there is one) fixed by the parties' agreement. . . .

The plaintiff who seeks to recover unreimbursed expenditures is required to deduct any loss that would have been incurred upon full performance of the contract. By contrast, the plaintiff who seeks the value of a partial performance is limited to recovery at the contract rate for what has been done, but is not charged with the further loss that would have been incurred had performance been completed. The result is that damages under § 38(2)(a) are limited by contractual expectancy, while damages under § 38(2)(b) are limited by the contract rate but not necessarily by expectancy. See Comment d. . . .

d.   *Losing contracts.* When a party who cannot prove expectation damages seeks instead to recover unreimbursed expenditures in reliance on the contract, it is an accepted rule that the award of damages may not shift to the defendant losses that the plaintiff would have realized on full performance. When the plaintiff who has been performing at a loss seeks damages measured by the value of performance, some authorities allow a recovery "off the contract," unlimited by the contract price; but this Restatement rejects that outcome. By capping the damage calculation at the contract rate (where such a rate may be determined), § 38(2)(b) prevents these plaintiffs as well from electing performance-based damages as a means of escape from an unfavorable bargain.

The contrary rule, allowing damages measured by the value of performance unlimited by the contract price, permits the injured party to reallocate or revalue risks that it is the function of contract to price and to assign. Such an outcome is contrary to fundamental objectives of contract law and inconsistent with the other remedies for breach of contract, all of which take the parties' agreement as the benchmark by which the plaintiff's remedies are measured.

A result that is plainly anomalous from a contract standpoint therefore came to be explained as a liability in unjust enrichment rather than contract. By the principles of this Restatement, however, performance of a valid and enforceable contract does not result in the unjust enrichment of the recipient. The argument to the contrary asserts that the defendant is unjustly enriched if he retains the benefit of a contract (goods or services on below-market terms) that he has failed to perform on his side. But the benefit to the defendant in such a case is the result of the contract, not of the breach. Assuming for the sake of argument that a breach of contract might be seen as a legal wrong, comparable to a tort—though the law does not generally so regard it. . .—the result of defendant's wrongdoing in such a case is not to benefit the defendant at the plaintiff's expense, but to benefit the plaintiff at the defendant's expense, by releasing the plaintiff from the expense of a further performance at a loss. In summary, the fact that the defendant has committed a material breach does not mean that the contract is to be disregarded, allowing the plaintiff to seek restitution as if there had never been a contract between the parties. Such precisely is the legal response where the contract was never valid to begin with, as in a case of rescission for fraud. It is not and has never been the remedy for breach of a valid and enforceable contract.

Accepting the contract price as a limit in a losing-contract case does not mean that expectation and performance-based damages are invariably the same. Because the plaintiff performing at a loss is allowed to cease performance (and terminate any remaining obligation) in response to the defendant's breach or repudiation, the plaintiff avoids the further loss that would have been sustained in completing performance. In other words, the loss that would have been realized by the plaintiff in completing performance of the contract is not subtracted from the plaintiff's recovery for partial performance. The result is explained by viewing the defendant's breach or repudiation as a gratuitous release of the plaintiff's further obligations under the contract. A defendant who wishes to be paid for releasing the plaintiff from an onerous obligation—a plausible resolution on the facts of some losing-contract cases—must negotiate with the plaintiff to settle the contract by agreement. If the rule were otherwise . . . the defendant would be in the position of imposing a unilateral modification or novation, on the terms most favorable to himself; and of doing so, moreover, by breach rather than by negotiation.

e. *Consequential harms.* Decisions authorizing "restitution" in excess of the contract price to parties who have been performing at a loss are found disproportionately in cases of long-term contracts for construction or manufacture that have been interrupted in the course of performance. Breach in such circumstances is particularly likely to subject the injured party to consequential harm; yet the plaintiff may face formidable difficulties in establishing the fact and amount of the resulting loss, if proof of damages must be made with rigorous specificity. If in such a setting the court perceives that the defendant has obtained a performance that was unexpectedly costly to the plaintiff—and if the evidence moreover suggests that the plaintiff's cost overruns may have their source in the defendant's breach—a judgment that the defendant is liable for the market value of the plaintiff's performance, although nominally explained on a theory of unjust enrichment, makes the plaintiff whole while avoiding the difficulties of proving the various elements of consequential or special damages. The practice in some jurisdictions of awarding damages in construction cases on a "total cost" basis relies on similar assumptions to achieve a similar result.

Because it prohibits a recovery in excess of the contract price for the work done, § 38 forecloses this use of a performance-based damage award; but plaintiffs may obtain the same compensation if they can prove the necessary elements of special damages. A jurisdiction that adopts the position of this Restatement should ensure that evidentiary requirements for proof of special damages caused by the defendant's breach are not unduly restrictive. . . .

§ 39. Profit from Opportunistic Breach

(1) If a deliberate breach of contract results in profit to the defaulting promisor and the available damage remedy affords inadequate protection to the promisee's contractual entitlement, the promisee has a claim to restitution of the profit realized by the promisor as a result of the breach. Restitution by the rule of this section is an alternative to a remedy in damages.

(2) A case in which damages afford inadequate protection to the promisee's contractual entitlement is ordinarily one in which damages will not permit the promisee to acquire a full equivalent to the promised performance in a substitute transaction.

(3) Breach of contract is profitable when it results in gains to the defendant (net of potential liability in damages) greater than the defendant would have realized from performance of the contract. Profits from breach include saved expenditure and consequential gains that the defendant would not have realized but for the breach, as measured by the rules that apply in other cases of disgorgement.

Comment:

a. General principles and scope; relation to other sections. In exceptional cases, a party's profitable breach of contract may be a source of unjust enrichment at the expense of the other contracting party. The law of restitution treats such cases in the same way that it treats other instances of intentional and profitable interference with another person's legally protected interests, authorizing a claim by the injured party to the measurable benefit realized as a result of the defendant's wrong. The claim described in this section is accordingly an instance of restitution for benefits wrongfully obtained (§ 3). . . .

Unlike §§ 37–38, which describe contract remedies that are independent of unjust enrichment, a primary object of § 39 is to prevent the unjust enrichment of the defendant at the expense of the plaintiff. Like the other rules of restitution for benefits wrongfully obtained, § 39 describes a disgorgement remedy: a claimant under this section may recover the defendant's profits from breach, even if they exceed the provable loss to the claimant from the defendant's defaulted performance. . . .

Judged by the usual presumptions of contract law, a recovery for breach that exceeds the plaintiff's provable damages is anomalous on its face. A breach of contract—whatever the actor's state of mind—is not usually treated in law as a wrong to the injured party of a sort comparable to a tort or breach of equitable duty. There is substantial truth, though not of course the whole story, in the Holmesian paradox according to which the legal obligation imposed by contract lies in a choice between performance and payment of damages. But the observation is most accurate where it matters least: in those transactional contexts where damages can be calculated with relative confidence as a full equivalent of performance. . . .

Compared to other forms of legal entitlement, contract rights may often be easier to value in money; but they would be vulnerable to the same risks of underenforcement if the exclusive remedy for breach were an action for money damages. Where a party's contractual entitlement would be inadequately protected by the legal remedy of damages for breach, a court will often reinforce the protection given to the claimant by an order of injunction or specific performance. Restitution affords comparable protection after the fact, awarding the gains from a profitable breach of a contract that the defendant can no longer be required to perform. . . .

b.   Opportunistic breach. The common rationale of every instance in which restitution allows a recovery of profits from wrongdoing, in the contractual context or any other, is the reinforcement of an entitlement that would be inadequately protected if liability for interference were limited to provable damages. Cases in which restitution reaches the profits from a breach of contract are those in which the promisee's contractual position is vulnerable to abuse. Vulnerability in this context stems from the difficulty that the promisee may face in recovering, as compensatory damages, a full equivalent of the performance for which the promisee has bargained. A promisor who was permitted to exploit the shortcomings of the promisee's damage remedy could accept the price of the promised performance, then deliver something less than what was promised. Such an outcome results in unjust enrichment as between the parties. The mere possibility of such an outcome undermines the stability of any contractual exchange in which one party's performance may be neither easily compelled nor easily valued.

A promisor who recognizes this possibility and attempts to profit by it commits what is here called an "oppor-

tunistic breach." The label suggests the reasons why a breach of this character is condemned, but there is no requirement under this section that the claimant prove the motivation of the breaching party.

In countering this form of opportunism, the rule of § 39 reinforces the contractual position of the vulnerable party and condemns a form of conscious advantage-taking that is the equivalent, in the contractual context, of an intentional and profitable tort. A restitution claim in response to a profitable tort typically operates to protect property from deliberate interference: standard examples include the claim to profits from trespass or infringement. See §§ 40 and 42. The rule of § 39 extends an analogous protection to contract rights, where what the wrongdoer seeks to acquire is not "property" but the modification or release of his own contractual obligation. The two situations have much in common. Confronted with a situation—in either context—in which the appropriate course of action would be to negotiate regarding legal entitlements, the wrongdoer takes without asking. The opportunistic calculation in either setting is that the wrongdoer's anticipated liability in damages is less than the anticipated cost of the entitlement, were it to be purchased from the claimant in a voluntary transaction. Restitution (through the disgorgement remedy) seeks to defeat this calculation, reducing the likelihood that the conscious disregard of another's entitlement can be more advantageous than its negotiated acquisition. See § 3, Comment c. . . .

Where the value of the promised performance is easily demonstrated—and substitutes are readily available—it may be plausible to attribute to the parties an understanding that the promisor shall be free, as a practical matter, to elect between performance and payment of damages. In other transactions. . . the proposition that the promisor should be free to choose whether or not to perform would be incompatible with fundamental objectives of the promisee, ultimately making it impossible to fix a price for the promisor's contractual obligation. Absent an enforceable agreement on liquidated damages, the bargain in question is then less likely to be made.

Not by coincidence, the contractual entitlements that are vulnerable in the manner just described are those for which the promisee would most often be entitled to protection by injunction, or to a remedy by specific performance; or in which well-advised parties would most often provide by contract (where permitted to do so) for liquidated damages or specific enforceability. Disgorgement by the rule of this section serves the same contract-reinforcing objectives as the devices just mentioned, at a different stage of contractual performance. . . .

d. *When disgorgement is available.* The cases in which the law allows disgorgement for breach of contract are susceptible of various particularized explanations; the purpose of § 39 is to frame a rule that will identify them all. It has been suggested, for example, that a contractual entitlement to acquire real property may sufficiently resemble ownership of the property (by the doctrine of equitable conversion or otherwise) that it is natural to treat a breach of the sales contract as an interference with the property right—thereby justifying recourse to the restitution claim that would be available in a case of interference with real property. . . . In cases of this kind, where specific performance is routinely available, it has long been assumed that damages are inadequate to protect the contractual entitlement of the promisee. Restitution gives the protection after the fact that specific performance would have given ahead of time.

In other contexts as well, contract rights may resemble noncontractual entitlements that are routinely protected against interference by a disgorgement remedy in restitution. Thus a promise not to disclose or utilize confidential information is the usual form by which trade secrets are protected; allowing restitution for breach of the contract is equivalent to restitution for misappropriation of the trade secret. Again, if one party's contractual obligation to another has a fiduciary or confidential character, disgorgement for breach of the contract might be justified by observing that it resembles a liability to account for profits derived from a breach of fiduciary duty. . . .

In a further set of cases, the nature of the underlying transaction makes it fair to surmise that the plaintiff has (in effect) paid the defendant in advance for a performance that the defendant has failed to render. If the circumstances of the transaction are such that the plaintiff can obtain neither rescission nor a meaningful remedy in damages, restitution by the rule of § 39 yields a monetary substitute for the performance the plaintiff paid for and should have received.

Illustrations:

. . . 5. Landowner and Mining Company enter a contract for strip-mining. The agreement authorizes Mining Company to remove coal from Blackacre in exchange for payment of a specified royalty per ton. A further provision of the agreement, included at Landowner's insistence, obliges Mining Company to restore the surface of Blackacre to its preexisting contours on the completion of mining operations. Mining Company removes the coal from Blackacre, pays the stipulated royalty, and repudiates its obligation to restore the land. In Landowner's action against Mining Company it is established that the cost of restoration would be $25,000, and that the diminution in the value of Blackacre if the restoration is not performed would be negligible. The contract is not affected by mistake or impracticability. The cost of restoration is in line with what Mining Company presumably anticipated, and the available comparisons suggest that Mining Company took this cost into account in calculating the contractual royalty. Landowner is entitled to recover $25,000 from Mining Company by the rule of this section. It is not a condition to Landowner's recovery in restitution that the money be used to restore Blackacre. . . .

e.   *Measure of recovery.* The purpose of the disgorgement remedy for breach of contract is to eliminate the possibility that an intentional and opportunistic breach will be more profitable to the performing party than negotiation with the party to whom performance is owed. For this reason, "profit realized . . . as a result of the breach" includes the gains that motivated the promisor's decision to breach the contract. If the defendant's liability in restitution were limited to the amount that might have been paid to obtain the necessary contractual modification in a voluntary transaction, there would be inadequate incentive to bargain over the entitlement in question.

While the rule of this section is intended to make breach unprofitable, it does not seek to punish a breach of contract by requiring forfeiture of the defendant's profit from the transaction as a whole. . . .

f.   *The exceptional nature of the claim.* Of the available remedies for breach of contract, the disgorgement claim described in § 39 is the least frequently encountered. The cumulative requirements of § 39 will exclude the great majority of contractual defaults. . . .

Even when breach is both profitable and deliberate—in the sense that it results from a conscious choice not to perform—there is no opportunism and no claim under this section if a damage remedy affords adequate protection to the promisee's contractual entitlement, by allowing the promisee "to acquire a full equivalent to the promised performance in a substitute transaction." . . .

h.   *Efficient breach.* Modern American contract scholarship devotes considerable attention to a hypothetical case in which breach of contract is "efficient." The scenario most often debated involves a seller who is offered a higher price for goods or services that he has sold but not yet delivered to the buyer. The seller—it is suggested—ought to breach the contract whenever the anticipated profits from resale at the higher price would be more than sufficient to pay the buyer's damages, thereby leaving some parties better off and nobody worse off. An efficient breach of contract by this definition is easy to hypothesize but difficult to find in real life. In a market context, gain to one party is normally offset or exceeded by loss to the other; while the test of efficiency will not be met unless the injured party is fully indemnified against the cost of resolving the resulting dispute. American practice regarding the allocation of litigation expense makes satisfaction of the latter condition especially unlikely. . . .

The rationale of the disgorgement liability in restitution, in a contractual context or any other, is inherently at odds with the idea of efficient breach in its usual connotation. Given the pervasive risk of undercompensation by standard damage measures, not to mention the deadweight loss from the cost of litigation, the law of restitution strongly favors voluntary over involuntary transactions in the adjustment of conflicts over any form of legal entitlement. A voluntary transaction in the present context requires a negotiated

261

release or modification of the existing obligation. The obligor who elects instead to take without asking—calculating that his anticipated liability for breach is less than the price he would have to pay to purchase the rights in question, and leaving the obligee to the chance of a recovery in damages—engages in precisely the conduct that the law of restitution normally condemns.

Whether the promisor's decision to modify or withhold a given performance infringes the contract rights of the promisee is a preliminary question of contract law and interpretation. If it does, the promisor's liability in restitution follows from the same principles as restitution for other instances of conscious and profitable interference with legally protected rights. The rule of § 39 does not automatically punish every "efficient breach" with a disgorgement remedy, because it applies only when a remedy in damages is inadequate to protect the promisee's entitlement. . . .

i. *Equitable limitations.* If a contract is one that a court would decline to enforce by specific performance or injunction on the ground that such relief would impose undue hardship or would otherwise be inequitable to the defaulting party, disgorgement by the rule of § 39 will be inappropriate for the same reasons, notwithstanding the fact that

the breach is both profitable and deliberate.

One important case in which equitable limitations preclude disgorgement involves the uncontroversial version of "efficient breach." Where contractual performance would be manifestly wasteful—imposing unexpected costs on the performing party that yield no corresponding (or bargained-for) benefit to the recipient—a court will refuse specific performance on the ground of disproportionate hardship. Under such circumstances, it is the party who insists on specific performance who is behaving opportunistically.

Even if a promised performance is fully within the scope of the parties' bargain, specific enforcement may be denied for policy reasons that would make it anomalous to order disgorgement after the fact. By contrast, some of the most frequent reasons for the unavailability of specific performance—either the burden of supervision, or the sheer difficulty of obtaining timely relief—have no application to a remedy via disgorgement after the fact. Unlike the all-or-nothing remedy of specific performance, moreover, a claim to disgorgement of profits under § 39 permits some shaping of the remedy to accord with the equities between the parties, if only in the measurement of the profits "realized . . . as a result of the breach." . . .

§ 49. Restitution in Money; Measures of Enrichment

(1) A claimant entitled to restitution may obtain a judgment for money in the amount of the defendant's unjust enrichment.

(2) Enrichment from a money payment is measured by the amount of the payment or the resulting increase in the defendant's net assets, whichever is less.

(3) Enrichment from the receipt of nonreturnable benefits may be measured by

(a) the value of the benefit in advancing the purposes of the defendant,

(b) the cost to the claimant of conferring the benefit,

(c)   the market value of the benefit, or

(d)   a price the defendant has expressed a willingness to pay, if the defendant's assent may be treated as valid on the question of price.

If the measures of enrichment available in a particular case yield different results, the choice between them is governed by the rules of §§ 50–52.

(4)   When restitution is intended to strip the defendant of a wrongful gain, the standard of liability is not the value of the benefit conferred but the amount of the profit wrongfully obtained. Unjust enrichment in such cases is measured by the rules of § 51(4)–(5).

(5)   Supplemental enrichment in the form of interest or use value, proceeds, and consequential gains is recognized as stated in § 53.

Comment:

a.   General principles and scope; relation to other sections. . . . The present section identifies six potentially different standards for measuring enrichment. The task is not as complicated as this might make it seem, however, because the circumstances of a given transaction will usually eliminate most choices—leaving only one or two means by which enrichment might plausibly be measured.

Many restitution cases pose no appreciable problem of measurement within the rule of this section. Enrichment resulting from a money payment is easily determined in most cases (§ 49(2)). When restitution aims to deprive the defendant of a wrongful gain, enrichment is measured as stated in § 51(4)–(5). The disgorgement rules involve complexities of their own, but they shift the focus of the remedy from measuring the value of a benefit to measuring the profits derived from wrongful conduct (§ 49(4)).

The measurement of enrichment from nonreturnable benefits is potentially more difficult (§ 49(3)), but the problem of choosing between conflicting measures of enrichment will not necessarily arise even here. Frequently the circumstances of the transaction are such that the defendant's unjust enrichment can plausibly be measured in only one way. At other times, two or more possible measures of enrichment will yield the same result. For example, when a professional recovers in restitution for the value of services rendered pursuant to an unenforceable contract (§ 31), there will not necessarily be a meaningful distinction between the value of the services to the recipient, their cost to the claimant, their market value, and a price fixed by the unenforceable agreement.

The significance of the different measures of enrichment from nonreturnable benefits, therefore, is not that they necessarily yield different amounts, but that they sometimes yield different amounts. When they do, the choice between them is dictated by general principles of unjust enrichment, turning chiefly on the innocence or blameworthiness of the defendant. . . .

b.   Liability, remedy, and defenses distinguished. The rules of the present section (and of the other sections within this Topic) address only the *extent* of a liability in restitution, once the question of liability has been decided by application of rules appearing elsewhere in this Restatement. The fact that a person has been demonstrably enriched at the expense of the claimant, by one of the measures identified in § 49, does not suffice to establish either unjust enrichment or liability in restitution. . . .

d.   *Value to the recipient.* This Restatement inherits the formula "value in advancing the purposes of the recipient" from Restatement of Restitution § 155 (1937). An expression such as "subjective value to the recipient" is often used to convey the same idea. The word "subjective" is potentially misleading in this context, because subjective values are often values that are entirely incapable of measurement. But restitution does not impose a liability in money for any enrichment that cannot be valued with reasonable confidence. The relevant comparison is normally between demonstrable value to the recipient, given what we know about the recipient's situation, and the available measures of market value between willing buyers and sellers.

So understood, "value to the recipient" is usually the most restrictive (and therefore the most favorable to the defendant) of the available measures of enrichment. Where this measure applies, a claimant will not necessarily succeed in demonstrating enrichment by showing that the benefits conferred have market value, or even that the recipient's illiquid assets have been increased by market measures, because restitution avoids subjecting the innocent recipient to a forced exchange. See § 2(4); § 9, Comment *a*; § 50(3). These protective features make "value to the recipient" the usual measure of enrichment in all cases where an innocent recipient has obtained unrequested, nonreturnable benefits. Given the potential inefficiency of most nonconsensual transactions—such as benefits conferred by mistake—either market value or cost to the claimant frequently exceeds value to the recipient. If the recipient is not at fault in the transaction, liability in restitution is limited to the least of these amounts (§ 50(2)(a)). Because the innocent recipient is protected against prejudice from the transaction, the claimant necessarily bears any loss that results from the difference between the cost and value of the benefit conferred.

In such circumstances, "value to the recipient" stands in sharp contrast to the other measures of enrichment; but there are cases in which the most natural approximation of "value to the recipient" may be cost of performance, market value, or even contract price. For example, market value is the usual measure of "value to the recipient" in cases of restitution for emergency services protecting life and health. . . . By contrast, where the beneficial nature of the services will not be presumed—as where the claimant acts in an emergency to preserve property, rather than life or health—the recipient will be liable in restitution for the amount of the loss avoided or for reasonable compensation to the claimant, whichever is less. . . . If the terms of the parties' unenforceable contract reveal the price that the defendant was willing to pay for a requested performance, the price so specified—although unenforceable by an action on the contract—may be the best evidence of "value to the recipient." . . .

e.   *Cost to the claimant.* Cost to the claimant recurs as the appropriate measure of enrichment in four kinds of cases:

(1)   When restitution is available for goods or services having no established market price, the cost of providing the benefit may furnish the best—or the only—means of measuring the recipient's enrichment.

(2)   If the value of an unrequested benefit exceeds its cost to the claimant, an innocent recipient will be liable only for the cost. See § 50(4). "Cost or value, whichever is less" is thus the standard recovery in cases of mistaken improvement, if restitution is available at all from an owner not at fault. . . .

(3) Conversely, where the measurable value of a benefit is less than the cost of conferring it, a recipient who is at fault in the transaction creating unjust enrichment may be liable to make restitution in the amount of the claimant's costs. . . .

(4) A court that allows recovery in restitution for performance under an unenforceable contract—where the reason for unenforceability is *malum prohibitum* such as regulatory noncompliance—will sometimes measure enrichment by the claimant's cost of performance, in preference to contract price or market value. . . .

f.   Market value. Liability in restitution for the market value of goods or services is the remedy traditionally known as quantum meruit. It is the usual measurement of enrichment in cases where nonreturnable benefits have been furnished at the defendant's request, but where the parties made no enforceable agreement as to price. See § 31, Comment *e.*

The measurement of unjust enrichment is significantly affected by the fact that the defendant requested the benefits in question and—implicitly, at least—expressed a willingness to pay for them. Where benefits are unrequested, their market value will be relevant (if at all) only as a way to demonstrate their value "in advancing the purposes of the defendant"—as when the claimant's performance has spared the defendant an otherwise necessary expense. . . . By contrast, benefits conferred at the defendant's request are presumed to have value to the recipient equal to the lesser of market value and a price the defendant has expressed a willingness to pay, unless the circumstances of the transaction make this valuation inappropriate. . . .

g.   Contract price. A price fixed by agreement does not conclusively establish the value of benefits conferred if the parties' contract is invalid or unenforceable under applicable law. But even an unenforceable contract may serve to establish value for restitution purposes, if the grounds of unenforceability do not draw into question the validity of the parties' agreement as to price.

Whether the contract price is ultimately acceptable as the measure of benefit for restitution purposes depends on the reasons why the claimant seeks a remedy in restitution rather than on the contract. A variety of circumstances may lead to a conclusion that the enrichment of the recipient from the claimant's contractual performance is something less than a price the recipient once offered to pay. See § 50, Comment *e.* Conversely, the innocent recipient of a contractual performance will in no case be liable in restitution for an amount exceeding the contract price. . . .

(Breach of contract does not ordinarily constitute the kind of legal wrong that would expose the recipient of performance to a liability in restitution exceeding the unpaid contract price. See § 2(2); § 44, Comment *a.* This Restatement recognizes a narrow exception to this rule in cases of profitable, opportunistic breach as described in § 39. Measurement of unjust enrichment in such a case is within the rule of § 51(4).)

If the claimant has rendered a conforming performance under a contract that is unenforceable solely for want of formality—the standard example being a contract that fails to satisfy the applicable Statute of Frauds—the value of the performance to the recipient is presumptively equal to the lesser of contract price and market value, two measures that are frequently identical (§ 50(2)(b)). . . . If instead of a price in money the same contract specifies a counterperformance that the recipient cannot be compelled to render, the implied price of the claimant's performance—and its presumptive value to the recipient, for restitution purposes—is the market rate for the performance in question. . . .

§ 50. Innocent Recipient

(1)   An "innocent recipient" is one who commits no misconduct in the transaction concerned (§ 51) and who bears no responsibility for the unjust enrichment in question (§ 52).

(2)   If nonreturnable benefits would be susceptible of different valuations by the standards identified in § 49(3), the liability of an innocent recipient is determined as follows:

  (a)   Unjust enrichment from unrequested benefits is measured by the standard that yields the smallest liability in restitution.

  (b)   Unjust enrichment from requested benefits is measured by their reasonable value to the recipient. Reasonable value is normally the lesser of market value and a price the recipient has expressed a willingness to pay.

  (c)   Reasonable value may be measured by a more restrictive standard if the validity of the recipient's assent is in question (§ 49(3)(d)); if the claimant has not performed as requested (§ 36); or if prevailing prices include an element of profit that the court decides to withhold from the claimant.

(3)   The liability in restitution of an innocent recipient of unrequested benefits may not leave the recipient worse off (apart from the costs of litigation) than if the transaction giving rise to the liability had not occurred.

(4)   The liability in restitution of an innocent recipient of unrequested benefits may not exceed the cost to the claimant of conferring the benefits in question, supplemented when appropriate by the rules of § 53.

(5)   An innocent recipient may be liable in an appropriate case for use value or proceeds, but not for consequential gains (§ 53).

Comment:

a.   *General principles and scope; relation to other sections.* Restitution may require a choice between two or more measures of the defendant's unjust enrichment, as set forth in § 49. The principles that determine this choice turn chiefly on the extent to which the defendant is at fault in the transaction concerned. . . .

b.   *Enrichment by money payment.* . . . The rule that limits recovery in restitution to the amount of the claimant's outlay (§ 50(4)) is consistent with the proposition that an innocent recipient is not liable in restitution for consequential gains (§ 50(5)). See § 53, Comment d. By contrast, there are circumstances in which the benefit derived by an innocent recipient from property of fluctuating value is most appropriately measured by the proceeds (in money) received on its eventual disposition. See § 53, Comment c . . .

c. Unrequested benefits. The sharpest contrasts between competing measures of enrichment appear in cases of unrequested, nonreturnable benefits, such as services conferred by mistake. A benefit that is costly to confer, with a substantial market value, may be of no value at all in advancing the purposes of the recipient. See § 49, Comment *d.* In such cases the unjust enrichment of an innocent recipient is ordinarily calculated by whichever of the available measures—as identified in § 49(3)—yields the smallest liability in restitution (§ 50(2)(a)). Because "value to the recipient" is usually the most restrictive measure of enrichment, it is the customary measure of the restitutionary liability of an innocent recipient of unrequested, nonreturnable benefits; though in particular contexts the rule of § 50(2)(a) yields the formula "cost or value, whichever is less." . . .

d. Requested benefits: reasonable value. Sometimes the defendant has requested the goods or services by which the defendant is unjustly enriched. Such cases arise when the claimant renders a contractual performance that—for one reason or another—yields no enforceable contract claim (§§ 31–36). In a distinct but closely related set of cases, a requested performance has been rendered in the mistaken belief that a contract exists, though in fact (as the court later determines) the parties never reached agreement. See § 9, Comment *f* . . . The fact that benefits were conferred in response to a valid request is potentially of great significance to the issue of valuation for restitution purposes. This is not because the logic of unjust enrichment is different in such cases, but because the recipient's prior request tends to reveal the value to the recipient of the benefits in question.

When the claimant's performance has been requested by the defendant, its value for restitution purposes is often said to be its "reasonable value."

. . . Reasonable value in such a case is uniformly determined by reference to a market price or "going rate," without consideration of alternatives such as cost to the claimant or value in advancing the purposes of the defendant (§ 49(3)). . . .

Combining these familiar results yields the rule of § 50(2)(b), whereby the "reasonable value" of a requested performance is normally the lesser of (i) its market value, and (ii) a price the defendant offered to pay for it. So if a defendant has requested benefits without specifying a price, "reasonable value" in restitution is presumptively fixed by market price. . . . But an innocent recipient who has offered to pay a given amount for a requested performance will not be required to pay a higher market value if the contract turns out to be unenforceable. . . . Conversely, the defendant's liability in restitution is not reduced by evidence that a validly requested performance, rendered as requested, has proved to be less valuable in advancing the defendant's purposes than the defendant expected. . . .

e. Requested benefits: restricted measures of enrichment. As stated in § 50(2)(c), the rule by which requested benefits are measured by their reasonable value—with the presumption by which "reasonable value" is normally determined by reference to a contract or market price—is subject to qualification in a number of circumstances.

Plainly, the fact of a prior request by the recipient will not be taken to establish value if the circumstances of the request deprive it of significance for this purpose. See Comment *d.* Invalidating factors such as fraud or incapacity may or may not have this effect in a particular case. . . . [T]he recipient's assent proves nothing about value of services for restitution purposes if the recipient has been deceived about the price or quality of what he is to receive.

If restitution is allowed in respect of benefits furnished to a recipient lacking capacity to contract (§ 33), the measure of enrichment is often the lesser of contract price or market value. But if the incapacitated party cannot be presumed to derive the usual advantage from the benefits in question—the basis of any market price—enrichment may be measured as if the benefits were unrequested. . . .

Recovery in restitution for requested benefits is sometimes restricted for other reasons. If the reason the parties' contract is unenforceable is a regulatory infraction by the claimant—such as a failure to obtain a license, or to adhere to a prescribed method of doing business—a court may be willing to allow a recovery in restitution (avoiding an entire forfeiture and the consequent unjust enrichment of the recipient), but not to value the benefit conferred by the claimant's performance at the contract or market price, since such a valuation would not impose any penalty for the infraction. One possibility in such a case is to allow recovery in the amount of the claimant's cost of performance, thereby eliminating the element of profit. . . .

f. Innocent recipients: protective rules. . . . The rules as stated [in subsections (3) and (4)] follow largely (though not entirely) from subsection (2)(a), making them to that extent redundant. The justification of these familiar limits derives from axiomatic propositions about the nature of liability in unjust enrichment.

First, because the basis of liability is the enrichment of the recipient, a judgment in restitution cannot be justified if it exceeds the defendant's enrichment, properly measured. It can be useful to ask whether a proposed outcome leaves the recipient worse off than if the entire transaction had not occurred, because the question directs our attention to the various ways in which the value of the benefit conferred—by the claimant's proposed measure—might be less than its value in advancing the purposes of the recipient. . . .

Second, in the unusual case in which the value to the recipient of an unrequested benefit exceeds the cost of conferring it, the restitutionary liability of an innocent recipient will not exceed the amount required to indemnify the claimant. The axiom underlying this second limitation has been variously expressed. It is often suggested that a person can be *unjustly* enriched only to the extent that the benefit in question has been conferred "at the expense of the claimant" . . . Once the claimant has been indemnified, there is—in the absence of contract—no reason why the innocent recipient of a benefit, however valuable, should pay anything more. . . .

The most common application of the rule stated in § 50(3) is to cases in which a claimant supplies unrequested goods or services whose value in advancing the purposes of the recipient is less than their value to a willing buyer. In such a case, § 50(3) states a rule of thumb that safeguards the innocent recipient against prejudice by assigning to the restitution claimant any loss from an inefficient noncontractual exchange. . . .

In circumstances where the value to the recipient of an unrequested benefit might plausibly exceed the cost to the claimant of conferring it, application of § 50(4) yields the familiar formula by which the recipient's liability is said to be "cost or benefit, whichever is less." . . .

§ 54. Rescission and Restitution

(1)   A person who has transferred money or other property is entitled to recover it by rescission and restitution if

(a)   the transaction is invalid or subject to avoidance for a reason identified in another section of this Restatement, and

(b)   the further requirements of this section may be satisfied.

(2)   Rescission requires a mutual restoration and accounting in which each party

(a)   restores property received from the other, to the extent such restoration is feasible,

(b)   accounts for additional benefits obtained at the expense of the other as a result of the transaction and its subsequent avoidance, as necessary to prevent unjust enrichment, and

(c)   compensates the other for loss from related expenditure as justice may require.

(3)   Rescission is limited to cases in which counter-restitution by the claimant will restore the defendant to the status quo ante, unless

(a)   the defendant is fairly compensated for any deficiencies in the restoration made by the claimant, or

(b)   the fault of the defendant or the assignment of risks in the underlying transaction makes it equitable that the defendant bear any uncompensated loss.

(4)   Rescission is appropriate when the interests of justice are served by allowing the claimant to reverse the challenged transaction instead of enforcing it. As a general rule:

(a)   If the claimant seeks to reverse a transfer induced by fraud or other conscious wrongdoing, the limitation described in subsection (3) is liberally construed in favor of the claimant.

(b)   If the claimant seeks rescission instead of damages as a remedy for material breach of contract (§ 37), the limitation described in subsection (3) is employed to prevent injustice to the defendant from the reversal of a valid and enforceable exchange.

(c)   If rescission would prejudice intervening rights of innocent third parties, the remedy will on that account be denied.

(5)   Restitution or a tender of restitution by the claimant is not a prerequisite of rescission if affirmative relief to the claimant can be reduced by (or made subject to) the claimant's reciprocal obligation of restitution.

(6)   Prejudicial or speculative delay by the claimant in asserting a right of rescission, or a change of circumstances unfairly prejudicial to the defendant, justifies denial of the remedy.

Comment:

a. General principles and scope; relation to other sections. Rescission is the common, shorthand name for a composite remedy (more fully, "rescission and restitution") that combines the avoidance of a transaction and the mutual restoration of performance thereunder. A judicial decree of rescission typically provides for (i) the nullification of a transfer of property between the claimant and the defendant, (ii) the restoration of performance on either side, and (iii) a mutual accounting in which each party pays for benefits received from the other in consequence of the underlying exchange and its subsequent reversal.

A party seeking rescission and restitution must first establish a substantive right to avoidance of the transaction in question. As a further requirement, the proponent of rescission must show that the unwinding of performance (as opposed to a remedy by money judgment) is both feasible and equitable on the facts of the case. . . .

Rescission as a remedy for unjust enrichment usually allows the claimant to recover property that has been transferred to the defendant pursuant to contract. Performance may be reversed when the contract proves to be invalid by reason of fraud, duress, undue influence, incapacity, or lack of authority (§§ 13–17), or when it is subject to avoidance on grounds such as mistake (§ 34) or breach of fiduciary duty (§ 43).

In a different set of cases, also arising in a contractual context, rescission and restitution may be available as an alternative to damages for material breach (§ 37). Rescission as a remedy for breach is available only in those circumstances indicated by § 37 (and subject to the express limitation of § 37(2)). . . .

b. The availability of rescission. A perfect rescission would restore both parties to the status quo ante by specific restitution of property previously transferred, leaving no unjust enrichment, no loss to either party (apart from the defendant's loss of bargain), and no need for the court to place a value on benefits conferred. . . . To the extent that the court must determine the money value of nonreturnable benefits, a remedy that attempts to unwind the transaction may be no more equitable (or administratively efficient) than enforcement by an award of damages.

Rescission is usually invoked in a contractual setting, where its effect is to release the claimant—with retroactive effect—from an exchange transaction with the other party. A claimant who is allowed to rescind has usually been given a choice between (i) dealing with the other party on the basis of their agreement, which the claimant was free to ratify and enforce, and (ii) dealing with the other party "off the contract," where benefits that either party may have derived at the expense of the other give rise to a liability in unjust enrichment. The divergence between contractual and extracontractual values means that rescission and damages will often lead to different results. The strategic possibilities of the choice between remedies, and the potential for hardship to the party against whom rescission is sought, explain the elaborate rules and the extensive case law regulating the availability of rescission as a remedial option.

The availability of rescission thus depends partly on the degree to which the parties' performance is capable of restoration in specie, and partly on the grounds of the claimant's entitlement to relief. Rescission will almost certainly be available when the claimant seeks to escape from an agreement that was induced by the other party's fraud or other wrongdoing. Even when a plaintiff seeks rescission as an alternative to damages for breach of a valid and enforceable contract, there are certain simplified situations in which the potential advantages of rescission over damages—in terms of fairness to the plaintiff as well as remedial efficiency—appear so evident that a plaintiff is uniformly permitted to pursue either remedy. Such cases typically involve breach or repudiation by a defendant who has obtained the plaintiff's performance without tendering any return. . . .

Factors relevant to this ultimate question are sometimes addressed directly. Elsewhere they are implicit in a judicial conclusion that rescission would not be equitable under the circumstances, or that it is not possible to place the parties *in statu quo.* Courts naturally consider the circumstances of the transaction; the quality of the parties' conduct; the relative ease or difficulty of compensating the claimant's injury in damages; and the fairness of limiting the claimant to a damage remedy. On the other side of the scale, they consider the difficulty of measuring noncontractual values; the burden to the defendant of being compelled to reverse a contractual exchange; and the extent of windfalls and forfeitures resulting from interim variation in the values being restored.

c. Restitution as a safeguard against forfeiture. . . . Rescission of a valid and enforceable contract overturns legitimate contractual expectations on which both parties may have significantly relied. The most notable form of reliance in this context is likely to consist in the defendant's performance (or preparation for performance), resulting in a change of position to the extent that any performance is not capable of restoration and subsequent resale. The consequences of invalidating the contractual exchange will not be adverse to the party seeking rescission, because the remedy is chosen at the claimant's election; but

they impose a potential forfeiture on the party in breach, who stands to lose not only the benefit of the bargain but also the sunk costs of performance.

The potentially inequitable consequences of rescission are therefore limited by the traditional requirement that the claimant make counter-restitution of property received under the contract, as a means of restoring both parties to the precontractual status quo. Such a rule reinforces significantly the stability of contractual price terms. If rescission were an optional remedy for any material breach of contract—with no requirement of restoration by the plaintiff—the plaintiff might elect in every case between (i) enforcing the bargain and (ii) dealing with the defendant (in restitution) as if no bargain had ever been made. Such an outcome would expand the implied conditions of the bargain beyond recognized limits, giving the party injured by material breach the right not only to terminate the contract (that is, to cease his own performance and recover damages) but, in the alternative, to set aside the contract whenever it was advantageous to do so. . . .

A claimant (such as a fraud victim) who has been an innocent party to a legally defective exchange will ordinarily be able to rescind on making restitution (in specie or in value) of any benefits conferred by the other party. Rescission is available on relatively liberal terms in such cases—especially if the defendant is a conscious wrongdoer—because the underlying exchange is ineffective to determine the parties' respective entitlements. . . . Rescission as a remedy for breach of contract is subject to more restrictive requirements because of its potential to destabilize the contractual exchange, imposing what may be an effective forfeiture as a penalty for breach. See Comment *e.* . . .

e.   *Rescission as a remedy for breach of contract.* . . . When rescission restores a performance rendered under a defective agreement—as when rescission unwinds an exchange that is invalid by reason of mistake, fraud, or duress—it can usually be understood as a remedy for unjust enrichment. By contrast, when rescission affords an alternative remedy for breach of a valid and enforceable contract (as permitted by the rule of § 37)—a breach, in other words, that might be remedied by damages or specific performance—the effect and the justification of the rescission remedy are significantly different. Rescission in such a case permits the injured party to make a fundamental election, choosing to go backward (to the status quo ante) instead of forward (by enforcement of the contractual exchange). The advantages to the party entitled to this remedial election are self-evident, but the court must determine whether rescission in place of enforcement serves the interests of justice. Unlike the case of rescission for fraud or mistake, the justification of rescission as an alternative remedy for breach is not the avoidance of unjust enrichment, but a concern with fairness to the injured party combined with remedial economy. . . .

i.   *Incidental or reliance loss.* Rescission of the parties' exchange may leave the claimant with losses from related expenditures (as distinct from payment of the price) made in reliance on the transaction that is being set aside. Compensation of such loss by an award of damages is a remedy different in kind from rescission and restitution, but the remedies are not necessarily inconsistent when the claimant's basic entitlement is to be restored to the status quo ante. Damages measured by the claimant's expenditure can be included in the accounting that accompanies rescission, in order to do complete justice in a single proceeding.

Recovery of what are commonly called "incidental damages" may thus be allowed in connection with rescission, consistent with the remedial objective of restoring the claimant to the precontractual position. . . . Reimbursement of other forms of reliance expenditure—as distinguished from restitution of the claimant's performance itself, in the form of the price paid—may likewise be included in the parties' accounting on rescission. . . .

The fact that rescission is consistent with reimbursement of the claimant's reliance expenditures in some cases should not be allowed to obscure the central distinction between avoidance of a contract and enforcement by an action for damages. Rescission contemplates a mutual restoration of performance without the need to compare contract and market values. Its most dramatic applications therefore permit a claimant to recover a prepaid price without proof of damages from the defendant's breach. . . . By contrast, no measure of *damages* for breach of contract—including performance-based damages measured by the claimant's expenditures—can be calculated without reference to contractual expectations. Because a nonfraudulent breach does not make the defendant a guarantor of the profitability of the claimant's bargain, damages measured by unreimbursed expenditures are reduced by losses the claimant would have incurred had there been full performance (§ 38(2)(a)). Accordingly, when the ground of rescission is breach of contract (§ 37), the claimant may not combine rescission with a claim to recover expenditures that would circumvent this fundamental limitation. . . .

j.   *Tender of restitution not a precondition.* Section 54(5) explicitly eliminates previous requirements that the claimant tender restitution to the other party as a precondition of rescission. No distinction is recognized between rescission "at law" and "in equity." The effect of former distinctions to govern the right to jury trial in a suit for rescission is a question outside the scope of this Restatement.

The requirement of a prior tender carried implicit safeguards to the defendant that the present section imposes more directly. It reduced the risk of a one-sided restitution, whereby the defendant might be compelled to restore what had been received in the transaction without obtaining restitution of what had been given. But there is no such danger when a judicial order can make restitution by one party conditional on counter-restitution by the other. . . .

[T]he requirement of prior tender imposed a procedural barrier as a proxy for a substantive rule, since it purported to bar from rescission all claimants who were unable (and had not merely neglected) to restore the other party to the status quo ante. This ostensibly simple rule, as already noted, engendered a host of exceptions. Section 54(3)(b) states a more realistic test, requiring the court to determine whether any loss that will be allocated by rescission is appropriately borne by the party against whom rescission is sought. . . .

§ 63.   Equitable Disqualification (Unclean Hands)

Recovery in restitution to which an innocent claimant would be entitled may be limited or denied because of the claimant's inequitable conduct in the transaction that is the source of the asserted liability.

Comment:

a.   General principles and scope; relation to other sections. . . . A court that encounters an instance of prima facie unjustified enrichment may decide that the usual consequence—a liability and remedy in restitution—is not what equity requires in the circumstances of the particular case. . . . The possibility that a court may refuse relief on this basis is classified within this Restatement, for convenience of organization, among the affirmative defenses to a liability in restitution. But the principle involved is in fact one of judicial forbearance, and its concern is with the disqualification of the claimant rather than the rightful position of the recipient.

Some prominent examples of equitable disqualification involve the denial of a claim for benefits conferred pursuant to certain illegal contracts. Because the possibility of disqualification is particularly salient in this context, it qualifies the affirmative

rule authorizing recovery (§ 32(3)). See Comment *b*.

There are cases in which the receipt of a benefit at the expense of a wrongdoer might be thought to constitute poetic justice rather than unjust enrichment. . . . The recipient escapes liability, not because of the recipient's equitable position, but because the court may deny the claimant a remedy to which an innocent party would be entitled as a matter of course. The idea is that a person who engages in inequitable conduct may forfeit the right to a judicial determination of what "equity and good conscience" require of the other party to the transaction. . . .

The rule of § 63 coincides in part, but only in part, with the equitable maxim that "he who comes into equity must come with clean hands." The affirmative defense described in this section is not restricted to claims that seek traditional forms of equitable relief; it may be interposed against claims that derive from the legal side of restitution as well. . . .

b.   Illicit contract between claimant and recipient. When a claimant seeks restitution for benefits conferred under a contract that is illegal or unenforceable for reasons of public policy, equitable disqualification by the rule of this section may be a decisive element in the resolution of the claim. See § 32(3). . . .

If the claimant has rendered a valuable performance to the recipient in a prohibited transaction, the court must decide—if the question is not governed by the language and objectives of the relevant statute—whether the appropriate sanctions for violation include forfeiture of what would otherwise be the claimant's entitlement to restitution. This question is frequently addressed by asking whether the claimant is equitably disqualified to assert the restitution claim. . . . The relative culpability of the claimant and the recipient in the transaction between them will sometimes, but not always, be taken into account. . . .

The consequences for restitution are the same when the claimant has conferred a benefit under an agreement with the recipient that (while not inherently wrongful) was entered into for a wrongful purpose. . . .

c.   Restitution from an innocent recipient. . . . The potential reach of equitable disqualification is . . . broader than a mere refusal to enforce or relieve against illegal transactions. Rather, the claimant's misconduct may lead a court to deny relief to which a claimant would ordinarily be entitled, based on any of the headings of liability in restitution. . . .

RESTATEMENT OF EMPLOYMENT LAW

(SELECTED SECTIONS)

§ 2.01 Default Rule of an At-Will Employment Relationship

Either party may terminate an employment relationship with or without cause unless the right to do so is limited by a statute, other law or public policy, or an agreement between the parties, a binding employer promise, or a binding employer policy statement (§ 2.02).

Comment: . . .

b.   *Rebuttable presumption of at-will employment.* At its core, employment is a contractual relationship. The law of contracts rests on a series of default rules that provide starting points for bargaining between the parties. These default rules control in the event neither the parties' agreement nor the applicable law prescribe different rules. . . .

The at-will presumption states a default rule that applies when the agreement between the parties or other binding employer promise or employer policy statement under § 2.02 does not provide for a definite term or contain a limit on the employer's power to terminate the relationship. The default rule is also subject to contrary statute, law, or public policy.

c.   *Contrary agreement; binding promise or statement.* Agreements and binding employer promises or employer policy statements that would overcome the presumption of at-will employment are discussed in § 2.02. . . .

Illustrations:

1.   Employer X and employee E enter into an employment agreement providing for a one-year term, renewable for an additional year if neither party serves the other with at least 30 days' notice prior to termination of the one-year period. Two months into the relationship, X terminates the agreement. X is subject to liability for breach of contract (10 months of pay subject to mitigation of damages), because the parties' agreement provides for a definite term, which overcomes the presumption of at-will employment. . . .

2.   Employer X and employee E enter into an employment agreement providing for a $50,000 "annual salary" plus benefits. Two months into the relationship, X serves E with notice of termination of the agreement. X is not, without more, in breach of contract because this agreement is presumed to provide only for at-will employment. The statement of employment at an annual rate of salary does not, standing alone, guarantee a year's employment or otherwise overcome the presumption of at-will status. . . .

f.   *Termination.* The at-will presumption applies not only to employer discharges of employees but also to other adverse employer actions or decisions falling short of discharge, including those that reasonably elicit a resignation from the employee. . . .

Illustration:

4.   Employer X and employee E enter into an at-will employment agreement, providing that E will work as a marketing representative

and will be paid at a rate of $50,000 per year plus benefits. Two months into the relationship, X announces that because of declining demand for X's product, E will henceforth be paid at the annual rate of $40,000 plus benefits. E continues to work and sues for breach. Because no contractual, statutory, or public-policy restriction applies, X has not breached the at-will agreement by reducing E's salary prospectively. (Note: This Illustration rests on the premise that the prior $50,000-per-year stated salary rate did not create a nonmodifiable right to that salary, see § 2.06.) The same result is reached if E quits and sues for breach. . . .

§ 2.02   Agreements and Binding Employer Promises or Statements Providing for Terms Other Than At-Will Employment

The employment relationship is not terminable at will by an employer if:

(a)   an agreement between the employer and the employee provides for (i) a definite term of employment, or (ii) an indefinite term of employment and requires cause (defined in § 2.04) to terminate the employment (§ 2.03); or

(b)   a promise by the employer to limit termination of employment reasonably induces detrimental reliance by the employee (§ 2.02, Comment c); or

(c)   a binding policy statement made by the employer limits termination of employment (§ 2.05); or

(d)   the implied duty of good faith and fair dealing applicable to all employment relationships (§ 2.07) limits termination of employment; or

(e)   other established principles recognized in the general law of contracts limit termination of employment (§ 2.02, Comment d).

Comment: . . .

c.   Promissory estoppel. Section 2.02(b) makes clear that an employer's promise that reasonably induces detrimental reliance by employees, or individuals about to become employees, is enforceable under the well-established doctrine of promissory estoppel under § 90 of the Restatement Second, Contracts. The promise must be definite enough to reasonably induce the action taken in reliance on the promise and must in fact induce such reliance. See id. and Comment *b*. If the conditions for promissory estoppel are present, then a promise may be enforceable even though an agreement itself would not be enforceable for lack of a written document. (Remedies for breach of promises enforceable under the doctrine are the subject of § 9.01(d) and Comment *i* of this Restatement.)

Illustrations:

1.   Spouses W and H are quality-control managers for Employer X. Because of a corporate reorganization, H's employment is terminated. W, a very successful employee at X, could readily obtain equivalent employment elsewhere. Knowing that H will be seeking employment with one of X's competitors, W speaks to her supervisor,

who responds, "your employment will not be affected if H goes to work for one of our competitors." Because of X's assurance, W turns down a better-paying offer of employment in the same industry. After H begins working for a competitor, X terminates W's employment for that reason. W has a valid claim in promissory estoppel.

2. Same facts as Illustration 1, except that W does not receive an offer of equivalent employment with another company. W does not have a valid claim in promissory estoppel because she cannot demonstrate detrimental reliance. . . .

§ 2.03 Agreements for a Definite or Indefinite Term

(a) An employer must have cause (§ 2.04) for terminating:

(1) an unexpired agreement for a definite term of employment; or

(2) an agreement for an indefinite term of employment requiring cause for termination.

(b) In the absence of an employee's express agreement providing otherwise, the employee is under no reciprocal obligation to have cause to terminate the employment relationship.

Comment: . . .

b. Agreements. Typically, agreements between employers and their employees involve an exchange of express promises, an offer contemplating acceptance by performance followed by such performance, or some other statement or conduct manifesting the employer's promise and the employee indication of assent, although no particular form of words is required. An agreement can provide for a definite term of employment whereby earlier termination of the agreement absent cause is a breach of contract (§ 2.03(a)(1)), or for an indefinite term yet require cause for termination such that termination without cause is a breach (§ 2.03(a)(2)), or for an indefinite term yet containing no limitation on termination (§ 2.01) except perhaps notice or a stipulated payment by the employer (§ 9.01(c)).

Illustrations:

1. Employer X and employee E enter into a contract providing for a one-year term, renewable for an additional year if neither party serves the other with 30 days' notice before the one-year term ends. Two months into the relationship, X serves E with notice of termination of the agreement effective before the end of the first year. X is in breach of contract.

2. X, eager to recruit E, a manager for a competitor in California, to a similar position at X's facility in Florida, promises E "permanent employment" and a starting annual salary of $100,000. E accepts the offer in a letter to X's president and starts the process of moving to Florida. Before E arrives in Florida, however, X announces that, because of a business downturn, X no longer requires E's services. Because E accepted X's offer, the parties entered into an enforceable agreement, and X's attempted termination is in breach of the agreement. (In effect, the promise of "permanent employment" requires X to provide "cause" for terminating E's employment; what constitutes "cause" sufficient to terminate such an agreement before the end of the agreed term is discussed in § 2.04.)

3. Same facts as Illustration 2, except that E does not verbally accept the offer but instead moves to Florida and begins work there for X, thus accepting the offer by performance. Because X's promise contemplated acceptance either by words or by beginning work in Florida pursuant to the offered terms, the parties entered into an enforceable agreement, and X's attempted termination is in breach of contract. . . .

d. Consideration or bargained-for exchange. The agreements that come under this Section must be enforceable under generally applicable contract law. . . . The general contract requirement of consideration or bargained-for exchange does not require identical or parallel consideration from both parties to the agreement. An employee's promise to work for the employer at stated terms is ordinarily sufficient to support a number of promises by the employer, including, for example, a promise to provide the employment on the stated terms and a promise not to terminate the relationship before the contract term ends except for cause.

e. Unilateral contracts. Some jurisdictions use a form of "unilateral contract" analysis to hold enforceable unilaterally promulgated employer statements that are provided to employees who then continue working after receiving those statements. Even in the majority of jurisdictions not relying on such analysis, certain employer policy statements (discussed in § 2.05) may give rise to binding obligations even in the absence of consideration or bargained-for exchange or a showing that the employee detrimentally relied on the statements. . . .

f. Mutuality. Mutuality of obligation is not required for employment agreements to be enforceable. Even if an employer agrees to a "cause" limit on the authority to discharge or impose other discipline and, as is typical, the employee does not agree to eschew the prerogative to quit the job at any time, with or without cause, the employment agreement is nevertheless enforceable. Even when an employee does agree to provide cause for a voluntary termination, the general rule is that specific performance is not available to enforce a "personal services" contract. . . . At the same time, the parties can provide for a reasonable period during which the departing employee will not solicit customers or employees for a competing business; such a promise in appropriate circumstances may be enforceable by injunction. . . . The parties can also require the employee to give advance notice of an intention to quit employment if the employee wishes to receive severance pay or other benefits that are not vested in the circumstances. . . .

g. Implied terms. In some cases, the parties to an otherwise enforceable employment agreement expressly or impliedly refer to stated policies or established practices of the employer or in the trade to supply omitted terms in the agreement.

Illustration:

5. P receives a letter from C, a local college, offering P a position as assistant professor of geometry on a year-to-year contract. Before P begins work for C, P and C had no communication about whether or when P might be eligible for tenure. ("Tenure" is a cause limitation on employment termination common in educational settings.) C's handbook for professors states that "assistant professors are eligible for tenure after 5 years of instruction." C's practice is to conduct a tenure review of assistant professors in their fifth year of teaching. C conducted no such review of P. Shortly before the end of P's fifth year, C notifies P that his contract will not be

renewed. C is in breach of contract. P's eligibility for a tenure review in his fifth year of instruction was an implied term of the employment agreement under C's established practices.

h. Indefinite-term agreements. Agreements that limit the employer's power to terminate the employment relationship can override the presumption of at-will employment even if the employment term is indefinite. This Section thus departs from decisions holding that contracts for indefinite employment should always be treated as contracts terminable at will or as tantamount to such contracts unless the employee can meet special proof burdens to defeat the at-will presumption. . . .

Illustrations:

6. At his August 1 job interview with X Corporation, E, a biochemist living in California, inquires about future job security if he were to accept a job with X. X's president responds that E would enjoy "permanent employment" and adds: "I hope you will stay forever." On August 31, X's president writes to E stating "this letter confirms our offer to you for employment as a biochemist at an initial salary of $50,000 per year." In October, E moves to Connecticut to begin work in X's facility there on November 1. On his first day on the job, E is given a copy of X's personnel manual. It states that X "reserves the right to hire, discharge for cause, promote, demote, reclassify, and assign work to employees." A year later, E is provided with an updated version of the manual that omits any reference to "for cause" in connection with any discharge or other personnel-management decisions. On these facts, the trier of fact can decide that X and E entered into an agreement for an indefinite term with a limitation on X's right to discharge E without "cause." The later manual's omission of the "for cause" language does not remove the cause limitation in the agreement between X and E.

7. Same facts as Illustration 6, except X's personnel manual when first provided to E on November 1 does not contain the "for cause" language. Because sophisticated parties would typically enter into a written agreement setting forth the terms of such an unusual agreement promising a prospective managerial employee essentially lifetime employment absent cause to terminate, X and E may well have understood that X's oral statements that E would have "permanent employment" and "stay forever" were not intended as a binding promise of lifetime employment absent cause. But E reasonably may have understood the statements in precisely those terms. If the terms of the parties' agreement are ambiguous, the trier of fact may consider the parties' bargaining history and the employer's relevant policies, procedures, or practices.

§ 2.04 Cause for Termination of Employment Agreements

Unless otherwise provided for in the agreement: . . .

(b) . . . [A]n employer has a ground for terminating an agreement for an indefinite term of employment requiring cause for termination when a significant change in the employer's economic circumstances means that the employer no longer has a business need for the employee's services.

Comment: . . .

c.   Indefinite-term agreements. When parties have negotiated an indefinite-term agreement containing a cause limitation on the employer's power to terminate, the definition of cause to which the parties have agreed controls. However, if the agreement is silent on the question, then given the potential length of indefinite-term agreements, the reasonable assumption is that the parties intended, in addition to the grounds stated in § 2.04(a), to include significant changes in the employer's economic circumstances.

d.   Factual cause. When the parties agree to a definite term of employment or for an indefinite term with a cause limitation on power to terminate, the reasonable assumption is that the parties intend any cause requirement to be undisputed or proven employee material breach, misconduct or malfeasance, or inability to perform the work due to long-term disability; and do not intend also to permit termination based on the employer's reasonable, good-faith but erroneous belief that there was cause for termination. This is in keeping with conventional views of cause as an objective concept. It is also consistent with the understanding that a good-faith but erroneous belief that early termination of a definite-term contract is justified, even if based on facts after an appropriate investigation, is not legally sufficient cause to terminate such an agreement.

Illustrations:

1.   X Corporation, eager to recruit E from E's managerial position with a competitor in California to work at X's facility in Florida, promises E in writing a four-year term of employment beginning with a $100,000 annual salary. E accepts the offer, moves to Florida, and begins working for X in Florida. Two years into the relationship, X announces that because of a business downturn, it is closing the Florida facility and terminating E's employment. Absent a specific agreement conditioning the full four-year term of employment on X's continuing its operations at the Florida facility, X is in breach of contract. X lacked cause for early termination of its obligations to E under the definite-term agreement absent E's material breach, misconduct or malfeasance, or inability to perform the work due to long-term disability. The employer's changed economic circumstances did not constitute cause for X's early termination of E's employment.

2.   Same facts as Illustration 1, except that X promises E "permanent employment . . . unless you screw up badly," rather than a definite term of employment. Two years into the relationship, X announces that because of a business downturn, it is closing its Florida facility and terminating E's employment. Absent evidence of an agreement to limit cause to terminate E's employment to the grounds stated in § 2.04(a), X has a legally sufficient business reason for terminating the indefinite-term employment agreement and is not in breach of contract.

3.   Same facts as Illustration 2, except that two years into the employment relationship, X determines in good faith and based upon facts obtained after reasonable investigation that E has sexually harassed X's employees in violation of X's policy and applicable law. X is in breach of contract if the trier of fact determines that E did not in fact engage in the claimed sexual harassment; even though X acted in good faith, X lacked cause for early termination of the agreement. . . .

§ 2.05   Binding Employer Policy Statements

Policy statements by an employer in documents such as employee manuals, personnel handbooks, and employment policy directives that are provided or made accessible to employees, whether by physical or electronic means, and that, reasonably read in context, establish limits on the employer's power to terminate the employment relationship, are binding on the employer until modified or revoked (as provided in § 2.06).

Comment:

a.   Scope and cross-references. As a general matter, employers of any size will make agreements (whether for a definite or indefinite term) that structure an employment relationship only with their higher-level employees. When an employer is dealing with a large number of similarly situated employees, the employer is likely to communicate the terms of the employment relationship through unilateral statements in documents such as employee manuals, personnel handbooks, and employment policy directives that are provided, or made accessible, to employees. Such statements, reasonably read in context, may limit the employer's power to terminate the employment relationship at will or may provide for other undertakings that are to apply uniformly to all similarly situated employees without further negotiation with individual employees. Under certain circumstances, such statements may give rise to an employment agreement under traditional contract principles. See § 2.03. In other situations, such statements may reasonably induce detrimental reliance under the promissory-estoppel doctrine. See § 2.02(b). But even if the elements of an enforceable agreement or promise are not present, these unilateral policy statements can bind the employer until properly modified or revoked. . . .

Unilateral employer statements may also establish, or purport to establish, employees' obligations to the employer. Statements filling out the duties expected of employees are generally enforceable only by the employer's power to terminate employment or administer discipline and do not provide an independent basis for imposing liability on the employee. . . .

b.   Rationale. Some courts have tried to fit this class of unilateral employer statements into a conventional contract-law framework, reasoning that employees "accept" or "rely on" these unilateral employer "offers" by continuing to provide services after the statements are disseminated. This has proved to be a conceptually awkward fit. Employees are rarely made aware, and even more rarely make themselves aware, of the content of such statements when they first accept employment, or later when statements are changed. That is particularly true when the employer does not provide the statements directly to employees but only to supervisors. Employees may only be able to read the statements in a personnel office or in summaries forwarded to the employee's paper or electronic-mail inbox. Such factual circumstances make it difficult to analogize this class of unilateral employer statements to unilateral-contract offers under the Restatement Second, Contracts § 45, Comment *a.*

Beyond that difficulty, traditional principles of consideration and bargained-for exchange rarely, if ever, apply when the employer's unilateral statements are not made in response to a prospective employee's expressed concerns or an employee's threat to resign. For similar reasons reasonable detrimental reliance by employees on such statements under the promissory-estoppel doctrine will be rare. Moreover, many jurisdictions adopting the unilateral-contract approach do not follow traditional contract analysis by permitting employers to unilaterally modify or rescind promises contained in handbooks or personnel manuals even when there is no consideration for the change and the employee does not consent to the change other than by continuing to work under the new terms.

Against that background, other courts, and this Restatement, rest the binding effect of unilateral employer statements on general estoppel principles. Employers make certain unilateral statements about personnel policy to govern the operational decisions of their supervisors and managers. Employers do so to serve their own interests in advancing productivity, improving employee morale, or achieving some other organizational objective. Absent contrary language in the statement, the employer's purpose in promulgating a unilateral policy statement is to have it govern operational decisions while the statement is in effect but not to bind the employer to continued adherence after changing the policy and giving reasonable notice to employees of the change. The courts reach this result in a number of ways: adjusting the unilateral-contract analysis to imply employees' "consent" to a new unilateral contract from the fact that employees continue to work under the new terms; allowing unilateral modification where employers have expressly reserved their right to change their unilateral policy statements; or invoking something akin to promissory-estoppel principles even in the absence of employee reliance or by conclusively presuming such reliance.

To avoid these analytical contortions, § 2.05 provides a general rule that unilateral employer policy statements that are not enforceable agreements or promises under § 2.02 may

still be enforceable but can be modified only on a prospective basis. Such statements are analogous to rules of practice promulgated by administrative agencies to govern their operational decisions. As a matter of administrative law, such rules bind the agency until properly modified or revoked on a theory of "administrative agency estoppel," even though no statute or regulation may have required their promulgation in the first place. Similarly, unilateral employer statements that, reasonably read in context, are intended to govern operational personnel decisions should be binding on the employer until properly modified or revoked. Modification or revocation of such statements is the subject of § 2.06.

c.   Reasonably read in context. Only certain unilateral employer policy statements are binding on the employer. It is often a question for the trier of fact whether a particular statement or set of statements, reasonably read in context, constitutes a binding policy statement. Several factors should inform this inquiry. First, the presence of a prominent disclaimer in the text of the statement may indicate that it is a hortatory pronouncement rather than a statement intended to govern the employer's operational personnel decisions. Any such disclaimer should be viewed, of course, in the context of the entire statement, other employer policies, and the employer's course of conduct. Second, the mode of dissemination may be relevant. Dissemination of a statement limited to supervisors, with no or limited access to the employees, suggests it is intended only as guidance to supervisors in exercising their discretion rather than as a rule or policy governing the workplace. Third, a workplace culture relying on bilateral agreements with employees may reduce the significance of unilateral employer statements. Other factors may also be relevant to determining whether a unilateral statement binds the employer.

Illustrations:

1. Employer X Corporation promulgates an employee handbook, distributed to all employees, containing a procedure that supervisors "should" follow before deciding to discharge an employee. The procedure includes a requirement of a prior warning, followed by an unpaid suspension from work for a repeated offense, and then by a "last chance" agreement in the event of a third offense. If those steps fail to correct the problem, the procedure culminates in termination of employment for violating the last-chance agreement. The procedure is "not applicable" where the employee has engaged in violence or theft, offenses for which immediate termination is indicated. Employee E has been absent from work on several Mondays following vacation days or holidays. E has received a warning for this absenteeism but no other discipline. When E is once again absent on a Monday, X's supervisor terminates E's employment. Because X promulgated the multistep disciplinary procedure in the hand-book to govern its supervisors' decisions on discipline for other than violence or theft, X has breached its contractual obligation to E.

2. Same facts as Illustration 1, except that the employee handbook contains a prominent disclaimer on the first page:

"The statements contained in this handbook are not intended to create a contractual obligation of any kind. Employment at X Corporation is at will. That means that, except as provided by law, you and your employer each has the right to terminate this relationship at any time, with or without cause or prior notice."

All employees are required to sign an acknowledgment of receipt of the handbook, immediately below the disclaimer on the first page, which E had signed. In view of this disclaimer, X may not have breached any binding commitment to E. In some circumstances, despite this disclaimer, there may still be a question of fact as to whether X limited its power of termination by other language in the handbook or other statements or course of conduct. . . .

§ 2.06 Modification or Revocation of Binding Employer Policy Statements

(a) An employer may prospectively modify or revoke its binding policy statements if it provides reasonable advance notice of, or reasonably makes accessible, the modified statement or revocation to the affected employees.

(b) Modifications and revocations apply to all employees hired, and all employees who continue working, after the notice is given and the modification or revocation becomes effective.

(c) Modifications and revocations cannot adversely affect vested or accrued employee rights that may have been created by the statement, an agreement based on the statement (covered by § 2.03), or reasonable detrimental reliance on a promise in the statement (covered by § 2.02, Comment c).

Comment:

a. Scope and cross-references. This Section deals with the issue of modification or revocation by employers of commitments made in previous unilateral statements. Absent an enforceable agreement under § 2.03 or an employer promise inducing the employee's detrimental reliance under § 2.02, Comment *c*, and except for vested or accrued employee rights created by the statement, undertakings in unilateral statements do not bind the employer for all time. It is not reasonable to assume that an employer intended permanently to circumscribe its operational policies through such non-bargained-for promulgations.

b. The special case of vested or accrued employee rights. An employer cannot by unilateral action modify or rescind employees' enforceable contractual rights. The terms "vested" or "accrued" are often used to indicate employee rights that cannot be reduced, taken away, or otherwise adversely changed absent the employee's consent, supported by consideration. . . . In appropriate circumstances, the employer's unilateral policy statement itself may have created vested or accrued employee rights, which, under this Section, cannot be unilaterally modified or rescinded. . . .

c. Modification or revocation. This Section provides that, in general, undertakings in an employer's policy statements are binding on the employer only from the date of distribution or a later-stated "effective date" until they are properly modified or revoked. Employment terminations that occur while the original statement is in place are governed by that statement; termi-nations that occur after modification takes effect are governed by the modified statement. . . .

e. Effectiveness of modification or revocation. A substantial number of courts have held that an employee who continues to work for the employer after receiving proper notice of a modification or revocation of a unilateral employer statement that makes a personnel policy less advantageous to the employees than the original statement are deemed to have "accepted" the change. A smaller number of courts have held that a changed personnel policy covers only those incumbent employees who have expressly agreed to the change. For these jurisdictions, it is not enough that an employee continues to work for the employer after receiving notice of the policy change.

This Restatement adopts the first position and rejects the second. A requirement that a modification or revocation of a unilateral employer statement can be made effective for incumbent employees only by a bilateral agreement is inconsistent with the basis for treating such statements as binding employer policy statements. That basis recognizes that the statements are self-imposed limitations on the employer's authority binding as a matter of equitable estoppel rather than contract principles of consideration, bargained-for exchange, or even promissory estoppel. Requiring employees expressly to agree to changes in employer statements would be unworkable for companies with large workforces and would lead to inconsistent treatment among similarly situated employees. . . .

§ 2.07 Implied Duty of Good Faith and Fair Dealing

(a) Each party to an employment relationship, including at-will employment, owes a nonwaivable duty of good faith and fair dealing to each other party, which includes a party's obligation not to hinder the other party's performance under, or to deprive the other party of the benefit of, their contractual relationship (§ 3.05(a)).

(b)   The implied duty of good faith and fair dealing applies to at-will employment relationships in manner consistent with the essential nature of such an at-will relationship.

(c)   In any employment relationship, including at-will employment, the employer's implied duty of good faith and fair dealing includes the duty not to terminate or seek to terminate the employment relationship for the purpose of:

(1)   preventing the vesting or accrual of an employee right or benefit; or

(2)   retaliating against the employee for performing the employee's obligations under the employment contract or law.

Comment: . . .

b.   Consistency with at-will contracts. As in all contracts, the implied duty of good faith and fair dealing serves as a supplementary aid in implementing the parties' reasonable expectations and should not be read as a means of overriding the basic terms of, or otherwise undermining the essential nature of, their contractual relationship. Jurisdictions that recognize the implied duty in the employment setting therefore also recognize that the duty applies to at-will employment in a manner consistent with the essential nature of such an at-will relationship— namely, except to the extent provided by law or public policy, either party may terminate the relationship with or without cause.

c.   Application in at-will employment: opportunistic firings. This Section sets out two principal (though not necessarily exclusive) applications of the implied duty of good faith and fair dealing in the employment context. The first addresses an employer's opportunistic use of its power to terminate the relationship as a means of preventing an employee right or benefit from vesting or accruing. . . . For example, if an employer provides a form of bonus tied to past performance but conditioned upon the employee's remaining on the payroll as of a certain date, discharge of the employee without cause prior to that date for the purpose of preventing vesting is a breach of the implied duty. The discharge will not be effective to prevent the vesting of the employee's bonus. This is not because the employer has a general obligation not to terminate employees without cause. Rather, in the context of this bonus plan, the employer's duty to cooperate means that once an employee has substantially performed, unless there is independent cause for termination, the employer cannot use its right to terminate without cause for the purpose of depriving the employee of the benefit of the contract. The implied duty enforces the parties' reasonable expectations in agreeing to the deferred-compensation bonus arrangement by requiring full payment of the amount owed. . . .

d.   Application in at-will employment: employer retaliation. The second principal application of the implied duty in at-will employment involves retaliatory discharge or other significant discipline of employees for performing their contractual or statutory duties. Although employers in at-will relationships are not required to have cause for termination of an employee, they are under an implied duty of cooperation that requires them not to terminate or otherwise discipline an employee for performing the employee's contractual obligations. Similarly, where employees are under a legal duty to act or refrain from acting in particular ways, employers violate the implied duty of good faith and fair dealing by using their at-will power to terminate or otherwise discipline employees for performing those legal obligations. In this context, a violation of the implied duty provides a basis for challenging the termination or other discipline.

e.   Nonwaivable duty. The implied duty of good faith and fair dealing is read into every contract as a matter of law, and in that sense is not subject to modification or waiver by the parties' agreement. The agreement frames the employee's job duties and the par-

ties' reasonable expectations, and informs the extent to which the implied duty applies in particular cases.

Illustration:

3. . . . E is X's manager of product quality control who hears "through the grapevine" that X is engaged in accounting improprieties. E sends a statement to X's president threatening "to go public" unless X addresses those accounting issues. In retaliation for that conduct, X fires E. E cannot claim a violation of the duty of good faith and fair dealing because the disclosure to X's president was unrelated to E's job duties; and E has no legal duty to issue the statement.

§ 8.06   Enforcement of Restrictive Covenants in Employment Agreements

Except as otherwise provided by other law or applicable professional rules, a covenant in an agreement between an employer and a former employee restricting the former employee's working activities is enforceable only if it is reasonably tailored in scope, geography, and time to further a protectable interest of the employer, as defined in § 8.07, unless:

(a)   the employer discharges the employee on a basis that makes enforcement of the covenant inequitable;

(b)   the employer acted in bad faith in requiring or invoking the covenant;

(c)   the employer materially breached the underlying employment agreement; or

(d)   in the geographic region covered by the restriction, a great public need for the special skills and services of the former employee outweighs any legitimate interest of the employer in enforcing the covenant.

Comment: . . .

b.   Types of restrictive covenants. The rule stated in this Section applies to many different types of postemployment restraints. So long as a restrictive covenant has the effect of substantially limiting employees from competing with their former employer, whether

completely or in a specific manner, the agreement must meet the requirements of this Section to be enforceable. In addition to noncompetition covenants, this Section also covers covenants that, rather than forbidding competition entirely, provide that certain competitive activity by a former employee will, for example, require specified payments by the former employee to the former employer. This Section also applies to covenants that prohibit postemployment solicitation of customers or solicitation or hiring of coworkers with whom the employee came in contact while employed.

Different types of restrictive covenants may be necessary to protect different types of employer interests, and courts should examine the asserted business justification for each specific limitation. The same general inquiry, however, applies to all restrictive covenants—namely, a court should determine whether the employer has a protectable interest, and whether the restrictive covenant is reasonably tailored to furthering that interest. . . .

c. *Reasonably tailored.* A court will enforce a restrictive covenant only if it is reasonably tailored to the protection of a legitimate interest of the employer as set forth in § 8.07. To be reasonably tailored, the covenant should be no more restrictive in duration, scope of activities, or geography than necessary to protect the legitimate interest at stake. Whether limitations are reasonable will vary depending on the circumstances of the case, including industry practices and the nature of the interest justifying the restrictive covenant. When confronted with a blanket contractual restriction on all competition—even if the restriction otherwise is of reasonable duration and geographical scope—courts will inquire whether the employer's legitimate interest could not be equally well served by a narrower restriction. For example, could the employer's interest in protecting customer relationships be satisfied by a reasonable nonsolicitation clause instead of a noncompete clause? In some circumstances, however, such as when it is especially difficult for an employer to determine whether a former employee is soliciting its customers, a nonsolicitation clause may not adequately protect the employer's

legitimate interests. Regardless of the nature of an employer's interest, the employer may not restrict employees from working in any market in which the employer does not do business.

The inquiry into the reasonableness of geographic, temporal, and scope-of-business limitations in restrictive covenants is context-sensitive and depends heavily on the nature of the legitimate interests at stake. Identical limitations will be reasonable to protect some interests but not others. A provision compensating the former employee during the term of the restrictive covenant (sometimes called "garden leave") may be a factor in favor of finding the restriction reasonable.

Illustrations: . . .

6.   Salesperson E agrees that, after he leaves X's employment, he will not compete with X in any state in which X services its customers. X services customers in 36 states, but E dealt with customers in only three states while working for X. The noncompetition agreement is not reasonably tailored to protect X from losing customer relationships that E developed with X's assistance. A narrower agreement, such as one prohibiting E from soliciting the customers whom E had serviced while working for X, would be sufficient to protect X's interest.

7.   E, a vice president of computer-data-storage company X, agrees not to compete with X anywhere in the world for six months. Both X and its competitors serve customers worldwide, and E has had extensive access to X's trade secrets, which apply worldwide. Because E's trade secrets have worldwide utility, the worldwide restriction is reasonably tailored to further a protectable interest of X. . . .

e.   Restrictive covenants agreed to after the start of the employment relationship. The majority rule is that continuing employment of an at-will employee is sufficient consideration to support the enforcement of an otherwise valid restrictive covenant. However, a significant minority of jurisdictions require "new" or "additional" consideration. Under either approach, the parties may enter into enforceable restrictive covenants after the start of an employment relationship. . . .

f.   Terminated employees. Reasonable restrictive covenants are generally enforceable against employees who have been discharged for cause. An opposite rule would have the perverse consequence of providing an incentive for an employee who wants relief from the restrictions of a reasonable covenant to perform badly and thus trigger a for-cause termination.

In contrast, restrictive covenants are generally unenforceable against employees who are terminated without cause or who quit employment for cause attributable to the employer (defined in the same way as cause for the termination of fixed-term agreements in § 2.04(a)). An opposite rule would have the perverse consequence of enabling an employer to terminate rather than retain an employee who is performing satisfactorily and then restrict the discharged employee's ability to secure new employment. By the same token, an employer should not be able to obtain enforcement of a restrictive covenant when the employer acts in bad faith, such as by securing the employee's execution of the covenant after planning to discharge the employee. . . .

g.   Employer's material breach of employment agreement. If the employer materially breaches the employment agreement, it cannot enforce an otherwise valid restrictive covenant contained in the agreement. . . .

§ 8.07   Protectable Interests for Restrictive Covenants

(a)   A restrictive covenant is enforceable only if the employer can demonstrate that the covenant furthers a legitimate interest of the employer.

(b)   An employer has a legitimate interest in protecting, by means of a reasonably tailored restrictive covenant with its employee, the employer's:

(1)   trade secrets, as defined in § 8.02, and other protectable confidential information that does not meet the definition of trade secret;

(2)   customer relationships;

(3)   investment in the employee's reputation in the market; or

(4)   purchase of a business owned by the employee.

Comment: . . .

b.   Confidential information. An employer's interest in protecting its trade secrets and other confidential information can justify a reasonable restrictive covenant. In general, most nonpublic information in which an employer has a protectable interest will be protectable as a trade secret . . . However, an employer may occasionally seek protection through contract of additional non-trade-secret information, often termed "confidential" or "proprietary," which is similarly nonpublic. Such arrangements may be in the form of noncompete agreements, whereby the employee is effectively barred from disclosing confidential information by not being able to take up employment with a competitor that will require disclosure of such information; or in the form of nondisclosure agreements, whereby the employer can seek damages or injunctive relief in the event of disclosure or imminent disclosure of the information covered by the agreement.

The determination of whether information is protectable as confidential or proprietary is inherently fact-specific, as it often turns on the language of the covenant at issue, the nature of the information to be protected, and the degree to which disclosure would unfairly benefit a competitor. Courts will generally protect nonpublic commercial information that provides a clear economic advantage to the employer by virtue of its confidentiality, provided that the restrictive covenant is otherwise reasonable under § 8.06 and the information has been treated as confidential by the employer. A justification for enforcing reasonable nondisclosure agreements that go beyond trade-secret protection is that the employee accused of violating the restrictive covenant was put on notice of which information the employer considered confidential and proprietary. An employer cannot protect as confidential any information in which it does not have a protectable interest, such as information that has entered the public domain and information that would be considered part of the general experience, knowledge, training, and skills that an employee acquires in the course of employment. . . .

c. Customer relationships. An employer often makes significant investments to foster relationships between its customers and its sales force and other employees. An employer has a legitimate interest in taking reasonable measures to protect that investment by barring employees from ap-

propriating customer relationships that the employer created and fostered by investing its resources. Because a covenant prohibiting former employees from soliciting customers with whom they dealt while employed will ordinarily fully protect this legitimate interest, a broader restriction barring all competition by former employees ordinarily is not enforceable. The length of time that employees worked for their employer is often relevant in determining the reasonableness of a restriction claimed to be necessary to preserve the former employer's customer relationships. For example, employees should not be bound by a broad restrictive covenant if they have worked for too short a time to have made use of or benefited from the type of customer relationships the employer would have a legitimate interest in protecting. . . .

f. Insufficient employer interests. An employer may have many economic reasons to attempt to restrict what its employees can do after termination of their employment. However, unless the employer can demonstrate a protectable interest under this Section, these reasons, standing alone, will not support an otherwise reasonable restrictive covenant because they are not sufficiently weighty to justify the social and individual costs inherent in restrictions on competition. For example, an interest in recouping investments in the training of employees may justify repayment obligations but would not justify a restriction on competition. Similarly, the desire of an employer to retain its talented, trained, or experienced employees is not an interest that can legitimately support a restrictive covenant. Finally, an employer's understandable wish to prevent competition by former employees is not, by itself, a protectable interest under this Section.

§ 8.08   Modification of Unreasonable Restrictive Covenant

A court may delete or modify provisions in an overbroad restrictive covenant in an employment agreement and then enforce the covenant as modified unless the agreement does not allow for modification or the employer lacked a reasonable and good-faith basis for believing the covenant was enforceable. Lack of a reasonable and good-faith basis for believing a covenant was enforceable may be manifested by its gross overbreadth alone, or by overbreadth coupled with other evidence that the employer sought to do more than protect its legitimate interests.

Comment:

a.   Scope and cross-references. Although unreasonable restrictive covenants should never be enforced as written, a court may modify an overly broad restrictive covenant into one that is reasonably tailored to the employer's protectable interest under § 8.07, and may thereafter enforce the modified covenant. Such modification, sometimes called "blue penciling," lies within the sound discretion of the court but that discretion should be exercised with care so as not to create an incentive for employers to draft overbroad restrictive covenants that in some instances will be taken by employees at face value as enforceable. On the other hand, a rule that forbids judicial modification and leaves courts with only a binary "enforce or reject" choice can also lead over time to a legal regime that provides employers with an incentive to draft overly broad covenants that employees will similarly regard as enforceable, due to judicial unwillingness to completely reject a covenant that is partially valid. For example, a court faced with a seven-month restriction when it thinks a six-month restriction is reasonable might uphold the greater restriction rather than strike it down completely. This would create a precedent that seven months is reasonable to which future employers might gravitate. The best approach, reflected in this Section, is for courts to refuse to modify an overly broad restrictive covenant when the employer lacked a reasonable good-faith belief that the covenant was enforceable. In some cases, lack of good faith can be shown by the covenant itself being so clearly overbroad that no reasonable employer would have believed it was reasonably tailored to protect the employer's legitimate interests. Other cases might require additional evidence of bad faith. Once overbreadth has been shown, the employer has the burden of demonstrating good faith in order to justify a modification.

b.   Overbreadth. To be enforceable, a restrictive covenant must be based on a protectable interest under § 8.07 and be reasonable in scope at the time of contracting and at the time of enforcement. A restrictive covenant that is either obtained in bad faith or objectively unreasonable at the time of contracting is unenforceable. Also, a change in circumstances between time of contracting and time of enforcement may in some cases so erode the employer's protectable interest as to render the covenant unenforceable. . . .

§ 9.01 Damages—Employer Termination in Breach of an Agreement for a Definite or Indefinite Term of Employment or of a Binding Employer Promise Limiting Termination of Employment

(a)   An employer who lacks cause for terminating the employment of an employee with an unexpired agreement for a definite term (§§ 2.03–2.04) is subject to liability to the discharged employee for:

(1)   all compensation that the employee would have received under the remaining term of the agreement, less mitigation of losses (such as the compensation earned and that reasonably could have been earned from comparable alternative employment during the remaining term);

(2)   reasonably foreseeable consequential damages; and

(3)   the expenses of reasonable efforts (whether or not successful) to mitigate losses.

(b)   An employer who lacks cause for terminating the employment of an employee with an agreement for an indefinite term requiring cause for termination (§§ 2.03–2.04) is subject to liability to the discharged employee for:

(1)   all compensation that the employee would have received under that agreement, less mitigation of losses (such as the compensation earned and that reasonably could have been earned from comparable alternative employment);

(2)   reasonably foreseeable consequential damages; and

(3)   the expenses of reasonable efforts (whether or not successful) to mitigate losses.

(c)   The employer and employee may specify in the agreement a reasonable amount to be paid by the employer for termination with or without cause in lieu of the measure of damages stated in (a) and (b).

(d)   An employer who breaches a promise that limits the employer's right to terminate employment and that induces reasonable and detrimental reliance by the employee (§ 2.02, Comment c) is subject to liability to the discharged employee for:

(1)   damages (including reasonably foreseeable consequential damages) caused by the employee's reasonable reliance on that promise;

(2)   less mitigation of losses (such as the compensation earned and that reasonably could have been earned from comparable alternative employment during the period covered by the promise); and

(3) the expenses of reasonable efforts (whether or not successful) to mitigate losses.

Comment:

a.   Termination of employment. For purposes of this Chapter, the phrase "termination of employment" includes not only express terminations effected by the employer, but also "constructive terminations" . . . .

b.   Agreement for a definite or indefinite term. The terminology here tracks that used in Chapter 2. An agreement between an employer and an employee is binding on both parties unless mutually rescinded or modified. It requires consideration or bargained-for exchange under the usual rules of contract formation . . . An agreement can provide for a definite term of employment whereby earlier termination of the agreement absent cause is a breach of contract (§ 2.03(a)(1)), or for an indefinite term requiring cause for termination so that a termination without cause is a breach (§ 2.03(a)(2)), or for an indefinite term with no limit on termination (§ 2.01) except perhaps notice or a stipulated payment by the employer (§ 9.01(c)).

Those jurisdictions that treat wrongful termination in violation of public policy as a contractual cause of action would look to § 9.01(b) for the measure of damages. . . .

d.   Would have received under the remaining term of the definite-term agreement. If the employer lacks cause to terminate a definite-term agreement, the usual remedy reflects the likelihood that employment would have continued for at least the stated term of the agreement. Even if there is some chance the employee might not have worked for the full term, the employer's termination without cause created that uncertainty. Courts generally allow the discharged employee to recover for the balance of the stated term, less income that was earned or should have been earned elsewhere (see Comment *f* below). Absent explicit language in the agreement, "cause" in a definite-term

agreement does not include changes in the economic condition of the employer (§ 2.04(a)). If the term of an oral employment contract exceeds one year, the agreement is likely to be unenforceable for lack of a writing under the applicable statute of frauds. . . .

e.   Would have received under the indefinite-term agreement. Unless otherwise agreed, the term "cause" in an indefinite-term agreement has a broader scope than in a definite-term agreement and includes significant changes in the economic condition of the employer (§ 2.04(b)). When the employer's discharge of the employee is without cause, determining what compensation the employee would have received under the agreement but for the employer's breach is necessarily a difficult inquiry. Both in cases governed by statute and by decisional law, the courts increasingly have allowed the issue of whether the proof establishes reasonably certain lost future income to go to the trier of fact under guidelines that place boundaries on the calculation. See § 9.05, Comment *e*. . . .

f.   Mitigation of losses or avoidable losses. Recovery for breach of any contractual obligation is limited to damages that could not have been "avoided without undue risk, burden or humiliation." Restatement Second, Contracts § 350(1). But the injured party is "not precluded from recovery . . . to the extent that he has made reasonable but unsuccessful efforts to avoid loss." Id. § 350(2). This is the rule of avoidable consequences, also known as the duty to mitigate damages. And of course the employee cannot recover for losses that actually are avoided, most commonly by accepting alternative employment. See generally id. §§ 347, 349. What the employee actually earns in alternative employment will often be the best measure of what the employee could have earned through reasonable effort. If actual earnings fall short of what reasonably could have been earned, the latter would constitute reasonable avoidance of losses under this Section.

Reasonable mitigation is not a "duty" in the sense that the employee is subject to liability for failure to mitigate. But the phrase is in common use, and "mitigation" and "avoidable losses" will be used interchangeably in this Chapter.

In employment cases, absent provision to the contrary in the applicable law, the employer has the burden of persuasion on failure to mitigate. The employer must show the employee failed to make reasonable efforts to mitigate losses and that such efforts would have succeeded. . . .

"Collateral source" income from private or social insurance is generally not deducted from damages.

Illustrations: . . .

8.   A is a famous cinema actress known for her singing, dancing, and musical comedy. Despite an agreement to employ her as the female lead in "Bloomer Girl," a motion-picture musical to be filmed in California where A lives and to pay her a guaranteed compensation of $100,000 a week for 10 weeks commencing January 1, 2013 for a total of $1,000,000, her producer X has decided not to produce "Bloomer Girl." Instead, X has offered A the female lead in "Big Country," a western movie, to be filmed in Australia. A would receive the same compensation for working in "Big Country," plus first-class travel and lodging accommodations. A declines the offer and sues X for the guaranteed compensation. A's requirement to reasonably mitigate losses does not require her to accept the "Big Country" offer. In the circumstances of this case, considering the reputational costs to A in appearing in a different type of motion picture for which she was not known and

which required work in a different part of the world, the "Big Country" film did not constitute comparable alternative employment.

9.   B, a well-known stunt man used in motion-picture musicals and dramas, entered into an agreement with producer X to provide stuntman services for the male lead in "Bloomer Girl" for a guaranteed compensation of $5000 per week for 10 weeks commencing January 1, 2013 for a total compensation of $50,000. When X decides not to produce "Bloomer Girl," he offers B employment (at the same compensation and to commence in the same time frame) in a western movie, "Midday Noon," to be produced in California. B declines the offer and does not engage in other efforts to obtain comparable employment. B has not reasonably mitigated his damages.

g.   Reasonable mitigation over time. When the discharged employee does not promptly obtain a comparable position after the termination, what constitutes reasonable mitigation changes over time. Soon after termination, and for a reasonable period thereafter, it is reasonable for the employee to seek only work involving comparable skill and working conditions. If the employee is unsuccessful in this pursuit, at some point it becomes reasonable to take similar work that is available, even if not as desirable as the previous employment. The decisions on this point outside of a statutory context are few but as courts have become more receptive to claims of reasonably certain future economic loss, see Comment *e*, courts should evaluate the reasonableness of mitigation efforts over time. . . .

i.   Promissory estoppel. Subsection (d) deals with employer promises to limit termination of employment that reasonably induce detrimental reliance by the promisee-employee. Such promises are enforceable under the Restatement Second, Contracts § 90(1). "The remedy granted for breach" of such promises "may be limited as justice requires." Id. The fundamental question is what the employer promised the employee or prospective employee. If the employer promised employment that could not be terminated except for cause and the employee reasonably relies to the employee's detriment on such a promise, the affected employee has a reliance-based claim for damages against the employer that is similar in scope and nature to a breach-of-contract claim under subsection (b). If, however, the employer promised the employee or prospective employee employment that, however attractive the compensation and other terms, would be terminable without cause, and the employee reasonably relies to his detriment on such a promise, the affected employee has a claim only for limited reliance damages, such as relocation costs, because no particular period of employment with the employer was promised. . . .

j.　Noneconomic damages. Damages for reputational harm and for emotional distress are generally not recoverable for breach of contract. Under § 353 of the Restatement Second, Contracts, "[r]ecovery for emotional disturbance will be excluded unless the breach also caused bodily harm or the contract or the breach is of such a kind that serious emotional disturbance was a particularly likely result." See id. § 353, Comment *a*.

k.　Consequential damages. . . . Losses that would otherwise be unforeseeable may become foreseeable and recoverable if the employer knows about these potential losses before entering into the employment agreement. Damages that stem from loss of income during the period between termination and the recovery of damages are generally not recoverable as consequential damages but, rather, are considered covered by interest on the judgment (and any prejudgment interest available under applicable law).

l.　Reasonable mitigation expenses. Reasonable mitigation expenses (whether successful or unsuccessful), such as retaining the services of a placement agency, are recoverable.

m.　Restitutionary relief. Restitutionary relief "off the contract" may be available in certain circumstances. Under § 31 of the Restatement Third, Restitution and Unjust Enrichment, "[a] person who renders performance under an agreement that cannot be enforced against the recipient by reason of (a) indefiniteness, or (b) the failure to satisfy an extrinsic requirement of enforceability such as the Statute of Frauds, has a claim in restitution against the recipient as necessary to prevent unjust enrichment." For instance, if an employee is discharged in violation of an oral agreement that is not enforceable for lack of a writing under the applicable statute of frauds, the employee may recover in quantum meruit for the reasonable value of services rendered.

§ 9.02　Damages—Employer Termination in Breach of a Binding Policy Statement Limiting Termination of Employment

An employer who breaches a binding employer policy statement that limits termination of employment (§ 2.05) is subject to liability to the discharged employee for:

(a)　all compensation the employee would have received under that policy statement, less mitigation of losses (such as the compensation the employee earned and could have obtained by reasonable efforts in comparable alternative employment, during the period of time covered by the policy statement (§ 2.06));

(b)   reasonably foreseeable consequential damages; and

(c)   the expenses of reasonable efforts (whether successful or not) to mitigate losses.

Comment:

a.   Binding employer policy statements. The terminology here tracks § 2.05, which provides that unilateral employer policy statements can be binding on employers while the statement remains in effect. The measure of damages stated here and in § 9.01(b) also applies in cases of discharge in violation of the implied duty of good faith and fair dealing or any other contract doctrine that limits the employer's right to terminate employment (§ 2.02).

b.   Would have received under that policy statement. Under § 2.06, the employer's obligation under a binding employer policy statement is generally limited to the period the policy remains in effect. If, however, the policy statement creates a nonmodifiable or vested term that cannot be adversely changed without the employee's agreement, supported by consideration, and that term limits the employer's power to terminate employment without cause, the measure of damages would be the same as under § 9.01(b). If that term creates an entitlement to compensation or benefits only, the measure of damages is treated in § 9.03.

§ 9.04   Injunctive Relief—Employer Breach

(a)   Except as otherwise provided by law, an employer's agreement, promise, or statement that it will hire or continue to employ an employee or job applicant will not be specifically enforced.

(b)   An employee may obtain injunctive relief to enforce any other term of an employment agreement (§ 2.03), binding employer promise (§ 2.02, Comment c), or binding employer policy statement (§ 2.05) if the employee satisfies the traditional requirements for equitable relief.

Comment: . . .

b.   Specific performance. It is a longstanding rule of equity that specific performance of promises to work (§ 9.08) or to provide employment will not be granted. See Restatement Second, Contracts § 367(1) ("A promise to render personal service will not be specifically enforced."). . . . The rule seeks to protect employees from performing compelled services, to protect employers from having to bring back unwanted employees into their organization, and to protect courts from the burden of enforcing and supervising the performance of affirmative duties in a continuing relationship already badly strained by the litigation and the dispute that led to it. The first purpose explains why employers cannot obtain such decrees; the second and third purposes explain why neither party can.

What equity will do, provided the traditional requirements stated in subsection (b) are met, is enforce positive decrees that do not require unduly burdensome judicial supervision (e.g., "pay the compensation owed") or negative decrees that require a party (usually the employee) to refrain from taking an action (e.g., "do not work for any competitor").

c.   Except as otherwise provided by law. Employment statutes often provide as a presumptive remedy reinstatement of employees to positions the employees held before their employment was unlawfully terminated (or instatement to positions that were unlawfully denied to them). . . . Sometimes reinstatement is not desired by the affected employee or is impractical; in such cases, courts under various statutes have interpreted their authority to award equitable relief to include a "front pay" remedy in lieu of reinstatement. In cases governed by common law, however, the courts as a general matter have not awarded reinstatement as a remedy. . . .

§ 9.07   Damages—Employee Breach of Agreement

(a)   An employee who breaches any obligation that the employment agreement clearly states is a basis for damages liability is subject to liability for that breach of contract. The employer may recover damages for foreseeable economic loss that the employer could not have reasonably avoided, including any reasonably foreseeable consequential damages and the expenses of reasonable efforts to mitigate damages.

(b)   Economic loss under subsection (a) does not include lost profits caused by the employee's breach unless the agreement expressly provides for such recovery or the employee knew or should have known that the employee would be held responsible for lost profits caused by the employee's breach. (For employees who have breached a tort-based or fiduciary duty to the employer, see § 9.09(b).)

Comment: . . .

b.   Basis for damages liability or actionable obligation. As a general matter, an employee's failure to meet the employee's contractual obligations to an employer is not redressable in an action for damages. In all employment relationships, the basic exchange is compensation and benefits to be paid the employee in return for the employee's competent, satisfactory performance of the requirements of the position. Unless otherwise agreed, if the employee performs poorly in the position, the employer's usual recourse is to terminate the employment relationship or implement discipline short of dismissal. Even when the employment relationship can be terminated only for cause, demonstrated poor performance constitutes cause for termination (see § 2.04).

Recognizing this background understanding of the parties to employment relationships, subsection (a) provides that absent language in the agreement that makes it clear that the parties intend what might be termed an "actionable obligation"—that is, an obligation the breach of which could result in employee liability for damages—employers do not have a cause of action for damages against an employee who breaches his or her contractual obligation to provide competent, satisfactory services. . . .

Illustrations:

3.   E . . . begins teaching mathematics at X County Elementary School in September 2012. Two weeks before the start of classes, X sends her a note listing X's "Performance Expectations for Our Teachers," which includes "effectively maintaining control in your classroom." On October 15, 2012, X terminates E's employment because "you

are not able effectively to maintain control in your classroom." Given the time constraints, X is compelled to hire Y at $80,000 plus benefits for the year. E has not breached an obligation that her employment agreement clearly states is a basis for damages liability. Even though the agreement contemplated E's competent performance of services and X had cause to terminate E's employment, E is not subject to liability for X's replacement costs.

4. Same facts as Illustration 3, except that the agreement states that "E expressly agrees to effectively teach mathematics and be responsible for any economic loss to X for my failure to do so." E is subject to damages liability for breach of contract under this Section, although X may have difficulty proving damages. X must make reasonable efforts to mitigate damages under subsection (a).

§ 9.08   Injunctive Relief—Employee Breach of Agreement

(a)   An employer may not obtain specific performance of the employee's promise to work.

(b)   An employer may obtain injunctive relief to enforce any other obligation expressly stated in the employment agreement if the employer satisfies the traditional requirements for obtaining equitable relief.

Comment:

a.   Scope and cross-references. This Section deals with injunctive relief against an employee's breach of contract. It is a longstanding rule of equity that courts will not grant specific performance of agreements or promises to work or provide employment (see § 9.04, Comment *b*). See Restatement Second, Contracts § 367(1) ("A promise to render personal service will not be specifically enforced."). This rule is supported not only by the difficulty courts would face monitoring compliance with a decree mandating the provision of services, but more fundamentally by the employee's generally protected interest in not being forced to provide services against the employee's will.

b.   Injunctions to enforce other contractual obligations. Injunctive relief is available in appropriate circumstances to restrain an employee from violating express or implied contractual obligations. This includes employees who are under an implied contractual duty of loyalty under § 8.01(a) or employees who have entered into reasonable restrictive covenants (§§ 8.06–8.08). . . . Recitals in agreements stipulating satisfaction of such requirements are given weight but are not determinative of whether the court should issue an injunction. . . .

UNIFORM COMMERCIAL CODE

(ARTICLES 1 AND 2)

COMPILERS' NOTE

The Uniform Commercial Code (UCC), a joint project of the National Conference of Commissioners on Uniform State Laws (also known as the Uniform Law Commission) and the American Law Institute, was originally promulgated in 1951 and has been amended a number of times in succeeding years. By the 1960s, it had been enacted in every state (although some Articles, including Article 2, were not enacted in Louisiana). Topics covered include sales of goods (Article 2), leases of goods (Article 2A), negotiable instruments (Article 3), bank deposits and collections (Article 4), funds transfers, (Article 4A), letters of credit (Article 5), documents of title (Article 7), investment securities (Article 8), and secured transactions (Article 9). In addition, Article 1 contains general provisions (including extensive definitions) that apply to all transactions within the scope of the UCC. Another Article (Article 6) dealt with bulk sales, but this Article has been repealed in all but a few states.

For purposes of the law of contracts, the two most important Articles of the UCC are Articles 1 and 2, the former containing general provisions that apply to all transactions within the scope of the UCC and the latter governing sales of goods. Both Articles were widely enacted by the 1960s (Article 1 was enacted in every state and Article 2 was enacted in every state except Louisiana), and remained quite stable for four decades, with the only amendments being minor changes to conform to revisions to other Articles. More recently, though, both Articles have been the subject of much change. In 2001, a revised text of Article 1 was promulgated by the Uniform Law Commission and the American Law Institute, and in 2003 those organizations promulgated substantial amendments to Article 2 and a revised version of Article 7 that include further revisions to some definitional provisions in Article 1. As of the publication of this volume, all 50 states and the District of Columbia had enacted the current version of Article 1 (i.e., through the 2003 amendments). In contrast to this successful modernization process, however, no states enacted the 2003 amendments to Article 2, and they were withdrawn in 2011.

Because Article 1 contains a number of provisions (including definitions) that are not relevant to Article 2 or contract law, the presentation of Article 1 in this volume is abridged by the omission of those provisions.

Sections of the Uniform Commercial Code are typically accompanied by "Official Comments" supplied by the drafters. These Comments, although not enacted by the legislature, have proven to be quite helpful and are often cited by judges. This volume contains a selection of those Comments.

UNIFORM COMMERCIAL CODE[1]

ARTICLE 1. GENERAL PROVISIONS (2003 OFFICIAL TEXT)* (ABRIDGED)

Table of Contents

PART 1. GENERAL PROVISIONS

---

* Article 1 was revised and reorganized in 2001, and slightly amended in 2003. The 2003 text of Article 1 has been enacted in all states and the District of Columbia. The enactment in several states, however, varies from the Official Text of Article 1 by retaining the pre-2001 definition of "good faith." See footnote a, *infra*.

PART 1   GENERAL PROVISIONS

§ 1–101.   Short Titles

(a)   This [Act] may be cited as the Uniform Commercial Code.

(b)   This article may be cited as Uniform Commercial Code—General Provisions.

§ 1–102.   Scope of Article

This article applies to a transaction to the extent that it is governed by another article of [the Uniform Commercial Code].

§ 1–103.   Construction of [Uniform Commercial Code] to Promote Its Purposes and Policies; Applicability of Supplemental Principles of Law

(a)   [The Uniform Commercial Code] must be liberally construed and applied to promote its underlying purposes and policies, which are:

(1)   to simplify, clarify, and modernize the law governing commercial transactions;

(2)   to permit the continued expansion of commercial practices through custom, usage, and agreement of the parties; and

(3)   to make uniform the law among the various jurisdictions.

(b)   Unless displaced by the particular provisions of [the Uniform Commercial Code], the principles of law and equity, including the law merchant and the law relative to capacity to contract, principal and agent, estoppel, fraud, misrepresentation, duress, coercion, mistake, bankruptcy, and other validating or invalidating cause supplement its provisions.

Official Comments

Source: Former Section 1–102 (1)–(2); Former Section 1–103.

Changes from former law: This section is derived from subsections (1) and (2) of former Section 1–102 and from former Section 1–103. Subsection (a) of this section combines subsections (1) and (2) of former Section 1–102. Except for changing the form of reference to the Uniform Commercial Code and minor stylistic changes, its language is the same as subsections (1) and (2) of former Section 1–102. Except for changing the form of reference to the Uniform Commercial Code and minor stylistic changes, subsection (b) of this section is identical to former Section 1–103. The provisions have been combined in this section to reflect the interrelationship between them.

1.   The Uniform Commercial Code is drawn to provide flexibility so that, since it is intended to be a semi-

permanent and infrequently-amended piece of legislation, it will provide its own machinery for expansion of commercial practices. It is intended to make it possible for the law embodied in the Uniform Commercial Code to be applied by the courts in the light of unforeseen and new circumstances and practices. The proper construction of the Uniform Commercial Code requires, of course, that its interpretation and application be limited to its reason.

Even prior to the enactment of the Uniform Commercial Code, courts were careful to keep broad acts from being hampered in their effects by later acts of limited scope. See Pacific Wool Growers v. Draper & Co., 158 Or. 1, 73 P.2d 1391 (1937), and compare Section 1–104. The courts have often recognized that the policies embodied in an act are applicable in reason to subject-matter that was not expressly included in the language of the act, Commercial Nat. Bank of New Orleans v. Canal-Louisiana Bank & Trust Co., 239 U.S. 520, 36 S.Ct. 194, 60 L.Ed. 417 (1916) (bona fide purchase policy of Uniform Warehouse Receipts Act extended to case not covered but of equivalent nature), and did the same where reason and policy so required, even where the subject-matter had been intentionally excluded from the act in general. Agar v. Orda, 264 N.Y. 248, 190 N.E. 479 (1934) (Uniform Sales Act change in seller's remedies applied to contract for sale of choses in action even though the general coverage of that Act was intentionally limited to goods "other than things in action.") They implemented a statutory policy with liberal and useful remedies not provided in the statutory text. They disregarded a statutory limitation of remedy where the reason of the limitation did not apply. Fiterman v. J. N. Johnson & Co., 156 Minn. 201, 194 N.W. 399 (1923) (requirement of return of the goods as a condition to rescission for breach of warranty; also, partial rescission allowed). Nothing in the Uniform Commercial Code stands in the way of the continuance of such action by the courts.

The Uniform Commercial Code should be construed in accordance with its underlying purposes and policies. The text of each section should be read in the light of the purpose and policy of the rule or principle in question, as also of the Uniform Commercial Code as a whole, and the application of the language should be construed narrowly or broadly, as the case may be, in conformity with the purposes and policies involved.

2. **Applicability of supplemental principles of law.** Subsection (b) states the basic relationship of the Uniform Commercial Code to supplemental bodies of law. The Uniform Commercial Code was drafted against the backdrop of existing bodies of law, including the common law and equity, and relies on those bodies of law to supplement it provisions in many important ways. At the same time, the Uniform Commercial Code is the primary source of commercial law rules in areas that it governs, and its rules represent choices made by its drafters and the enacting legislatures about the appropriate policies to be furthered in the transactions it covers. Therefore, while principles of common law and equity may supplement provisions of the Uniform Commercial Code, they may not be used to supplant its provisions, or the purposes and policies those provisions reflect, unless a specific provision of the Uniform Commercial Code provides otherwise. In the absence of such a provision, the Uniform Commercial Code preempts principles of common law and equity that are inconsistent with either its provisions or its purposes and policies.

The language of subsection (b) is intended to reflect both the concept of supplementation and the concept of preemption. Some courts, however, had difficulty in applying the identical language of former Section 1–103 to determine when other law appropriately may be applied to supplement the Uniform Commercial Code, and when that law has been displaced by the Code. Some decisions applied other law in situations in which that application, while not inconsistent with the text of any particular provision of the Uniform Commercial Code, clearly was inconsistent with the underlying purposes and policies reflected in the relevant provisions of the Code. See, e.g., Sheerbonnet, Ltd. v. American Express Bank, Ltd., 951 F. Supp. 403 (S.D.N.Y. 1995). In part, this difficulty arose from Comment 1 to former Section 1–103, which stated that "this section indicates the continued applicability to commercial contracts of all supplemental bodies of law except insofar as they are explicitly displaced by this Act." The "explicitly displaced" language of that Comment did not accurately reflect the proper scope of Uniform Commercial Code preemption, which extends to displacement of other law that is inconsistent with the purposes and policies of the Uniform Commercial Code, as well as with its text.

3. **Application of subsection (b) to statutes.** The primary focus of Section 1–103 is on the relationship between the Uniform Commercial Code and principles of common law and equity as developed by the courts. State law, however, increasingly is statutory. Not only are there a growing number of state statutes addressing specific issues that come within the scope of the Uniform Commercial Code, but in some States many general principles of common law and equity have been codified. When the other law relating to a matter within the scope of the Uniform Commercial Code is a statute, the principles of subsection (b) remain relevant to the court's analysis of the relationship between that statute and the Uniform Commercial Code, but other principles of statutory interpretation that specifically address the in-

terrelationship between statutes will be relevant as well. In some situations, the principles of subsection (b) still will be determinative. For example, the mere fact that an equitable principle is stated in statutory form rather than in judicial decisions should not change the court's analysis of whether the principle can be used to supplement the Uniform Commercial Code—under subsection (b), equitable principles may supplement provisions of the Uniform Commercial Code only if they are consistent with the purposes and policies of the Uniform Commercial Code as well as its text. In other situations, however, other interpretive principles addressing the interrelationship between statutes may lead the court to conclude that the other statute is controlling, even though it conflicts with the Uniform Commercial Code. This, for example, would be the result in a situation where the other statute was specifically intended to provide additional protection to a class of individuals engaging in transactions covered by the Uniform Commercial Code.

4. **Listing not exclusive.** The list of sources of supplemental law in subsection (b) is intended to be merely illustrative of the other law that may supplement the Uniform Commercial Code, and is not exclusive. No listing could be exhaustive. Further, the fact that a particular section of the Uniform Commercial Code makes express reference to other law is not intended to suggest the negation of the general application of the principles of subsection (b). Note also that the word "bankruptcy" in subsection (b), continuing the use of that word from former Section 1–103, should be understood not as a specific reference to federal bankruptcy law but, rather as a reference to general principles of insolvency, whether under federal or state law.

§ 1–106. Use of Singular and Plural; Gender

In [the Uniform Commercial Code], unless the statutory context otherwise requires:

    (1) words in the singular number include the plural, and those in the plural include the singular; and

    (2) words of any gender also refer to any other gender.

§ 1–107. Section Captions

Section captions are part of [the Uniform Commercial Code].

§ 1–108. Relation to Electronic Signatures in Global and National Commerce Act

This article modifies, limits, and supersedes the federal Electronic Signatures in Global and National Commerce Act, 15 U.S.C. Section 7001 et seq., except that nothing in this article modifies, limits, or supersedes Section 7001(C) of that Act or authorizes electronic delivery of any of the notices described in Section 7003(B) of that Act.

PART 2

GENERAL DEFINITIONS AND PRINCIPLES OF INTERPRETATION

§ 1–201. General Definitions [Selections]

    (a) Unless the context otherwise requires, words or phrases defined in this section, or in the additional definitions contained in other articles of [the Uniform Commercial Code] that apply to particular articles or parts thereof, have the meanings stated.

    (b) Subject to definitions contained in other articles of [the Uniform Commercial Code] that apply to particular articles or parts thereof:

    (1) "Action", in the sense of a judicial proceeding, includes recoupment, counterclaim, set-off, suit in equity, and any other proceeding in which rights are determined.

    (2) "Aggrieved party" means a party entitled to pursue a remedy.

    (3) "Agreement", as distinguished from "contract", means the bargain of the parties in fact, as found in their language or inferred from other circumstances, including course of performance, course of dealing, or usage of trade as provided in Section 1–303.

    (4) "Bank" means a person engaged in the business of banking and includes a savings bank, savings and loan association, credit union, and trust company.

(6) "Bill of lading" means a document of title evidencing the receipt of goods for shipment issued by a person engaged in the business of directly or indirectly transporting or forwarding goods. The term does not include a warehouse receipt.

(8) "Burden of establishing" a fact means the burden of persuading the trier of fact that the existence of the fact is more probable than its nonexistence.

(9) "Buyer in ordinary course of business" means a person that buys goods in good faith, without knowledge that the sale violates the rights of another person in the goods, and in the ordinary course from a person, other than a pawnbroker, in the business of selling goods of that kind. A person buys goods in the ordinary course if the sale to the person comports with the usual or customary practices in the kind of business in which the seller is engaged or with the seller's own usual or customary practices. A person that sells oil, gas, or other minerals at the wellhead or minehead is a person in the business of selling goods of that kind. A buyer in ordinary course of business may buy for cash, by exchange of other property, or on secured or unsecured credit, and may acquire goods or documents of title under a preexisting contract for sale. Only a buyer that takes possession of the goods or has a right to recover the goods from the seller under Article 2 may be a buyer in ordinary course of business. "Buyer in ordinary course of business" does not include a person that acquires goods in a transfer in bulk or as security for or in total or partial satisfaction of a money debt.

(10) "Conspicuous", with reference to a term, means so written, displayed, or presented that a reasonable person against which it is to operate ought to have noticed it. Whether a term is "conspicuous" or not is a decision for the court. Conspicuous terms include the following:

   (A) a heading in capitals equal to or greater in size than the surrounding text, or in contrasting type, font, or color to the surrounding text of the same or lesser size; and

   (B) language in the body of a record or display in larger type than the surrounding text, or in contrasting type, font, or color to the surrounding text of the same size, or set off from surrounding text of the same size by symbols or other marks that call attention to the language.

(11) "Consumer" means an individual who enters into a transaction primarily for personal, family, or household purposes.

306

(12) "Contract", as distinguished from "agreement", means the total legal obligation that results from the parties' agreement as determined by [the Uniform Commercial Code] as supplemented by any other applicable laws.

(13) "Creditor" includes a general creditor, a secured creditor, a lien creditor, and any representative of creditors, including an assignee for the benefit of creditors, a trustee in bankruptcy, a receiver in equity, and an executor or administrator of an insolvent debtor's or assignor's estate.

(15) "Delivery", with respect to an electronic document of title means voluntary transfer of control and with respect to an instrument, a tangible document of title, or chattel paper, means voluntary transfer of possession.

(16) "Document of title" means a record (i) that in the regular course of business or financing is treated as adequately evidencing that the person in possession or control of the record is entitled to receive, control, hold, and dispose of the record and the goods the record covers and (ii) that purports to be issued by or addressed to a bailee and to cover goods in the bailee's possession which are either identified or are fungible portions of an identified mass. The term includes a bill of lading, transport document, dock warrant, dock receipt, warehouse receipt, and order for delivery of goods. An electronic document of title is evidenced by a record consisting of information stored in an electronic medium. A tangible document of title is evidenced by a record consisting of information that is inscribed on a tangible medium.

(17) "Fault" means a default, breach, or wrongful act or omission.

(18) "Fungible goods" means:

    (A) goods of which any unit, by nature or usage of trade, is the equivalent of any other like unit; or

    (B) goods that by agreement are treated as equivalent.

(20) "Good faith," except as otherwise provided in Article 5, means honesty in fact and the observance of reasonable commercial standards of fair dealing.[a]

(21) "Holder" means:

    (A) the person in possession of a negotiable instrument that is payable either to bearer or to an identified person that is the person in possession;

---

[a] The following states have retained the prior definition of "good faith," which does not include a reference to "the observance of reasonable commercial standards of fair dealing": Alabama, Arizona, Hawaii, Idaho, Illinois, Indiana, Maryland, Michigan, Nebraska, New York, Rhode Island, Utah, and Virginia.

    (B) the person in possession of a negotiable tangible document of title if the goods are deliverable either to bearer or to the order of the person in possession; or

    (C) a person in control of a negotiable electronic document of title.

(23) "Insolvent" means:

    (A) having generally ceased to pay debts in the ordinary course of business other than as a result of bona fide dispute;

    (B) being unable to pay debts as they become due; or

    (C) being insolvent within the meaning of federal bankruptcy law.

(24) "Money" means a medium of exchange currently authorized or adopted by a domestic or foreign government. The term includes a monetary unit of account established by an intergovernmental organization or by agreement between two or more countries.

(26) "Party", as distinguished from "third party", means a person that has engaged in a transaction or made an agreement subject to [the Uniform Commercial Code].

(27) "Person" means an individual, corporation, business trust, estate, trust, partnership, limited liability company, association, joint venture, government, governmental subdivision, agency, or instrumentality, public corporation, or any other legal or commercial entity.

(29) "Purchase" means taking by sale, lease, discount, negotiation, mortgage, pledge, lien, security interest, issue or reissue, gift, or any other voluntary transaction creating an interest in property.

(30) "Purchaser" means a person that takes by purchase.

(31) "Record" means information that is inscribed on a tangible medium or that is stored in an electronic or other medium and is retrievable in perceivable form.

(32) "Remedy" means any remedial right to which an aggrieved party is entitled with or without resort to a tribunal.

(34) "Right" includes remedy.

(35) "Security interest" means an interest in personal property or fixtures which secures payment or performance of an obligation. "Security interest" includes any interest of a consignor and a buyer of accounts, chattel paper, a payment intangible, or a promissory note in a transaction that is subject to Article

9. "Security interest" does not include the special property interest of a buyer of goods on identification of those goods to a contract for sale under Section 2–401, but a buyer may also acquire a "security interest" by complying with Article 9. Except as otherwise provided in Section 2–505, the right of a seller or lessor of goods under Article 2 or 2A to retain or acquire possession of the goods is not a "security interest", but a seller or lessor may also acquire a "security interest" by complying with Article 9. The retention or reservation of title by a seller of goods notwithstanding shipment or delivery to the buyer under Section 2–401 is limited in effect to a reservation of a "security interest." Whether a transaction in the form of a lease creates a "security interest" is determined pursuant to Section 1–203.

(36) "Send" in connection with a writing, record, or notice means:

    (A) to deposit in the mail or deliver for transmission by any other usual means of communication with postage or cost of transmission provided for and properly addressed and, in the case of an instrument, to an address specified thereon or otherwise agreed, or if there be none to any address reasonable under the circumstances; or

    (B) in any other way to cause to be received any record or notice within the time it would have arrived if properly sent.

(37) "Signed" includes using any symbol executed or adopted with present intention to adopt or accept a writing.

(40) "Term" means a portion of an agreement that relates to a particular matter.

(43) "Writing" includes printing, typewriting, or any other intentional reduction to tangible form. "Written" has a corresponding meaning.

Official Comments

. . .

10. "Conspicuous." . . . This definition states the general standard that to be conspicuous a term ought to be noticed by a reasonable person. Whether a term is conspicuous is an issue for the court. Subparagraphs (A) and (B) set out several methods for making a term conspicuous. Requiring that a term be conspicuous blends a notice function (the term ought to be noticed) and a planning function (giving guidance to the party relying on the term regarding how that result can be achieved). Although these paragraphs indicate some of the methods for making a term attention-calling, the test is whether attention can reasonably be expected to be called to it. The statutory language should not be construed to permit a result that is inconsistent with that test.

§ 1–202.　Notice; Knowledge

(a)　Subject to subsection (f), a person has "notice" of a fact if the person:

    (1)　has actual knowledge of it;

    (2)　has received a notice or notification of it; or

    (3)　from all the facts and circumstances known to the person at the time in question, has reason to know that it exists.

(b)　"Knowledge" means actual knowledge. "Knows" has a corresponding meaning.

(c)　"Discover", "learn", or words of similar import refer to knowledge rather than to reason to know.

(d)　A person "notifies" or "gives" a notice or notification to another person by taking such steps as may be reasonably required to inform the other person in ordinary course, whether or not the other person actually comes to know of it.

(e)　Subject to subsection (f), a person "receives" a notice or notification when:

    (1)　it comes to that person's attention; or

    (2)　it is duly delivered in a form reasonable under the circumstances at the place of business through which the contract was made or at another location held out by that person as the place for receipt of such communications.

(f)　Notice, knowledge, or a notice or notification received by an organization is effective for a particular transaction from the time it is brought to the attention of the individual conducting that transaction and, in any event, from the time it would have been brought to the individual's attention if the organization had exercised due diligence. An organization exercises due diligence if it maintains reasonable routines for communicating significant information to the person conducting the transaction and there is reasonable compliance with the routines. Due diligence does not require an individual acting for the organization to communicate information unless the communication is part of the individual's regular duties or the individual has reason to know of the transaction and that the transaction would be materially affected by the information.

§ 1–204.　Value

Except as otherwise provided in Articles 3, 4, [and] 5, [and 6], a person gives value for rights if the person acquires them:

    (1)　in return for a binding commitment to extend credit or for the extension of immediately available credit, whether or not drawn upon and whether or not a charge-back is provided for in the event of difficulties in collection;

(2)   as security for, or in total or partial satisfaction of, a preexisting claim;

(3)   by accepting delivery under a preexisting contract for purchase; or

(4)   in return for any consideration sufficient to support a simple contract.

§ 1–205.   Reasonable Time; Seasonableness

(a)   Whether a time for taking an action required by [the Uniform Commercial Code] is reasonable depends on the nature, purpose, and circumstances of the action.

(b)   An action is taken seasonably if it is taken at or within the time agreed or, if no time is agreed, at or within a reasonable time.

PART 3

TERRITORIAL APPLICABILITY AND GENERAL RULES

§ 1–302.   Variation By Agreement

(a)   Except as otherwise provided in subsection (b) or elsewhere in [the Uniform Commercial Code], the effect of provisions of [the Uniform Commercial Code] may be varied by agreement.

(b)   The obligations of good faith, diligence, reasonableness, and care prescribed by [the Uniform Commercial Code] may not be disclaimed by agreement. The parties, by agreement, may determine the standards by which the performance of those obligations is to be measured if those standards are not manifestly unreasonable. Whenever [the Uniform Commercial Code] requires an action to be taken within a reasonable time, a time that is not manifestly unreasonable may be fixed by agreement.

(c)   The presence in certain provisions of [the Uniform Commercial Code] of the phrase "unless otherwise agreed", or words of similar import, does not imply that the effect of other provisions may not be varied by agreement under this section.

Official Comments

Source: Former Sections 1–102(3)–(4) and 1–204(1).

Changes: This section combines the rules from subsections (3) and (4) of former Section 1–102 and subsection (1) of former Section 1–204. No substantive changes are made.

1.   Subsection (a) states affirmatively at the outset that freedom of contract is a principle of the Uniform Commercial Code: "the effect" of its provisions may be varied by "agreement." The meaning of the statute itself must be found in its text, including its definitions, and in appropriate extrinsic aids; it cannot be varied by

agreement. But the Uniform Commercial Code seeks to avoid the type of interference with evolutionary growth found in pre-Code cases such as Manhattan Co. v. Morgan, 242 N.Y. 38, 150 N.E. 594 (1926). Thus, private parties cannot make an instrument negotiable within the meaning of Article 3 except as provided in Section 3–104; nor can they change the meaning of such terms as "bona fide purchaser," "holder in due course," or "due negotiation," as used in the Uniform Commercial Code. But an agreement can change the legal consequences that would otherwise flow from the provisions of the Uniform Commercial Code. "Agreement" here includes the effect given to course of dealing, usage of trade and course of performance by Sections 1–201 and 1–303; the effect of an agreement on the rights of third parties is left to specific provisions of the Uniform Commercial Code and to supplementary principles applicable under Section 1–103. The rights of third parties under Section 9–317 when a security interest is unperfected, for example, cannot be destroyed by a clause in the security agreement.

This principle of freedom of contract is subject to specific exceptions found elsewhere in the Uniform Commercial Code and to the general exception stated here. The specific exceptions vary in explicitness: the statute of frauds found in Section 2–201, for example, does not explicitly preclude oral waiver of the requirement of a writing, but a fair reading denies enforcement to such a waiver as part of the "contract" made unenforceable; Section 9–602, on the other hand, is a quite explicit limitation on freedom of contract. Under the exception for "the obligations of good faith, diligence, reasonableness and care prescribed by [the Uniform Commercial Code]," provisions of the Uniform Commercial Code prescribing such obligations are not to be disclaimed. However, the section also recognizes the prevailing practice of having agreements set forth standards by which due diligence is measured and explicitly provides that, in the absence of a showing that the standards manifestly are unreasonable, the agreement controls. In this connection, Section 1–303 incorporating into the agreement prior course of dealing and usages of trade is of particular importance.

Subsection (b) also recognizes that nothing is stronger evidence of a reasonable time than the fixing of such time by a fair agreement between the parties. However, provision is made for disregarding a clause which whether by inadvertence or overreaching fixes a time so unreasonable that it amounts to eliminating all remedy under the contract. The parties are not required to fix the most reasonable time but may fix any time which is not obviously unfair as judged by the time of contracting.

2. An agreement that varies the effect of provisions of the Uniform Commercial Code may do so by stating the rules that will govern in lieu of the provisions varied. Alternatively, the parties may vary the effect of such provisions by stating that their relationship will be governed by recognized bodies of rules or principles applicable to commercial transactions. Such bodies of rules or principles may include, for example, those that are promulgated by intergovernmental authorities such as UNCITRAL or Unidroit (see, e.g., Unidroit Principles of International Commercial Contracts), or non-legal codes such as trade codes.

3. Subsection (c) is intended to make it clear that, as a matter of drafting, phrases such as "unless otherwise agreed" have been used to avoid controversy as to whether the subject matter of a particular section does or does not fall within the exceptions to subsection (b), but absence of such words contains no negative implication since under

subsection (b) the general and residual rule is that the effect of all provisions of the Uniform Commercial Code may be varied by agreement.

§ 1–303. Course of Performance, Course of Dealing, and Usage of Trade

(a) A "course of performance" is a sequence of conduct between the parties to a particular transaction that exists if:

(1) the agreement of the parties with respect to the transaction involves repeated occasions for performance by a party; and

(2) the other party, with knowledge of the nature of the performance and opportunity for objection to it, accepts the performance or acquiesces in it without objection.

(b) A "course of dealing" is a sequence of conduct concerning previous transactions between the parties to a particular transaction that is fairly to be regarded as establishing a common basis of understanding for interpreting their expressions and other conduct.

(c) A "usage of trade" is any practice or method of dealing having such regularity of observance in a place, vocation, or trade as to justify an expectation that it will be observed with respect to the transaction in question. The existence and scope of such a usage must be proved as facts. If it is established that such a usage is embodied in a trade code or similar record, the interpretation of the record is a question of law.

(d) A course of performance or course of dealing between the parties or usage of trade in the vocation or trade in which they are engaged or of which they are or should be aware is relevant in ascertaining the meaning of the parties' agreement, may give particular meaning to specific terms of the agreement, and may supplement or qualify the terms of the agreement. A usage of trade applicable in the place in which part of the performance under the agreement is to occur may be so utilized as to that part of the performance.

(e) Except as otherwise provided in subsection (f), the express terms of an agreement and any applicable course of performance, course of dealing, or usage of trade must be construed whenever reasonable as consistent with each other. If such a construction is unreasonable:

(1) express terms prevail over course of performance, course of dealing, and usage of trade;

(2) course of performance prevails over course of dealing and usage of trade; and

(3) course of dealing prevails over usage of trade.

(f) Subject to Section 2–209, a course of performance is relevant to show a waiver or modification of any term inconsistent with the course of performance.

313

(g)   Evidence of a relevant usage of trade offered by one party is not admissible unless that party has given the other party notice that the court finds sufficient to prevent unfair surprise to the other party.

Official Comments

Source: Former   Sections   1–205, 2–208, and Section 2A–207.

Changes from former law: This section integrates the "course of performance" concept from Articles 2 and 2A into the principles of former Section 1–205, which deals with course of dealing and usage of trade. In so doing, the section slightly modifies the articulation of the course of performance rules to fit more comfortably with the approach and structure of former Section 1–205. There are also slight modifications to be more consistent with the definition of "agreement" in former Section 1–201(3). It should be noted that a course of performance that might otherwise establish a defense to the obligation of a party to a negotiable instrument is not available as a defense against a holder in due course who took the instrument without notice of that course of performance.

1.   The   Uniform   Commercial Code rejects both the "lay-dictionary" and the "conveyancer's" reading of a commercial agreement. Instead the meaning of the agreement of the parties is to be determined by the language used by them and by their action, read and interpreted in the light of commercial practices and other surrounding circumstances. The measure and background for interpretation are set by the commercial context, which may explain and supplement even the language of a formal or final writing.

2.   "Course of dealing," as defined in subsection (b), is restricted, literally, to a sequence of conduct between the parties previous to the agreement. A sequence of conduct after or under the agreement, however, is a "course of performance." "Course of dealing" may enter the agreement either by explicit provisions of the agreement or by tacit recognition.

3.   The   Uniform   Commercial Code deals with "usage of trade" as a factor in reaching the commercial meaning of the agreement that the parties have made. The language used is to be interpreted as meaning what it may fairly be expected to mean to parties involved in the particular commercial transaction in a given locality or in a given vocation or trade. By adopting in this context the term "usage of trade," the Uniform Commercial Code expresses its intent to reject those cases which see evidence of "custom" as representing an effort to displace or negate "established rules of law." A distinction is to be drawn between mandatory rules of law such as the Statute of Frauds provisions of Article 2 on Sales whose very office is to control and restrict the actions of the parties, and which cannot be abrogated by agreement, or by a usage of trade, and those rules of law (such as those in Part 3 of Article 2 on Sales) which fill in points which the parties have not considered and in fact agreed upon. The latter rules hold "unless otherwise agreed" but yield to the contrary agreement of the parties. Part of the agreement of the parties to which such rules yield is to be sought for in the usages of trade which furnish the background and give particular meaning to the language used, and are the framework of common understanding controlling any general rules of law which hold only when there is no such understanding.

4.   A usage of trade under subsection (c) must have the "regularity of observance" specified. The ancient English tests for "custom" are abandoned in this connection. Therefore, it is not required that a usage of trade be "ancient or immemorial," "universal,"

or the like. Under the requirement of subsection (c) full recognition is thus available for new usages and for usages currently observed by the great majority of decent dealers, even though dissidents ready to cut corners do not agree. There is room also for proper recognition of usage agreed upon by merchants in trade codes.

5. The policies of the Uniform Commercial Code controlling explicit unconscionable contracts and clauses (Sections 1–304, 2–302) apply to implicit clauses that rest on usage of trade and carry forward the policy underlying the ancient requirement that a custom or usage must be "reasonable." However, the emphasis is shifted. The very fact of commercial acceptance makes out a prima facie case that the usage is reasonable, and the burden is no longer on the usage to establish itself as being reasonable. But the anciently established policing of usage by the courts is continued to the extent necessary to cope with the situation arising if an unconscionable or dishonest practice should become standard.

6. Subsection (d), giving the prescribed effect to usages of which the parties "are or should be aware," reinforces the provision of subsection (c) requiring not universality but only the described "regularity of observance" of the practice or method. This subsection also reinforces the point of subsection (c) that such usages may be either general to trade or particular to a special branch of trade.

7. Although the definition of "agreement" in Section 1–201 includes the elements of course of performance, course of dealing, and usage of trade, the fact that express reference is made in some sections to those elements is not to be construed as carrying a contrary intent or implication elsewhere. Compare Section 1–302(c).

8. In cases of a well established line of usage varying from the general rules of the Uniform Commercial Code where the precise amount of the variation has not been worked out into a single standard, the party relying on the usage is entitled, in any event, to the minimum variation demonstrated. The whole is not to be disregarded because no particular line of detail has been established. In case a dominant pattern has been fairly evidenced, the party relying on the usage is entitled under this section to go to the trier of fact on the question of whether such dominant pattern has been incorporated into the agreement.

9. Subsection (g) is intended to insure that this Act's liberal recognition of the needs of commerce in regard to usage of trade shall not be made into an instrument of abuse.

§ 1–304. Obligation of Good Faith

Every contract or duty within [the Uniform Commercial Code] imposes an obligation of good faith in its performance and enforcement.

Official Comments

Source: Former Section 1–203.

Changes from former law: Except for changing the form of reference to the Uniform Commercial Code, this section is identical to former Section 1–203.

1. This section sets forth a basic principle running throughout the Uniform Commercial Code. The principle is that in commercial transactions good faith is required in the performance and enforcement of all agreements or duties. While this duty is explicitly stated in some provisions of the Uniform Commercial Code, the applicabil-

ity of the duty is broader than merely these situations and applies generally, as stated in this section, to the performance or enforcement of every contract or duty within this Act. It is further implemented by Section 1–303 on course of dealing, course of performance, and usage of trade. This section does not support an independent cause of action for failure to perform or enforce in good faith. Rather, this section means that a failure to perform or enforce, in good faith, a specific duty or obligation under the contract, constitutes a breach of that contract or makes unavailable, under the particular circumstances, a remedial right or power. This distinction makes it clear that the doctrine of good faith merely directs a court towards interpreting contracts within the commercial context in which they are created, performed, and enforced, and does not create a separate duty of fairness and reasonableness which can be independently breached.

2.   "Performance and enforcement" of contracts and duties within the Uniform Commercial Code include the exercise of rights created by the Uniform Commercial Code.

§ 1–305.   Remedies to Be Liberally Administered

(a)   The remedies provided by [the Uniform Commercial Code] must be liberally administered to the end that the aggrieved party may be put in as good a position as if the other party had fully performed but neither consequential or special damages nor penal damages may be had except as specifically provided in [the Uniform Commercial Code] or by other rule of law.

(b)   Any right or obligation declared by [the Uniform Commercial Code] is enforceable by action unless the provision declaring it specifies a different and limited effect.

Official Comments

Source: Former Section 1–106.

Changes from former law: Other than changes in the form of reference to the Uniform Commercial Code, this section is identical to former Section 1–106.

1.   Subsection (a) is intended to effect three propositions. The first is to negate the possibility of unduly narrow or technical interpretation of remedial provisions by providing that the remedies in the Uniform Commercial Code are to be liberally administered to the end stated in this section. The second is to make it clear that compensatory damages are limited to compensation. They do not include consequential or special damages, or penal damages; and the Uniform Commercial Code elsewhere makes it clear that dam-ages must be minimized. Cf. Sections 1–304, 2–706(1), and 2–712(2). The third purpose of subsection (a) is to reject any doctrine that damages must be calculable with mathematical accuracy. Compensatory damages are often at best approximate: they have to be proved with whatever definiteness and accuracy the facts permit, but no more. Cf. Section 2–204(3).

2.   Under subsection (b), any right or obligation described in the Uniform Commercial Code is enforceable by action, even though no remedy may be expressly provided, unless a particular provision specifies a different and limited effect. Whether specific performance or other equitable relief is available is determined not by this section but by specific provisions and by supplementary principles. Cf. Sections 1–103, 2–716.

3. "Consequential" or "special" damages and "penal" damages are not defined in the Uniform Commercial Code; rather, these terms are used in the sense in which they are used outside the Uniform Commercial Code.

§ 1–306. Waiver or Renunciation of Claim or Right After Breach

A claim or right arising out of an alleged breach may be discharged in whole or in part without consideration by agreement of the aggrieved party in an authenticated record.

Official Comments

Source: Former Section 1–107.

Changes from former law: This section changes former law in two respects. First, former Section 1–107, requiring the "delivery" of a "written waiver or renunciation" merges the separate concepts of the aggrieved party's agreement to forego rights and the manifestation of that agreement. This section separates those concepts, and explicitly requires agreement of the aggrieved party. Second, the revised section reflects developments in electronic commerce by providing for memorialization in an authenticated record. In this context, a party may "authenti-cate" a record by (i) signing a record that is a writing or (ii) attaching to or logically associating with a record that is not a writing an electronic sound, symbol or process with the present intent to adopt or accept the record. See Sections 1–201(b)(37) and 9–102(a)(7).

1. This section makes consideration unnecessary to the effective renunciation or waiver of rights or claims arising out of an alleged breach of a commercial contract where the agreement effecting such renunciation is memorialized in a record authenticated by the aggrieved party. Its provisions, however, must be read in conjunction with the section imposing an obligation of good faith. (Section 1–304).

§ 1–308. Performance or Acceptance Under Reservation of Rights

(a) A party that with explicit reservation of rights performs or promises performance or assents to performance in a manner demanded or offered by the other party does not thereby prejudice the rights reserved. Such words as "without prejudice," "under protest," or the like are sufficient.

(b) Subsection (a) does not apply to an accord and satisfaction.

Official Comments

Source: Former Section 1–207.

Changes from former law: This section is identical to former Section 1–207.

1. This section provides machinery for the continuation of performance along the lines contemplated by the contract despite a pending dispute, by adopting the mercantile device of going ahead with delivery, acceptance, or payment "without prejudice," "under protest," "under reserve," "with reservation of all our rights," and the like. All of these phrases completely reserve all rights within the meaning of this section. The section therefore contemplates that limited as well as general reservations and acceptance by a party may be made "subject to satisfaction of

our purchaser," "subject to acceptance by our customers," or the like.

2.   This section does not add any new requirement of language of reservation where not already required by law, but merely provides a specific measure on which a party can rely as that party makes or concurs in any interim adjustment in the course of performance. It does not affect or impair the provisions of this Act such as those under which the buyer's remedies for defect survive acceptance without being expressly claimed if notice of the defects is given within a reasonable time. Nor does it disturb the policy of those cases which restrict the effect of a waiver of a defect to reasonable limits under the circumstances, even though no such reservation is expressed.

The section is not addressed to the creation or loss of remedies in the ordinary course of performance but rather to a method of procedure where one party is claiming as of right something which the other believes to be unwarranted.

3.   Subsection (b) states that this section does not apply to an accord and satisfaction. Section 3–311 governs if an accord and satisfaction is attempted by tender of a negotiable instrument as stated in that section. If Section 3–311 does not apply, the issue of whether an accord and satisfaction has been effected is determined by the law of contract. Whether or not Section 3–311 applies, this section has no application to an accord and satisfaction.

§ 1–309.   Option to Accelerate at Will

A term providing that one party or that party's successor in interest may accelerate payment or performance or require collateral or additional collateral "at will" or when the party "deems itself insecure," or words of similar import, means that the party has power to do so only if that party in good faith believes that the prospect of payment or performance is impaired. The burden of establishing lack of good faith is on the party against which the power has been exercised.

Official Comments

Source: Former Section 1–208.

Changes from former law: Except for minor stylistic changes, this section is identical to former Section 1–208.

1.   The common use of acceleration clauses in many transactions governed by the Uniform Commercial Code, including sales of good on credit notes payable at a definite time, and secured transactions, raises an issue as to the effect to be given to a clause that seemingly grants the power to accelerate at the whim and caprice of one party. This section is intended to make clear that despite language that

might be so construed and which further might be held to make the agreement void as against public policy or to make the contract illusory or too indefinite for enforcement, the option is to be exercised only in the good faith belief that the prospect of payment or performance is impaired.

Obviously this section has no application to demand instruments or obligations whose very nature permits call at any time with or without reason. This section applies only to an obligation of payment or performance which in the first instance is due at a future date.

ARTICLE 2. SALES

Table of Contents

PART 1. SHORT TITLE, GENERAL CONSTRUCTION AND SUBJECT MATTER

PART 2. FORM, FORMATION AND READJUSTMENT OF CONTRACT

PART 3. GENERAL OBLIGATION AND CONSTRUCTION OF CONTRACT

ARTICLE 2. SALES

PART 1

SHORT TITLE, GENERAL CONSTRUCTION AND SUBJECT MATTER

§ 2–101.   Short Title

This Article shall be known and may be cited as Uniform Commercial Code—Sales.

§ 2–102.   Scope; Certain Security and Other Transactions Excluded From This Article

Unless the context otherwise requires, this Article applies to transactions in goods; it does not apply to any transaction which although in the form of an unconditional contract to sell or present sale is intended to operate only as a security transaction nor does this Article impair or repeal any statute regulating sales to consumers, farmers or other specified classes of buyers.

Definitional Cross References: "Present sale". Section 2–106.

"Contract". Section 1–201.   "Sale". Section 2–106.

"Contract for sale". Section 2–106.

§ 2–103.   Definitions and Index of Definitions

(1)   In this Article unless the context otherwise requires

   (a)   "Buyer" means a person who buys or contracts to buy goods.

[(b) "Good faith" in the case of a merchant means honesty in fact and the observance of reasonable commercial standards of fair dealing in the trade.][b]

(c)   "Receipt" of goods means taking physical possession of them.

(d)   "Seller" means a person who sells or contracts to sell goods.

(2)   Other definitions applying to this Article or to specified Parts thereof, and the sections in which they appear are:

"Acceptance". Section 2–606.

"Banker's credit". Section 2–325.

"Between merchants". Section 2–104.

"Cancellation". Section 2–106(4).

"Commercial unit". Section 2–105.

"Confirmed credit". Section 2–325.

"Conforming to contract". Section 2–106.

"Contract for sale". Section 2–106.

"Cover". Section 2–712.

"Entrusting". Section 2–403.

"Financing agency". Section 2–104.

"Future goods". Section 2–105.

"Goods". Section 2–105.

"Identification". Section 2–501.

"Installment contract". Section 2–612.

"Letter of Credit". Section 2–325.

"Lot". Section 2–105.

"Merchant". Section 2–104.

"Overseas". Section 2–323.

"Person in position of seller". Section 2–707.

"Present sale". Section 2–106.

"Sale". Section 2–106.

"Sale on approval". Section 2–326.

"Sale or return". Section 2–326.

"Termination". Section 2–106.

---

[b] The bracketed definition of "good faith" is retained in the states that did not enact the definition of "good faith" in the Official Text of UCC § 1–201(b)(20). See footnote a, supra. The bracketed provision is deleted in other states.

(3)　The following definitions in other Articles apply to this Article:

"Check". Section 3–104.

"Consignee". Section 7–102.

"Consignor". Section 7–102.

"Consumer goods". Section 9–102.

"Control". Section 7–106.

"Dishonor". Section 3–502.

"Draft". Section 3–104.

(4)　In addition Article 1 contains general definitions and principles of construction and interpretation applicable throughout this Article.

Definitional Cross Reference:

"Person". Section 1–201.

§ 2–104.　Definitions; "Merchant"; "Between Merchants"; "Financing Agency"

(1)　"Merchant" means a person who deals in goods of the kind or otherwise by his occupation holds himself out as having knowledge or skill peculiar to the practices or goods involved in the transaction or to whom such knowledge or skill may be attributed by his employment of an agent or broker or other intermediary who by his occupation holds himself out as having such knowledge or skill.

(2)　"Financing agency" means a bank, finance company or other person who in the ordinary course of business makes advances against goods or documents of title or who by arrangement with either the seller or the buyer intervenes in ordinary course to make or collect payment due or claimed under the contract for sale, as by purchasing or paying the seller's draft or making advances against it or by merely taking it for collection whether or not documents of title accompany or are associated with the draft. "Financing agency" includes also a bank or other person who similarly intervenes between persons who are in the position of seller and buyer in respect to the goods (Section 2–707).

(3)　"Between merchants" means in any transaction with respect to which both parties are chargeable with the knowledge or skill of merchants.

Official Comment

Prior Uniform Statutory Provision: None. But see Sections 15(2), (5), 16(c), 45(2) and 71, Uniform Sales Act, and Sections 35 and 37, Uniform Bills of Lading Act for examples of the policy expressly provided for in this Article.

Purposes:

1.　This Article assumes that transactions between professionals in a given field require special and clear rules which may not apply to a casual or inexperienced seller or buyer. It thus adopts a policy of expressly stating rules applicable "between merchants" and "as against a merchant", wherever they are needed instead of making them depend upon the circumstances of each case as in the statutes cited above. This section lays the foundation of this policy by defining those who are to be regarded as professionals or "merchants" and by stating when a transaction is deemed to be "between merchants".

2. The term "merchant" as defined here roots in the "law merchant" concept of a professional in business. The professional status under the definition may be based upon specialized knowledge as to the goods, specialized knowledge as to business practices, or specialized knowledge as to both and which kind of specialized knowledge may be sufficient to establish the merchant status is indicated by the nature of the provisions.

The special provisions as to merchants appear only in this Article and they are of three kinds. Sections 2–201(2), 2–205, 2–207 and 2–209 dealing with the statute of frauds, firm offers, confirmatory memoranda and modification rest on normal business practices which are or ought to be typical of and familiar to any person in business. For purposes of these sections almost every person in business would, therefore, be deemed to be a "merchant" under the language "who . . . by his occupation holds himself out as having knowledge or skill peculiar to the practices . . . involved in the transaction . . ." since the practices involved in the transaction are non-specialized business practices such as answering mail. In this type of provision, banks or even universities, for example, well may be "merchants." But even these sections only apply to a merchant in his mercantile capacity; a lawyer or bank president buying fishing tackle for his own use is not a merchant.

On the other hand, in Section 2–314 on the warranty of merchantability, such warranty is implied only "if the seller is a merchant with respect to goods of that kind." Obviously this qualification restricts the implied warranty to a much smaller group than everyone who is engaged in business and requires a professional status as to particular kinds of goods. The exception in Section 2–402(2) for retention of possession by a merchant-seller falls in the same class; as does Section 2–403(2) on entrusting of possession to a merchant "who deals in goods of that kind".

A third group of sections includes 2–103(1)(b), which provides that in the case of a merchant "good faith" includes observance of reasonable commercial standards of fair dealing in the trade; 2–327(1)(c), 2–603 and 2–605, dealing with responsibilities of merchant buyers to follow seller's instructions, etc.; 2–509 on risk of loss, and 2–609 on adequate assurance of performance. This group of sections applies to persons who are merchants under either the "practices" or the "goods" aspect of the definition of merchant.

3. The "or to whom such knowledge or skill may be attributed by his employment of an agent or broker . . ." clause of the definition of merchant means that even persons such as universities, for example, can come within the definition of merchant if they have regular purchasing departments or business personnel who are familiar with business practices and who are equipped to take any action required.

Cross References:

Point 1: See Sections 1–102 and 1–203.

Point 2: See Sections 2–314, 2–315 and 2–320 to 2–325, of this Article, and Article 9.

Definitional Cross References:

"Bank". Section 1–201.

"Buyer". Section 2–103.

§ 2–105. Definitions: Transferability; "Goods"; "Future" Goods; "Lot"; "Commercial Unit"

(1) "Goods" means all things (including specially manufactured goods) which are movable at the time of identification to the contract for sale other than the money in which the price is to be paid, investment securities (Article 8) and things in action. "Goods" also includes the unborn young of animals and growing crops and other identified things attached to realty as described in the section on goods to be severed from realty (Section 2–107).

(2) Goods must be both existing and identified before any interest in them can pass. Goods which are not both existing and identified are "future" goods. A purported present sale of future goods or of any interest therein operates as a contract to sell.

(3) There may be a sale of a part interest in existing identified goods.

(4) An undivided share in an identified bulk of fungible goods is sufficiently identified to be sold although the quantity of the bulk is not determined. Any agreed proportion of such a bulk or any quantity thereof agreed upon by number, weight or other measure may to the extent of the seller's interest in the bulk be sold to the buyer who then becomes an owner in common.

(5) "Lot" means a parcel or a single article which is the subject matter of a separate sale or delivery, whether or not it is sufficient to perform the contract.

(6) "Commercial unit" means such a unit of goods as by commercial usage is a single whole for purposes of sale and division of which materially impairs its character or value on the market or in use. A commercial unit may be a single article (as a machine) or a set of articles (as a suite of furniture or an assortment of sizes) or a quantity (as a bale, gross, or carload) or any other unit treated in use or in the relevant market as a single whole.

Definitional Cross References:

§ 2–106. Definitions: "Contract"; "Agreement"; "Contract for Sale"; "Sale"; "Present Sale"; "Conforming" to Contract; "Termination"; "Cancellation"

(1)   In this Article unless the context otherwise requires "contract" and "agreement" are limited to those relating to the present or future sale of goods. "Contract for sale" includes both a present sale of goods and a contract to sell goods at a future time. A "sale" consists in the passing of title from the seller to the buyer for a price (Section 2–401). A "present sale" means a sale which is accomplished by the making of the contract.

(2)   Goods or conduct including any part of a performance are "conforming" or conform to the contract when they are in accordance with the obligations under the contract.

(3)   "Termination" occurs when either party pursuant to a power created by agreement or law puts an end to the contract otherwise than for its breach. On "termination" all obligations which are still executory on both sides are discharged but any right based on prior breach or performance survives.

(4)   "Cancellation" occurs when either party puts an end to the contract for breach by the other and its effect is the same as that of "termination" except that the cancelling party also retains any remedy for breach of the whole contract or any unperformed balance.

Definitional Cross References:

"Agreement". Section 1–201.

"Buyer". Section 2–103.

"Contract". Section 1–201.

"Goods". Section 2–105.

"Party". Section 1–201.

"Remedy". Section 1–201.

"Rights". Section 1–201.

"Seller". Section 2–103.

§ 2–107. Goods to Be Severed From Realty: Recording

(1)   A contract for the sale of minerals or the like (including oil and gas) or a structure or its materials to be removed from realty is a contract for the sale of goods within this Article if they are to be severed by the seller but until severance a purported present sale thereof which is not effective as a transfer of an interest in land is effective only as a contract to sell.

(2)   A contract for the sale apart from the land of growing crops or other things attached to realty and capable of severance without material harm thereto but not described in subsection (1) or of timber to be cut is a contract for the sale of goods within this Article whether the subject matter is to be severed by the buyer or by the seller even though it forms part of the realty at the time of contracting, and the parties can by identification effect a present sale before severance.

(3)   The provisions of this section are subject to any third party rights provided by the law relating to realty records, and the contract for sale may be executed and recorded as a document transferring an interest in land and shall then constitute notice to third parties of the buyer's rights under the contract for sale.

Definitional Cross References:	"Party". Section 1–201.
"Buyer". Section 2–103.	"Present sale". Section 2–106.
"Contract". Section 1–201.	"Rights". Section 1–201.
"Contract for sale". Section 2–106.	"Seller". Section 2–103.
"Goods". Section 2–105.	

PART 2

FORM, FORMATION AND READJUSTMENT OF CONTRACT

§ 2–201.   Formal Requirements; Statute of Frauds

(1)   Except as otherwise provided in this section a contract for the sale of goods for the price of $500 or more is not enforceable by way of action or defense unless there is some writing sufficient to indicate that a contract for sale has been made between the parties and signed by the party against whom enforcement is sought or by his authorized agent or broker. A writing is not insufficient because it omits or incorrectly states a term agreed upon but the contract is not enforceable under this paragraph beyond the quantity of goods shown in such writing.

(2)   Between merchants if within a reasonable time a writing in confirmation of the contract and sufficient against the sender is received and the party receiving it has reason to know its contents, it satisfies the requirements of subsection (1) against such party unless written notice of objection to its contents is given within ten days after it is received.

(3)   A contract which does not satisfy the requirements of subsection (1) but which is valid in other respects is enforceable

(a)   if the goods are to be specially manufactured for the buyer and are not suitable for sale to others in the ordinary course of the seller's business and the seller, before notice of repudiation is received and under circumstances which reasonably indicate that the goods are for the buyer, has made either a substantial beginning of their manufacture or commitments for their procurement; or

(b)   if the party against whom enforcement is sought admits in his pleading, testimony or otherwise in court that a contract for sale was made, but the contract is not enforceable under this provision beyond the quantity of goods admitted; or

(c)   with respect to goods for which payment has been made and accepted or which have been received and accepted (Sec. 2–606).

Official Comment

Prior Uniform Statutory Provision: Section 4, Uniform Sales Act (which was based on Section 17 of the Statute of 29 Charles II).

Changes: Completely rephrased; restricted to sale of goods. See also Sections 1–206, 8–319 and 9–203.

Purposes of Changes: The changed phraseology of this section is intended to make it clear that:

1.   The required writing need not contain all the material terms of the contract and such material terms as are stated need not be precisely stated. All that is required is that the writing afford a basis for believing that the offered oral evidence rests on a real transaction. It may be written in lead pencil on a scratch pad. It need not indicate which party is the buyer and which the seller. The only term which must appear is the quantity term which need not be accurately stated but recovery is limited to the amount stated. The price, time and place of payment or delivery, the general quality of the goods, or any particular warranties may all be omitted.

Special emphasis must be placed on the permissibility of omitting the price term in view of the insistence of some courts on the express inclusion of this term even where the parties have contracted on the basis of a published price list. In many valid contracts for sale the parties do not mention the price in express terms, the buyer being bound to pay and the seller to accept a reasonable price which the trier of the fact may well be trusted to determine. Again, frequently the price is not mentioned since the parties have based their agreement on a price list or catalogue known to both of them

and this list serves as an efficient safeguard against perjury. Finally, "market" prices and valuations that are current in the vicinity constitute a similar check. Thus if the price is not stated in the memorandum it can normally be supplied without danger of fraud. Of course if the "price" consists of goods rather than money the quantity of goods must be stated.

Only three definite and invariable requirements as to the memorandum are made by this subsection. First, it must evidence a contract for the sale of goods; second, it must be "signed", a word which includes any authentication which identifies the party to be charged; and third, it must specify a quantity.

2.   "Partial performance" as a substitute for the required memorandum can validate the contract only for the goods which have been accepted or for which payment has been made and accepted.

Receipt and acceptance either of goods or of the price constitutes an unambiguous overt admission by both parties that a contract actually exists. If the court can make a just apportionment, therefore, the agreed price of any goods actually delivered can be recovered without a writing or, if the price has been paid, the seller can be forced to deliver an apportionable part of the goods. The overt actions of the parties make admissible evidence of the other terms of the contract necessary to a just apportionment. This is true even though the actions of the parties are not in themselves inconsistent with a different transaction such as a consignment for resale or a mere loan of money.

Part performance by the buyer requires the delivery of something by him that is accepted by the seller as such performance. Thus, part payment may be made by money or check, accepted by the seller. If the agreed price consists of goods or services, then they must also have been delivered and accepted.

3.   Between merchants, failure to answer a written confirmation of a contract within ten days of receipt is tantamount to a writing under subsection (2) and is sufficient against both parties under subsection (1). The only effect, however, is to take away from the party who fails to answer the defense of the Statute of Frauds; the burden of persuading the trier of fact that a contract was in fact made orally prior to the written confirmation is unaffected. Compare the effect of a failure to reply under Section 2–207.

4.   Failure to satisfy the requirements of this section does not render the contract void for all purposes, but merely prevents it from being judicially enforced in favor of a party to the contract. For example, a buyer who takes possession of goods as provided in an oral contract which the seller has not meanwhile repudiated, is not a trespasser. Nor would the Statute of Frauds provisions of this section be a defense to a third person who wrongfully induces a party to refuse to perform an oral contract, even though the injured party cannot maintain an action for damages against the party so refusing to perform.

5.   The requirement of "signing" is discussed in the comment to Section 1–201.

6.   It is not necessary that the writing be delivered to anybody. It need not be signed or authenticated by both parties but it is, of course, not sufficient against one who has not signed it. Prior to a dispute no one can determine which party's signing of the memorandum may be necessary but from the time of contracting each party should be aware that to him it is signing by the other which is important.

7.   If the making of a contract is admitted in court, either in a written pleading, by stipulation or by oral statement before the court, no additional writing is necessary for protection against fraud. Under this section it is no longer possible to admit the contract in court and still treat the Statute as a defense. However, the contract is not thus conclusively established. The admission so made by a party is itself evidential against him of the truth of the facts so admitted and of nothing more; as against the other party, it is not evidential at all.

Cross References:

See Sections 1–201, 2–202, 2–207, 2–209 and 2–304.

Definitional Cross References:

"Action". Section 1–201.

"Between merchants". Section 2–104.

"Buyer". Section 2–103.

"Contract". Section 1–201.

"Contract for sale". Section 2–106.

"Goods". Section 2–105.

"Notice". Section 1–202.

"Party". Section 1–201.

"Reasonable time". Section 1–205.

"Sale". Section 2–106.

"Seller". Section 2–103.

§ 2–202.   Final Written Expression: Parol or Extrinsic Evidence

Terms with respect to which the confirmatory memoranda of the parties agree or which are otherwise set forth in a writing intended by the parties as a final expression of their agreement with respect to such terms as are included therein may not be contradicted by evidence of any prior agreement or of a contemporaneous oral agreement but may be explained or supplemented

(a) by course of performance, course of dealing, or usage of trade (Section 1–303); and

(b) by evidence of consistent additional terms unless the court finds the writing to have been intended also as a complete and exclusive statement of the terms of the agreement.

Official Comment

Prior Uniform Statutory Provisions: None.

Purposes:

1. This section definitely rejects:

(a) Any assumption that because a writing has been worked out which is final on some matters, it is to be taken as including all the matters agreed upon;

(b) The premise that the language used has the meaning attributable to such language by rules of construction existing in the law rather than the meaning which arises out of the commercial context in which it was used; and

(c) The requirement that a condition precedent to the admissibility of the type of evidence specified in paragraph (a) is an original determination by the court that the language used is ambiguous.

2. Paragraph (a) makes admissible evidence of course of dealing, usage of trade and course of performance to explain or supplement the terms of any writing stating the agreement of the parties in order that the true understanding of the parties as to the agreement may be reached. Such writings are to be read on the assumption that the course of prior dealings between the parties and the usages of trade were taken for granted when the document was phrased. Unless carefully negated they have become an element of the meaning of the words used. Similarly, the course of actual performance by the parties is considered the best indication of what they intended the writing to mean.

3. Under paragraph (b) consistent additional terms, not reduced to writing, may be proved unless the court finds that the writing was intended by both parties as a complete and exclusive statement of all the terms. If the additional terms are such that, if agreed upon, they would certainly have been included in the document in the view of the court, then evidence of their alleged making must be kept from the trier of fact.

Cross References:

Point 3: Sections 1–303, 2–207, 2–302 and 2–316.

Definitional Cross References:

"Agreed" and "agreement". Section 1–201.

"Course of dealing". Section 1–303.

"Course of performance". Section 1–303.

"Party". Section 1–201.

"Term". Section 1–201.

"Usage of trade". Section 1–303.

"Written" and "writing". Section 1–201.

§ 2–203. Seals Inoperative

The affixing of a seal to a writing evidencing a contract for sale or an offer to buy or sell goods does not constitute the writing a sealed instrument and the law with respect to sealed instruments does not apply to such a contract or offer.

Definitional Cross References: "Goods". Section 2–105.

"Contract for sale". Section 2–106.   "Writing". Section 1–201.

§ 2–204. Formation in General

(1) A contract for sale of goods may be made in any manner sufficient to show agreement, including conduct by both parties which recognizes the existence of such a contract.

(2) An agreement sufficient to constitute a contract for sale may be found even though the moment of its making is undetermined.

(3) Even though one or more terms are left open a contract for sale does not fail for indefiniteness if the parties have intended to make a contract and there is a reasonably certain basis for giving an appropriate remedy.

Official Comment

Purposes of Changes

Subsection (1) continues without change the basic policy of recognizing any manner of expression of agreement, oral, written or otherwise. The legal effect of such an agreement is, of course, qualified by other provisions of this Article.

Under subsection (1) appropriate conduct by the parties may be sufficient to establish an agreement. Subsection (2) is directed primarily to the situation where the interchanged correspondence does not disclose the exact point at which the deal was closed, but the actions of the parties indicate that a binding obligation has been undertaken.

Subsection (3) states the principle as to "open terms" underlying later sections of the Article. If the parties intend to enter into a binding agreement, this subsection recognizes that agreement as valid in law, despite missing terms, if there is any reasonably certain basis for granting a remedy. The test is not certainty as to what the parties were to do nor as to the exact amount of damages due the plaintiff. Nor is the fact that one or more terms are left to be agreed upon enough of itself to defeat an otherwise adequate agreement. Rather, commercial standards on the point of "indefiniteness" are intended to be applied, this Act making provision elsewhere for missing terms needed for performance, open price, remedies and the like.

The more terms the parties leave open, the less likely it is that they have intended to conclude a binding agreement, but their actions may be frequently conclusive on the matter despite the omissions.

Definitional Cross References:

"Agreement". Section 1–201.

"Contract". Section 1–201.

"Contract for sale". Section 2–106.

"Goods". Section 2–105.

"Party". Section 1–201.

"Remedy". Section 1–201.   "Term". Section 1–201.

§ 2–205.   Firm Offers

An offer by a merchant to buy or sell goods in a signed writing which by its terms gives assurance that it will be held open is not revocable, for lack of consideration, during the time stated or if no time is stated for a reasonable time, but in no event may such period of irrevocability exceed three months; but any such term of assurance on a form supplied by the offeree must be separately signed by the offeror.

Official Comment

Prior Uniform Statutory Provision: Sections 1 and 3, Uniform Sales Act.

Changes: Completely rewritten by this and other sections of this Article.

Purposes of Changes:

1.   This section is intended to modify the former rule which required that "firm offers" be sustained by consideration in order to bind, and to require instead that they must merely be characterized as such and expressed in signed writings.

2.   The primary purpose of this section is to give effect to the deliberate intention of a merchant to make a current firm offer binding. The deliberation is shown in the case of an individualized document by the merchant's signature to the offer, and in the case of an offer included on a form supplied by the other party to the transaction by the separate signing of the particular clause which contains the offer. "Signed" here also includes authentication but the reasonableness of the authentication herein allowed must be determined in the light of the purpose of the section. The circumstances surrounding the signing may justify something less than a formal signature or initialing but typically the kind of authentication involved here would consist of a minimum of initialing of the clause involved. A handwritten memorandum on the writer's letterhead purporting in its terms to "confirm" a firm offer already made would be enough to satisfy this section, although not subscribed, since under the circumstances it could not be considered a memorandum of mere negotiation and it would adequately show its own authenticity. Similarly, an authorized telegram will suffice, and this is true even though the original draft contained only a typewritten signature. However, despite settled courses of dealing or usages of the trade whereby firm offers are made by oral communication and relied upon without more evidence, such offers remain revocable under this Article since authentication by a writing is the essence of this section.

3.   This section is intended to apply to current "firm" offers and not to long term options, and an outside time limit of three months during which such offers remain irrevocable has been set. The three month period during which firm offers remain irrevocable under this section need not be stated by days or by date. If the offer states that it is "guaranteed" or "firm" until the happening of a contingency which will occur within the three month period, it will remain irrevocable until that event. A promise made for a longer period will operate under this section to bind the offeror only for the first three months of the period but may of course be renewed. If supported by consideration it may continue for as long as the parties specify. This section deals only with the offer which is not supported by consideration.

4.   Protection is afforded against the inadvertent signing of a firm offer when contained in a form prepared by the offeree by requiring that such a clause be separately authenticated. If the offer clause is called to the offeror's attention and he separately authenticates it, he will be bound; Section 2–302 may operate, however, to prevent an unconscionable result which otherwise would flow from other terms appearing in the form.

5.   Safeguards are provided to offer relief in the case of material mistake by virtue of the requirement of good faith and the general law of mistake.

Cross References:

Point 1: Section 1–102.

Point 2: Section 1–102.

Point 3: Section 2–201.

Point 5: Section 2–302.

Definitional Cross References:

"Goods". Section 2–105.

"Merchant". Section 2–104.

"Signed". Section 1–201.

"Writing". Section 1–201.

§ 2–206.   Offer and Acceptance in Formation of Contract

(1)   Unless otherwise unambiguously indicated by the language or circumstances

(a)   an offer to make a contract shall be construed as inviting acceptance in any manner and by any medium reasonable in the circumstances;

(b)   an order or other offer to buy goods for prompt or current shipment shall be construed as inviting acceptance either by a prompt promise to ship or by the prompt or current shipment of conforming or non-conforming goods, but such a shipment of non-conforming goods does not constitute an acceptance if the seller seasonably notifies the buyer that the shipment is offered only as an accommodation to the buyer.

(2)   Where the beginning of a requested performance is a reasonable mode of acceptance an offeror who is not notified of acceptance within a reasonable time may treat the offer as having lapsed before acceptance.

Official Comment

Prior Uniform Statutory Provision: Sections 1 and 3, Uniform Sales Act.

Changes: Completely rewritten in this and other sections of this Article.

Purposes of Changes: To make it clear that:

1.   Any reasonable manner of acceptance is intended to be regarded as available unless the offeror has made quite clear that it will not be acceptable. Former technical rules as to acceptance, such as requiring that telegraphic offers be accepted by telegraphed acceptance, etc., are rejected and a criterion that the acceptance be "in any manner and by any medium reasonable under the circumstances," is substituted. This section is intended to remain flexible and its applicability to be enlarged as new media of communication develop or as the more time-saving present day media come into general use.

2. Either shipment or a prompt promise to ship is made a proper means of acceptance of an offer looking to current shipment. In accordance with ordinary commercial understanding the section interprets an order looking to current shipment as allowing acceptance either by actual shipment or by a prompt promise to ship and rejects the artificial theory that only a single mode of acceptance is normally envisaged by an offer. This is true even though the language of the offer happens to be "ship at once" or the like. "Shipment" is here used in the same sense as in Section 2–504; it does not include the beginning of delivery by the seller's own truck or by messenger. But loading on the seller's own truck might be a beginning of performance under subsection (2).

3. The beginning of performance by an offeree can be effective as acceptance so as to bind the offeror only if followed within a reasonable time by notice to the offeror. Such a beginning of performance must unambiguously express the offeree's intention to engage himself. For the protection of both parties it is essential that notice follow in due course to constitute acceptance.

Nothing in this section however bars the possibility that under the common law performance begun may have an intermediate effect of temporarily barring revocation of the offer, or at the offeror's option, final effect in constituting acceptance.

4. Subsection (1)(b) deals with the situation where a shipment made following an order is shown by a notification of shipment to be referable to that order but has a defect. Such a nonconforming shipment is normally to be understood as intended to close the bargain, even though it proves to have been at the same time a breach. However, the seller by stating that the shipment is non-conforming and is offered only as an accommodation to the buyer keeps the shipment or notification from operating as an acceptance.

Definitional Cross References:

"Buyer". Section 2–103.

"Conforming". Section 2–106.

"Contract". Section 1–201.

"Goods". Section 2–105.

"Notifies". Section 1–202.

"Reasonable time". Section 1–205.

§ 2–207. Additional Terms in Acceptance or Confirmation

(1) A definite and seasonable expression of acceptance or a written confirmation which is sent within a reasonable time operates as an acceptance even though it states terms additional to or different from those offered or agreed upon, unless acceptance is expressly made conditional on assent to the additional or different terms.

(2) The additional terms are to be construed as proposals for addition to the contract. Between merchants such terms become part of the contract unless:

   (a) the offer expressly limits acceptance to the terms of the offer;

   (b) they materially alter it; or

   (c) notification of objection to them has already been given or is given within a reasonable time after notice of them is received.

(3) Conduct by both parties which recognizes the existence of a contract is sufficient to establish a contract for sale although the writings of

the parties do not otherwise establish a contract. In such case the terms of the particular contract consist of those terms on which the writings of the parties agree, together with any supplementary terms incorporated under any other provisions of this Act.

Official Comment

Prior Uniform Statutory Provision: Sections 1 and 3, Uniform Sales Act.

Changes: Completely rewritten by this and other sections of this Article.

Purposes of Changes:

1.   This section is intended to deal with two typical situations. The one is the written confirmation, where an agreement has been reached either orally or by informal correspondence between the parties and is followed by one or both of the parties sending formal memoranda embodying the terms so far as agreed upon and adding terms not discussed. The other situation is offer and acceptance, in which a wire or letter expressed and intended as an acceptance or the closing of an agreement adds further minor suggestions or proposals such as "ship by Tuesday," "rush," "ship draft against bill of lading inspection allowed," or the like. A frequent example of the second situation is the exchange of printed purchase order and acceptance (sometimes called "acknowledgment") forms. Because the forms are oriented to the thinking of the respective drafting parties, the terms contained in them often do not correspond. Often the seller's form contains terms different from or additional to those set forth in the buyer's form. Nevertheless, the parties proceed with the transaction. [Comment 1 was amended in 1966.]

2.   Under this Article a proposed deal which in commercial understanding has in fact been closed is recognized as a contract. Therefore, any additional matter contained in the confirmation or in the acceptance falls within subsection (2) and must be regarded as a proposal for an added term unless the acceptance is made conditional on the acceptance of the additional or different terms. [Comment 2 was amended in 1966.]

3.   Whether or not additional or different terms will become part of the agreement depends upon the provisions of subsection (2). If they are such as materially to alter the original bargain, they will not be included unless expressly agreed to by the other party. If, however, they are terms which would not so change the bargain they will be incorporated unless notice of objection to them has already been given or is given within a reasonable time.

4.   Examples of typical clauses which would normally "materially alter" the contract and so result in surprise or hardship if incorporated without express awareness by the other party are: a clause negating such standard warranties as that of merchantability or fitness for a particular purpose in circumstances in which either warranty normally attaches; a clause requiring a guaranty of 90% or 100% deliveries in a case such as a contract by cannery, where the usage of the trade allows greater quantity leeways; a clause reserving to the seller the power to cancel upon the buyer's failure to meet any invoice when due; a clause requiring that complaints be made in a time materially shorter than customary or reasonable.

5.   Examples of clauses which involve no element of unreasonable surprise and which therefore are to be incorporated in the contract unless notice of objection is seasonably given are: a clause setting forth and perhaps enlarging slightly upon the seller's exemption due to supervening causes

beyond his control, similar to those covered by the provision of this Article on merchant's excuse by failure of pre-supposed conditions or a clause fixing in advance any reasonable formula of proration under such circumstances; a clause fixing a reasonable time for complaints within customary limits, or in the case of a purchase for sub-sale, providing for inspection by the sub-purchaser; a clause providing for interest on overdue invoices or fixing the seller's standard credit terms where they are within the range of trade practice and do not limit any credit bargained for; a clause limiting the right of rejection for defects which fall within the customary trade tolerances for acceptance "with adjustment" or otherwise limiting remedy in a reasonable manner (see Sections 2–718 and 2–719).

6. If no answer is received within a reasonable time after additional terms are proposed, it is both fair and commercially sound to assume that their inclusion has been assented to. Where clauses on confirming forms sent by both parties conflict each party must be assumed to object to a clause of the other conflicting with one on the confirmation sent by himself. As a result the requirement that there be notice of objection which is found in subsection (2) is satisfied and the conflicting terms do not become a part of the contract. The contract then consists of the terms originally expressly agreed to, terms on which the confirmations agree, and terms supplied by his Act, including subsection (2). The written confirmation is also subject to Section 2–201. Under that section a failure to respond permits enforcement of a prior oral agreement; under this section a failure to respond permits additional terms to become part of the agreement. [Comment 6 was amended in 1966.]

7. In many cases, as where goods are shipped, accepted and paid for before any dispute arises, there is no question whether a contract has been made. In such cases, where the writings of the parties do not establish a contract, it is not necessary to determine which act or document constituted the offer and which the acceptance. See Section 2–204. The only question is what terms are included in the contract, and subsection (3) furnishes the governing rule. [Comment 7 was added in 1966.]

Cross References:

See generally Section 2–302.

Point 5: Sections 2–513, 2–602, 2–607, 2–609, 2–612, 2–614, 2–615, 2–616, 2–718 and 2–719.

Point 6: Sections 1–102 and 2–104.

Definitional Cross References:

"Between merchants". Section 2–104.

"Contract". Section 1–201.

"Notification". Section 1–202.

"Reasonable time". Section 1–205.

"Seasonably". Section 1–205.

"Send". Section 1–201.

"Term". Section 1–201.

"Written". Section 1–201.

§ 2–208. Course of Performance or Practical Construction[c]

§ 2–209. Modification, Rescission and Waiver

(1) An agreement modifying a contract within this Article needs no consideration to be binding.

[c] This section is deleted in the 2003 Official Text of the Uniform Commercial Code in light of UCC § 1–303 (2003), which covers the same point. Although all states have enacted the 2003 text of Article 1, some of those states have nonetheless redundantly retained this section.

(2) A signed agreement which excludes modification or rescission except by a signed writing cannot be otherwise modified or rescinded, but except as between merchants such a requirement on a form supplied by the merchant must be separately signed by the other party.

(3) The requirements of the statute of frauds section of this Article (Section 2–201) must be satisfied if the contract as modified is within its provisions.

(4) Although an attempt at modification or rescission does not satisfy the requirements of subsection (2) or (3) it can operate as a waiver.

(5) A party who has made a waiver affecting an executory portion of the contract may retract the waiver by reasonable notification received by the other party that strict performance will be required of any term waived, unless the retraction would be unjust in view of a material change of position in reliance on the waiver.

Official Comment

Prior Uniform Statutory Provision: Subsection (1)—Compare Section 1, Uniform Written Obligations Act; Subsections (2) to (5)—none.

Purposes of Changes and New Matter:

1. This section seeks to protect and make effective all necessary and desirable modifications of sales contracts without regard to the technicalities which at present hamper such adjustments.

2. Subsection (1) provides that an agreement modifying a sales contract needs no consideration to be binding.

However, modifications made thereunder must meet the test of good faith imposed by this Act. The effective use of bad faith to escape performance on the original contract terms is barred, and the extortion of a "modification" without legitimate commercial reason is ineffective as a violation of the duty of good faith. Nor can a mere technical consideration support a modification made in bad faith.

The test of "good faith" between merchants or as against merchants includes "observance of reasonable commercial standards of fair dealing in the trade" (Section 2–103), and may in some situations require an objectively demonstrable reason for seeking a modification. But such matters as a market shift which makes performance come to involve a loss may provide such a reason even though there is no such unforeseen difficulty as would make out a legal excuse from performance under Sections 2–615 and 2–616.

3. Subsections (2) and (3) are intended to protect against false allegations of oral modifications. "Modification or rescission" includes abandonment or other change by mutual consent, contrary to the decision in Green v. Doniger, 300 N.Y. 238, 90 N.E.2d 56 (1949); it does not include unilateral "termination" or "cancellation" as defined in Section 2–106.

The Statute of Frauds provisions of this Article are expressly applied to modifications by subsection (3). Under those provisions the "delivery and acceptance" test is limited to the goods which have been accepted, that is, to the past. "Modification" for the future cannot therefore be conjured up by oral testimony if the price involved is $500.00 or more since such modification must be shown at least by an authenticated memo. And since a memo is limited in its effect to the quantity of goods set forth in it there is safeguard against oral evidence.

Subsection (2) permits the parties in effect to make their own Statute of Frauds as regards any future modification of the contract by giving effect to a clause in a signed agreement which expressly requires any modification to be by signed writing. But note that if a consumer is to be held to such a clause on a form supplied by a merchant it must be separately signed.

4.   Subsection (4) is intended, despite the provisions of subsections (2) and (3), to prevent contractual provisions excluding modification except by a signed writing from limiting in other respects the legal effect of the parties' actual later conduct. The effect of such conduct as a waiver is further regulated in subsection (5).

Cross References:

Point 1: Section 1–203.

Point 2: Sections 1–201, 1–203, 2–615 and 2–616. Point 3: Sections 2–106, 2–201 and 2–202.

Point 4: Sections 2–202 and 2–208.

Definitional Cross References:

"Agreement". Section 1–201.

"Between merchants". Section 2–104.

"Contract". Section 1–201.

"Notification". Section 1–202.

"Signed". Section 1–201.

"Term". Section 1–201.

"Writing". Section 1–201.

§ 2–210.   Delegation of Performance; Assignment of Rights

(1)   A party may perform his duty through a delegate unless otherwise agreed or unless the other party has a substantial interest in having his original promisor perform or control the acts required by the contract. No delegation of performance relieves the party delegating of any duty to perform or any liability for breach.

(2)   Except as otherwise provided in Section 9–406, unless otherwise agreed all rights of either seller or buyer can be assigned except where the assignment would materially change the duty of the other party, or increase materially the burden or risk imposed on him by his contract, or impair materially his chance of obtaining return performance. A right to damages for breach of the whole contract or a right arising out of the assignor's due performance of his entire obligation can be assigned despite agreement otherwise.

(3)   The creation, attachment, perfection, or enforcement of a security interest in the seller's interest under a contract is not a transfer that materially changes the duty of or increases materially the burden or risk imposed on the buyer or impairs materially the buyer's chance of obtaining return performance within the purview of subsection (2) unless, and then only to the extent that, enforcement actually results in a delegation of material performance of the seller. Even in that event, the creation, attachment, perfection, and enforcement of the security interest remains effective, but (i) the seller is liable to the buyer for damages caused by the delegation to the extent that the damages could not reasonably be prevented by the buyer, and (ii) a court having jurisdiction may grant other

appropriate relief, including cancellation of the contract for sale or an injunction against enforcement of the security interest or consummation of the enforcement.

(4) Unless the circumstances indicate the contrary a prohibition of assignment of "the contract" is to be construed as barring only the delegation to the assignee of the assignor's performance.

(5) An assignment of "the contract" or of "all my rights under the contract" or an assignment in similar general terms is an assignment of rights and unless the language or the circumstances (as in an assignment for security) indicate the contrary, it is a delegation of performance of the duties of the assignor and its acceptance by the assignee constitutes a promise by him to perform those duties. This promise is enforceable by either the assignor or the other party to the original contract.

(6) The other party may treat any assignment which delegates performance as creating reasonable grounds for insecurity and may without prejudice to his rights against the assignor demand assurances from the assignee (Section 2–609).

Definitional Cross References:

"Agreement". Section 1–201.

"Buyer". Section 2–103.

"Contract". Section 1–201.

"Party". Section 1–201.

"Rights". Section 1–201.

"Seller". Section 2–103.

"Term". Section 1–201.

PART 3

GENERAL OBLIGATION AND CONSTRUCTION OF CONTRACT

§ 2–301. General Obligations of Parties

The obligation of the seller is to transfer and deliver and that of the buyer is to accept and pay in accordance with the contract.

Definitional Cross References:

"Buyer". Section 2–103.

"Contract". Section 1–201.

"Party". Section 1–201.

"Seller". Section 2–103.

§ 2–302. Unconscionable Contract or Clause

(1) If the court as a matter of law finds the contract or any clause of the contract to have been unconscionable at the time it was made the court may refuse to enforce the contract, or it may enforce the remainder of the contract without the unconscionable clause, or it may so limit the application of any unconscionable clause as to avoid any unconscionable result.

(2) When it is claimed or appears to the court that the contract or any clause thereof may be unconscionable the parties shall be afforded a reasonable opportunity to present evidence as to its commercial setting, purpose and effect to aid the court in making the determination.

Official Comment

Prior Uniform Statutory Provision: None.

Purposes:

1. This section is intended to make it possible for the courts to police explicitly against the contracts or clauses which they find to be unconscionable. In the past such policing has been accomplished by adverse construction of language, by manipulation of the rules of offer and acceptance or by determinations that the clause is contrary to public policy or to the dominant purpose of the contract. This section is intended to allow the court to pass directly on the unconscionability of the contract or particular clause therein and to make a conclusion of law as to its unconscionability. The basic test is whether, in the light of the general commercial background and the commercial needs of the particular trade or case, the clauses involved are so one-sided as to be unconscionable under the circumstances existing at the time of the making of the contract. Subsection (2) makes it clear that it is proper for the court to hear evidence upon these questions. The principle is one of the prevention of oppression and unfair surprise (Cf. Campbell Soup Co. v. Wentz, 172 F.2d 80, 3d Cir.1948) and not of disturbance of allocation of risks because of superior bargaining power. The underlying basis of this section is illustrated by the results in cases such as the following:

Kansas City Wholesale Grocery Co. v. Weber Packing Corporation, 93 Utah 414, 73 P.2d 1272 (1937), where a clause limiting time for complaints was held inapplicable to latent defects in a shipment of catsup which could be discovered only by microscopic analysis; Hardy v. General Motors Acceptance Corporation, 38 Ga.App. 463, 144 S.E. 327 (1928), holding that a disclaimer of warranty clause applied only to express warranties, thus letting in a fair implied warranty; Andrews Bros. v. Singer & Co. (1934 CA) 1 K.B. 17, holding that where a car with substantial mileage was delivered instead of a "new" car, a disclaimer of warranties, including those "implied," left unaffected an "express obligation" on the description, even though the Sale of Goods Act called such an implied warranty; New Prague Flouring Mill Co. v. G.A. Spears, 194 Iowa 417, 189 N.W. 815 (1922), holding that a clause permitting the seller, upon the buyer's failure to supply shipping instructions, to cancel, ship, or allow delivery date to be indefinitely postponed 30 days at a time by the inaction, does not indefinitely postpone the date of measuring damages for the buyer's breach, to the seller's advantage; and Kansas Flour Mills Co. v. Dirks, 100 Kan. 376, 164 P. 273 (1917), where under a similar clause in a rising market the court permitted the buyer to measure his damages for non-delivery at the end of only one 30 day postponement; Green v. Arcos, Ltd. (1931 CA) 47 T.L.R. 336, where a blanket clause prohibiting rejection of shipments by the buyer was restricted to apply to shipments where discrepancies represented merely mercantile variations; Meyer v. Packard Cleveland Motor Co., 106 Ohio St. 328, 140 N.E. 118 (1922), in which the court held that a "waiver" of all agreements not specified did not preclude implied warranty of fitness of a rebuilt dump truck for ordinary use as a dump truck; Austin Co. v. J.H. Tillman Co., 104 Or. 541, 209 P. 131 (1922), where a clause limiting the buyer's remedy to return was held to be applicable only if the seller had delivered a machine needed for a construction job which reasonably met the contract description; Bekkevold v. Potts, 173 Minn. 87, 216 N.W. 790, 59 A.L.R. 1164 (1927), refusing to allow warranty of fitness for purpose imposed by law to be negated by clause excluding all warranties "made" by the seller; Robert A. Munroe & Co. v. Meyer (1930) 2 K.B. 312, holding that the warranty of description overrides a clause reading "with all faults and defects" where adulterated meat not up to the contract description was delivered.

2.   Under this section the court, in its discretion, may refuse to enforce the contract as a whole if it is perme-ated by the unconscionability, or it may strike any single clause or group of clauses which are so tainted or which are contrary to the essential purpose of the agreement, or it may simply limit unconscionable clauses so as to avoid unconscionable results.

3.   The present section is addressed to the court, and the decision is to be made by it. The commercial evidence referred to in subsection (2) is for the court's consideration, not the jury's. Only the agreement which results from the court's action on these matters is to be submitted to the general triers of the facts.

Definitional Cross Reference:

"Contract". Section 1–201.

§ 2–303.   Allocation or Division of Risks

Where this Article allocates a risk or a burden as between the parties "unless otherwise agreed", the agreement may not only shift the allocation but may also divide the risk or burden.

Definitional Cross References:

"Agreement". Section 1–201.

"Party". Section 1–201.

§ 2–304.   Price Payable in Money, Goods, Realty, or Otherwise

(1)   The price can be made payable in money or otherwise. If it is payable in whole or in part in goods each party is a seller of the goods which he is to transfer.

(2)   Even though all or part of the price is payable in an interest in realty the transfer of the goods and the seller's obligations with reference to them are subject to this Article, but not the transfer of the interest in realty or the transferor's obligations in connection therewith.

§ 2–305.   Open Price Term

(1)   The parties if they so intend can conclude a contract for sale even though the price is not settled. In such a case the price is a reasonable price at the time for delivery if

(a)   nothing is said as to price; or

(b)   the price is left to be agreed by the parties and they fail to agree; or

(c)   the price is to be fixed in terms of some agreed market or other standard as set or recorded by a third person or agency and it is not so set or recorded.

(2)   A price to be fixed by the seller or by the buyer means a price for him to fix in good faith.

(3)   When a price left to be fixed otherwise than by agreement of the parties fails to be fixed through fault of one party the other may at his option treat the contract as cancelled or himself fix a reasonable price.

(4)   Where, however, the parties intend not to be bound unless the price be fixed or agreed and it is not fixed or agreed there is no contract. In such a case the buyer must return any goods already received or if unable so to do must pay their reasonable value at the time of delivery and the seller must return any portion of the price paid on account.

Official Comment

Prior Uniform Statutory Provision: Sections 9 and 10, Uniform Sales Act.

Changes: Completely rewritten.

Purposes of Changes:

1.   This section applies when the price term is left open on the making of an agreement which is nevertheless intended by the parties to be a binding agreement. This Article rejects in these instances the formula that "an agreement to agree is unenforceable" if the case falls within subsection (1) of this section, and rejects also defeating such agreements on the ground of "indefiniteness". Instead this Article recognizes the dominant intention of the parties to have the deal continue to be binding upon both. As to future performance, since this Article recognizes remedies such as cover (Section 2–712), resale (Section 2–706) and specific performance (Section 2–716) which go beyond any mere arithmetic as between contract price and market price, there is usually a "reasonably certain basis for granting an appropriate remedy for breach" so that the contract need not fail for indefiniteness.

2.   Under some circumstances the postponement of agreement on price will mean that no deal has re-

ally been concluded, and this is made express in the preamble of subsection (1) ("The parties if they so intend") and in subsection (4). Whether or not this is so is, in most cases, a question to be determined by the trier of fact.

3.   Subsection (2), dealing with the situation where the price is to be fixed by one party rejects the uncommercial idea that an agreement that the seller may fix the price means that he may fix any price he may wish by the express qualification that the price so fixed must be fixed in good faith. Good faith includes observance of reasonable commercial standards of fair dealing in the trade if the party is a merchant. (Section 2–103). But in the normal case a "posted price" or a future seller's or buyer's "given price," "price in effect," "market price," or the like satisfies the good faith requirement.

4.   The section recognizes that there may be cases in which a particular person's judgment is not chosen merely as a barometer or index of a fair price but is an essential condition to the parties' intent to make any contract at all. For example, the case where a known and trusted expert is to "value" a particular painting for which there is no market standard differs sharply from the situation where a named expert is to determine the grade

of cotton, and the difference would support a finding that in the one the parties did not intend to make a binding agreement if that expert were unavailable whereas in the other they did so intend. Other circumstances would of course affect the validity of such a finding.

5.　　Under subsection (3), wrongful interference by one party with any agreed machinery for price fixing in the contract may be treated by the other party as a repudiation justifying cancellation, or merely as a failure to take cooperative action thus shifting to the aggrieved party the reasonable leeway in fixing the price.

6.　　Throughout the entire section, the purpose is to give effect to the agreement which has been made. That effect, however, is always conditioned by the requirement of good faith action which is made an inherent part of all contracts within this Act. (Section 1–203).

Cross References:

Point 1: Sections 2–204(3), 2–706, 2–712 and 2–716.

Point 3: Section 2–103.

Point 5: Sections 2–311 and 2–610.

Point 6: Section 1–203.

Definitional Cross References:

"Agreement". Section 1–201.

"Burden of establishing". Section 1–201.

"Buyer". Section 2–103.

"Cancellation". Section 2–106.

"Contract". Section 1–201.

"Contract for sale". Section 2–106.

"Fault". Section 1–201.

"Goods". Section 2–105.

"Party". Section 1–201.

"Receipt of goods". Section 2–103.

"Seller". Section 2–103.

"Term". Section 2–201.

§ 2–306.　Output, Requirements and Exclusive Dealings

(1)　A term which measures the quantity by the output of the seller or the requirements of the buyer means such actual output or requirements as may occur in good faith, except that no quantity unreasonably disproportionate to any stated estimate or in the absence of a stated estimate to any normal or otherwise comparable prior output or requirements may be tendered or demanded.

(2)　A lawful agreement by either the seller or the buyer for exclusive dealing in the kind of goods concerned imposes unless otherwise agreed an obligation by the seller to use best efforts to supply the goods and by the buyer to use best efforts to promote their sale.

Official Comment

Prior Uniform Statutory Provision: None.

Purposes:

1.　　Subsection (1) of this section, in regard to output and requirements, applies to this specific problem the general approach of this Act which requires the reading of commercial background and intent into the language of any agreement and demands good faith in the performance of that agreement. It applies to such contracts of nonproducing establishments such as dealers or distributors as well as to manufacturing concerns.

2. Under this Article, a contract for output or requirements is not too indefinite since it is held to mean the actual good faith output or requirements of the particular party. Nor does such a contract lack mutuality of obligation since, under this section, the party who will determine quantity is required to operate his plant or conduct his business in good faith and according to commercial standards of fair dealing in the trade so that his output or requirements will approximate a reasonably foreseeable figure. Reasonable elasticity in the requirements is expressly envisaged by this section and good faith variations from prior requirements are permitted even when the variation may be such as to result in discontinuance. A shut-down by a requirements buyer for lack of orders might be permissible when a shut-down merely to curtail losses would not. The essential test is whether the party is acting in good faith. Similarly, a sudden expansion of the plant by which requirements are to be measured would not be included within the scope of the contract as made but normal expansion undertaken in good faith would be within the scope of this section. One of the factors in an expansion situation would be whether the market price had risen greatly in a case in which the requirements contract contained a fixed price. Reasonable variation of an extreme sort is exemplified in Southwest Natural Gas Co. v. Oklahoma Portland Cement Co., 102 F.2d 630 (C.C.A.10, 1939). This Article takes no position as to whether a requirements contract is a provable claim in bankruptcy.

3. If an estimate of output or requirements is included in the agreement, no quantity unreasonably disproportionate to it may be tendered or demanded. Any minimum or maximum set by the agreement shows a clear limit on the intended elasticity. In similar fashion, the agreed estimate is to be regarded as a center around which the parties intend the variation to occur.

4. When an enterprise is sold, the question may arise whether the buyer is bound by an existing output or requirements contract. That question is outside the scope of this Article, and is to be determined on other principles of law. Assuming that the contract continues, the output or requirements in the hands of the new owner continue to be measured by the actual good faith output or requirements under the normal operation of the enterprise prior to sale. The sale itself is not grounds for sudden expansion or decrease.

5. Subsection (2), on exclusive dealing, makes explicit the commercial rule embodied in this Act under which the parties to such contracts are held to have impliedly, even when not expressly, bound themselves to use reasonable diligence as well as good faith in their performance of the contract. Under such contracts the exclusive agent is required, although no express commitment has been made, to use reasonable effort and due diligence in the expansion of the market or the promotion of the product, as the case may be. The principal is expected under such a contract to refrain from supplying any other dealer or agent within the exclusive territory. An exclusive dealing agreement brings into play all of the good faith aspects of the output and requirement problems of subsection (1). It also raises questions of insecurity and right to adequate assurance under this Article.

Cross References:

Point 4: Section 2–210.

Point 5: Sections 1–203 and 2–609.

Definitional Cross References:

"Agreement". Section 1–201.

"Buyer". Section 2–103.

"Contract for sale". Section 2–106.

"Good faith". Section 1–201.

"Goods". Section 2–105.

"Party". Section 1–201.

"Term". Section 1–201.

"Seller". Section 2–103.

§ 2–307.　Delivery in Single Lot or Several Lots

Unless otherwise agreed all goods called for by a contract for sale must be tendered in a single delivery and payment is due only on such tender but where the circumstances give either party the right to make or demand delivery in lots the price if it can be apportioned may be demanded for each lot.

Definitional Cross References:

"Contract for sale". Section 2–106.

"Goods". Section 2–105.

"Lot". Section 2–105.

"Party". Section 1–201.

"Rights". Section 1–201.

§ 2–308.　Absence of Specified Place for Delivery

Unless otherwise agreed

(a)　the place for delivery of goods is the seller's place of business or if he has none his residence; but

(b)　in a contract for sale of identified goods which to the knowledge of the parties at the time of contracting are in some other place, that place is the place for their delivery; and

(c)　documents of title may be delivered through customary banking channels.

Definitional Cross References:

"Contract for sale". Section 2–106.

"Delivery". Section 1–201.

"Document of title". Section 1–201.

"Goods". Section 2–105.

"Party". Section 1–201.

"Seller". Section 2–103.

§ 2–309.　Absence of Specific Time Provisions; Notice of Termination

(1)　The time for shipment or delivery or any other action under a contract if not provided in this Article or agreed upon shall be a reasonable time.

(2)　Where the contract provides for successive performances but is indefinite in duration it is valid for a reasonable time but unless otherwise agreed may be terminated at any time by either party.

(3)　Termination of a contract by one party except on the happening of an agreed event requires that reasonable notification be received by the other party and an agreement dispensing with notification is invalid if its operation would be unconscionable.

Official Comment

Prior Uniform Statutory Provision: Subsection (1)—see Sections 43(2), 45(2), 47(1) and 48, Uniform Sales Act, for policy continued under this Article; Subsection (2)—none; Subsection (3)—none.

Changes: Completely different in scope.

Purposes of Changes and New Matter:

1.   Subsection (1) requires that all actions taken under a sales contract must be taken within a reasonable time where no time has been agreed upon. The reasonable time under this provision turns on the criteria as to "reasonable time" and on good faith and commercial standards set forth in Sections 1–203, 1–204 and 2–103. It thus depends upon what constitutes acceptable commercial conduct in view of the nature, purpose and circumstances of the action to be taken. Agreement as to a definite time, however, may be found in a term implied from the contractual circumstances, usage of trade or course of dealing or performance as well as in an express term. Such cases fall outside of this subsection since in them the time for action is "agreed" by usage.

2.   The time for payment, where not agreed upon, is related to the time for delivery; the particular problems which arise in connection with determining the appropriate time of payment and the time for any inspection before payment which is both allowed by law and demanded by the buyer are covered in Section 2–513.

3.   The facts in regard to shipment and delivery differ so widely as to make detailed provision for them in the text of this Article impracticable. The applicable principles, however, make it clear that surprise is to be avoided, good faith judgment is to be protected, and notice or negotiation to reduce the uncertainty to certainty is to be favored.

4.   When the time for delivery is left open, unreasonably early offers of or demands for delivery are intended to be read under this Article as expressions of desire or intention, requesting the assent or acquiescence of the other party, not as final positions which may amount without more to breach or to create breach by the other side. See Sections 2–207 and 2–609.

5.   The obligation of good faith under this Act requires reasonable notification before a contract may be treated as breached because a reasonable time for delivery or demand has expired. This operates both in the case of a contract originally indefinite as to time and of one subsequently made indefinite by waiver.

When both parties let an originally reasonable time go by in silence, the course of conduct under the contract may be viewed as enlarging the reasonable time for tender or demand of performance. The contract may be terminated by abandonment.

6.   Parties to a contract are not required in giving reasonable notification to fix, at peril of breach, a time which is in fact reasonable in the unforeseeable judgment of a later trier of fact. Effective communication of a proposed time limit calls for a response, so that failure to reply will make out acquiescence. Where objection is made, however, or if the demand is merely for information as to when goods will be delivered or will be ordered out, demand for assurances on the ground of insecurity may be made under this Article pending further negotiations. Only when a party insists on undue delay or on rejection of the other party's reasonable proposal is there a question of flat breach under the present section.

7.   Subsection (2) applies a commercially reasonable view to resolve

347

the conflict which has arisen in the cases as to contracts of indefinite duration. The "reasonable time" of duration appropriate to a given arrangement is limited by the circumstances. When the arrangement has been carried on by the parties over the years, the "reasonable time" can continue indefinitely and the contract will not terminate until notice.

8.   Subsection (3) recognizes that the application of principles of good faith and sound commercial practice normally call for such notification of the termination of a going contract relationship as will give the other party reasonable time to seek a substitute arrangement. An agreement dispensing with notification or limiting the time for the seeking of a substitute arrangement is, of course, valid under this subsection unless the results of putting it into operation would be the creation of an unconscionable state of affairs.

9.   Justifiable cancellation for breach is a remedy for breach and is not the kind of termination covered by the present subsection.

10.   The requirement of notification is dispensed with where the contract provides for termination on the happening of an "agreed event." "Event" is a term chosen here to contrast with "option" or the like.

Cross References:

Point 1: Sections 1–203, 1–204 and 2–103.

Point 2: Sections 2–320, 2–321, 2–504, and 2–511 through 2–514.

Point 5: Section 1–203.

Point 6: Section 2–609.

Point 7: Section 2–204.

Point 9: Sections 2–106, 2–318, 2–610 and 2–703.

Definitional Cross References:

"Agreement". Section 1–201.

"Contract". Section 1–201.

"Notification". Section 1–202.

"Party". Section 1–201.

"Reasonable time". Section 1–205.

"Termination". Section 2–106.

§ 2–310.   Open Time for Payment or Running of Credit; Authority to Ship Under Reservation

Unless otherwise agreed

(a)   payment is due at the time and place at which the buyer is to receive the goods even though the place of shipment is the place of delivery; and

(b)   if the seller is authorized to send the goods he may ship them under reservation, and may tender the documents of title, but the buyer may inspect the goods after their arrival before payment is due unless such inspection is inconsistent with the terms of the contract (Section 2–513); and

(c)   if delivery is authorized and made by way of documents of title otherwise than by subsection (b) then payment is due regardless of where the goods are to be received (i) at the time and place at which the buyer is to receive delivery of the tangible documents or (ii) at the time the buyer is to receive delivery of the electronic documents and at the seller's place of business or if none, the seller's residence; and

(d)   where the seller is required or authorized to ship the goods on credit the credit period runs from the time of shipment but post-dating the invoice or delaying its dispatch will correspondingly delay the starting of the credit period.

Definitional Cross References:

"Buyer". Section 2–103.

"Delivery". Section 1–201.

"Document of title". Section 1–201.

"Goods". Section 2–105.

"Receipt of goods". Section 2–103.

"Seller". Section 2–103.

"Send". Section 1–201.

"Term". Section 1–201.

§ 2–311.   Options and Cooperation Respecting Performance

(1)   An agreement for sale which is otherwise sufficiently definite (subsection (3) of Section 2–204) to be a contract is not made invalid by the fact that it leaves particulars of performance to be specified by one of the parties. Any such specification must be made in good faith and within limits set by commercial reasonableness.

(2)   Unless otherwise agreed specifications relating to assortment of the goods are at the buyer's option and except as otherwise provided in subsections (1)(c) and (3) of Section 2–319 specifications or arrangements relating to shipment are at the seller's option.

(3)   Where such specification would materially affect the other party's performance but is not seasonably made or where one party's cooperation is necessary to the agreed performance of the other but is not seasonably forthcoming, the other party in addition to all other remedies

(a)   is excused for any resulting delay in his own performance; and

(b)   may also either proceed to perform in any reasonable manner or after the time for a material part of his own performance treat the failure to specify or to cooperate as a breach by failure to deliver or accept the goods.

Definitional Cross References:

"Agreement". Section 1–201.

"Buyer". Section 2–103.

"Contract for sale". Section 2–106.

"Goods". Section 2–105.

"Party". Section 1–201.

"Remedy". Section 1–201.

"Seasonably". Section 1–205.

"Seller". Section 2–103.

§ 2–312.   Warranty of Title and Against Infringement; Buyer's Obligation Against Infringement

(1)   Subject to subsection (2) there is in a contract for sale a warranty by the seller that

(a)   the title conveyed shall be good, and its transfer rightful; and

349

(b) the goods shall be delivered free from any security interest or other lien or encumbrance of which the buyer at the time of contracting has no knowledge.

(2) A warranty under subsection (1) will be excluded or modified only by specific language or by circumstances which give the buyer reason to know that the person selling does not claim title in himself or that he is purporting to sell only such right or title as he or a third person may have.

(3) Unless otherwise agreed a seller who is a merchant regularly dealing in goods of the kind warrants that the goods shall be delivered free of the rightful claim of any third person by way of infringement or the like but a buyer who furnishes specifications to the seller must hold the seller harmless against any such claim which arises out of compliance with the specifications.

Definitional Cross References:

"Buyer". Section 2–103.

"Contract for sale". Section 2–106.

"Goods". Section 2–105.

"Person". Section 1–201.

"Right". Section 1–201.

"Seller". Section 2–103.

§ 2–313.   Express Warranties by Affirmation, Promise, Description, Sample

(1) Express warranties by the seller are created as follows:

(a) Any affirmation of fact or promise made by the seller to the buyer which relates to the goods and becomes part of the basis of the bargain creates an express warranty that the goods shall conform to the affirmation or promise.

(b) Any description of the goods which is made part of the basis of the bargain creates an express warranty that the goods shall conform to the description.

(c) Any sample or model which is made part of the basis of the bargain creates an express warranty that the whole of the goods shall conform to the sample or model.

(2) It is not necessary to the creation of an express warranty that the seller use formal words such as "warrant" or "guarantee" or that he have a specific intention to make a warranty, but an affirmation merely of the value of the goods or a statement purporting to be merely the seller's opinion or commendation of the goods does not create a warranty.

Official Comment

Prior Uniform Statutory Provision: Sections 12, 14 and 16, Uniform Sales Act.

Changes: Rewritten.

Purposes of Changes: To consolidate and systematize basic principles with the result that:

1. "Express" warranties rest on "dickered" aspects of the individual bargain, and go so clearly to the es-

sence of that bargain that words of disclaimer in a form are repugnant to the basic dickered terms. "Implied" warranties rest so clearly on a common factual situation or set of conditions that no particular language or action is necessary to evidence them and they will arise in such a situation unless unmistakably negated.

This section reverts to the older case law insofar as the warranties of description and sample are designated "express" rather than "implied".

2. Although this section is limited in its scope and direct purpose to warranties made by the seller to the buyer as part of a contract for sale, the warranty sections of this Article are not designed in any way to disturb those lines of case law growth which have recognized that warranties need not be confined either to sales contracts or to the direct parties to such a contract. They may arise in other appropriate circumstances such as in the case of bailments for hire, whether such bailment is itself the main contract or is merely a supplying of containers under a contract for the sale of their contents. The provisions of Section 2–318 on third party beneficiaries expressly recognize this case law development within one particular area. Beyond that, the matter is left to the case law with the intention that the policies of this Act may offer useful guidance in dealing with further cases as they arise.

3. The present section deals with affirmations of fact by the seller, descriptions of the goods or exhibitions of samples, exactly as any other part of a negotiation which ends in a contract is dealt with. No specific intention to make a warranty is necessary if any of these factors is made part of the basis of the bargain. In actual practice affirmations of fact made by the seller about the goods during a bargain are regarded as part of the description of those

goods; hence no particular reliance on such statements need be shown in order to weave them into the fabric of the agreement. Rather, any fact which is to take such affirmations, once made, out of the agreement requires clear affirmative proof. The issue normally is one of fact.

4. In view of the principle that the whole purpose of the law of warranty is to determine what it is that the seller has in essence agreed to sell, the policy is adopted of those cases which refuse except in unusual circumstances to recognize a material deletion of the seller's obligation. Thus, a contract is normally a contract for a sale of something describable and described. A clause generally disclaiming "all warranties, express or implied" cannot reduce the seller's obligation with respect to such description and therefore cannot be given literal effect under Section 2–316.

This is not intended to mean that the parties, if they consciously desire, cannot make their own bargain as they wish. But in determining what they have agreed upon good faith is a factor and consideration should be given to the fact that the probability is small that a real price is intended to be exchanged for a pseudo-obligation.

5. Paragraph (1)(b) makes specific some of the principles set forth above when a description of the goods is given by the seller.

A description need not be by words. Technical specifications, blueprints and the like can afford more exact description than mere language and if made part of the basis of the bargain goods must conform with them. Past deliveries may set the description of quality, either expressly or impliedly by course of dealing. Of course, all descriptions by merchants must be read against the applicable trade usages with the general rules as to merchantability resolving any doubts.

6.   The basic situation as to statements affecting the true essence of the bargain is no different when a sample or model is involved in the transaction. This section includes both a "sample" actually drawn from the bulk of goods which is the subject matter of the sale, and a "model" which is offered for inspection when the subject matter is not at hand and which has not been drawn from the bulk of the goods.

Although the underlying principles are unchanged, the facts are often ambiguous when something is shown as illustrative, rather than as a straight sample. In general, the presumption is that any sample or model just as any affirmation of fact is intended to become a basis of the bargain. But there is no escape from the question of fact. When the seller exhibits a sample purporting to be drawn from an existing bulk, good faith of course requires that the sample be fairly drawn. But in mercantile experience the mere exhibition of a "sample" does not of itself show whether it is merely intended to "suggest" or to "be" the character of the subject-matter of the contract. The question is whether the seller has so acted with reference to the sample as to make him responsible that the whole shall have at least the values shown by it. The circumstances aid in answering this question. If the sample has been drawn from an existing bulk, it must be regarded as describing values of the goods contracted for unless it is accompanied by an unmistakable denial of such responsibility. If, on the other hand, a model of merchandise not on hand is offered, the mercantile presumption that it has become a literal description of the subject matter is not so strong, and particularly so if modification on the buyer's initiative impairs any feature of the model.

7.   The precise time when words of description or affirmation are made or samples are shown is not material. The sole question is whether the language or samples or models are fairly to be regarded as part of the contract. If language is used after the closing of the deal (as when the buyer when taking delivery asks and receives an additional assurance), the warranty becomes a modification, and need not be supported by consideration if it is otherwise reasonable and in order (Section 2–209).

8.   Concerning affirmations of value or a seller's opinion or commendation under subsection (2), the basic question remains the same: What statements of the seller have in the circumstances and in objective judgment become part of the basis of the bargain? As indicated above, all of the statements of the seller do so unless good reason is shown to the contrary. The provisions of subsection (2) are included, however, since common experience discloses that some statements or predictions cannot fairly be viewed as entering into the bargain. Even as to false statements of value, however, the possibility is left open that a remedy may be provided by the law relating to fraud or misrepresentation.

Cross References:

Point 1: Section 2–316.

Point 2: Sections 1–102(3) and 2–318.

Point 3: Section 2–316(2)(b).

Point 4: Section 2–316.

Point 5: Sections 1–205(4) and 2–314.

Point 6: Section 2–316.

Point 7: Section 2–209.

Point 8: Section 1–103.

Definitional Cross References:

"Buyer". Section 2–103.

"Conforming". Section 2–106.

"Goods". Section 2–105.

"Seller". Section 2–103.

§ 2–314. Implied Warranty: Merchantability; Usage of Trade

(1)   Unless excluded or modified (Section 2–316), a warranty that the goods shall be merchantable is implied in a contract for their sale if the seller is a merchant with respect to goods of that kind. Under this section the serving for value of food or drink to be consumed either on the premises or elsewhere is a sale.

(2)   Goods to be merchantable must be at least such as

(a)   pass without objection in the trade under the contract description; and

(b)   in the case of fungible goods, are of fair average quality within the description; and

(c)   are fit for the ordinary purposes for which such goods are used; and

(d)   run, within the variations permitted by the agreement, of even kind, quality and quantity within each unit and among all units involved; and

(e)   are adequately contained, packaged, and labeled as the agreement may require; and

(f)   conform to the promises or affirmations of fact made on the container or label if any.

(3)   Unless excluded or modified (Section 2–316) other implied warranties may arise from course of dealing or usage of trade.

Official Comment

Prior Uniform Statutory Provision: Section 15(2), Uniform Sales Act.

Changes: Completely rewritten.

Purposes of Changes: This section, drawn in view of the steadily developing case law on the subject, is intended to make it clear that:

1.   The seller's obligation applies to present sales as well as to contracts to sell subject to the effects of any examination of specific goods. (Subsection (2) of Section 2–316). Also, the warranty of merchantability applies to sales for use as well as to sales for resale.

2.   The question when the warranty is imposed turns basically on the meaning of the terms of the agreement as recognized in the trade. Goods delivered under an agreement made by a merchant in a given line of trade must be of a quality comparable to that generally acceptable in that line of trade under the description or other designation of the goods used in the agreement. The responsibility imposed rests on any merchant-seller, and the absence of the words "grower or manufacturer or not" which appeared in Section 15(2) of the Uniform Sales Act does not restrict the applicability of this section.

3.   A specific designation of goods by the buyer does not exclude the seller's obligation that they be fit for the general purposes appropriate to such goods. A contract for the sale of second-hand goods, however, involves only such obligation as is appropriate to such goods for that is their contract description. A person making an isolated sale of goods is not a "merchant"

within the meaning of the full scope of this section and, thus, no warranty of merchantability would apply. His knowledge of any defects not apparent on inspection would, however, without need for express agreement and in keeping with the underlying reason of the present section and the provisions on good faith, impose an obligation that known material but hidden defects be fully disclosed.

4.   Although a seller may not be a "merchant" as to the goods in question, if he states generally that they are "guaranteed" the provisions of this section may furnish a guide to the content of the resulting express warranty. This has particular significance in the case of second-hand sales, and has further significance in limiting the effect of fine-print disclaimer clauses where their effect would be inconsistent with large-print assertions of "guarantee".

5.   The second sentence of subsection (1) covers the warranty with respect to food and drink. Serving food or drink for value is a sale, whether to be consumed on the premises or elsewhere. Cases to the contrary are rejected. The principal warranty is that stated in subsections (1) and (2)(c) of this section.

6.   Subsection (2) does not purport to exhaust the meaning of "merchantable" nor to negate any of its attributes not specifically mentioned in the text of the statute, but arising by usage of trade or through case law. The language used is "must be at least such as . . .," and the intention is to leave open other possible attributes of merchantability.

7.   Paragraphs (a) and (b) of subsection (2) are to be read together. Both refer, as indicated above, to the standards of that line of the trade which fits the transaction and the seller's business. "Fair average" is a term directly appropriate to agricultural bulk products and means goods centering around the middle belt of quality, not the least or the worst that can be understood in the particular trade by the designation, but such as can pass "without objection." Of course a fair percentage of the least is permissible but the goods are not "fair average" if they are all of the least or worst quality possible under the description. In cases of doubt as to what quality is intended, the price at which a merchant closes a contract is an excellent index of the nature and scope of his obligation under the present section.

8.   Fitness for the ordinary purposes for which goods of the type are used is a fundamental concept of the present section and is covered in paragraph (c). As stated above, merchantability is also a part of the obligation owing to the purchaser for use. Correspondingly, protection, under this aspect of the warranty, of the person buying for resale to the ultimate consumer is equally necessary, and merchantable goods must therefore be "honestly" resalable in the normal course of business because they are what they purport to be.

9.   Paragraph (d) on evenness of kind, quality and quantity follows case law. But precautionary language has been added as a remainder of the frequent usages of trade which permit substantial variations both with and without an allowance or an obligation to replace the varying units.

10.   Paragraph (e) applies only where the nature of the goods and of the transaction require a certain type of container, package or label. Paragraph (f) applies, on the other hand, wherever there is a label or container on which representations are made, even though the original contract, either by express terms or usage of trade, may not have required either the labelling or the representation. This follows from the general obligation of good faith which requires that a buyer should not be

placed in the position of reselling or using goods delivered under false representations appearing on the package or container. No problem of extra consideration arises in this connection since, under this Article, an obligation is imposed by the original contract not to deliver mislabeled articles, and the obligation is imposed where mercantile good faith so requires and without reference to the doctrine of consideration.

11. Exclusion or modification of the warranty of merchantability, or of any part of it, is dealt with in the section to which the text of the present section makes explicit precautionary references. That section must be read with particular reference to its subsection (4) on limitation of remedies. The warranty of merchantability, wherever it is normal, is so commonly taken for granted that its exclusion from the contract is a matter threatening surprise and therefore requiring special precaution.

12. Subsection (3) is to make explicit that usage of trade and course of dealing can create warranties and that they are implied rather than express warranties and thus subject to exclusion or modification under Section 2–316. A typical instance would be the obligation to provide pedigree papers to evidence conformity of the animal to the contract in the case of a pedigreed dog or blooded bull.

13. In an action based on breach of warranty, it is of course necessary to show not only the existence of the warranty but the fact that the warranty was broken and that the breach of the warranty was the proximate cause of the loss sustained. In such an action an affirmative showing by the seller that the loss resulted from some action or event following his own delivery of the goods can operate as a defense. Equally, evidence indicating that the seller exercised care in the manufacture, processing or selection of the goods is relevant to the issue of whether the warranty was in fact broken. Action by the buyer following an examination of the goods which ought to have indicated the defect complained of can be shown as matter bearing on whether the breach itself was the cause of the injury.

Cross References:

Point 1: Section 2–316.

Point 3: Sections 1–203 and 2–104.

Point 5: Section 2–315.

Point 11: Section 2–316.

Point 12: Sections 1–201, 1–205 and 2–316.

Definitional Cross References:

"Agreement". Section 1–201.

"Contract". Section 1–201.

"Contract for sale". Section 2–106.

"Goods". Section 2–105.

"Merchant". Section 2–104.

"Seller". Section 2–103.

§ 2–315. Implied Warranty: Fitness for Particular Purpose

Where the seller at the time of contracting has reason to know any particular purpose for which the goods are required and that the buyer is relying on the seller's skill or judgment to select or furnish suitable goods, there is unless excluded or modified under the next section an implied warranty that the goods shall be fit for such purpose.

Official Comment

Prior Uniform Statutory Provision: Section 15(1), (4), (5), Uniform Sales Act.

Changes: Rewritten.

Purposes of Changes:

1. Whether or not this warranty arises in any individual case is basically a question of fact to be determined by the circumstances of the contracting. Under this section the buyer need not bring home to the seller actual knowledge of the particular purpose for which the goods are intended or of his reliance on the seller's skill and judgment, if the circumstances are such that the seller has reason to realize the purpose intended or that the reliance exists. The buyer, of course, must actually be relying on the seller.

2. A "particular purpose" differs from the ordinary purpose for which the goods are used in that it envisages a specific use by the buyer which is peculiar to the nature of his business whereas the ordinary purposes for which goods are used are those envisaged in the concept of merchantability and go to uses which are customarily made of the goods in question. For example, shoes are generally used for the purpose of walking upon ordinary ground, but a seller may know that a particular pair was selected to be used for climbing mountains.

A contract may of course include both a warranty of merchantability and one of fitness for a particular purpose.

The provisions of this Article on the cumulation and conflict of express and implied warranties must be considered on the question of inconsistency between or among warranties. In such a case any question of fact as to which warranty was intended by the parties to apply must be resolved in favor of the warranty of fitness for particular purpose as against all other warranties except where the buyer has taken upon himself the responsibility of furnishing the technical specifications.

3. In connection with the warranty of fitness for a particular purpose the provisions of this Article on the allocation or division of risks are particularly applicable in any transaction in which the purpose for which the goods are to be used combines requirements both as to the quality of the goods themselves and compliance with certain laws or regulations. How the risks are divided is a question of fact to be determined, where not expressly contained in the agreement, from the circumstances of contracting, usage of trade, course of performance and the like, matters which may constitute the "otherwise agreement" of the parties by which they may divide the risk or burden.

4. The absence from this section of the language used in the Uniform Sales Act in referring to the seller, "whether he be the grower or manufacturer or not," is not intended to impose any requirement that the seller be a grower or manufacturer. Although normally the warranty will arise only where the seller is a merchant with the appropriate "skill or judgment," it can arise as to non-merchants where this is justified by the particular circumstances.

5. The elimination of the "patent or other trade name" exception constitutes the major extension of the warranty of fitness which has been made by the cases and continued in this Article. Under the present section the existence of a patent or other trade name and the designation of the article by that name, or indeed in any other definite manner, is only one of the facts to be considered on the question of whether the buyer actually relied on the seller, but it is not of itself decisive of the issue. If the buyer himself is insisting on a particular brand he is not relying

on the seller's skill and judgment and so no warranty results. But the mere fact that the article purchased has a particular patent or trade name is not sufficient to indicate nonreliance if the article has been recommended by the seller as adequate for the buyer's purposes.

6. The specific reference forward in the present section to the following section on exclusion or modification of warranties is to call attention to the possibility of eliminating the warranty in any given case. However it must be noted that under the following section the warranty of fitness for a particular purpose must be excluded or modified by a conspicuous writing.

Cross References:

Point 2: Sections 2–314 and 2–317.

Point 3: Section 2–303.

Point 6: Section 2–316.

Definitional Cross References:

"Buyer". Section 2–103.

"Goods". Section 2–105.

"Seller". Section 2–103.

§ 2–316. Exclusion or Modification of Warranties

(1) Words or conduct relevant to the creation of an express warranty and words or conduct tending to negate or limit warranty shall be construed wherever reasonable as consistent with each other; but subject to the provisions of this Article on parol or extrinsic evidence (Section 2–202) negation or limitation is inoperative to the extent that such construction is unreasonable.

(2) Subject to subsection (3), to exclude or modify the implied warranty of merchantability or any part of it the language must mention merchantability and in case of a writing must be conspicuous, and to exclude or modify any implied warranty of fitness the exclusion must be by a writing and conspicuous. Language to exclude all implied warranties of fitness is sufficient if it states, for example, that "There are no warranties which extend beyond the description on the face hereof."

(3) Notwithstanding subsection (2)

(a) unless the circumstances indicate otherwise, all implied warranties are excluded by expressions like "as is", "with all faults" or other language which in common understanding calls the buyer's attention to the exclusion of warranties and makes plain that there is no implied warranty; and

(b) when the buyer before entering into the contract has examined the goods or the sample or model as fully as he desired or has refused to examine the goods there is no implied warranty with regard to defects which an examination ought in the circumstances to have revealed to him; and

(c) an implied warranty can also be excluded or modified by course of dealing or course of performance or usage of trade.

(4)   Remedies for breach of warranty can be limited in accordance with the provisions of this Article on liquidation or limitation of damages and on contractual modification of remedy (Sections 2–718 and 2–719).

Official Comment

Prior Uniform Statutory Provision: None. See sections 15 and 71, Uniform Sales Act.

Purposes:

1.   This section is designed principally to deal with those frequent clauses in sales contracts which seek to exclude "all warranties, express or implied." It seeks to protect a buyer from unexpected and unbargained language of disclaimer by denying effect to such language when inconsistent with language of express warranty and permitting the exclusion of implied warranties only by conspicuous language or other circumstances which protect the buyer from surprise.

2.   The seller is protected under this Article against false allegations of oral warranties by its provisions on parol and extrinsic evidence and against unauthorized representations by the customary "lack of authority" clauses. This Article treats the limitation or avoidance of consequential damages as a matter of limiting remedies for breach, separate from the matter of creation of liability under a warranty. If no warranty exists, there is of course no problem of limiting remedies for breach of warranty. Under subsection (4) the question of limitation of remedy is governed by the sections referred to rather than by this section.

3.   Disclaimer of the implied warranty of merchantability is permitted under subsection (2), but with the safeguard that such disclaimers must mention merchantability and in case of a writing must be conspicuous.

4.   Unlike the implied warranty of merchantability, implied warranties of fitness for a particular purpose may be excluded by general language, but only if it is in writing and conspicuous.

5.   Subsection (2) presupposes that the implied warranty in question exists unless excluded or modified. Whether or not language of disclaimer satisfies the requirements of this section, such language may be relevant under other sections to the question whether the warranty was ever in fact created. Thus, unless the provisions of this Article on parol and extrinsic evidence prevent, oral language of disclaimer may raise issues of fact as to whether reliance by the buyer occurred and whether the seller had "reason to know" under the section on implied warranty of fitness for a particular purpose.

6.   The exceptions to the general rule set forth in paragraphs (a), (b) and (c) of subsection (3) are common factual situations in which the circumstances surrounding the transaction are in themselves sufficient to call the buyer's attention to the fact that no implied warranties are made or that a certain implied warranty is being excluded.

7.   Paragraph (a) of subsection (3) deals with general terms such as "as is," "as they stand," "with all faults," and the like. Such terms in ordinary commercial usage are understood to mean that the buyer takes the entire risk as to the quality of the goods involved. The terms covered by paragraph (a) are in fact merely a particularization of paragraph (c) which provides for exclusion or modification of implied warranties by usage of trade.

8.   Under paragraph (b) of subsection (3) warranties may be excluded or modified by the circumstances where the buyer examines the goods or a sample or model of them before entering into the contract. "Examina-

tion" as used in this paragraph is not synonymous with inspection before acceptance or at any other time after the contract has been made. It goes rather to the nature of the responsibility assumed by the seller at the time of the making of the contract. Of course if the buyer discovers the defect and uses the goods anyway, or if he unreasonably fails to examine the goods before he uses them, resulting injuries may be found to result from his own action rather than proximately from a breach of warranty. See Sections 2–314 and 2–715 and comments thereto.

In order to bring the transaction within the scope of "refused to examine" in paragraph (b), it is not sufficient that the goods are available for inspection. There must in addition be a demand by the seller that the buyer examine the goods fully. The seller by the demand puts the buyer on notice that he is assuming the risk of defects which the examination ought to reveal. The language "refused to examine" in this paragraph is intended to make clear the necessity for such demand.

Application of the doctrine of "caveat emptor" in all cases where the buyer examines the goods regardless of statements made by the seller is, however, rejected by this Article. Thus, if the offer of examination is accompanied by words as to their merchantability or specific attributes and the buyer indicates clearly that he is relying on those words rather than on his examination, they give rise to an "express" warranty. In such cases the question is one of fact as to whether a warranty of merchantability has been expressly incorporated in the agreement. Disclaimer of such an express warranty is governed by subsection (1) of the present section.

The particular buyer's skill and the normal method of examining goods in the circumstances determine what defects are excluded by the examination. A failure to notice defects which are obvious cannot excuse the buyer. However, an examination under circumstances which do not permit chemical or other testing of the goods would not exclude defects which could be ascertained only by such testing. Nor can latent defects be excluded by a simple examination. A professional buyer examining a product in his field will be held to have assumed the risk as to all defects which a professional in the field ought to observe, while a nonprofessional buyer will be held to have assumed the risk only for such defects as a layman might be expected to observe.

9. The situation in which the buyer gives precise and complete specifications to the seller is not explicitly covered in this section, but this is a frequent circumstance by which the implied warranties may be excluded. The warranty of fitness for a particular purpose would not normally arise since in such a situation there is usually no reliance on the seller by the buyer. The warranty of merchantability in such a transaction, however, must be considered in connection with the next section on the cumulation and conflict of warranties. Under paragraph (c) of that section in case of such an inconsistency the implied warranty of merchantability is displaced by the express warranty that the goods will comply with the specifications. Thus, where the buyer gives detailed specifications as to the goods, neither of the implied warranties as to quality will normally apply to the transaction unless consistent with the specifications.

Cross References:

Point 2: Sections 2–202, 2–718 and 2–719.

Point 7: Sections 1–205 and 2–208.

Definitional Cross References:

"Agreement". Section 1–201.

"Buyer". Section 2–103.

"Contract". Section 1–201.

"Course of dealing". Section 1–303.

"Goods". Section 2–105.

"Remedy". Section 1–201.

"Seller". Section 2–103.

"Usage of trade". Section 1–303.

§ 2–317.　Cumulation and Conflict of Warranties Express or Implied

Warranties whether express or implied shall be construed as consistent with each other and as cumulative, but if such construction is unreasonable the intention of the parties shall determine which warranty is dominant. In ascertaining that intention the following rules apply:

(a) Exact or technical specifications displace an inconsistent sample or model or general language of description.

(b) A sample from an existing bulk displaces inconsistent general language of description.

(c) Express warranties displace inconsistent implied warranties other than an implied warranty of fitness for a particular purpose.

Definitional Cross Reference:

"Party". Section 1–201.

§ 2–318.　Third Party Beneficiaries of Warranties Express or Implied

Note: If this Act is introduced in the Congress of the United States this section should be omitted. (States to select one alternative.)

Alternative A

A seller's warranty whether express or implied extends to any natural person who is in the family or household of his buyer or who is a guest in his home if it is reasonable to expect that such person may use, consume or be affected by the goods and who is injured in person by breach of the warranty. A seller may not exclude or limit the operation of this section.

Alternative B

A seller's warranty whether express or implied extends to any natural person who may reasonably be expected to use, consume or be affected by the goods and who is injured in person by breach of the warranty. A seller may not exclude or limit the operation of this section.

Alternative C

A seller's warranty whether express or implied extends to any person who may reasonably be expected to use, consume or be affected by the goods and who is injured by breach of the warranty.

A seller may not exclude or limit the operation of this section with respect to injury to the person of an individual to whom the warranty extends.

Official Comment

Prior Uniform Statutory Provision: None.

Purposes:

1. The last sentence of this section does not mean that a seller is precluded from excluding or disclaiming a warranty which might otherwise arise in connection with the sale provided such exclusion or modification is permitted by Section 2–316. Nor does that sentence preclude the seller from limiting the remedies of his own buyer and of any beneficiaries, in any manner provided in Sections 2–718 or 2–719. To the extent that the contract of sale contains provisions under which warranties are excluded or modified, or remedies for breach are limited, such provisions are equally operative against beneficiaries of warranties under this section. What this last sentence forbids is exclusion of liability by the seller to the persons to whom the warranties which he has made to his buyer would extend under this section.

2. The purpose of this section is to give certain beneficiaries the benefit of the same warranty which the buyer received in the contract of sale, thereby freeing any such beneficiaries from any technical rules as to "privity." It seeks to accomplish this purpose without any derogation of any right or remedy resting on negligence. It rests primarily upon the merchant-seller's warranty under this Article that the goods sold are merchantable and fit for the ordinary purposes for which such goods are used rather than the warranty of fitness for a particular purpose. Implicit in the section is that any beneficiary of a warranty may bring a direct action for breach of warranty against the seller whose warranty extends to him [As amended in 1966].

3. The first alternative expressly includes as beneficiaries within its provisions the family, household, and guests of the purchaser. Beyond this, the section in this form is neutral and is not intended to enlarge or restrict the developing case law on whether the seller's warranties, given to his buyer who resells, extend to other persons in the distributive chain. The second alternative is designed for states where the case law has already developed further and for those that desire to expand the class of beneficiaries. The third alternative goes further, following the trend of modern decisions as indicated by Restatement of Torts 2d § 402A (Tentative Draft No. 10, 1965) in extending the rule beyond injuries to the person.

§ 2–319. F.O.B. and F.A.S. Terms

(1) Unless otherwise agreed the term F.O.B. (which means "free on board") at a named place, even though used only in connection with the stated price, is a delivery term under which

(a) when the term is F.O.B. the place of shipment, the seller must at that place ship the goods in the manner provided in this Article (Section 2–504) and bear the expense and risk of putting them into the possession of the carrier; or

(b) when the term is F.O.B. the place of destination, the seller must at his own expense and risk transport the goods to that place and there tender delivery of them in the manner provided in this Article (Section 2–503);

(c)   when under either (a) or (b) the term is also F.O.B. vessel, car or other vehicle, the seller must in addition at his own expense and risk load the goods on board. If the term is F.O.B. vessel the buyer must name the vessel and in an appropriate case the seller must comply with the provisions of this Article on the form of bill of lading (Section 2–323).

(2)   Unless otherwise agreed the term F.A.S. vessel (which means "free alongside") at a named port, even though used only in connection with the stated price, is a delivery term under which the seller must

(a)   at his own expense and risk deliver the goods alongside the vessel in the manner usual in that port or on a dock designated and provided by the buyer; and

(b)   obtain and tender a receipt for the goods in exchange for which the carrier is under a duty to issue a bill of lading.

(3)   Unless otherwise agreed in any case falling within subsection (1) (a) or (c) or subsection (2) the buyer must seasonably give any needed instructions for making delivery, including when the term is F.A.S. or F.O.B. the loading berth of the vessel and in an appropriate case its name and sailing date. The seller may treat the failure of needed instructions as a failure of cooperation under this Article (Section 2–311). He may also at his option move the goods in any reasonable manner preparatory to delivery or shipment.

(4)   Under the term F.O.B. vessel or F.A.S. unless otherwise agreed the buyer must make payment against tender of the required documents and the seller may not tender nor the buyer demand delivery of the goods in substitution for the documents.

Definitional Cross References:

"Agreed". Section 1–201.

"Bill of lading". Section 1–201.

"Buyer". Section 2–103.

"Goods". Section 2–105.

"Seasonably". Section 1–205.

"Seller". Section 2–103.

"Term". Section 1–201.

§ 2–320.   C.I.F. and C. & F. Terms

(1)   The term C.I.F. means that the price includes in a lump sum the cost of the goods and the insurance and freight to the named destination. The term C. & F. or C.F. means that the price so includes cost and freight to the named destination.

(2)   Unless otherwise agreed and even though used only in connection with the stated price and destination, the term C.I.F. destination or its equivalent requires the seller at his own expense and risk to

(a)   put the goods into the possession of a carrier at the port for shipment and obtain a negotiable bill or bills of lading covering the entire transportation to the named destination; and

(b)   load the goods and obtain a receipt from the carrier (which may be contained in the bill of lading) showing that the freight has been paid or provided for; and

(c)   obtain a policy or certificate of insurance, including any war risk insurance, of a kind and on terms then current at the port of shipment in the usual amount, in the currency of the contract, shown to cover the same goods covered by the bill of lading and providing for payment of loss to the order of the buyer or for the account of whom it may concern; but the seller may add to the price the amount of the premium for any such war risk insurance; and

(d)   prepare an invoice of the goods and procure any other documents required to effect shipment or to comply with the contract; and

(e)   forward and tender with commercial promptness all the documents in due form and with any indorsement necessary to perfect the buyer's rights.

(3)   Unless otherwise agreed the term C. & F. or its equivalent has the same effect and imposes upon the seller the same obligations and risks as a C.I.F. term except the obligation as to insurance.

(4)   Under the term C.I.F. or C. & F. unless otherwise agreed the buyer must make payment against tender of the required documents and the seller may not tender nor the buyer demand delivery of the goods in substitution for the documents.

Definitional Cross References:

"Bill of lading". Section 1–201.

"Buyer". Section 2–103.

"Contract". Section 1–201.

"Goods". Section 2–105.

"Rights". Section 1–201.

"Seller". Section 2–103.

"Term". Section 1–201.

§ 2–321.   C.I.F. or C. & F.: "Net Landed Weights"; "Payment on Arrival"; Warranty of Condition on Arrival

Under a contract containing a term C.I.F. or C. & F.

(1)   Where the price is based on or is to be adjusted according to "net landed weights", "delivered weights", "out turn" quantity or quality or the like, unless otherwise agreed the seller must reasonably estimate the price. The payment due on tender of the documents called for by the contract is the amount so estimated, but after final adjustment of the price a settlement must be made with commercial promptness.

(2)   An agreement described in subsection (1) or any warranty of quality or condition of the goods on arrival places upon the seller the risk of ordinary deterioration, shrinkage and the like in transportation but has no effect on the place or time of identification to the contract for sale or delivery or on the passing of the risk of loss.

(3)   Unless otherwise agreed where the contract provides for payment on or after arrival of the goods the seller must before payment allow such preliminary inspection as is feasible; but if the goods are lost delivery of the documents and payment are due when the goods should have arrived.

Definitional Cross References:

"Agreement". Section 1–201.

"Contract". Section 1–201.

"Delivery". Section 1–201.

"Goods". Section 2–105.

"Seller". Section 2–103.

"Term". Section 1–201.

§ 2–322.   Delivery "Ex-Ship"

(1)   Unless otherwise agreed a term for delivery of goods "ex-ship" (which means from the carrying vessel) or in equivalent language is not restricted to a particular ship and requires delivery from a ship which has reached a place at the named port of destination where goods of the kind are usually discharged.

(2)   Under such a term unless otherwise agreed

(a)   the seller must discharge all liens arising out of the carriage and furnish the buyer with a direction which puts the carrier under a duty to deliver the goods; and

(b)   the risk of loss does not pass to the buyer until the goods leave the ship's tackle or are otherwise properly unloaded.

Definitional Cross References:

"Buyer". Section 1–103.

"Goods". Section 2–105.

"Seller". Section 2–103.

"Term". Section 1–201.

§ 2–323.   Form of Bill of Lading Required in Overseas Shipment; "Overseas"

(1)   Where the contract contemplates overseas shipment and contains a term C.I.F. or C. & F. or F.O.B. vessel, the seller unless otherwise agreed must obtain a negotiable bill of lading stating that the goods have been loaded on board or, in the case of a term C.I.F. or C. & F., received for shipment.

(2)   Where in a case within subsection (1) a tangible bill of lading has been issued in a set of parts, unless otherwise agreed if the documents are not to be sent from abroad the buyer may demand tender of the full set; otherwise only one part of the bill of lading need be tendered. Even if the agreement expressly requires a full set

(a)   due tender of a single part is acceptable within the provisions of this Article on cure of improper delivery (subsection (1) of Section 2–508); and

(b)   even though the full set is demanded, if the documents are sent from abroad the person tendering an incomplete set may nevertheless require payment upon furnishing an indemnity which the buyer in good faith deems adequate.

(3) A shipment by water or by air or a contract contemplating such shipment is "overseas" insofar as by usage of trade or agreement it is subject to the commercial, financing or shipping practices characteristic of international deep water commerce.

Definitional Cross References:

"Bill of lading". Section 1–201.

"Buyer". Section 2–103.

"Contract". Section 1–201.

"Delivery". Section 1–201.

"Financing agency". Section 2–104.

"Person". Section 1–201.

"Seller". Section 2–103.

"Send". Section 1–201.

"Term". Section 1–201.

§ 2–324. "No Arrival, No Sale" Term

Under a term "no arrival, no sale" or terms of like meaning, unless otherwise agreed,

(a) the seller must properly ship conforming goods and if they arrive by any means he must tender them on arrival but he assumes no obligation that the goods will arrive unless he has caused the non-arrival; and

(b) where without fault of the seller the goods are in part lost or have so deteriorated as no longer to conform to the contract or arrive after the contract time, the buyer may proceed as if there had been casualty to identified goods (Section 2–613).

Definitional Cross References:

"Buyer". Section 2–103.

"Conforming". Section 2–106.

"Contract". Section 1–201.

"Fault". Section 1–201.

"Goods". Section 2–105.

"Sale". Section 2–106.

"Seller". Section 2–103.

"Term". Section 1–201.

§ 2–325. "Letter of Credit" Term; "Confirmed Credit"

(1) Failure of the buyer seasonably to furnish an agreed letter of credit is a breach of the contract for sale.

(2) The delivery to seller of a proper letter of credit suspends the buyer's obligation to pay. If the letter of credit is dishonored, the seller may on seasonable notification to the buyer require payment directly from him.

(3) Unless otherwise agreed the term "letter of credit" or "banker's credit" in a contract for sale means an irrevocable credit issued by a financing agency of good repute and, where the shipment is overseas, of good international repute. The term "confirmed credit" means that the

credit must also carry the direct obligation of such an agency which does business in the seller's financial market.

§ 2–326.   Sale on Approval and Sale or Return; Rights of Creditors

(1) Unless otherwise agreed, if delivered goods may be returned by the buyer even though they conform to the contract, the transaction is

    (a) a "sale on approval" if the goods are delivered primarily for use, and

    (b) a "sale or return" if the goods are delivered primarily for resale.

(2) Goods held on approval are not subject to the claims of the buyer's creditors until acceptance; goods held on sale or return are subject to such claims while in the buyer's possession.

(3) Any "or return" term of a contract for sale is to be treated as a separate contract for sale within the statute of frauds section of this Article (Section 2–201) and as contradicting the sale aspect of the contract within the provisions of this Article on parol or extrinsic evidence (Section 2–202).

§ 2–327.   Special Incidents of Sale on Approval and Sale or Return

(1) Under a sale on approval unless otherwise agreed

    (a) although the goods are identified to the contract the risk of loss and the title do not pass to the buyer until acceptance; and

    (b) use of the goods consistent with the purpose of trial is not acceptance but failure seasonably to notify the seller of election to return the goods is acceptance, and if the goods conform to the contract acceptance of any part is acceptance of the whole; and

(c)   after due notification of election to return, the return is at the seller's risk and expense but a merchant buyer must follow any reasonable instructions.

(2)   Under a sale or return unless otherwise agreed

(a)   the option to return extends to the whole or any commercial unit of the goods while in substantially their original condition, but must be exercised seasonably; and

(b)   the return is at the buyer's risk and expense.

Definitional Cross References:

"Agreed". Section 1–201.

"Buyer". Section 2–103.

"Commercial unit". Section 2–105.

"Conform". Section 2–106.

"Contract". Section 1–201.

"Goods". Section 2–105.

"Merchant". Section 2–104.

"Notifies". Section 1–202.

"Notification". Section 1–202.

"Sale on approval". Section 2–326.

"Sale or return". Section 2–326.

"Seasonably". Section 1–205.

"Seller". Section 2–103.

§ 2–328.   Sale by Auction

(1)   In a sale by auction if goods are put up in lots each lot is the subject of a separate sale.

(2)   A sale by auction is complete when the auctioneer so announces by the fall of the hammer or in other customary manner. Where a bid is made while the hammer is falling in acceptance of a prior bid the auctioneer may in his discretion reopen the bidding or declare the goods sold under the bid on which the hammer was falling.

(3)   Such a sale is with reserve unless the goods are in explicit terms put up without reserve. In an auction with reserve the auctioneer may withdraw the goods at any time until he announces completion of the sale. In an auction without reserve, after the auctioneer calls for bids on an article or lot, that article or lot cannot be withdrawn unless no bid is made within a reasonable time. In either case a bidder may retract his bid until the auctioneer's announcement of completion of the sale, but a bidder's retraction does not revive any previous bid.

(4)   If the auctioneer knowingly receives a bid on the seller's behalf or the seller makes or procures such a bid, and notice has not been given that liberty for such bidding is reserved, the buyer may at his option avoid the sale or take the goods at the price of the last good faith bid prior to the completion of the sale. This subsection shall not apply to any bid at a forced sale.

Definitional Cross References:

"Buyer". Section 2–103.

"Good faith". Section 1–201.

"Goods". Section 2–105.

"Lot". Section 2–105.

"Notice". Section 1–202.

PART 4

TITLE, CREDITORS AND GOOD FAITH PURCHASERS

§ 2–401. **Passing of Title; Reservation for Security; Limited Application of This Section**

Each provision of this Article with regard to the rights, obligations and remedies of the seller, the buyer, purchasers or other third parties applies irrespective of title to the goods except where the provision refers to such title. Insofar as situations are not covered by the other provisions of this Article and matters concerning title become material the following rules apply:

(1)   Title to goods cannot pass under a contract for sale prior to their identification to the contract (Section 2–501), and unless otherwise explicitly agreed the buyer acquires by their identification a special property as limited by this Act. Any retention or reservation by the seller of the title (property) in goods shipped or delivered to the buyer is limited in effect to a reservation of a security interest. Subject to these provisions and to the provisions of the Article on Secured Transactions (Article 9), title to goods passes from the seller to the buyer in any manner and on any conditions explicitly agreed on by the parties.

(2)   Unless otherwise explicitly agreed title passes to the buyer at the time and place at which the seller completes his performance with reference to the physical delivery of the goods, despite any reservation of a security interest and even though a document of title is to be delivered at a different time or place; and in particular and despite any reservation of a security interest by the bill of lading

(a)   if the contract requires or authorizes the seller to send the goods to the buyer but does not require him to deliver them at destination, title passes to the buyer at the time and place of shipment; but

(b)   if the contract requires delivery at destination, title passes on tender there.

(3)   Unless otherwise explicitly agreed where delivery is to be made without moving the goods,

(a)   if the seller is to deliver a tangible document of title, title passes at the time when and the place where he delivers such documents and if the seller is to deliver an electronic document of title, title passes when the seller delivers the document; or

(b) if the goods are at the time of contracting already identified and no documents are to be delivered, title passes at the time and place of contracting.

(4) A rejection or other refusal by the buyer to receive or retain the goods, whether or not justified, or a justified revocation of acceptance revests title to the goods in the seller. Such revesting occurs by operation of law and is not a "sale".

Definitional Cross References:

"Agreement". Section 1–201.

"Bill of lading". Section 1–201.

"Buyer". Section 2–103.

"Contract". Section 1–201.

"Contract for sale". Section 2–106.

"Delivery". Section 1–201.

"Document of title". Section 1–201.

"Good faith". Section 1–201.

"Goods". Section 2–105.

"Party". Section 1–201.

"Purchaser". Section 1–201.

"Receipt" of goods. Section 2–103.

"Remedy". Section 1–201.

"Rights". Section 1–201.

"Sale". Section 2–106.

"Security interest". Section 1–201.

"Seller". Section 2–103.

"Send". Section 1–201.

§ 2–402. Rights of Seller's Creditors Against Sold Goods

(1) Except as provided in subsections (2) and (3), rights of unsecured creditors of the seller with respect to goods which have been identified to a contract for sale are subject to the buyer's rights to recover the goods under this Article (Sections 2–502 and 2–716).

(2) A creditor of the seller may treat a sale or an identification of goods to a contract for sale as void if as against him a retention of possession by the seller is fraudulent under any rule of law of the state where the goods are situated, except that retention of possession in good faith and current course of trade by a merchant-seller for a commercially reasonable time after a sale or identification is not fraudulent.

(3) Nothing in this Article shall be deemed to impair the rights of creditors of the seller

(a) under the provisions of the Article on Secured Transactions (Article 9); or

(b) where identification to the contract or delivery is made not in current course of trade but in satisfaction of or as security for a pre-existing claim for money, security or the like and is made under circumstances which under any rule of law of the state where the goods are situated would apart from this Article constitute the transaction a fraudulent transfer or voidable preference.

Definitional Cross References:

"Contract for sale". Section 2–106.

"Creditor". Section 1–201.

"Good faith". Section 1–201.

"Goods". Section 2–105.

"Merchant". Section 2–104.

"Money". Section 1–201.

"Reasonable time". Section 1–204.

"Rights". Section 1–201.

"Sale". Section 2–106.

"Seller". Section 2–103.

§ 2–403. Power to Transfer; Good Faith Purchase of Goods; "Entrusting"

(1) A purchaser of goods acquires all title which his transferor had or had power to transfer except that a purchaser of a limited interest acquires rights only to the extent of the interest purchased. A person with voidable title has power to transfer a good title to a good faith purchaser for value. When goods have been delivered under a transaction of purchase the purchaser has such power even though

    (a) the transferor was deceived as to the identity of the purchaser, or

    (b) the delivery was in exchange for a check which is later dishonored, or

    (c) it was agreed that the transaction was to be a "cash sale", or

    (d) the delivery was procured through fraud punishable as larcenous under the criminal law.

(2) Any entrusting of possession of goods to a merchant who deals in goods of that kind gives him power to transfer all rights of the entruster to a buyer in ordinary course of business.

(3) "Entrusting" includes any delivery and any acquiescence in retention of possession regardless of any condition expressed between the parties to the delivery or acquiescence and regardless of whether the procurement of the entrusting or the possessor's disposition of the goods have been such as to be larcenous under the criminal law.

(4) The rights of other purchasers of goods and of lien creditors are governed by the Articles on Secured Transactions (Article 9), Bulk Transfers (Article 6) and Documents of Title (Article 7).

Definitional Cross References:

"Buyer in ordinary course of business". Section 1–201.

"Good faith". Section 1–201.

"Goods". Section 2–105.

"Person". Section 1–201.

"Purchaser". Section 1–201.

"Signed". Section 1–201.

"Term". Section 1–201.

"Value". Section 1–204.

PART 5

PERFORMANCE

§ 2–501. Insurable Interest in Goods; Manner of Identification of Goods

(1) The buyer obtains a special property and an insurable interest in goods by identification of existing goods as goods to which the contract refers even though the goods so identified are non-conforming and he has an option to return or reject them. Such identification can be made at any time and in any manner explicitly agreed to by the parties. In the absence of explicit agreement identification occurs

(a) when the contract is made if it is for the sale of goods already existing and identified;

(b) if the contract is for the sale of future goods other than those described in paragraph (c), when goods are shipped, marked or otherwise designated by the seller as goods to which the contract refers;

(c) when the crops are planted or otherwise become growing crops or the young are conceived if the contract is for the sale of unborn young to be born within twelve months after contracting or for the sale of crops to be harvested within twelve months or the next normal harvest season after contracting whichever is longer.

(2) The seller retains an insurable interest in goods so long as title to or any security interest in the goods remains in him and where the identification is by the seller alone he may until default or insolvency or notification to the buyer that the identification is final substitute other goods for those identified.

(3) Nothing in this section impairs any insurable interest recognized under any other statute or rule of law.

Definitional Cross References:

"Agreement". Section 1–201.

"Contract". Section 1–201.

"Contract for sale". Section 2–106.

"Future goods". Section 2–105.

"Goods". Section 2–105.

"Notification". Section 1–202.

"Party". Section 1–201.

"Sale". Section 2–106.

"Security interest". Section 1–201.

"Seller". Section 2–103.

§ 2–502. Buyer's Right to Goods on Seller's Repudiation, Failure to Deliver, or Insolvency

(1) Subject to subsections (2) and (3) and even though the goods have not been shipped a buyer who has paid a part or all of the price of goods in which he has a special property under the provisions of the immedi-

ately preceding section may on making and keeping good a tender of any unpaid portion of their price recover them from the seller if:

(a)   in the case of goods bought for personal, family, or household purposes, the seller repudiates or fails to deliver as required by the contract; or

(b)   in all cases, the seller becomes insolvent within ten days after receipt of the first installment on their price.

(2)   The buyer's right to recover the goods under subsection (1)(a) vests upon acquisition of a special property, even if the seller had not then repudiated or failed to deliver.

(3)   If the identification creating his special property has been made by the buyer he acquires the right to recover the goods only if they conform to the contract for sale.

Definitional Cross References:

"Buyer". Section 2–103.

"Conform". Section 2–106.

"Contract for sale". Section 2–106.

"Goods". Section 2–105.

"Insolvent". Section 1–201.

"Right". Section 1–201.

"Seller". Section 2–103.

§ 2–503.   Manner of Seller's Tender of Delivery

(1)   Tender of delivery requires that the seller put and hold conforming goods at the buyer's disposition and give the buyer any notification reasonably necessary to enable him to take delivery. The manner, time and place for tender are determined by the agreement and this Article, and in particular

(a)   tender must be at a reasonable hour, and if it is of goods they must be kept available for the period reasonably necessary to enable the buyer to take possession; but

(b)   unless otherwise agreed the buyer must furnish facilities reasonably suited to the receipt of the goods.

(2)   Where the case is within the next section respecting shipment tender requires that the seller comply with its provisions.

(3)   Where the seller is required to deliver at a particular destination tender requires that he comply with subsection (1) and also in any appropriate case tender documents as described in subsections (4) and (5) of this section.

(4)   Where goods are in the possession of a bailee and are to be delivered without being moved

(a)   tender requires that the seller either tender a negotiable document of title covering such goods or procure acknowledgment by the bailee of the buyer's right to possession of the goods; but

(b)   tender to the buyer of a non-negotiable document of title or of a record directing the bailee to deliver is sufficient tender unless the buyer seasonably objects, and except as otherwise provided in Article 9 receipt by the bailee of notification of the buyer's rights fixes those rights as against the bailee and all third persons; but risk of loss of the goods and of any failure by the bailee to honor the non-negotiable document of title or to obey the direction remains on the seller until the buyer has had a reasonable time to present the document or direction, and a refusal by the bailee to honor the document or to obey the direction defeats the tender.

(5)   Where the contract requires the seller to deliver documents

(a)   he must tender all such documents in correct form, except as provided in this Article with respect to bills of lading in a set (subsection (2) of Section 2–323); and

(b)   tender through customary banking channels is sufficient and dishonor of a draft accompanying or associated with the documents constitutes non-acceptance or rejection.

Definitional Cross References:

"Agreement". Section 1–201.

"Bill of lading". Section 1–201.

"Buyer". Section 2–103.

"Conforming". Section 2–106.

"Contract". Section 1–201.

"Delivery". Section 1–201.

"Dishonor". Section 3–508.

"Document of title". Section 1–201.

"Draft". Section 3–104.

"Goods". Section 2–105.

"Notification". Section 1–202.

"Reasonable time". Section 1–205.

"Receipt of goods". Section 2–103.

"Rights". Section 1–201.

"Seasonably". Section 1–205.

"Seller". Section 2–103.

"Written". Section 1–201.

§ 2–504.   Shipment by Seller

Where the seller is required or authorized to send the goods to the buyer and the contract does not require him to deliver them at a particular destination, then unless otherwise agreed he must

(a)   put the goods in the possession of such a carrier and make such a contract for their transportation as may be reasonable having regard to the nature of the goods and other circumstances of the case; and

(b)   obtain and promptly deliver or tender in due form any document necessary to enable the buyer to obtain possession of the goods or otherwise required by the agreement or by usage of trade; and

(c)   promptly notify the buyer of the shipment.

Failure to notify the buyer under paragraph (c) or to make a proper contract under paragraph (a) is a ground for rejection only if material delay or loss ensues.

Definitional Cross References:

"Agreement". Section 1–201.

"Buyer". Section 2–103.

"Contract". Section 1–201.

"Delivery". Section 1–201.

"Goods". Section 2–105.

"Notifies". Section 1–201.

"Seller". Section 2–103.

"Send". Section 1–201.

"Usage of trade". Section 1–303.

§ 2–505.   Seller's Shipment Under Reservation

(1)   Where the seller has identified goods to the contract by or before shipment:

(a)   his procurement of a negotiable bill of lading to his own order or otherwise reserves in him a security interest in the goods. His procurement of the bill to the order of a financing agency or of the buyer indicates in addition only the seller's expectation of transferring that interest to the person named.

(b)   a non-negotiable bill of lading to himself or his nominee reserves possession of the goods as security but except in a case of conditional delivery (subsection (2) of Section 2–507) a non-negotiable bill of lading naming the buyer as consignee reserves no security interest even though the seller retains possession or control of the bill of lading.

(2)   When shipment by the seller with reservation of a security interest is in violation of the contract for sale it constitutes an improper contract for transportation within the preceding section but impairs neither the rights given to the buyer by shipment and identification of the goods to the contract nor the seller's powers as a holder of a negotiable document of title.

Definitional Cross References:

"Bill of lading". Section 1–201.

"Buyer". Section 2–103.

"Consignee". Section 7–102.

"Contract". Section 1–201.

"Contract for sale". Section 2–106.

"Delivery". Section 1–201.

"Financing agency". Section 2–104.

"Goods". Section 2–105.

"Holder". Section 1–201.

"Person". Section 1–201.

"Security interest". Section 1–201.

"Seller". Section 2–103.

§ 2–506.   Rights of Financing Agency

(1)   A financing agency by paying or purchasing for value a draft which relates to a shipment of goods acquires to the extent of the payment or purchase and in addition to its own rights under the draft and any document of title securing it any rights of the shipper in the goods

including the right to stop delivery and the shipper's right to have the draft honored by the buyer.

(2) The right to reimbursement of a financing agency which has in good faith honored or purchased the draft under commitment to or authority from the buyer is not impaired by subsequent discovery of defects with reference to any relevant document which was apparently regular.

Definitional Cross References:

"Buyer". Section 2–103.

"Document of title". Section 1–201.

"Draft". Section 3–104.

"Financing agency". Section 2–104.

"Good faith". Section 1–201.

"Goods". Section 2–105.

"Purchase". Section 1–201.

"Rights". Section 1–201.

"Value". Section 1–204.

§ 2–507. Effect of Seller's Tender; Delivery on Condition

(1) Tender of delivery is a condition to the buyer's duty to accept the goods and, unless otherwise agreed, to his duty to pay for them. Tender entitles the seller to acceptance of the goods and to payment according to the contract.

(2) Where payment is due and demanded on the delivery to the buyer of goods or documents of title, his right as against the seller to retain or dispose of them is conditional upon his making the payment due.

Definitional Cross References:

"Buyer". Section 2–103.

"Contract". Section 1–201.

"Delivery". Section 1–201.

"Document of title". Section 1–201.

"Goods". Section 2–105.

"Rights". Section 1–201.

"Seller". Section 2–103.

§ 2–508. Cure by Seller of Improper Tender or Delivery; Replacement

(1) Where any tender or delivery by the seller is rejected because non-conforming and the time for performance has not yet expired, the seller may seasonably notify the buyer of his intention to cure and may then within the contract time make a conforming delivery.

(2) Where the buyer rejects a non-conforming tender which the seller had reasonable grounds to believe would be acceptable with or without money allowance the seller may if he seasonably notifies the buyer have a further reasonable time to substitute a conforming tender.

Official Comment

Prior Uniform Statutory Provision: None.

Purposes:

1. Subsection (1) permits a seller who has made a non-conforming tender in any case to make a conforming delivery within the contract time upon seasonable notification to the buyer. It

applies even where the seller has taken back the non-conforming goods and refunded the purchase price. He may still make a good tender within the contract period. The closer, however, it is to the contract date, the greater is the necessity for extreme promptness on the seller's part in notifying of his intention to cure, if such notification is to be "seasonable" under this subsection.

The rule of this subsection, moreover, is qualified by its underlying reasons. Thus if, after contracting for June delivery, a buyer later makes known to the seller his need for shipment early in the month and the seller ships accordingly, the "contract time" has been cut down by the supervening modification and the time for cure of tender must be referred to this modified time term.

2.   Subsection (2) seeks to avoid injustice to the seller by reason of a surprise rejection by the buyer. However, the seller is not protected unless he had "reasonable grounds to believe" that the tender would be acceptable. Such reasonable grounds can lie in prior course of dealing, course of performance or usage of trade as well as in the particular circumstances surrounding the making of the contract. The seller is charged with commercial knowledge of any factors in a particular sales situation which require him to comply strictly with his obligations under the contract as, for example, strict conformity of documents in an overseas shipment or the sale of precision parts or chemicals for use in manufacture. Further, if the buyer gives notice either implicitly, as by a prior course of dealing involving rigorous inspections, or expressly, as by the deliberate inclusion of a "no replacement" clause in the contract, the seller is to be held to rigid compliance. If the clause appears in a "form" contract evidence that it is out of line with trade usage or the prior course of dealing and was not called to the seller's attention may be sufficient to show that the seller had reasonable grounds to believe that the tender would be acceptable.

3.   The words "a further reasonable time to substitute a conforming tender" are intended as words of limitation to protect the buyer. What is a "reasonable time" depends upon the attending circumstances. Compare Section 2–511 on the comparable case of a seller's surprise demand for legal tender.

4.   Existing trade usages permitting variations without rejection but with price allowance enter into the agreement itself as contractual limitations of remedy and are not covered by this section.

Definitional Cross References:

"Buyer". Section 2–103.

"Conforming". Section 2–106.

"Contract". Section 1–201.

"Money". Section 1–201.

"Notifies". Section 1–202.

"Reasonable time". Section 1–205.

"Seasonably". Section 1–205.

"Seller". Section 2–103.

§ 2–509.   Risk of Loss in the Absence of Breach

(1)   Where the contract requires or authorizes the seller to ship the goods by carrier

(a)   if it does not require him to deliver them at a particular destination, the risk of loss passes to the buyer when the goods are duly delivered to the carrier even though the shipment is under reservation (Section 2–505); but

(b)   if it does require him to deliver them at a particular destination and the goods are there duly tendered while in the possession of the carrier, the risk of loss passes to the buyer when the goods are there duly so tendered as to enable the buyer to take delivery.

(2)   Where the goods are held by a bailee to be delivered without being moved, the risk of loss passes to the buyer

(a)   on his receipt of possession or control of a negotiable document of title covering the goods; or

(b)   on acknowledgment by the bailee of the buyer's right to possession of the goods; or

(c)   after his receipt of possession or control of a non-negotiable document of title or other direction to deliver in a record, as provided in subsection (4)(b) of Section 2–503.

(3)   In any case not within subsection (1) or (2), the risk of loss passes to the buyer on his receipt of the goods if the seller is a merchant; otherwise the risk passes to the buyer on tender of delivery.

(4)   The provisions of this section are subject to contrary agreement of the parties and to the provisions of this Article on sale on approval (Section 2–327) and on effect of breach on risk of loss (Section 2–510).

Definitional Cross References:

"Agreement". Section 1–201.

"Buyer". Section 2–103.

"Contract". Section 1–201.

"Delivery". Section 1–201.

"Document of title". Section 1–201.

"Goods". Section 2–105.

"Merchant". Section 2–104.

"Party". Section 1–201.

"Receipt" of goods. Section 2–103.

"Sale on approval". Section 2–326.

"Seller". Section 2–103.

§ 2–510.   Effect of Breach on Risk of Loss

(1)   Where a tender or delivery of goods so fails to conform to the contract as to give a right of rejection the risk of their loss remains on the seller until cure or acceptance.

(2)   Where the buyer rightfully revokes acceptance he may to the extent of any deficiency in his effective insurance coverage treat the risk of loss as having rested on the seller from the beginning.

(3)   Where the buyer as to conforming goods already identified to the contract for sale repudiates or is otherwise in breach before risk of their loss has passed to him, the seller may to the extent of any deficiency in his effective insurance coverage treat the risk of loss as resting on the buyer for a commercially reasonable time.

Definitional Cross References:

"Buyer". Section 2–103.

"Conform". Section 2–106.

"Contract for sale". Section 2–106.

"Goods". Section 2–105.   "Seller". Section 2–103.

§ 2–511.   Tender of Payment by Buyer; Payment by Check

(1)   Unless otherwise agreed tender of payment is a condition to the seller's duty to tender and complete any delivery.

(2)   Tender of payment is sufficient when made by any means or in any manner current in the ordinary course of business unless the seller demands payment in legal tender and gives any extension of time reasonably necessary to procure it.

(3)   Subject to the provisions of this Act on the effect of an instrument on an obligation (Section 3–802), payment by check is conditional and is defeated as between the parties by dishonor of the check on due presentment.

Definitional Cross References: "Party". Section 1–201.

"Buyer". Section 2–103.   "Reasonable time". Section 1–205.

"Check". Section 3–104.   "Seller". Section 2–103.

"Dishonor". Section 3–508.

§ 2–512.   Payment by Buyer Before Inspection

(1)   Where the contract requires payment before inspection non-conformity of the goods does not excuse the buyer from so making payment unless

(a)   the non-conformity appears without inspection; or

(b)   despite tender of the required documents the circumstances would justify injunction against honor under the provisions of this Act (Section 5–114).

(2)   Payment pursuant to subsection (1) does not constitute an acceptance of goods or impair the buyer's right to inspect or any of his remedies.

Definitional Cross References: "Financing agency". Section 2–104.

"Buyer". Section 2–103.   "Goods". Section 2–105.

"Conform". Section 2–106.   "Remedy". Section 1–201.

"Contract". Section 1–201.   "Rights". Section 1–201.

§ 2–513.   Buyer's Right to Inspection of Goods

(1)   Unless otherwise agreed and subject to subsection (3), where goods are tendered or delivered or identified to the contract for sale, the buyer has a right before payment or acceptance to inspect them at any reasonable place and time and in any reasonable manner. When the seller is required or authorized to send the goods to the buyer, the inspection may be after their arrival.

(2)   Expenses of inspection must be borne by the buyer but may be recovered from the seller if the goods do not conform and are rejected.

(3)   Unless otherwise agreed and subject to the provisions of this Article on C.I.F. contracts (subsection (3) of Section 2–321), the buyer is not entitled to inspect the goods before payment of the price when the contract provides

(a)   for delivery "C.O.D." or on other like terms; or

(b)   for payment against documents of title, except where such payment is due only after the goods are to become available for inspection.

(4)   A place or method of inspection fixed by the parties is presumed to be exclusive but unless otherwise expressly agreed it does not postpone identification or shift the place for delivery or for passing the risk of loss. If compliance becomes impossible, inspection shall be as provided in this section unless the place or method fixed was clearly intended as an indispensable condition failure of which avoids the contract.

Definitional Cross References:

"Buyer". Section 2–103.

"Conform". Section 2–106.

"Contract". Section 1–201.

"Contract for sale". Section 2–106.

"Document of title". Section 1–201.

"Goods". Section 2–105.

"Party". Section 1–201.

"Presumed". Section 1–201.

"Reasonable time". Section 1–205.

"Rights". Section 1–201.

"Seller". Section 2–103.

"Send". Section 1–201.

"Term". Section 1–201.

§ 2–514.   When Documents Deliverable on Acceptance; When on Payment

Unless otherwise agreed documents against which a draft is drawn are to be delivered to the drawee on acceptance of the draft if it is payable more than three days after presentment; otherwise, only on payment.

Definitional Cross References: "Draft". Section 3–104.

"Delivery". Section 1–201.

§ 2–515.   Preserving Evidence of Goods in Dispute

In furtherance of the adjustment of any claim or dispute

(a)   either party on reasonable notification to the other and for the purpose of ascertaining the facts and preserving evidence has the right to inspect, test and sample the goods including such of them as may be in the possession or control of the other; and

(b)   the parties may agree to a third party inspection or survey to determine the conformity or condition of the goods and may agree that the findings shall be binding upon them in any subsequent litigation or adjustment.

PART 6

BREACH, REPUDIATION AND EXCUSE

§ 2–601.   Buyer's Rights on Improper Delivery

Subject to the provisions of this Article on breach in installment contracts (Section 2–612) and unless otherwise agreed under the sections on contractual limitations of remedy (Sections 2–718 and 2–719), if the goods or the tender of delivery fail in any respect to conform to the contract, the buyer may

(a)   reject the whole; or

(b)   accept the whole; or

(c)   accept any commercial unit or units and reject the rest.

§ 2–602.   Manner and Effect of Rightful Rejection

(1)   Rejection of goods must be within a reasonable time after their delivery or tender. It is ineffective unless the buyer seasonably notifies the seller.

(2)   Subject to the provisions of the two following sections on rejected goods (Sections 2–603 and 2–604),

(a)   after rejection any exercise of ownership by the buyer with respect to any commercial unit is wrongful as against the seller; and

(b)   if the buyer has before rejection taken physical possession of goods in which he does not have a security interest under the provisions of this Article (subsection (3) of Section 2–711), he is under a duty after rejection to hold them with reasonable care at the seller's disposition for a time sufficient to permit the seller to remove them; but

(c)   the buyer has no further obligations with regard to goods rightfully rejected.

(3)   The seller's rights with respect to goods wrongfully rejected are governed by the provisions of this Article on Seller's remedies in general (Section 2–703).

Definitional Cross References:

"Buyer". Section 2–103.

"Commercial unit". Section 2–105.

"Goods". Section 2–105.

"Merchant". Section 2–104.

"Notifies". Section 1–202.

"Reasonable time". Section 1–205.

"Remedy". Section 1–201.

"Rights". Section 1–201.

"Seasonably". Section 1–205.

"Security interest". Section 1–201.

"Seller". Section 2–103.

§ 2–603. Merchant Buyer's Duties as to Rightfully Rejected Goods

(1) Subject to any security interest in the buyer (subsection (3) of Section 2–711), when the seller has no agent or place of business at the market of rejection a merchant buyer is under a duty after rejection of goods in his possession or control to follow any reasonable instructions received from the seller with respect to the goods and in the absence of such instructions to make reasonable efforts to sell them for the seller's account if they are perishable or threaten to decline in value speedily. Instructions are not reasonable if on demand indemnity for expenses is not forthcoming.

(2) When the buyer sells goods under subsection (1), he is entitled to reimbursement from the seller or out of the proceeds for reasonable expenses of caring for and selling them, and if the expenses include no selling commission then to such commission as is usual in the trade or if there is none to a reasonable sum not exceeding ten per cent on the gross proceeds.

(3) In complying with this section the buyer is held only to good faith and good faith conduct hereunder is neither acceptance nor conversion nor the basis of an action for damages.

Definitional Cross References:

"Buyer". Section 2–103.

"Good faith". Section 1–201.

"Goods". Section 2–105.

"Merchant". Section 2–104.

"Security interest". Section 1–201.

"Seller". Section 2–102.

§ 2–604. Buyer's Options as to Salvage of Rightfully Rejected Goods

Subject to the provisions of the immediately preceding section on perishables if the seller gives no instructions within a reasonable time after notification of rejection the buyer may store the rejected goods for the seller's account or reship them to him or resell them for the seller's account with reimbursement as provided in the preceding section. Such action is not acceptance or conversion.

Definitional Cross References:

"Buyer". Section 2–103.

"Notification". Section 1–202.

"Reasonable time". Section 1–205.

"Seller". Section 2–103.

§ 2–605. Waiver of Buyer's Objections by Failure to Particularize

(1) The buyer's failure to state in connection with rejection a particular defect which is ascertainable by reasonable inspection precludes him from relying on the unstated defect to justify rejection or to establish breach

    (a) where the seller could have cured it if stated seasonably; or

    (b) between merchants when the seller has after rejection made a request in writing for a full and final written statement of all defects on which the buyer proposes to rely.

(2) Payment against documents made without reservation of rights precludes recovery of the payment for defects apparent in the documents.

Definitional Cross References:

"Between merchants". Section 2–104.

"Buyer". Section 2–103.

"Seasonably". Section 1–205.

"Seller". Section 2–103.

"Writing" and "written". Section 1–201.

§ 2–606. What Constitutes Acceptance of Goods

(1) Acceptance of goods occurs when the buyer

    (a) after a reasonable opportunity to inspect the goods signifies to the seller that the goods are conforming or that he will take or retain them in spite of their nonconformity; or

    (b) fails to make an effective rejection (subsection (1) of Section 2–602), but such acceptance does not occur until the buyer has had a reasonable opportunity to inspect them; or

    (c) does any act inconsistent with the seller's ownership; but if such act is wrongful as against the seller it is an acceptance only if ratified by him.

(2) Acceptance of a part of any commercial unit is acceptance of that entire unit.

Definitional Cross References:

"Buyer". Section 2–103.

"Commercial unit". Section 2–105.

"Goods". Section 2–105.

"Seller". Section 2–103.

§ 2–607. Effect of Acceptance; Notice of Breach; Burden of Establishing Breach After Acceptance; Notice of Claim or Litigation to Person Answerable Over

(1) The buyer must pay at the contract rate for any goods accepted.

(2) Acceptance of goods by the buyer precludes rejection of the goods accepted and if made with knowledge of a non-conformity cannot be re-

voked because of it unless the acceptance was on the reasonable assumption that the non-conformity would be seasonably cured but acceptance does not of itself impair any other remedy provided by this Article for non-conformity.

(3) Where a tender has been accepted.

(a) the buyer must within a reasonable time after he discovers or should have discovered any breach notify the seller of breach or be barred from any remedy; and

(b) if the claim is one for infringement or the like (subsection (3) of Section 2–312) and the buyer is sued as a result of such a breach he must so notify the seller within a reasonable time after he receives notice of the litigation or be barred from any remedy over for liability established by the litigation.

(4) The burden is on the buyer to establish any breach with respect to the goods accepted.

(5) Where the buyer is sued for breach of a warranty or other obligation for which his seller is answerable over

(a) he may give his seller written notice of the litigation. If the notice states that the seller may come in and defend and that if the seller does not do so he will be bound in any action against him by his buyer by any determination of fact common to the two litigations, then unless the seller after seasonable receipt of the notice does come in and defend he is so bound.

(b) if the claim is one for infringement or the like (subsection (3) of Section 2–312) the original seller may demand in writing that his buyer turn over to him control of the litigation including settlement or else be barred from any remedy over and if he also agrees to bear all expense and to satisfy any adverse judgment, then unless the buyer after seasonable receipt of the demand does turn over control the buyer is so barred.

(6) The provisions of subsection (3), (4) and (5) apply to any obligation of a buyer to hold the seller harmless against infringement or the like (subsection (3) of Section 2–312).

Definitional Cross References:

"Burden of establishing". Section 1–201.

"Buyer". Section 2–103.

"Conform". Section 2–106.

"Contract". Section 1–201.

"Goods". Section 2–105.

"Notifies". Section 1–202.

"Reasonable time". Section 1–205.

"Remedy". Section 1–201.

"Seasonably". Section 1–205.

§ 2–608.   Revocation of Acceptance in Whole or in Part

(1)   The buyer may revoke his acceptance of a lot or commercial unit whose non-conformity substantially impairs its value to him if he has accepted it

(a)   on the reasonable assumption that its non-conformity would be cured and it has not been seasonably cured; or

(b)   without discovery of such non-conformity if his acceptance was reasonably induced either by the difficulty of discovery before acceptance or by the seller's assurances.

(2)   Revocation of acceptance must occur within a reasonable time after the buyer discovers or should have discovered the ground for it and before any substantial change in condition of the goods which is not caused by their own defects. It is not effective until the buyer notifies the seller of it.

(3)   A buyer who so revokes has the same rights and duties with regard to the goods involved as if he had rejected them.

Definitional Cross References:

"Buyer". Section 2–103.

"Commercial unit". Section 2–105.

"Conform". Section 2–106.

"Goods". Section 2–105.

"Lot". Section 2–105.

"Notifies". Section 1–202.

"Reasonable time". Section 1–205.

"Rights". Section 1–201.

"Seasonably". Section 1–205.

"Seller". Section 2–103.

§ 2–609.   Right to Adequate Assurance of Performance

(1)   A contract for sale imposes an obligation on each party that the other's expectation of receiving due performance will not be impaired. When reasonable grounds for insecurity arise with respect to the performance of either party the other may in writing demand adequate assurance of due performance and until he receives such assurance may if commercially reasonable suspend any performance for which he has not already received the agreed return.

(2)   Between merchants the reasonableness of grounds for insecurity and the adequacy of any assurance offered shall be determined according to commercial standards.

(3)   Acceptance of any improper delivery or payment does not prejudice the aggrieved party's right to demand adequate assurance of future performance.

(4)   After receipt of a justified demand failure to provide within a reasonable time not exceeding thirty days such assurance of due performance as is adequate under the circumstances of the particular case is a repudiation of the contract.

Official Comment

Prior Uniform Statutory Provision: See Sections 53, 54(1)(b), 55 and 63(2), Uniform Sales Act.

Purposes:

1. The section rests on the recognition of the fact that the essential purpose of a contract between commercial men is actual performance and they do not bargain merely for a promise, or for a promise plus the right to win a lawsuit and that a continuing sense of reliance and security that the promised performance will be forthcoming when due, is an important feature of the bargain. If either the willingness or the ability of a party to perform declines materially between the time of contracting and the time for performance, the other party is threatened with the loss of a substantial part of what he has bargained for. A seller needs protection not merely against having to deliver on credit to a shaky buyer, but also against having to procure and manufacture the goods, perhaps turning down other customers. Once he has been given reason to believe that the buyer's performance has become uncertain, it is an undue hardship to force him to continue his own performance. Similarly, a buyer who believes that the seller's deliveries have become uncertain cannot safely wait for the due date of performance when he has been buying to assure himself of materials for his current manufacturing or to replenish his stock of merchandise.

2. Three measures have been adopted to meet the needs of commercial men in such situations. First, the aggrieved party is permitted to suspend his own performance and any preparation therefor, with excuse for any resulting necessary delay, until the situation has been clarified. "Suspend performance" under this section means to hold up performance pending the outcome of the demand, and includes also the holding up of any preparatory action. This is the same principle which governs the ancient law of stoppage and seller's lien, and also of excuse of a buyer from prepayment if the seller's actions manifest that he cannot or will not perform. (Original Act, Section 63(2).)

Secondly, the aggrieved party is given the right to require adequate assurance that the other party's performance will be duly forthcoming. This principle is reflected in the familiar clauses permitting the seller to curtail deliveries if the buyer's credit becomes impaired, which when held within the limits of reasonableness and good faith actually express no more than the fair business meaning of any commercial contract.

Third, and finally, this section provides the means by which the aggrieved party may treat the contract as broken if his reasonable grounds for insecurity are not cleared up within a reasonable time. This is the principle underlying the law of anticipatory breach, whether by way of defective part performance or by repudiation. The present section merges these three principles of law and commercial practice into a single theory of general application to all sales agreements looking to future performance.

3. Subsection (2) of the present section requires that "reasonable" grounds and "adequate" assurance as used in subsection (1) be defined by commercial rather than legal standards. The express reference to commercial standards carries no connotation that the obligation of good faith is not equally applicable here.

Under commercial standards and in accord with commercial practice, a ground for insecurity need not arise from or be directly related to the contract in question. The law as to "dependence" or "independence" of promises within a single contract does not control the application of the present section.

Thus a buyer who falls behind in "his account" with the seller, even though the items involved have to do with separate and legally distinct contracts, impairs the seller's expectation of due performance. Again, under the same test, a buyer who requires precision parts which he intends to use immediately upon delivery, may have reasonable grounds for insecurity if he discovers that his seller is making defective deliveries of such parts to other buyers with similar needs. Thus, too, in a situation such as arose in Jay Dreher Corporation v. Delco Appliance Corporation, 93 F.2d 275 (C.C.A. 2, 1937), where a manufacturer gave a dealer an exclusive franchise for the sale of his product but on two or three occasions breached the exclusive dealing clause, although there was no default in orders, deliveries or payments under the separate sales contract between the parties, the aggrieved dealer would be entitled to suspend his performance of the contract for sale under the present section and to demand assurance that the exclusive dealing contract would be lived up to. There is no need for an explicit clause tying the exclusive franchise into the contract for the sale of goods since the situation itself ties the agreements together.

The nature of the sales contract enters also into the question of reasonableness. For example, a report from an apparently trustworthy source that the seller had shipped defective goods or was planning to ship them would normally give the buyer reasonable grounds for insecurity. But when the buyer has assumed the risk of payment before inspection of the goods, as in a sales contract on C.I.F. or similar cash against documents terms, that risk is not to be evaded by a demand for assurance. Therefore no ground for insecurity would exist under this section unless the report went to a ground which would excuse payment by the buyer.

4.   What constitutes "adequate" assurance of due performance is subject to the same test of factual conditions. For example, where the buyer can make use of a defective delivery, a mere promise by a seller of good repute that he is giving the matter his attention and that the defect will not be repeated, is normally sufficient. Under the same circumstances, however, a similar statement by a known corner-cutter might well be considered insufficient without the posting of a guaranty or, if so demanded by the buyer, a speedy replacement of the delivery involved. By the same token where a delivery has defects, even though easily curable, which interfere with easy use by the buyer, no verbal assurance can be deemed adequate which is not accompanied by replacement, repair, money-allowance, or other commercially reasonable cure.

A fact situation such as arose in Corn Products Refining Co. v. Fasola, 94 N.J.L. 181, 109 A. 505 (1920) offers illustration both of reasonable grounds for insecurity and "adequate" assurance. In that case a contract for the sale of oils on 30 days' credit, 2% off for payment within-10 days, provided that credit was to be extended to the buyer only if his financial responsibility was satisfactory to the seller. The buyer had been in the habit of taking advantage of the discount but at the same time that he failed to make his customary 10 day payment, the seller heard rumors, in fact false, that the buyer's financial condition was shaky. Thereupon, the seller demanded cash before shipment or security satisfactory to him. The buyer sent a good credit report from his banker, expressed willingness to make payments when due on the 30 day terms and insisted on further deliveries under the contract. Under this Article the rumors, although false, were enough to make the buyer's financial condition "unsatisfactory" to the seller under the contract clause. Moreover, the buyer's practice of taking the cash discounts is enough, apart from the contract clause, to lay a commercial foundation for suspicion when the practice is suddenly stopped. These matters, however, go only to the justification of the seller's demand for security, or his "reasonable grounds for insecurity".

The adequacy of the assurance given is not measured as in the type of "satisfaction" situation affected with intangibles, such as in personal service cases, cases involving a third party's judgment as final, or cases in which the whole contract is dependent on one party's satisfaction, as in a sale on approval. Here, the seller must exercise good faith and observe commercial standards. This Article thus approves the statement of the court in James B. Berry's Sons Co. of Illinois v. Monark Gasoline & Oil Co., Inc., 32 F.2d 74 (C.C.A.8, 1929), that the seller's satisfaction under such a clause must be based upon reason and must not be arbitrary or capricious; and rejects the purely personal "good faith" test of the Corn Products Refining Co. case, which held that in the seller's sole judgment, if for any reason he was dissatisfied, he was entitled to revoke the credit. In the absence of the buyer's failure to take the 2% discount as was his custom, the banker's report given in that case would have been "adequate" assurance under this Act, regardless of the language of the "satisfaction" clause. However, the seller is reasonably entitled to feel insecure at a sudden expansion of the buyer's use of a credit term, and should be entitled either to security or to a satisfactory explanation.

The entire foregoing discussion as to adequacy of assurance by way of explanation is subject to qualification when repeated occasions for the application of this section arise. This Act recognizes that repeated delinquencies

must be viewed as cumulative. On the other hand, commercial sense also requires that if repeated claims for assurance are made under this section, the basis for these claims must be increasingly obvious.

5.   A failure to provide adequate assurance of performance and thereby to re-establish the security of expectation, results in a breach only "by repudiation" under subsection (4). Therefore, the possibility is continued of retraction of the repudiation under the section dealing with that problem, unless the aggrieved party has acted on the breach in some manner.

The thirty day limit on the time to provide assurance is laid down to free the question of reasonable time from uncertainty in later litigation.

6.   Clauses seeking to give the protected party exceedingly wide powers to cancel or readjust the contract when ground for insecurity arises must be read against the fact that good faith is a part of the obligation of the contract and not subject to modification by agreement and includes, in the case of a merchant, the reasonable observance of commercial standards of fair dealing in the trade. Such clauses can thus be effective to enlarge the protection given by the present section to a certain extent, to fix the reasonable time within which requested assurance must be given, or to define adequacy of the assurance in any commercially reasonable fashion. But any clause seeking to set up arbitrary standards for action is ineffective under this Article. Acceleration clauses are treated similarly in the Articles on Commercial Paper and Secured Transactions.

Cross References:

Point 3: Section 1–203.

Point 5: Section 2–611.

Point 6: Sections 1–203 and 1–208 and Articles 3 and 9.

Definitional Cross References:

"Aggrieved party". Section 1–201.

"Between merchants". Section 2–104.

"Contract". Section 1–201.

"Contract for sale". Section 2–106.

"Party". Section 1–201.

"Reasonable time". Section 1–205.

"Rights". Section 1–201.

"Writing". Section 1–201.

§ 2–610.　Anticipatory Repudiation

When either party repudiates the contract with respect to a performance not yet due the loss of which will substantially impair the value of the contract to the other, the aggrieved party may

    (a)　for a commercially reasonable time await performance by the repudiating party; or

    (b)　resort to any remedy for breach (Section 2–703 or Section 2–711), even though he has notified the repudiating party that he would await the latter's performance and has urged retraction; and

    (c)　in either case suspend his own performance or proceed in accordance with the provisions of this Article on the seller's right to identify goods to the contract notwithstanding breach or to salvage unfinished goods (Section 2–704).

Definitional Cross References:

"Aggrieved party". Section 1–201.

"Contract". Section 1–201.

"Party". Section 1–201.

"Remedy". Section 1–201.

Official Comment

1.　With the problem of insecurity taken care of by the preceding section and with provision being made in this Article as to the effect of a defective delivery under an installment contract, anticipatory repudiation centers upon an overt communication of intention or an action which renders performance impossible or demonstrates a clear determination not to continue with performance.

Under the present section when such a repudiation substantially impairs the value of the contract, the aggrieved party may at any time resort to his remedies for breach, or he may suspend his own performance while he negotiates with, or awaits performance by, the other party. But if he awaits performance beyond a commercially reasonable time he cannot recover resulting damages which he should have avoided.

2.　It is not necessary for repudiation that performance be made literally and utterly impossible. Repudiation can result from action which reasonably indicates a rejection of the continuing obligation. And, a repudiation automatically results under the preceding section on insecurity when a party fails to provide adequate assurance of due future performance within thirty days after a justifiable demand therefor has been made. Under the language of this section, a demand by one or both parties for more than the contract calls for in the way of counter-performance is not in itself a repudiation nor does it invalidate a plain expression of desire for future performance. However, when under a fair reading it amounts to a statement of intention not to perform except on conditions which go beyond the contract, it becomes a repudiation.

§ 2–611. Retraction of Anticipatory Repudiation

(1) Until the repudiating party's next performance is due he can retract his repudiation unless the aggrieved party has since the repudiation cancelled or materially changed his position or otherwise indicated that he considers the repudiation final.

(2) Retraction may be by any method which clearly indicates to the aggrieved party that the repudiating party intends to perform, but must include any assurance justifiably demanded under the provisions of this Article (Section 2–609).

(3) Retraction reinstates the repudiating party's rights under the contract with due excuse and allowance to the aggrieved party for any delay occasioned by the repudiation.

Definitional Cross References:

"Aggrieved party". Section 1–201.

"Cancellation". Section 2–106.

"Contract". Section 1–201.

"Party". Section 1–201.

"Rights". Section 1–201.

§ 2–612. "Installment Contract"; Breach

(1) An "installment contract" is one which requires or authorizes the delivery of goods in separate lots to be separately accepted, even though the contract contains a clause "each delivery is a separate contract" or its equivalent.

(2) The buyer may reject any installment which is non-conforming if the non-conformity substantially impairs the value of that installment and cannot be cured or if the non-conformity is a defect in the required documents; but if the non-conformity does not fall within subsection (3) and the seller gives adequate assurance of its cure the buyer must accept that installment.

(3) Whenever non-conformity or default with respect to one or more installments substantially impairs the value of the whole contract there is a breach of the whole. But the aggrieved party reinstates the contract if he accepts a non-conforming installment without seasonably notifying of cancellation or if he brings an action with respect only to past installments or demands performance as to future installments.

Definitional Cross References:

"Action". Section 1–201.

"Aggrieved party". Section 1–201.

"Buyer". Section 2–103.

"Cancellation". Section 2–106.

"Conform". Section 2–106.

"Contract". Section 1–201.

"Lot". Section 2–105.

"Notifies". Section 1–202.

"Seasonably". Section 1–205.

"Seller". Section 2–103.

§ 2–613.   Casualty to Identified Goods

Where the contract requires for its performance goods identified when the contract is made, and the goods suffer casualty without fault of either party before the risk of loss passes to the buyer, or in a proper case under a "no arrival, no sale" term (Section 2–324) then

(a)   if the loss is total the contract is avoided; and

(b)   if the loss is partial or the goods have so deteriorated as no longer to conform to the contract the buyer may nevertheless demand inspection and at his option either treat the contract as avoided or accept the goods with due allowance from the contract price for the deterioration or the deficiency in quantity but without further right against the seller.

Definitional Cross References: "Goods". Section 2–105.

"Buyer". Section 2–103.   "Party". Section 1–201.

"Conform". Section 2–106.   "Rights". Section 1–201.

"Contract". Section 1–201.   "Seller". Section 2–103.

"Fault". Section 1–201.

§ 2–614.   Substituted Performance

(1)   Where without fault of either party the agreed berthing, loading, or unloading facilities fail or an agreed type of carrier becomes unavailable or the agreed manner of delivery otherwise becomes commercially impracticable but a commercially reasonable substitute is available, such substitute performance must be tendered and accepted.

(2)   If the agreed means or manner of payment fails because of domestic or foreign governmental regulation, the seller may withhold or stop delivery unless the buyer provides a means or manner of payment which is commercially a substantial equivalent. If delivery has already been taken, payment by the means or in the manner provided by the regulation discharges the buyer's obligation unless the regulation is discriminatory, oppressive or predatory.

Definitional Cross References: "Party". Section 1–201.

"Buyer". Section 2–103.   "Seller". Section 2–103.

"Fault". Section 1–201.

§ 2–615.   Excuse by Failure of Presupposed Conditions

Except so far as a seller may have assumed a greater obligation and subject to the preceding section on substituted performance:

(a)   Delay in delivery or non-delivery in whole or in part by a seller who complies with paragraphs (b) and (c) is not a breach of his duty under a contract for sale if performance as agreed has been made impracticable by the occurrence of a contingency the non-occurrence of which was a basic assumption on which the contract was made or by compliance in good faith with any applicable foreign or domestic governmental regulation or order whether or not it later proves to be invalid.

(b) Where the causes mentioned in paragraph (a) affect only a part of the seller's capacity to perform, he must allocate production and deliveries among his customers but may at his option include regular customers not then under contract as well as his own requirements for further manufacture. He may so allocate in any manner which is fair and reasonable.

(c) The seller must notify the buyer seasonably that there will be delay or non-delivery and, when allocation is required under paragraph (b), of the estimated quota thus made available for the buyer.

Official Comment

Prior Uniform Statutory Provision: None.

Purposes:

1. This section excuses a seller from timely delivery of goods contracted for, where his performance has become commercially impracticable because of unforeseen supervening circumstances not within the contemplation of the parties at the time of contracting. The destruction of specific goods and the problem of the use of substituted performance on points other than delay or quantity, treated elsewhere in this Article, must be distinguished from the matter covered by this section.

2. The present section deliberately refrains from any effort at an exhaustive expression of contingencies and is to be interpreted in all cases sought to be brought within its scope in terms of its underlying reason and purpose.

3. The first test for excuse under this Article in terms of basic assumption is a familiar one. The additional test of commercial impracticability (as contrasted with "impossibility," "frustration of performance" or "frustration of the venture") has been adopted in order to call attention to the commercial character of the criterion chosen by this Article.

4. Increased cost alone does not excuse performance unless the rise in cost is due to some unforeseen contingency which alters the essential nature of the performance. Neither is a rise or a collapse in the market in itself a justification, for that is exactly the type of business risk which business contracts made at fixed prices are intended to cover. But a severe shortage of raw materials or of supplies due to a contingency such as war, embargo, local crop failure unforeseen shutdown of major sources of supply or the like, which either causes a marked increase in cost or altogether prevents the seller from securing supplies necessary to his performance, is within the contemplation of this section. (See Ford & Sons, Ltd. v. Henry Leetham & Sons, Ltd., 21 Com.Cas. 55 (1915, K.B.D.).)

5. Where a particular source of supply is exclusive under the agreement and fails through casualty, the present section applies rather than the provision on destruction or deterioration of specific goods. The same holds true where a particular source of supply is shown by the circumstances to have been contemplated or assumed by the parties at the time of contracting. (See Davis Co. v. Hoffmann-LaRoche

Chemical Works, 178 App.Div. 855, 166 N.Y.S. 179 (1917) and International Paper Co. v. Rockefeller, 161 App. Div. 180, 146 N.Y.S. 371 (1914).) There is no excuse under this section, however, unless the seller has employed all due measures to assure himself that his source will not fail. (See Canadian Industrial Alcohol Co., Ltd. v. Dunbar Molasses Co., 258 N.Y. 194, 179 N.E. 383, 80 A.L.R. 1173 (1932) and Washington Mfg. Co. v. Midland Lumber Co., 113 Wash. 593, 194 P. 777 (1921).)

In the case of failure of production by an agreed source for causes beyond the seller's control, the seller should, if possible, be excused since production by an agreed source is without more a basic assumption of the contract. Such excuse should not result in relieving the defaulting supplier from liability nor in dropping into the seller's lap an unearned bonus of damages over. The flexible adjustment machinery of this Article provides the solution under the provision on the obligation of good faith. A condition to his making good the claim of excuse is the turning over to the buyer of his rights against the defaulting source of supply to the extent of the buyer's contract in relation to which excuse is being claimed.

6.   In situations in which neither sense nor justice is served by either answer when the issue is posed in flat terms of "excuse" or "no excuse," adjustment under the various provisions of this Article is necessary, especially the sections on good faith, on insecurity and assurance and on the reading of all provisions in the light of their purposes, and the general policy of this Act to use equitable principles in furtherance of commercial standards and good faith.

7.   The failure of conditions which go to convenience or collateral values rather than to the commercial practicability of the main performance does not amount to a complete excuse.

However, good faith and the reason of the present section and of the preceding one may properly be held to justify and even to require any needed delay involved in a good faith inquiry seeking a readjustment of the contract terms to meet the new conditions.

8.   The provisions of this section are made subject to assumption of greater liability by agreement and such agreement is to be found not only in the expressed terms of the contract but in the circumstances surrounding the contracting, in trade usage and the like. Thus the exemptions of this section do not apply when the contingency in question is sufficiently foreshadowed at the time of contracting to be included among the business risks which are fairly to be regarded as part of the dickered terms, either consciously or as a matter of reasonable, commercial interpretation from the circumstances. (See Madeirense Do Brasil, S.A. v. Stulman-Emrick Lumber Co., 147 F.2d 399 (C.C.A., 2 Cir., 1945).) The exemption otherwise present through usage of trade under the present section may also be expressly negated by the language of the agreement. Generally, express agreements as to exemptions designed to enlarge upon or supplant the provisions of this section are to be read in the light of mercantile sense and reason, for this section itself sets up the commercial standard for normal and reasonable interpretation and provides a minimum beyond which agreement may not go.

Agreement can also be made in regard to the consequences of exemption as laid down in paragraphs (b) and (c) and the next section on procedure on notice claiming excuse.

9.   The case of a farmer who has contracted to sell crops to be grown on designated land may be regarded as falling either within the section on casualty to identified goods or this section, and he may be excused, when

there is a failure of the specific crop, either on the basis of the destruction of identified goods or because of the failure of a basic assumption of the contract.

Exemption of the buyer in the case of a "requirements" contract is covered by the "Output and Requirements" section both as to assumption and allocation of the relevant risks. But when a contract by a manufacturer to buy fuel or raw material makes no specific reference to a particular venture and no such reference may be drawn from the circumstances, commercial understanding views it as a general deal in the general market and not conditioned on any assumption of the continuing operation of the buyer's plant. Even when notice is given by the buyer that the supplies are needed to fill a specific contract of a normal commercial kind, commercial understanding does not see such a supply contract as conditioned on the continuance of the buyer's further contract for outlet. On the other hand, where the buyer's contract is in reasonable commercial understanding conditioned on a definite and specific venture or assumption as, for instance, a war procurement subcontract known to be based on a prime contract which is subject to termination, or a supply contract for a particular construction venture, the reason of the present section may well apply and entitle the buyer to the exemption.

10. Following its basic policy of using commercial practicability as a test for excuse, this section recognizes as of equal significance either a foreign or domestic regulation and disregards any technical distinctions between "law," "regulation," "order" and the like. Nor does it make the present action of the seller depend upon the eventual judicial determination of the legality of the particular governmental action. The seller's good faith belief in the validity of the regulation is the test under this Article and the best evidence of his good faith is the general commercial acceptance of the regulation. However, governmental interference cannot excuse unless it truly "supervenes" in such a manner as to be beyond the seller's assumption of risk. And any action by the party claiming excuse which causes or colludes in inducing the governmental action preventing his performance would be in breach of good faith and would destroy his exemption.

11. An excused seller must fulfill his contract to the extent which the supervening contingency permits, and if the situation is such that his customers are generally affected he must take account of all in supplying one. Subsections (a) and (b), therefore, explicitly permit in any proration a fair and reasonable attention to the needs of regular customers who are probably relying on spot orders for supplies. Customers at different stages of the manufacturing process may be fairly treated by including the seller's manufacturing requirements. A fortiori, the seller may also take account of contracts later in date than the one in question. The fact that such spot orders may be closed at an advanced price causes no difficulty, since any allocation which exceeds normal past requirements will not be reasonable. However, good faith requires, when prices have advanced, that the seller exercise real care in making his allocations, and in case of doubt his contract customers should be favored and supplies prorated evenly among them regardless of price. Save for the extra care thus required by changes in the market, this section seeks to leave every reasonable business leeway to the seller.

Cross References:

Point 1: Sections 2–613 and 2–614.

Point 2: Section 1–102.

Point 5: Sections 1–203 and 2–613.

Point 6: Sections 1–102, 1–203 and 2–609.

Point 7: Section 2–614.

Point 8: Sections 1–201, 2–302 and 2–616.

Point 9: Sections 1–102, 2–306 and 2–613.

Definitional Cross References:

"Between merchants". Section 2–104.

"Buyer". Section 2–103.

"Contract". Section 1–201.

"Contract for sale". Section 2–106.

"Good faith". Section 1–201.

"Merchant". Section 2–104.

"Notifies". Section 1–202.

"Seasonably". Section 1–205.

"Seller". Section 2–103.

§ 2–616.   Procedure on Notice Claiming Excuse

(1)   Where the buyer receives notification of a material or indefinite delay or an allocation justified under the preceding section he may by written notification to the seller as to any delivery concerned, and where the prospective deficiency substantially impairs the value of the whole contract under the provisions of this Article relating to breach of installment contracts (Section 2–612), then also as to the whole,

(a)   terminate and thereby discharge any unexecuted portion of the contract; or

(b)   modify the contract by agreeing to take his available quota in substitution.

(2)   If after receipt of such notification from the seller the buyer fails so to modify the contract within a reasonable time not exceeding thirty days the contract lapses with respect to any deliveries affected.

(3)   The provisions of this section may not be negated by agreement except in so far as the seller has assumed a greater obligation under the preceding section.

Definitional Cross References:

"Buyer". Section 2–103.

"Contract". Section 1–201.

"Installment contract". Section 2–612.

"Notification". Section 1–202.

"Reasonable time". Section 1–205.

"Seller". Section 2–103.

"Termination". Section 2–106.

"Written". Section 1–201.

PART 7

REMEDIES

§ 2–701.   Remedies for Breach of Collateral Contracts Not Impaired

Remedies for breach of any obligation or promise collateral or ancillary to a contract for sale are not impaired by the provisions of this Article.

Definitional Cross References: "Remedy". Section 1–201.

"Contract for sale". Section 2–106.

§ 2–702. Seller's Remedies on Discovery of Buyer's Insolvency

(1) Where the seller discovers the buyer to be insolvent he may refuse delivery except for cash including payment for all goods theretofore delivered under the contract, and stop delivery under this Article (Section 2–705).

(2) Where the seller discovers that the buyer has received goods on credit while insolvent he may reclaim the goods upon demand made within ten days after the receipt, but if misrepresentation of solvency has been made to the particular seller in writing within three months before delivery the ten day limitation does not apply. Except as provided in this subsection the seller may not base a right to reclaim goods on the buyer's fraudulent or innocent misrepresentation of solvency or of intent to pay.

(3) The seller's right to reclaim under subsection (2) is subject to the rights of a buyer in ordinary course or other good faith purchaser under this Article (Section 2–403). Successful reclamation of goods excludes all other remedies with respect to them.

Definitional Cross References:

"Buyer". Section 2–103.

"Buyer in ordinary course of business". Section 1–201.

"Contract". Section 1–201.

"Good faith". Section 1–201.

"Goods". Section 2–105.

"Insolvent". Section 1–201.

"Person". Section 1–201.

"Purchaser". Section 1–201.

"Receipt" of goods. Section 2–103.

"Remedy". Section 1–201.

"Rights". Section 1–201.

"Seller". Section 2–103.

"Writing". Section 1–201.

§ 2–703. Seller's Remedies in General

Where the buyer wrongfully rejects or revokes acceptance of goods or fails to make a payment due on or before delivery or repudiates with respect to a part or the whole, then with respect to any goods directly affected and, if the breach is of the whole contract (Section 2–612), then also with respect to the whole undelivered balance, the aggrieved seller may

(a) withhold delivery of such goods;

(b) stop delivery by any bailee as hereafter provided (Section 2–705);

(c) proceed under the next section respecting goods still unidentified to the contract;

(d) resell and recover damages as hereafter provided (Section 2–706);

(e)   recover damages for non-acceptance (Section 2–708) or in a proper case the price (Section 2–709);

(f)   cancel.

Official Comment

Prior Uniform Statutory Provision: No comparable index section. See Section 53, Uniform Sales Act.

Purposes:

1.   This section is an index section which gathers together in one convenient place all of the various remedies open to a seller for any breach by the buyer. This Article rejects any doctrine of election of remedy as a fundamental policy and thus the remedies are essentially cumulative in nature and include all of the available remedies for breach. Whether the pursuit of one remedy bars another depends entirely on the facts of the individual case.

2.   The buyer's breach which occasions the use of the remedies under this section may involve only one lot or delivery of goods, or may involve all of the goods which are the subject matter of the particular contract. The right of the seller to pursue a remedy as to all the goods when the breach is as to only one or more lots is covered by the section on breach in installment contracts. The present section deals only with the remedies available after the goods involved in the breach have been determined by that section.

3.   In addition to the typical case of refusal to pay or default in payment, the language in the preamble, "fails to make a payment due," is intended to cover the dishonor of a check on due presentment, or the non-acceptance of a draft, and the failure to furnish an agreed letter of credit.

4.   It should also be noted that this Act requires its remedies to be liberally administered and provides that any right or obligation which it declares is enforceable by action unless a different effect is specifically prescribed (Section 1–106).

Cross References:

Point 2: Section 2–612.

Point 3: Section 2–325.

Point 4: Section 1–106.

Definitional Cross References:

"Aggrieved party". Section 1–201.

"Buyer". Section 2–103.

"Cancellation". Section 2–106.

"Contract". Section 1–201.

"Goods". Section 2–105.

"Remedy". Section 1–201.

"Seller". Section 2–103.

§ 2–704.   Seller's Right to Identify Goods to the Contract Notwithstanding Breach or to Salvage Unfinished Goods

(1)   An aggrieved seller under the preceding section may

(a)   identify to the contract conforming goods not already identified if at the time he learned of the breach they are in his possession or control;

(b)   treat as the subject of resale goods which have demonstrably been intended for the particular contract even though those goods are unfinished.

(2)   Where the goods are unfinished an aggrieved seller may in the exercise of reasonable commercial judgment for the purposes of avoiding loss and of effective realization either complete the manufacture and wholly identify the goods to the contract or cease manufacture and resell for scrap or salvage value or proceed in any other reasonable manner.

Definitional Cross References:

"Aggrieved party". Section 1–201.

"Conforming". Section 2–106.

"Contract". Section 1–201.

"Goods". Section 2–105.

"Rights". Section 1–201.

"Seller". Section 2–103.

§ 2–705.   Seller's Stoppage of Delivery in Transit or Otherwise

(1)   The seller may stop delivery of goods in the possession of a carrier or other bailee when he discovers the buyer to be insolvent (Section 2–702) and may stop delivery of carload, truckload, planeload or larger shipments of express or freight when the buyer repudiates or fails to make a payment due before delivery or if for any other reason the seller has a right to withhold or reclaim the goods.

(2)   As against such buyer the seller may stop delivery until

(a)   receipt of the goods by the buyer; or

(b)   acknowledgment to the buyer by any bailee of the goods except a carrier that the bailee holds the goods for the buyer; or

(c)   such acknowledgment to the buyer by a carrier by reshipment or as a warehouse; or

(d)   negotiation to the buyer of any negotiable document of title covering the goods.

(3)(a)   To stop delivery the seller must so notify as to enable the bailee by reasonable diligence to prevent delivery of the goods.

(b)   After such notification the bailee must hold and deliver the goods according to the directions of the seller but the seller is liable to the bailee for any ensuing charges or damages.

(c)   If a negotiable document of title has been issued for goods the bailee is not obliged to obey a notification to stop until surrender of possession or control of the document.

(d)   A carrier who has issued a non-negotiable bill of lading is not obliged to obey a notification to stop received from a person other than the consignor.

Definitional Cross References:

"Buyer". Section 2–103.

"Contract for sale". Section 2–106.

"Document of title". Section 1–201.

"Goods". Section 2–105.

"Insolvent". Section 1–201.

"Notification". Section 1–202.

"Receipt" of goods. Section 2–103.

"Rights". Section 1–201.   "Seller". Section 2–103.

§ 2–706.   Seller's Resale Including Contract for Resale

(1)   Under the conditions stated in Section 2–703 on seller's remedies, the seller may resell the goods concerned or the undelivered balance thereof. Where the resale is made in good faith and in a commercially reasonable manner the seller may recover the difference between the resale price and the contract price together with any incidental damages allowed under the provisions of this Article (Section 2–710), but less expenses saved in consequence of the buyer's breach.

(2)   Except as otherwise provided in subsection (3) or unless otherwise agreed resale may be at public or private sale including sale by way of one or more contracts to sell or of identification to an existing contract of the seller. Sale may be as a unit or in parcels and at any time and place and on any terms but every aspect of the sale including the method, manner, time, place and terms must be commercially reasonable. The resale must be reasonably identified as referring to the broken contract, but it is not necessary that the goods be in existence or that any or all of them have been identified to the contract before the breach.

(3)   Where the resale is at private sale the seller must give the buyer reasonable notification of his intention to resell.

(4)   Where the resale is at public sale

(a)   only identified goods can be sold except where there is a recognized market for a public sale of futures in goods of the kind; and

(b)   it must be made at a usual place or market for public sale if one is reasonably available and except in the case of goods which are perishable or threaten to decline in value speedily the seller must give the buyer reasonable notice of the time and place of the resale; and

(c)   if the goods are not to be within the view of those attending the sale the notification of sale must state the place where the goods are located and provide for their reasonable inspection by prospective bidders; and

(d)   the seller may buy.

(5)   A purchaser who buys in good faith at a resale takes the goods free of any rights of the original buyer even though the seller fails to comply with one or more of the requirements of this section.

(6)   The seller is not accountable to the buyer for any profit made on any resale. A person in the position of a seller (Section 2–707) or a buyer who has rightfully rejected or justifiably revoked acceptance must account for any excess over the amount of his security interest, as hereinafter defined (subsection (3) of Section 2–711).

Definitional Cross References:

"Buyer". Section 2–103.

"Contract". Section 1–201.

"Contract for sale". Section 2–106.

"Good faith". Section 1–201.

"Goods". Section 2–105.

"Merchant". Section 2–104.

"Notification". Section 1–202.

"Person in position of seller". Section 2–707.

"Purchase". Section 1–201.

"Rights". Section 1–201.

"Sale". Section 2–106.

"Security interest". Section 1–201.

"Seller". Section 2–103.

§ 2–707. "Person in the Position of a Seller"

(1) A "person in the position of a seller" includes as against a principal an agent who has paid or become responsible for the price of goods on behalf of his principal or anyone who otherwise holds a security interest or other right in goods similar to that of a seller.

(2) A person in the position of a seller may as provided in this Article withhold or stop delivery (Section 2–705) and resell (Section 2–706) and recover incidental damages (Section 2–710).

Definitional Cross References:

"Consignee". Section 7–102.

"Consignor". Section 7–102.

"Goods". Section 2–105.

"Security interest". Section 1–201.

"Seller". Section 2–103.

§ 2–708. Seller's Damages for Non-Acceptance or Repudiation

(1) Subject to subsection (2) and to the provisions of this Article with respect to proof of market price (Section 2–723), the measure of damages for non-acceptance or repudiation by the buyer is the difference between the market price at the time and place for tender and the unpaid contract price together with any incidental damages provided in this Article (Section 2–710), but less expenses saved in consequence of the buyer's breach.

(2) If the measure of damages provided in subsection (1) is inadequate to put the seller in as good a position as performance would have done then the measure of damages is the profit (including reasonable overhead) which the seller would have made from full performance by the buyer, together with any incidental damages provided in this Article (Section 2–710), due allowance for costs reasonably incurred and due credit for payments or proceeds of resale.

Definitional Cross References:

"Buyer". Section 2–103.

"Contract". Section 1–201.

"Seller". Section 2–103.

§ 2–709. Action for the Price

(1) When the buyer fails to pay the price as it becomes due the seller may recover, together with any incidental damages under the next section, the price

399

(a) of goods accepted or of conforming goods lost or damaged within a commercially reasonable time after risk of their loss has passed to the buyer; and

(b) of goods identified to the contract if the seller is unable after reasonable effort to resell them at a reasonable price or the circumstances reasonably indicate that such effort will be unavailing.

(2) Where the seller sues for the price he must hold for the buyer any goods which have been identified to the contract and are still in his control except that if resale becomes possible he may resell them at any time prior to the collection of the judgment. The net proceeds of any such resale must be credited to the buyer and payment of the judgment entitles him to any goods not resold.

(3) After the buyer has wrongfully rejected or revoked acceptance of the goods or has failed to make a payment due or has repudiated (Section 2–610), a seller who is held not entitled to the price under this section shall nevertheless be awarded damages for non-acceptance under the preceding section.

Definitional Cross References:

"Action". Section 1–201.

"Buyer". Section 2–103.

"Conforming". Section 2–106.

"Contract". Section 1–201.

"Goods". Section 2–105.

"Seller". Section 2–103.

§ 2–710. Seller's Incidental Damages

Incidental damages to an aggrieved seller include any commercially reasonable charges, expenses or commissions incurred in stopping delivery, in the transportation, care and custody of goods after the buyer's breach, in connection with return or resale of the goods or otherwise resulting from the breach.

Definitional Cross References:

"Aggrieved party". Section 1–201.

"Buyer". Section 2–103.

"Goods". Section 2–105.

"Seller". Section 2–103.

§ 2–711. Buyer's Remedies in General; Buyer's Security Interest in Rejected Goods

(1) Where the seller fails to make delivery or repudiates or the buyer rightfully rejects or justifiably revokes acceptance then with respect to any goods involved, and with respect to the whole if the breach goes to the whole contract (Section 2–612), the buyer may cancel and whether or not he has done so may in addition to recovering so much of the price as has been paid

(a) "cover" and have damages under the next section as to all the goods affected whether or not they have been identified to the contract; or

(b) recover damages for non-delivery as provided in this Article (Section 2–713).

(2) Where the seller fails to deliver or repudiates the buyer may also

(a) if the goods have been identified recover them as provided in this Article (Section 2–502); or

(b) in a proper case obtain specific performance or replevy the goods as provided in this Article (Section 2–716).

(3) On rightful rejection or justifiable revocation of acceptance a buyer has a security interest in goods in his possession or control for any payments made on their price and any expenses reasonably incurred in their inspection, receipt, transportation, care and custody and may hold such goods and resell them in like manner as an aggrieved seller (Section 2–706).

Definitional Cross References:

"Aggrieved party". Section 1–201.

"Buyer". Section 2–103.

"Cancellation". Section 2–106.

"Contract". Section 1–201.

"Cover". Section 2–712.

"Goods". Section 2–105.

"Notifies". Section 1–202.

"Receipt" of goods. Section 2–103.

"Remedy". Section 1–201.

"Security interest". Section 1–201.

"Seller". Section 2–103.

§ 2–712. "Cover"; Buyer's Procurement of Substitute Goods

(1) After a breach within the preceding section the buyer may "cover" by making in good faith and without unreasonable delay any reasonable purchase of or contract to purchase goods in substitution for those due from the seller.

(2) The buyer may recover from the seller as damages the difference between the cost of cover and the contract price together with any incidental or consequential damages as hereinafter defined (Section 2–715), but less expenses saved in consequence of the seller's breach.

(3) Failure of the buyer to effect cover within this section does not bar him from any other remedy.

Official Comment

Prior Uniform Statutory Provision: None.

Purposes:

1. This section provides the buyer with a remedy aimed at enabling him to obtain the goods he needs thus meeting his essential need. This remedy is the buyer's equivalent of the seller's right to resell.

2. The definition of "cover" under subsection (1) envisages a series of contracts or sales, as well as a single

contract or sale; goods not identical with those involved but commercially usable as reasonable substitutes under the circumstances of the particular case; and contracts on credit or delivery terms differing from the contract in breach, but again reasonable under the circumstances. The test of proper cover is whether at the time and place the buyer acted in good faith and in a reasonable manner, and it is immaterial that hindsight may later prove that the method of cover used was not the cheapest or most effective.

The requirement that the buyer must cover "without unreasonable delay" is not intended to limit the time necessary for him to look around and decide as to how he may best effect cover. The test here is similar to that generally used in this Article as to reasonable time and seasonable action.

3.   Subsection (3) expresses the policy that cover is not a mandatory remedy for the buyer. The buyer is always free to choose between cover and damages for non-delivery under the next section.

However, this subsection must be read in conjunction with the section which limits the recovery of consequential damages to such as could not have been obviated by cover. Moreover, the operation of the section on specific performance of contracts for "unique" goods must be considered in this connection for availability of the goods to the particular buyer for his particular needs is the test for that remedy and inability to cover is made an express condition to the right of the buyer to replevy the goods.

4.   This section does not limit cover to merchants, in the first instance. It is the vital and important remedy for the consumer buyer as well. Both are free to use cover: the domestic or non-merchant consumer is required only to act in normal good faith while the merchant buyer must also observe all reasonable commercial standards of fair dealing in the trade, since this falls within the definition of good faith on his part.

Cross References:

Point 1: Section 2–706.

Point 2: Section 1–204.

Point 3: Sections 2–713, 2–715 and 2–716.

Point 4: Section 1–203.

Definitional Cross References:

"Buyer". Section 2–103.

"Contract". Section 1–201.

"Good faith". Section 1–201.

"Goods". Section 2–105.

"Purchase". Section 1–201.

"Remedy". Section 1–201.

"Seller". Section 2–103.

§ 2–713.   Buyer's Damages for Non-Delivery or Repudiation

(1)   Subject to the provisions of this Article with respect to proof of market price (Section 2–723), the measure of damages for non-delivery or repudiation by the seller is the difference between the market price at the time when the buyer learned of the breach and the contract price together with any incidental and consequential damages provided in this Article (Section 2–715), but less expenses saved in consequence of the seller's breach.

(2)   Market price is to be determined as of the place for tender or, in cases of rejection after arrival or revocation of acceptance, as of the place of arrival.

Official Comment

Prior Uniform Statutory Provision: Section 67(3), Uniform Sales Act.

Changes: Rewritten.

Purposes of Changes: To clarify the former rule so that:

1. The general baseline adopted in this section uses as a yardstick the market in which the buyer would have obtained cover had he sought that relief. So the place for measuring damages is the place of tender (or the place of arrival if the goods are rejected or their acceptance is revoked after reaching their destination) and the crucial time is the time at which the buyer learns of the breach.

2. The market or current price to be used in comparison with the contract price under this section is the price for goods of the same kind and in the same branch of trade.

3. When the current market price under this section is difficult to prove the section on determination and proof of market price is available to permit a showing of a comparable market price or, where no market price is available, evidence of spot sale prices is proper. Where the unavailability of a market price is caused by a scarcity of goods of the type involved, a good case is normally made for specific performance under this Article. Such scarcity conditions, moreover, indicate that the price has risen and under the section providing for liberal administration of remedies, opinion evidence as to the value of the goods would be admissible in the absence of a market price and a liberal construction of allowable consequential damages should also result.

4. This section carries forward the standard rule that the buyer must deduct from his damages any expenses saved as a result of the breach.

5. The present section provides a remedy which is completely alternative to cover under the preceding section and applies only when and to the extent that the buyer has not covered.

Cross References:

Point 3: Sections 1–106, 2–716 and 2–723.

Point 5: Section 2–712.

Definitional Cross References:

"Buyer". Section 2–103.

"Contract". Section 1–201.

"Seller". Section 2–103.

§ 2–714. Buyer's Damages for Breach in Regard to Accepted Goods

(1) Where the buyer has accepted goods and given notification (subsection (3) of Section 2–607) he may recover as damages for any non-conformity of tender the loss resulting in the ordinary course of events from the seller's breach as determined in any manner which is reasonable.

(2) The measure of damages for breach of warranty is the difference at the time and place of acceptance between the value of the goods accepted and the value they would have had if they had been as warranted, unless special circumstances show proximate damages of a different amount.

(3) In a proper case any incidental and consequential damages under the next section may also be recovered.

Definitional Cross References:

"Buyer". Section 2–103.

"Conform". Section 2–106.

"Goods". Section 1–201.

"Notification". Section 1–202.

"Seller". Section 2–103.

§ 2–715. Buyer's Incidental and Consequential Damages

(1) Incidental damages resulting from the seller's breach include expenses reasonably incurred in inspection, receipt, transportation and care and custody of goods rightfully rejected, any commercially reasonable charges, expenses or commissions in connection with effecting cover and any other reasonable expense incident to the delay or other breach.

(2) Consequential damages resulting from the seller's breach include

(a) any loss resulting from general or particular requirements and needs of which the seller at the time of contracting had reason to know and which could not reasonably be prevented by cover or otherwise; and

(b) injury to person or property proximately resulting from any breach of warranty.

Official Comment

Purposes of Changes and New Matter:

1. Subsection (1) is intended to provide reimbursement for the buyer who incurs reasonable expenses in connection with the handling of rightfully rejected goods or goods whose acceptance may be justifiably revoked, or in connection with effecting cover where the breach of the contract lies in nonconformity or non-delivery of the goods. The incidental damages listed are not intended to be exhaustive but are merely illustrative of the typical kinds of incidental damage.

2. Subsection (2) operates to allow the buyer, in an appropriate case, any consequential damages which are the result of the seller's breach. The "tacit agreement" test for the recovery of consequential damages is rejected. Although the older rule at common law which made the seller liable for all consequential damages of which he had "reason to know" in advance is followed, the liberality of that rule is modified by refusing to permit recovery unless the buyer could not reasonably have prevented the loss by cover or otherwise. Subparagraph (2) carries forward the provisions of the prior uniform statutory provision as to consequential damages resulting from breach of warranty, but modifies the rule by requiring first that the buyer attempt to minimize his damages in good faith, either by cover or otherwise.

3. In the absence of excuse under the section on merchant's excuse by failure of presupposed conditions, the seller is liable for consequential damages in all cases where he had reason to know of the buyer's general or particular requirements at the time of contracting. It is not necessary that there be a conscious acceptance of an insurer's liability on the seller's part, nor is his obligation for consequential damages limited to cases in which he fails to use due effort in good faith.

Particular needs of the buyer must generally be made known to the seller while general needs must rarely be made known to charge the seller with knowledge.

Any seller who does not wish to take the risk of consequential damages has available the section on contractual limitation of remedy.

4. The burden of proving the extent of loss incurred by way of consequential damage is on the buyer, but the section on liberal administration of remedies rejects any doctrine of certainty which requires almost mathematical precision in the proof of loss. Loss may be determined in any manner which is reasonable under the circumstances.

5. Subsection (2)(b) states the usual rule as to breach of warranty, allowing recovery for injuries "proximately" resulting from the breach. Where the injury involved follows the use of goods without discovery of the defect causing the damage, the question of "proximate" cause turns on whether it was reasonable for the buyer to use the goods without such inspection as would have revealed the defects. If it was not reasonable for him to do so, or if he did in fact discover the defect prior to his use, the injury would not proximately result from the breach of warranty.

6. In the case of sale of wares to one in the business of reselling them, resale is one of the requirements of which the seller has reason to know within the meaning of subsection (2)(a).

Definitional Cross References:

"Cover". Section 2–712.

"Goods". Section 1–201.

"Person". Section 1–201.

"Receipt" of goods. Section 2–103.

"Seller". Section 2–103.

§ 2–716. Buyer's Right to Specific Performance or Replevin

(1) Specific performance may be decreed where the goods are unique or in other proper circumstances.

(2) The decree for specific performance may include such terms and conditions as to payment of the price, damages, or other relief as the court may deem just.

(3) The buyer has a right of replevin for goods identified to the contract if after reasonable effort he is unable to effect cover for such goods or the circumstances reasonably indicate that such effort will be unavailing or if the goods have been shipped under reservation and satisfaction of the security interest in them has been made or tendered. In the case of goods bought for personal, family, or household purposes, the buyer's right of replevin vests upon acquisition of a special property, even if the seller had not then repudiated or failed to deliver.

Official Comment

Prior Uniform Statutory Provision: Section 68, Uniform Sales Act.

Changes: Rephrased.

Purposes of Changes: To make it clear that:

1. The present section continues in general prior policy as to specific performance and injunction against breach. However, without intending to impair in any way the exercise of the court's sound discretion in the matter, this Article seeks to further a more liberal attitude than some courts have shown in connection with the specific performance of contracts of sale.

2. In view of this Article's emphasis on the commercial feasibility of

replacement, a new concept of what are "unique" goods is introduced under this section. Specific performance is no longer limited to goods which are already specific or ascertained at the time of contracting. The test of uniqueness under this section must be made in terms of the total situation which characterizes the contract. Output and requirements contracts involving a particular or peculiarly available source or market present today the typical commercial specific performance situation, as contrasted with contracts for the sale of heirlooms or priceless works of art which were usually involved in the older cases. However, uniqueness is not the sole basis of the remedy under this section for the relief may also be granted "in other proper circumstances" and inability to cover is strong evidence of "other proper circumstances".

3.   The legal remedy of replevin is given to the buyer in cases in which cover is reasonably unavailable and goods have been identified to the contract. This is in addition to the buyer's right to recover identified goods under Section 2–502. For consumer goods, the buyer's right to replevin vests upon the buyer's acquisition of a special property, which occurs upon identification of the goods to the contract. See Section 2–501. Inasmuch as a secured party normally acquires no greater rights in its collateral that its debtor had or had power to convey, see Section 2–403(1) (first sentence), a buyer who acquires a right of replevin under subsection (3) will take free of a security interest created by the seller if it attaches to the goods after the goods have been identified to the contract. The buyer will take free, even if the buyer does not buy in ordinary course and even if the security interest is perfected. Of course, to the extent that the buyer pays the price after the security interest attaches, the payments will constitute proceeds of the security interest.

4.   This section is intended to give the buyer rights to the goods comparable to the seller's rights to the price.

5.   If a negotiable document of title is outstanding, the buyer's right of replevin relates of course to the document not directly to the goods. See Article 7, especially Section 7–602.

Cross References:

Point 3: Section 2–502.

Point 4: Section 2–709.

Point 5: Article 7.

Definitional Cross References:

"Buyer". Section 2–103.

"Goods". Section 1–201.

"Rights". Section 1–201.

§ 2–717.   Deduction of Damages From the Price

The buyer on notifying the seller of his intention to do so may deduct all or any part of the damages resulting from any breach of the contract from any part of the price still due under the same contract.

Definitional Cross References: "Notifies". Section 1–202.

"Buyer". Section 2–103.

§ 2–718.   Liquidation or Limitation of Damages; Deposits

(1)   Damages for breach by either party may be liquidated in the agreement but only at an amount which is reasonable in the light of the anticipated or actual harm caused by the breach, the difficulties of proof of loss, and the inconvenience or non-feasibility of otherwise obtaining an

adequate remedy. A term fixing unreasonably large liquidated damages is void as a penalty.

(2)   Where the seller justifiably withholds delivery of goods because of the buyer's breach, the buyer is entitled to restitution of any amount by which the sum of his payments exceeds

(a)   the amount to which the seller is entitled by virtue of terms liquidating the seller's damages in accordance with subsection (1), or

(b)   in the absence of such terms, twenty per cent of the value of the total performance for which the buyer is obligated under the contract or $500, whichever is smaller.

(3)   The buyer's right to restitution under subsection (2) is subject to offset to the extent that the seller establishes

(a)   a right to recover damages under the provisions of this Article other than subsection (1), and

(b)   the amount or value of any benefits received by the buyer directly or indirectly by reason of the contract.

(4)   Where a seller has received payment in goods their reasonable value or the proceeds of their resale shall be treated as payments for the purposes of subsection (2); but if the seller has notice of the buyer's breach before reselling goods received in part performance, his resale is subject to the conditions laid down in this Article on resale by an aggrieved seller (Section 2–706).

Definitional Cross References:

"Aggrieved party". Section 1–201.	"Goods". Section 2–105.
"Agreement". Section 1–201.	"Action". 1–201.
"Buyer". Section 2–103.	"Seller". Section 2–103.
	"Term". Section 1–201.

§ 2–719.   Contractual Modification or Limitation of Remedy

(1)   Subject to the provisions of subsections (2) and (3) of this section and of the preceding section on liquidation and limitation of damages,

(a)   the agreement may provide for remedies in addition to or in substitution for those provided in this Article and may limit or alter the measure of damages recoverable under this Article, as by limiting the buyer's remedies to return of the goods and repayment of the price or to repair and replacement of non-conforming goods or parts; and

(b)   resort to a remedy as provided is optional unless the remedy is expressly agreed to be exclusive, in which case it is the sole remedy.

(2)   Where circumstances cause an exclusive or limited remedy to fail of its essential purpose, remedy may be had as provided in this Act.

(3)   Consequential damages may be limited or excluded unless the limitation or exclusion is unconscionable. Limitation of consequential

damages for injury to the person in the case of consumer goods is prima facie unconscionable but limitation of damages where the loss is commercial is not.

Official Comment

Purposes:

1.   Under this section parties are left free to shape their remedies to their particular requirements and reasonable agreements limiting or modifying remedies are to be given effect.

However, it is of the very essence of a sales contract that at least minimum adequate remedies be available. If the parties intend to conclude a contract for sale within this Article they must accept the legal consequence that there be at least a fair quantum of remedy for breach of the obligations or duties outlined in the contract. Thus any clause purporting to modify or limit the remedial provisions of this Article in an unconscionable manner is subject to deletion and in that event the remedies made available by this Article are applicable as if the stricken clause had never existed. Similarly, under subsection (2), where an apparently fair and reasonable clause because of circumstances fails in its purpose or operates to deprive either party of the substantial value of the bargain, it must give way to the general remedy provisions of this Article.

2.   Subsection (1)(b) creates a presumption that clauses prescribing remedies are cumulative rather than exclusive. If the parties intend the term to describe the sole remedy under the contract, this must be clearly expressed.

3.   Subsection (3) recognizes the validity of clauses limiting or excluding consequential damages but makes it clear that they may not operate in an unconscionable manner. Actually such terms are merely an allocation of unknown or undeterminable risks. The seller in all cases is free to disclaim warranties in the manner provided in Section 2–316.

Definitional Cross References:

"Agreement". Section 1–201.

"Buyer". Section 2–103.

"Conforming". Section 2–106.

"Contract". Section 1–201.

"Goods". Section 2–105.

"Remedy". Section 1–201.

"Seller". Section 2–103.

§ 2–720.   Effect of "Cancellation" or "Rescission" on Claims for Antecedent Breach

Unless the contrary intention clearly appears, expressions of "cancellation" or "rescission" of the contract or the like shall not be construed as a renunciation or discharge of any claim in damages for an antecedent breach.

Definitional Cross References:

"Cancellation". Section 2–106.

"Contract". Section 1–201.

§ 2–721.   Remedies for Fraud

Remedies for material misrepresentation or fraud include all remedies available under this Article for non-fraudulent breach. Neither rescission or a claim for rescission of the contract for sale nor rejection or return of the goods shall bar or be deemed inconsistent with a claim for damages or other remedy.

Definitional Cross References:

"Contract for sale". Section 2–106.

"Goods". Section 1–201.

"Remedy". Section 1–201.

§ 2–722. Who Can Sue Third Parties for Injury to Goods

Where a third party so deals with goods which have been identified to a contract for sale as to cause actionable injury to a party to that contract

    (a) a right of action against the third party is in either party to the contract for sale who has title to or a security interest or a special property or an insurable interest in the goods; and if the goods have been destroyed or converted a right of action is also in the party who either bore the risk of loss under the contract for sale or has since the injury assumed that risk as against the other;

    (b) if at the time of the injury the party plaintiff did not bear the risk of loss as against the other party to the contract for sale and there is no arrangement between them for disposition of the recovery, his suit or settlement is, subject to his own interest, as a fiduciary for the other party to the contract;

    (c) either party may with the consent of the other sue for the benefit of whom it may concern.

Definitional Cross References:

"Action". Section 1–201.

"Buyer". Section 2–103.

"Contract for sale". Section 2–106.

"Goods". Section 2–105.

"Party". Section 1–201.

"Rights". Section 1–201.

"Security interest". Section 1–201.

§ 2–723. Proof of Market Price: Time and Place

    (1) If an action based on anticipatory repudiation comes to trial before the time for performance with respect to some or all of the goods, any damages based on market price (Section 2–708 or Section 2–713) shall be determined according to the price of such goods prevailing at the time when the aggrieved party learned of the repudiation.

    (2) If evidence of a price prevailing at the times or places described in this Article is not readily available the price prevailing within any reasonable time before or after the time described or at any other place which in commercial judgment or under usage of trade would serve as a reasonable substitute for the one described may be used, making any proper allowance for the cost of transporting the goods to or from such other place.

    (3) Evidence of a relevant price prevailing at a time or place other than the one described in this Article offered by one party is not admis-

sible unless and until he has given the other party such notice as the court finds sufficient to prevent unfair surprise.

Definitional Cross References:

"Action". Section 1–201.

"Aggrieved party". Section 1–201.

"Goods". Section 2–105.

"Notifies". Section 1–202.

"Party". Section 1–201.

"Reasonable time". Section 1–205.

"Usage of trade". Section 1–303.

§ 2–724. Admissibility of Market Quotations

Whenever the prevailing price or value of any goods regularly bought and sold in any established commodity market is in issue, reports in official publications or trade journals or in newspapers or periodicals of general circulation published as the reports of such market shall be admissible in evidence. The circumstances of the preparation of such a report may be shown to affect its weight but not its admissibility.

Definitional Cross Reference:

"Goods". Section 2–105.

§ 2–725. Statute of Limitations in Contracts for Sale

(1) An action for breach of any contract for sale must be commenced within four years after the cause of action has accrued. By the original agreement the parties may reduce the period of limitation to not less than one year but may not extend it.

(2) A cause of action accrues when the breach occurs, regardless of the aggrieved party's lack of knowledge of the breach. A breach of warranty occurs when tender of delivery is made, except that where a warranty explicitly extends to future performance of the goods and discovery of the breach must await the time of such performance the cause of action accrues when the breach is or should have been discovered.

(3) Where an action commenced within the time limited by subsection (1) is so terminated as to leave available a remedy by another action for the same breach such other action may be commenced after the expiration of the time limited and within six months after the termination of the first action unless the termination resulted from voluntary discontinuance or from dismissal for failure or neglect to prosecute.

(4) This section does not alter the law on tolling of the statute of limitations nor does it apply to causes of action which have accrued before this Act becomes effective.

Definitional Cross References:

"Action". Section 1–201.

"Aggrieved party". Section 1–201.

"Agreement". Section 1–201.

"Contract for sale". Section 2–106.

"Goods". Section 2–105.

"Party". Section 1–201.

"Remedy". Section 1–201.

"Term". Section 1–201.

"Termination". Section 2–106.

ARTICLE 3.   NEGOTIABLE INSTRUMENTS

(SELECTED SECTIONS)

§ 3–303.   Value and Consideration

(a)   An instrument is issued or transferred for value if:

(1)   the instrument is issued or transferred for a promise of performance, to the extent the promise has been performed;

(2)   the transferee acquires a security interest or other lien in the instrument other than a lien obtained by judicial proceeding;

(3)   the instrument is issued or transferred as payment of, or as security for, an antecedent claim against any person, whether or not the claim is due;

(4)   the instrument is issued or transferred in exchange for a negotiable instrument; or

(5)   the instrument is issued or transferred in exchange for the incurring of an irrevocable obligation to a third party by the person taking the instrument.

(b)   "Consideration" means any consideration sufficient to support a simple contract. The drawer or maker of an instrument has a defense if the instrument is issued without consideration. If an instrument is issued for a promise of performance, the issuer has a defense to the extent performance of the promise is due and the promise has not been performed. If an instrument is issued for value as stated in subsection (a), the instrument is also issued for consideration.

§ 3–311.   Accord and Satisfaction by Use of Instrument

(a)   If a person against whom a claim is asserted proves that (i) that person in good faith tendered an instrument to the claimant as full satisfaction of the claim, (ii) the amount of the claim was unliquidated or subject to a bona fide dispute, and (iii) the claimant obtained payment of the instrument, the following subsections apply.

(b)   Unless subsection (c) applies, the claim is discharged if the person against whom the claim is asserted proves that the instrument or an accompanying written communication contained a conspicuous statement to the effect that the instrument was tendered as full satisfaction of the claim.

(c)   Subject to subsection (d), a claim is not discharged under subsection (b) if either of the following applies:

(1)   The claimant, if an organization, proves that (i) within a reasonable time before the tender, the claimant sent a conspicuous state-

ment to the person against whom the claim is asserted that communications concerning disputed debts, including an instrument tendered as full satisfaction of a debt, are to be sent to a designated person, office, or place, and (ii) the instrument or accompanying communication was not received by that designated person, office, or place.

(2) The claimant, whether or not an organization, proves that within 90 days after payment of the instrument, the claimant tendered repayment of the amount of the instrument to the person against whom the claim is asserted. This paragraph does not apply if the claimant is an organization that sent a statement complying with paragraph (1) (i).

(d) A claim is discharged if the person against whom the claim is asserted proves that within a reasonable time before collection of the instrument was initiated, the claimant, or an agent of the claimant having direct responsibility with respect to the disputed obligation, knew that the instrument was tendered in full satisfaction of the claim.

ARTICLE 9

(SELECTED SECTIONS ADDRESSING
ASSIGNMENT OF RIGHTS TO PAYMENT)

§ 9–102. Definitions and Index of Definitions.

(a) [Article 9 definitions.] In this article:

. . .

(2) "Account", except as used in "account for", means a right to payment of a monetary obligation, whether or not earned by performance, (i) for property that has been or is to be sold, leased, licensed, assigned, or otherwise disposed of, (ii) for services rendered or to be rendered, (iii) for a policy of insurance issued or to be issued, (iv) for a secondary obligation incurred or to be incurred, (v) for energy provided or to be provided, (vi) for the use or hire of a vessel under a charter or other contract, (vii) arising out of the use of a credit or charge card or information contained on or for use with the card, or (viii) as winnings in a lottery or other game of chance operated or sponsored by a State, governmental unit of a State, or person licensed or authorized to operate the game by a State or governmental unit of a State. The term includes health-care-insurance receivables. The term does not include (i) rights to payment evidenced by chattel paper or an instrument, (ii) commercial tort claims, (iii) deposit accounts, (iv) investment property, (v) letter-of-credit rights or letters of credit, or (vi) rights to payment for money or funds advanced or sold, other than rights arising out of the use of a credit or charge card or information contained on or for use with the card.

(3) "Account debtor" means a person obligated on an account, chattel paper, or general intangible. The term does not include persons obligated to pay a negotiable instrument, even if the instrument constitutes part of chattel paper.

. . .

(7) "Authenticate" means:

(A) to sign; or

(B) to execute or otherwise adopt a symbol, or encrypt or similarly process a record in whole or in part, with the present intent of the authenticating person to identify the person and adopt or accept a record with present intent to adopt or accept a record, to attach to or logically associate with the record an electronic sound, symbol, or process.

. . .

(11) "Chattel paper" means a record or records that evidence both a monetary obligation and a security interest in specific goods, a security interest in specific goods and software used in the goods, a security interest in specific goods and license of software used in the goods, a lease of specific goods, or a lease of specific goods and license of software used in the goods. In this paragraph, "monetary obligation" means a monetary obligation secured by the goods or owed under a lease of the goods and includes a monetary obligation with respect to software used in the goods. The term does not include (i) charters or other contracts involving the use or hire of a vessel or (ii) records that evidence a right to payment arising out of the use of a credit or charge card or information contained on or for use with the card. If a transaction is evidenced by records that include an instrument or series of instruments, the group of records taken together constitutes chattel paper.

(12) "Collateral" means the property subject to a security interest or agricultural lien. The term includes:

(A)　proceeds to which a security interest attaches;

(B)　accounts, chattel paper, payment intangibles, and promissory notes that have been sold; and

(C)　goods that are the subject of a consignment.

. . .

(28) "Debtor" means:

(A)　a person having an interest, other than a security interest or other lien, in the collateral, whether or not the person is an obligor;

(B)　a seller of accounts, chattel paper, payment intangibles, or promissory notes; or

(C)　a consignee.

. . .

(42) "General intangible" means any personal property, including things in action, other than accounts, chattel paper, commercial tort claims, deposit accounts, documents, goods, instruments, investment property, letter-of-credit rights, letters of credit, money, and oil, gas, or other minerals before extraction. The term includes payment intangibles and software.

. . .

(46) "Health-care-insurance receivable" means an interest in or claim under a policy of insurance which is a right to payment of a monetary obligation for health-care goods or services provided or to be provided.

(47) "Instrument" means a negotiable instrument or any other writing that evidences a right to the payment of a monetary obligation, is not itself a security agreement or lease, and is of a type that in ordinary course of business is transferred by delivery with any necessary indorsement or assignment. The term does not include (i) investment property, (ii) letters of credit, or (iii) writings that evidence a right to payment arising out of the use of a credit or charge card or information contained on or for use with the card.

. . .

(61) "Payment intangible" means a general intangible under which the account debtor's principal obligation is a monetary obligation.

. . .

(65) "Promissory note" means an instrument that evidences a promise to pay a monetary obligation, does not evidence an order to pay, and does not contain an acknowledgment by a bank that the bank has received for deposit a sum of money or funds.

. . .

(70) "Record", except as used in "for record", "of record", "record or legal title", and "record owner", means information that is inscribed on a tangible medium or which is stored in an electronic or other medium and is retrievable in perceivable form.

. . .

(73) "Secured party" means:

(A) a person in whose favor a security interest is created or provided for under a security agreement, whether or not any obligation to be secured is outstanding;

(B) a person that holds an agricultural lien;

(C) a consignor;

(D) a person to which accounts, chattel paper, payment intangibles, or promissory notes have been sold;

(E) a trustee, indenture trustee, agent, collateral agent, or other representative in whose favor a security interest or agricultural lien is created or provided for; or

(F) a person that holds a security interest arising under Section 2–401, 2–505, 2–711(3), 2A–508(5), 4–210, or 5–118.

(74) "Security agreement" means an agreement that creates or provides for a security interest.

. . .

(79) "Tangible chattel paper" means chattel paper evidenced by a record or records consisting of information that is inscribed on a tangible medium.

§ 9–109.   Scope.

(a)   **[General scope of article.]** Except as otherwise provided in subsections (c) and (d), this article applies to:

(1)   a transaction, regardless of its form, that creates a security interest in personal property or fixtures by contract;

(2)   an agricultural lien;

(3)   a sale of accounts, chattel paper, payment intangibles, or promissory notes;

(4)   a consignment;

(5)   a security interest arising under Section 2–401, 2–505, 2–711(3), or 2A–508(5), as provided in Section 9–110; and

(6)   a security interest arising under Section 4–210 or 5–118.

(b)   **[Security interest in secured obligation.]** The application of this article to a security interest in a secured obligation is not affected by the fact that the obligation is itself secured by a transaction or interest to which this article does not apply.

(c)   **[Extent to which article does not apply.]** This article does not apply to the extent that:

(1)   a statute, regulation, or treaty of the United States preempts this article;

(2)   another statute of this State expressly governs the creation, perfection, priority, or enforcement of a security interest created by this State or a governmental unit of this State;

(3)   a statute of another State, a foreign country, or a governmental unit of another State or a foreign country, other than a statute generally applicable to security interests, expressly governs creation, perfection, priority, or enforcement of a security interest created by the State, country, or governmental unit; or

(4)   the rights of a transferee beneficiary or nominated person under a letter of credit are independent and superior under Section 5–114.

(d)   **[Inapplicability of article.]** This article does not apply to:

(1)   a landlord's lien, other than an agricultural lien;

(2)   a lien, other than an agricultural lien, given by statute or other rule of law for services or materials, but Section 9–333 applies with respect to priority of the lien;

(3) an assignment of a claim for wages, salary, or other compensation of an employee;

(4) a sale of accounts, chattel paper, payment intangibles, or promissory notes as part of a sale of the business out of which they arose;

(5) an assignment of accounts, chattel paper, payment intangibles, or promissory notes which is for the purpose of collection only;

(6) an assignment of a right to payment under a contract to an assignee that is also obligated to perform under the contract;

(7) an assignment of a single account, payment intangible, or promissory note to an assignee in full or partial satisfaction of a preexisting indebtedness;

(8) a transfer of an interest in or an assignment of a claim under a policy of insurance, other than an assignment by or to a health-care provider of a health-care-insurance receivable and any subsequent assignment of the right to payment, but Sections 9–315 and 9–322 apply with respect to proceeds and priorities in proceeds;

(9) an assignment of a right represented by a judgment, other than a judgment taken on a right to payment that was collateral;

(10) a right of recoupment or set-off, but:

(A) Section 9–340 applies with respect to the effectiveness of rights of recoupment or set-off against deposit accounts; and

(B) Section 9–404 applies with respect to defenses or claims of an account debtor;

(11) the creation or transfer of an interest in or lien on real property, including a lease or rents thereunder, except to the extent that provision is made for:

(A) liens on real property in Sections 9–203 and 9–308;

(B) fixtures in Section 9–334;

(C) fixture filings in Sections 9–501, 9–502, 9–512, 9–516, and 9–519; and

(D) security agreements covering personal and real property in Section 9–604;

(12) an assignment of a claim arising in tort, other than a commercial tort claim, but Sections 9–315 and 9–322 apply with respect to proceeds and priorities in proceeds; or

(13) an assignment of a deposit account in a consumer transaction, but Sections 9–315 and 9–322 apply with respect to proceeds and priorities in proceeds.

Official Comments

. . .

4. Sales of Accounts, Chattel Paper, Payment Intangibles, Promissory Notes, and Other Receivables. Under subsection (a)(3), as under former Section 9–102, this Article applies to sales of accounts and chattel paper. This approach generally has been successful in avoiding difficult problems of distinguishing between transactions in which a receivable secures an obligation and those in which the receivable has been sold outright. In many commercial financing transactions the distinction is blurred.

Subsection (a)(3) expands the scope of this Article by including the sale of a "payment intangible" (defined in Section 9–102 as "a general intangible under which the account debtor's principal obligation is a monetary obligation") and a "promissory note" (also defined in Section 9–102). To a considerable extent, this Article affords these transactions treatment identical to that given sales of accounts and chattel paper. In some respects, however, sales of payment intangibles and promissory notes are treated differently from sales of other receivables. See, e.g., Sections 9–309 (automatic perfection upon attachment), 9–408 (effect of restrictions on assignment). By virtue of the expanded definition of "account" (defined in Section 9–102), this Article now covers sales of (and other security interests in) "health-care-insurance receivables" (also defined in Section 9–102). Although this Article occasionally distinguishes between outright sales of receivables and sales that secure an obligation, neither this Article nor the definition of "security interest" (Section 1–201(37)) delineates how a particular transaction is to be classified. That issue is left to the courts.

5. Transfer of Ownership in Sales of Receivables. A "sale" of an account, chattel paper, a promissory note, or a payment intangible includes a sale of a right in the receivable, such as a sale of a participation interest. The term also includes the sale of an enforcement right. For example, a "[p]erson entitled to enforce" a negotiable promissory note (Section 3–301) may sell its ownership rights in the instrument. See Section 3–203, Comment 1 ("Ownership rights in instruments may be determined by principles of the law of property, independent of Article 3, which do not depend upon whether the instrument was transferred under Section 3–203."). Also, the right under Section 3–309 to enforce a lost, destroyed, or stolen negotiable promissory note may be sold to a purchaser who could enforce that right by causing the seller to provide the proof required under that section. This Article rejects decisions reaching a contrary result, e.g., *Dennis Joslin Co. v. Robinson Broadcasting*, 977 F.Supp. 491 (D.D.C.1997).

Nothing in this section or any other provision of Article 9 prevents the transfer of full and complete ownership of an account, chattel paper, an instrument, or a payment intangible in a transaction of sale. However, as mentioned in Comment 4, neither this Article nor the definition of "security interest" in Section 1–201 provides rules for distinguishing sales transactions from those that create a security interest securing an obligation. This Article applies to both types of transactions. The principal effect of this coverage is to apply this Article's perfection and priority rules to these sales transactions. Use of terminology such as "security interest," "debtor," and "collateral" is merely a drafting convention adopted to reach this end, and its use has no relevance to distinguishing sales from other transactions. See PEB Commentary No. 14.

Following a debtor's outright sale and transfer of ownership of a receivable, the debtor-seller retains no legal or equitable rights in the receivable that has been sold. See Section 9–318(a). This is so whether or not the buyer's security interest is perfected. (A security interest arising from the sale of a promissory note or payment intangible is perfected upon attachment without further action. See Section 9–309.) However, if the buyer's interest in accounts or chattel paper is unperfected, a subsequent lien creditor, perfected secured party, or qualified buyer can reach the sold receivable and achieve priority over (or take free of) the buyer's unperfected security interest under Section 9–317. This is so not because the seller of a receivable retains rights in the property sold; it does not. Nor is this so because the seller of a receivable is a "debtor" and

the buyer of a receivable is a "secured party" under this Article (they are). It is so for the simple reason that Sections 9–318(b), 9–317, and 9–322 make it so, as did former Sections 9–301 and 9–312. Because the buyer's security interest is unperfected, for purposes of determining the rights of creditors of and purchasers for value from the debtor-seller, under Section 9–318(b) the debtor-seller is deemed to have the rights and title it sold. Section 9–317 subjects the buyer's unperfected interest in accounts and chattel paper to that of the debtor-seller's lien creditor and other persons who qualify under that section.

. . .

§ 9–203. Attachment and Enforceability of Security Interest; Proceeds; Supporting Obligations; Formal Requisites.

(a)   **[Attachment.]** A security interest attaches to collateral when it becomes enforceable against the debtor with respect to the collateral, unless an agreement expressly postpones the time of attachment.

(b)   **[Enforceability.]** Except as otherwise provided in subsections (c) through (i), a security interest is enforceable against the debtor and third parties with respect to the collateral only if:

(1)   value has been given;

(2)   the debtor has rights in the collateral or the power to transfer rights in the collateral to a secured party; and

(3)   one of the following conditions is met:

(A)   the debtor has authenticated a security agreement that provides a description of the collateral and, if the security interest covers timber to be cut, a description of the land concerned;

(B)   the collateral is not a certificated security and is in the possession of the secured party under Section 9–313 pursuant to the debtor's security agreement;

(C)   the collateral is a certificated security in registered form and the security certificate has been delivered to the secured party under Section 8–301 pursuant to the debtor's security agreement; or

(D)   the collateral is deposit accounts, electronic chattel paper, investment property, or letter-of-credit rights, and the secured party has control under Section 9–104, 9–105, 9–106, or 9–107 pursuant to the debtor's security agreement.

(c)   **[Other UCC provisions.]** Subsection (b) is subject to Section 4–210 on the security interest of a collecting bank, Section 5–118 on the security interest of a letter-of-credit issuer or nominated person, Section 9–110 on a security interest arising under Article 2 or 2A, and Section 9–206 on security interests in investment property.

(d)   **[When person becomes bound by another person's security agreement.]** A person becomes bound as debtor by a security agreement entered into by another person if, by operation of law other than this article or by contract:

     (1)   the security agreement becomes effective to create a security interest in the person's property; or

     (2)   the person becomes generally obligated for the obligations of the other person, including the obligation secured under the security agreement, and acquires or succeeds to all or substantially all of the assets of the other person.

(e)   **[Effect of new debtor becoming bound.]** If a new debtor becomes bound as debtor by a security agreement entered into by another person:

     (1)   the agreement satisfies subsection (b)(3) with respect to existing or after-acquired property of the new debtor to the extent the property is described in the agreement; and

     (2)   another agreement is not necessary to make a security interest in the property enforceable.

(f)   **[Proceeds and supporting obligations.]** The attachment of a security interest in collateral gives the secured party the rights to proceeds provided by Section 9–315 and is also attachment of a security interest in a supporting obligation for the collateral.

(g)   **[Lien securing right to payment.]** The attachment of a security interest in a right to payment or performance secured by a security interest or other lien on personal or real property is also attachment of a security interest in the security interest, mortgage, or other lien.

(h)   **[Security entitlement carried in securities account.]** The attachment of a security interest in a securities account is also attachment of a security interest in the security entitlements carried in the securities account.

(i)   **[Commodity contracts carried in commodity account.]** The attachment of a security interest in a commodity account is also attachment of a security interest in the commodity contracts carried in the commodity account.

§ 9–308. When Security Interest or Agricultural Lien is Perfected; Continuity of Perfection.

(a) **[Perfection of security interest.]** Except as otherwise provided in this section and Section 9–309, a security interest is perfected if it has attached and all of the applicable requirements for perfection in Sections 9–310 through 9–316 have been satisfied. A security interest is perfected when it attaches if the applicable requirements are satisfied before the security interest attaches.

(b) **[Perfection of agricultural lien.]** An agricultural lien is perfected if it has become effective and all of the applicable requirements for perfection in Section 9–310 have been satisfied. An agricultural lien is perfected when it becomes effective if the applicable requirements are satisfied before the agricultural lien becomes effective.

(c) **[Continuous perfection; perfection by different methods.]** A security interest or agricultural lien is perfected continuously if it is originally perfected by one method under this article and is later perfected by another method under this article, without an intermediate period when it was unperfected.

(d) **[Supporting obligation.]** Perfection of a security interest in collateral also perfects a security interest in a supporting obligation for the collateral.

(e) **[Lien securing right to payment.]** Perfection of a security interest in a right to payment or performance also perfects a security interest in a security interest, mortgage, or other lien on personal or real property securing the right.

(f) **[Security entitlement carried in securities account.]** Perfection of a security interest in a securities account also perfects a security interest in the security entitlements carried in the securities account.

(g) **[Commodity contract carried in commodity account.]** Perfection of a security interest in a commodity account also perfects a security interest in the commodity contracts carried in the commodity account.

§ 9–309. Security Interest Perfected Upon Attachment.

The following security interests are perfected when they attach:

(1) a purchase-money security interest in consumer goods, except as otherwise provided in Section 9–311(b) with respect to consumer goods that are subject to a statute or treaty described in Section 9–311(a);

(2) an assignment of accounts or payment intangibles which does not by itself or in conjunction with other assignments to the same assignee transfer a significant part of the assignor's outstanding accounts or payment intangibles;

(3)   a sale of a payment intangible;

(4)   a sale of a promissory note;

(5)   a security interest created by the assignment of a health-care-insurance receivable to the provider of the health-care goods or services;

(6)   a security interest arising under Section 2–401, 2–505, 2–711(3), or 2A–508(5), until the debtor obtains possession of the collateral;

(7)   a security interest of a collecting bank arising under Section 4–210;

(8)   a security interest of an issuer or nominated person arising under Section 5–118;

(9)   a security interest arising in the delivery of a financial asset under Section 9–206(c);

(10) a security interest in investment property created by a broker or securities intermediary;

(11) a security interest in a commodity contract or a commodity account created by a commodity intermediary;

(12) an assignment for the benefit of all creditors of the transferor and subsequent transfers by the assignee thereunder;

(13) a security interest created by an assignment of a beneficial interest in a decedent's estate; and

(14) a sale by an individual of an account that is a right to payment of winnings in a lottery or other game of chance.

Official Comments

. . .

4.   **Rights to Payment.** Paragraph (2) expands upon former Section 9–302(1)(e) by affording automatic perfection to certain assignments of payment intangibles as well as accounts. The purpose of paragraph (2) is to save from ex post facto invalidation casual or isolated assignments-assignments which no one would think of filing. Any person who regularly takes assignments of any debtor's accounts or payment intangibles should file. In this connection Section 9–109(d)(4) through (7), which excludes certain transfers of accounts, chattel paper, payment intangibles, and promissory notes from this Article, should be consulted.

Paragraphs (3) and (4), which are new, afford automatic perfection to sales of payment intangibles and promissory notes, respectively. They reflect the practice under former Article 9. Under that Article, filing a financing statement did not affect the rights of a buyer of payment intangibles or promissory notes, inasmuch as the former Article did not cover those sales. To the extent that the exception in paragraph (2) covers outright sales of payment intangibles, which automatically are perfected under paragraph (3), the exception is redundant.

Paragraph (14), which is new, affords automatic perfection to sales by individuals of an "account" (as defined in Section 9–102) consisting of the right to winnings in a lottery or other game of chance. Payments on these accounts typically extend for periods of twenty years or more. It would be unduly burdensome for the secured party, who would have no other reason to maintain contact with the seller, to monitor the seller's whereabouts for such a length of time. This paragraph was added in 2001. It applies to a sale of an account described in it, even if the sale was entered into before the effective date of the paragraph. However, if the relative priorities of conflicting claims to the account were established before the paragraph took effect, Article 9 as in effect immediately prior to the date the paragraph took effect determines priority.

5. **Health-Care-Insurance Receivables.** Paragraph (5) extends automatic perfection to assignments of health-care-insurance receivables if the assignment is made to the health-care provider that provided the health-care goods or services. The primary effect is that, when an individual assigns a right to payment under an insurance policy to the person who provided health-care goods or services, the provider has no need to file a financing statement against the individual. The normal filing requirements apply to other assignments of health-care-insurance receivables covered by this Article, e.g., assignments from the health-care provider to a financer.

. . .

§ 9–310. When Filing Required to Perfect Security Interest or Agricultural Lien; Security Interests and Agricultural Liens to Which Filing Provisions Do Not Apply.

(a) **[General rule: perfection by filing.]** Except as otherwise provided in subsection (b) and Section 9–312(b), a financing statement must be filed to perfect all security interests and agricultural liens.

(b) **[Exceptions: filing not necessary.]** The filing of a financing statement is not necessary to perfect a security interest:

(1) that is perfected under Section 9–308(d), (e), (f), or (g);

(2) that is perfected under Section 9–309 when it attaches;

(3) in property subject to a statute, regulation, or treaty described in Section 9–311(a);

(4) in goods in possession of a bailee which is perfected under Section 9–312(d)(1) or (2);

(5) in certificated securities, documents, goods, or instruments which is perfected without filing or possession under Section 9–312(e), (f), or (g);

(6) in collateral in the secured party's possession under Section 9–313;

(7) in a certificated security which is perfected by delivery of the security certificate to the secured party under Section 9–313;

(8)   in deposit accounts, electronic chattel paper, investment property, or letter-of-credit rights which is perfected by control under Section 9–314;

(9)   in proceeds which is perfected under Section 9–315; or

(10) that is perfected under Section 9–316.

(c)   **[Assignment of perfected security interest.]** If a secured party assigns a perfected security interest or agricultural lien, a filing under this article is not required to continue the perfected status of the security interest against creditors of and transferees from the original debtor.

§ 9–401.   Alienability of Debtor's Rights.

(a)   **[Other law governs alienability; exceptions.]** Except as otherwise provided in subsection (b) and Sections 9–406, 9–407, 9–408, and 9–409, whether a debtor's rights in collateral may be voluntarily or involuntarily transferred is governed by law other than this article.

(b)   **[Agreement does not prevent transfer.]** An agreement between the debtor and secured party which prohibits a transfer of the debtor's rights in collateral or makes the transfer a default does not prevent the transfer from taking effect.

§ 9–403.   Agreement Not to Assert Defenses Against Assignee.

(a)   **["Value."]** In this section, "value" has the meaning provided in Section 3–303(a).

(b)   **[Agreement not to assert claim or defense.]** Except as otherwise provided in this section, an agreement between an account debtor and an assignor not to assert against an assignee any claim or defense that the account debtor may have against the assignor is enforceable by an assignee that takes an assignment:

(1)   for value;

(2)   in good faith;

(3)   without notice of a claim of a property or possessory right to the property assigned; and

(4)   without notice of a defense or claim in recoupment of the type that may be asserted against a person entitled to enforce a negotiable instrument under Section 3–305(a).

(c)   **[When subsection (b) not applicable.]** Subsection (b) does not apply to defenses of a type that may be asserted against a holder in due course of a negotiable instrument under Section 3–305(b).

(d)   **[Omission of required statement in consumer transaction.]** In a consumer transaction, if a record evidences the account debtor's obligation, law other than this article requires that the record include a statement to the effect that the rights of an assignee are subject to claims or defenses that the account debtor could assert against the original obligee, and the record does not include such a statement:

(1)   the record has the same effect as if the record included such a statement; and

(2)   the account debtor may assert against an assignee those claims and defenses that would have been available if the record included such a statement.

(e)   **[Rule for individual under other law.]** This section is subject to law other than this article which establishes a different rule for an account debtor who is an individual and who incurred the obligation primarily for personal, family, or household purposes.

(f)   **[Other law not displaced.]** Except as otherwise provided in subsection (d), this section does not displace law other than this article which gives effect to an agreement by an account debtor not to assert a claim or defense against an assignee.

Official Comments

. . .

2.   **Scope and Purpose.** Subsection (b), like former Section 9–206, generally validates an agreement between an account debtor and an assignor that the account debtor will not assert against an assignee claims and defenses that it may have against the assignor. These agreements are typical in installment sale agreements and leases. However, this section expands former Section 9–206 to apply to all account debtors; it is not limited to account debtors that have bought or leased goods. This section applies only to the obligations of an "account debtor," as defined in Section 9–102. Thus, it does not determine the circumstances under which and the extent to which a person who is obligated on a negotiable instrument is disabled from asserting claims and defenses. Rather, Article 3 must be consulted. See, e.g., Sections 3–305, 3–306. Article 3 governs even when the negotiable instrument constitutes part of chattel paper. See Section 9–102 (an obligor on a negotiable instrument constituting part of chattel paper is not an "account debtor").

3.   **Conditions of Validation; Relationship to Article 3.** Subsection (b) validates an account debtor's agreement only if the assignee takes an assignment for value, in good faith, and without notice of conflicting claims to the property assigned or of certain claims or defenses of the account debtor. Like former Section 9–206, this section is designed to put the assignee in a position that is no better and no worse than that of a holder in due course of a negotiable instrument under Article 3. However, former Section 9–206 left open certain issues, e.g., whether the section incorporated the special Article 3 definition of "value" in Section 3–303 or the generally applicable definition in Section 1–201(44). Subsection (a) addresses this question; it provides that "value" has the meaning specified in Section 3–303(a). Similarly, subsection (c) provides that subsection (b) does not validate an agreement with respect to defenses that could be asserted against a holder in due course under Section 3–305(b) (the so-called "real" defenses). In 1990, the definition of "holder in due course" (Section 3–302) and the articulation of the rights of a holder in due course (Sections 3–305 and 3–306) were revised substantially. This sec-

tion tracks more closely the rules of   . . .
Sections 3–302, 3–305, and 3–306.

§ 9–404. Rights Acquired by Assignee; Claims and Defenses Against Assignee.

(a) **[Assignee's rights subject to terms, claims, and defenses; exceptions.]** Unless an account debtor has made an enforceable agreement not to assert defenses or claims, and subject to subsections (b) through (e), the rights of an assignee are subject to:

(1) all terms of the agreement between the account debtor and assignor and any defense or claim in recoupment arising from the transaction that gave rise to the contract; and

(2) any other defense or claim of the account debtor against the assignor which accrues before the account debtor receives a notification of the assignment authenticated by the assignor or the assignee.

(b) **[Account debtor's claim reduces amount owed to assignee.]** Subject to subsection (c) and except as otherwise provided in subsection (d), the claim of an account debtor against an assignor may be asserted against an assignee under subsection (a) only to reduce the amount the account debtor owes.

(c) **[Rule for individual under other law.]** This section is subject to law other than this article which establishes a different rule for an account debtor who is an individual and who incurred the obligation primarily for personal, family, or household purposes.

(d) **[Omission of required statement in consumer transaction.]** In a consumer transaction, if a record evidences the account debtor's obligation, law other than this article requires that the record include a statement to the effect that the account debtor's recovery against an assignee with respect to claims and defenses against the assignor may not exceed amounts paid by the account debtor under the record, and the record does not include such a statement, the extent to which a claim of an account debtor against the assignor may be asserted against an assignee is determined as if the record included such a statement.

(e) **[Inapplicability to health-care-insurance receivable.]** This section does not apply to an assignment of a health-care-insurance receivable.

Official Comments

. . .

2. **Purpose; Rights of Assignee in General.** Subsection (a), like former Section 9–318(1), provides that an assignee generally takes an assignment subject to defenses and claims of an account debtor. Under subsection (a)(1), if the account debtor's defenses on an assigned claim arise from the transaction that gave rise to the contract with the assignor, it makes no difference whether the defense or claim accrues before or after the account debtor is notified of the assignment. Under subsection (a)(2), the assignee takes subject to other defenses or claims only if they ac-

crue before the account debtor has been notified of the assignment. Of course, an account debtor may waive its right to assert defenses or claims against an assignee under Section 9–403 or other applicable law. Subsection (a) tracks Section 3–305(a)(3) more closely than its predecessor.

3. **Limitation on Affirmative Claims.** Subsection (b) is new. It limits the claim that the account debtor may assert against an assignee. Borrowing from Section 3–305(a)(3) and cases construing former Section 9–318, subsection (b) generally does not afford the account debtor the right to an affirmative recovery from an assignee.

4. **Consumer Account Debtors; Relationship to Federal Trade Commission Rule.** Subsections (c) and (d) also are new. Subsection (c) makes clear that the rules of this section are subject to other law establishing special rules for consumer account debtors. An "account debtor who is an individual" as used in subsection (c) includes individuals who are jointly or jointly and severally obligated. Subsection (d) applies to rights evidenced by a record that is required to contain, but does not contain, the notice set forth in Federal Trade Commission Rule 433, 16 C.F.R. Part 433 (the "Holder-in-Due-Course Regulations"). Under subsection (d), a consumer account debtor has the same right to an affirmative recovery from an assignee of such a re-

cord as the consumer would have had against the assignee had the record contained the required notice.

5. **Scope; Application to "Account Debtor."** This section deals only with the rights and duties of "account debtors"-and for the most part only with account debtors on accounts, chattel paper, and payment intangibles. Subsection (e) provides that the obligation of an insurer with respect to a health-care-insurance receivable is governed by other law. References in this section to an "account debtor" include account debtors on collateral that is proceeds. Neither this section nor any other provision of this Article, including Sections 9–408 and 9–409, provides analogous regulation of the rights and duties of other obligors on collateral, such as the maker of a negotiable instrument (governed by Article 3), the issuer of or nominated person under a letter of credit (governed by Article 5), or the issuer of a security (governed by Article 8). Article 9 leaves those rights and duties untouched; however, Section 9–409 deals with the special case of letters of credit. When chattel paper is composed in part of a negotiable instrument, the obligor on the instrument is not an "account debtor," and Article 3 governs the rights of the assignee of the chattel paper with respect to the issues that this section addresses. See, e.g., Section 3–601 (dealing with discharge of an obligation to pay a negotiable instrument).

§ 9–406. **Discharge of Account Debtor; Notification of Assignment; Identification and Proof of Assignment; Restrictions on Assignment of Accounts, Chattel Paper, Payment Intangibles, and Promissory Notes Ineffective.**

(a) **[Discharge of account debtor; effect of notification.]** Subject to subsections (b) through (i), an account debtor on an account, chattel paper, or a payment intangible may discharge its obligation by paying the assignor until, but not after, the account debtor receives a notification, authenticated by the assignor or the assignee, that the amount due or to become due has been assigned and that payment is to be made to the assignee. After receipt of the notification, the account debtor may discharge its obligation by paying the assignee and may not discharge the obligation by paying the assignor.

(b)   **[When notification ineffective.]** Subject to subsection (h), notification is ineffective under subsection (a):

(1)   if it does not reasonably identify the rights assigned;

(2)   to the extent that an agreement between an account debtor and a seller of a payment intangible limits the account debtor's duty to pay a person other than the seller and the limitation is effective under law other than this article; or

(3)   at the option of an account debtor, if the notification notifies the account debtor to make less than the full amount of any installment or other periodic payment to the assignee, even if:

(A)   only a portion of the account, chattel paper, or payment intangible has been assigned to that assignee;

(B)   a portion has been assigned to another assignee; or

(C)   the account debtor knows that the assignment to that assignee is limited.

(c)   **[Proof of assignment.]** Subject to subsection (h), if requested by the account debtor, an assignee shall seasonably furnish reasonable proof that the assignment has been made. Unless the assignee complies, the account debtor may discharge its obligation by paying the assignor, even if the account debtor has received a notification under subsection (a).

(d)   **[Term restricting assignment generally ineffective.]** Except as otherwise provided in subsections (e) and (k) and Sections 2A–303 and 9–407, and subject to subsection (h), a term in an agreement between an account debtor and an assignor or in a promissory note is ineffective to the extent that it:

(1)   prohibits, restricts, or requires the consent of the account debtor or person obligated on the promissory note to the assignment or transfer of, or the creation, attachment, perfection, or enforcement of a security interest in, the account, chattel paper, payment intangible, or promissory note; or

(2)   provides that the assignment or transfer or the creation, attachment, perfection, or enforcement of the security interest may give rise to a default, breach, right of recoupment, claim, defense, termination, right of termination, or remedy under the account, chattel paper, payment intangible, or promissory note.

(e)   **[Inapplicability of subsection (d) to certain sales.]** Subsection (d) does not apply to the sale of a payment intangible or promissory note, other than a sale pursuant to a disposition under Section 9–610 or an acceptance of collateral under Section 9–620.

(f) **[Legal restrictions on assignment generally ineffective.]** Except as otherwise provided in subsection (k) and Sections 2A–303 and 9–407 and subject to subsections (h) and (i), a rule of law, statute, or regulation that prohibits, restricts, or requires the consent of a government, governmental body or official, or account debtor to the assignment or transfer of, or creation of a security interest in, an account or chattel paper is ineffective to the extent that the rule of law, statute, or regulation:

(1) prohibits, restricts, or requires the consent of the government, governmental body or official, or account debtor to the assignment or transfer of, or the creation, attachment, perfection, or enforcement of a security interest in the account or chattel paper; or

(2) provides that the assignment or transfer or the creation, attachment, perfection, or enforcement of the security interest may give rise to a default, breach, right of recoupment, claim, defense, termination, right of termination, or remedy under the account or chattel paper.

(g) **[Subsection (b)(3) not waivable.]** Subject to subsection (h), an account debtor may not waive or vary its option under subsection (b)(3).

(h) **[Rule for individual under other law.]** This section is subject to law other than this article which establishes a different rule for an account debtor who is an individual and who incurred the obligation primarily for personal, family, or household purposes.

(i) **[Inapplicability to health-care-insurance receivable.]** This section does not apply to an assignment of a health-care-insurance receivable.

(j) **[Section prevails over specified inconsistent law.]** This section prevails over any inconsistent provisions of the following statutes, rules, and regulations:

[List here any statutes, rules, and regulations containing provisions inconsistent with this section.]

(k) **[Inapplicability to interests in certain entities.]** Subsections (d), (f), and (j) do not apply to a security interest in an ownership interest in a general partnership, limited partnership, or limited liability company.

Official Comments

. . .

2. **Account Debtor's Right to Pay Assignor Until Notification.** Subsection (a) provides the general rule concerning an account debtor's right to pay the assignor until the account debtor receives appropriate notification. The revision makes clear that once the account debtor receives the notification, the account debtor cannot discharge its obligation by paying the assignor. It also makes explicit that payment to the assignor before notification, or payment to the assignee after notification, discharges the obligation. No change in meaning from former Section 9–318 is intended. Nothing in this section conditions the effectiveness

of a notification on the identity of the person who gives it. An account debtor that doubts whether the right to payment has been assigned may avail itself of the procedures in subsection (c). See Comment 4.

An effective notification under subsection (a) must be authenticated. This requirement normally could be satisfied by sending notification on the notifying person's letterhead or on a form on which the notifying person's name appears. In each case the printed name would be a symbol adopted by the notifying person for the purpose of identifying the person and adopting the notification. See Section 9–102 (defining "authenticate").

Subsection (a) applies only to account debtors on accounts, chattel paper, and payment intangibles. (Section 9–102 defines the term "account debtor" more broadly, to include those obligated on all general intangibles.) Although subsection (a) is more precise than its predecessor, it probably does not change the rule that applied under former Article 9. Former Section 9–318(3) referred to the account debtor's obligation to "pay," indicating that the subsection was limited to account debtors on accounts, chattel paper, and other payment obligations.

3. **Limitations on Effectiveness of Notification.** Subsection (b) contains some special rules concerning the effectiveness of a notification under subsection (a).

Subsection (b)(1) tracks former Section 9–318(3) by making ineffective a notification that does not reasonably identify the rights assigned. A reasonable identification need not identify the right to payment with specificity, but what is reasonable also is not left to the arbitrary decision of the account debtor. If an account debtor has doubt as to the adequacy of a notification, it may not be safe in disregarding the notification unless it notifies the assignee

with reasonable promptness as to the respects in which the account debtor considers the notification defective.

Subsection (b)(2), which is new, applies only to sales of payment intangibles. It makes a notification ineffective to the extent that other law gives effect to an agreement between an account debtor and a seller of a payment intangible that limits the account debtor's duty to pay a person other than the seller. Payment intangibles are substantially less fungible than accounts and chattel paper. In some (e.g., commercial bank loans), account debtors customarily and legitimately expect that they will not be required to pay any person other than the financial institution that has advanced funds.

It has become common in financing transactions to assign interests in a single obligation to more than one assignee. Requiring an account debtor that owes a single obligation to make multiple payments to multiple assignees would be unnecessarily burdensome. Thus, under subsection (b)(3), an account debtor that is notified to pay an assignee less than the full amount of any installment or other periodic payment has the option to treat the notification as ineffective, ignore the notice, and discharge the assigned obligation by paying the assignor. Some account debtors may not realize that the law affords them the right to ignore certain notices of assignment with impunity. By making the notification ineffective at the account debtor's option, subsection (b)(3) permits an account debtor to pay the assignee in accordance with the notice and thereby to satisfy its obligation pro tanto. Under subsection (g), the rights and duties created by subsection (b)(3) cannot be waived or varied.

4. **Proof of Assignment.** Subsection (c) links payment with discharge, as in subsection (a). It follows former Section 9–318(3) in referring to

the right of the account debtor to pay the assignor if the requested proof of assignment is not seasonably forthcoming. Even if the proof is not forthcoming, the notification of assignment would remain effective, so that, in the absence of reasonable proof of the assignment, the account debtor could discharge the obligation by paying either the assignee or the assignor. Of course, if the assignee did not in fact receive an assignment, the account debtor cannot discharge its obligation by paying a putative assignee who is a stranger. The observations in Comment 3 concerning the reasonableness of an identification of a right to payment also apply here. An account debtor that questions the adequacy of proof submitted by an assignor assignee would be well advised to promptly inform the assignor assignee of the defects.

An account debtor may face another problem if its obligation becomes due while the account debtor is awaiting reasonable proof of the assignment that it has requested from the assignee. This section does not excuse the account debtor from timely compliance with its obligations. Consequently, an account debtor that has received a notification of assignment and who has requested reasonable proof of the assignment may discharge its obligation by paying the assignor at the time (or even earlier if reasonably necessary to avoid risk of default) when a payment is due, even if the account debtor has not yet received a response to its request for proof. On the other hand, after requesting reasonable proof of the assignment, an account debtor may not discharge its obligation by paying the assignor substantially in advance of the time that the payment is due unless the assignee has failed to provide the proof seasonably.

5. **Contractual Restrictions on Assignment.** Former Section 9–318(4) rendered ineffective an agreement between an account debtor and

an assignor which prohibited assignment of an account (whether outright or to secure an obligation) or prohibited a security assignment of a general intangible for the payment of money due or to become due. Subsection (d) essentially follows former Section 9–318(4), but expands the rule of free assignability to chattel paper (subject to Sections 2A–303 and 9–407) and promissory notes and explicitly overrides both restrictions and prohibitions of assignment. The policies underlying the ineffectiveness of contractual restrictions under this section build on common-law developments that essentially have eliminated legal restrictions on assignments of rights to payment as security and other assignments of rights to payment such as accounts and chattel paper. Any that might linger for accounts and chattel paper are addressed by new subsection (f). See Comment 6.

Former Section 9–318(4) did not apply to a sale of a payment intangible (as described in the former provision, "a general intangible for money due or to become due") but did apply to an assignment of a payment intangible for security. Subsection (e) continues this approach and also makes subsection (d) inapplicable to sales of promissory notes. Section 9–408 addresses anti-assignment clauses with respect to sales of payment intangibles and promissory notes.

Like former Section 9–318(4), subsection (d) provides that anti-assignment clauses are "ineffective." The quoted term means that the clause is of no effect whatsoever; the clause does not prevent the assignment from taking effect between the parties and the prohibited assignment does not constitute a default under the agreement between the account debtor and assignor. However, subsection (d) does not override terms that do not directly prohibit, restrict, or require consent to an assignment but which might, nonetheless, present a practical impairment of the assignment. Properly read, however, subsection (d) reaches only covenants that prohibit, restrict, or require consents to assignments; it does not override all terms that might "impair" an assignment in fact.

Example: Buyer enters into an agreement with Seller to buy equipment that Seller is to manufacture according to Buyer's specifications. Buyer agrees to make a series of prepayments during the construction process. In return, Seller agrees to set aside the prepaid funds in a special account and to use the funds solely for the manufacture of the designated equipment. Seller also agrees that it will not assign any of its rights under the sale agreement with Buyer. Nevertheless, Seller grants to Secured Party a security interest in its accounts. Seller's anti-assignment agreement is ineffective under subsection (d); its agreement concerning the use of prepaid funds, which is not a restriction or prohibition on assignment, is not. However, if Secured Party notifies Buyer to make all future payments directly to Secured Party, Buyer will be obliged to do so under subsection (a) if it wishes the payments to discharge its obligation. Unless Secured Party releases the funds to Seller so that Seller can comply with its use-of-funds covenant, Seller will be in breach of that covenant.

In the example, there appears to be a plausible business purpose for the use-of-funds covenant. However, a court may conclude that a covenant with no business purpose other than imposing an impediment to an assignment actually is a direct restriction that is rendered ineffective by subsection (d).

6. **Legal Restrictions on Assignment.** Former Section 9–318(4), like subsection (d) of this section, addressed only contractual restrictions on assignment. The former section was grounded on the reality that legal, as opposed to contractual, restrictions on assignments of rights to payment had largely disappeared. New subsection (f) codifies this principle of free assignability for accounts and chattel paper. For the most part the discussion of contractual restrictions in Comment 5 applies as well to legal restrictions rendered ineffective under subsection (f).

7. **Multiple Assignments.** This section, like former Section 9–318, is not a complete codification of the law of assignments of rights to payment. In particular, it is silent concerning many of the ramifications for an account debtor in cases of multiple assignments of the same right. For example, an assignor might assign the same receivable to multiple assignees (which assignments could be either inadvertent or wrongful). Or, the assignor could assign the receivable to assignee-1, which then might re-assign it to assignee-2, and so forth. The rights and duties of an account debtor in the face of multiple assignments and in other circumstances not resolved in the statutory text are left to the common-law rules. See, e.g., Restatement (2d), Contracts §§ 338(3), 339. The failure of former Article 9 to codify these rules does not appear to have caused problems.

8. **Consumer Account Debtors.** Subsection (h) is new. It makes clear that the rules of this section are subject to other law establishing special rules for consumer account debtors.

9. **Account Debtors on Health-Care-Insurance Receivables.** Subsection (i) also is new. The obligation of an insurer with respect to a health-care-insurance receivable is governed by other law. Section 9–408 addresses contractual and legal restrictions on the assignment of a health-care-insurance receivable.

§ 9–408. Restrictions on Assignment of Promissory Notes, Health-Care-Insurance Receivables, and Certain General Intangibles Ineffective.

(a) **[Term restricting assignment generally ineffective.]** Except as otherwise provided in subsection (b), a term in a promissory note or in an agreement between an account debtor and a debtor which relates to a health-care-insurance receivable or a general intangible, including a contract, permit, license, or franchise, and which term prohibits, restricts, or requires the consent of the person obligated on the promissory note or the account debtor to, the assignment or transfer of, or creation, attachment, or perfection of a security interest in, the promissory note, health-care-insurance receivable, or general intangible, is ineffective to the extent that the term:

(1) would impair the creation, attachment, or perfection of a security interest; or

(2) provides that the assignment or transfer or the creation, attachment, or perfection of the security interest may give rise to a default, breach, right of recoupment, claim, defense, termination, right of termination, or remedy under the promissory note, health-care-insurance receivable, or general intangible.

(b) **[Applicability of subsection (a) to sales of certain rights to payment.]** Subsection (a) applies to a security interest in a payment intangible or promissory note only if the security interest arises out of a sale of the payment intangible or promissory note, other than a sale pursuant to a disposition under Section 9–610 or an acceptance of collateral under Section 9–620.

(c) **[Legal restrictions on assignment generally ineffective.]** A rule of law, statute, or regulation that prohibits, restricts, or requires the consent of a government, governmental body or official, person obligated on a promissory note, or account debtor to the assignment or transfer of, or creation of a security interest in, a promissory note, health-care-insurance receivable, or general intangible, including a contract, permit, license, or franchise between an account debtor and a debtor, is ineffective to the extent that the rule of law, statute, or regulation:

(1) would impair the creation, attachment, or perfection of a security interest; or

(2) provides that the assignment or transfer or the creation, attachment, or perfection of the security interest may give rise to a default, breach, right of recoupment, claim, defense, termination, right of termination, or remedy under the promissory note, health-care-insurance receivable, or general intangible.

(d) **[Limitation on ineffectiveness under subsections (a) and (c).]** To the extent that a term in a promissory note or in an agreement between an account debtor and a debtor which relates to a health-care-insurance receivable or general intangible or a rule of law, statute, or regulation described in subsection (c) would be effective under law other than this article but is ineffective under subsection (a) or (c), the creation, attachment, or perfection of a security interest in the promissory note, health-care-insurance receivable, or general intangible:

(1)   is not enforceable against the person obligated on the promissory note or the account debtor;

(2)   does not impose a duty or obligation on the person obligated on the promissory note or the account debtor;

(3)   does not require the person obligated on the promissory note or the account debtor to recognize the security interest, pay or render performance to the secured party, or accept payment or performance from the secured party;

(4)   does not entitle the secured party to use or assign the debtor's rights under the promissory note, health-care-insurance receivable, or general intangible, including any related information or materials furnished to the debtor in the transaction giving rise to the promissory note, health-care-insurance receivable, or general intangible;

(5)   does not entitle the secured party to use, assign, possess, or have access to any trade secrets or confidential information of the person obligated on the promissory note or the account debtor; and

(6)   does not entitle the secured party to enforce the security interest in the promissory note, health-care-insurance receivable, or general intangible.

(e)   **[Section prevails over specified inconsistent law.]** This section prevails over any inconsistent provisions of the following statutes, rules, and regulations:

[List here any statutes, rules, and regulations containing provisions inconsistent with this section.]

(f)   **[Inapplicability to interests in certain entities.]** This section does not apply to a security interest in an ownership interest in a general partnership, limited partnership, or limited liability company.

Official Comments

. . .

2.   **Free Assignability.** This section makes ineffective any attempt to restrict the assignment of a general intangible, health-care-insurance receivable, or promissory note, whether the restriction appears in the terms of a promissory note or the agreement between an account debtor and a debtor (subsection (a)) or in a rule of law, including a statute or governmental rule or regulation (subsection (c)). This result allows the creation, attachment, and perfection of a security interest in a general intangible, such as an agreement for the nonexclusive license of software, as well as sales of certain receivables, such as a health-care-insurance receivable (which is an "account"), payment intangible, or promissory note, without giving rise to a default or breach by the assignor or from trigger-

ing a remedy of the account debtor or person obligated on a promissory note. This enhances the ability of certain debtors to obtain credit. On the other hand, subsection (d) protects the other party-the "account debtor" on a general intangible or the person obligated on a promissory note-from adverse effects arising from the security interest. It leaves the account debtor's or obligated person's rights and obligations unaffected in all material respects if a restriction rendered ineffective by subsection (a) or (c) would be effective under law other than Article 9.

Example 1: A term of an agreement for the nonexclusive license of computer software prohibits the licensee from assigning any of its rights as licensee with respect to the software. The agreement also provides that an attempt to assign rights in violation of the restriction is a default entitling the licensor to terminate the license agreement. The licensee, as debtor, grants to a secured party a security interest in its rights under the license and in the computers in which it is installed. Under this section, the term prohibiting assignment and providing for a default upon an attempted assignment is ineffective to prevent the creation, attachment, or perfection of the security interest or entitle the licensor to terminate the license agreement. However, under subsection (d), the secured party (absent the licensor's agreement) is not entitled to enforce the license or to use, assign, or otherwise enjoy the benefits of the licensed software, and the licensor need not recognize (or pay any attention to) the secured party. Even if the secured party takes possession of the computers on the debtor's default, the debtor would remain free to remove the software from the computer, load it on another computer, and continue to use it, if the license so permits. If the debtor does not remove the software, other law may require the secured party to remove it before disposing of

the computer. Disposition of the software with the computer could violate an effective prohibition on enforcement of the security interest. See subsection (d).

3. **Nature of Debtor's Interest.** Neither this section nor any other provision of this Article determines whether a debtor has a property interest. The definition of the term "security interest" provides that it is an "interest in personal property." See Section 1–201(b)(35). Ordinarily, a debtor can create a security interest in collateral only if it has "rights in the collateral." See Section 9–203(b). Other law determines whether a debtor has a property interest ("rights in the collateral") and the nature of that interest. For example, the nonexclusive license addressed in Example 1 may not create any property interest whatsoever in the intellectual property (e.g., copyright) that underlies the license and that effectively enables the licensor to grant the license. The debtor's property interest may be confined solely to its interest in the promises made by the licensor in the license agreement (e.g., a promise not to sue the debtor for its use of the software).

4. **Scope: Sales of Payment Intangibles and Other General Intangibles; Assignments Unaffected by this Section.** Subsections (a) and (c) render ineffective restrictions on assignments only "to the extent" that the assignments restrict the "creation, attachment, or perfection of a security interest," including sales of payment intangibles and promissory notes. This section does not render ineffective a restriction on an assignment that does not create a security interest. For example, if the debtor in Comment 2, Example 1 purported to assign the license to another entity that would use the computer software itself, other law would govern the effectiveness of the anti-assignment provisions.

Subsection (a) applies to a security interest in payment intangibles only if the security interest arises out of sale of the payment intangibles. Contractual restrictions directed to security interests in payment intangibles which secure an obligation are subject to Section 9–406(d). Subsection (a) also deals with sales of promissory notes which also create security interests. See Section 9–109(a). Subsection (c) deals with all security interests in payment intangibles or promissory notes, whether or not arising out of a sale.

Subsection (a) does not render ineffective any term, and subsection (c) does not render ineffective any law, statute or regulation, that restricts outright sales of general intangibles other than payment intangibles. They deal only with restrictions on security interests. The only sales of general intangibles that create security interests are sales of payment intangibles.

5. **Terminology: "Account Debtor"; "Person Obligated on a Promissory Note."** This section uses the term "account debtor" as it is defined in Section 9–102. The term refers to the party, other than the debtor, to a general intangible, including a permit, license, franchise, or the like, and the person obligated on a health-care-insurance receivable, which is a type of account. The definition of "account debtor" does not limit the term to persons who are obligated to *pay* under a general intangible. Rather, the term includes all persons who are obligated on a general intangible, including those who are obligated to render performance in exchange for payment. In some cases, e.g., the creation of a security interest in a franchisee's rights under a franchise agreement, the principal payment obligation may be owed *by* the debtor (franchisee) *to* the account debtor (franchisor). This section also refers to a "person obligated on a promissory note," inasmuch as those

persons do not fall within the definition of "account debtor."

Example 2: A licensor and licensee enter into an agreement for the nonexclusive license of computer software. The licensee's interest in the license agreement is a general intangible. If the licensee grants to a secured party a security interest in its rights under the license agreement, the licensee is the debtor and the licensor is the account debtor. On the other hand, if the licensor grants to a secured party a security interest in its right to payment (an account) under the license agreement, the licensor is the debtor and the licensee is the account debtor. (This section applies to the security interest in the general intangible but not to the security interest in the account, which is not a health-care-insurance receivable.)

6. **Effects on Account Debtors and Persons Obligated on Promissory Notes.** Subsections (a) and (c) affect two classes of persons. These subsections affect account debtors on general intangibles and health-care-insurance receivables and persons obligated on promissory notes. Subsection (c) also affects governmental entities that enact or determine rules of law. *However, subsection (d) ensures that these affected persons are not affected adversely.* That provision removes any burdens or adverse effects on these persons for which any rational basis could exist to restrict the effectiveness of an assignment or to exercise any remedies. For this reason, the effects of subsections (a) and (c) are immaterial insofar as those persons are concerned.

Subsection (a) does not override terms that do not directly prohibit, restrict, or require consent to an assignment but which might, nonetheless, present a practical impairment of the assignment. Properly read, however, this section, like Section 9–406(d), reaches only covenants that prohibit, restrict, or require consents to assignments; it does not override all terms that might "impair" an assignment in fact.

Example 3: A licensor and licensee enter into an agreement for the non-exclusive license of valuable business software. The license agreement includes terms (i) prohibiting the licensee from assigning its rights under the license, (ii) prohibiting the licensee from disclosing to anyone certain information relating to the software and the licensor, and (iii) deeming prohibited assignments and prohibited disclosures to be defaults. The licensee wishes to obtain financing and, in exchange, is willing to grant a security interest in its rights under the license agreement. The secured party, reasonably, refuses to extend credit unless the licensee discloses the information that it is prohibited from disclosing under the license agreement. The secured party cannot determine the value of the proposed collateral in the absence of this information. Under this section, the terms of the license prohibiting the assignment (grant of the security interest) and making the assignment a default are ineffective. However, the nondisclosure covenant is not a term that prohibits the assignment or creation of a security interest in the license. Consequently, the nondisclosure term is enforceable even though the *practical* effect is to restrict the licensee's ability to use its rights under the license agreement as collateral.

The nondisclosure term also would be effective in the factual setting of Comment 2, Example 1. If the secured party's possession of the computers loaded with software would put it in a position to discover confidential information that the debtor was prohibited from disclosing, the licensor should be entitled to enforce its rights against the secured party. Moreover, the licensor could have required the debtor to obtain the secured party's agreement that (i) it would immediately return all copies of software loaded on the computers and that (ii) it would not examine or otherwise acquire any information contained in the software. This section does not prevent an account debtor from protecting by agreement its independent interests that are unrelated to the "creation, attachment, or perfection" of a security interest. In Example 1, moreover, the secured party is not in possession of copies of software by virtue of its security interest or in connection with enforcing its security interest *in the debtor's license of the software*. Its possession is incidental to its possession of the computers, in which it has a security interest. Enforcing against the secured party a restriction relating to the software in no way interferes with its security interest in the computers.

. . .

EXCERPTS FROM THE REPORT OF THE SUBCOMMITTEE ON BUNDLED HARDWARE, SOFTWARE, AND SERVICE TRANSACTIONS TO THE JOINT COMMITTEE OF THE AMERICAN LAW INSTITUTE AND THE UNIFORM LAW COMMISSION ON THE UNIFORM COMMERCIAL CODE AND EMERGING TECHNOLOGIES (2020)

Determination as to Whether Bundled Transactions Are Governed by Article 2 or Article 2A Generally

Background: In a dispute arising out of a contract (traditionally referred to as a "mixed" or "hybrid" transaction and more recently often referred to as a "bundled transaction") in which the vendor provides both goods and non-goods (especially technological services, including support, consulting or cloud services), most states apply a "predominant purpose" test to determine whether (i) the contract is governed by the UCC Articles about goods (Article 2 or Article 2A, as applicable), or (ii) by non-goods law outside the UCC. But not all disputes are alike. In some cases, the dispute concerns the contract taken as a whole (such as whether an enforceable contract was formed), while in other cases the dispute may involve only one aspect of the transaction. Such a dispute may involve only the goods aspect of the transaction (such as when the claim is that the goods do not conform to contractual specifications) or only the non-goods aspect (such as a claim about support services). Many members of the subcommittee indicated that it would be preferable, in the case of a dispute involving only one aspect of the transaction, for the law governing the disputed issue to be the UCC law of goods when a dispute about the goods is the gravamen of the dispute, and for the law governing the disputed issue be non-UCC law when a dispute about the non-goods aspect of the transaction is the gravamen of the dispute.

Proposed resolution: In a bundled transaction involving both goods and non-goods, in deciding whether the parties' rights are determined under Article 2/2A (as applicable) or other law (typically the common law of contracts), the predominant purpose test should be applied in most cases. However, if a matter arises that relates solely to the goods, Article 2/2A should be applied to that matter even if the goods aspect of the transaction does not predominate.

REPORT OF THE SUBCOMMITTEE ON BUNDLED HARDWARE, SOFTWARE, AND SERVICE TRANSACTIONS

Illustrations:

1. Vendor entered into negotiations with Truck Mechanic to provide Truck Mechanic with computerized diagnostic services that can enable her to repair efficiently the newest generation of trucks that contain many "smart" components that continuously upload information as part of the Internet of Things (IoT). The transaction that is the subject of the negotiations would involve vendor supplying specialized diagnostic software to Truck Mechanic along with highly-trained personnel to utilize the software and also supplying a terminal on which the software will reside and which can be used to transmit diagnostic information to specialists at Vendor's headquarters. When major issues concerning the proposed transaction were resolved, Truck Mechanic sent Vendor a "purchase order" for the diagnostic services. Vendor replied with an "order acknowledgement" that seemed to express acceptance of the purchase order but which contained some terms additional to those in the purchase order and others that were different from those in the purchase order. Before Vendor started providing the diagnostic services a dispute arose. Vendor claims that there is no contract with Truck Mechanic for the computerized diagnostic services, while Truck Mechanic claims that a contract exists. In the applicable jurisdiction, UCC § 2-207 has been enacted but the jurisdiction's common law of contracts follows the "mirror image rule" under which a purported acceptance of an offer operates as a rejection and counter-offer if the purported acceptance contains terms additional to or different from those offered. Because the non-goods aspect of this transaction predominates, the determination of whether the exchange of purchase order and order acknowledgment created a contract should be made under the rules of the jurisdiction's common law of contracts.

2. Customer and Newspaper enter into a contract pursuant to which, for a one-year period, Newspaper is to provide Customer with full access to Newspaper's website and a physical copy of each day's newspaper. The contract provides that the ink used in printing the physical copy of the paper to be delivered to Customer will be non-allergenic, which is important to Customer because many members of his family have an uncommon allergy to certain frequently-used newspaper inks. The contract price is $500 per year. One day, as a result of a mistake by Newspaper, the issue delivered to Customer is printed with ink that can trigger allergies. As a result, when Customer's grandson, who has the uncommon allergy, read that day's paper while visiting Customer's house, he suffered dermatological injuries that were caused by the allergy. Whether the benefit of the Newspaper's promise that the ink would be non-allergenic extends to the grandson is determined by the jurisdiction's enactment of UCC § 2-318 whether or not the predominant purpose of the contract is the furnishing of the physical copy of the newspaper each day or the provision of the access to Newspaper's website. This is because the matter that arose relates solely to the goods and was unrelated to the website access.

REPRESENTATIVE STATUTES OF FRAUDS

CALIFORNIA

Civil Code § 1624. Statute of Frauds.

(a)   The following contracts are invalid, unless they, or some note or memorandum thereof, are in writing and subscribed by the party to be charged or by the party's agent:

(1)   An agreement that by its terms is not to be performed within a year from the making thereof.

(2)   A special promise to answer for the debt, default, or miscarriage of another, except in the cases provided for in Section 2794.

(3)   An agreement for the leasing for a longer period than one year, or for the sale of real property, or of an interest therein; such an agreement, if made by an agent of the party sought to be charged, is invalid, unless the authority of the agent is in writing, subscribed by the party sought to be charged.

(4)   An agreement authorizing or employing an agent, broker, or any other person to purchase or sell real estate, or to lease real estate for a longer period than one year, or to procure, introduce, or find a purchaser or seller of real estate or a lessee or lessor of real estate where the lease is for a longer period than one year, for compensation or a commission.

(5)   An agreement that by its terms is not to be performed during the lifetime of the promisor.

(6)   An agreement by a purchaser of real property to pay an indebtedness secured by a mortgage or deed of trust upon the property purchased, unless assumption of the indebtedness by the purchaser is specifically provided for in the conveyance of the property.

(7)   A contract, promise, undertaking, or commitment to loan money or to grant or extend credit, in an amount greater than one hundred thousand dollars ($100,000), not primarily for personal, family, or household purposes, made by a person engaged in the business of lending or arranging for the lending of money or extending credit. For purposes of this section, a contract, promise, undertaking, or commitment to loan money secured solely by residential property consisting of one to four dwelling units shall be deemed to be for personal, family, or household purposes.

(b)   Notwithstanding paragraph (1) of subdivision (a):

(1) An agreement or contract that is valid in other respects and is otherwise enforceable is not invalid for lack of a note, memorandum, or other writing and is enforceable by way of action or defense, provided that the agreement or contract is a qualified financial contract as defined in paragraph (2) and one of the following apply:

(A) There is, as provided in paragraph (3), sufficient evidence to indicate that a contract has been made.

(B) The parties thereto by means of a prior or subsequent written contract, have agreed to be bound by the terms of the qualified financial contract from the time they reached agreement (by telephone, by exchange of electronic messages, or otherwise) on those terms.

(2) For purposes of this subdivision, a "qualified financial contract" means an agreement as to which each party thereto is other than a natural person and that is any of the following:

(A) For the purchase and sale of foreign exchange, foreign currency, bullion, coin, or precious metals on a forward, spot, next-day value or other basis.

(B) A contract (other than a contract for the purchase of a commodity for future delivery on, or subject to the rules of, a contract market or board of trade) for the purchase, sale, or transfer of any commodity or any similar good, article, service, right, or interest that is presently or in the future becomes the subject of a dealing in the forward contract trade, or any product or byproduct thereof, with a maturity date more than two days after the date the contract is entered into.

(C) For the purchase and sale of currency, or interbank deposits denominated in United States dollars.

(D) For a currency option, currency swap, or cross-currency rate swap.

(E) For a commodity swap or a commodity option (other than an option contract traded on, or subject to the rules of, a contract market or board of trade).

(F) For a rate swap, basis swap, forward rate transaction, or an interest rate option.

(G) For a security-index swap or option, or a security or securities price swap or option.

(H) An agreement that involves any other similar transaction relating to a price or index (including, without limitation, any transaction or agreement involving any combination of the foregoing, any cap, floor, collar, or similar transaction with respect to a rate, commodity price, commodity index, security or securities price, security index, other price index, or loan price).

(I)   An option with respect to any of the foregoing.

(3)   There is sufficient evidence that a contract has been made in any of the following circumstances:

(A)   There is evidence of an electronic communication (including, without limitation, the recording of a telephone call or the tangible written text produced by computer retrieval), admissible in evidence under the laws of this state, sufficient to indicate that in the communication a contract was made between the parties.

(B)   A confirmation in writing sufficient to indicate that a contract has been made between the parties and sufficient against the sender is received by the party against whom enforcement is sought no later than the fifth business day after the contract is made (or any other period of time that the parties may agree in writing) and the sender does not receive, on or before the third business day after receipt (or the other period of time that the parties may agree in writing), written objection to a material term of the confirmation. For purposes of this subparagraph, a confirmation or an objection thereto is received at the time there has been an actual receipt by an individual responsible for the transaction or, if earlier, at the time there has been constructive receipt, which is the time actual receipt by that individual would have occurred if the receiving party, as an organization, had exercised reasonable diligence. For the purposes of this subparagraph, a "business day" is a day on which both parties are open and transacting business of the kind involved in that qualified financial contract that is the subject of confirmation.

(C)   The party against whom enforcement is sought admits in its pleading, testimony, or otherwise in court that a contract was made.

(D)   There is a note, memorandum, or other writing sufficient to indicate that a contract has been made, signed by the party against whom enforcement is sought or by its authorized agent or broker.

For purposes of this paragraph, evidence of an electronic communication indicating the making in that communication of a contract, or a confirmation, admission, note, memorandum, or writing is not insufficient because it omits or incorrectly states one or more material terms agreed upon, as long as the evidence provides a reasonable basis for concluding that a contract was made.

(4)   For purposes of this subdivision, the tangible written text produced by telex, telefacsimile, computer retrieval, or other process by which electronic signals are transmitted by telephone or otherwise shall constitute a writing, and any symbol executed or adopted by a

party with the present intention to authenticate a writing shall constitute a signing. The confirmation and notice of objection referred to in subparagraph (B) of paragraph (3) may be communicated by means of telex, telefacsimile, computer, or other similar process by which electronic signals are transmitted by telephone or otherwise, provided that a party claiming to have communicated in that manner shall, unless the parties have otherwise agreed in writing, have the burden of establishing actual or constructive receipt by the other party as set forth in subparagraph (B) of paragraph (3).

(c) This section does not apply to leases subject to Division 10 (commencing with Section 10101) of the Commercial Code.

(d) An electronic message of an ephemeral nature that is not designed to be retained or to create a permanent record, including, but not limited to, a text message or instant message format communication, is insufficient under this title to constitute a contract to convey real property, in the absence of a written confirmation that conforms to the requirements of subparagraph (B) of paragraph (3) of subdivision (b).

Civil Code § 1624.5. Written contract; sale of personal property exceeding $5000; exceptions.

(a) Except in the cases described in subdivision (b), a contract for the sale of personal property is not enforceable by way of action or defense beyond five thousand dollars ($5,000) in amount or value of remedy unless there is some record, as defined in subdivision (m) of Section 1633.2, but solely to the extent permitted by applicable law, that indicates that a contract for sale has been made between the parties at a defined or stated price, reasonably identifies the subject matter, and is signed, including by way of electronic signature, as defined in subdivision (h) of Section 1633.2, but solely to the extent permitted by applicable law, by the party against whom enforcement is sought or by his or her authorized agent.

(b) Subdivision (a) does not apply to contracts governed by the Commercial Code, including contracts for the sale of goods (Section 2201 of the Commercial Code), contracts for the sale of securities (Section 8113 of the Commercial Code), and security agreements (Sections 9201 and 9203 of the Commercial Code).

(c) Subdivision (a) does not apply to a qualified financial contract as that term is defined in paragraph (2) of subdivision (b) of Section 1624 if either of the following exists:

(1) There is, as provided in paragraph (3) of subdivision (b) of Section 1624, sufficient evidence to indicate that a contract has been made.

(2) The parties thereto, by means of a prior or subsequent written contract, have agreed to be bound by the terms of the qualified financial contract from the time they reach agreement (by telephone, by exchange of electronic messages, or otherwise) on those terms.

NEW YORK

General Obligations Law § 5–701. Agreements Required to be in Writing.

a. Every agreement, promise or undertaking is void, unless it or some note or memorandum thereof be in writing, and subscribed by the party to be charged therewith, or by his lawful agent, if such agreement, promise or undertaking:

1. By its terms is not to be performed within one year from the making thereof or the performance of which is not to be completed before the end of a lifetime;

2. Is a special promise to answer for the debt, default or miscarriage of another person;

3. Is made in consideration of marriage, except mutual promises to marry;

[4. Repealed]

5. Is a subsequent or new promise to pay a debt discharged in bankruptcy;

6. Notwithstanding section 2–201 of the uniform commercial code, if the goods be sold at public auction, and the auctioneer at the time of the sale, enters in a sale book, a memorandum specifying the nature and price of the property sold, the terms of the sale, the name of the purchaser, and the name of the person on whose account the sale was made, such memorandum is equivalent in effect to a note of the contract or sale, subscribed by the party to be charged therewith;

[7., 8. Repealed]

9. Is a contract to assign or an assignment, with or without consideration to the promisor, of a life or health or accident insurance policy, or a promise, with or without consideration to the promisor, to name a beneficiary of any such policy. This provision shall not apply to a policy of industrial life or health or accident insurance.

10. Is a contract to pay compensation for services rendered in negotiating a loan, or in negotiating the purchase, sale, exchange, renting or leasing of any real estate or interest therein, or of a business opportunity, business, its good will, inventory, fixtures or an interest therein, including a majority of the voting stock interest in a corporation and including the creating of a partnership interest. "Negotiating" includes procuring an introduction to a party to the transaction or assisting in the negotiation or consummation of the transaction. This provision shall apply to a contract implied in fact or in law to pay reasonable compensation but shall not apply to a contract to pay compensation to an auctioneer, an attorney at law, or a duly licensed real estate broker or real estate salesman.

b.   Notwithstanding paragraph one of subdivision a of this section:

1.   An agreement, promise, undertaking or contract, which is valid in other respects and is otherwise enforceable, is not void for lack of a note, memorandum or other writing and is enforceable by way of action or defense provided that such agreement, promise, undertaking or contract is a qualified financial contract as defined in paragraph two of this subdivision and (a) there is, as provided in paragraph three of this subdivision, sufficient evidence to indicate that a contract has been made, or (b) the parties thereto, by means of a prior or subsequent written contract, have agreed to be bound by the terms of such qualified financial contract from the time they reach agreement (by telephone, by exchange of electronic messages, or otherwise) on those terms.

2.   For purposes of this subdivision, a "qualified financial contract" means an agreement as to which each party thereto is other than a natural person and which is:

(a)   for the purchase and sale of foreign exchange, foreign currency, bullion, coin or precious metals on a forward, spot, next-day value or other basis;

(b)   a contract (other than a contract for the purchase and sale of a commodity for future delivery on, or subject to the rules of, a contract market or board of trade) for the purchase, sale or transfer of any commodity or any similar good, article, service, right, or interest which is presently or in the future becomes the subject of dealing in the forward contract trade, or any product or byproduct thereof, with a maturity date more than two days after the date the contract is entered into;

(c)   for the purchase and sale of currency, or interbank deposits denominated in United States dollars;

(d)   for a currency option, currency swap or cross-currency rate swap;

(e)   for a commodity swap or a commodity option (other than an option contract traded on, or subject to the rules of a contract market or board of trade);

(f)   for a rate swap, basis swap, forward rate transaction, or an interest rate option;

(g)   for a security-index swap or option or a security (or securities) price swap or option;

(h)   an agreement which involves any other similar transaction relating to a price or index (including, without limitation, any transaction or agreement involving any combination of the foregoing, any cap, floor, collar or similar transaction with respect to a rate, commodity price, commodity index, security (or securities) price, security-index or other price index);

(i) for the assignment, sale, trade, participation or exchange of indebtedness or claims relating thereto arising in the course of the claimant's business or profession (including but not limited to commercial and/or bank loans, choses in action arising under or in connection with loan agreements and private notes, and including forward sales), but only to the extent that such indebtedness or obligation was not incurred by a natural person primarily for personal, family or household purposes; or

(j) an option with respect to any of the foregoing.

3. There is sufficient evidence that a contract has been made if:

(a) There is evidence of electronic communication (including, without limitation, the recording of a telephone call or the tangible written text produced by computer retrieval), admissible in evidence under the laws of this state, sufficient to indicate that in such communication a contract was made between the parties;

(b) A confirmation in writing sufficient to indicate that a contract has been made between the parties and sufficient against the sender is received by the party against whom enforcement is sought no later than the fifth business day after such contract is made (or such other period of time as the parties may agree in writing) and the sender does not receive, on or before the third business day after such receipt (or such other period of time as the parties may agree in writing), written objection to a material term of the confirmation; for purposes of this subparagraph, a confirmation or an objection thereto is received at the time there has been actual receipt by an individual responsible for the transaction or, if earlier, at the time there has been constructive receipt which is the time actual receipt by such an individual would have occurred if the receiving party, as an organization, has exercised reasonable diligence; and a "business day" for the purposes of this subparagraph is a day on which both parties are open and transacting business of the kind involved in that qualified financial contract which is the subject of the confirmation;

(c) The party against whom enforcement is sought admits in its pleading, testimony or otherwise in court that a contract was made; or

(d) There is a note, memorandum or other writing sufficient to indicate that a contract has been made, signed by the party against whom enforcement is sought or by its authorized agent or broker.

For purposes of this paragraph evidence of an electronic communication indicating the making therein of a contract or a confirmation, admission, note, memorandum or writing is not insufficient because it omits or incorrectly states one or more material terms agreed upon, so long as such evidence provides a reasonable basis for concluding that a contract was made.

4.   For purposes of this subdivision, the tangible written text produced by telex, telefacsimile, computer retrieval or other process by which electronic signals are transmitted by telephone or otherwise shall constitute a writing and any symbol executed or adopted by a party with the present intention to authenticate a writing shall constitute a signing. The confirmation and notice of objection referred to in subparagraph (b) of paragraph three of this subdivision may be communicated by means of telex, telefacsimile, computer or other similar process by which electronic signals are transmitted by telephone or otherwise, provided that a party claiming to have communicated in such a manner shall, unless the parties have otherwise agreed in writing, have the burden of establishing actual or constructive receipt by the other party as set forth in subparagraph (b) of paragraph three of this subdivision.

General Obligations Law § 5–703. Conveyances and contracts concerning real property required to be in writing.

1.   An estate or interest in real property, other than a lease for a term not exceeding one year, or any trust or power, over or concerning real property, or in any manner relating thereto, cannot be created, granted, assigned, surrendered or declared, unless by act or operation of law, or by a deed or conveyance in writing, subscribed by the person creating, granting, assigning, surrendering or declaring the same, or by his lawful agent, thereunto authorized by writing. But this subdivision does not affect the power of a testator in the disposition of his real property by will; nor prevent any trust from arising or being extinguished by implication or operation of law, nor any declaration of trust from being proved by a writing subscribed by the person declaring the same.

2.   A contract for the leasing for a longer period than one year, or for the sale, of any real property, or an interest therein, is void unless the contract or some note or memorandum thereof, expressing the consideration, is in writing, subscribed by the party to be charged, or by his lawful agent thereunto authorized by writing.

3.   A contract to devise real property or establish a trust of real property, or any interest therein or right with reference thereto, is void unless the contract or some note or memorandum thereof is in writing and subscribed by the party to be charged therewith, or by his lawfully authorized agent.

4.   Nothing contained in this section abridges the powers of courts of equity to compel the specific performance of agreements in cases of part performance.

OHIO

R.C. § 1335.04. Interest in land to be granted in writing.

No lease, estate, or interest, either of freehold or term of years, or any uncertain interest of, in, or out of lands, tenements, or hereditaments, shall be assigned or granted except by deed, or note in writing, signed by the party assigning or granting it, or his agent thereunto lawfully authorized, by writing, or by act and operation of law.

R.C. § 1335.05. Certain agreements to be in writing.

No action shall be brought whereby to charge the defendant, upon a special promise, to answer for the debt, default, or miscarriage of another person; nor to charge an executor or administrator upon a special promise to answer damages out of his own estate; nor to charge a person upon an agreement made upon consideration of marriage, or upon a contract or sale of lands, tenements, or hereditaments, or interest in or concerning them, or upon an agreement that is not to be performed within one year from the making thereof; unless the agreement upon which such action is brought, or some memorandum or note thereof, is in writing and signed by the party to be charged therewith or some other person thereunto by him or her lawfully authorized.

No action shall be brought to charge a person licensed by Chapter 4731. of the Revised Code to practice medicine or surgery, osteopathic medicine or surgery, or podiatric medicine and surgery in this state, upon any promise or agreement relating to a medical prognosis unless the promise or agreement is in writing and signed by the party to be charged therewith.

TEXAS

Business and Commerce Code § 26.01. Promise or Agreement Must be in Writing.

(a)   A promise or agreement described in Subsection (b) of this section is not enforceable unless the promise or agreement, or a memorandum of it, is

(1)   in writing; and

(2)   signed by the person to be charged with the promise or agreement or by someone lawfully authorized to sign for him.

(b)   Subsection (a) of this section applies to:

(1)   a promise by an executor or administrator to answer out of his own estate for any debt or damage due from his testator or intestate;

(2)   a promise by one person to answer for the debt, default, or miscarriage of another person;

(3)   an agreement made on consideration of marriage or on consideration of nonmarital conjugal cohabitation;

(4)   a contract for the sale of real estate;

(5)   a lease of real estate for a term longer than one year;

(6)   an agreement which is not to be performed within one year from the date of making the agreement;

(7)   a promise or agreement to pay a commission for the sale or purchase of:

    (A)   an oil or gas mining lease;

    (B)   an oil or gas royalty;

    (C)   minerals; or

    (D)   a mineral interest; and

(8)   an agreement, promise, contract, or warranty of cure relating to medical care or results thereof made by a physician or health care provider as defined in Section 74.001, Civil Practice and Remedies Code. This section shall not apply to pharmacists.

FEDERAL ARBITRATION ACT
(EXCERPT)

§ 2. (9 U.S.C. § 2)

A written provision in any maritime transaction or a contract evidencing a transaction involving commerce to settle by arbitration a controversy thereafter arising out of such contract or transaction, or the refusal to perform the whole or any part thereof, or an agreement in writing to submit to arbitration an existing controversy arising out of such a contract, transaction, or refusal, shall be valid, irrevocable, and enforceable, save upon such grounds as exist at law or in equity for the revocation of any contract.

(July 30, 1947, c. 392, 61 Stat. 670.)

PRINCIPLES OF THE LAW OF SOFTWARE CONTRACTS

(SELECTED SECTIONS)

CHAPTER 1. DEFINITIONS, SCOPE, AND GENERAL TERMS

TOPIC 1. DEFINITIONS

§ 1.01 Definitions

As used in these Principles

. . .

(k) Standard Form and Standard Term

(1) A "standard form" is a record regularly used to embody terms of agreements of the same type.

(2) A "standard term" is a term appearing in a standard form and relating to a particular matter.

(*l*) Standard-Form Transfer of Generally Available Software

A "standard-form transfer of generally available software" is a transfer using a standard form of

(1) a small number of copies of software to an end user; or

(2) the right to access software to a small number of end users

if the software is generally available to the public under substantially the same standard terms.

Comment:

a. Generally. Standard-form transfers of generally available software target retail-like transactions. Transfers of a small number of copies of software are consistent with the quantity of software transferred in a typical retail sale. However, the definition includes some transfers not usually considered retail transactions, such as some transfers of open-source software, shareware, and freeware.

An end user under this definition intends to use the software for business, personal, or family reasons, and includes large and small businesses and consumers. But end users under this definition do not intend to offer the software commercially to third parties.

Section 2.02, Comment a, discusses the reasons for including businesses in the treatment of small-quantity standard-form transfers. Section 2.01, on formation, governs standard-form transfers if the quantity of copies transferred is not small. Section 2.01 also applies if the software is not generally available to the public under the same standard terms.

Software is not generally available to the public if it is customized more than insignificantly. Similarly, software is not available to the public under substantially the same standard terms if the terms differ from those offered in the general market more than insignificantly due to negotiation or otherwise. Software is "generally available to the public" even if certain subsets of the public are excluded from obtaining it, such as people under 18 years of age. Further, software is "generally available to the public" even if software marketing targets particular groups, such as foreign speakers or particular services or industries, so long as the software is available to the general public.

CHAPTER 2.　FORMATION AND ENFORCEMENT

TOPIC 1.　FORMATION, GENERALLY

§ 2.01　Formation, Generally

(a)　Subject to § 2.02, a contract may be formed in any manner sufficient to show an agreement, including by offer and acceptance and by conduct.

(b)　A contract may be formed under subsection (a) even though

(1)　one or more terms are left open, if there is a reasonably certain basis for granting an appropriate remedy in the event of a breach; or

(2)　the parties' records are different. In such a case, the terms of the contract are

(A)　terms, whether in a record or not, to which both parties agree;

(B)　terms that appear in the records of both parties; and

(C)　terms supplied by these Principles or other law.

Comment:

. . . b.　*General rule.* . . . Providers of custom software or those transferring a large number of copies of software sometimes present standard forms to the transferee on a take-it-or-leave-it basis. A transferor may present the standard form in a manner called "shrinkwrap" because the terms appear on or inside the software package after the transferee has paid for the software. Or a transferor may present terms electronically as part of a "browsewrap" transaction, in which the transferee views a screen that refers to terms that can be found elsewhere before downloading the software electronically. The act of downloading or some other act is considered acceptance of the terms. Finally, transferors may employ a "clickwrap" presentation, in which the end user, who downloads software electronically, must click "I agree" to terms presented electronically in order to complete the transaction.

Section 2.01 governs the enforcement of contracts formed in any of these manners if the transfer is of a large number of copies of the software or the software is not generally available under the same standard terms. Transferees in such transactions may consist of sophisticated businesses that should be expected to insist on access to the standard form, to read and understand the form, and even, in some instances, to bargain successfully for better terms. Even if a transferee business is small and less sophisticated, large-quantity or custom-software transactions should constitute a red flag that the standard form is important and should be read. The Principles therefore take the position that such transferees do not need the special safeguards of § 2.02. See § 2.02, Comment a. Further, § 2.01 does not rule out enforcement of any of the standard-form presentations so long as the circumstances show that both parties intended to form an agreement and the transferee had reasonable notice of the terms.

Nevertheless, courts applying § 2.01 to any standard-form transaction should be especially vigilant about the formation process on the theory that even in large-quantity, standard-form transactions or custom-software transactions transferees may have little or no bargaining power or choice. In fact, some evidence suggests that within particular software markets standard-form transferors can dictate terms and adopt dubious, retail-like strategies even when the transferee is a business and the number of copies of software is large or the software is custom engineered. It is also clear that transferors include in their forms very stringent limitations of liability and broad reservations of ownership rights in the software in retail and other business markets alike. Software transferors may have ample reasons for including such terms, but in some circumstances their existence tends to show that transferors have superior bargaining power at the expense of businesses acquiring custom software or large quantities of software.

There are several possible explanations for transferor bargaining power in this context. An obvious reason is that some transferors have few competitors. The market may be highly concentrated. In addition, liability limitations may be extremely important because of the uncertain, but potentially large damages that can result from defective software. Retaining property rights in the software and restrictions on use also may be crucial because of the ease of copying and transferring software. The importance of such boilerplate may signal to transferees the unwillingness of transferors to make concessions. Further, if the subject matter is standard software that the transferee downloads from the Internet, the transferee likely will neither seek nor be able to extract concessions from the transferor despite a large-quantity transaction. These considerations do not mean that standard forms should be unenforceable in this setting, only that courts should not exempt them from scrutiny simply because the transfer is large or of custom software. Even such business transferees may have little or no bargaining power and therefore may fail to read the standard form.

In applying the objective test of assent of subsection (a), courts should therefore consider factors not unlike those set forth in § 2.02(c), infra, including whether the transferee received adequate notice of and access to the standard form before and at the time of the transfer, the likelihood that the transferee will read the standard form, and its comprehensibility. . . .

d. Different records. Subsection (b)(2) follows U.C.C. § 2–207 and amended U.C.C. §§ 2–206 and 2–207 in rejecting the common-law mirror-image rule, which barred formation of a contract if an acceptance was not identical to the offer. If under § 2.01(a) the circumstances show that the parties intended to contract, a contract can be formed even though the parties' records are different. For example, the parties can form a contract in the "battle-of-the-forms" context if their subsequent performance shows that they made an agreement and intended to ignore the contradictory terms in their communications.

U.C.C. § 2–207(1) and (2) cause confusion because subsection (1) refers to "additional or different terms," but subsection (2) refers only to "additional" terms. Further, § 2–207 defines neither "additional" nor "different." Section 2.01(b)(2) of these Principles applies if the parties' records do not establish a contract because the records are "different," here meaning that the terms are not the same in each record. Records are "different" therefore if one record contains a term that does not appear in the other record or one record changes a term in the other record.

In cases of contracts formed under subsections (a) and (b)(2), § 2.01(b)(2)(A) through (C) determine the terms. These subsections follow the approach of amended § 2–207 because it is clearer and simpler than original § 2–207 and is party neutral. (Original § 2–207 favored the party who sent an offer because material changes in the acceptance would not become part of the contract. If neither party read the other's form, but goods were delivered and accepted, there seems to be little reason to favor either party.) Under § 2.01(b)(2) of these Principles, the terms consist of terms common to both records, other terms the parties agreed to, and supplemental terms supplied by these Principles and outside law. Thus, if the parties' records differ insubstantially, courts can enforce the common terms under § 2.01(b)(2)(B).

CHAPTER 2.　FORMATION AND ENFORCEMENT

TOPIC 2.　STANDARD-FORM TRANSFERS OF GENERALLY AVAILABLE SOFTWARE; ENFORCEMENT OF THE STANDARD FORM

§ 2.02　Standard-Form Transfers Of Generally Available Software; Enforcement Of The Standard Form

(a)　This Section applies to standard-form transfers of generally available software as defined in § 1.01(l).

(b)　A transferee adopts a standard form as a contract when a reasonable transferor would believe the transferee intends to be bound to the form.

(c)　A transferee will be deemed to have adopted a standard form as a contract if

(1)　the standard form is reasonably accessible electronically prior to initiation of the transfer at issue;

(2)　upon initiating the transfer, the transferee has reasonable notice of and access to the standard form before payment or, if there is no payment, before completion of the transfer;

(3)　in the case of an electronic transfer of software, the transferee signifies agreement at the end of or adjacent to the electronic standard form, or in the case of a standard form printed on or attached to packaged software or separately wrapped from the software, the transferee does not exercise the opportunity to return the software unopened for a full refund within a reasonable time after the transfer; and

(4)   the transferee can store and reproduce the standard form if presented electronically.

(d)   Subject to § 1.10 (public policy), § 1.11 (unconscionability), and other invalidating defenses supplied by these Principles or outside law, a standard term is enforceable if reasonably comprehensible.

(e)   If a transferee asserts that it did not adopt a standard form as a contract under subsection (b) or asserts a failure of the transferor to comply with subsection (c) or (d), the transferor has the burden of production and persuasion on the issue of compliance with the subsections.

Comment:

a.   *Scope.* Section 2.02 applies to standard-form transfers of generally available software (defined in § 1.01(l)) only. These include electronic and pre-packaged software transfers.

Section 2.02(b) adopts the general contract-law objective test of contract formation. See Comment b. Subsection (c) enumerates factors that ensure enforcement of a standard form under the objective test of formation. Subsection (d) requires clarity of standard terms, and subsection (e) deals with burdens of proof.

Section 2.02 applies whether the transferee is a consumer or a large-or small-business end user, so long as the software is available to the general public under substantially the same terms and the quantity of copies transferred is small, meaning consistent with a retail sale. See § 1.01(l), Comment a. Restricting the reach of this Section to consumers would create hardship for many small businesses, who essentially are in the same position as consumers downloading software over the Internet. Even large businesses (who less regularly shop for software in a retail market) may have difficulty overseeing their employees' processing of small-quantity software transactions, especially if there is no opportunity to peruse the terms prior to a transaction. Further, drawing lines between what constitutes a large or small business or between businesses in the same position as consumers and businesses with a better bargaining position would be difficult and largely arbitrary. In addition, enlarging the scope of the Section to include businesses should increase the incentive of drafters to write reasonable terms because businesses are more likely to read disclosed terms. Perhaps most important, because the elements of § 2.02 are largely in the nature of disclosure and not onerous for transferors, a "one size fits all" approach is sure to reach all of those worthy of disclosure protection without unduly burdening software transferors.

Transferees that acquire a large number of copies of software or gain the right to access software for a large number of users pursuant to a standard form do not come under § 2.02. Nor do transferees of custom software even if the quantity is small. Such transferees do not necessarily need the special considerations of this Section because they often consist of sophisticated businesses that should be expected to insist on access to and to read and understand the standard form, and even in some instances, to bargain successfully for better terms. Even if the transferee's business is small and less sophisticated, large-quantity and often expensive custom-software transactions should constitute a red flag that the standard form is important and should be read. Nonetheless, as developed more fully in Comment b to § 2.01, courts applying that Section should be especially vigilant about the formation process and the substantive terms on the theory that even in large-quantity, standard-form transactions or custom-software transactions transferees may have little or no bargaining power and the standard form may contain suspect terms. . . .

b. General rule. Section 2.02(b) adopts the flexible contract-law approach to contract formation that bases formation on the objective test of whether a reasonable transferor would believe the transferee intends to be bound. Notwithstanding this approach, in many instances, failure to satisfy subsection (c), which consists of transferor best practices, may mean that the standard form will not be enforceable because a reasonable transferor would not believe the transferee intends to be bound to the form. In such cases, if the transfer has not been terminated, the terms of the contract consist of those terms in which the parties agree, the terms supplied by these Principles, and outside-law default rules. Cf. § 2.01(b)(2).

Subsection (b) also applies subject to other Sections of these Principles, such as § 1.11 (unconscionability), and outside law also may bar the formation of a contract or enforcement of some of its terms. Nor does subsection (b) preempt consumer-protection law. See § 1.12.

Electronic transfers of software

Section 2.02(b) is consistent with the general emerging approach to e-standard forms that allows for various kinds of acceptable electronic presentations of the standard form. For example, under current technology, if a transferee clicks on an "I agree" icon located at the end of a standard form, a reasonable transferor would believe the transferee intends to adopt the standard form as a contract. The same result may follow even if the terms are accessible via a hyperlink or a scroll-down window located near the "I agree" icon provided that the transferee must click "I agree" or the like. Other presentations may be more problematic. For example, mere reference to standard terms found on another page (browse-wrap) may be insufficient under the reasonable-transferor test unless the transferee is already well-acquainted with the terms, for example, from previous notices and transactions.

For several reasons, § 2.02(b) does not establish a bright-line rule for enforcement requiring, for example, clicking "I agree" at the end of an electronic standard form. First, as already mentioned, case law already presents a wide variety of formation types that are not easily captured by a narrow rule and, for the most part, handle the issues in an effective manner. These include situations in which the transferee is aware of the terms because of a course of dealing or because the transferor delivered an update of previously downloaded software. The safeguard of requiring a click at the end of the form does not seem necessary in either case. Second, open-source transfers rarely follow the current click-wrap model, and these Principles should not upset an established custom unless problematic. Third, certain publishers of software, such as shareware, may have difficulty ensuring that Internet distributors of their software abide by bright-line formation requirements. Fourth, some transactions simply may be too cumbersome yet sufficiently insignificant to require scrolling through a standard form before agreeing to the form. Nevertheless, in the usual case, transferors should adopt the best practices of subsection (c) to ensure enforcement of the form, which include presenting the standard form in a manner that requires clicking "I agree" or the like at the end of or adjacent to the standard form. See Comment c.

Illustration:

> ... 3. B, a consumer, downloads a single copy of word-processing software manufactured by A, a software publisher. Before paying with a credit card, B clicks "I agree to the terms" on a computer screen that also states: "Please read the License because it includes important terms governing your use of the software." The quoted language constitutes a hyperlink that takes the transferee to the terms. If B was unaware of the terms because of the lack of previous dealings with A or otherwise, a court may find that a reasonable transferor would not believe B intended to be bound to the terms.

Packaged Software

In a typical transfer of packaged software, often called a "shrinkwrap transaction," the transferee acquires the packaged software either at a store or by placing an order on an Internet site or over the telephone and pays with a credit card. The first opportunity to read the terms, usually contained in the package or presented electronically upon downloading and installing the software, occurs after the transferee brings the software package home or the software is delivered. Shrinkwrap agreements obviously exacerbate the problem of standard forms by requiring payment before the transferee sees the terms.

Courts first considering the shrinkwrap process (many of the cases, both old and recent, involve hard goods such as computers) did not favor shrinkwrap terms because of their unavailability until after payment. Commentators criticized UCITA for taking a contrary position. Under UCITA § 112(a), shrinkwrap terms are enforceable if a person "manifests assent" after an "opportunity to review" the terms. Under § 113(a), "[a] person has an opportunity to review" a term if it is "made available in a manner that ought to call it to the attention of a reasonable person and permit review." Under § 113(c), in shrinkwrap situations, with some exceptions, a "person has an opportunity to review only if it has a right to a return if it rejects the record." Writers thought that copyholders who brought their software home might delay opening the package or returning the software, or might decide not to return it because of their needs, the cost of returning it, or their unhappiness with only a few terms. In any of these situations, a copyholder probably would be bound to the terms under UCITA's test. Despite these criticisms of shrinkwrap presentations, many courts and commentators note the value and popularity of the shrinkwrap method of doing business.

Subsection (b) allows for various methods of packaged-software contract formation, based on when a reasonable transferor would believe the transferee intends to be bound. For example, if a printed standard form is not separately wrapped from the software, a transferee may adopt the standard form as a contract by failing to exercise the opportunity to return the software opened or unopened for a full refund within a reasonable time after the transfer. If the transferee can read the standard form before opening the software because, for example, the standard form is printed on or attached to the package or the standard form and the software are separately wrapped within the package, a reasonable transferor may believe that the transferee intends to be bound upon opening the software wrapper.

Methods of notice and presentation of a printed standard form that fall between these examples require a case-by-case judicial analysis of what is reasonable under the circumstances. Notwithstanding the open-endedness of subsection (b), subsection (c) prescribes best practices that ensure enforcement of the standard form.

Illustration:

. . . 4. B, a consumer, acquires a copy of a word-processing program at a retail store. A is the manufacturer of the software. The software package contains a paper copy of the standard form attached to the package that is accessible without opening the software. A court may find that a reasonable transferor would believe that B intends to be bound to the standard form if B opens the software wrapper. A can ensure enforcement by following the requirements of subsection (c).

c. *Best practices.* Subsection (c) prescribes best practices and constitutes a safe-harbor provision for transferors. Compliance with subsection (c) should assure a transferor of the enforcement of the standard form, but failure to comply does not absolutely bar a transferor from otherwise proving transferee assent. Unsophisticated transferors who may not have knowledge of the requirements of subsection (c) or cannot prove whether or what type of standard form was posted at the time of contracting should not be precluded from establishing the transferee's intention to be bound based on subsection (b). See also Comment b. Further, when appropriate, an objective of the Principles is to present courts with perspectives on best practices, not to prescribe flat rules. Notwithstanding the nature of subsection (c), in many instances, failure to comply with the subsection should mean that the standard form will not be enforceable because it fails the reasonable-transferor test of subsection (b).

Subsection (c) presents several requirements. The standard form must be reasonably accessible electronically prior to any particular transaction (regardless of whether the standard form is electronic or printed); upon initiation of a transaction, the transferee must receive reasonable notice of and access to the standard form prior to payment or completion of the transaction; the transferee must signify agreement at the end of or adjacent to an e-standard form or, in the case of a standard form printed on or attached to a package or separately wrapped from the software, must fail to exercise the opportunity to return the packaged software unopened for a full refund within a reasonable time; the terms must be reasonably comprehensible; and electronic terms must be capable of storage and reproduction, such as by printing a hard copy.

Under subsection (c)(1), a standard form must be reasonably accessible electronically prior to initiation of the transaction at issue. Initiation of a transfer occurs when, viewed objectively, the transferee intends to contract and begins that process, such as by clicking on a "purchase" icon that precedes elicitation of payment information or by bringing packaged software to the check-out line in a retail store. Based on current technology, a transferor therefore can satisfy this aspect of subsection (c)(1) by maintaining an Internet presence and by posting its terms prior to the initiation of any particular transfer so that transferees can read and compare terms without entering a transaction at all. Accessibility issues under subsection (c)(1) also include the sufficiency of notice on the website of the standard form's availability, who must display the standard form, the manner of presentation, and when the standard form is available to read.

For example, notice on the transferor's homepage of the availability of the standard form should be sufficient if a visitor to the site could not help but see the notice. Based on current technology, the standard form should be reasonably accessible from the website of the party asserting enforcement of the standard form against the transferee. This will usually be the software manufacturer or access provider, but it also may be a retail vendor with a web presence. It is hard to imagine that a software manufacturer would not already have a presence on the Internet but, at any rate, creating and maintaining a homepage should not be costly. Nor should disclosure of terms on the website be expensive.

Based on current technology, reasonable accessibility with respect to the manner of presentation means, for example, that the standard form should not disappear after appearing on a computer screen and should be conspicuously displayed. In addition, standard terms should be on the homepage or only a few clicks away because transferees may become discouraged and lose interest if they must search too far to reach their Internet destination.

Reasonable accessibility with respect to time means that the standard form is on display for a reasonable time prior to initiation of a transaction. A "reasonable time" depends on the circumstances, but would ordinarily mean that the terms are available during the period a typical shopper would look for them prior to a transaction.

Subsection (c)(2)'s notice and access requirements are different from the requirements of (c)(1). Subsection (c)(1) requires a transferor to maintain a web presence and to post its terms prior to any particular transaction. A transferee could then see terms without entering any transaction at all. Subsection (c)(2), on the other hand, applies to a transaction in progress and requires a presentation so that the transferee

cannot help but become aware of the terms.

In an electronic transfer of software, for example, subsection (c)(2)'s notice and access requirements require first that the notice is conspicuous both in terms of placement and size so that a transferee cannot help but see the notice. Further, the notice should constitute a hyperlink that leads directly to the standard form or, at minimum, the standard form should be only a few clicks away from the notice. The standard form itself also must be conspicuously displayed.

In the case of packaged software ordered by telephone, subsection (c)(2) would be satisfied by an announcement of the form's availability on the Internet. Although a transferee is unlikely to terminate the telephone call to access and read the standard form, a transferee should be made aware of that opportunity before payment. As mentioned in the Summary Overview to Topic 2, "[i]ncreasing the opportunity to read supports autonomy reasons for enforcing software standard forms. . . ." If the transferee is physically present in a store, the store can satisfy the requirements of subsection (c)(2) by posting or distributing the standard form or by making a computer available to view the terms online. Reasonable accessibility also requires the store to furnish adequate notice of the availability of the terms. Adequate notice requires that a reasonable shopper would understand that the terms are available on paper or by using a store computer prior to a transaction. Standard forms printed on or attached to the software package ordinarily are reasonably accessible as well. In the case of orders placed over the Internet for packaged software, the provider can present the terms electronically.

Under subsection (c)(3), to signify acceptance and to complete an electronic transfer of software, a transferee must click "I agree" or the like after terms are presented on a screen, just as a transferee must sign a paper standard form. Subsection (c)(3) would be satisfied, for example, if the "I agree" icon is adjacent to a scroll-down window that contains the standard form. This form of clickwrap closely resembles traditional modes of agreeing to paper standard forms. Under subsection (c)(3), a mere screen reference to terms that can be found somewhere else on the site would be insufficient as would a scroll-down window containing the standard form if the "I agree" icon is not at the end of or adjacent to the standard form.

In the case of packaged software, under current marketing processes, at least in theory, a transferee in a shrinkwrap transaction can return software for a full refund after opening the software package and reviewing the terms. However, in reality many, perhaps most, retailers refuse to accept returns of software if the package is opened, presumably at least in part because transferees can easily make a copy of the software before returning it. Further, monitoring and policing the transferee to deter copying is problematic. In addition, some retailers have begun charging a "restocking fee" for returns.

To satisfy subsection (c)(3), the standard form must be accessible without opening the software package. In fact, under § 2.02(c), a transferee has several opportunities to read the standard form before opening the software package. Therefore, a transferee can return packaged software and receive a refund for a reasonable time, but only if the package is unopened. Under this approach, the transferor does not have to monitor or police transferee copying before returning the software. Further, the subsection should create incentives for transferors to make their standard forms separately accessible. Section 2.02(b) governs the question of a trans-

feree's adoption of a standard form if the transferee opens a software package in which the standard form is not separately accessible on or in the package.

Sales of Computers with Pre-loaded Software

Under current conditions, a purchaser of a computer with pre-loaded software usually cannot use the software until the purchaser clicks on an "I agree" icon after turning on the computer for the first time and accessing the software. Subsections (c)(1) and (c)(2) apply to this mode of transfer, so that if the software transferor does not make the terms available before the computer-buyer decides to purchase the computer and again upon initiating the purchase, whether by telephone, Internet, or in a store, the transaction would not come within the best practices of (c)(1) and (c)(2) (and enforcement of the software terms would depend on subsection (b)). However, subsection (c)(3) should not apply in the case of software loaded on a new computer. In such a case, (c)(3) would raise intractable questions regarding the transferee's right to return the computer because of dissatisfaction with the software terms and regarding the allocation of expenses for doing so. Further, so long as the transferor satisfies subsections (c)(1) and (c)(2), the computer purchaser has ample opportunity to see the software terms. A purchaser of a new car likely cannot rescind the deal because of dissatisfaction with the warranty terms for the tires. Further, if the purchaser had reasonable access to the tire warranties before the purchase, the purchaser probably should be bound to the terms. These Principles take the position that a software transferee who purchases a new computer with pre-loaded software should be treated no differently.

Under current technology, subsection (c)(4) is satisfied if the transferee can print a hard copy of the electronic terms and save them on the transferee's hard drive.

Illustrations:

5. B, a consumer, downloads a single copy of word-processing software manufactured by A, a software transferor. The standard form is reasonably accessible on the homepage of A's website prior to B's selection of A's software. B clicks "I agree" at the bottom of a standard form presented on a computer screen before the download begins. Section 2.02(c)(1) through (3) are satisfied.

6. B, a consumer, downloads a single copy of word-processing software from A, a software transferor. The standard form is reasonably accessible on the homepage of A's website prior to B's selection of A's software. B clicks "I agree to the terms" on a computer screen that states: "Please read the License because it includes important terms governing your use of the software." The quoted language constitutes a hyperlink that takes the transferee to the terms. Section 2.02(c)(3) is not satisfied.

7. B, a merchant in business for herself, downloads from A, a software manufacturer, a single copy of a software "plug-in" that serves to enhance the user's browser capabilities. The standard-form licensing agreement is available on A's homepage prior to the transaction. However, the license appears in a scroll-down window for two minutes and then disappears. Further, the standard form occupies such a small part of the screen that the form is not readable without special attention. The standard form is not reasonably accessible for both reasons, and § 2.02(c)(1) is not satisfied.

8. B, a small mortgage lender with three employees, telephones A, a software manufacturer, and orders one copy of computer software to assist in the preparation and management of loan-closing documents. B pays by credit card. The software is available to the general public under the same terms. The packaged software delivered to B includes a paper copy of the standard-form licensing agreement that is accessible without opening the software. The terms are not reasonably accessible on A's website prior to the transfer. A has not satisfied § 2.02(c)(1) of these Principles.

d. Comprehensibility. Subsection (d) follows current law in striking incomprehensible terms. Incomprehensible terms are "unintelligible" or ambiguous, use "obscure terminology," conflict with each other, or lack certainty, even after the admission of extrinsic evidence. General contract law asks whether a reasonable person of average intelligence and education can understand the language with ordinary effort, and this test should be applied here.

Illustration:

9. B, a merchant with three employees, downloads a single copy of word-processing software from A, a software transferor. The standard form is reasonably accessible on the homepage of A's website prior to the transaction. B clicks "I agree" at the bottom of a standard form presented on a computer screen before the download begins. Nevertheless, the standard form, in garbled language, fails to clarify that A has conditioned B's access to the word-processing software on B accepting another program consisting of spyware that will monitor B's Internet activity and supply information to a third party. Under § 2.02(d), the spyware terms are not reasonably

SOFTWARE CONTRACTS

comprehensible and therefore not enforceable.

e.   Benefits of website disclosure. These Principles adopt website disclosure as part of a package of best practices because it may be the best strategy for minimizing the problem of market failures in the retail-like, standard-form market for software. Transferors should follow the set of best practices to ensure enforcement of their standard forms and because disclosure is inexpensive. At the same time, at least in theory, transferors will be unable to ignore the increased number of readers of standard forms and shoppers for terms. Transferors will also be mindful of watchdog groups that can easily access the standard form and can spread the word about the use of unsavory terms. Transferors therefore may be moved to write fair terms to preserve their reputations and market shares. Further, website disclosure enables transferees to read and compare terms before the excitement of a particular transaction deflects their focus from the terms. Software transferors will be unable to segregate readers and offer them better terms because of the large number of readers. Businesses in non-competitive industries also may want to write reasonable terms because of the volume of readers. In theory, prices should adequately reflect the quality of the terms.

Section 2.02(c) also supports economic-liberty reasons for enforcing contracts. The idea of individual assent is obviously more robust when transferees have a reasonable opportunity to read and compare terms. As Karl Llewellyn suggested, such transferees have given their blanket assent to reasonable standard terms, regardless of whether they decide to read and shop for terms.

As the primary strategy for dealing with market failures, website disclosure also avoids difficult questions, such as the need to distinguish transferees who should be relieved of their standard-form obligations from those who should remain bound. It is no surprise that transferees exhibit many different emotions and attitudes when they are e-shopping. The law cannot effectively distinguish those software shoppers who are capable of fending for themselves from those who, because of emotional or cognitive deficiencies, may fail to understand adverse terms.

f.   Costs of website disclosure. Website disclosure should be relatively inexpensive. The costs of maintaining a web homepage and displaying a standard form should be insignificant, especially because virtually all software transferors have or soon will have a web page. Nor should enforcement costs be high. . . .

h.   Will website disclosure succeed? The website-disclosure provisions of subsection (c), if followed, will fail to motivate transferors to write reasonable standard terms if transferees still do not read and shop for terms or watchdog groups fail to spread the word or are otherwise ineffectual. Many commentators are not optimistic about disclosure as a remedy for market failures in standard-form contracting. They have observed the relative failure of truth-in-lending and other disclosure legislation. In addition, they have noted that, notwithstanding disclosure, people still have rational reasons for failing to read their forms, decisionmaking processes that deter careful reading, and a limited ability to process all of the information they do read. In the software-contract setting, transferees also exhibit impatience and exuberance that stand in the way of a measured response to disclosed terms. In fact, if a transferee is not contemplating an immediate transaction, she may find reading terms especially tedious and worthless. Further, the barrage of new information that disclosure will make available on the Internet

464

may only increase the problem of information overload.

In addition, watchdog groups may be ill-equipped to police unsavory terms, either because they fail to identify particularly problematic terms or because they fail to spread the word adequately because of their lack of influence or the lack of exposure of their websites.

Perhaps the most ominous possibility is that website disclosure will fail to increase transferee reading of terms, but will create a safe haven for businesses to draft marginal ones. Most courts contemplating the enforcement of standard terms under doctrines such as unconscionability look for problems with the bargaining process and with the substantive unfairness of the terms. The more outrageous the bargaining process, the more likely a court will strike a substantive term, and vice versa. In light of the judicial acceptance of such a sliding scale, marginal terms that do not quite meet the test of substantive abuse may be enforceable because of their disclosure on the website. In fact, there may be some justice to this approach, especially if competitors of the transferor offered better terms so that the transferee had a choice. After all, if a term is not substantively unconscionable, is fully disclosed, and the transferee had options, on what grounds should it be stricken? Indeed, § 1.11 of these Principles adopts the traditional sliding-scale approach of unconscionability because of its soundness.

Nonetheless, increasing the enforcement of some marginal terms is a real concern. Still, affording transferees the opportunity to read and compare terms prior to a transaction as well as during or, in the case of shrinkwrap, sometimes even after a transaction is likely the most promising of many imperfect solutions. Other methods of dealing with market failures run into numerous problems of their own. See supra the Summary Overview to Topic 2 of this Chapter. Further, disclosure is inexpensive and unlikely to impede commerce even if it fails to resolve market imperfections. In addition, including businesses in the coverage of § 2.02 should increase the incentive of drafters to write reasonable terms because businesses are more likely to read disclosed terms. And even if, in the short run, software transferors rely on § 2.02(b) instead of (c) or benefit from disclosure more than transferees, eventually the word should get out about a transferor who fails to disclose terms on its website and who continues to employ unsavory terms. Such a transferor's incentives should change as it loses market share.

Illustration:

11. B, a consumer, downloads a single copy of virus-protection software from A, a software transferor. The governing standard form is reasonably accessible on the homepage of A's website prior to B's selection of A's software. B clicks "I agree," at the end of a computer screen presenting the standard form before the download begins. A standard term allows the software transferor to "collect nonpersonal information about B's web surfing and computer use." The term may be substantively suspect, but its disclosure prior to the transaction makes a determination of unconscionability problematic. Nevertheless, in the long run, A may replace the provision because of adverse publicity and the loss of market share.

RESTATEMENT OF THE LAW
CONSUMER CONTRACTS

TENTATIVE DRAFT
(APRIL 18, 2019)[*]

Reporters' Introduction: Consumer contracts present a fundamental challenge to the law of contracts, arising from the asymmetry in information, sophistication, and stakes between the parties to these contracts—the business and the consumers. On one side stands a well-informed and counseled business party, entering numerous identical transactions, with the tools and sophistication to understand and draft detailed legal terms and design practices that serve its commercial goals. On the other side stand consumers who are informed only about some core aspects of the transaction, but rarely about the list of standard terms. These consumers enter the transaction solely for personal or household purposes, without any professional understanding of its legal contours. It is both irrational and infeasible for most consumers to keep up with the increasingly complex terms provided by businesses in the multitude of transactions, large and small, entered into daily.

There are many benefits to standard-form contracting, even in such asymmetric environments. The efficiencies of mass production and mass distribution of products and services would be hindered if the terms of each transaction with each consumer had to be individually negotiated. These efficiencies can benefit all market participants, and the law has accordingly viewed standard-form contracting favorably, enforcing such contracts without mounting special impediments.

But the benefits of standard-form contracting are not without risks. Because consumers typically lack the information, sophistication, and incentive to monitor the terms appended to their transactions, there is a concern that businesses will include terms that are unreasonably one-sided, unfair, and inefficient. In the absence of scrutiny from their customers, businesses might overreach and draft terms of agreement that undermine some of the value that consumers reasonably expected. Such overreaching might persist even in competitive environments.

In dealing with this fundamental challenge of potential abuse in asymmetric contracting environments, consumer-contract law deploys several policing techniques. The first set of techniques fit within the doctrine of mutual assent—the rules that determine how a contract is formed, which

[*] As of the date of publication, this Draft has not been considered by the members of The American Law Institute and does not represent the position of the Institute on any of the issues with which it deals. The action, if any, taken by the members with respect to this Draft may be ascertained by consulting the Annual Proceedings of the Institute, which are published following each Annual Meeting.

terms are adopted into the agreement, and what processes a business must follow to alert consumers to the terms being introduced and to the consequences of their adoption. The second set of techniques involve mandatory restrictions over the substance of the deal—rules that limit the discretion of the business in drafting contract terms and set boundaries to the permissible terms of contracts.

Questions relating to these policing techniques have emerged at the forefront of consumer-contract case law in recent decades. In the area of contract formation, technological advances have made it easier for business parties to draft and disseminate lengthy documents with (often self-serving) contractual terms at the initiation phases of consumer transactions and to modify those terms periodically. Whereas shopping at a grocery store in the brick and mortar world entails very few standard contract terms (and many legally supplied gap-fillers), shopping at the online outlet of that store now entails a lengthy list of standard terms. The proliferation of lengthy standard-term contracts, mostly in digital form, makes it practically impossible for consumers to scrutinize the terms and evaluate them prior to manifesting assent. A signature at the bottom of the form, or a click "I Accept" is, at best, a declaration "I know I am agreeing to something, but I don't know to what. I trust that if something really bad is buried in the fine print, the law will protect me from its bite." In such environments, whether the lengthy terms are presented to the consumer before or after the decision to enter the transaction has little bearing on the consumer's awareness or understanding of the terms, as the process of review-and-scrutiny has become largely impractical.

Likewise, questions relating to the second set of policing techniques—the limits of permissible contracting—have emerged at the other forefront of consumer-contract law. As standard-form contracts increasingly replace longstanding default rules with provisions drafted by business entities, courts have been called upon to police their reach. Whether the terms are excessively one-sided and unfair, or merely diverge from the consumer's reasonable expectations as shaped by the business's marketing practices, common-law courts and consumer-protection statutes establish a framework for marking the boundaries. Traditional doctrines like unconscionability and misrepresentation have been applied to police suspect practices and terms relating to the subject matter of the transaction, to the remedies that consumers or the business may seek when the transaction fails, to choices of law and forum, to the business's discretion to specify and adjust contractual obligations, and to many other areas of contracting.

Common-law courts have sought to address the concern for potential abuse in asymmetric contracting environments through both techniques—the assent doctrine and mandatory limits over permissible contracting. Courts have established some minimum requirements relating to the manner in which the agreements are presented to consumers and to the conspicuousness of the alerts that consumers receive. At the same time, courts have developed standards that prohibit various intolerable or deceptive terms even if those terms pass through the filter of mutual assent.

Because the imbalance between businesses and consumers is so great, the application of contract law's general rules of mutual assent alone are not likely to level the playing field. In a world of lengthy standard forms, which consumers are unlikely to read, more restrictive assent rules that demand more disclosures, more notifications and alerts, and more structured templates for manifesting assent are unlikely to produce substantial benefit for consumers. Similarly, outside the common law, the Uniform Commercial Code's rule that disclaimers of implied warranties become effective and are adopted as part of the contract only if made in a conspicuous manner induced lengthy disclaimer paragraphs in ALL CAPS typeface, but again without curing the imbalance between the business and the consumer. As the length and incidence of standard-form contracts have grown, it has become all the less plausible to expect consumers to read and take informed account of the contracts' provisions. In these environments, strengthening the disclosure requirements emanating from contract law's general rules of mutual assent would not prompt consumers to read the terms, to carefully weigh them, and to ultimately make more prudent contracting decisions. Since advance disclosure of standard terms generally does not render the assent process any more meaningful, the "opportunity to read" technique, which courts have embraced, is quite ineffective in consumer contracts. Some observers have even argued that mandating more disclosures might "backfire" by creating a false presumption of meaningful assent, thus undercutting the second policing technique—the ex post scrutiny of contract terms.

Despite the limited effectiveness of the assent doctrine and of advance disclosure rules in producing environments of informed consent, courts have—without exception—endorsed and enforced standard form contracts, as long as some necessary requirements are met. This Restatement states the requirements developed by common-law courts for the adoption of standard contract terms into consumer contracts. The requirements focus on the timing, format of presentation, context, and substance of the notifications consumers receive regarding the existence of terms applying to the transaction. The goal of these court-developed requirements is to afford consumers a meaningful opportunity to review the terms and to avoid the transaction. While some variation exists among courts and jurisdictions concerning the necessary substance and scope of the notifications accompanying the presentation of standard contract terms, this Restatement presents a comprehensive set of requirements unifying this common-law jurisprudence. Satisfaction of such requirements does not impose significant burdens on businesses or consumers interested in quick, streamlined completion of transactions. Adherence

469

by businesses to these procedures would provide certainty surrounding the process of adoption of standard contract terms.

In addition to the rules governing the adoption of standard contract terms, this Restatement unifies and presents the primary common-law mandatory restrictions over the substance of those terms. One category of restrictions, which common-law courts have developed primarily under the unconscionability doctrine, protects consumers against egregiously unfair terms. Another category of restrictions protects consumers from standard contract terms that negate or undermine consumers' reasonably expected benefits from the bargain. At the center of this second safeguard stand rules that give effect to representations, affirmations, and promises made to consumers, even when meticulous language in the standard contract terms purports to undo such effect.

In recent decades, an important question regarding the scope of the unconscionability safeguard is the effect of limits (stipulated in standard contract terms) on the ability of consumers to pursue a complaint or to seek reasonable redress, particularly by channeling all disputes to arbitration or barring class actions. Many courts have held that imposing express or de facto class-action bars on consumers is unconscionable, because such limitations render the enforcement of consumer contractual rights impractical. Recently, however, the enforceability of these terms has turned also on the provisions of various federal statutes. One such statute is the Federal Arbitration Act (FAA), which has been held by the U.S. Supreme Court to preempt, in some cases, the application of the common-law doctrine of unconscionability to arbitration clauses.

The interpretation of the FAA and of other federal rules that regulate the procedures for consumers' access to justice is outside the scope of the common law of consumer contracts. This Restatement states the principles that, in the absence of constraints of federal law, guide the application of the doctrine of unconscionability under state law. It takes no position on the proper application of the Federal Arbitration Act or other statutes governing enforceability of or limits on arbitration provisions, and the way such statutes affect the application of the unconscionability standard.

The ex post scrutiny of permissible contracting, as well as the scrutiny of standard contract terms that conflict with other promises and representations made to consumers, are not intended to be (nor can they feasibly operate as) a replacement for private ordering. Parties are allowed to design their transactions, and standard contract terms—despite being invisible to most consumers—are an indispensable part of the transaction. Parties may agree to bargain-basement terms, if they so wish, and for the right price. The ex post scrutiny by courts is only intended to uproot terms so unfair that they would be unlikely to survive in an environment of meaningful free choice, or that stealthily peel off the value that consumers bargained for.

Consumer-contract law as developed by courts reflects Karl Llewellyn's familiar model: a fairly streamlined adoption of standard contract terms (the "supplementary boilerplate," in Llewellyn's words), along with rigorous scrutiny to protect the spirit of the bargained-for deal ("the dickered terms"). Llewellyn captured this with the concept of "blanket assent" to "any not unreasonable or indecent terms." He recognized then—an insight that has become all the more relevant in the digital era—that the manifestation of assent to a consumer contract results in the adoption of standard contract terms but does not imply meaningful informed consent to these terms. Llewellyn recognized that common-law courts scrutinize and uproot unfair terms and enforce the standard contract terms only if they "do not alter or eviscerate the reasonable meaning of the dickered terms." Karl N. Llewellyn, The Common Law Tradition: Deciding Appeals 370 (New York: Little, Brown, 1960).

This Restatement offers a roadmap to the implementation of Llewellyn's approach, which continues to accurately characterize the approach taken by courts. This Restatement reflects the common-law "blanket assent" principle, whereby courts allow businesses to draft and affix standard contract terms to the transaction, as long as they provide consumers with adequate notices and opportunity to review the terms, as well as a meaningful opportunity to avoid the transaction. At the same time, this Restatement identifies the doctrines and rules arising from common-law jurisprudence, which restrict the effect of standard contract terms by prohibiting businesses from imposing intolerable terms or undermining the core bargain presented to consumers either as part of the dickered terms or in precontractual communications.

In drafting the rules that apply contract law to consumer contracts, this Restatement relies on two main sources. The first and primary source informing this Restatement are the common-law principles that have been guiding courts in adjudicating consumer-contract disputes. Those principles were originally found in the Restatement of the Law Second, Contracts (and often reflect the statutory provisions of the Uniform Commercial Code), but have evolved in particular and important directions that are specific to consumer contracts. When appropriate and consistent with the common law of contracts and the UCC, the rules of this Restatement also reflect the principles of fairness and antideception guiding consumer-protection statutes and regulations. The principles that guide this latter body of law are manifested in several Sections of this Restatement that protect consumers by enforcing the bargain as presented to them, even when some elements are missing from, or qualified in, the standard contract terms. The two bodies of law that address consumer contracts—the general common law of contracts and statutory and regulatory consumer-protection law—appear together in many litigated cases. The present document promotes a greater conceptual unity across these two bodies of law.

The challenges posed by consumer contracts have heightened over the past generation, as courts have adapted traditional contract-law rules to consumer contracts. To track this development, this Restatement follows the traditional ALI methodology and bolsters it with an additional layer of transparency. Primarily, this Restatement follows leading court decisions, eliciting from them the guiding rationales. It clarifies the policy goals underlying the rules applied by courts, and develops their conceptual implications to accord them greater clarity and coherence. In addition, and in order to confirm that the rules identified through this primary method indeed reflect the "law in action," the Reporters read the entire body of contract-law decisions relating to consumer contracts and the rules of this Restatement—higher-court as well as lower-court decisions, both state-court and federal-court cases, published and unpublished, and holdings as well as dicta, made available in online legal-research directories and from secondary sources. By looking at all the information flowing from case law and carefully organizing it according to outcomes, rationales, and influence, this methodology made it possible to examine with greater subtlety the emerging rules, their impact, and their prominence. It decreases the possibility that important or well-reasoned cases may have been missed, and allows a closer consideration of the evolution of the doctrine to better understand how courts address key issues. We thus present a Restatement that reflects the rules as elicited from the most influential and persuasive court decisions, along with the assurance that these rules are indeed widely accepted by the courts in the many jurisdictions within the United States. It is important to emphasize that the examination of the entire body of case law does not replace nor modify the traditional legal analysis—the craft of discovering the DNA of the law through experienced and informed reading of persuasive sources. Rather, the full landscape view bolsters the traditional approach with an added measure of comprehensiveness and transparency. The traditional method of legal reasoning is reflected in the black letter and explicated in the Comments to the Sections of this Restatement. The comprehensive analysis of the entire case law is explained and reported in Reporters' Notes accompanying the relevant Sections.

As explained above, this Restatement draws on common-law principles that have antecedents in the Restatement of the Law Second, Contracts. The application of those principles in the area of consumer contracts produced the rules that are restated here. In restating these rules in the consumer context, the present document seeks to provide courts with more tailored guidance in adjudicating consumer-contract disputes than the Restatement Second of Contracts offers, reflecting developments in consumer-contract law since the completion of the Restatement Second of Contracts. Importantly, this Restatement does not purport to cover all possible aspects of a consumer-contracts case. The Restatement Second of Contracts continues to provide valuable guidance on general contract-law questions in the consumer context that are not covered in this Restatement.

This Restatement is organized as follows. Section 1 defines key terms. The first substantive rule is the Adoption of Standard Contract Terms provision in § 2. The rule reflects an approach, widely embraced by a large majority of courts, that enables businesses to design the terms of the transaction, as long as they provide reasonable notice and meaningful opportunity to review the terms and to avoid the transaction. This rule is complemented by a related provision in § 3, extending similar principles to modifications of standard contract terms.

The remaining Sections comprise a set of rules that rely on ex post scrutiny by courts to limit the risk of abuse. Section 4 addresses the problem of open-ended terms, which grant the business unrestricted discretion to specify and adjust its obligations. Section 5 is the unconscionability rule, providing the framework for invalidating terms that unreasonably favor the business party and unfairly surprise the consumer. Section 6 deals with the problem of deception, whereby the standard contract terms conflict with explicit affirmations or promises made to the consumer. Section 7 includes the rules regarding precontractual affirmations and promises. Section 8 creates presumptions of integration for standard contract terms (under the Parol Evidence Rule) and explains how such presumptions are rebutted by prior affirmations of fact or promises. And § 9 completes this list of anti-abuse provisions by stipulating the effects of striking terms out of contracts.

§ 1. Definitions and Scope

(a) Definitions:

(1) "Consumer"—An individual acting primarily for personal, family, or household purposes.

(2) "Business"—An individual or entity other than a consumer that regularly participates in or solicits, directly or indirectly, transactions with consumers.

(3) "Contract"—A promise or set of promises for the breach of which the law gives a remedy, or the performance of which the law in some way recognizes as a duty.

(4) "Consumer contract"—A contract between a business and a consumer other than an employment contract.

(5) "Standard contract term"—A term, relating to a consumer contract, that has been drafted prior to the transaction for use in multiple transactions between the business and consumer parties.

(6) "Affirmation of fact or promise"—Any statement about the transaction, including but not limited to statements about quantity, quality, characteristics, utility, price, discount, comparative cost, ser-

vice, and remedy, intended to reach consumers, including in negotiations, advertising, brochures, or labels, or in any record accompanying the transaction, but excluding statements that would be reasonably understood by consumers as "puffing" or statements of belief not founded on fact.

(7) "Good faith"—Honesty in fact and the observance of reasonable commercial standards of fair dealing.

(b) Scope: This Restatement applies to consumer contracts, except to the extent that a matter is governed by statute or regulation. It restates contract-law principles under state law and takes no position on the proper relationship between statutory or regulatory requirements and these principles.

Comment:

... *4. "Standard contract terms" defined.* The definition of "standard contract term" focuses on the pre-drafting factor, which captures a key feature of consumer contracts: their multi-transaction application. Pre-drafting also implies that there is no negotiation between the business and the consumer over the language of those terms. In some cases, negotiation of the standard contract terms is present, as when the consumer may choose which version of the standard terms applies, or choose to avoid a particular set of terms. In other cases, tailoring of the standard contract terms is present, as when the terms are tailored per consumer based on personal information known to the business. Such negotiated or tailored terms are considered "standard contract terms" despite the absence of uniform content, because of the multi-transaction application.

Illustrations:

1. A credit-card issuer includes a pre-drafted arbitration clause in the terms that it offers to all of its consumer customers. The arbitration clause is a standard contract term, as defined in subsection (a)(5), even if the consumer can prevent it from becoming part of the contract by a notice to the business.

2. An insurer offers different, non-negotiated premiums to different policyholders based on a formula that rates each policyholder's risk. The premium is not negotiable. The term setting the premium is a standard contract term, as defined in subsection (a)(5).

5. *Core deal terms versus boilerplate.* Standard contract terms may include both terms that consumers readily identify as characterizing the transaction, or "core deal terms," as well as terms that are usually appended to the transaction in fine print, or "boilerplate." The criteria for adoption and legal enforceability may vary according to the classification of the standard contract term or the circumstances in which the term is provided to the consumer, and thus some rules of this Restatement may apply differently to core deal terms versus boilerplate (for example, rules relating to adoption of terms under §§ 2 and 3, unconscionability under § 5, deception under § 6, disclaimers under § 7(c), and integration under § 8).

Illustration:

3. A product is sold online for a fixed price. The listing of the product contains a description of the product, the price, the delivery charge, and a "30-day money-back" statement, as well as a link to the

seller's website, where additional terms of sale are posted. All are standard contract terms as defined in subsection (a)(5), even though only some of them (the price, the description of the goods, the delivery charge, and the "30-day money-back" statement) are core deal terms.

6. *"Affirmation of fact or promise" defined.* The definition of "affirmation of fact or promise" includes express statements, as well as reasonable interpretations of express statements, and implications that reasonably flow from express statements or acts. Affirmations and promises can be found, for example, on a business's website, on packaging materials, and in advertisements. The definition does not include statements that should be reasonably understood as "puffing" or statements of belief not founded on fact. (Compare Restatement of the Law Second, Contracts §§ 168–169; UCC § 2–313(2).) As explained in §§ 6 to 8, an affirmation or promise can result in nonenforcement of inconsistent standard contract terms (§ 6), can create an obligation that becomes part of the consumer contract (§ 7), and can rebut the presumption of partial or complete integration of the standard contract terms (§ 8).

7. *"Good faith" defined.* The definition of "good faith" follows the Uniform Commercial Code § 1–201(b)(20), which has evolved since the original version of the Uniform Commercial Code. Although various formulations and explications of the duty of good faith have been adopted in different sources of law, they all share the same ultimate goal. The duty of good faith is intended to capture and weed out various forms of opportunistic behavior— including unfair advantage-taking, hold up, and dishonesty—that reduce the value of contracting and require costly precautions. Good-faith performance or enforcement of a contract em-

phasizes faithfulness to an agreed common purpose and consistency with the justified expectations of the other party. The element of "observance of reasonable commercial standards of fair dealing" is particularly necessary when businesses operate through agents and deal with numerous consumers. In these settings, unfair advantage-taking may occur even without dishonesty in fact. Compare Restatement of the Law Second, Contracts § 205, Comment *a*. This definition does not intend to change the meaning of the implied covenant of good faith and fair dealing.

. . . 9. *Contracts over data and privacy.* A "consumer contract" is defined by the type of parties that enter it, not by the subject matter that it governs. Consumer contracts could govern a variety of topics, including the business's data and privacy policies. Indeed, consumer transactions often involve attempts by the business to form agreements governing the business's treatment of consumers' personal information, including the business's collection, use, sharing, protection, or other handling of personal information. Such matters have become an important economic component of many consumer transactions. While some privacy notices are required by law and some reflect obligations that are not contractual in their nature, and while the legal treatment of such aspects of the agreement may be subject to additional area-specific rules (see, e.g., Principles of the Law, Data Privacy, Introductory Note), the business's rights and obligations could also be governed by contract law and by the rules of this Restatement. Accordingly, this Restatement is not intended to determine which data or privacy policies or terms constitute or become part of contracts, but merely to provide principles of contract law for those that do. Specifically, if the data and privacy terms are presented to consumers in a manner that satisfies the definitions of "contract" and "consumer contract," courts should apply the rules of this Restatement (as well as other contract-law rules, but subject to specific rules of data-privacy law) to determine the formation, scope, and consequences of an agreement over data.

Illustration:

4. A consumer uses a business's website to order a product. Before the purchase is complete, the website refers the consumer to two sets of standard contract terms that the website says will apply to the transaction. The first set of terms is titled "Terms of Service" and covers several issues including warranties, remedies, choice of law and forum, and intellectual-property rights. The second set of terms is titled "Privacy Policy" and states the agreements of the parties with respect to the scope of personal data collection, use, sharing, and security. The provisions of § 2 of this Restatement that determine whether the "Terms of Service" are adopted into the agreement also determine whether the Privacy Policy is adopted into the agreement.

10. *Relation to the Uniform Commercial Code and other statutory law.* This Restatement restates the rules of the common law of consumer contracts. A significant number of consumer contracts are governed by statutes. Importantly, sales or leases of goods are governed extensively (but not completely) by Articles 2 and 2A of the Uniform Commercial Code (UCC), and other consumer contracts are within the scope of other UCC articles. Of course, the common-law rules set out in this Restatement cannot override statutory provisions of the UCC, and this point is made explicit in subsection (b), and explained here. But the UCC does not create complete legal systems for contracts within its scope, and the common-law rules restated here apply to issues not addressed by the partic-

ular provisions of the statute. Indeed, the UCC provides that common-law principles supplement the UCC unless displaced by particular provisions of the UCC. (See UCC § 1–103(b) and Comment 2 to that Section). In some cases, the UCC is silent as to an issue. In other cases, even when there is a UCC rule generally applicable to a particular issue, the UCC rule does not answer all the questions that may arise in connection with that issue. Thus, many of the common-law rules set out in this Restatement, in addition to applying to non-UCC transactions, will have application to contracts within the scope of the UCC when no particular provisions of the UCC address or displace them. In addition, many of the common-law rules set out in this Restatement are drawn directly from UCC provisions and from case law interpreting them that reflects a widely shared view as to the meaning and application of the UCC.

Certain other subsets of consumer contracts, e.g., credit transactions, insurance contracts, real-estate contracts, or contracts involving investments in securities, are governed by specific federal or state statutes. Consumer contracts for the sale of goods are also governed by the Magnuson-Moss Warranty Act. Many consumer contracts are covered by additional statutes and regulations, including the Federal Trade Commission Act and state Unfair and Deceptive Acts and Practices statutes. This Restatement provides common-law rules that supplement and implement the provisions of these enactments, but in case of conflict or displacement by statute, the statutory rules apply. The statutory rules take precedence also when the statute supplants the common law. The existence of a statute, however, does not, in and of itself, supplant or displace the common-law rules restated herein.

476

In addition, this Restatement takes no position on the proper application of the Federal Arbitration Act or other statutory or regulatory requirements that may affect the enforceability of or limits on arbitration provisions, and the way such requirements may affect application of the stated contract principles. It includes some Illustrations and, in the Reporters' Notes, some case citations, that reference arbitration clauses in consumer contracts. Those references are intended to clarify the principles that guide the application of the doctrine of unconscionability or other contract principles. They are not intended to address the question how these principles align vis-à-vis the law of arbitration.

Parties to a consumer contract are also subject to additional common-law rules. See, for example, the Restatement of the Law Third, Torts: Liability for Economic Harm, and the Restatement of the Law, Liability Insurance. In case of conflict, sector-specific common-law rules may take precedence over the general common-law rules of consumer contracts that are restated herein.

§ 2. Adoption of Standard Contract Terms

(a) A standard contract term is adopted as part of a consumer contract if the consumer manifests assent to the transaction after receiving:

(1) a reasonable notice of the standard contract term and of the intent to include the term as part of the consumer contract, and

(2) a reasonable opportunity to review the standard contract term.

(b) When a standard contract term is available for review only after the consumer manifests assent to the transaction, the standard contract term is adopted as part of the consumer contract if:

(1) before manifesting assent to the transaction, the consumer receives a reasonable notice regarding the existence of the standard contract term intended to be provided later and to be part of the consumer contract, informing the consumer about the opportunity to review and terminate the contract, and explaining that the failure to terminate would result in the adoption of the standard contract term;

(2) after manifesting assent to the transaction, the consumer receives a reasonable opportunity to review the standard contract term; and

(3) after the standard contract term is made available for review, the consumer has a reasonable opportunity to terminate the transaction without unreasonable cost, loss of value, or personal burden, and does not exercise that power.

(c) If the consumer manifests assent to the transaction, a contract exists even if some of the standard contract terms are not adopted. In such case, the terms of the contract are those adopted under subsections (a) and (b), and, if the consumer elects, the unadopted standard terms, along with any terms supplied by law.

Comment:

1. General. This Section describes the procedures for adoption of standard contract terms into consumer contracts. It operates in a reality in which consumers are fully aware of some "core" aspects of the transaction but are unlikely to read and exercise meaningful informed consent to the non-core standard contract terms. The adoption rules seek to preserve the convenience of streamlined contracting while providing consumers reasonable opportunity to scrutinize the standard contract terms and avoid unwanted transactions. Accordingly, this Section identifies minimum requirements for contracting procedures that result in the adoption of standard contract terms. Recognizing, however, that despite these procedures, consumers often enter into contracts without appreciating the effect of the standard contract terms, other Sections of this Restatement provide additional layers of protection against surprising and unfair outcomes.

2. Adoption of standard terms may be separate from manifestation of assent to the transaction. A consumer contract is not formed unless the consumer manifests assent to the transaction. A consumer may manifest assent to the transaction proposed by the business in any manner and by any medium reasonable in the circumstances. Once the transaction is formed, this Section determines which standard contract terms are adopted. While in many instances, the manifestation of assent to the transaction and the adoption of standard contract terms happen at the same time, in other instances they may be done separately. Because the review of the entire body of standard contract terms is an uncommon practice for the great majority of consumers, and because convenience in the method of delivery of the terms benefits consumers and businesses alike, the adoption of standard contract terms can be made either together with or separate from the act of manifesting assent to the transaction. Standard contract terms may be presented to the consumer before the consumer manifests assent to the transaction, at the same time that the consumer manifests assent to the transaction but before the product is delivered or the service is rendered, or when the product is delivered or the service commences. Standard contract terms may also be presented in some combination of the foregoing. Accordingly, a single consumer contract may contain several "packets" of standard contract terms, each adopted in a different manner and at a different time (see Comment 7). Manifesting assent to the transaction as a whole generally involves adoption of at least some standard contract terms—the core deal terms (see § 1, Comment 5; see also Comment 3 to this Section); other standard contract terms may then be adopted separately from those that are adopted concurrently with the manifestation of assent.

Illustration:

1. A consumer rents a car at an airport counter and concludes the transaction by signing a printed sheet titled "Rental Contract." The price and description of the vehicle are prominently displayed on the front of the sheet. The consumer's signature manifests assent to the transaction and constitutes the adoption of the core deal terms (which, in car-rental contracts, typically include the price, the description of the vehicle, and the type of insurance provided). Additional standard contract terms are presented on the back of the sheet, and a statement referring to their inclusion is posted adjacent to the signature line in a prominent fashion. Those terms are adopted concurrently with the manifestation of assent to the transaction via

478

the signature. If, in addition, other standard contract terms are presented to the consumer after the time of signature—for example, in an email sent to the consumer some time later—those terms may be adopted under subsection (b) separately from the manifestation of assent to the transaction (see Comment 5), but only if the requirements of subsection (b) are met.

3. Manifesting assent to the transaction. A consumer may manifest assent to the transaction proposed by the business in any manner and by any medium reasonable in the circumstances. In inviting the consumer to enter a transaction, the business may establish how the assent may be manifested, as long as the manner and medium are reasonable in the circumstances and reasonably communicated to the consumer as manifesting assent. (Compare Restatement of the Law Second, Contracts §§ 30, 50.) Most often, assent to the transaction is manifested by signing an agreement, paying, or clicking "Purchase Now" or "I Agree" after the consumer has been put on reasonable notice that such actions would result in the formation of a legal obligation. Absent such effective communication—for example, when the consumer may reasonably think that proceeding with the activity does not create a set of legally binding obligations—the consumer does not manifest assent to a consumer contract. When manifesting assent, the consumer is usually aware only of the core deal terms. Such core deal terms often include price and payment methods, a shorthand description of the product, key delivery arrangements, and a few successfully communicated legal limitations (for example, the nonrefundable classification of some airline fares or the duration commitment in some service contracts). In assenting to the transaction, the consumer simultaneously adopts those core deal terms—

many of which are standard contract terms under the definition in § 1(a)(5), but some may be nonstandard—as part of the contract.

4. Adoption of terms reasonably available for review prior to manifesting assent to the transaction. When the consumer manifests assent to the transaction, a consumer contract is formed. The consumer contract includes the core deal terms (those which, from the perspective of the consumer, characterize the bargain), as well as other standard and nonstandard contract terms reasonably available for review prior to manifesting assent. Some of these standard contract terms may be explicitly acknowledged by the consumer in the course of manifesting assent to the transaction (see Illustrations 2–4). Other standard contract terms may not be explicitly acknowledged, but as long as the consumer receives reasonable notice of them, including reasonable notice that they are intended to be part of the transaction and that manifesting assent would constitute a legally binding adoption of those terms, and has a reasonable opportunity to review them, they are adopted when the consumer manifests assent to the transaction (see Illustrations 5–6). The standards for reasonable notice and opportunity to review that apply to terms that are not explicitly acknowledged in the course of affirmatively manifesting assent may be more exacting (see Comment 9).

Illustrations:

2. A consumer uses a business's website to purchase a product. To complete the transaction, the website asks the consumer to read the Terms and Conditions that are provided in a scroll-down text box and to click "I Agree." The website does not allow the consumer to complete the purchase without clicking "I Agree." The consumer manifests assent to the transaction

by clicking the button. The terms in the scroll-down box are adopted as part of the contract under subsection (a).

3. Same facts as in Illustration 2, but the Terms and Conditions incorporate by reference a separate list of Privacy Policy terms. The following statement appears in clear type in the first paragraph of the Terms and Conditions: "Additional binding terms related to our Privacy Policy are available here," linking to another webpage with the Privacy Policy terms. The consumer's manifestation of assent to the transaction (by clicking "I Agree") encompasses the additional Privacy Policy terms, and those terms are adopted as part of the contract under subsection (a).

4. A consumer opens an account with a web retailer and clicks an "I Agree" button immediately below the Terms of Service but does not make any purchase. The Terms of Service appear in a text box in the middle of the page and state prominently that they apply to all subsequent purchases made by the consumer using the account. Later, the consumer makes a purchase on this website using the account, without assenting to any terms other than the description of the goods, the price, and the delivery method. The Terms of Service are part of the contract formed under subsection (a) at the time of the purchase because they were available for review in a reasonable manner before the consumer manifested assent to the transaction (see Comment 9).

5. A consumer uses a website to order a product. During the checkout process, the consumer is presented with the core deal terms—the description of the product, the price, and the shipping arrangement. The consumer

manifests assent to the transaction by entering payment information and clicking "Purchase Now." Located immediately in the vicinity of the "Purchase Now" button is an underlined link, in large font and contrasting color, titled "Additional Terms of Sale Applying to Your Purchase." If clicked, the link opens a new webpage containing additional standard contract terms. When the consumer clicks "Purchase Now," the linked terms are adopted as part of the contract under subsection (a) because reasonable notice of the terms and the intent to include them in the consumer contract, as well as a reasonable opportunity to read them, have been given.

6. A consumer enters a dry-cleaner's store. At the entrance, a large sign is posted in such a way that any consumer entering the store will see it and be able to read its terms. The sign states that the store is not responsible for damage to items occurring in the ordinary course of the cleaning process. When the consumer manifests assent to the transaction by completing the drop-off process and receiving an acknowledgment of the order, the standard contract term posted on the sign is adopted as part of the contract under subsection (a).

5. *Adoption of terms after manifesting assent to the transaction.* Subsection (b) identifies an alternative process for the adoption of standard contract terms, under which terms may be made available for review for the first time after the consumer manifests assent to the transaction. The process of replacing the opportunity to read prior to assent with a reasonable post-assent review period and termination right allows the parties to enter transactions with greater ease and without sacrificing any meaningful protection that advance reading of the contract bestows. Subsection (b) vali-

dates this process, under which terms are adopted if the consumer receives: (1) reasonable notice before manifesting assent to the transaction that additional standard contract terms will be presented after manifesting assent to the transaction, including reasonable notice that such terms are intended to be part of the transaction; (2) reasonable opportunity to review the terms upon their arrival; and (3) the opportunity to terminate the entire transaction without unreasonable cost, risk, or personal burden. The majority of courts do not require all the notices listed in subsection (b)(1), focusing instead on the opportunity to review and terminate in subsections (b)(2) and (3). To avoid surprising the consumer with unexpected terms, this Restatement endorses the more restrictive approach, adopted by a minority of courts, requiring that before manifesting assent to the transaction, the consumer must be reasonably notified about the opportunity to review the newly available standard contract terms and to terminate the transaction, and that failure to terminate would result in the adoption of the standard contract terms.

Illustration:

7. A consumer orders a product from a business by signing an agreement that contains the core deal terms and making a payment. On the form, a clearly visible statement immediately above the signature line informs the consumer that additional standard contract terms will be arriving with the product and will become part of the contract if the consumer does not return the product. Later, along with the delivered product, the consumer receives the additional standard contract terms that include an express warranty statement and limitations on remedies. The terms appear inside an envelope labeled "Terms and Conditions" and are affixed to the

product. They contain a clear, upfront statement that the consumer has a right to return the product within 30 days if she does not agree with the terms, and that reasonable return shipping costs will be paid by the business. The standard terms are adopted as part of the contract under subsection (b). The same result applies if the Terms and Conditions arrive separately from the product, e.g., with a welcome letter delivered by mail, as long as such letter provides reasonable notice that it is related to the purchase of the product and that it contains terms that govern that transaction, as well as a reasonable notice of the opportunity to terminate the transaction.

6. *Adoption of terms by entry to, or use of, a proprietary environment of the business.* Standard contract terms governing the proprietary environment of the business—whether physical or digital—may be adopted as part of a consumer contract upon entry to, or continued use of, that environment, even if no purchase is concluded while in the environment. The deliberate act of entering the business's proprietary environment and remaining in it long enough to gain access to the content and benefits it confers constitutes a manifestation of assent by the consumer to a transaction. The transaction consists of the right to use the proprietary environment and receive the benefits it is reasonably expected to confer, under the terms specified by the business, including terms that specify the rights of the business and the obligations of the consumer, as long as the consumer has reason to know that the use of the proprietary environment was offered subject to those terms. The consumer has a reason to know if a reasonable notice is provided that use of the proprietary environment (including the use upon recurring entries) is governed by legally binding standard

contract terms, which the consumer then has a reasonable opportunity to review (see Comment 9). If such notice and opportunity to review are provided to the consumer prior to entry, the standard contract terms are adopted upon entry. If, instead, the notice and opportunity to review are provided only after entry (for example, when the consumer enters the business's website and only then is able to access a link governing the use of the website), the manifestation of assent to the transaction and the adoption of the terms occur upon the continued use of the proprietary environment and the receipt of its benefits. In such case, the consumer must receive a reasonable notice that continued use will constitute adoption of the terms, a reasonable opportunity to review the terms, and a reasonable opportunity to exit without being bound to the terms. In some contexts, market norms and course of dealings may provide sufficient notice to the consumer that additional standard contract terms are intended to apply to the transaction (see Comment 9). Compare Restatement of the Law Second, Contracts § 69(1)(a), in which the taking of the benefit of offered services can serve as a manifestation of assent by the recipient. Assent to the transaction and adoption of the standard contract terms are effective only if the consumer has a reasonable opportunity to terminate the transaction without being bound (thereby satisfying the "reasonable opportunity to reject" requirement of § 69(1)(a)).

Illustrations:

8.   A consumer parks her car in a private parking lot. A prominent sign at the entrance to the lot states that a $10 per hour charge will be collected upon exit from the lot and that the business is not responsible for damage to the vehicle while parked in the lot. By entering the lot, the consumer manifests as-sent to the transaction concerning the use of the parking lot, and the terms posted on the sign are adopted under subsection (a).

9.   A consumer visits a department store. A prominent sign posted at the entrance to the store's parking lot states that parking is free while visiting the store, and that the store is not responsible for damage to the vehicle while parked in the lot. The consumer parks the car in the lot and browses the store's aisles but does not make any purchase. Upon exit, the consumer discovers that the car was damaged. By entering the lot, the consumer manifests assent to the transaction concerning the use of the parking lot and the terms posted on the sign are adopted under subsection (a).

10.   A consumer enters an information-service website's homepage for the purpose of gaining access to its information content, without creating an account or making a purchase, and without checking a box or clicking a link evidencing assent to any agreement. At the top of the homepage, a notice is posted in large font, underlined, and in contrasting color: "By continuing past this page, you agree to abide by the Terms of Use for this site." The phrase "Terms of Use" is under-lined and highlighted. If clicked, it directs the consumer to a page that contains the full Terms of Use. By continuing past the homepage, the consumer manifests assent to the transaction concerning the use of the website and the Terms of Use are adopted under subsection (a).

11.   A consumer is directed from Website A, a search platform where users can search and access information from numerous sources, to linked content appearing on Website B, a separate information-service website. Initially, when

clicking on the link that appears on Website A, only the first paragraph of the content on Website B's page is visible, with a "Read More" button obscuring the remainder of the content. A notice prominently appearing near the "Read More" button states that the use of Website B is governed by standard contract terms. Clicking on the "Read More" button allows the consumer to enter and to access the full content of Website B's page. By clicking "Read More" the consumer manifests assent to the transaction with Website B governing the access to the content posted on the page. If the consumer can view the terms prior to clicking "Read More" (for example, if a link to the terms appears within the notice), the standard contract terms are adopted under subsection (a). If, instead, the consumer can only view the terms after clicking "Read More" (for example, a prominent link to them appears at the bottom of the full-content page), the terms may be adopted under subsection (b), but only if the consumer has an opportunity to reject the application of the terms by exiting the full page of Website B, and does not do so.

7. *The possibility of multiple contracts.* A single manifestation of assent could result in multiple contracts, if the requirements of this Section are satisfied for each of those contracts. The additional contract is formed only if it conforms to the reasonable expectations of the consumer, so as to avoid imposing on the consumer an unwanted additional contractual relationship. The consumer must be specifically notified, and thus must reasonably expect, that by manifesting assent to the transaction an additional contract with this or another party will be created.

In particular, in connection with a purchase at a retail store, it is possible and convenient for the consum-er to enter, by one act of manifesting assent, into two contracts—one contract with the retailer and a second contract with the manufacturer of the purchased product (and thus avoid the inconvenience of multiple affirmative acts of manifesting assent). At times, the terms governing the second contract, offered by the manufacturer of the product, are available for review prior to the manifestation of assent, for example, when they are presented to the consumer as part of the description of the product before checkout and payment to a retailer. In such cases, subsection (a) determines whether the terms are adopted. Other times, the terms provided by the manufacturer are available to review for the first time only after the consumer manifests assent to the transaction. In such cases, subsection (b) determines whether the terms are adopted. Under either case, the terms offered by the manufacturer are adopted if the consumer receives reasonable notice, before manifesting assent to the transaction, that a separate contract with the manufacturer will be formed and that the manifestation of assent to the transaction will apply also to this additional contract. And, under either case, the requirements of either subsection (a) or subsection (b) must also be met in order for the standard contract terms offered by the manufacturer to be adopted. An attempt to impose on the consumer a contractual relationship with a third party, if that contractual relationship does not satisfy the requirements of this Section and conflicts with the consumer's reasonable expectations, may also be deceptive under § 6.

Illustrations:

12. A consumer purchases a product at an online store and, at the checkout screen, manifests assent to a list of standard contract terms governing the transaction with the retailer, which are promi-

nently offered for review prior to the transaction. In addition, a notice on the screen titled "Additional Terms of Sale" appears in a manner reasonably visible to the consumer, instructing that by clicking "Purchase Now" the consumer is accepting terms stipulated by the manufacturer, which are available in a printed booklet inside the box. In the booklet, at the top of the first page, the consumer is informed of her right to return the product within 30 days at no cost if she does not agree with the terms. In this scenario, two consumer contracts are formed by manifesting assent to the purchase at the retail outlet. The first contract is with the retailer, and contains the core deal terms as well as the standard contract terms that the retailer has specified, in accordance with subsection (a). The second contract is with the manufacturer, assent to which is also manifested at the time of purchase. It contains the standard contract terms specified by the manufacturer, and they are adopted at the end of the 30-day return period, in accordance with subsection (b).

13. A consumer purchases from a dealer a new car, which is delivered with a three-month trial subscription for satellite radio. When the consumer manifests assent to the purchase, no reference is made concerning a separate contract with a satellite-radio service and the intent to adopt terms governing that service. A month after the purchase, the consumer receives a Service Agreement by mail from the satellite-radio business, notifying the consumer about the standard contract terms governing the service. Since the customer had no notice prior to the manifestation of assent to the transaction with the dealer that such manifestation of assent would apply also to a sep-

arate contract governing the satellite-radio service and that the standard contract terms governing this service would be mailed, no contract is formed between the consumer and the satellite-radio business. The standard contract terms mailed to the consumer concerning the satellite-radio service are not adopted.

8. *Combined use of different adoption processes.* A business might use different adoption processes for different sets of terms within a single consumer contract. For instance, the business may present some standard contract terms in advance and ask the consumer to explicitly acknowledge them in the course of manifesting assent to the transaction (e.g., by clicking "I Agree"), and may present other standard contract terms in a separate format, which the consumer is not asked to affirmatively acknowledge (e.g., the other terms may be posted on a website, or packaged with the product). Thus, it is possible to adopt some standard contract terms under subsection (a) and others under subsection (b). The combined adoption of different sets of terms occurs if the requirements for adoption under either subsection (a) or (b) are fully satisfied for each set of terms.

Illustration:

14. A consumer in State A uses a website to create a service account. The consumer is asked to click "I Agree" at the bottom of a scroll box titled "Terms of Service" in which some standard contract terms are presented. Immediately adjacent to the "I Agree" button appears a clearly labeled, easily identifiable statement: "Additional terms relating to subscribers in State A will be sent to you within 72 hours. They will become part of your contract with us unless you notify us within 14 days of your decision to cancel your account."

By clicking "I Agree" the consumer manifests assent to the transaction and adopts the terms presented in the scroll box under subsection (a). The additional terms are adopted under subsection (b) if the consumer does not cancel the account within 14 days of their presentation.

9. *Notice and opportunity to review.* The consumer must receive reasonable notice of the existence of the standard contract terms, including reasonable indication that they are intended to be part of a legally binding transaction to which the consumer is manifesting assent, and a reasonable opportunity to review the terms. In some contexts, market norms, or course of dealing, may provide sufficient notice to the consumer that additional standard contract terms are intended to apply to the transaction. The characteristics of the contracting parties may also be taken into account when evaluating the reasonableness of the notice (e.g., when a product or service is offered to a small segment of especially sophisticated consumers). These requirements of notice and opportunity to review apply when the terms are available for review prior to the manifestation of assent to the transaction and are adopted under subsection (a), as well as when the terms are available for review only after the manifestation of assent to the transaction under subsection (b). (Compare UCC § 1–202 (defining "Notice").)

Illustrations:

15. A consumer visits a business's website to purchase a product. During the checkout process, the consumer enters her credit-card information and shipping address, and is then required to click "I agree to purchase." The business places a link to Terms and Conditions at the bottom of every one of its webpages, including at the bottom of the checkout page. The link is in a font smaller than the one used in the rest of the website, and on the checkout page the link can only be seen and accessed by scrolling down the page, otherwise it is not visible when the consumer clicks "I agree to purchase." The link does not provide reasonable notice, and therefore the linked terms are not adopted as part of the contract. If, instead, there is a prominent, stand-alone notice in a central portion of the checkout page, in contrasting, large font, not blended with other notices, stating that the transaction is subject to Terms and Conditions that are noticeably linked for the consumer to access, all visible when the consumer clicks "I agree to purchase," then the terms are adopted as part of the contract under subsection (a).

16. A purchase agreement is drafted by the business to be presented to consumers on the business's website, but is sometimes presented to consumers as a paper printout at the business's service desk in a department store. On the online version, the consumer is asked to click "I Agree" at the bottom, and on the paper-printout version the consumer is asked to affix a signature next to the "I Agree" box. Immediately above the location of the "I Agree" click, there is a phrase stating "Additional Terms." In the online version, the phrase "Additional Terms" appears as a link, in distinct color font, which, if clicked, opens a page with the additional terms. In the paper-printout version, the phrase "Additional Terms" appears in an underlined, pale font, and no other information is provided as to what this phrase implies or how to access the additional terms. The link appearance in the online version provides the consumer reasonable notice and opportunity to review, and the additional terms

485

are adopted once the consumer manifests assent to the transaction, under subsection (a). The underlined phrase in the paper-printout version does not provide the consumer reasonable notice and opportunity to review, and the terms are not adopted under subsection (a). If, however, along with the printout version the consumer receives an explicit explanation that the Additional Terms apply to the transaction and could be obtained by asking the sales clerk for a readily available copy for the consumer to review, the terms are adopted under subsection (a).

17. A consumer purchases a product at a retail store. During checkout, the consumer signs a form titled "Agreement" which includes the store's General Terms and Conditions. Later, upon unpacking the product, the consumer finds attached a brochure from the manufacturer that contains the manufacturer's standard contract terms, including an End User License Agreement for the software installed on the product. No advance notice was given to the consumer about these "terms in the box" either during the purchase process with the retailer or on the box presented to the consumer prior to purchase. Because such notice is lacking, the terms in the brochure are not adopted as part of the consumer contract. If, instead, there was a prominent notice, either on the box or presented by the retailer, that further terms were available for review once the consumer opened the box, the notice requirement would be satisfied. In such case, the terms in the brochure would be adopted under subsection (b) (subject to notice to the consumer of the consumer's right to terminate the transaction within a reasonable

time after reviewing the terms; see also Comment 10.)

18. A consumer visits a business's website to order a service. During the checkout process, the consumer is presented with a scroll window with the heading "Service Agreement" in which the first two lines of the agreement's text are visible. Below the scroll window, a paragraph in bold text explains that by clicking "Accept and Continue" the consumer authorizes the business to obtain the consumer's personal credit profile from a third party. It does not state that by clicking "Accept and Continue" the consumer also adopts the "Service Agreement." The consumer manifests assent to the transaction by clicking the "Accept and Continue" button. The terms in the "Service Agreement" are not adopted as part of the contract because the consumer did not receive adequate notice that assent applies to the "Service Agreement."

19. A consumer purchases a product at a retail store. During checkout, the consumer is presented with a 120-page brochure titled "Operation Manual." The brochure contains instructions from the manufacturer on how to use the product. It also contains, on page 97, an arbitration agreement applying to the contract with the manufacturer. Because the presentation of the brochure as a "Manual" does not include any language indicating that standard contract terms affecting the consumer's rights are included in the Manual, there is no reasonable notice of the existence of the standard contract terms and they are not adopted as part of the contract under subsection (a).

20. A consumer signs up for in-flight Wi-Fi service. On the "create account" page, immediately be-

low the boxes in which the consumer is instructed to enter personal information, appears a prominent "NEXT" button that takes the consumer to a webpage on which the consumer is instructed to enter credit-card information. Above the "NEXT" button, the following statement appears in small font that is not distinguished—by size, color, or typeface—from other text on the screen: "By clicking 'NEXT' I agree to the *terms of use* and *privacy policy*." The words "terms of use" and "privacy policy" are hyperlinks and, if clicked, would take the consumer to webpages that include the business's terms of use and privacy policy, respectively. The consumer clicks "NEXT," completes the registration process, and proceeds to use the in-flight Wi-Fi service. There is no reasonable notice of the existence of the standard contract terms and they are not adopted as part of the contract under subsection (a). If instead the statement above the "NEXT" button was made conspicuous through the use of large, different colored font (or large, bold-faced font), the notice requirement would be satisfied and the terms of use would be adopted under subsection (a).

21. A consumer installs an application on a smartphone and is prompted to enter personal information in a sequence of screens. In the middle of the last screen, where the consumer is asked to provide payment information, appears a conspicuous "Register" button that the consumer must click to complete the installation. Immediately below that button and in large, contrasting, and conspicuous font, against an otherwise uncluttered background, there is a statement notifying the consumer that by clicking the "Register" button the consumer is agreeing to the Terms of Service

and Privacy Policy, both of which are hyperlinked and underlined in contrasting colors. There is reasonable notice of the Terms of Service and Privacy Policy under subsection (a) because their placement makes them easy to find, and the design, placement, and language of the adjacent text make it clear that the standard terms are intended to be part of the transaction when the consumer chooses to register with the website.

10. *Opportunity to terminate.* Under subsection (b), the consumer must be given a reasonable opportunity to terminate the transaction and a reasonable notice of the right to terminate. The duration of the review-and-terminate period has to be reasonable, providing sufficient time for the consumer who is interested in reviewing the terms to complete a meaningful review. In addition, the consumer's opportunity to terminate the transaction after receiving the terms must not place unreasonable cost, loss of value, or personal burden on the consumer. If a reasonable right to terminate is granted, the consumer's choice not to terminate constitutes the adoption of the standard contract terms. Effective termination by the consumer discharges the contract to which the consumer manifested assent.

Illustrations:

22. A consumer visits a store to purchase a product. Upon payment at the cash register, the consumer is handed a receipt prominently referencing additional terms and noting that these additional terms can be readily obtained on site at the customer-service desk. If the service desk is nearby and readily accessible without undue delay or hardship, and if the store allows the consumer to terminate the transaction after receiving the additional terms (and reasonably

notifies the consumer of the right to terminate), then they are adopted under subsection (b). If, however, the additional terms are not readily available upon the consumer's request, or if the consumer is not allowed to reasonably terminate the transaction after payment, or allowed but not reasonably notified about the right to terminate, the additional terms are not adopted as part of the consumer contract.

23. A consumer purchases a computer online for $500. Prior to the purchase, a notice that satisfies the requirements of subsection (b) (1) is provided. When the computer is installed, a set of standard contract terms is displayed on-screen. The terms, which are lengthy and complex, allow the consumer five days to return the computer and avoid being bound by the terms. The standard contract terms are not adopted as part of the contract because five days is not a reasonable time to perform the logistics required in the return of a computer.

24. Same facts as in Illustration 23, but the consumer has 30 days to return the computer. The terms further specify that, if the consumer returns the computer, the refund will be only partial, as the business reserves the right to charge a 15 percent restocking fee. While a restocking fee may be reasonable from the seller's standpoint in light of the handling and depreciation costs, it nevertheless restricts the opportunity of the consumer to terminate the contract upon review of the terms. Accordingly, the standard contract terms are not adopted as part of the contract.

25. Same facts as in Illustration 23, but the consumer has 30 days to return the computer and there is no restocking fee. The terms further specify that, if the consumer

returns the computer, the consumer will bear the return shipping cost. The shipping cost may be reasonable, but it nevertheless restricts the opportunity of the consumer to terminate the contract upon review of the terms. Accordingly, the standard contract terms are not adopted as part of the contract.

26. Same facts as in Illustration 23, but the consumer purchases the computer at the business's local retail store (rather than online) and the terms specify that the consumer may return the computer to the local retail store for a full refund within 60 days. Even though driving back to the retail store imposes some cost or burden on the consumer, this cost or burden is not unreasonable. In such case, the "opportunity to terminate" requirement of subsection (b)(3) is satisfied. If, however, the store only accepts returns during limited hours, or only when the box is unopened, the opportunity to terminate is unreasonably restrictive and the standard contract terms are not adopted as part of the contract.

11. *Legal consequences of nonadopted terms.* Standard terms that fail to conform to the adoption-process requirements of subsections (a) or (b) do not become part of the consumer contract. In such a case, under subsection (c), there is a contract that contains the terms—standard and nonstandard—that were effectively adopted, supplemented by gap-fillers supplied by law. A consumer, however, has no obligation to assert that standard contract terms were not adopted. Because the requirements of this Section are intended to provide consumers a reasonable opportunity to review the terms, a consumer may waive these protections and may choose to get the benefit of the standard contract terms. If the consumer so chooses, the business may not assert that its standard contract terms were not adopted. (Compare § 7 for the

consumer's right to enforce as part of the consumer contract an affirmation of fact or promise that does not appear in the standard contract terms.)

Illustrations:

> 27. Same facts as in Illustration 23, but the standard contract terms include a statement by the business that information about the transaction will not be provided to any other third party. The business, in violation of that statement, provides information about the transaction to a third party, to the detriment of the consumer. While the standard contract terms are not adopted as part of the contract, the consumer may assert a claim for breach of a contractual promise as embodied in the nonadopted statement.

12. Mandatory rule. The rules restated in this Section specify mandatory requirements of assent, notice, and opportunity to terminate, and cannot be excluded or derogated from by agreement. A business is free to specify the precise manner or medium that the manifestation of assent, notice, and termination take, as long as they are reasonable in the circumstances. If the business specifies a process for adopting standard terms that does not meet these mandatory requirements, that process is not effective and the standard terms it purports to adopt are not adopted as part of the contract. (Compare § 9.)

13. Relation to other Sections. The adoption rules in this Section reflect the reality in which the consumer's consent to the standard contract terms is rarely informed. In classic contract law, the requirement of assent was regarded as a meaningful mechanism that protects the contracting party, under the premise that this party, with full knowledge of the terms and with sufficient understanding of their impact, would manifest assent only to a

contract that promotes his or her interests. The length and complexity of standard-form contracts, and the large number of such contracts consumers enter into, have diluted the effectiveness and plausibility of such front-end self-protection. Accordingly, it is widely recognized that adoption procedures designed to achieve informed consent would yield relatively little value to, and might even impose burdensome transaction costs upon, the typical consumer. Courts have thus recognized the importance of safeguards in consumer-contract law. Primary among these are the rules that strike down unconscionable terms and other standard contract terms that undermine consumers' benefit of the bargain (§ 5). Adding to the protection afforded by the unconscionability doctrine are the good-faith duties that govern contract modification and open discretionary terms (§§ 3 and 4) and rules that police deception and enforce precontractual affirmations and promises (§§ 6 to 8). If, despite reasonably communicated disclosures, consumers are not expected to scrutinize the legal terms up front, courts should scrutinize them ex post. The ex post scrutiny is intended to uproot terms that are so extreme that they would be unlikely to survive in an environment of meaningful assent, or that peel off the value that consumers bargained for.

14. Relation to the Uniform Commercial Code and to the Restatement of the Law Second, Contracts. The common-law rules restated herein are consistent with, and elaborate on, the general principles of contract formation, as articulated in Restatement of the Law Second, Contracts, Chapter 3, and how a majority of courts have interpreted UCC § 2–204 in this context. With respect to adoption of terms after manifesting assent to the transaction (subsection (b)), some courts have interpreted UCC § 2–207 to bar adoption of those terms as part of the consumer contract. Most courts, however, reject that interpretation of UCC § 2–207 and, as those courts have determined that no other provisions of Article 2 address the question of which post-purchase terms become part of the contract, apply instead UCC § 2–204 and—through the gateway provided by UCC § 1–103(b)—general common-law principles. With respect to the adoption of standard contract terms by entry to or continued use of a proprietary environment, the rule of this Section is consistent with Restatement of the Law Second, Contracts § 69(1)(a), which allows silence to operate as an acceptance when the offeree "takes the benefit of offered services with reasonable opportunity to reject them and reason to know that they were offered with the expectation of compensation." See Comment *6* to this Section.

§ 3. Modification of Standard Contract Terms

(a)   A standard contract term in a consumer contract governing an ongoing relationship is modified if:

(1)   the consumer receives a reasonable notice of the proposed modified term and a reasonable opportunity to review it;

(2)   the consumer receives a reasonable opportunity to reject the proposed modified term and continue the contractual relationship under the existing term, and a reasonable notice of this opportunity; and

(3)   the consumer either:

(A)   manifests assent to the modified term or

(B)   does not reject the proposed modified term and continues the contractual relationship after the expiration of the rejection period provided in the proposal.

(b)   A consumer contract governing an ongoing relationship may provide for a reasonable procedure under which the business may propose a modification of the standard contract terms, but may not, to the detriment of the consumer, exclude the application of subsection (a), except that the established procedure may replace the reasonable opportunity to reject the proposed modified term with a reasonable opportunity to terminate the transaction without unreasonable cost, loss of value, or personal burden.

(c)   A modification of a standard contract term in a consumer contract is enforceable only if it is proposed in good faith and if it does not have the effect of undermining an affirmation or promise made by the business that was made part of the basis of the original bargain between the business and the consumer.

Comment:

1.   General. Standard contract terms in consumer contracts governing ongoing relationships, like other species of contracts, are often modified. This Section focuses on the adoption of modifications to the standard contract terms. Similar principles may apply to the modification of nonstandard terms. Many modifications may be justified by changes in the economic or legal environment, by revisions in the service itself, or by the realization of other unexpected contingencies. There is a concern, however, that businesses will make self-serving, opportunistic modifications in standard contract terms once consumers are already locked into the service. Accordingly, for a modification to be adopted, it is not enough that consumers have manifested their assent to the modified standard terms after the terms have been presented to them. Consumers may manifest such assent reluctantly, if termination of the contract would squander some acquired value, would unreasonably undermine their reliance investments, or would be practically infeasible. Thus, this Section provides two necessary safeguards, procedural and substantive. First, procedurally, under subsection (a), the process of adoption of a modification must satisfy requirements of assent analogous to those in § 2 (including the requirement, analogous to that in § 2(b), that the consumer receive a reasonable opportunity to reject the modification and continue the contract on the original terms). Subsection (b) allows the parties, usually at the instance of the business, to establish in the initial contract a reasonable modification procedure that implements these assent requirements, although it may replace the opportunity to reject with a reasonable opportunity to terminate the transaction entirely (see Comment 6). Second, substantively, under subsection (c), the modification may not undermine the benefit of the bargain secured in the pre-modification contract.

2. Modification versus independent contract. New terms proposed by the business are, depending on the circumstances, either an attempt to modify the terms of an existing contract within an ongoing relationship (governed by this Section) or an attempt to form a new, independent, contract, alongside or in succession to the original contract (governed by § 2).

Illustrations:

1. A consumer uses a website without creating an account or making a purchase. The website has a link to Terms of Use in large, contrasting font on the lower portion of the site, which the consumer can see immediately upon opening the page and without scrolling down the page. The consumer can review the terms by clicking on the link and there is a clear notice that the terms are intended to become part of the contract governing the current use of the website. The consumer visits the website regularly. The business changes the Terms of Use from time to time. The current standard terms may be adopted as a new contract each time the consumer visits the website, if the requirements of § 2 are satisfied each time, and do not constitute a modification of a prior contract.

2. A consumer opens a checking account with a bank and signs a user agreement. The bank seeks to change the terms of the agreement occasionally and sends notices to the consumer in advance of each such change. Each change of terms is a proposed modification under this Section, not a new contract. This is so even if the original agreement allows the bank to terminate the contract at any time, as long as the bank did not effectively terminate the original contract.

3. A consumer signs up for an ongoing web-based service, creating an account and manifesting assent to the transaction by agreeing to pay the monthly service fee and providing credit-card information. The website displays links to Terms of Use, which are referred to during the sign-up process and are adopted as part of the consumer contract upon the initial formation of the contract under § 2(a). The consumer

491

can review the terms by clicking on the links. The business changes the Terms of Use from time to time and sends the consumer notices upon each such change. Each change is a proposed modification governed by this Section.

4. A consumer signs up for a one-year service period with a business. If the contract requires fresh assent to renew the service at the end of the year, new terms sent upon renewal are not a modification; their adoption is governed by § 2. If, instead, the contract provides for auto-renewal for a second year, unless the consumer explicitly terminates the service, the original contract continues to govern during the second year, and any different or additional terms sent upon the renewal or during the second year are a proposed modification of the original contract and are governed by this Section.

3. Notice and opportunity to review. As with the adoption of original terms under § 2, modified standard contract terms may be adopted only if the consumer receives reasonable notice of the new terms and a reasonable opportunity to review them. In addition, the consumer must receive reasonable notice of the opportunity to reject the modified terms, along with a reasonable notice that continuing the contractual relationship without rejecting the modified terms will result in the modifications becoming legally binding. The appearance, placement, and timing of the notice are factors that determine whether the notice and opportunity to review are reasonable.

Illustrations:

5. A consumer entered into a two-year service contract online. At the time of the original contract formation, standard contract terms were adopted by satisfying all the requirements of § 2(a), including reasonable notice of the Terms and Conditions. The business later posts a modified version of the Terms and Conditions on its website, revising the heading in the page on which the terms are posted and entitling it "Revised Terms and Conditions." If the business does not provide the consumer with a distinct or separate notice of the modification, describing specific changes to the agreement and the effective date of those changes, the new terms are not adopted as a binding modification. It is not reasonable to expect consumers to revisit and check the Terms and Conditions webpage regularly, and, in the absence of an affirmative, reasonable alert, the consumer does not have a reasonable opportunity to review the proposed modification as required by subsection (a)(1).

6. A consumer opens a checking account with a bank and signs a 20-page user agreement. The bank seeks to change the terms of the agreement occasionally and sends notices to the consumer in advance of each change. Each such notice arrives with a monthly statement sent to the consumer, on a separate sheet titled "Change of Terms" describing specific changes to the agreement and the effective date of those changes. The presentation of the proposed modification in this manner satisfies the requirement of subsection (a)(1).

7. Same facts as in Illustration 6, but the bank seeks to change the terms by attaching to the monthly statement the revised version of the 20-page agreement entitled "Revised Agreement," which includes most of the terms in the original agreement as well as some additional or different ones. There is no explanation as to which terms are being changed or added. The presentation of the proposed modi-

fication in this manner does not satisfy the requirement of subsection (a)(1), because consumers cannot meaningfully compare and analyze two such lengthy and technical documents and thus cannot effectively review the proposed modification.

4. *Opportunity to reject the modification.* A modification is binding only if the consumer has a meaningful opportunity to reject it. Subsection (a)(2) requires that modified terms not be adopted unless the business gives the consumer a reasonable opportunity (with reasonable notice) to reject the modification and continue the relationship without the new terms. There is a close conceptual relationship between adoption of standard terms after the consumer manifests assent to the transaction under § 2(b) and modification of standard terms under this Section—in both settings, the standard contract terms are presented to the consumer after a decision to enter into the transaction was already made. Accordingly, the adoption of the standard contract terms in both settings has to satisfy a similar requirement—the existence of a reasonable opportunity to reject (which, in turn, requires affording the consumer a reasonable time period in which to exercise such rejection).

Illustrations:

8. A consumer attempts to log in to an online web service that the consumer joined as a member at an earlier time. The consumer is unable to log in without first clicking "I Accept" to a list of new terms that are presented as a modification of the original contract. Since the consumer is not given an opportunity to reject the modification, the terms are not adopted.

9. A consumer receives a clearly labeled notice by mail regarding a change of the data-privacy terms governing an ongoing service. The notice informs the consumer that continued use of the service would constitute acceptance of the terms and a modification of the agreement. It also explains that the change of terms will not apply and the original terms will remain in place if the consumer requests an opt-out within 30 days, by signing and submitting a pre-addressed opt-out form provided in the notice. The specified procedure for rejection of the modification is reasonable and the requirement of subsection (a)(2) is satisfied.

5. *Adoption of the modified standard contract terms.* With the receipt of a reasonable notice of the proposed modification and a reasonable opportunity to reject it, the modification is effective if the consumer either affirmatively manifests assent to it or continues to take the benefit of the relationship (without rejecting the proposed modification). Subsection (a)(3) thus recognizes that the consumer can adopt the modified terms by conduct that can fairly be treated as constituting acceptance. It maintains the dual adoption framework of § 2, under which terms may be adopted either by an affirmative act of acceptance or by continuation of the relationship once the terms are presented. In some cases, the conduct that adopts the modification is the consumer's continued participation in the contractual relationship, e.g., in a credit-card contract when the consumer makes new purchases using the credit card. In such cases, the modification is adopted through acceptance by performance. See Restatement of the Law Second, Contracts §§ 30, 62.

Illustration:

10. A consumer enters a pay-as-you-go agreement with a fitness club. Months later, the business sends the consumer a notice by mail titled "Change of Terms of Service" describing particular changes to the agreement and giving the consum-

er 30 days to opt out of the modified terms (and retain the original terms). If the consumer does not exercise the opt-out option, the new terms are adopted as a modification as soon as the 30-day, opt-out period elapses.

6.   *Agreed procedures for modification.* Businesses often include in consumer contracts "modification clauses" that specify procedures for subsequent modifications. Such clauses may give concrete effect to the requirements of subsection (a), but cannot derogate from them, except that the agreed procedure for modification may replace the opportunity to reject in subsection (a) (2) with a reasonable opportunity to terminate the transaction entirely. An opportunity to terminate is reasonable if it does not impose unreasonable cost, loss of value, or personal burden on the consumer. If termination of the contractual relationship by the consumer is not feasible or practicable—for example, because such termination would impose a significant loss of value acquired by the consumer prior to the proposed modification; would force the consumer to incur a significant financial or other burden to enter a substitute contract; would squander a substantial investment in the relationship; or would undermine the consumer's reasonable, forward-looking expectation from the relationship—then the consumer does not have a reasonable opportunity to terminate. In such a case, the modified standard terms are usually not adopted, even if the consumer manifested assent to the modification. In evaluating whether the costs imposed on the consumer by the modification are reasonable, courts may take into account the circumstances that prompted the business to propose the modification, including an increase in the business's costs; changes in market, technology, or regulatory environments; and improvements to the service provided by the business. If the modified terms confer

substantial benefits, as in the example of new terms that are needed to accommodate an upgrade to the business's computer systems, the evaluation of the reasonableness of the opportunity to terminate must consider those benefits in relation to any cost, loss of value, or personal burden that a termination would impose on those consumers who prefer the original terms.

Modification clauses that grant the business power to modify standard terms without meeting the mandatory requirements of this Section are ineffective, and any modification attempted under such clauses is unenforceable by the business. See § 9.

Illustrations:

11.   A consumer attempts to log in to an online web service that the consumer joined as a member at an earlier time. The original contract includes a modification procedure. The consumer is unable to log in without first clicking "I Accept" to a list of new terms that are presented as a modification of the original contract. Since the consumer is not given an opportunity to reject the modification, the terms are not adopted unless the consumer is provided a meaningful opportunity to cancel the membership (for example, by clicking on a separate hyperlink that takes the consumer to a "Service Cancellation" page), and unless such termination can be done without the consumer incurring unreasonable cost, loss of value, or personal burden.

12.   Same facts as in Illustration 8, but the cancellation options—although clearly posted and processed without delay—trigger an early-termination fee (adopted as part of the original contract). Because of the imposition of such termination fee, the consumer is not offered a reasonable opportunity to

terminate the transaction, and so the new terms are not adopted.

13. A consumer purchases a home-surveillance-camera system. At the same time, the consumer enters a one-year service agreement that allows the consumer to stream the images recorded by the camera to a handheld device through an integrated streaming service separately provided by the business. The agreements include a modification procedure. A few months later, the business sends the consumer a notice explaining that the Terms of Service for the service agreement will be modified in 30 days, that continuing the service will constitute acceptance of the new terms, and that the terms may be rejected by cancelling the service before the end of the 30 days. Despite the reasonable notice and cancellation method, the opportunity to terminate the contractual relationship is not reasonable under subsection (b) because termination of the service agreement would impose a significant loss of value of the camera equipment.

14. A consumer entered a six-month service agreement with a snow-removal company to plow the consumer's driveway after each snowfall for a fixed price of $100. The agreement includes a modification procedure. Two months into the contract, the consumer receives a letter stating "Due to the high demand for plowing services, we are modifying the contract with you by raising the price for plowing your driveway after each snowfall to $150. If you do not want to pay us $150, you may terminate our relationship by sending us an email to that effect within 14 days." Because termination of the transaction would entail a loss of value, the opportunity to terminate is not reasonable under subsection (b),

and thus the consumer's failure to terminate the transaction within 14 days does not create an enforceable modification. In addition, the modification is separately unenforceable under subsection (c) because modification would have the effect of undermining the promise to plow for $100, which is part of the basis of the original bargain. Agreements incorporating a flexible price formula may be enforceable. See § 9.

15. Same facts as in Illustration 14, except that the agreement does not include a modification procedure. The modification would be unenforceable under subsection (a) because the consumer is not provided with a reasonable opportunity to reject the modification. In addition, the modification is separately unenforceable under subsection (c) because modification would have the effect of undermining the promise to plow for $100, which is part of the basis of the original bargain.

16. A consumer subscribes to a web-based service that provides a no-charge, ad-free platform for posting and sharing photographs. The original agreement includes a clause stating that the ad-free feature of the service may be revised in the future. It also includes a modification clause that permits the business to change the terms of service any time in the future, subject to providing the consumers an opportunity to terminate the subscription upon such change. Later, in order to ensure its commercial viability, the business decides to switch to a personalized-advertisement model that uses subscribers' personal data. It proposes a modification explaining the change and the type of data that will be collected. The offer to modify gives the consumer an option to accept the new terms or terminate the contract by deleting the account. The opportunity to terminate is

reasonable despite imposing inconvenience on consumers who choose to delete the account.

7. *Good faith.* Modifications must be made in good faith. See Restatement of the Law Second, Contracts § 89 (adopting the related "fair and equitable" test) and UCC § 2–209. A modification affects the performance of the contract, and it is thus governed by the general obligation to perform contracts in good faith. See Restatement of the Law Second, Contracts § 205 and UCC § 1–304. It is restated in subsection (c) because of the heightened role that it plays in policing modifications of consumer contracts. Subsection (c) is intended to ensure that the modification does not unduly disadvantage the consumer, even if the requirements of subsections (a) and (b) have been met. It seeks, in particular, to prevent opportunistic modifications that purport to take advantage of locked-in consumers who have already invested in the contractual relationship. Thus, a modification of a standard contract term is not enforceable if it undermines the benefit of the bargain guaranteed by the original contract, as when it contradicts an affirmation of fact or promise by the business that has been made part of the basis of the original bargain between the business and the consumer. Such contradiction may occur, for example, when the business has promised in the original agreement or in a precontractual representation (see Comment 8) that the standard contract term will not change for a fixed period of time. See also Illustrations 17 and 18. Even if the consumer is afforded the opportunity to terminate the relationship without unreasonable cost, loss of value, or personal burden (in line with an agreed-upon modification procedure under subsection (b)), the modification is not enforceable if the termination undermines the benefit of the bargain guaranteed by the original contract. In general, a modification is more likely to satisfy subsection (c) if the modified standard terms are simultaneously being offered, as original terms, to new customers. Then, there is less concern that the modification intends to take advantage of consumers who are locked in by the cost of changing the deal. Nevertheless, because the same term may affect entrenched consumers differently than new ones, it may be enforceable as part of the contract with new consumers but not as a modification. Thus, an important implication of subsection (c) is that some standard terms that may be acceptable if presented as part of the original contract may not be enforceable if presented as part of a proposed modification. Further, subsection (c) will generally bar the modification of contracts fully performed, or of short-term contracts such as a one-shot purchase-of-product contract, unless circumstances are present that were not anticipated by the parties when the contract was made.

Illustrations:

17. A consumer opens a checking account with a bank and signs a standard-form checking agreement. The agreement specifies a fixed fee to be charged whenever a consumer draws a check from an account with insufficient funds. Later, the bank proposes a modification that would raise this fee, prospectively. The consumer manifested assent to the modified term, or the agreement provided an appropriate procedure for the proposal of modifications, such that the requirements of subsection (a)(3)(A) or of subsection (b) are satisfied. The amount by which the bank may propose to increase the processing fee is limited by subsection (c).

18. A consumer purchases and downloads hundreds of song tracks from an online music store, along with software that is necessary to

play the tracks. The initial contract adopted as part of the purchase of the tracks states that the consumer may load the tracks to seven different devices. Later, together with a mandatory software update, the business proposes a modification that allows the consumer to load the tracks only to five devices. If the new, five-device clause applies only to prospective track purchases by the consumer, it does not violate subsection (c). If, instead, the new clause applies also to tracks already paid for, it violates subsection (c) because it retroactively reduces the consumer's benefit from the bargain and partially squanders the consumer's investment in previously purchased tracks.

8. *Modification adopted using a more passive process.* It is not uncommon for the standard terms to be adopted, initially, through one adoption process, such as requiring the consumer to click "I Agree" to the terms, and then modified through a different process that does not require a similar affirmative action by the consumer. Terms modified in such a way can be adopted as part of the contract as long as the requirements of subsection (a) are met. There is concern, however, that when the initial terms are adopted through a particular active process, the consumer would expect the same or a similar process for modifications of the standard terms. Similarly, if the business employed a particular process for prior modifications, the consumer would expect the same or a similar process for future modifications. A shift to a more passive process triggers a heightened notice requirement.

9. *Legal consequences of nonadopted terms.* A consumer has no obligation to assert that terms offered by the business as modifications were not adopted and may instead choose to get the benefit of the modified terms. If the consumer so chooses, the business may not assert that its modified contract terms were not adopted. (Compare § 2, Comment *11*.)

Illustration:

19. A business posts a "New Privacy Policy" on its website, without giving consumers a notice that the standard contract terms in this new policy purport to modify the existing contract. The New Privacy Policy is not adopted as a modification. As part of the New Privacy Policy, the business states that none of the consumers' personal information collected by the business will be shared with the government. A consumer may enforce the business's statement as a binding contractual promise, despite the fact that the New Privacy Policy is not adopted as an enforceable modification of the original contract.

10. *Relation to the Uniform Commercial Code and to the Restatement of the Law Second, Contracts.* The rule of subsection (c), that modifications of standard terms are enforceable only if they are made in good faith and if they do not undermine an affirmation or promise made by the business that has been made part of the basis of the bargain, is consistent with a principal element of UCC § 2–209 and with Restatement of the Law Second, Contracts § 89 (see also Comment 7). UCC § 2–309 provides that a contract of indefinite duration is valid for a reasonable time and can be terminated on reasonable notice.

§ 4. Discretionary Obligations

(a) A contract or any term that grants the business discretion to determine its rights and obligations must be interpreted, when reasonably susceptible to such interpretation, to provide that such discretion will be exercised in good faith.

(b) A term in a contract that purports to grant the business absolute and unlimited discretion to determine its contractual rights and obligations unconstrained by the good-faith obligation is unenforceable by the business.

Comment:

1. *Discretionary terms.* A consumer contract may include provisions that grant the business discretion to specify or adjust its contractual obligations. There are two types of discretion-granting terms: (1) terms that grant the business discretion to resolve an issue that was left open in the initial contract, e.g., when the initial contract states that any dispute will be settled by arbitration, does not specify the arbitration forum, and grants the business discretion to choose the arbitration forum; and (2) terms that grant the business discretion to adjust or change obligations that were specified in the initial contract, e.g., when the initial contract states that any dispute will be settled by arbitration in Arbitration Forum A and grants the business discretion to replace Arbitration Forum A with another arbitration forum. This Section applies to both types of discretion-granting terms. Discretion-granting terms of type (2) are modification clauses and thus governed also by § 3 (see Comment 4).

2. *Discretionary terms restricted by good faith.* When a consumer contract includes a provision that grants the business absolute and unlimited discretion to specify or adjust its contractual obligations, the contract lacks consideration because it fails the basic requirement of mutuality—that each party make a commitment to the other (Restatement of the Law Second, Contracts § 77). But, following a long tradition in contract law, subsection (a) establishes that such open-ended language does not ordinarily lead to nonenforcement if it can reasonably be read not to exclude the implied limitation that the business is required to exercise its discretion in good faith. Such implied limitation is consistent with the approach taken by the Uniform Commercial Code (for example, in §§ 2–305 and 2–306)—to supplement discretionary terms by an obligation to exercise the discretion in good faith. The implied duty of good faith applies more broadly in shaping the performance obligation of both parties (see Restatement of the Law Second, Contracts § 205 and UCC § 1–304). It is emphasized here because of the central role that it plays in policing otherwise facially unlimited discretionary terms in consumer contracts and rendering contracts that contain them enforceable.

Illustrations:

1. A contract contains a clause requiring disputes between a business and a consumer to be resolved in a particular forum. It grants the business the power to set a forum and procedures at its own discretion, and does not contain any express limitation on such discretion. The term is enforceable, but the business must exercise its discretion in good faith, choosing a forum and procedures that conform to commercial standards of fair dealing in the circumstances.

2. A contract contains a clause applying to the entire agreement, stating that the business "reserves the right at any time to modify, revoke, suspend, terminate, or change any or all terms of the contract, in whole or in part." The

clause is enforceable, but the business must exercise its powers under this clause in good faith. Any subsequent modifications of the contract attempted under this clause would be enforceable if consistent with § 3.

3. *Discretionary terms in violation of the good-faith restriction.* When a term in the contract purports to grant the business absolute and unlimited discretion to specify contractual obligations in a way that cannot be reconciled with or that explicitly conflicts with the good-faith restriction, the business's promises as expressed in those terms are often labeled by courts as "illusory" because by failing to constrain its discretion the business made no meaningful commitment to the consumer with respect to the matters subject to the discretionary rights. Such a term, or—if it is not severable—the entire contract, is an illusory promise and is not enforceable by the business (but may be enforceable by the consumer; see Comment 7). The term or contract may also be substantively unconscionable under § 5.

Illustrations:

3. A consumer enters into an agreement for a cruise service with a business that operates cruise ships, pays a nonrefundable deposit to reserve a cabin on a specific cruise, and agrees to pay the remainder of the price by a specified date. The standard contract terms allow the business to cancel the reservation at any time and for any reason, without prior notice and without providing any explanation or compensation. The contract is unenforceable by the business because the business's promise is illusory. This conclusion does not change even if the business must return the deposit upon such termination.

4. A consumer purchases a hot tub along with a two-year service agreement. The service component is priced separately, but marketed as an important complement to the sale and as part of a single, unified transaction. The standard contract terms allow the business to cancel the service component at any time and for any reason, by mailing back the remaining balance of the prepaid service price. The entire contract is unenforceable by the business, including the hot-tub sale, because a significant source of value can be eliminated by the business without any limitation.

4. *Unilateral modification clauses.* Businesses sometimes include, in their standard terms, a clause that purports to grant the business unrestricted discretion to modify the terms of service. When reasonably susceptible of such an interpretation, such clauses should be interpreted to allow only good-faith modification, in accordance with this Section and § 3. When the explicit language of the modification clause precludes such an interpretation, the clause is not consistent with subsection (a) and is thus unenforceable by the business under subsection (b). The clause may also be substantively unconscionable under § 5. The effects of such an attempt to derogate from the good-faith restriction are described in § 9.

Illustration:

5. A contract between an airline and a consumer allows the airline to modify the frequent-flyer program at its discretion. The provision is enforceable, and any subsequent modification is enforceable, if it is adopted in accordance with the requirements of § 3, as long as it is done in good faith. A modification that unreasonably reduces the value of previously acquired perks is inconsistent with the good-faith requirement of this Section, and it may also violate the requirement of

§ 3(a) if the airline does not afford the consumer a meaningful opportunity to reject it. But a modification that reduces the value of prospectively acquired miles does not conflict with the good-faith requirement.

5. *Discretionary terms and course of performance.* A contract or a term that grants the business wide discretion is unenforceable by the business if the business exhibits a pattern of conduct under which the discretion is exercised in bad faith. Similarly, a modification clause that grants the business wide discretion to modify the terms of the contract is unenforceable by the business if the business attempts to modify the contract with retroactive effect or otherwise in bad faith. Those results apply even if, in the absence of such courses of performance, the discretion or modification terms would be enforceable under subsection (a) because it is subject to the implied obligation of good faith. In effect, the ability to invoke the implied obligation of good faith to save the term is negated when there is a course of performance that is inconsistent with a good-faith exercise of the business's discretion, and in the absence of such an implied restriction the discretionary term is unenforceable by the business.

Illustration:

6. A contract contains an arbitration clause that allows the business to select the arbitration body and procedure at its discretion. Under subsection (a), the clause is enforceable, because the discretion is subject to an obligation to exercise it in good faith. Invoking this power, the business refers consumers' disputes to an arbitration body that is inaccessible to most consumers, despite the existence of more readily accessible and more reasonable alternatives. Such exercise of discretion by the business

violates the good-faith duty and is not enforceable. Depending on the circumstances, it may render the entire arbitration clause unenforceable by the business. (See also § 9.)

6. *No requirement of symmetry.* Discretionary terms, by their nature, allocate contractual rights in an asymmetric manner. Such allocations are a regular feature of contracting and require no special justification. Thus, asymmetry alone does not make a contract unenforceable. As long as the discretionary power is bounded by the requirement of good faith (and by other equivalent contractual restrictions), it does not pose a problem of mutuality.

Illustration:

7. A consumer contract contains a choice-of-forum clause that requires all consumer complaints to be resolved in a specified forum, but gives the business discretion to pursue its own complaints in a different forum. The asymmetry alone does not render the clause unenforceable by the business.

7. *Legal consequences of unenforceable discretionary terms.* Terms that provide for the exercise of discretion without good faith are inconsistent with subsection (a) and are unenforceable by the business under subsection (b). If such terms can be severed from the rest of the agreement, they are replaced with gap-fillers, as described in § 9. If severance or restriction of the terms cannot be accomplished by reformation or augmentation of the contract without undue burden (for example, when the unenforceable term is the price or the quantity), the entire contract is unenforceable by the business. Discretionary terms in explicit violation of the good-faith restriction may also render the contract substantively unconscionable under § 5. Discretionary terms intended to provide value to the consumer may be enforced by the consumer, replacing the business's dis-

cretion with gap-fillers, as described in § 9.

Illustration:

8. A contract for installation of a home-alarm system provides for one-year, on-site service in the event that the system malfunctions, at no additional charge. The service term in the contract grants the business unlimited discretion to schedule any requested service at its own convenience. It specifies that delayed scheduling of the repair would not give rise to any claim against the business. Such unlimited discretion is not consistent with this Section. The consumer may enforce the on-site service promise, stripped of the business's unlimited scheduling discretion. The consumer's contractual right under the sev-ered agreement is to receive on-site service within a reasonable time.

8. *Relation to the Uniform Commercial Code and to the Restatement of the Law Second, Contracts.* The rule of this Section is consistent with Restatement of the Law Second, Contracts § 77, which deems discretionary terms illusory when the discretion is not limited (by the doctrine of good faith or otherwise). It is also consistent with the approach of UCC §§ 2–305, 2–306, 2–309, and 2–311(1), which impose good-faith limitations on discretionary terms. UCC § 1–302(b) specifies that the duty of good faith may not be disclaimed by agreement, but that the parties may agree on "the standards by which the performance of [the good-faith obligation] is to be measured if those standards are not manifestly unreasonable."

§ 5. Unconscionability

(a) An unconscionable contract or term is unenforceable, to the extent stated in § 9.

(b) A contract or a term is unconscionable if at the time the contract is made it is:

(1) substantively unconscionable, namely fundamentally unfair or unreasonably one-sided, and

(2) procedurally unconscionable, because it results in unfair surprise or results from the absence of meaningful choice on the part of the consumer.

In determining that a contract or a term is unconscionable, a greater degree of one of the elements in this subsection means that a lesser degree of the other element is sufficient to establish unconscionability.

(c) Without limiting the scope of subsection (b)(1), a contract term is substantively unconscionable if its effect is to:

(1) unreasonably exclude or limit the business's liability or the consumer's remedies that would otherwise be applicable for:

(A) death or personal injury for which, in the absence of a contractual provision in the consumer contract, the business would be liable, or

(B) any loss to the consumer caused by an intentional or negligent act or omission of the business;

(2)   unreasonably expand the consumer's liability, the business's remedies, or the business's enforcement powers that would otherwise be applicable in the event of breach of contract by the consumer; or

(3)   unreasonably limit the consumer's ability to pursue or express a complaint or seek reasonable redress for a violation of a legal right.

(d)   In determining whether a contract or a term is unconscionable, the court should afford the parties a reasonable opportunity to present evidence as to its commercial setting, purpose, and effect.

Comment:

1.   The two prongs of unconscionability. The doctrine of unconscionability has the primary goal of protecting contracting parties against fundamentally unfair and unreasonably one-sided terms. It thus represents one of the primary safeguards necessary in an environment in which complex terms are adopted without meaningful scrutiny by consumers. Because consumers rarely read or review the non-core, standard contract terms, and because such faintly reviewed terms may nevertheless be adopted under the principles developed in the case law and reflected in §§ 2 and 3 of this Restatement, the doctrine of unconscionability is a primary tool against the inclusion of intolerable terms in the consumer contract. While the principal element of the unconscionability doctrine is the substantive prong that identifies such intolerable terms, the doctrine recognizes that sometimes consumers may choose to accept harsh terms in exchange for another benefit (such as low price). The doctrine asks whether consumers in fact meaningfully chose to accept a harsh term by also requiring (except in rare circumstances) a showing of some quantum of procedural unconscionability. In determining whether a contract or a term is unconscionable, a court has to examine its expected effects as they appear at the time that the contract was made (compare Restatement of the Law Second, Contracts § 208 and Uniform Commercial Code (UCC) § 2–302).

2.   Sliding scale. In general, both the substantive and the procedural prongs are necessary for a finding of unconscionability. But they need not be present in the same degree. Under subsection (b), the two prongs are viewed in tandem and a sliding-scale approach is applied: a large quantum of one prong means that a relatively small quantum of the other is sufficient to establish unconscionability. Because the ultimate goal of the unconscionability doctrine is to deny enforcement to contract terms that are fundamentally unfair, in appropriate circumstances a high degree of substantive unconscionability is sufficient to find that a standard contract term, ordinarily not one of the core-deal terms of which most consumers are aware, is unconscionable.

3.   Substantive unconscionability. The substantive-unconscionability test in subsection (b)(1) addresses the unfairness and one-sidedness of a contract term that potentially undermines the consumer's benefit from the bargain, and for which the business cannot show a reasonable justification. There are various ways to characterize the required severity of the substantive unconscionability—e.g., "shock the conscience," "oppressive," "unreasonably harsh," or "fundamentally unfair." Those tests, as articulated by courts and in the Uniform Commercial Code, are all intended to capture a limiting criterion, that the doctrine is to be used only when the one-sidedness of a term in the contract is extreme.

In general, it is impossible to evaluate the one-sidedness of a particular term at the time the contract is made without looking at the contract as a whole, including the price, and the context surrounding the contract. What might appear as unfair may be merely a bargain-basement deal in which the pro-business term is matched by a pro-consumer price or other consumer advantage. Thus, for example, a contract that provides few rights to a consumer may not be problematic if a low price reflects those minimal rights, but might be problematic without the corresponding benefit of a low price. Likewise, an extreme pro-business term may not be unfair if, in the context surrounding the contract, it reflects or offsets a large risk taken by the business. While the presence of a competitive market environment may suggest that, in ordinary commerce, pro-business terms would lead to more favorable prices or other terms for consumers, it does not preclude a legal finding that a term is substantively unconscionable.

4. *Contract terms that are substantively unconscionable.* Subsection (c) provides a nonexhaustive list of categories of standard contract terms that are substantively unconscionable, if their effect is to impose:

(a). *Unreasonable limit on the business's liability or the consumer's remedies.* Subsection (c)(1) establishes that it is unconscionable to unreasonably exclude or limit the business's liability or the consumer's remedies that would otherwise be applicable for (A) death or personal injury for which, in the absence of a contractual provision in the consumer contract, the business would be liable, or (B) any loss to the consumer caused by an intentional or negligent act or omission of the business. Subsection (c)(1) applies both to limits on the consumer's remedies and to limits on the business's liability, including disclaimers of implied warranties. Standard contract terms stating that the liability or remedy limitations are specifically agreed upon, or that conduct that would otherwise be regarded by law as negligent is contractually agreed upon to be non-negligent, do not necessarily render the limit on liability reasonable. A limit on liability for personal injury may be reasonable, for example, in situations in which the consumer is well positioned to prevent the loss or in which the activity is broadly known to involve significant physical risks. But even then the waiver may not apply if the business failed to take cost-effective measures to reduce the risk.

Illustrations:

1. A consumer purchases fitness equipment for her household use. The contract contains standard terms that release the seller from liability for all risk of personal injury arising from the use of the equipment, including injuries arising from defects in the equipment that would otherwise constitute breach of warranty. This limitation of consequential damages is substantively unconscionable. See also UCC § 2–719(3), which states that this limitation is prima facie substantively unconscionable.

2. A consumer enters an agreement with a fitness club that uses the same equipment as in Illustration 1. The agreement contains standard contract terms releasing the club from liability for all risks of personal injury, including injuries arising from defective or poorly maintained equipment. While this service contract does not come under UCC § 2–719(3), the same principle of unconscionability applies under this Restatement. The release from liability is substantively unconscionable if, in the absence of such standard contract terms, the business would be liable.

3. A consumer purchases a lift ticket at a ski resort. The ticket recites standard contract terms that disclaim the resort's liability for personal injuries to the consumer while the consumer is using the skiing facilities. The disclaimer is not substantively unconscionable because skiing is an activity broadly known to involve significant risk of death or personal injury and the disclaimer is thus not unreasonable. Nevertheless, the application of the disclaimer to risks caused not by an inherent risk of skiing but directly by the resort's negligence—such as negligently allowing fallen logs to remain on the ski runs, or failing to prevent malfunctions of the ski lifts—is substantively unconscionable under subsection (c)(1)(B).

(b). Unreasonable expansion of the consumer's liability, the business's remedies, or the business's enforcement powers. Subsection (c)(2) establishes that consumers' liability for breach may not unreasonably exceed the liability that would otherwise apply, and that consumers may not be subject to enforcement measures that unreasonably expand the enforcement measures that would otherwise apply. What is reasonable depends on the lost profit incurred by the business, the difficulty of obtaining redress, and the value of the unpaid-for benefits the consumer enjoyed before breach. Under longstanding case law and statutes in many jurisdictions, excessive liquidated damages and early-termination fees are not enforceable, even if they do not rise to the level of substantive unconscionability. (See Restatement of the Law Second, Contracts § 356; UCC § 2–718(1).) Other instances in which expansion of a business's remedies and enforcement tactics may be substantively unconscionable include, but are not limited to, cross-collateral clauses, waiver-of-defense clauses, and debt-collection clauses. They are un-

conscionable under consumer-contract law even if, at the same time, they may also be prohibited under other legal rules. A finding of substantive unconscionability can be avoided by showing that the remedial provision is reasonable, for example, when the consumer received some front-end value in exchange for the expanded remedies.

Illustrations:

4. A cellphone-service provider enters into a two-year contract with a consumer. The consumer does *not* receive any meaningful, up-front benefit, like a subsidized device or a lower-than-market rate for the service. The contract stipulates that a consumer who exits the relationship before the end of the two-year commitment period must pay a fee of $250, regardless of the timing of exit. The termination fee satisfies the substantive-unconscionability test. It may also be an unenforceable penalty for breach (see Restatement of the Law Second, Contracts § 356). If, however, the consumer receives meaningful, up-front benefits for agreeing to the two-year commitment, the termination fee may not be unreasonable and therefore not substantively unconscionable.

5. A car dealership enters into a three-year lease contract with a consumer. The contract stipulates that a consumer who terminates the lease prematurely must pay damages that exceed the sum of the remaining payments under the lease contract. The liquidated-damages clause is substantively unconscionable. See also UCC §§ 2A–504 and 2A–528(1).

6. An online news source enters into a three-year subscription with a consumer. The contract stipulates that a consumer who terminates the subscription prematurely must pay damages that exceed the

sum of remaining payments under the subscription. The liquidated-damages clause is substantively unconscionable because it unreasonably expands the consumer's liability that would otherwise apply, above the business's lost profit.

(c). Unreasonable limit on consumer's ability to enforce a legal right. Subsection (c)(3) establishes that it is substantively unconscionable to specify an excessively burdensome redress mechanism and, by doing so, to unreasonably limit consumers' ability to enforce their legal rights. Such limitations are unconscionable because they undermine the substantive rights consumers acquired under the contract. They are substantively unconscionable for the same reason that limitations on remedies are—that it is the essence of a contract that at least minimum adequate recovery for breach be available (UCC § 2–719, Official Comment 1). A business may try to limit consumers' reasonable redress through unreasonable choice-of-forum clauses, choice-of-law clauses, or arbitration arrangements that in each case impose unreasonably high costs on consumers; waivers of aggregate-litigation processes in situations in which individual suits are impractical; unreasonably short limitations periods; unjustified denial of statutory damages and attorneys' fees; and more. While consumers may agree to limit their process rights, the agreed-upon arrangements must enable some reasonably effective pursuit of legally available redress for breach of contract or for violation of legal rights that govern the contractual relationship. A limit on the consumer's ability to enforce a legal right is not substantively unconscionable if it is not too severe or if it serves to screen meritless claims, or when the consumer received some value in return for it.

Subsection (c)(3) states a principle of consumer-contract law and does not express a preference for a particular mode of dispute resolution, such as litigation, arbitration, or mediation. The requirement that a consumer's right to seek redress not be unreasonably hindered may be further strengthened or weakened by other laws and regulations governing the choice of law and forum. For example, it may be bolstered by the doctrine of "effective vindication" in arbitration law, or by laws that prohibit pre-dispute arbitration agreements in specific sectors. And, conversely, the requirement in subsection (c)(3) may be weakened by federal law's preference for some forms of dispute resolution, even if those erode the right to seek redress. In stating a principle of consumer-contract law, subsection (c)(3) does not address the possible interaction of such a contract-law principle with federal law, and specifically, it does not address its possible preemption under the Federal Arbitration Act.

Illustrations:

7.   A business's standard contract terms include a dispute-resolution term specifying a forum in a distant location, such that the consumer would have to bear travel and accommodation expenses exceeding the value of the remedy sought. The dispute-resolution forum requires a nonrefundable filing fee exceeding the value of the remedy sought. Either one of these two features unreasonably limits the consumer's ability to enforce legal rights and renders the dispute-resolution clause substantively unconscionable. That result applies to any type of dispute-resolution forum that imposes such an unreasonable cost or personal burden, be it a public court or a private arbitration tribunal.

8.   A business's standard contract terms include a class-action waiver. A common grievance for consumers entering this contract involves low damages, no more than a few dollars each. A court

may determine that the class-action waiver is substantively unconscionable if the waiver unreasonably limits consumers' ability to enforce low-stakes legal rights. This result applies regardless of the type of dispute-resolution forum specified in the contract, be it a public (small-claims) court or a private arbitration tribunal.

9. A business's standard contract terms require that all claims against the business be made within three months after the conclusion of the transaction. The clause is substantively unconscionable to the extent that it covers claims arising from latent defects. (Compare UCC § 2–725(1).)

(d). Limits on consumers' ability to pursue or express a complaint. In the same spirit, it is substantively unconscionable for the business to unreasonably limit the consumer's ability to express or pursue a complaint, or to restrict the ability of the consumer to engage in review, assessment, or analysis of the business's performance. (Compare the Consumer Review Fairness Act of 2016, 15 U.S.C. § 45b.)

Illustration:

10. A business includes in its standard-form contract a clause that charges a high monetary penalty every time a consumer posts a negative review of the business online or obligates the consumer to indemnify the business for any loss caused by the negative review. This "anti-disparagement" clause is substantively unconscionable, because it unreasonably limits the consumer's ability to pursue or express a complaint about the product.

5. *Substantive unconscionability versus statutory standards.* The substantive-unconscionability standard may capture contract terms that are considered "unfair acts or practices" under the Federal Trade Commission (FTC) Act and state Unfair and Deceptive Acts and Practices (UDAP) statutes. The extensive jurisprudence identifying such unfair acts and practices ought to continue to guide courts in evaluating unfair standard contract terms under the unconscionability doctrine. In addition, the Dodd-Frank Wall Street Reform and Consumer Protection Act prohibits "abusive acts or practices" (12 U.S.C. §§ 5531, 5536(a)). Practices defined by regulatory and enforcement agencies as unfair or abusive may also be substantively unconscionable when authorized in the standard contract terms. However, a finding of substantive unconscionability requires a degree of fundamental unfairness (or abusiveness) that may be higher than the level of unfairness (or abusiveness) that supports some claims under those consumer-protection statutes. Compliance with statutory standards would ordinarily support a finding that a term is not substantively unconscionable, but in proper circumstances would not bar a finding of substantive unconscionability.

Illustrations:

11. A retail installment-sales contract includes a grant of a non-possessory security interest in household goods of the consumer other than those acquired in the transaction (a "cross-collateral" clause). The term is unfair under the FTC Credit Practices Rule, 16 C.F.R. § 444.2. It is also substantively unconscionable.

12. A sales contract contains a waiver-of-defenses clause, under which the consumer promises not to assert against any assignee of the contract any defense the consumer might have against the seller. The term is unfair under § 5 of the FTC Act and the FTC Preservation of Consumers' Claims and Defenses Rule, 16 C.F.R. § 433. It is also sub-

stantively unconscionable. (Compare UCC § 9–403(d).)

13. A dance studio solicits a client to commit to a large number of dance classes, more than the client can use, and at a price that does not reflect a significant bulk discount. The arrangement is unfair under state UDAP case law. It is also substantively unconscionable.

6. *Procedural unconscionability.*

(a). Identifying procedural unconscionability; sliding scale. The procedural prong of the unconscionability doctrine refers to some defects in the bargaining *process*, like a surprising and unexpected term, or lack of meaningful choice. A finding of procedural unconscionability based solely on the fact that a term was presented in standard, non-negotiable form, without more, constitutes the lowest quantum of procedural unconscionability and would have to be matched with a high degree of substantive unconscionability to render the contract or term unenforceable.

(b). Consumer awareness; market context. The procedural-unconscionability test may look to consumer awareness of the term in a market context. The question would be whether ordinary consumers would be aware of the term or would expect its inclusion, and thus would be more likely to take it into account when making contracting decisions. When consumers expect or are aware of a term, the term can (but does not always) affect their contracting decisions. In those situations, the reasons for intervention in the substance of the deal are diminished. One question, then, in applying the procedural unconscionability test, is whether a term is likely to affect the contracting decisions of a large enough number of consumers. (If the market is segmented, the question is whether a term is likely to affect the contracting

decisions of a large enough number of consumers in the relevant segment.)

A term that affects the contracting decisions of a substantial number of consumers is more likely to be subject to forces of market competition, even if it is not negotiated and even if it appears in the contracts of all businesses in the relevant market. Such a term may be policed by market forces, and so policing by courts—through the unconscionability doctrine—may be less necessary and may lead to undesirable results, including a reduction in consumer choice. On the other hand, when drafting terms that do not affect consumers' contracting decisions, the business is not subject to market discipline, and so the unconscionability doctrine is all the more necessary to police such terms.

The prevalence, in the relevant market, of similar pro-business terms does not negate a finding of procedural unconscionability. Indeed, if a term does not affect consumers' contracting decisions, all businesses might be tempted to draft a similar term in a one-sided, pro-business fashion.

(c). Market forces and non-core standard contract terms. Ordinarily, non-core standard contract terms do not affect the contracting decisions of a substantial number of consumers. This observation applies most forcefully when the standard contract term is part of a long list of fine-print terms. Non-core standard contract terms do not affect the contracting decisions of consumers even if they are presented in larger font or positioned in a prominent place in the form contract, because it is exceedingly common for consumers to be unaware even of such bolstered disclosure. In contrast, when the standard contract term is part of the core-deal terms, e.g., a bottom-line price or delivery fee, it ordinarily affects the contracting decisions of consumers. Moreover, some non-core standard con-

tract terms may affect the contracting decisions.

In determining whether a standard contract term affects the contracting decisions of a substantial number of consumers, courts ought to look at factors like consumers' limited sophistication, the business's use of incomprehensible language in the standard contract terms, the business's use of high-pressure sales tactics, and the existence of external circumstances (not created by the business) that compelled consumers to execute the contract. In addition, in situations of extreme inequality in bargaining power between the business and the consumer, when consumers are compelled to transact with the business regardless of the standard contract term, the term is unlikely to affect the contracting decisions of many consumers. Of course, a business may demonstrate that a term does affect consumers' contracting decisions with appropriate evidentiary support, for example by survey evidence (as commonly used in litigation involving aspects of unfair competition), or by any other indicia suggesting that the affected term was noticeably communicated in the course of the precontractual representations.

Illustrations:

14. A fitness center advertises two membership plans: Plan 1 charges a lower membership fee but requires a two-year commitment and imposes an early-termination fee. Plan 2, titled "No Contract," charges a higher membership fee, but allows consumers to terminate with no penalty anytime. The zero-termination-fee feature is made explicit in the marketing of the "No Contract" plan. By virtue of the explicit advertising, the possibility and cost of early termination become known to consumers. Consumers can reasonably weigh the value of the choice. Accordingly, the

termination penalty in Plan 1 is not procedurally unconscionable.

15. A sales contract includes a nonpossessory security-interest clause, like the substantively unconscionable one presented in Illustration 11. The clause is part of a long "boilerplate" form, presented to the consumer during the closing of the transaction, which the consumer must sign to complete the transaction. In circumstances in which consumers have limited financial sophistication, the clause is procedurally unconscionable.

7. *Procedural unconscionability—related concepts.*

(a). Subjective knowledge. Subjective knowledge of an individual consumer does not preclude a finding of procedural unconscionability, if the finding of procedural unconscionability is based on the objective test of consumer awareness. Subjective knowledge does not cure the market failure caused when a term does not affect the contracting decisions of a substantial number of consumers.

(b). Disclosure. The procedural-unconscionability inquiry should be distinguished from a conspicuousness test. It is not enough that the harsh terms were disclosed in larger typeface or that a ritual of a separate affirmation of assent to the harsh terms was mechanically followed. While such enhanced presentation may satisfy other rules mandating disclosure (e.g., Magnuson-Moss Warranty Act, 15 U.S.C. § 2301) and may be a factor in determining whether there was a "surprising and unexpected term," it does not establish a safe harbor against a finding of procedural unconscionability. Because of the length, complexity, and accumulation of standard-form contracts, an enhanced-format disclosure of a term does not guarantee that consumers will not be surprised and thus does not guarantee meaningful choice.

The harsh effect of the standard terms can continue to be hidden even in full daylight, given that consumers rarely read those terms and, even if they do, often may not understand or appreciate their effect at the time of contracting. In particular, the display of standard contract terms in ALL CAPS or other enhanced typeface does not, in and of itself, avoid procedural unconscionability. The Uniform Commercial Code provides guidance in this area. While a disclaimer may be conspicuous under UCC § 2–316(2) by virtue of the typeface used to display it (UCC § 1–201(b)(10)), it may still be ineffective under the UCC and procedurally unconscionable. While the UCC stipulates that a conspicuous disclaimer of warranties is effective, it also explains that the underlying purpose is to "protect the buyer from surprise," namely to deny enforcement to "unexpected and unbargained language" (UCC § 2–316(2) and Official Comment 1). As long as the disclosure is not effective in protecting the consumer from surprise and the disclosed term is not likely to affect the contracting decisions of a substantial number of consumers entering such a transaction, it does not preclude a finding of procedural unconscionability.

Illustration:

16. Goods purchased by a consumer are found to be totally worthless. The standard terms include a disclaimer of the implied warranty of merchantability in large font and in a manner that satisfies the requirements of UCC § 2–316 and of the Magnuson-Moss Warranty Act. If a court finds that the disclaimer is substantively unconscionable, the court may also find that the disclaimer was procedurally unconscionable on grounds that it was "surprising and unexpected" and refuse to enforce it, even if the disclaimer was printed in conspicuous font.

8. *Unconscionable price.* The substantive unconscionability test can be applied to scrutinize the contract price, but this should be done with extra care. An excessively high price, substantially in excess of the price at which similar products are obtainable in similar consumer transactions by like consumers, or bearing no reasonable relationship to the cost of providing the good or service, may be found to be substantively unconscionable. The procedural-unconscionability test may be more difficult to satisfy because the price is usually the most prominent element of a transaction and a critical factor in the consumer's contracting decision (see Comment 6). Still, an egregiously high price may be held unconscionable by courts if it occurs in connection with unfair surprise or the absence of meaningful choice. A price term itself may surprise consumers, for example when a product is sold via a complex pricing scheme. A consumer may be unfairly surprised when the price is multidimensional and certain price dimensions do not affect the contracting decisions. A consumer may also be unfairly surprised when the price is contingent or deferred and the consumer underestimates the likelihood of triggering the relevant price or the importance of certain deferred price dimensions (e.g., a long-term interest rate that replaces a low teaser rate after a long introductory period, or the long-term, overall price of a repeatedly rolled-over short-term loan), and thus underestimates the true cost of the contract. An egregiously high price may also result from absence of meaningful choice when there are market imperfections that make it less likely that the price was set by a freely competitive market to reflect the cost or the fair value of the product. And it may arise in situations in which the consumer's levels of literacy and numeracy or urgency of needs impede the exercise of the sophisticated, prudent judgment needed to evaluate the price.

In those circumstances, a court might find that the price term is procedurally unconscionable. When the price, or some element of the price, is hidden from consumers, it may also be policed under § 6 (Deception).

Illustrations:

17. A consumer contracts for a two-year home-security plan, when a one-year plan with much lower monthly payments is available to the consumer from the same business. The business does not advise the consumer of the availability of the one-year plan. It is substantively unconscionable to contract for the two-year plan, which provides no benefit to the consumer relative to the cheaper one-year plan. It is procedurally unconscionable to withhold information about the clearly superior (from the consumer's perspective) one-year plan.

18. A business promises to help a consumer obtain a $14,000 unclaimed surplus from a real-estate foreclosure sale in exchange for half the surplus, i.e., for a $7,000 fee. In the circumstances, the consumer is aware that the surplus is obtainable, but does not know that it could be easily obtained by visiting the court's help desk (which is easy to find and use), without paying any fee. The $7,000 fee is substantively unconscionable. The procedural-unconscionability test is also satisfied, because the availability of the court's help desk was withheld from the consumer and a typical consumer dealing with such a business and accepting such advice would not have known that the surplus could be obtained easily and without cost at the court's help desk. The outcome would be different if the business had to expend substantial resources in identifying consumers with such unclaimed surpluses—consumers who, without this contract, would have received nothing.

19. A set of cookware is sold, by home solicitation, for $375 in an area where a set of comparable quality is readily available for $125 or less. The high price satisfies the substantive-unconscionability test. The procedural-unconscionability test is satisfied if the high-pressure, door-to-door sales method prevented the consumer from obtaining information on the prevailing market price.

20. A consumer borrows $5,000 under a three-year unsecured loan contract carrying an interest rate of 135%. The interest rate is substantively unconscionable if, under the facts of the case, it is excessive relative to the cost of credit the consumer can obtain on a comparable loan elsewhere, or relative to the expected cost for the business of supplying the credit, taking into account the risk of default. The procedural-unconscionability test is satisfied if the interest-rate term was obscured at the time of entering the contract, or if the consumer was under pressure to enter the contract.

9. *Noncommercial activity.* The rule of this Section does not draw a distinction between commercial and noncommercial activity. Some courts, for example, have held that the rule of subsection (c)(1) does not apply when the business that supplies the standard contract terms is operating not for profit, or applies those terms only to its noncommercial activity. The black letter rejects this approach. However, the noncommercial nature of the transaction or the presence of a not-for-profit participant may be taken into account by a court in determining whether a contract or a term satisfies the definition of "unconscionable."

10. *Effects of unconscionability.* Under subsection (a), an unconsciona-

ble contract or term is unenforceable to the extent stated in § 9. In particular, § 9 restates the power of a court to choose between not enforcing the unconscionable term or contract in its entirety or merely limiting the application of any unconscionable clause so as to avoid any unconscionable result.

11. Illegality. The doctrine of unconscionability is related to but distinct from the doctrine of illegality or unenforceability on grounds of public policy. A contract or a term is unenforceable if its performance is inconsistent with statutory or regulatory law or with public policy. See Restatement of the Law Second, Contracts § 178. The legal implications of unenforceability are restated in § 9 of this Restatement.

Illustration:

21. Same facts as in Illustration 10. The "anti-disparagement" clause, in addition to being substantively unconscionable, may also be unenforceable under the doctrine of illegality or on grounds of public policy.

12. Shield versus sword. An unconscionability claim can be used as a defense ("shield"). For example, if a business sues to collect money charged to, but unpaid by, the consumer, the consumer can defend by showing that the charge is unconscionable. The same unconscionability claim can be made by the consumer as a plaintiff, if, for example, an unconscionable charge was already collected by the business, and the consumer is suing to recover it. In that procedural posture, it is sometimes said that the unconscionability claim is used as a "sword." That description is misleading. The unconscionability claim is used to challenge the business's exercise of an alleged contractual right, as in the traditional "shield" cases. A true "sword" application would arise if the consumer has a cause of action for the mere inclusion of an unconscionable term in the contract. Some state consumer-protection laws create an unconscionability-based affirmative right of action and allow consumers to sue for statutory damages. Such statutory claims fall outside the scope of this Restatement.

13. Relation to the Uniform Commercial Code and to the Restatement of the Law Second, Contracts. The rules restated herein are consistent with Restatement of the Law Second, Contracts § 208 and UCC § 2–302, as applied by courts. The unconscionability doctrine has long been understood as being comprised of a procedural prong and a substantive prong. Even in sales-of-goods transactions, warranty disclaimers and limitations of remedies are tested not only against the specific rules of UCC §§ 2–316(2) and 2–719(3), but also against the general overarching unconscionability norm of UCC § 2–302. Such scrutiny may add additional circumstances under which provisions may be found unconscionable, beyond those stipulated in the specific rules.

§ 6. Deception

(a) A contract or a term adopted as a result of a deceptive act or practice by the business is unenforceable by the business to the extent stated in § 9.

(b) Without limiting the scope of subsection (a), an act or practice is deceptive if it has the effect of:

(1) contradicting or unreasonably limiting in the standard contract terms a material affirmation of fact or promise made by the business before the consumer assented to the transaction; or

(2)   obscuring a charge to be paid by the consumer or the overall cost to the consumer.

§ 7. Affirmations of Fact and Promises That Are Part of the Consumer Contract

(a)   An affirmation of fact or promise made by the business that creates a reasonable expectation by a reasonable consumer who is its intended audience that the subject matter of the contract will have the described attribute becomes part of the consumer contract.

(b)   An affirmation of fact or promise made by a third party that creates a reasonable expectation by a reasonable consumer who is its intended audience that the subject matter of the contract will have the described attribute:

(1)   becomes part of the contract between the business and the consumer if:

(A)   the business knew or reasonably should have known of it, and

(B)   the consumer could have reasonably believed that the business intended to stand behind the affirmation or promise; and

(2)   creates a contractual obligation of the third party to the consumer, even if the third party did not transact directly with the consumer, so long as the third party has an appreciable financial interest in the contract between the business and the consumer.

(c)   Standard contract terms that purport to negate or limit affirmations of fact or promises that become part of the consumer contract under subsections (a) and (b) are not enforceable.

§ 8. Standard Contract Terms and the Parol Evidence Rule

A standard contract term that contradicts, unreasonably limits, or fails to give the reasonably intended effect to a prior affirmation of fact or promise by the business does not constitute a final expression of the agreement regarding the subject matter of that term and does not have the effect under the parol evidence rule of discharging obligations that would otherwise arise as a result of the prior affirmation of fact or promise.

Comment:

1.   *Balancing two interests.* Consumer contracts, like all contracts, are subject to the parol evidence rule (Restatement of the Law Second, Contracts §§ 209–218). As that rule is stated in § 213 of the Restatement of the Law Second, Contracts, a conclusion that an agreement is partially or complete-ly integrated—that is, that the agreement consists of a writing (including in electronic form) that constitutes a final expression of one or more terms of an agreement—has the effect of discharging prior agreements. In consumer contracts, the finality provided by the parol evidence rule protects an important interest of the business in certain-

ty and security. But such finality might undermine the interest of consumers in enforcing their reasonable expectations, as formed by affirmations of fact or promises made outside the standard contract terms. Since the standard contract terms do not result from a combined effort by both parties to draft a negotiated agreement, there is less justification to view them as a joint affirmative memorialization of a mutually designed agreement, and thus less reason to allow them to override affirmations of fact or promises made to the consumer. Accordingly, when standard contract terms are inconsistent with prior affirmations of fact or promises, this Section denies those terms the preclusive effect of the parol evidence rule. It accomplishes this by negating the prerequisite for finding an integrated agreement—the conclusion that the standard contract terms constitute a final expression of those terms. This is consistent with § 7, which holds that such affirmations of fact or promises are part of the contract and cannot be undone by standard contract terms (see § 7(c)). Indeed, an attempt to use standard contract terms to contradict or unreasonably limit an affirmation or promise is deceptive under § 6. The result stated in this Section is, therefore, a logical corollary of §§ 6 and 7.

Illustrations:

1. A consumer who lives in an area with frequent, heavy snowfalls enters into a contract with a snow-removal business to shovel her sidewalk the day following snowfalls of two inches or more. During the negotiations, the business's representative assures the consumer that all snow removal will be completed by 10 a.m. on the day of removal. This is important to the consumer because a local ordinance requires sidewalks to be shoveled by that time. The written

agreement signed by the consumer and the business, however, contains a standard contract term stating that the business promises only to complete snow removal by sunset on the day of removal. That standard contract term contradicts the prior promise that snow will be removed by 10 a.m. Accordingly, the "snow removal by sunset" term in the written agreement does not constitute the parties' final expression of the timing term.

2. A consumer enters a dealership to buy a vehicle and, after identifying a satisfactory model for purchase, the dealer promises that delivery will occur within 10 weeks. The time of delivery is important for the consumer because he will be borrowing a vehicle until delivery, but such option is available only for a short amount of time. The consumer manifests assent to the transaction by signing the dealership's Contract for Sale. That document makes no reference to delivery obligations by the seller. It contains a merger clause. The absence of a statement or any reference to the promised delivery does not discharge the obligation of the business that arose from the promise to deliver within 10 weeks.

3. A consumer visits a health club with an interest in becoming a member. After an agent for the club gives the consumer a tour of the facilities and explains membership fees and costs of said membership, the consumer expresses interest in joining, but requests an additional period to make a final decision. The agent presents the consumer with a Membership Contract to sign, but assures the consumer that it will not go into effect upon signing, promising that the consumer may take additional time to make a final decision and give express approval. The standard contract terms con-

tain an initiation term that contradicts the agent's assurance that the agreement will not be effective immediately. The initiation term in the written agreement does not constitute the parties' final expression of agreement regarding the effective date when the membership and resulting obligations will begin.

2. Demonstrating prior affirmations of fact or promises. A consumer may demonstrate that a standard contract term contradicts, unreasonably limits, or fails to give the reasonably intended effect to a prior affirmation of fact or promise by the business even when the standard contract term is unambiguous. Accordingly, in consumer contracts, the "four corners test" does not apply, and a determination of integration must be informed by the alleged prior affirmations of fact or promises. (See Restatement of the Law Second, Contracts § 209, Comment *c*.)

3. Merger clauses. Consumer contracts often contain "merger claus-
es" stating that there are no affirmations of fact, promises, or agreements between the parties except those found in the writing. Because consumers are not likely to notice, read, or understand the effect of such merger clauses, they do not control the conclusion of whether the standard contract terms constitute a partially or completely integrated agreement, and thus do not preclude a finding that the standard contract terms do not constitute the parties' final expression of a particular matter.

4. Relation to the Restatement of the Law Second, Contracts, and the Uniform Commercial Code. The rule of this Section supplements the approach taken by Restatement of the Law Second, Contracts § 213. Uniform Commercial Code (UCC) §§ 2–202 and 2A–202, which are similar in effect to § 213 (although they employ a different structure and different terminology), are also triggered by a "final expression." As a result, this Section can be used to supplement those UCC provisions.

§ 9. Effects of Derogation from Mandatory Rules

(a) If a court finds that a contract or any term excludes, limits, or violates any mandatory rule, the court should do one of the following:

(1) refuse to enforce the contract,

(2) enforce the remainder of the contract without the derogating term, or

(3) limit the application of the derogating term.

(b) If the court enforces the remainder of the contract without the derogating term, the court may replace the derogating term with:

(1) a term that is reasonable in the circumstances,

(2) a term that effects the minimal correction necessary to bring the contract into compliance with the mandatory rule, or

(3) if the contravening term was placed by the business in bad faith, a term that is calculated to give the business an incentive to avoid placing such terms in consumer contracts.

ALI-ELI PRINCIPLES FOR A DATA ECONOMY—DATA TRANSACTIONS AND DATA RIGHTS

TENTATIVE DRAFT NO. 2 (12 APRIL 2021)[*]
EXCERPTS

INTRODUCTORY NOTE

The law governing trades in commerce in the United States and in Europe has historically focused on trade in items that are either real property, goods, or intangible assets such as shares, receivables, intellectual property rights, licenses, *etc.* With the emergence of the data economy, however, tradeable items often cannot readily be classified as such goods or rights, and they are arguably not services. They are often simply 'data'. Both in the U.S. and in Europe, uncertainty as to the applicable rules and doctrines to govern the data economy is beginning to trouble stakeholders (such as data-driven industries, micro, small and medium-sized enterprises, as well as consumers). This uncertainty undermines the predictability necessary for efficient transactions in data, may inhibit innovation and growth, and may lead to market failure and manifest unfairness, in particular for the weaker party in a commercial relationship.

A. Why Principles on data transactions and data rights?

The application of traditional legal doctrines to trades in data is not well-developed, often does not fit the trade, and is not always useful or appropriate or even accomplished in a consistent manner. At the bottom of this uncertainty lies the fact that data is different from other resources in several ways, such as by being what has come to be called a 'non-rivalrous resource', i.e. data can be multiplied at basically no cost and can be used in parallel for a variety of different purposes by many different people at the same time. Where A sells a machine to B, A will no longer have the machine in the end, but where A sells data to B, both A and B can have and use the data, and the multiplication of the data does not in any way reduce its practical utility (without prejudice to the fact that the

---

[*] As of this date, this Draft has not been considered by the members of the American Law Institute and the European Law Institute and does not represent the position of the Institutes on any of the issues with which it deals. The action, if any, taken by members of the American Law Institute with respect to this Draft may be ascertained by consulting the Annual Proceedings of the Institute, which are published following each Annual Meeting.

market value of data may decrease rapidly with increasing numbers of persons having the data). Also, the way data can be shared or supplied differs significantly from the way goods are made available to others, and many transactions in the data economy do not have an analogy in traditional commerce. If A allows B to access data in a secure space on A's servers with an algorithm to run certain processing activities, this would be a very common type of transaction in the data economy, but there is no established body of applicable contract law that would fit precisely this type of transaction.

However, data is also different from intellectual property as, in the transactions usually considered to be part of the 'data economy', what is 'sold' is not the permission to utilise an intangible but rather binary impulses with a particular meaning, usually as 'bulk' or 'serial' data. This focus on binary impulses in large batches, which may be stored, transmitted, processed with the help of machines, etc., is also what differentiates transactions in the data economy from traditional information services. Where A pays B for gathering information on election outcomes in a foreign country the focus is on B *doing* something (i.e. telling A, even if A and B have agreed B must give A the information in a particular format, such as by email). By contrast, where A pays B for real time transmission of exit poll data to be displayed on A's news channel the focus is on B *delivering* something (i.e. a large batch of binary impulses with a particular meaning in a particular format).

The fact that data is different is the reason why it has become necessary to draft principles for data transactions and data rights instead of merely referring to the existing law of, say, sale and lease of goods, or of services. It is important to note that the legal analysis depends to a great degree on whether the relevant data is protected under rules such as intellectual property law or trade secret law and/or rules that limit certain types of conduct (such as data privacy/data protection law and consumer protection law).

This project seeks to propose a set of principles that might be implemented in any kind of legal environment, and to work in conjunction with any kind of data privacy/data protection law, intellectual property law or trade secret law, without addressing or seeking to change any of the substantive rules of these bodies of law.

B. Players and relations in the data ecosystem

These Principles cannot provide a complete set of standards for any sort of dealings within the data economy. This is so for a variety of reasons, including the special dynamics of the data economy as a fast-moving field, the desire to reduce complexity and focus the Principles on some central points, and the need to produce something that works in vastly differing legal environments in different regions of the world.

The Principles have taken the basic types of players and relations which we find in data ecosystems as a starting point. The central player in all data ecosystems is the controller (often also called the 'holder') of data, i.e. the person that is in a position to access the data and that decides about the purposes and means of their processing. That controller may exercise control all by itself or share it with co-controllers, such as under a data pooling arrangement. A (mere) processor of data, on the other hand, is a service provider that processes data on a controller's behalf.

There is also a variety of different parties contributing in different ways to the generation of data. One important way of contributing to the generation of data is by being the individual or legal entity that is the subject of the information recorded in the data. Another way of contributing to the generation of data is by being a data producer, i.e. generating data in the sense of recording information that had previously not been recorded. There are also parties that do not produce data in this sense, but create added value by assembling data in some meaningful ways, and parties that contribute in more remote roles. The parties that contribute to the generation of data may provide the data to the controller (provided data). Data may be produced by the controller itself through observing the parties (observed data). The controller may also obtain derived or inferred data from data that has been observed or provided.

A controller of data often supplies the data to third party data recipients, in particular under contractual or other data sharing arrangements. Recipients of data may become new controllers where data is fully transferred to them, or they may receive only access to the data, such as where they are permitted to process data with a mobile software agent on the supplier's server. Needless to say, an important part of the data economy consists in using data for creating new value, such as by developing and marketing data-based products and services; marketing these products and services is, however, not covered by these Principles.

In addition to the parties mentioned there is an increasing number of different types of data intermediaries, such as data trustees, data escrowees, or data marketplace providers. They facilitate the transactions between the different actors, in particular between parties generating data and data controllers, and between data suppliers and data recipients, such as by acting as trusted third party.

. . .

C. Structure of the Principles

a. Part I: General Provisions. The first Part sets out the purpose and scope of the Principles and provides definitions of key terms that they utilize, such as 'data', 'copy', 'processing', 'control of data' and 'supply' of data. In defining these terms, efforts have been made to ensure consistency with both established terminology worldwide and other ALI and

ELI work. Part I also includes an outline of some basic values and ideas guiding the interpretation and application of the Principles.

b. Part II: Data Contracts. The second Part of the Principles is devoted to contracts with regard to data, establishing, in the first place, sets of default terms that seem appropriate for different basic types of data transactions. While focussing on contracts, the default terms apply, with appropriate adjustments, also to the governing principles of similar arrangements, such as where a company or other legal entity is established instead (e.g. for a data pooling arrangement). Part II begins by setting out, in Chapter A, some general provisions on the rules and principles governing data contracts.

Chapter B is more specifically about contracts for supply or sharing of data. The Principles identify, as a first step, typical contractual promises in the data economy that involve different types and modalities of provision of data and show how these transactions in the data economy can be systematized, with a view to analysing the rights and obligations of the parties to the transaction. These rights and obligations may be very different, depending on whether, *e.g.*, a party has promised to fully transfer data to a medium within the recipient's sphere of control, or only to grant access to a medium on which data is stored or maybe even only to consent to the collecting and processing of data by the other party to the transaction while refusing to take any responsibility for what the other party ultimately receives. Where data is not just provided by a supplier to a recipient, but where two or several parties decide to contribute data to a data pool or closed platform each of them has access to, this again may require a somewhat different set of rules. It should be noted that the terms 'supply' and 'sharing' may, by and large, be used interchangeably, even though 'supply' fits better to describe a one-way provision of data. Among the policy choices recommended by these Principles in the context of supply or sharing of data is the default position that data supplied may be used by the recipient for any lawful purpose that does not infringe the rights of third parties ('sales approach' as opposed to a 'license approach'). Because, however, the Principles provide a wide berth for private ordering, including provisions that emphasize freedom of contract except when limited by a mandatory rule of the applicable jurisdiction, parties will remain able to agree on arrangements close to a 'data license', as is frequently found in model agreements and in data contracts even where data is not protected by intellectual property law.

Chapter C deals with contracts whose focus is not the provision of data by one party to another, or the sharing of data among various parties, but rather the provision of services with regard to data. The most important contract type in this regard is contracts for the processing of data, including any cloud storage of data and any data analytics. Another type of contract addressed in Chapter C is a type that has been labeled, for lack of a better term, 'data trust contracts', although that term should not be taken as encompassing the specific legal implications of the common law concept of trusts, and a related type of contract labeled 'data escrow contracts'. Also, data marketplace contracts, which are essentially about the facilitation of data transactions and the matchmaking between parties, are dealt with under this Part.

. . .

Part I: General Provisions

Principle 1: Purpose of these Principles

(1) The Principles for a Data Economy are intended for use in legal systems in Europe, the United States, and elsewhere. They are designed to

    (a) bring coherence to, and move toward harmonization of, existing law and legal concepts relevant for the data economy;

    (b) be used as a source to inspire and guide the further development of the law by courts and legislators worldwide;

    (c) inform the development of best practices and guide the development of emerging standards, including standards or trade codes that are specific to a particular industry or industry sector;

    (d) facilitate the drafting of model agreements or provisions to be used on a voluntary basis by parties in the data economy;

    (e) govern contracts or complement the law that governs them to the extent that they provide default rules or that parties to a transaction have incorporated them into their contract or have otherwise designated them to govern; and

    (f) guide the deliberations of tribunals in arbitration.

(2) These Principles recommend a legal framework that is intended to work with any form of data privacy or data protection law, intellectual property law, or trade secrets law. These Principles are not intended to amend or create any such law, but they may inform the development of such other law. In the event of any inconsistency between these Principles and such other law that cannot be overcome by interpretation, the other law should prevail.

Comment:

a.   Addressees and added value.
These Principles address a fast-emerging but already major sector of the economy. Yet, this sector has developed largely without a legal framework that recognizes and reflects many of the sector's important and unique attributes in order to govern it in a way that thoughtfully balances and facilitates both the public interest and the private interests of the parties. These Principles are the result of collaborative work of lawyers from Europe and the U.S. They are designed to provide guidance as to the basic principles to be applied to data transactions and related matters irrespective of the otherwise applicable legal framework (whether that of a U.S. state or one of the European legal systems), and thereby seek to develop a consistent, general approach across national borders and legal disciplines.

The purpose of these Principles is to provide guidance to and to inform parties, practitioners, arbitral tribunals, standardization bodies, courts, and legislators worldwide. They seek to promote the enhancement and better adaptation of the law to the data economy as an ever more important part of the economy at large and to identify guiding principles in dealing with data as an asset and tradeable item. By doing so, they facilitate the further development of the law by courts and legislators worldwide and the review of existing law and soft law instruments by, in particular, legislative bodies, standardization agencies, or bodies developing codes of conduct. The Principles are also designed to facilitate the drafting of model agreements or provisions to be used on a voluntary basis by parties in the data economy. Equally, they may govern contracts or complement the law that governs contracts to the extent that they provide default rules or that parties to a transaction have incorporated them into their contract or have otherwise designated them to govern. The Principles may, in a similar vein, guide the deliberations of tribunals in arbitration. Depending on the specific needs and characteristics of a particular industry these Principles may provide the basis for adaptation or extension for the development of industry-specific standards.

By their very nature, some Parts of these Principles are addressed to particular players more than to others. For instance, Part II on data transactions is addressed both to parties in the data economy (and to counsel advising these parties), bringing some clarity as to the main types of transactions and suggesting rules that could typically be considered reasonable and fair, and to courts, which must deal with incomplete agreements and provide appropriate 'gap fillers' when parties have failed to deal with important issues. Part III on Data Rights is predominantly addressed to legislators and bodies developing standards and codes of conduct. However, it is also addressed to parties, their legal advisers, and to courts dealing with issues that involve the relationship between, e.g., the users of goods, digital content or services and the manufacturer, or between the manufacturer and suppliers of components. Part IV may be seen to be addressed primarily to legislators considering issues raised by the data economy, and to courts that have been called upon by a party, e.g., because that party claims its rights have been infringed by some data activity. The same would hold true for Part V dealing with cross-border issues. However, none of the Parts is exclusively targeted at the specific audiences just mentioned, and these Principles seek to provide added value to as broad a variety of actors as possible.

b.   Relationship with specific areas of the law not addressed by these Principles. The data economy is a subject that touches upon and cuts across many areas of the law. Most notably, data may in many instances be protected by copyright or other intellectual property rights. In addition, to the extent that data is personal data (i.e. is identified, or identifiable, to a particular natural person), data privacy/ data protection law provides for an ever more comprehensive set of rules. Another area of the law with a firmly established framework that addresses the protection of information and data is trade secret law. While these Principles cannot entirely avoid referring to these areas of the law, they do not seek to restate what the rules in those areas are or should be. Rather, they take those areas of the law as more or less given.

For example, these Principles propose rules to govern transactions in non-personal data as well as personal data, recognizing that the latter type of data may be subject to data privacy/data protection regimes. The Principles, in some cases, address some implications of such regimes for trade in data. But the Principles do not deal with issues fully covered by data privacy/data protection law, such as when consent is necessary and/or can be withdrawn.

Illustration:

1.   Business S supplies an online video game and holds a broad range of personal data from users playing that game, much of which is protected under data privacy regimes such as the California Consumer Privacy Act (CCPA) or the General Data Protection Regulation (GDPR). S 'sells' the data of 20,000 users to data analytics business R in a way that is in conformity with the relevant data privacy regimes. Shortly after the data is transferred to B, 5,000 users from the EU withdraw their consent to the processing of the data. As a reaction, R demands return of 25% of the price

paid to S. As these Principles do not seek to restate or revise data privacy/data protection law, they do not deal with questions such as whether the users' consent may be withdrawn at any time, or whether the users have a right to object to the sale by clicking a button stating 'Do not sell my data' or the like. Rather, user rights under data privacy/data protection law are left to the applicable rules, considering also the territorial scope of those rules. The Principles do, however, address the effect of data privacy/data protection regimes, and of rights exercised under such regimes, on the rights of parties to a data transaction such as the transaction between S and B, e.g., whether S would have been under a duty to make R aware of this risk and whether R has any rights against S because R ultimately lost 25% of what R had bargained for.

Sometimes, the validity of a transaction dealt with under these Principles will depend on such other law, e.g. where a transaction is blatantly inconsistent with data privacy/data protection law that may, depending on the circumstances, mean the transaction is illegal and thus void or voidable under the applicable law. That, too, is not a matter for these Principles to deal with.

Illustration:

2.   Assuming that, in a scenario such as that in Illustration 1, a large number of users had failed to give their consent, or had really clicked the button 'Do not sell my data', and thus 'sale' and transfer of the data by S to R was really against the law, and both S and R were aware of that. Whether that affects in any way the validity of the contract between S and R should not be for these Principles to deal with. However, these Principles will then deal with what the unwinding

of the transaction means with regard to the data.

Sometimes, different aspects of the same activity may be the subject of these Principles as well as other bodies of law. For instance, data porting (portability) rights are dealt with under Part III of these Principles, but they may also be an element of data protection law, consumer protection law, or competition law. It is, in particular, in those grey zones that the other bodies of law would prevail in the event of any inescapable inconsistency between them and these Principles, but still these Principles might inform the development of these other bodies of law and point at directions of development that might be more favorable for a flourishing data economy than others. For example, a major challenge for the data economy is that there is hardly any data pool that does not implicate potential issues arising from data privacy/protection law (e.g. because some data in the pool is personal data, or can be de-anonymized in the future), intellectual property law (e.g. because some snippets of text might be protected by copyright) or trade secrets law (e.g. because aggregated machine data allow conclusions about business operations). This leads to reluctance on the part of businesses to share their data with others as such sharing might indirectly expose them to requests for erasure, claims for damages and other adverse consequences. The law should take these considerations into account when accommodating these diverse needs, and Principles 34, 36 and 37 in particular make some suggestions as to how this could be achieved.

c. Relationship with contract rules and doctrines. The relationship of the Data Economy Principles to existing law of sales and service contracts, such as can be found in European civil codes or statutes or in the Uniform Commercial Code, is an entirely different story. There is a clear overlap between such areas of the law and these Principles, such as with regard to contractual rights and obligations of the parties. These Principles are inspired by those bodies of law and are guided by them, sometimes clarifying application of existing principles in the data context while other times providing a roadmap for future development. They seek to identify standards that, if adopted, would take priority over existing rules in these areas by tailoring their application to data transactions. The same holds true for unfair competition law, which, however, normally does not specifically deal with data or information and would be informed by these Principles only with regard to data economy scenarios.

These Principles do not address general legal doctrines such as those governing formation of contracts or protections provided to consumers in consumer contracts, leaving those matters to existing law. Thus, these Principles do not differentiate between consumers and businesses as customers. Rather than create new protective doctrines unique to this context, these Principles instead provide guidance as to the application in a data setting of existing protective rules and doctrines, which often differentiate between consumers and businesses. Whenever these Principles refer to 'contract' or 'contractual' this automatically implies that all general contract law doctrines, whether from statute or common law, apply, and that, where the contracting parties are a business and a consumer, all applicable consumer protection standards remain unaffected. These doctrines and standards vary from jurisdiction to jurisdiction (e.g. notions of 'unconscionabilty' and 'unfairness' in business-to-business transactions may mean very different things in different jurisdictions), and it is not the purpose of these Principles to change, with regard to data, a more general approach taken by the contract law of a particular jurisdiction on these matters.

d.   Relationship with property law. These Principles do not address whether rights in data are to be characterised as 'ownership' or 'property' (except, of course, when other law, such as intellectual property law or the like, affirmatively creates property rights), nor do they take any position in the controversy between more privacy-oriented and more property-oriented theories of data law. Rather, they describe the attributes of rights with regard to data without addressing the issue of 'proper' doctrinal characterisation as the one or the other.

Principle 2: Scope of these Principles

(1)   **These Principles address matters with regard to digital data. The primary focus of the Principles is on records of larger quantities of information as an asset, resource or tradeable commodity. The Principles do not address functional data and representative data.**

(2)   **Subject to paragraph 3, these Principles address**

    (a)   **data contracts,**

    (b)   **data rights, and**

    (c)   **third party aspects of points (a) and (b).**

(3)   **These Principles are not designed to apply to public bodies insofar as such bodies are engaging in the exercise of sovereign powers.**

Comment:

a.   Restriction to digital data. The definition of 'data' in Principle 3(1)(a) is broad. Applying the Principles to all rights and transactions about data (as so defined) would result in application of the Principles beyond their intended context. Accordingly, Principle 2(1) provides that these Principles are concerned only with digital data (as defined in Principle 3(1)(c)). These Principles may also be appropriate for application by analogy to other recorded information in some circumstances depending on, inter alia, the way the information is recorded and the manner in which it is to be used.

Illustration:

3.   Employee E of business B (unlawfully) 'sells' B's customer database to competitor C. However, due to specific IT security measures taken by B, it turns out to be easier for E to print the customer data on paper to deliver to C than to store the information on a digital medium or transmit it online to C. C will immediately scan the prints and convert the data into a digital format. In a setting like this it would not seem appropriate to restrict the application of these Principles—such as the Principles on unauthorized access and what it means for a downstream recipient—to the phases when the customer data is in digital format. (Note that issues of criminal and other liability on the part of E are beyond the scope of the Principles).

b.   Focus on information. The Principles (as well as the terms 'data contracts', 'data rights' etc.) should be understood as covering only issues that have a primary focus on records of larger quantities of information. They should not cover cases where, e.g., the focus is on the medium itself, or on an entirely different aspect of data. This flexible approach allows for these Principles to be applied to the whole transaction, to a particular part or aspect of a transaction, or not applied at all when the 'records of information' aspect is not the focus of the subject matter.

Illustrations:

4.   A simple contract between a law firm and a client pursuant to which the law firm will represent the client in contract negotiations would not be within the scope of the Principles even where it is anticipated that the law firm will transmit proposed drafts of transactional documents in digital form through an electronic message system. This is because the focus of the contract between the law firm and the client is not the records of information, but rather the legal advice as such. Of course, a wider relationship between a law firm and a client may include aspects that are within the scope of these Principles, and that relationship may include, e.g., access to data or processing of data within the meaning of the Principles.

The distinction between a primary focus on records of (larger quantities of) information and a different focus is particularly relevant when it comes to digital phenomena that are not primarily considered as 'data' even though, technically speaking, they have the same or a very similar nature. A computer program, for example, is primarily seen as a set of commands delivering particular functionalities ('functional data' as defined in Principle 3(1)(d)). Cryptocurrencies and other tokens may be seen as, amongst others, data packets, but clearly the focus is not on any value inherent in the information recorded in the token, but rather on the off-ledger asset represented by them ('representative data' as defined

in Principle 3(1)(e)) or the on-ledger asset generated by the fact that other members of a community are prepared to trade them for value. This is why Principle 2(1) clarifies that the Principles do not address functional data or representative data.

Illustrations:

5.   A transfer of Bitcoins from wallet holder A to wallet holder B is not a 'data transaction' for purposes of these Principles because the transaction is primarily about a transfer of value represented by a virtual token and documented on the blockchain. Likewise, in-game purchase of a weapon or superpower would not be a 'data transaction' and would not be covered by the Principles because the focus is on the functionality, not on the information.

The fact that a set of digital data normally serves the purpose to deliver certain functionalities does not exclude the possibility that the same set of data may also be used without reference to those functionalities, in which case the data could be within the scope of these Principles.

c.   Asset, resource or tradeable commodity. Information has always been subject to a variety of different contracts, in particular service contracts, and information rights have always been included in a wide range of different legal regimes. Many of these issues fall outside the scope of these Principles already because they are not about 'digital' data, or because the information is not the focus of the transaction. However, there are cases where the law provides that, e.g., particular information must be given to a consumer with particular digital means, or where two parties agree in a contract that one party will disclose and publish all its conflicts-of-interest on the company's website. In these cases, the legal rules are about digital data, and they are about the information aspect, but still such rules would not be within the focus of these Principles. This is because these Principles are not primarily concerned with single pieces of information provided with the aim of immediately making another party know something, but more about 'bulk' or 'serial' data, usually to be processed with the help of machines, and used as an asset, resource or tradeable commodity. Accordingly, supplying data within the meaning of these Principles is not so much about doing something, but more about *delivering* something.

d. *Issues addressed.* The development and identification of clear and certain principles that promote a data economy that is both efficient and fair is of fundamental importance to the development of that economy. Law governs the data economy in a wide variety of ways. These include the allocation of private rights with respect to transactions and the data to which the transactions relate, unfair competition and antitrust law, privacy and data protection law, etc. These Principles do not address that entire range of legal issues but, rather, focus on data contracts and data rights, and on the third-party aspects of such contracts and rights, as far as these are relevant in the context. In addition, the Principles provide for some limited guidance as to multi-state issues with regard to data contracts and data rights, without providing a full set of choice-of-law rules.

e. *Public bodies.* The control and processing of data by public bodies in the exercise of sovereign powers afforded to them by the applicable law is an extremely important topic which is, however, beyond the boundaries of these Principles. The Principles therefore apply only to the extent that exercise of sovereign powers is not implicated (but even where the Principles could be applied to activities of public bodies, other, more specific, rules for dealings with the government or government agencies may also apply).

Illustration:

6. A public prosecutor's authority collects data on a group of individuals suspected of having committed cybercrimes. This activity is one in the exercise of sovereign powers, and suspects might not, e.g., rely on any of the Principles concerning data rights in co-generated data. However, where that authority enters into a contract with a private company for data analytics services, the Principles might apply, because the authority would not exercise any sovereign powers vis-à-vis that company.

References to a 'public body' in these Principles include public administrations and judges as well as civil law notaries and any kind of body insofar as such bodies are engaging in the exercise of sovereign powers, be it directly or by means of delegation to any other authorities, official professionals or mixed bodies.

Even though these Principles do not apply to public bodies insofar as such bodies are engaging in the exercise of sovereign powers, the Principles may still apply to situations where public bodies have collected data in the exercise of sovereign powers, but are now making this data available under schemes of open public sector data and the like, because sharing data in that manner is not in itself exercise of sovereign powers.

Principle 3: Definitions

(1) **For the purposes of these Principles the following definitions shall apply:**

(a) 'Data' means information recorded in any form or medium or as it is being transmitted;

(b) 'Copy' means any physical manifestation of data in any form or medium;

(c) 'Digital data' means information recorded in digital form;

(d) 'Functional data' means data the main purpose of which is to deliver particular functionalities, such as a computer programme;

(e) 'Representative data' means data the main purpose of which is to represent other assets or value, such as crypto-assets;

(f) 'Processing data' means any operation or set of operations that is performed on data, whether or not by automated means; it includes, inter alia, the structuring, alteration, storage, retrieval, transmission, combination, aggregation or erasure of data;

(g) 'Access to data' means being in a position to read the data and utilize it, with or without having control of that data;

(h) 'Control of data' means being in a position to access the data and determine the purposes and means of its processing;

(i) 'Controller' means the person that, alone or jointly with other persons, has control of data;

(j) 'Processor' means a person that, without being a controller, processes data on a controller's behalf;

(k) 'Co-generated data' means data to the generation of which a person other than the controller has contributed, such as by being the subject of the information or the owner or operator of that subject, by pursuing a data-generating activity or owning or operating a data-generating device, or by producing or developing a data-generating product or service;

(l) 'Derived data' means data generated by processing other data and includes aggregated data and data inferred from other data with the help of external decision rules;

(m) 'Data contract' means a contract the subject of which is data;

(n) 'Data right' means a right against a controller of data that is specific to the nature of data and that arises from the way the data is generated, or from the law for reasons of public interest;

(o) 'Data activities' means activities by a person with respect to data, such as collection, acquisition, control, processing and other activities including onward supply of data;

(p) 'Supply' of data means providing access to data to another person or putting another person in control of data;

(q) 'Supplier' of data means a party who supplies data to another party, or undertakes to do so;

(r) 'Recipient' of data means a party to whom data is supplied, or to be supplied;

(s) 'Transfer' of data means supply of data by way of which the supplier puts the recipient in control of the data, whether or not the supplier retains control of the data;

(t) 'Porting' data means initiating the transfer of data controlled by another party to oneself or to a designated third party;

(u) 'Erasure of data' means taking steps to assure, as far as is reasonably possible, that the data is permanently inaccessible or otherwise unreadable; and

(v) 'Notice' means having knowledge of a fact or, from all the facts and circumstances of which a person has knowledge, being in a position that the person can reasonably be expected to have known of the fact.

(2) The terms 'contract for the transfer of data', 'contract for simple access to data, 'contract for exploitation of a data source', 'contract for authorization to access', 'contract for data pooling', 'contract for the processing of data', 'data trust contract', 'data escrow contract' and 'data marketplace contract', and any terms denoting the parties to such contracts, have the meanings given to them in Principles 7 to 15.

(3) References to a 'person' include natural and legal persons, private or public. References to an operation or activity shall include operations or activities carried out with the help of other persons or of machines, including any artificial intelligence.

Comment:

a.   'Data' and 'copy'. The term 'data' has multiple facets in common parlance. In fact, lawyers frequently talk past each other when using the term because they are referring to different facets or concepts of 'data'. Much confusion has been caused, in particular, by the varying use of the terms 'information' on the one hand and 'data' on the other. These Principles use 'data' to refer to information recorded in any form or medium, or being in a state of transmission. In the case of digital data, this means that data is more than the binary electrical impulse stored or being transmitted, as it includes context and semantics. Context and semantics are to be found in metadata, domain tables etc.

The term 'data' as defined in paragraph (1)(a) has more than one layer. For apart from the semantic layer, i.e. the layer that constitutes meaning, it can be understood as referring to the code as such (e.g. a characteristic binary string of '0s' and '1s') or its physical manifestation on a particular medium. The former can be 'coded', 'modified', 'decompiled' etc, while the latter can be 'stored', 'damaged', 'erased' etc. In order to make this distinction more transparent these Principles restrict the term 'data' to the former, i.e. to the code as such (including context and semantics), while the physical manifestation on a medium is called a 'copy'. A term that is often used with a similar meaning is 'file', which, however, seems also to arouse some associations that are not intended in this context.

Illustration:

7. Business B collects data concerning B's transactions with its customers, such as A, on a local hard disk drive, but there is a backup on a cloud server provided by C. The fact that A has bought a specified commodity from B on a specified date is the information. This information is recorded in the form of coded binary impulses, i.e. a characteristic string of '0s' and '1s', which constitutes the data. This string can be found as a physical manifestation both on B's local hard disk drive and on C's cloud server, so there exist two copies of the data (or really even more, as there will be redundancies, and as there may be transitional copies in the cache of several devices).

Of course, the definition of the term 'copy' applies only as the term is used in these Principles. The definition here is not intended to resolve issues about the meaning of that term in other areas of the law, such as copyright law.

b. *'Digital data', 'functional data' and 'representative data'.* 'Digital data', as referred to in Principle 2(1), is defined as data recorded in digital form. 'Digital' should be interpreted broadly to cover non-digital technologies (such as analog computing and, perhaps, quantum computing) when those technologies enable comparable sorts of operations to be performed on the data by automated means, i.e. where data is recorded in other machine-readable formats suitable for automated processing. 'Functional data' and 'representative data', as likewise referred to in Principle 2(1) as types of data not covered by the Principles, are defined as data the main purpose of which is to deliver certain functionalities, such as a computer program, or to represent other assets or value, such as crypto-assets.

c. *'Processing data' and 'access to data'.* A central term is 'processing' data, which is defined to include any operation or set of operations that is performed on data. Thus 'processing' includes operations such as organising, structuring, storing, adapting or altering, retrieving, transmitting, aligning or combining, restricting, erasing or destroying data. Some of these operations directly target the data as such, while others target the data only indirectly by targeting one or all existing copies. Defining the term generically to cover all of these operations is useful because, given the multitude of different ways in which data can be handled or used, it would be quite unwieldy to utilize different terminology for each of them and, given the pace at which

528

technology is developing, any terminology defined today may be incomplete or inappropriate tomorrow.

'Access to data' and processing of data are closely related notions. 'Access' means being in a position to read the data and utilize it, in unspecified or specified ways, and with or without having control of that data. Processing of data usually requires access to the data. Access, conversely, often includes some kind of processing, but not necessarily so; merely reading data on a screen would amount to access but normally not to processing, at least not in the more narrow sense adopted by these Principles.

Illustration:

8.   Business B in Illustration 7 processes transactional data by structuring them, analyzing them, and by way of many other operations. Assuming B checks its transactions with A because A has filed a complaint (e.g. A claims never to have received a commodity for which he has been billed), retrieving transactional data from either the local drive or the cloud and making it visible on a screen on one of B's devices amounts to processing (but it is also a form of taking access). If B lets A take a look at the screen and read the information about A's shopping history this is a situation where access (on the part of A) is not accompanied by processing.

d.   *'Control of data', 'controller' and 'processor'.* Another central notion is that of 'control of data'. 'Control of data' means being in a position to access the data and to determine the purposes and means of its processing, with or without having a right to do so. A 'controller' means the natural or legal person, public authority, agency or other body that, alone or jointly with others, has control of data.

Illustration:

9.   Business B in Illustration 7 has its business data stored in cloud space on servers operated by C. B has the access credentials required to access and process the data as B deems appropriate. Even though B is not in 'physical' control of the medium, B has, for the purposes of these Principles, control of the data and qualifies as controller. C does not qualify as a controller insofar as there are features in place, be they of a technical or legal nature, that prevent C from determining the processing of its customers' data.

Control does not necessarily mean being in a position to determine any possible kind of processing, e.g. a person may have access to a set of data and may be in a position to transfer it to someone else, but the data may be protected against modification. Also, 'control' does not necessarily imply that the 'controller' actually seeks access to the data or has the technical capabilities that are necessary for actually accessing the data, as long as there are technical or legal features that would allow that party, without unreasonable effort, to access the data if the party wished to do so.

Illustration:

10.   Company N runs a news website. Use of the website by each visitor is, with the consent of N, closely monitored and recorded by data broker B (B paying a remuneration to N). While company N itself never takes an interest in collecting the visitors' data, and may not even have made any technical arrangements that would allow such collection, it would not require unreasonable effort on N's part to do so. N therefore has control of the visitors' data because it could access the data at any time if it so wished and because N determines the means

and purposes of their processing by allowing B to harvest the data.

Frequently, controllers enter into contractual arrangements with other persons about the processing of data to be carried out by those other persons, while keeping full control because processing is carried out on their behalf and according to their directions. Such other person is a processor, which means that, in some contexts—such as when it comes to the question who has to comply with duties under Principle 32 or whose position counts for rightfulness under Principle 28—it is only the controller on whose behalf the processor is acting who counts. Being a processor and processing data on behalf of a controller does not constitute control of data, so the roles of 'processor' and of 'controller' are normally mutually exclusive.

Illustrations:

11. Business B decides to outsource payroll services with regard to B's employees and hires company P to perform these services. For this purpose, relevant data (such as the employees' names, wages, bank accounts or tax numbers) is processed by P on B's behalf. P is not free in determining the means and, in particular, not the purposes for which the employee data is processed, but rather has to follow B's directions. P is therefore not a controller, but a processor.

12. Business B allows financial consulting firm A to access B's business data in order to analyse B's business situation. A is not entirely free to determine the means and the purposes of processing B's business data (e.g. A would not be allowed to disclose the data to B's competitors), which could mean A is only a processor. However, A is not strictly subject to B's directions either (e.g. B would not be allowed to direct A that A ignores certain

data in order to paint a more optimistic picture of B's business situation than is the reality). Therefore it is more convincing to qualify A as controller, albeit as a controller that is subject to quite rigid restrictions when it comes to the purposes of the processing.

Employees or similar persons integrated in the controller's organisational framework and through whom the controller exercises control would not even be considered 'processors'. When the controller is a legal entity it can act only through its employees and other agents, anyway. Accordingly, when an employee is merely executing decisions made by the employer, any activity of the employee with regard to data should be attributed exclusively to the employer.

e. *'Co-generated data' and 'derived data'.* 'Co-generated data' means data to the generation of which a person has contributed, such as by being the subject of the information or the owner or operator of that subject, by pursuing a data-generating activity or owning or operating a data-generating device, or by producing or developing a data-generating product or service. The term is used in the context of a particular type of data rights dealt with under Chapter B of Part III. The term is designed to indicate that, usually, a number of different persons have contributed to the generation of data, sometimes in very different roles. Needless to say there may be situations where only one person has contributed, at least in a meaningful way, to the generation of data. In this situation the term 'co-generated' may not be fully appropriate, but, of course, such a person would (a fortiori) have the rights under Chapter B of Part III.

While the term 'co-generated data' refers to the parties who had a share in the generation of data the term 'derived data' refers to the fact that data develops in a dynamic way and is often generated on the basis of other data. Only an exact copy of a particular set of data would count as the 'same' data, and even minor modifications would make a set of data a 'different' set of data. In these Principles, 'derived data' means any data which the relevant controller has generated by processing other data, i.e. by modifying, reducing, extrapolating other data or drawing inferences from other data. Given that there are many different ways in which data can be generated on the basis of other data and that it is so difficult to draw a clear line and provide a coherent and complete set of classifications, these Principles adopt a broad notion of 'derived'. In particular, they do not differentiate between 'derived' and 'inferred' data (i.e. data generated from other data with the help of external decision rules).

Illustration:

13.   When opening a user account for an online game run by business G, users provide to G their name, email address and credit card data, and G collects all sorts of other user data, such as about the user's gaming behavior, typing pace etc. G then re-structures the data, fills gaps in the data and infers, with the help of algorithms and other knowledge not contained in the collected data, new information from the observed data, e.g. predictions about a party's disposition to suffer from depression. The restructured data, the completed data as well as the data inferred all count as derived data.

f.   *'Data contracts', 'data rights' and 'data activities'*. These Principles are about data contracts and data rights, so these two terms are quite important for the proper understanding of the whole draft. Both terms are to be understood broadly. A 'data contract' is a contract the subject of which is data, either in the sense that data is the ob-

ject of the transaction between two parties (i.e. the data is to be transferred, disclosed, otherwise shared etc.) or in the sense that one party promises to do something with regard to the data (i.e. the data is to be collected, processed, secured, etc.).

A 'data right' means a right against a controller of certain data that is specific to the nature of data as a non-rivalrous resource and that arise from the way the data is generated (see Principles 18 to 23), or from the law for reasons of public interest (see Principles 24 to 27). It may, in particular, be a right to access to or porting of this data, to correction of this data or desistance from data use, or, very exceptionally, to an economic share in profits derived from using the data. Data rights are, in a certain way, the data-specific corollary to the ownership rights we find in the tangible world or with regard to intellectual property.

'Data activities' is a term referred to in various places in these Principles, in particular in Part IV with regard to affected third parties. It means any activities by a person with respect to data, such as collection, acquisition, control, processing and other activities including onward supply of data. The term is to be understood broadly, and as comprising activities of a more factual (e.g. actually disclosing data to another party) as well as of a more legal nature (e.g. making a contract with another party about access to data).

g.   *'Supply', 'supplier' and 'recipient'.* It is in particular in data transactions based on contract that 'supply' of data comes into play. The person who supplies data is the 'supplier' and the other person is the 'recipient.' 'Supply' of data should be understood very broadly. In particular, it is sufficient that the recipient gains access to the data, while it is not necessary that the recipient also gains control.

Illustrations:

14. Company N runs a news website, offering access to world news to any visitor without a pay-wall. N collects a wide range of data concerning the search requests and browsing habits of its visitors and 'sells' and transfers the data to business B who will use the data for profiling and scoring purposes. This involves a twofold supply: First, the news to which visitors to the website of N are given access constitutes 'data,' and the granting of access to that news is 'supply' of data. Second, the transfer of the data to B qualifies as 'supply' of the visitor data.

15. Assume that company N in Illustration 14 does not collect the visitors' data itself but only allows B to collect the data on N's site. Despite the fact that N does not physically transmit any data to B, N still enables B to access the data, and to gain control of the data, and therefore qualifies as a 'supplier' under these Principles.

h. *'Transfer', 'porting' and 'erasure'.* While 'supply' of data is a very broad and rather generic term, it is often necessary to be more specific and to differentiate between different types of supply. An important type of supply is 'transfer' of data, in which the supplier puts the recipient in control of the data supplied (as contrasted with simple access). This normally implies that data is to be physically stored on a medium within the recipient's sphere of control. Note that 'transfer' does not imply that copies of the data are subsequently erased by the supplier.

Illustration:

16. Supply to data broker B in both Illustrations 14 and 15 would qualify as 'transfer' as B gets full control of the data. However, supply of the news items to visitors in Illustration no. 14 would not qualify as 'transfer' because the visitors to the news site only get access to the data and not control of the data (unless a download option is offered).

'Porting' data, which is frequently also referred to as 'portability' of data, means requesting or otherwise initiating the transfer of data controlled by another party to oneself or to a particular third party. 'Porting' and 'transfer' are thus closely related, with the main difference being that of perspective, as 'porting' clearly takes the perspective of the recipient exercising a right, while 'transfer' is more neutral and describes an activity of the supplier. 'Porting' tends to suggests to a certain extent that the person requesting the transfer has a data right, i.e. that the data is, in one way or another, that persons' data.

Illustration:

17. Supply of the data collected by N to B in Illustration no. 14 would be described as a 'transfer' (and not as 'porting') because it is supplier N who collects the data and who then initiates transfer to B. However, where B is allowed to harvest data from the site in Illustration no. 15 and store the harvested data on B's own medium that would be described as 'porting' rather than as 'transfer', because the active part is rather played by recipient B.

In particular contexts, 'erasure' of data (one type of 'processing' data) may become relevant. This means taking reasonable steps to assure that the data is permanently inaccessible or otherwise unreadable. What counts as 'reasonable' depends on the individual circumstances and the purposes of erasure. It may, in an individual case, mean deleting all copies of the data that are accessible to the person erasing the data, and, as far as possible, deleting all copies accessible to third parties to whom that person has supplied the data. This is because, given the nature of data, there may exist an indefinite number of copies worldwide. Sometimes it may be sufficient to press a 'delete' button even though, strictly speaking, the data would then still remain to be retrievable until the relevant storage space has been fully overwritten, and possibly even after that point. But normally, more sophisticated technical measures would be required.

i. *Notice.* A term that is used in various places throughout the Principles is 'notice'. 'Notice' means having knowledge of a fact, but it also covers constellation where, from all the facts and circumstances of which a person has knowledge, the person can reasonably be expected to have known of the fact. It certainly includes what is often referred to as 'wilful blindness'. Where a person has notice of a fact (e.g. of the fact that processing data was wrongful) that often gives rise to an expectation that the person takes action or desists from particular actions accordingly, and if the person fails to react as can reasonably be expected, this often triggers adverse legal consequences.

j. *Definitions in other Principles.* Paragraph (2) reminds us that only those terms are defined in Principle 3 that are used in various places throughout the Principles. There are other terms that require a definition but that are used only in one Principle, or in one specific context, and that are thus better defined in the relevant context itself. This concerns, in particular, the different types of data transactions identified in Part II.

k. *References to 'person'.* Paragraph (3) clarifies that reference to 'person' includes any natural or legal person, or group of persons. What may be more important is that reference to any operation or activity includes operations and activities carried out by human auxiliaries and, more and more importantly, by machines. Machines include any artificial intelligence, i.e.

it is irrelevant for the application of the Principles whether, e.g., a data contract was concluded by way of two individuals exchanging offer and acceptance or whether offer and acceptance were articulated and received by 'autonomous' software agents.

Needless to say, where a contract is concluded by machines some concepts used in these Principles may require adaptation. For example, these Principles frequently refer to a party having 'notice' of a fact. Where there is not a human but a machine that carries out relevant operations or activities the concept of 'notice' may have to be adapted.

Illustration:

18. A contract for the transfer of particular data is made with the help of two different autonomous software agents operated by supplier S and recipient R. S had received the data from third party T under another contract, and under that contract S had promised not to forward or disclose the data to any other person. According to Principle 34, T may have remedies against R where R had 'knowledge' or could be expected to have knowledge of S's breach vis-à-vis T and further conditions are met. Where R used an autonomous software agent and that agent was unable to process information as to restrictions of that kind, R cannot hide behind the agent and claim to have been in good faith.

Equally, any reference to intent or to standards of care, due diligence etc. may have to be understood in a way that is suitable for machine-to-machine dealings. However, this is not in any way different from machine-to-machine dealings other than in the context of data rights and transactions, which is why these Principles do not spell out in detail how general concepts are to be adapted.

Principle 4: Remedies

(1) **Remedies with respect to data contracts and data rights, including with respect to any protection of third parties in the context of data activities, should generally be determined by the applicable law.**

(2) **Where these Principles or applicable law would mandate the return or surrender of data by a party (the defendant) to another person (the claimant), the defendant should be able to satisfy the obligation to return or surrender the data by, instead, erasing all of the defendant's copies of the data. If the claimant has not retained a copy of the data, the defendant must put the claimant in control of the data before erasing it.**

Comment:

a. Remedies. These Principles do not generally address remedial matters, leaving that to applicable law. Often, applicable law assesses money damages or monetary restitution as the remedy. However, there are also a number of cases where the applicable law may require specific performance, and some jurisdictions, in particular in continental Europe, may have a general tendency towards preferring specific performance over money damages.

b. Return as part of a remedy. Sometimes, applicable rules or principles would require the return of an item, including data, that had been delivered to a party—for example, when data has been supplied by mistake, or when a contract was avoided or cancelled after data had already been supplied. Return is an elusive concept for data, of which there can be many copies. Hence, paragraph (2) reflects the unique character of data and adjusts the duty to return accordingly. It provides that data may be 'returned' by erasing all copies of the data that the recipient may still have under control. Where the supplier had not retained a copy, e.g., because the parties had agreed that the recipient would have exclusive control and the supplier had undertaken to erase all of its copies, the recipient must put the supplier in

control of a copy again before erasing its copies.

Illustration:

19. Employees of a department of company S transmit industrial data to company R in the erroneous belief that a contract between S and R about the supply of the data has been concluded. (Actually, negotiations had failed at the very last moment.) If applicable law would otherwise require R to return the mistakenly-supplied data, R may instead erase all copies of the data of which it has control. If the employees of S had erased all S's copies of the data—perhaps because that was a term of the (failed) contract—R must put S in control of the data before erasing it.

There will be many situations where application of general remedial principles would lead to the conclusion that data that has already been processed must be returned by the recipient. This may not be reasonable and fair under all circumstances, such as, for example, when the data has been processed so as to integrate it with other data in a manner that makes separation unfeasible. Generally speaking, when return by erasure is unreasonable in light of the circumstances mandating the return and the legitimate interests of the claimant as well as any protected third party, a court should instead make a reasonable allowance in money to be paid to the supplier. Broadly speaking, this is analogous to a situation in which there would be an obligation to return building materials but, because the building materials have been incorporated into a structure, it would be impractical to order return of the building materials so a monetary remedy is given instead.

Illustration:

20. If in Illustration no. 19 company R has already processed the data erroneously supplied by S by way of integrating it with data from other sources and reformatting and restructuring so that the data is now in the form of a searchable database from which the data supplied by S cannot be separated without significant burden and expense, it may be unreasonable and unfair to require R to bear that burden and expense or to erase the database. However, in such a case it would equally be unfair if R were allowed to keep and market the database without having to pay a reasonable amount for it, so R should be required to pay S a reasonable amount of money in lieu of returning the data.

For an application of this concept in the context of wrongful processing see Principle 36(2).

Part II: Data Contracts

Chapter A: Rules and Principles Governing Data Contracts

Principle 5: Application of these Principles to data contracts

Data contracts under Part II should be governed, in the following order of priority, by:

(a) rules of law that cannot be derogated from by agreement;

(b) the agreement of the parties;

(c) any rules of the law other than those referred to in paragraph (a) that have been developed for application to data transactions of the relevant kind;

(d) the terms included in the contracts by operation of Principles 7 to 15;

(e) application by analogy of default rules and principles of law that are not directly applicable to data transactions of the relevant kind but that would govern analogous transactions; and

(f) general principles of law.

Comment:

This Principle provides a general hierarchy for determining the rules governing data contracts.

At the top of that hierarchy are mandatory rules of applicable law that cannot be varied by agreement. Such mandatory rules differ from jurisdiction to jurisdiction. Examples of such rules include doctrines of unconscionability or unfairness control, obligations of good faith and fair dealing that cannot be disclaimed, prohibitions on excessively large liquidated damages, and also certain mandatory requirements to be included in contracts between controllers and processors under the law of some jurisdictions.

Next in priority is the agreement of the parties. This is because principles of party autonomy present in most legal systems give parties to a contract wide leeway to determine the terms of their relationship. Of course, what counts as the 'agreement of the parties' is partly an issue of fact and partly the result of applying the rules of the applicable legal system as to what constitutes an agreement and how binding agreements are formed, as well as rules that determine which communications are to be treated as part of an agreement when varying communications, oral as well as written or electronic, have been exchanged.

Many data transactions are the subject of extensive negotiations and careful contract drafting, while others are entered into with significantly less individualized attention. Disputes about the rights and obligations of parties do not typically arise when the subject of the dispute is covered by express agreement of the parties. Rather, they arise more often with respect to issues not covered in that agreement. All agreements are inevitably incomplete, with the result that, in the event of dispute, law is called upon to fill the gaps. In some cases, the issue may be one that was simply not addressed by the parties; in other cases, the parties may have thought the resolution was implicit in their agreement. For issues of this sort that arise with some frequency, contract law often deals with this phenomenon by providing for terms that are 'automatically' included in a contract unless derogated from by agreement of the parties. Such terms are usually referred to as 'default'

terms or 'implied' terms. Paragraphs (c)-(e) of this Principle set out, in order of priority, how law fills the gaps in parties' agreements in determining their rights and obligations.

First, paragraph (c) defers to contract law rules of the relevant jurisdiction insofar as they have been developed for application to data transactions of the relevant kind. Some states may have such data-specific rules, while others may not. Next, paragraph (d) refers to Principles 7 through 15, which develop recommended default rules for nine types of data transactions. Finally, paragraph (e) provides for the application of default rules and principles that apply to analogous transactions. As it is often difficult to identify contract law principles to govern a contract by analogy, Principles 7 to 15 also supply a list of factors a court should consider when deciding whether to adopt rules by analogy in the context of the particular types of data transactions addressed in those Principles. In applying rules by analogy under paragraph (e), terms in those rules should of course be adjusted to the context of data transactions. So, for example, references to ownership in such rules must sometimes be replaced by references to control of the data, references to use or the like replaced by references to access to data, and references to delivery or the like should sometimes be read as referring to the provision of control or access. For matters not addressed in paragraphs (c) to (e), paragraph (f) of this Principle ultimately defers to general principles of law to fill remaining gaps. These general principles will, in the first place, be general principles of contract law, but could equally be general principles of other bodies of law.

Principle 6: Interpretation and application of contract law

In interpreting and applying rules and principles of contract law, the following factors, among others, should be considered:

(a) the fact that data is a combination of (i) physical manifestations on a medium or in a state of being transmitted, and (ii) information recorded;

(b) the nature of data as a resource of which there may be multiple copies and which can be used in parallel by various parties for a multitude of different purposes;

(c) the fact that data is usually derived from other data, and that the original data set and a multitude of derived data sets that resemble the original data set to a larger or lesser extent may co-exist;

(d) the fact that, while the physical location of data storage may change quickly and easily, data is normally utilized by way of remote access and the physical location of data storage is typically of little importance; and

(e) the high significance of cumulative effects and effects of scale.

Comment:

a.   General observations. The subject of data contracts is different, in many ways, from the subject of most other contracts. Because of those differences between the subject of data contracts and that of many other contracts, application of general principles of contract law, often designed for those other contexts, should be sensitive to those differences. In some cases, this will involve interpretation of general principles in a manner that is consistent with the context in which they are to be applied. In other cases, it guides and constrains analogies to principles of law that govern different subjects.

Principle 6 comes into play at several of the levels within the hierarchy of rules mentioned in Principle 5. Where there are mandatory rules of law, i.e. rules of law that cannot be derogated from by agreement, within the meaning of Principle 5(a) those mandatory rules may have been drafted with traditional transactions about traditional

resources (such as goods or rights) in mind. When they need to be applied to a data contract, the specificities of data must be taken into account. Even more so, where default rules and principles of law that are not directly applicable to data transactions of the relevant kind are applied by analogy, within the meaning of Principle 5(e), those rules and principles will normally have to be adapted to fit in the data context. The same holds true for general principles of law, including contract law, within the meaning of Principle 5(f).

b.   Factors to be considered. Principle 6 lists some factors that ought to be considered when applying contract law that has not originally been drafted with data transactions in mind. The most important special feature of data is the fact that data is a combination of binary impulses that may be physically manifest on a medium or be transmitted, and the information recorded in those binary impulses. This means that, e.g., the act of supplying data is somewhat in between 'delivering' and 'doing', and, accordingly, a contract to supply data is somewhat in between a sale contract and a service contract.

Illustration:

21. If A sells a machine to B that transaction can be described as being about delivering something, and if A promises to provide legal advice to B that is clearly a service. However, where A shares data with B that is somewhat in between delivering something to B (i.e. the binary impulses, by way of transmission) and doing something for B (i.e. triggering a change in the state of B's storage device), which makes it difficult, for instance, to seek proper analogies.

Another important feature that makes data different from almost all other resources is its non-rivalrous nature, i.e. the fact that there may be multiple copies of one and the same set of data, which can be used in parallel by various parties for a multitude of different purposes.

Illustration:

22. Where A sells a machine to B, A will no longer have the machine in the end, but where A sells data to B, both A and B can have and use the data, and the multiplication of the data does not in any way reduce its practical utility (without prejudice to the fact that the market value of data may decrease rapidly with increasing numbers of persons having the data). This may affect the way in which a court would apply rules and doctrines such as on the passing of risk, because if data is lost or destroyed while being transmitted from the supplier to the recipient the supplier is able to transmit another copy at no or only negligible cost.

A similar feature of data is that data can be changed within fractions of a second, and that almost all data is derived from other data, with the changed or derived set of data often existing in parallel with all the previous versions, partly coinciding with previous versions, and partly not.

Illustration:

23. If A rents a cow to B it is clear that, when the contract period comes to an end, B will have to return the cow, and, if the cow has meanwhile given birth to a calf, possibly the calf (depending on the applicable contract and property law). If A gives access to data to B for a particular access period the law will not only have to mandate that B erases any copies of the data B may have retained (on which see the previous point as well as Principle 4(2)), but will also have to decide which data sets that have, in one way or the other, been derived from A's data set, are included in the duty to return.

Another characteristic feature of data is the fact that, while the physical location of data storage may change within fractions of a second the data is normally utilised by way of remote access and the storage location is of little relevance.

Illustration:

24. If A sells a machine to B, contract law may provide for rules on the place of performance, e.g. the default rule might be that the place of performance is the place of establishment of seller A, but that it is the establishment of C if the machine is currently in the possession of C. However, if A supplies data to B, it may not necessarily make sense to identify the place of performance according to the same rules, in particular as, with cloud-based storage, the location of data may no longer play any meaningful role. Indeed, the concept of a "place" of per-

formance may have little meaning in this context.

Last but not least, it is the unusually high significance of cumulative effects and effects of scale that make data different from other resources in that the value of data depends largely on which other data they can be combined with, who has access to the data, and similar factors.

Chapter B: Contracts for Supply or Sharing of Data

Principle 7: Contracts for the transfer of data

(1) A contract for the transfer of data is a transaction under which the supplier undertakes to put the recipient in control of particular data by transferring the data to a medium within the recipient's control or by delivering to the recipient a medium on which the data is stored.

(2) Subject to agreement of the parties and to rules that take priority pursuant to Principle 5, the law should provide that the following terms are included in a contract for the transfer of data:

  (a) With regard to the manner in which the supplier is to perform its undertaking described in paragraph (1), the data is to be transferred electronically to a medium indicated by the recipient, or to a medium from which the recipient can download the data to a medium of the recipient's choice, unless either that mode of delivery or the medium indicated is unreasonable in the light of data security concerns in which case the supplier should promptly notify the recipient of those concerns so that the recipient may indicate a substitute mode of delivery or medium.

  (b) With regard to the characteristics of the data supplied, including with regard to nature, quantity, accuracy, currentness, integrity, granularity, and formats, as well as with regard to the inclusion of metadata, domain tables and other specifications required for data utilization, and to frequency of supply and any updates:

  (i) The supplied data must conform to any material descriptions or representations concerning the data made or adopted by the supplier, and to any samples or models provided;

  (ii) If the supplier has notice of the recipient's particular purpose for obtaining the data and that the recipient is relying on the supplier's skill or judgment in selecting the supplied data, the supplied data must be fit for the recipient's particular purpose; and

(iii) If the supplier is in the business of supplying data of the sort that is the subject of the contract or otherwise holds itself out as having expertise with respect to data of that sort, the supplied data must be of a quality that would reasonably be expected in a transaction of the relevant kind.

(c) With regard to the control of, and other data activities with regard to, the supplied data:

(i) If the supplied data is protected by intellectual property law or a similar regime, the supplier must place the recipient in the position of having a legal right, effective against third parties, that is sufficient to result in the recipient's control of the data, or other data activities in which the controller had notice that the recipient could reasonably expect to engage in, not constituting infringement; if putting the recipient in that position requires additional steps to be taken by the supplier, such as execution or recordation of a required document, the supplier must take those additional steps;

(ii) The supplier must place the recipient in a position, at the time the data is supplied, of being able rightfully to exercise control over the data and rightfully to engage in other data activities in which the controller had notice that the recipient could reasonably expect to engage in; if, after the data has been supplied, the recipient's control of the data or other data activities become wrongful this does not of itself give rise to a claim by the recipient against the supplier;

(iii) The supplier must co-operate, to the extent reasonably necessary, in actions that may be required to comply with legal requirements with respect to control of the data or other data activities in which the controller had notice that the recipient could reasonably expect to engage in. In addition, the supplier must provide to the recipient information about any legal requirements with respect to any such data activities of which the supplier has notice and of which the recipient cannot be expected to be aware;

(iv) The recipient may utilize the data and any derived data, including by onward supply to others, for any lawful purpose and in any way that does not infringe the rights of the supplier or third parties, and that

does not violate any obligations the supplier has vis-à-vis third parties provided the recipient had notice of these obligations at the time the contract for the transfer of data was concluded;

(v) **As between the parties, new intellectual property rights or similar rights created by the recipient with the use of the supplied data belong to the recipient; and**

(vi) **The supplier may retain a copy of the data and may continue using the data, including by supplying it to third parties.**

(3) **In determining which rules and principles should apply by way of analogy to contracts for the transfer of data, as provided in Principle 5, factors to be taken into account should include, among others:**

(a) **whether the contract provides for the recipient to be in control of the data for an unlimited period of time or for a limited period of time; and**

(b) **whether the contract is for a single supply of data, repeated supply, or continuous supply over a period of time.**

Comment:

a. *Scope.* Principle 7 is the first of a series of Principles setting out default provisions for contracts concerning different types of data transactions. The type of data transaction addressed in Principle 7 is called a 'contract for the transfer of data'. A contract for the transfer of data is a transaction under which the supplier undertakes to supply particular data to a recipient, and, in doing so, to put the recipient in control of that data by transferring the data to a medium within the recipient's control or by delivering to the recipient a medium on which the data is stored. This type of contract may involve data of any kind, whether raw or derived, and whether or not protected by intellectual property law or a similar regime.

Illustration:

25. Supplier S operates an online shop and holds large amounts of customer data. S promises to recipient R to supply specified types of data (name, email address, goods bought, search requests made) regarding the shopping behavior of a specified number (20,000) of customers from specified regions (U.S. and EU) that has accumulated over a specified period (24 months) and to transfer the data to a medium within R's control. The purpose of this deal is to enable R to engage in targeted advertising campaigns. This would be a contract for the transfer of data under this Principle.

A medium within the recipient's control may be the recipient's server. It may also be a cloud space to which the supplier gives the recipient the access credentials if the intention is to allow the recipient to download the data from the cloud space onto a medium within the recipient's control, or if the cloud space is intended to remain within the recipient's control.

b.   *Default terms as to the mode of supply.* The parties to a contract for the transfer of data will typically agree how the data should be supplied to the recipient. If the contract is silent regarding the mode of supply of the data, paragraph (7)(2)(a) provides relevant default terms. The default terms provide that, generally speaking, the data is to be supplied electronically and to a medium indicated by the recipient. Instead of transferring the data directly to a medium controlled by the recipient, the supplier may also upload the data to a medium to which the recipient has or is given access and from which the recipient may download the data to a medium of the recipient's choice. However, that mode of transfer is not required if either that mode of delivery or the medium indicated by the recipient is unreasonable in the light of data security concerns.

Illustration:

26.   Assume that, in the transaction described in Illustration 25, recipient R has directed supplier S to transfer the customer-related data to particular cloud space, but this cloud space is insecure and, thus, not a reasonable mode of transfer. S is not obligated to transfer the data to the insecured cloud space. (This protects S from the possibility that S itself might be in breach of contractual and statutory duties if customer data is transferred to insecure storage space.)

Where the mode of delivery or the medium indicated by the recipient is unreasonable in the light of data security concerns the supplier should promptly notify the recipient of those concerns so that the recipient may indicate a substitute mode of delivery or medium.

c.   *Default terms as to the characteristics of the data.* When the default terms relate to characteristics of the data that is the subject of the transaction, these terms are usually referred to as 'warranties'. Characteristics of data have many facets, some of the most important being: nature (including whether the data are personal data or non-personal data according to the applicable law), accurateness, currentness, integrity, granularity, and formats, as well as the inclusion of meta data, domain tables and other specifications (such as ontologies) required for data utilization, and frequency of supply and any updates. The warranty terms set out in this Principle are analogous to warranty terms included as default terms in contracts for the sale of goods.

First, in some cases, even though the parties have not expressly stated in the contract the nature, quantity and quality of the data, descriptions or representations concerning the data have been made or adopted by the supplier. When these descriptions or representations are have become part of the basis of the bargain, this Principle incorporates them into the contract. In those cases, it is appropriate for the supplier to be bound by those descriptions or representations as though they were expressly stated in the agreement of the parties. The same holds true if the supplier has provided the recipient with samples (such as a sample dataset) or models (such as the structure in which the information will be presented).

Illustrations:

27.   Assume that, in the negotiation of the transaction described in Illustration 25, supplier S had stated that the data sets have been updated within the last six months. Therefore, the contract includes a requirement that the data has, in

fact, been updated within that period.

28. If, during the negotiations, supplier S has provided recipient R with sample datasets of 100 typical customers, and in these datasets the names were complete and all the fields, even the non-mandatory fields, filled in, the contract would include a term that all datasets are as complete as the sample.

Second, if the supplier has notice of the recipient's particular purpose for obtaining the data and that the recipient is relying on the supplier's skill or judgment in selecting the supplied data, the supplied data must be fit for the recipient's particular purpose. In the data world, this is probably an exceptional situation that is not the norm. Indeed, selecting and furnishing data in such circumstances can easily be seen as an implicit statement by the supplier that the data is fit for that purpose.

Illustration:

29. Assume that, in a situation of the kind described in Illustration 25, recipient R has developed a new smart service that functions in conjunction with fitness bracelets from a defined range of manufacturers. R is interested in having access to customers who have bought such bracelets and might thus be interested in R's new service. R approaches supplier S, disclosing to S this purpose and indicating that it is relying on S in selecting appropriate data sets. S then declares that S has appropriate datasets for R, and the two enter into a contract for the transfer of customer data. It is a term of the contract that the datasets supplied are fit for the purpose disclosed by R.

Third, according to paragraph (2) (b)(ii) a default term that the supplied data must be of a quality that would reasonably be expected in a transaction of the relevant kind becomes part of the contract if 'the supplier is in the business of supplying data of the sort that is the subject of the contract or otherwise holds itself out as having expertise with respect to data of that sort'. This condition to the presence of the default term is included because it is fair to require the supplier to stand behind the quality of data in situations in which the marketplace has that expectation in light of the characteristics of the supplier. This is not a mandatory term, but the burden is on a supplier that does not want to have this responsibility for the quality of the data to negate the default term in the contract. This arrangement of responsibilities is similar to responsibilities for the quality of goods in many legal systems. One context is when the supplier is a business that collects large amounts of data as part of its business, such as a social network or a search engine provider. Another context occurs when a company that manufactures goods or provides services accumulates a substantial amount of data as part of is operations and goes into the separate business of selling that data.

Illustrations:

30. Shoe manufacturer S manufactures custom-made shoes for customers who supply foot measurements via a specially-designed app. Accordingly, S has accumulated a large amount of data about foot sizes that is not available elsewhere. S concludes that there is a market for this sort of data among other shoe manufacturers, suppliers of orthopedic equipment, etc., and markets the foot-size data to companies in those industries. There is so much demand for this data that S makes significant profits every year supplying it. S is 'in the business of supplying data of the sort that is the subject of the contract'. Accord-

ingly the contracts for the transfer of data include the default term in Principle 7(2)(b)(ii).

31. If, in a situation of the kind described in Illustration 25, supplier S has made trade in customer data part of its business and regularly engages in this to generate additional income, S can be expected to make sure the data is of the quality that is normal in transactions of the relevant kind. For example, where in the relevant industry and under the relevant circumstances the normal expectation would be that not more than about 15 percent of customer email addresses will fail at the point in time when the data is transferred, the contract includes a term that the email addresses will conform to that expectation.

32. If, conversely, in a situation of the kind described in Illustration 25, supplier S simply runs an online shop and has just accumulated customer data for S's own purposes, but then is approached by R whether S might be prepared to sell the customer data (which S would initially not have planned, but is happy to do in order to generate additional income), the term that the email addresses will conform to the expectations in the relevant industry is not included in the contract.

d. *Default terms with regard to control of, and other data activities with regard to, the supplied data.* A third group of default terms concerns control and use of the supplied data by the recipient.

First, when the supplied data is protected under intellectual property law or a similar regime (such as EU investment protection for databases), the supply of that data would have little value if it did not include an appropriate legal right to use that data. After all, the parties' intention is normally focused on the granting or assignment of a legal right that allows the grantee or assignee to have rightful control of that particular set of data, and that allows the recipient to engage in all data activities in which the controller had notice that the recipient could reasonably expect to engage in, and that is effective vis-à-vis the rightholder and other third parties.

This Principle does not address whether and to what extent the supply of copyright-protected software should be characterized as a license contract or as a sale, and the Principle applies under either characterization. The nature and extent of the right to be provided (e.g. whether it is a license for limited or for unlimited time, on how many servers the data may be stored and run, how many people may use the data at the same time), if not specified by the parties, should be broad enough to enable the use contemplated by the contract. If the right provided is insufficient for such use, the supplier's actions fall short of what this term requires and the supplier is liable for breach. Because some domestic intellectual property regimes require licenses to be memorialized in a writing or record or require recordation of the writing or record (or a reference to it), Paragraph (2)(c)(i) also addresses that situation.

Illustration:

33. The customer data that supplier S promises to transfer to recipient R in a situation of the kind described in Illustration 25 includes some photo material that customers have uploaded to share their experience with other customers and which is protected by intellectual property law. Even if not expressly agreed, the contract includes a term according to which S must make sure R gets a license that allows R to do at least what R intends to do with the data when the contract is

concluded, i.e. analyse the data for purposes of targeted advertising.

Even where data is not protected by intellectual property law, the usefulness of data to the recipient would be undermined if the recipient did not obtain rightful control over the data at the time it is supplied, or could not engage in other data activities in which the controller had notice that the recipient could reasonably expect to engage in. Thus, paragraph (2)(c)(ii) states a default term mandating that the recipient shall obtain such control. The supplier must therefore ensure that, for example, there are no legal barriers that would prevent the recipient from rightfully gaining control. Legal barriers could be barriers stemming, e.g., from data privacy/data protection law, from intellectual property law, or from trade secrets law. The methods by which the supplier ensures the absence of legal barriers will depend on the individual circumstances. They could, e.g., include the seeking of valid consent or other forms of waiver of rights, or technical measures such as anonymization of data.

Illustration:

34. Assume that, in a situation of the kind described in Illustration 25, the agreement between supplier S and recipient R is silent as to whether S is responsible for assuring that the customers, who are protected by a data privacy regime, have given all necessary consents to transfer of control of the data to R. S supplies the data, but 5,000 of the customers have not given their consent to the transfer of control of the data, with the result that, under the applicable data privacy regime, control of the data by R would be wrongful. S has violated its obligation under paragraph 2(c)(i) to enable the recipient rightfully to exercise control over the data at the time it is supplied.

Unless the parties have agreed otherwise, subsequent facts rendering control or other data activities by the recipient wrongful (and possibly triggering a duty of the supplier to inform the recipient under Principle 32(2)), do not, as such, give rise to a claim by the recipient against the supplier.

Illustration:

35. Same facts as Illustration 34 except that, at the time of transfer, the customers had all given consent to the transfer of control of the data. After the data is supplied, however, 5,000 customers protected by a data privacy regime withdraw their consent to the processing, with the result that, under the applicable data privacy regime, any future control or processing of these data by R would be wrongful. S has not violated its obligation under paragraph 2(c)(i) to enable the recipient rightfully to exercise control over the data at the time it is supplied.

Third, there may be other legal requirements with respect to control and use of the data. Paragraph (2)(c)(iii) provides, as a default term, important obligations of the supplier with respect to such requirements. In particular, the supplier is obliged to provide the sort of support that can reasonably be expected in order to comply with legal requirements governing control and use of the data. In addition, although a recipient can be expected to be aware of the sort of legal requirements that apply to the control and use of data generally, paragraph 2(c)(ii) includes a default term requiring the supplier to disclose any legal requirements that the recipient cannot be expected to be aware of, as far as the supplier has notice of them, and provide support to the recipient in complying with them.

Illustration:

36. In a situation of the kind described in Illustration 25, recip-

ient R can be expected to be sufficiently aware of the general fact that both customers from the U.S. (e.g. those resident in California) and customers from the EU may be protected by data privacy regimes because this is a fact that should be known to anyone engaging in a data transaction. However, if it is not evident that some of the customer data qualifies as health data and is therefore subject to a much stricter regime, and R (who is not a very sophisticated recipient) cannot be expected to be aware of this stricter regime, S is under an obligation to inform R of this fact if S has notice.

Fourth, unless the parties have agreed to the contrary, it is appropriate to treat the contract as one that does not place any limits on how the recipient may utilize the data (including by passing it on), so a default rule to that effect is included. Thus, among the policy choices for default rules recommended by these Principles is that data supplied may be used by the recipient for any lawful purpose that does not infringe the rights of the supplier or of third parties, including any obligations the supplier has vis-à-vis third parties provided the recipient had notice of these obligations. With regard to data that is not protected by intellectual property law, these Principles thus take a 'sale' approach (i.e. freedom of the recipient is the default position, and limitations must be agreed upon), and not a 'license' approach (which would mean that, as a default rule, the recipient may engage only in the data activities agreed upon).

Illustration:

37. As a default position, R would, in a situation of the kind described in Illustration 25, be allowed to utilize the customer data for any purpose R deems fit as long as this purpose utilization does not infringe any rights of S or of third

parties, including in particular the customers under an applicable data privacy regime. So, provided the data privacy law so allows, and there are no other specific restrictions on the use of the data (such as a duty of S of which R had notice when the contract was concluded), R would be free to change its mind slowly and no longer (just) engage in targeted advertising, but instead (also) use the data for developing a new online reputation system.

In practice, however, it is quite common that parties supply data under a contract labelled a 'license' even where they have really concluded a contract for the transfer of data, and specify in that 'license' the conditions under which the supplied data may be used. Where the data is not protected by intellectual property law, or no longer protected due to exhaustion (first sale doctrine), this is a contract covered by Principle 7 without regard to how the parties label it. Where the parties make further agreements about the purposes for which the recipient may or may not process the data, about the number of people to whom the data may be disclosed, or about the duration of use by the recipient, they create, by virtue of freedom of contract, independent contractual obligations of the recipient to refrain from particular operations.

Illustration:

38. If the parties in a situation of the kind in Illustration 25 so wish they may describe, in some detail, the types of data use recipient R may or may not engage in. In particular, they may agree that R must not compete with S on particular markets, or pass the data on to third parties. R is bound by this contractual restriction on data utilization.

In this context, it is important to highlight the connection between Principles 7 through 15 and Principles 32

546

through 34 inasmuch as the latter deal with the supplier's obligation to pass on certain restrictions and obligations to the recipient and to alert the recipient, (e.g., if subsequent events occur that are relevant for the recipient's legal position). In particular, Principle 32(1) obliges the supplier to impose particular contractual duties and restrictions on the recipient to the extent that these duties and restrictions must be complied with for the benefit of a protected party within the meaning of Part IV Chapter A.

Fifth, the question of allocation of intellectual property rights created with supplied data is something parties to a transaction should normally agree on in advance, inasmuch as that allocation may have important economic effects. Under this Principle there is a default term that these new intellectual property rights belong to the recipient. As with all default terms, this is subject to mandatory legal rules that cannot be derogated from by contract, and to agreement between the parties to the transaction. For example, applicable law might provide that new intellectual property rights are vested in a third party such as in an employee of the recipient.

Illustration:

39. Assume that in a situation of the kind described in Illustration 25 R would indeed use the data for developing a new online reputation system, which in itself would be protected by copyright. As a default position, S would not hold any rights in that system, and all intellectual property rights would be vested in R. This is, however, just as between the parties, so if the law provides that, really, the intellectual property rights should be vested in independent coder C this is to be respected.

Sixth and finally, a contract for the transfer of data is not usually intended to deprive the supplier of the continuing right to use that data. Accordingly, paragraph (2)(c)(vi) provides a default rule to the effect that supplier may retain a copy of the data and may continue using it, including by supplying it to third parties, i.e., any utilization rights of the recipient are normally non-exclusive.

Illustration:

40. In a situation of the kind described in Illustration 25, no one would expect supplier S to delete all its customer data after having transferred them to recipient R. But there may be scenarios where this is less self-evident, e.g. where the data relate to a type of goods S wishes to stop offering on the market, while R wants to invest a lot into selling precisely this type of goods. Still, in the absence of an agreement to the contrary, S would not be required to delete the data after the transfer.

e.   Application of other law by analogy. Principle 5 provides that default rules and principles that are not directly applicable to the transaction at hand but that would govern a type of transaction akin to the transaction at hand may be applied to the transaction at hand by analogy.

Since a contract for the transfer of data under which the recipient may use the data for an unlimited period of time will very often have many important characteristics of a sale, inasmuch as unlimited use transfers the economic value of the data to the recipient, the closest analogy may often be to the law of sale of goods, unless the relevant jurisdiction provides for specific rules on the supply of digital content. Where, however, the recipient may use the data only for a limited period of time the more appropriate analogy may sometimes be the law of lease contracts, or similar bodies of the law. Also, different sets of legal rules may apply depending on whether the contract is for a one-off exchange or for repeated or continuous supply.

The list of criteria to take into account when deciding which rules and principles to apply by analogy provided in paragraph (3) is not exhaustive. Other criteria that may be useful, depending on the circumstances, include the nature of the data and of any third-party rights in the data, and whether the supplier also promises, under the same contract, to customise the data sets that are to be supplied, which may recommend an analogy to the law of services contracts.

Principle 8: Contracts for simple access to data

(1) **A contract for simple access to data is one under which the supplier undertakes to provide to the recipient access to particular data on a medium within the supplier's control and which is not a contract for the transfer of data under Principle 7. This includes contracts where the supplier, in addition to enabling the recipient to read the data, undertakes to put the recipient in a position to process the data on the medium within the supplier's control, or port data.**

(2) **Subject to agreement of the parties and to rules that take priority under Principle 5, the law should provide that the following terms are included in a contract for simple access to data:**

    (a) **With regard to the mode of the recipient's access to the data:**

        (i) **The supplier must provide the recipient with the necessary access credentials and remove any technical barriers to access whose removal could reasonably be expected in a transaction of the relevant kind;**

        (ii) **The supplier must make the data accessible in a structured and machine-readable format of a sort that can reasonably be expected in a transaction of the relevant kind;**

        (iii) **The supplier must enable the data to be accessed remotely by the recipient unless this is unreasonable in the light of data security concerns;**

        (iv) **The recipient may process the data to which the recipient is given access only for purposes consistent with any purposes agreed in the contract;**

        (v) **The recipient may port data to which it is given access in the contract only when the porting of such data can reasonably be expected in a transaction of the relevant kind and may port data derived from the recipient's processing activities carried out in** accordance with the contract (e.g., data derived from data analytics); and

(vi) The recipient may read the data, process or port the data, as applicable, by any means, including automated means, and may do so as often as the recipient wishes during the access period agreed.

(b) With regard to the characteristics of the data to which access is provided, the terms listed in Principle 7(2)(b) for contracts for transfer of data also apply in a contract for simple access to data.

(c) With regard to the control of any data ported by the recipient in accordance with the contract, and other data activities, the terms listed in Principle 7(2)(c) for contracts for transfer of data also apply in a contract for simple access to data.

(3) In determining which rules and principles to apply by way of analogy, as provided in Principle 5, to contracts for simple access to data, consideration should be given in particular to the degree to which the recipient may only view the data, may process data on the medium within the supplier's control, or may port data.

Comment:

a.   Scope This Principle covers contracts where the obligation assumed by the supplier is to give the recipient access to data on a medium within the supplier's control. Parties may wish to choose a contract for simple access to data where they do not want the recipient obtaining full control of (all) the data that are the object of the bargain. This can be for data privacy/protection, data security or other reasons, in particular in light of the fact that data that has once been transferred to a recipient can hardly be recovered if used or passed on by the recipient in breach of the terms agreed. Contracts for simple access to data do not fall under Principle 7, but are covered in Principle 8 (and, to a certain extent, in Principle 9). The main difference between contracts within Principle 7 and those within this Principle is that, under the latter, the supplier does not transfer the data to a medium under the control of the recipient but, rather, gives the recipient access to a medium under the supplier's control on which the data is stored.

Illustration:

41.   Car manufacturer S conducts intensive research on the development of new car models, collecting vast amounts of test data on various prototypes and their components. The data would enable engine manufacturer R to learn better how its engines operate and how they can be improved. S is willing to enter into a contract with R that would enable R to obtain that benefit but, in light of the vast investment made by S into the research and the risk that any data transferred to R will be passed on to competitors or hacked by third parties, S is reluctant to transfer the test data to R. Rather, the parties agree that R will have access to a defined class of test data on S's servers. The contract effectuating this agree-

ment is a contract for simple access to data under this Principle.

42. Same facts as Illustration 41 except that the contract requires S to upload the data to R's server. The contract is a contract for the transfer of data under Principle 7.

Contracts for simple access to data can involve situations in which the recipient is provided read-only access, as well as those in which the recipient may process the data on the medium within the supplier's control or port particular data. As the key motivation for suppliers to enter into a contract for simple access to data covered by Principle 8 rather than into a contract for the transfer of data covered by Principle 7 is typically for the supplier to remain in full control of the data, this motivation may be served best if access is provided to the recipient on a read-only basis. However, a read-only basis is often not sufficiently useful for the recipient. This is why parties frequently agree that the recipient is permitted not only to read the data but also to process the data on the medium within the supplier's control or port particular data. Such contracts also fall under Principle 8.

Illustration:

43. In order to benefit from the test data and be able to improve its engines, R in Illustration 41 would need to conduct its own research using the data. Accordingly, S and R agree that R may run its own data analytics on S's servers, thus engaging in data processing on a medium controlled by S. Because R wants to use the results of such data analytics in R's own factory, S and R agree that R may port the results of data analytics, transferring those results to R's own servers. The contract is a contract for simple access to data under this Principle.

Obviously, the greater the portion of data the recipient is allowed to port the more similar in effect the transaction will be to a contract for the transfer of data under Principle 7.

b.   *Terms with regard to the mode of the recipient's access to the data.* The default terms in Principle 8(2)(a) regarding the mode of the recipient's access to the data are necessarily more complex than the terms stated in Principle 7 with respect to the mode of supply.

First, since the access will typically be secure, Principle 8(2)(a)(i) states that the supplier must provide the recipient with the necessary access credentials and remove any technical barriers whose removal could reasonably be expected in a transaction of the relevant kind.

Illustration:

44. Assume that, in Illustration 41, S provides R with the access credentials, but when R tries to access the data it turns out that R can read the data, which is encrypted, only if R is prepared to buy very special and expensive decryption software used by S but not common in R's industry. S could easily decrypt the data itself. R has a right against S that S remove the technical barrier posed by the encryption.

Second, Principle 8(2)(a)(ii) supplies a default term as to the format in which the data is to be accessible. Under that term, the data must be accessible in a structured and machine-readable format that can reasonably be expected in transactions of the relevant kind.

Third, the default term in Principle 8(2)(a)(iii) provides that the recipient may access the data remotely unless this is unreasonable in the light of data security concerns. Of course, in some cases the parties may agree that the recipient is allowed to view the data only locally, e.g. where the data is saved on a server without internet connection.

Illustration:

45.   Assume that in a situation such as the one in Illustration 41, when R requests remote access to S's server for the first time, S denies access, claiming that its internal security policies only allow such data to be accessed locally. Instead, S insists that R's employees must travel to S's premises whenever R intends to access the data. According to the default term in Principle 8(2)(a) (ii), S is allowed to deny access to R only if remote access was, in light of the sensitivity of the data and the inherent insecurity of the internet connections available to R, objectively unreasonable, and not just according to S's internal policies.

Fourth, Principle 8(2)(a)(iv) provides that the recipient may process the data to which the recipient is given access only for purposes that are consistent with the purposes agreed in the contract. This default term is clearly different from the default term provided in Principle 8(2)(c) for data to be ported (the latter being the same as under Principle 7(2)(c)(iv)). The reason is that the main motivation for parties to enter into a contract for simple access to data under this Principle instead of in a contract for the transfer of data under Principle 7 is that the supplier wants to remain in control, in particular due to data security or data privacy/ data protection concerns, or any other necessity to remain on top of data activities with regard to the data in question.

Illustration:

46.   Assume that in a situation such as the one in Illustration 41, the parties originally envisaged in their contract that R would engage in certain processing activities to learn better how its engines oper-

ate and how they can be improved. However, when analyzing the data, R realizes that there is huge potential in the data for developing a new recommender system for connected cars. Given that this purpose is different from the purpose agreed in the contract, and might potentially harm S's interests (e.g., if S itself is developing such a service), R cannot simply process the data for that purpose but has to seek an extended agreement with S.

Fifth, Principle 8(2)(a)(v) addresses which data the recipient is allowed to port. Given that porting data is likely to undermine the motivation of the parties for choosing a contract under this Principle instead of a contract for the transfer of data under Principle 7, this default term is rather restrictive. Under this term, the recipient may port only such data as the recipient could reasonably expect to be allowed to port in a transaction of the relevant kind. Principle 8(2)8a)(v) also supplies a default term that, if the recipient is entitled to process the data (e.g. by analyzing it) on the supplier's medium, the recipient may also port the derived data.

Illustration:

47.   According to the contract between S and R in Illustration 41, R is allowed to run its own data analytics with its own software in a workspace on S's servers in order to learn more about the performance of its engines. However, after the data analytics has been completed and R asks S for the credentials required for porting the results S claims that porting of any data had never been part of the contract and that R would be allowed to port the results of the analytics only if R is prepared to pay a significant extra sum of money. Even if the contract is silent, R has a right to port the

data derived from its own process-ing activities.

Sixth, Principle 8(2)(a)(vi) provides a default term that, as is typical in con-tracts for simple access to data, the re-cipient may read, process, or port the data by any means, including automat-ed means, and as often as the recipient wishes during the agreed access period.

Illustration:

48. Assume that in a situation such as the one in Illustration 41 R accesses the data with the help of advanced artificial intelligence, which, within only very few hours, analyses all the data made accessi-ble to R. S had not anticipated this and claims that this sort of access was improper and that, if R had dis-closed its intentions during the ne-gotiations, the price for the access would have been much higher. As the parties have left this point open the default position is that R was entitled to access the data with the help of AI.

c. *Terms with regard to the char-acteristics of the data supplied.* Prin-ciple 8(2)(b) indicates that, with re-spect to the characteristics of the data supplied, the supplier has the same responsibilities as it would have in a contract for the transfer of data. See Principle 7(2)(b). This reflects the view that there are no policy reasons for dif-ferentiating between a contract for the transfer of data and a contract for sim-

ple access to data with respect to these issues. As with the default terms stat-ed in Principle 8(2)(a), the parties are free to vary from these terms by agree-ment.

d. *Terms with regard to legal rights and obligations with respect to any data ported by the recipient.* As with the rules with respect to char-acteristics of data supplied, Principle 8(2)(c) indicates that the supplier in a contract for simple access to data has, as far as data ported by the recipient in accordance with the contract is con-cerned, the same responsibility with regard to legal rights and obligations as it would have in a contract for the transfer of data. See Principle 7(2)(c).

e. *Application of other law by analogy.* Principle 5 provides that de-fault rules and principles not directly applicable to the transaction at hand but that would govern a type of trans-action akin to the transaction at hand may be applied to the transaction at hand by analogy. Principle 8(3) pro-vides additional guidance in the con-text of contracts for simple access to data. Under the law of most jurisdic-tions, the closest analogy will often be that of some kind of services contract, the service being to enable the recipi-ent to access the data. However, de-pending on the circumstances, and in particular on the extent to which the recipient may port data, appropriate analogies may also be a sale or lease (see Principle 7).

Principle 9: Contracts for exploitation of a data source

(1) **A contract for exploitation of a data source is one under which the supplier undertakes to provide to the recipient access to data by providing access to a particular device or facility by which data is collected or otherwise generated (the 'data source') enabling the recipient to read the data, process or port data from the data source.**

(2) **Subject to agreement of the parties and to rules that take priority under Principle 5, the law should provide that the**

following terms in addition to those provided in Principle 8 are included in a contract for exploitation of a data source:

(a) With regard to the mode of the recipient's access to the data on the data source:

    (i) The recipient may port all data collected or generated by the data source; and

    (ii) Access to the data is provided in real time as the data is collected or generated by the data source.

(b) With regard to the characteristics of the data, there is no requirement that the recipient will receive data of a particular quality or quantity.

(3) In determining which rules and principles to apply by way of analogy, as provided in Principle 5, to contracts for exploitation of a data source, consideration should be given in particular to:

(a) the degree and duration of control which the recipient is to receive over the data source; and

(b) whether, and the degree to which, the recipient may port data.

Comment:	Illustrations:

a. Scope. Under a contract for exploitation of a data source within the meaning of Principle 9 the supplier undertakes to provide to the recipient access to data by giving the recipient access to a device or facility by which data is collected or otherwise generated. A contract for exploitation of a data source is thus a special type of a contract for access to data, focussing on access to, and usually processing and/or porting of, data collected or generated by the data source. Thus, the focus of the transaction is the data source rather than the characteristics of the data. If a contract is about access to particular (existing) data, it is not a contract for exploitation of a data source addressed by this Principle, but a contract for the simple access to data under Principle 8. Contracts for the exploitation of a data source are rather common in the data economy.

49. Car manufacturer C makes a contract with business B under which B is granted access to the data generated by the connected cars' windshield wipers and headlights, which in turn enables B to provide exact weather reports even for areas where no other weather sensor data is available. Neither C nor B know how much the car owners will drive their cars and where and when they will drive them, and C does not make any promise to B in that regard. Since B is granted access to the facility by which data is produced and the contract is not one for access to data under Principle 8, the contract is thus one for exploitation of a data source.

50. Company N runs a news website. Use of the website by every visitor is, under contractual agreements with N, closely monitored and recorded by data broker B. B will use the data for profiling and

scoring purposes. The agreement between N and B is a contract for exploitation of a data source because neither N nor B knows exactly how many visitors will use the website and there is no requirement that there be any particular number of visitors.

The technical arrangements for providing the recipient with access to the device or facility as described in paragraph (1) may vary. In particular, it is not necessary that the supplier gives the recipient access to the 'original' data source. Very often, the parties will agree that the data may be transferred from the original data source to a kind of 'duplicate' of that source, to which the recipient is then provided access.

Illustration:

51. In a case such as the one described in Illustration 49, car manufacturer C does not wish to give B direct access to its car fleet. Rather, the parties agree to an arrangement according to which C initiates automatic and continuous transfer of any data generated by the windshield wipers and headlights to a server space to which B is then granted access. While this server space is not really the 'data source,' the parties have made it a 'duplicate' of the original data source. Accordingly, the contract is one for exploitation of a data source.

b. Default terms. The default terms included in a contract for exploitation of a data source are, as a starting point, the same as under Principle 8. However, there are three additional terms complementing or concretising the terms listed in Principle 8(2). In particular, where the default terms in Principle 8(2) refer to what can 'reasonably be expected in a transaction of the relevant kind', the fact that the nature of the transaction is one for exploitation of a data source rather than one for access to particular

data is very relevant in determining those reasonable expectations. More precisely, in a contract for exploitation of a data source under this Principle, there are two specific default terms, i.e. that the recipient (i) is permitted to access and port all data generated by the data source, and (ii) be given real-time access to the data as the data is generated, or as close to real time access as is reasonably possible.

Illustration:

52. Assume that, in Illustration 51, a certain part of the data generated by the windshield wipers is not transferred by car manufacturer C provides to the medium made accessible to B because C is afraid that this part of the data might disclose details about a new feature C is developing (activation of windshield wipers by the driver's facial expression). Unless this was agreed between B and C, pruning the data by C would be in breach of the default terms incorporated under Principle 9(2)(a)(i).

53. Assume further that, in Illustration 51, a certain part of the data generated by the windshield wipers is made available to B only with a time lag of up to 30 minutes. Unless this was agreed between B and C, this deviation from real-time access would be inconsistent with the reasonable expectations of parties in a transaction of this kind and C would be in breach of the default terms incorporated under Principle 9(2)(a)(ii).

Another key difference between contracts for simple access to particular data under Principle 8 and contracts for exploitation of a data source under Principle 9 concerns terms as to the characteristics and quantity of data: Unless the parties have agreed otherwise, the supplier in a contract governed by this Principle has no obligation with respect to the quality or quantity of data to which the recipient will have access. Of course, parties will sometimes deviate from this default rule and agree, e.g., that the recipient will be enabled to harvest a particular minimum quantity of data and/or data of a particular minimum quality. But if both the quality and the quantity of data are clearly defined in the agreement, the transaction would often be one in which recipient is granted access to 'particular data' and the contract would be subject only to Principle 8. It is to be noted that the terms in Principle 8(2)(a)(i) and (ii) still apply and, thus, for example, material descriptions or representations would still be relevant.

Illustrations:

54.   Assume that, in Illustration 49, business B approaches car manufacturer C, describes to C its plans to develop a smart weather report service for remote areas, and asks C whether there is any data generated by C's cars that would be suitable for this purpose. C then offers to B access to the connected cars' windshield wipers and headlights, to which B agrees. It turns out, however, that the headlights do not at all react to different weather conditions, but run in the same mode irrespective of whether rain is pouring or the sun shining, and that the windshield wipers are automatically activated also where there is dust on the windshield, rendering the windshield wiper data much less useful for B's purposes. As C had notice of B's particular purpose for obtaining the data and that B was relying on C's skill or judgment in selecting the data source, the data source must be fit for the recipient's particular purposes. However, unless the parties have agreed otherwise, B would not be entitled to a particular quantity of headlight or windshield wiper data and,

for example, B would not have any rights against C where it turns out that buyers of C's cars are becoming more and more climate-aware and use their cars less and less often.

As to terms with regard to control or use of any data ported by the recipient in accordance with the contract, the same default rules apply as under a contract for access to data under Principle 8.

Illustration:

55.   In Illustration 50, company N would be under an obligation vis-à-vis B to seek valid consent from the visitors to the website or to ensure otherwise that relevant data privacy/data protection legislation is complied with. However, unless otherwise agreed N would be under no obligation to B that there will be a particular number of clicks from a particular number of visitors.

c.   Application of other law by analogy. Contracts for the access to a data source do not readily analogize to other well-developed sets of contract law rules. A functional analogy might be that of a lease of the medium, device or facility to which the recipient is granted access, where the recipient gets a significant degree of (temporary) control over that source. This device or facility is often owned or otherwise run by the supplier, so if the supplier contracts for the use of that facility by the recipient for the purpose of the collecting and further processing of data it is not far-fetched to analyze this as a form of lease or a contract akin to lease. This analysis may be useful where, for instance, a court needs to fill a gap in the contract.

Illustration:

56.   In Illustration 50, company N enters into a contract with B to allow it to use the news website, for a specified amount of time, for mon-

itoring and recording the browsing behavior of visitors. N's obligation vis-à-vis B to enable it to pursue its activities during that time period could be analogized to the obligation of a lessor to enable a lessee to use a leased facility. Accordingly, should B claim that it accessed the data only during a small portion of that time and, thus, should not have to pay for the portion of the access period that it did not utilize, that claim would not succeed, just as a lessee of a facility must pay the full lease price without regard to how often it used the leased goods during the term of the lease.

In jurisdictions where there is a difference between such lease contracts where the lessee is allowed only to use the leased object, and lease contracts where the lessee may derive and keep the fruits of the leased object (such as the crop yielded by a farm or the profit yielded by a restaurant) the appropriate analogy would be rather the latter, depending on whether and to what extent the recipient is allowed to port and keep data.

Principle 10: Contracts for authorization to access

(1) A contract for authorization to access data is one under which the supplier (referred to in this Principle as the 'authorizing party') authorizes the access to data or a data source by the recipient, including usually processing or porting of the data, but where, in the light of the passive nature of the authorizing party's anticipated conduct under the contract and the authorizing party's lack of meaningful influence on the transaction, the authorizing party cannot reasonably be expected to undertake any responsibilities of the sort described in Principles 7 to 9.

(2) Subject to agreement of the parties and to rules that take priority under Principle 5, the law should provide that in a contract for authorization to access:

   (a) With regard to the mode of the recipient's access, a term that the authorizing party will facilitate or assist the recipient in gaining access is not included, and the authorizing party may continue using the data or data source in any way, even if this impairs the recipient's access or even renders it impossible;

   (b) With regard to the characteristics of the data, there is no requirement that the recipient will receive data of a particular quality or quantity;

   (c) With regard to control of the data and any other data activities the recipient may engage in, the authorizing party has no obligation to assure that the recipient will have any particular rights

   (d) As between the authorizing party and the recipient, the recipient is responsible for compliance with any duties vis-à-vis third parties under Part IV, including the duties incumbent on a supplier of data under Principle 32; and

(e) The recipient must indemnify the authorizing party for any liability vis-à-vis third parties that follows from the authorizing party's authorization to access the data unless such liability could not reasonably be foreseen by the recipient.

(3) In determining which rules and principles to apply by way of analogy, as provided in Principle 5, to contracts for authorization to access data, consideration should be given to whether the focus of the agreement between the parties is on the access to the data or on the supply of another commodity (such as a digital service) in the course of which access to the data occurs.

Comment:

a. *Scope.* Principle 10 addresses data transactions in which the authorizing party provides the recipient with access and allows processing but undertakes no obligations with respect to that data. In contrast to a contract for access to particular data under Principle 8 or for access to a data source under Principle 9, the authorizing party does not in any way undertake to support the recipient in accessing or processing the data or to remove any technical or legal barriers.

b. *Default terms.* As set out in paragraph (2), the default terms in a contract for authorization to access are rather minimal, putting no obligations on the authorizing party. In particular, subject to contrary agreement of the parties as far as such contrary agreement is consistent with mandatory law (see Principle 5), the supplier (who, in order to contrast the position of the parties in the contracts governed by this Principle with those covered by Principles 7 to 9, is referred to as 'authorizing party') does not undertake to facilitate or assist the recipient in gaining access. Also, the authorizing party may continue using the data or data source (e.g., an electronic device) as the authorizing party wishes, even if this impairs the recipient's access or

renders it impossible (e.g., because the device is disconnected from the Internet). Accordingly, the authorizing party does not warrant that the recipient will receive data of a particular quality, fitness for purpose, or quantity, nor that the recipient will have a particular legal position with regard to the data.

Illustration:

57. Provider M provides a messenger application and service 'for free'. In return, users authorize the processing of personal data on the device on which the application is installed for a variety of purposes that are in M's commercial interest. In this passive access situation, the users are under no obligation actually to use the messenger service, to produce a minimum quantity of user-generated data, or to produce data of a particular quality (e.g. data that reveals the actual identity of the individuals with whom the users correspond). Users are also free to delete the application, thus making any further access to the data source on the part of M impossible.

c. *Duties with respect to third parties.* Unlike the contracts described in Principles 7 to 9 above, where the

557

default terms primarily impose duties on the supplier, Principle 10 contains default terms that impose significant duties on the recipient. If the authorizing party were to qualify as a normal 'supplier', it would be subject both to any duties it owes vis-à-vis third parties under Principle 32 and to potential liability where these duties are breached; but in a contract for authorization to access, those costs should not ordinarily be borne by the authorizing party, whose role is quite passive. Accordingly, Principle 10(2)(d) supplies a default term stating that the recipient is, as between the authorizing party and the recipient, responsible for complying with the duties under Principle 32. Also, under Principle 10(2)(d), the recipient must indemnify the authorizing party for any liability vis-à-vis third parties that follows from authorization to processing unless such liability was not reasonably foreseeable by the recipient.

Illustration:

58. Assuming that provider M in Illustration 57 not only instigates user C to permit processing of C's own personal data, but also to 'authorize' the processing of personal data of all individuals displayed under C's contacts on the mobile device. Even though it is still primarily C who remains responsible vis-à-vis his friends, M has to assume responsibility for making sure C is allowed to pass on his friends' data and for complying with all duties under Principle 32, and in case C is sued by one of his friends, to indemnify C for all liability.

d. Application of other law by analogy. In deciding which law to apply by analogy within the meaning of Principle 5, the focus of the parties' agreement should be considered. In some transactions, access to the data may be the main subject matter of the agreement. More often, however, access to the data is not what the agreement, as reflected in the parties' declarations and any contract documents, is mainly about, but, rather, is an incidental element within a wider transaction about something else, such as provision of some digital service (e.g. search engine service, navigation service, messenger service) by the recipient of the data to whom authorization to access is granted. Where this is the case, authorization to access is best seen not as the defining characteristic of the transaction but, rather, as a substitute for payment in money for the digital service.

Illustrations:

59. In Illustration 57, user C allows provider M to use C's devices (e.g. a mobile phone and messenger application) for the collection of personal data. A court might, where relevant in a domestic legal system, analyze this as a case of consideration other than money.

60. Farm corporation F buys a 'smart' tractor from seller S, which has been manufactured by manufacturer T. The tractor comes with digital services, including weather forecasts, soil analyses, targeted recommendations concerning the use of particular fertilizers and insecticides, and predictive maintenance, to be provided by T and companies U and V that cooperate with T. T, U and V will normally use the data that is collected by the sensors of the tractor for their own commercial purposes. Economically speaking, T, U and V will consider the value of the data they will probably receive, and the profits they can derive from exploiting the data, when calculating the price to be charged for the tractor and any digital service provided.

The insight that authorizing the processing of user-generated data amounts to a form of payment, at least from an economic point of view, may be relevant in a number of different contexts. E.g., where a jurisdiction provides different rules for gratuitous contracts and for non-gratuitous con- tracts, the fact that data is provided in lieu of a sum of money may mean that the contract should be treated as a non-gratuitous contract.

Principle 11: Contracts for data pooling

(1) A contract for data pooling is one under which two or more parties (the 'data partners') undertake to share data in a data pool by

(a) transferring particular data to a medium that is jointly controlled by the data partners or that is controlled by a data trustee or escrowee or other third party acting on behalf of the data partners; or

(b) granting each other access to particular data or the possibility to exploit particular data sources, with or without the involvement of a third party.

(2) This Principle applies, with appropriate adjustments, to the governing principles of any entity created pursuant to a data pooling contract.

(3) Subject to agreement of the parties and to rules that take priority pursuant to Principle 5, the law should provide that the following terms are included in a contract for data pooling:

(a) A data partner may utilize data from the data pool, or data derived from such data, only

(i) for purposes agreed upon between the data partners in the contract for data pooling;

(ii) for purposes which the relevant data partner could reasonably expect to be accepted by the other data partners, unless these purposes are inconsistent with an agreement referred to in subparagraph (i); or

(iii) as necessary to comply with applicable law;

(b) A data partner may engage data processors, but may otherwise pass data from the data pool, or data derived from such data, on to third parties only under the conditions agreed upon between the data partners or required by applicable law;

(c) As between the data partners, new intellectual property rights or similar rights created with the use of data from the data pool belong to the partner or partners who conducted the activity leading to the creation of the new right;

  (d) If a data partner leaves the data pool, the data supplied by that data partner must be returned to the relevant data partner, but data derived from the data, unless essentially identical with the original data, remains in the pool. Upon leaving the data pool, a data partner is entitled to a copy of any data in the pool that has been derived, in whole or in substantial part, from data supplied by that data partner.

(4) In determining which rules and principles to apply by way of analogy, as provided in Principle 5, to contracts for data pooling, consideration should be given to whether the relationship between the data partners is one characterized by mutual trust and confidence, such that the data partners owe each other fiduciary obligations, or, rather, whether it is characterized by arm's length transactions with no fiduciary obligations.

Comment:

  a. *Scope.* Principle 11 applies to a phenomenon under which separate parties, which are here called the 'data partners', agree to share data in a way that there is not a 'supplier' and a 'recipient' but that each of the parties is, at the same time, both supplier and recipient with regard to data shared in a data pool. Often, such arrangements are referred to as 'closed data platforms', with 'closed' indicating that the data pool is accessible only to the data partners involved and not to a wider public, such as under open data schemes. The technical and legal arrangements in place may vary. Very often, the data partners will transfer data to a medium (or a defined sector of such a medium, such as cloud space) that is controlled jointly by all partners or by a third party. The third party may, in particular, be a data trustee within the meaning of Principle 13, or an escrowee within the meaning of Principle 14, or a new company established and held jointly by the data partners specifically for the purpose of managing and exploiting the data pool. But it is also possible that the data pool is held in a decentralized manner on media controlled by each of the data partners, who then give access to that data to the other data partners within the meaning of Principle 8. Often, the data partners will focus on the exploitation of particular data sources within the meaning of Principle 9 rather than on particular data. All these arrangements may be qualified as contracts for data pooling.

Illustration:

  61. Tractor manufacturers M, N and O agree to pool, and therefore to grant each other access to, a particular type of data generated by their respective smart tractors with the aim of better enabling each of them to provide a smart service, such as recommendations as to optimal use of insecticides, to farmers. If M, N and O transfer particular data sets from the past to a server controlled jointly by M, N and O, this is a contract for data pooling based on data transfer (Principle 7). If M, N and O provide each other with access credentials to particular data sets stored on their respective servers, this is a contract for data pooling based on data access (Principle 8). If M, N and O promise each other access to all the data

produced by their fleet of tractors, which will be transferred in real time to a server controlled jointly by M, N and O, this is a contract for data pooling based on exploitation of data sources (Principle 9).

b.   Default terms. As with other contracts addressed in this Chapter, parties to contracts for data pooling will likely negotiate and draft contractual language to cover important business terms, but it may still be essential to determine the parties' rights and responsibilities with respect to matters that were not the subject of explicit agreement. Paragraphs (3) and (4) of this Principle address some of these issues.

The application of paragraph (3) depends on which of the three types of data pooling contract is present. In cases in which the contract provides for the transfer of data to a closed platform that is jointly controlled by the data partners or that is controlled by a third party acting on behalf of the data partners, the default rules in Principle 7 are applicable. In cases in which the contract provides for the parties granting each other access to the data, the default rules in Principle 8 are applicable. Finally, in cases in which the contract provides for the parties granting each other the right to exploit particular data sources, the default rules in Principle 9 are applicable. In addition to incorporating default rules from Principles 7 to 9, paragraph (3) adds five more default rules.

First, in contrast with the 'sales' approach chosen by Principle 7 and, as far as data rightfully ported are concerned, by Principles 8 and 9, Principle 11 opts for a 'license' approach. This means that a data partner may utilize data from the data pool only for the purposes agreed upon between the data partners or required by law. As the parties may not be able to think of all eventualities, paragraph 3(a) clarifies that a data partner may also use data from the data pool for purposes that data partner could reasonably expect to be accepted by all the other data partners.

Illustration:

62.   Assume that M, N and O in Illustration no. 61 agree that the pooled tractor data may be used for improving the data bases for an enumerative list of precision farming services. N decides to engage also in real estate services, arranging deals between buyers and sellers of farmland and providing services in this context. Without an additional agreement between M, N and O to that end, N would not be allowed to use data from the data pool (other than the data N itself contributed) for this new purpose. N would not be able to rely on a reasonable expectation that the other partners would accept this, as it significantly enhances the data pool's utility for N, at the expense of M and O, which might have had similar plans, or might even get into trouble with the farmers using their tractors. Where, on the other hand, N wishes to report on the new data pool at its annual shareholder meeting and to show some slides with statistical data derived from the data in the pool, and the data does not disclose anyone's business secrets, N could reasonably expect that this would be accepted by M and O.

Second, in line with this 'license approach' paragraph (3)(b) states that a data partner may engage data processors, but may otherwise pass data from the data pool, or data derived from such data, on to third parties only under the conditions agreed upon between the data partners or mandated by law. After all, it can be expected that the data partners are agreeing to share among themselves and would want the right to prevent others who are not parties to the contract from obtaining access to the data.

Third, the default rules in paragraph (3)(c) address the topic of ownership of new intellectual property rights or similar rights created with use of the shared data. Paragraph (3)(c) provides, as a default rule, that new intellectual property rights or similar rights created with the use of data retrieved from the platform shall belong, as between the data partners, to the partner or partners who conducted the activity leading to the creation of the new right. With this as a default rule, the parties will have an incentive to bargain explicitly if they want a different allocation of such new rights. While paragraph (3)(c) provides a default rule for ownership of those new rights, it should be noted that applicable intellectual property law might require the parties to execute an instrument transferring those rights from whoever would own them under that law to those who are to own them under the contract.

Illustration:

63.   Assume that N and O in Illustration no. 61, with the help of data from the pool and in line with the purposes agreed upon between all three partners, develop, with the help of their respective R&D departments, a new smart service with significantly more granular recommendations as to the type and optimal amount of insecticides required. As between the three data partners, the intellectual property rights in this new smart service (the type of which, such as copyright or a patent right, would depend on the applicable intellectual property regime) would belong to N and O, who have invested in the development of the new service, unless M, N, and O have agreed otherwise. If the applicable intellectual property regime assigns rights in a different

manner, there would, by default, be a contractual obligation to bring the situation, as between the data partners, into line with paragraph (3)(c).

Fourth, paragraph (3)(d) together with Principle 4(2) and (3) provides that if a data partner leaves the data pool, the data supplied by that data partner must be erased or, where erasure of the data would be unreasonable under the circumstances within the meaning of Principle 4(3), an allowance be made in money. Upon leaving the data pool, a data partner is entitled to a copy of any data in the pool that has been derived, in whole or to a substantial part, from data supplied by that data partner. (Naturally, where the whole data pooling contract is terminated and all data partners leave the pool, this applies to all of the partners.).

Illustration:

64.   Assume that O in Illustration no. 61 decides to leave the data pooling contract, which is silent as to the further destiny of the data. In this case, paragraph (3)(d) provides that the data generated by all smart tractors produced by O must be returned to O and must be erased from the pool. Where data has been derived from that data, and the derived data is not essentially identical with the data contributed by O (such as in Illustration no. 63 where O's data has been aggregated with N's data to create added value) the derived data may remain in the pool, but O is entitled to a copy.

c.   Application of other law by analogy. When deciding which other law to apply—either directly or by analogy—the first question that needs to be asked is whether or not a company under company law has been established, in which case many issues, such as the contributions to be made by the partners, and the benefits to be derived by the partners, would be regulated directly by company law. Generally speaking, consideration should be given to whether the relationship between the data partners is one characterized by mutual trust and confidence, such that the data partners owe each other fiduciary obligations, or, rather, whether it is characterized by arm's length transactions with no fiduciary obligations.

Chapter C: Contracts for Services with regard to Data

Principle 12: Contracts for the processing of data

(1) A contract for the processing of data is one under which a processor undertakes to process data on behalf of the controller. Such processing may include, inter alia:

  (a) the collection and recording of data (e.g., data scraping);

  (b) storage or retrieval of data (e.g., cloud space provision);

  (c) analysis of data (e.g., data analytics services);

  (d) organization, structuring, presentation, alteration or combination of data (e.g., data management services); or

  (e) erasure of data.

(2) Subject to agreement of the parties and to rules that take priority under Principle 5, the law should provide that the following terms are included in a contract for the processing of data:

  (a) The processor must follow the controller's directions and act consistently with the controller's stated purposes for the processing;

  (b) The processor must ensure at least the same level of data security and of protection for the rights of third parties as the controller was under an obligation to ensure, and must support the controller in complying with any legal obligations for the protection of third parties that could reasonably be expected in a situation of the relevant kind or of which the processor had notice when the contract was made;

  (c) The processor must not pass the data on to third parties;

  (d) The processor may not process the data for the processor's own purposes, except to the extent reasonably necessary to improve the quality or efficiency of the relevant service, so long as this does not harm the controller's legitimate interests; and

  (e) Upon full performance or termination of the contract, the processor must transfer to the controller any data resulting from the processing that has not already been transferred. The processor must subsequently erase any data retained, except to the extent reasonably necessary for existing or likely litigation or to the extent that the processor has a legal right or obligation independent of these Principles to keep the data beyond that time.

(3) In determining which rules and principles to apply directly or by way of analogy, as provided in Principle 5, to contracts for processing of data, consideration should be given to the nature of the service, such as to whether the focus is on changing the data or on keeping it safe.

Comment:

a.   Scope. Contracts for the processing of data, as described in paragraph (1), are very common. Given the broad definition of 'processing' under Principle 3(1)(e), these contracts may appear in an extremely broad variety of forms. Contracts for processing of data may relate to the collection and recording of data (e.g. data scraping), to its storage or retrieval (e.g. cloud space provision), to analysis of it (e.g. data analytics services), to its organisation, structuring, presentation, alteration or combination (e.g. data management services), or to its erasure.

Illustration:

65. Real property business C hires the services of company P to create digital twins of C's buildings for facilitating maintenance. This includes the processing of a broad range of data, including data collected by a variety of sensors in the buildings and photographic data collected by drones. In this situation, C defines the means and purposes of the collecting and other processing of the data and P's motivation for processing the data is to fulfill its contract with C, so C is the controller, and P qualifies as processor and the contract is one for the processing of data within the meaning of Principle 12.

The description of 'contract for processing', in Principle 12(1) should be read in conjunction with the limitation in Principle 2(1) to matters for which 'the primary focus of the matter is on records of larger quantities of information as an asset, resource or tradeable commodity.' Accordingly, although Principle 12(1) could be read in isolation as covering some contracts involving the processing of data but where the focus of the transaction is not related to these Principles (e.g. a photographer's services, proofreading a manuscript, etc.), such contracts are not within the scope of Principle 12.

Given the very broad definition of 'processing' under Principle 3(1)(e), situations where a contracting partner engages in some sort of processing activities while fulfilling contractual duties will be very common even within the general scope of the Principles. However, Principle 12 should apply only where the focus of the agreement is on the processing activities as such, not where processing is necessary merely to fulfill an obligation of a different nature. For example, where the operator of a data marketplace contract within the meaning of Principle 15, in order to fulfil its obligations under the data marketplace contract by facilitating a transaction between the client and other parties, processes some data provided by the client (e.g. in order to transfer it to the client's contracting party), this still should be treated as a contract under Principle 15, and not under Principle 12; however, as far as the processing activities are concerned, the default terms under Principle 12 might still prove to be useful. Where, on the other hand, data storage and storage management are important aspects of the contractual obligations of a data trustee within the meaning of Principle 13, it may be justified to apply both Principles 12 and 13 for the respective aspects of the bundle of obligations.

b.   Default terms applicable to contracts for processing of data. Paragraph 2(a) is straightforward—a contract for the processing of data has, as a default term, an obligation of the processor both to follow the controller's directions and to act consistently with the controller's stated purposes for the processing.

Illustration:

66.   If, in a situation such as the one in Illustration no. 65, real property business C directs company P not to create a digital twin of a particular building (e.g. because of security concerns raised by a State authority that is a tenant in that building), P must comply with that direction, even if there is no explicit clause to that end in the contract. Whether or not P has a claim to be paid for creating a digital twin of that building, if the building was included in the initial contract, is a different question and depends on the applicable contract law.

In the event of a conflict, the controller's directions typically should prevail, but where the processor is more sophisticated and realises that the controller's directions are inconsistent with the purpose the processor may reasonably be expected to warn the controller.

Under paragraph 2(b), the processor has a duty to provide the same level of data protection and data security for protecting the rights of third parties as the controller is under an obligation to ensure, and similarly must support the controller in complying with its legal obligations in this regard. Generally speaking, these duties are present only if such obligations could reasonably be expected in a situation of the relevant kind or if the processor had notice of the controller's obligations.

Illustration:

67.   Assume that C in Illustration no. 65 may create a digital twin of all buildings, but is under an obligation vis-à-vis a State authority that is a tenant of one of C's buildings to treat any data of that building with a particular degree of data security. If P has notice of these requirements when the contract is made, or if the requirements could reasonably be expected, P is under an obligation to apply the same level of security to the data produced.

Paragraph (2)(c) provides that the processor must not pass data on to third parties because such action by the processor may harm the legitimate interests both of the controller and of third parties to whom the controller is responsible. There may, of course, be situations where the processor has a legitimate interest in passing data on, e.g. where the processor needs to engage a subcontractor. However, because paragraph 2(c) is only a default term, the processor and controller are free to agree on appropriate conditions for the engagement and duties of a subcontractor.

Illustration:

68.   In the situation described in Illustration no. 67, P may require the services of independent company P to produce the digital twins. If this is the case, P must raise this point in the negotiations with C. P would need to procure C's agreement to the use of the independent company as a subcontractor. C and P might agree, for example, that the subcontractor is allowed so long as the same level of protection is en-

sured, plus that P remains fully responsible for what the subcontractor does.

Paragraph (2)(d) provides that the processor must refrain from any processing of the data for the processor's own purposes. This should not be interpreted as implying that the experience gained by the processor cannot benefit the processor in subsequent contracts. For instance, where the processor, in the course of fulfilling its duties under the contract for processing with the controller, uses AI, and that AI becomes better by being run on the controller's data, the processor may of course keep the improved AI and may benefit from that when dealing with the next customer. As this is just an incidental effect of fulfilling the contract with the controller and does not harm the controller's interests it is not prohibited by the default term under (2) (d). This is why (2)(d) contains an exception where use of the data is reasonably necessary to improve the quality or efficiency of the relevant service, so long as this does not harm the controller's legitimate interests.

Illustration:

69. Assume that P in Illustration no. 65 wants to process the data produced for C for two additional purposes, on which the contract document is silent: (a) analyzing it immediately for internal quality control and optimization of drone trajectories while the contract is still being performed, and (b) retaining the data in a form that is still attributable to C to promote P's services. Use of the data for purpose (a) is permitted by this default term because it is for the benefit of the controller, while purpose (b) would not be permitted by this default term because it is not C's legitimate interests.

Paragraph (2)(e) addresses situations that may differentiate a contract for the processing of data from other service contracts. While a service provider who undertakes to apply fresh paint to a house, or to repair a car, or to transport goods from one place to another, has little opportunity to retain the materials provided by the other party after the contract has been performed, the situation is different with respect to data. In a contract for the processing of data, the processor would easily be able to retain a copy of the data without the controller's knowledge and at low cost for storage, etc., creating a temptation to use the data for a separate commercial purpose of the processor. Accordingly, paragraph 2(e) supplies a default term of the contract to the effect that the processor must erase any data retained by the processor after the contract has been performed and the processed data has been provided to the controller. There may be some circumstances, however, where retention of a copy of the data for a short period of time after the contract has been performed is not improper and is justified, e.g., by the processor's interest in defending itself in pending or imminent litigation. Even in those circumstances, however, retention of a copy would be a breach of the supplier's obligation if the terms of the contract indicate that retention of a copy is not allowed for this purpose (subject to rules of law that cannot be derogated from by agreement, such as doctrines of unconscionability).

Illustration:

70. Company P in no. 65 retains the data on its servers after having finished its service for C. Retaining the controller's data is normally not in conformity with the terms of the contract. However, where C has already announced it will withhold payment because the photographic material was not in conformity with the contract, P may have a legitimate interest in retain-

ing the material in order to use it in potential litigation.

Of course, under law governing the litigation process a party may have a duty to preserve copies. In such as case, such a mandatory rule would govern.

c.   *Rules applicable to contracts for processing of data.* A contract for the processing of data under Principle 12 is a service contract. Legal systems typically do not differentiate between services in the brick-and-mortar world and services with regard to data. This is why paragraph (3) limits itself to stating that, in determining which rules and principles to apply directly or by way of analogy, as provided in Principle 5, to contracts for processing of data, consideration should be given to the nature of the service, such as to whether the focus is on changing the data or on keeping it safe.

Principle 13: Data trust contracts

(1)   A data trust contract is a contract among one or more controllers of data (the 'entrusters') and a third party under which the entrusters empower the third party (the 'data trustee') to make certain decisions about use or onward supply of data (the 'entrusted data') on their behalf, in the furtherance of stated purposes that may benefit the entrusters or a wider group of stakeholders (such entrusters or stakeholders being referred to as the 'beneficiaries').

(2)   A data trust contract and the relationships it creates need not conform to any particular organizational structure and need not include the characteristics and duties associated with a common law trust. This Principle applies, with appropriate adjustments, to the governing principles of any entity created pursuant to a data trust contract.

(3)   Subject to agreement of the parties and to rules that take priority under Principle 5, the law should provide that the following terms are included in a data trust contract or are incorporated into the governing principles of any entity created pursuant to the data trust contract:

(a)   The data trustee is, subject to subparagraphs (b) and (c), empowered to make and implement all decisions with regard to use or onward supply of the entrusted data, including decisions concerning intellectual property rights and rights based on data privacy/data protection law;

(b)   The data trustee must act in furtherance of the stated purposes of the data trust contract for the benefit of the beneficiaries and, even if the entrusters are not the beneficiaries, in a manner that is not inconsistent with the legitimate interests of the entrusters of which the data trustee has notice;

(c) The data trustee must follow any directions given by the entrusters, except to the extent that the data trustee has notice that the directions are incompatible with the stated or manifestly obvious purposes of the data trust;

(d) The data trustee must refrain from any use of the entrusted data for its own purposes and must avoid any conflict-of-interest;

(e) The entrusters may terminate the data trustee's power with regard to the data entrusted by them at any time; however, this right may be limited to the extent necessary to take into account reliance and similar legitimate interests of the beneficiaries; and

(f) If the data trustee has retained any data entrusted, or any data derived from such data, after the contract has come to an end (by termination or otherwise) the data trustee must return the data to the entrusters, and, when reasonable, take steps to prevent further use of the data by onward recipients.

(4) In determining which rules and principles to apply by way of analogy, as provided in Principle 5, to data trust contracts, consideration should be given in particular to

(a) the stated purposes of the data trust contract and the nature of the data and of the parties involved;

(b) whether the purposes of the data trust contract are primarily for the benefit of the entrusters or broader constituencies; and

(c) the organizational structure of the relationships created by the data trust contract.

Comment:

a. Scope. This Principle provides a general overview of the legal principles recommended for data trust contracts. As noted in paragraph (2), notwithstanding the use of the term 'trust' in the nomenclature describing these arrangements, the arrangements need not include the characteristics and duties associated with a common law trust. Principle 13 is stated at a high level of generality because both the subject of data trust arrangements and the nature of those arrangements can vary widely. Moreover, data trust arrangements are an emerging concept,

with new subjects and mechanisms constantly arising. The purpose of this Principle, as of most other Principles, is facilitative. Thus, the description of types of data trust contracts, and the recommended rules to govern them, are not limited to arrangements that are common today; rather, they are designed to be flexible enough to accommodate arrangements that may emerge in the future.

Data trust arrangements within the meaning of Principle 13 are often combined with arrangements for the processing of data within the meaning of Principle 12, as the data trustee's activities under the data trust arrangements would often include storage of data and similar data processing activities. When this is the case, both Principles 12 and 13 would apply, with Principle 13 more specifically dealing with the power of decision making, i.e. a power that rests with the controller of data, and not with the processor. A data trustee is thus a person to whom one or more controllers of data delegate (some of) their powers as controllers, while possibly engaging the same party to provide other services under Principle 12.

Data trust arrangements are typically contracts that create a continuing relationship of a particular or indefinite duration. While, theoretically, any contract dealt with under these Principles could be either a one-time exchange or a continuing relationship, the contracts dealt with under Principle 13, as well as some other Principles, are more often entered into for a particular or indefinite period of time.

b. Typical data trust arrangements. Under this Principle, a wide variety of arrangements may be governed as data trust contracts. All that is needed is a contract of the sort described in paragraph (1) among an entruster or entrusters and a data trustee under which the data trustee is empowered and directed to make decisions about use and onward supply of the data in furtherance of the stated purpose. Despite this generality, and the wide-open possibilities that it suggests, some types of data trust contracts that are found at present can be identified and described.

For example, one common type of data trust contract (as that term is used in this Principle) is a data management contract, under which one party undertakes to manage data on behalf of another party. An example is provided by personal information management services (PIMS), also some-

times known as personal data stores, personal data spaces, or personal data vaults, under which the party undertaking to manage the data (the 'data trustee' under the nomenclature of this Principle) is empowered to make decisions on behalf of the entruster with respect to intellectual property issues, data protection, etc. Such arrangements involve a requirement that the data trustee manage the data for the interest of the entrusters and follow directions that they may give, subject to the entruster's right to withdraw from the arrangement at any time. In some ways, such an arrangement is akin to an agency arrangement, with the entruster as principal and the data trustee as agent.

Illustration:

71.   Individuals I1 to In contract with a service provider M under an arrangement in which I1 to In provide to M access to certain personal information collected by and stored on their respective mobile devices. M is given the power to interact with website operators that seek personal information from visitors to their websites and disclose only such information under such conditions as meets criteria established in the contract. The contract is a data trust contract.

Another common type of data trust arrangement is an arrangement under which one party (the data trustee) undertakes to control data it has been entrusted with for a stated purpose, e.g. data donation for health research. As with the data management contract, the greater expertise of the data trustee is a motivating factor in entering into the arrangement.

Illustration:

72.   A large number of health care providers H1 to Hn contract with data trustee T to transfer to the trustee access to data about

cases of certain infectious diseases so that the trustee can manage the data and make it available under specified terms to inform disease-control programs in order to target interventions and improve health service coverage. This contract is a data trust contract.

c. *Structure.* The arrangement created by a data trust contract can take many forms. In some cases, the data trust contract may result in the formation of a common law trust (in jurisdictions where that concept exists), but this is not necessary. Similarly, the data trust contract may result in the creation of other arrangements that use trust nomenclature even though they are not common law trusts, such as a 'Massachusetts Business Trust' or a Delaware Statutory Trust or Purpose Trust, but this is not necessary either. Rather, the distinguishing feature of the data trust contract is the agreement pursuant to which decisions about access to and use of data are to be made collectively in furtherance of the stated purposes and for the benefit of the beneficiaries. The form of such an agreement, and the decision making structure that results from it, is not constrained by these Principles; of course, other law, such as competition law and data privacy/data protection law, may apply and, in some cases, place limits.

d. *Distinguishing between the data trust contract and legal structures it may create.* It is important to distinguish the data trust contract—the contract among the entrusters and the data trustee under which the governing structure is created—from law governing the structure itself. For example, if the agreement calls for the formation of a common law trust, with a trustee holding the data for the benefit of beneficiaries to whom the trustee owes a fiduciary duty, the law applicable to such common law trusts applies. Similarly, if the data trust contract calls for the formation of a typical for-profit corporation or a public benefit corporation, the law governing such corporations governs their internal affairs. It should be noted, however, that the law governing structures that may be created by a data trust contract often provides for a substantial role for private ordering by agreement among stakeholders. Examples include shareholder agreements with respect to a corporation and the terms of the trust instrument in the case of a trust. The data trust contract can be seen, therefore, not only as the agreement to create a particular structure but also as an agreement among the stakeholders in the context of that structure.

Thus, while the default terms provided by this Principle do not impose fiduciary duties in data trust arrangements, the form or structure selected by the parties to effectuate their data trust arrangement may do so. In such cases, the fiduciary duties are those created by the law governing the form or structure, and those duties augment the duties imposed by this Principle.

e. *Default terms.* The default terms for a data trust contract as described in this Principle are necessarily general in light of the variety of situations in which such a contract may be utilized and the variety of arrangements that the parties may devise.

First, subparagraph (a) provides a term relating to the power to make decisions with regard to use and onward supply of the entrusted data. Under this term, the data trustee is, by default, given the power to make all types of decisions with regard to the data, i.e. in the event of doubt the power vested in the trustee is broader rather than narrower. However, that power is always subject to terms (b) and (c), i.e. to the furtherance of the stated purpose of the data trust contract and the benefit of the beneficiaries and the legitimate interests of the entrusters, as well as to any specific directions given by the entrusters.

Illustration:

> 73.   Assume that in a scenario such as the one in Illustration no. 72 the agreement between the health care providers and trustee T does not specify clearly which kind of decisions T may take with regard to the data, i.e. it is unclear whether T may pass the data on only to public bodies or may also sell the data to private companies. Under Principle 13(3)(a) the trustee may make such decisions, subject to Principle 13(3)(b) and (c).

Second, subparagraph (b) provides that the data's trustee's primary obligation is to act in furtherance of the stated purposes of the data trust contract for the benefit of the beneficiaries. This is a critical point inasmuch as it means that gaps or incompleteness in the data trust contract will be filled with terms that are primarily guided by the purpose of the contract (which may differ from the private interests of the parties).

Third, subparagraph (c) provides a default rule directing the data trustee to follow directions given by the entrusters. This rule has an important limit, however; the trustee need not (or even must not) follow directions where the trustee could reasonably be expected to realise that the directions are incompatible with the stated purposes of the data trust. Thus, unless otherwise agreed, the stated purposes of the trust serve as an outside limit on the power of entrusters to direct the data trustee.

Illustration:

> 74.   If T in Illustration no. 73, by selling the data to private companies, would be jeopardizing the legitimate interests of the health care providers, e.g. by potentially disclosing very sensitive data about

the patients treated by those health care providers and putting the health care providers at risk of being sued by their patients for breach of confidentiality, the power vested in T does not include the power to sell the data to the private companies as this would be incompatible with Principle 13(3)(b). The health care providers could, in addition, give binding directions to T under Principle 13(3)(c) to refrain from selling the data. However, they could not give directions to T to sell the data if this is in violation of the stated purposes of the data trust contract (e.g. if that stated or manifestly obvious purpose includes protection of patients' rights).

Fourth, subparagraph (d) provides a default rule that protects entrusters from data trustees who might use their position to benefit themselves rather than the entrusters. This rule prohibits the trustee from using the data to serve its own ends rather than the purposes of the entrusters; more generally, this rule directs data trustees to avoid conflicts of interest with respect to the data and its stewardship. This is so irrespective of whether the use of the data would also be in violation of the default term under Principle 13(3)(b).

Illustration:

> 75.   If T in Illustration no. 73 decided to form a research company and use the data it has been entrusted with for that company's own research, T would be violating the default term under Principle 13(3)(d).

Fifth, subparagraph (e) addresses the ability of the entrusters to terminate the powers of the data trustee. The term proposed enables the entrusters to terminate the powers of the data trustee at any time (much like termination without cause in the corporate context). This right, however, is limited to the extent necessary to take into account legitimate interests of the beneficiaries of the data trust.

Finally, subparagraph (f) states that, upon termination, the data trustee must return any entrusted data the trustee has retained, or any data derived from such data, and, when reasonable, take steps to prevent further use of the data by any onward recipients. This provision is similar to that of Principle 12(2)(e) and if the data trustee may also be considered a processor under Principle 12 (which may or may not be the case), the obligation to erase might follow from both Principles.

Illustration:

76. If in Illustration no. 71, health care provider Hx, which is among the health care providers entrusting T with their data, decides that it no longer wishes to participate in the arrangement, it may, under Principle 13(3)(e), terminate the arrangement with T at any time. This would mean T may no longer take any decisions with regard to Hx's data. If Hx had transferred the data to storage space within T's control, T would have to erase that data. If T has passed the data on to others, the question whether T must also take steps to prevent further use of the data by those onward recipients depends on whether that is reasonable. What counts as 'reasonable' depends on many factors, including applicable law (such as data protection/data privacy law), any potential adverse effects on the entrusters and the terms of the contractual arrangements T has entered into with the onward recipients in fulfilment of its duties as data trustee.

f. *Incorporation of default terms into governing principles of structure of the data trust.* In light of the fact that, as noted in comment d, a data trust contract often calls for the creation of a structure, such as a corporation or common law trust, that has its own governance principles that allow for the autonomy of the parties to shape their relationship, paragraph (3) also provides that the default terms may be effectuated by being incorporated into the governing principles of an entity created pursuant to the data trust contract rather than into the data trust contract itself.

g. *Analogies.* As noted in paragraph (4), this Principle suggests two approaches to identifying analogies as the source of rules to govern data trust contracts. The first is to take into account whether the purposes of the data trust contract are primarily for the benefit of the entrusters or broader constituencies. Law has, for quite a long time, often taken different approaches to arrangements that are primarily for private benefit and those whose primary purpose is to advance public interests rather than solely the private interests of the parties. Thus, if the purpose of the data trust contract is public benefit, appropriate analogies should be drawn. Second, the nature of any organizational structure created by the data trust contract can supply analogies. For example, if the data trust contract contemplates the creation of a corporation that will manage and exploit the data on behalf of the entrusters, an analogy to shareholder agreements in corporations would be useful.

Principle 14: Data escrow contracts

(1) **A data escrow contract is a contract among one or more parties planning to use data (the 'contracting parties') and a third party (the 'escrowee') under which the escrowee un-**

dertakes to make sure the powers and abilities of some or all of the contracting parties with respect to the data are restricted (the 'restricted parties') so as to avoid conflict with legal requirements, such as those imposed by antitrust law or data privacy/data protection law.

(2) A data escrow contract and the relationships it creates need not conform to any particular organizational structure. This Principle applies, with appropriate adjustments, to the governing principles of any entity created pursuant to a data escrow contract.

(3) Subject to agreement of the parties and to other principles that take priority under Principle 5, the law should provide that the following terms are included in a data escrow contract or are incorporated into the governing principles of any entity created pursuant to the data escrow contract:

(a) The escrowee has such powers with regard to the data as are necessary for the stated purpose of the data escrow contract;

(b) The escrowee must act in furtherance of the stated purposes of the data escrow contract even if such action is inconsistent with interests of the contracting parties that are distinct from the stated purpose of the data escrow contract;

(c) The escrowee must not follow any direction given by a contracting party that is incompatible with the stated or manifestly obvious purpose of the data escrow contract;

(d) The escrowee must refrain from any use or onward supply of the entrusted data for its own purposes and must avoid any conflict of interest; and

(e) If the data escrow contract is terminated, each party has an obligation during the winding-up of the relationship not to take actions that undermine the stated purposes of the data escrow contract.

(4) In determining which rules and principles to apply by way of analogy, as provided in Principle 5, to data escrow contracts, consideration should be given in particular to

(a) The stated purpose of the data escrow contract and the nature of the data and of the parties involved; and

(b) The organizational structure of the relationships created by the data escrow contract.

Principle 14

Comments:

a. *Scope.* This Principle provides a general overview of the legal principles recommended for data escrow contracts. It is stated at a high level of generality because, as with the case of data trust contracts, both the subject of data escrow contracts and their nature can vary widely and data escrow contracts are still an emerging concept. The main difference between a data escrow contract under Principle 14 and a data trust contract under Principle 13 is that the purpose of a data escrow contract is to limit the powers of some or all parties contracting with the escrowee, whereas under a data trust contract the trustee must, at the end of the day, follow the directions and defer to the powers of the entrusters. This difference entails several consequences, resulting in a set of default terms that is quite distinct from that under Principle 13.

b. *Purposes of data escrow arrangements.* The essence of a data escrow contract is that the restricted parties either divest themselves of (full) control of data they hold, transferring that control to a third party (the escrowee), or take steps to ensure they will never get (full) control of particular data. It might seem anomalous for a party to voluntarily surrender or renounce control. There are, however, situations in which, for regulatory reasons or the like, it is important for a person with rights or powers with respect to data to surrender or renounce control of that data. Antitrust considerations (and related demands of competition law) are one example of such a situation; another example is provided by data privacy and data protection law. In such cases, the parties can avoid running afoul of important legal rules by renouncing control of data that they would otherwise have.

Illustration:

77. European company C would like to use a customer management system, run by U.S. software company S. In order to comply with European data protection law, C must ensure its customers' personal data are not transferred to the U.S. unless there are sufficient guarantees in place that ensure U.S. authorities cannot access the data merely upon a request made to S. In order to be able to make the deal, C and S therefore enter into an agreement with trusted third party E, according to which customer data will be transferred to S only in encrypted form, and it will be only with the help of keys held by E that it will be possible to decrypt the customer data. The arrangement between S and E is a data escrow contract.

c. *Structure.* The arrangement created by a data escrow contract can take many forms. In some cases, especially in legal systems in which escrow arrangements are common and well-understood, the arrangement may be created by an agreement that spells out the terms of the escrow arrangement. In other cases, however, the data escrow contract may provide for the formation of an entity of sorts to hold the escrowed data. It is important to distinguish the data escrow contract—the contract among the contracting parties and the escrowee under which the governing structure is created—from law governing the structure itself. For example, if the agreement calls for the formation of a public benefit corporation, the law governing such corporations governs its internal affairs. It should be noted, however, that the law governing structures that may be created by a data escrow contract often provides for a substantial role for private ordering by agreement among stakeholders. Examples include shareholder agreements with respect to a corporation and the terms of the trust instrument in the case of a trust. The data escrow contract can be seen, therefore, not only as the agreement to create a particular structure but also as an agreement among the stakeholders in the context of that structure.

d. Default terms. The default terms for a data escrow contract as described in this Principle are necessarily general in light of the variety of situations in which such a contract may be utilized and the variety of arrangements that the parties may devise. Accordingly, paragraph (3) identifies only a small number of default terms, which are applicable to all of these arrangements in case the contract is silent, and leave it to the parties to adapt the arrangement to their relevant data trust model in detail.

First, subparagraph (a) provides the key governing principle—the escrowee has whatever powers are necessary for accomplishment of the stated purposes of the data escrow contract.

Second, subparagraph (b) provides that the escrowee's primary obligation is to act in furtherance of the stated or manifestly obvious purposes of the data escrow contract. This is a critical point inasmuch as it means that gaps or incompleteness in the data trust contract will be filled with terms that are primarily guided by the purpose of the contract (which may differ from the private interests of the parties). Moreover, subparagraph (b) provides that the escrowee has this obligation even if its actions would be inconsistent with interests of the contracting parties that are distinct from the stated purpose of the data escrow contract.

It follows from this rule that subparagraph (c) provides that the escrowee must not follow directions from contracting parties where the directions are inconsistent with the stated or manifestly obvious purpose of the arrangement.

Illustration:

78.   S and E in Illustration no. 77 did not agree on the exact conditions under which S may, as far as necessary for software maintenance, get access to particular sample datasets. This gap is to be closed by reference to the purpose of the data escrow contract, which is compliance with European data protection law. So E must take whatever steps are needed to ensure that the requirements of European data protection law are fulfilled. This is so even where S (or even both S and C) directs E to transfer particular datasets to the U.S.

Fourth, subparagraph (d) provides a default rule that protects contracting parties from escrowees who might use their position to benefit themselves rather than the position of the contracting parties. This rule prohibits the escrowee from using the data to serve its own ends rather than the purposes of the contracting parties.

Finally, subparagraph (e) provides that if the data escrow contract is terminated, the winding-up of the relationship must not occur in a way that poses a threat to the stated purposes of the data escrow contract. In some circumstances, particularly when the purpose of the data escrow contract is to ensure that the restricted parties do not have (full) control of the data, this may mean that a substitute escrowee should succeed to the interest of the original escrowee, or that some other mechanism be created to ensure that the purpose of the arrangement is not undermined, rather than having control revert to restricted parties.

Illustration:

79.   If the contract with E in Illustration no. 77 is terminated for whatever reason, this does not mean that the data can simply be made accessible to S without en-

cryption, because this granting of access would be in breach of the stated purpose. Instead, compliance with applicable data protection law would have to be ensured by other means.

e.   Incorporation into governing principles of data escrow structure. In light of the fact that, as noted in comment c, a data escrow contract often calls for the creation of a structure, such as a corporation or common law trust, that has its own governance principles that allow for the autonomy of the parties to shape their relationship, paragraph (3) also provides that the default terms of a data escrow contract may be effectuated by being incorporated into the governing principles of an entity created pursuant to the data escrow contract rather than into the data escrow contract itself.

f.   Analogies. As noted in paragraph (4), this Principle suggests two approaches to identifying analogies as the source of rules to govern data escrow contracts. The first approach is to take into account the stated purpose of the data escrow contract and the nature of the data and of the parties involved. The focus on the stated purpose is particularly apt in light of the purposes for which data escrow arrangements are typically established, as described in comment b. Second, the nature of any organizational structure created by the data escrow contract can supply analogies. For example, if the data escrow contract contemplates the creation of a corporation that will manage and exploit the data, an analogy to shareholder agreements or proxies in corporations would be useful.

Principle 15: Data marketplace contracts

(1)   **A data marketplace contract is a contract between a party seeking to enter into a data transaction (the 'client') and a data marketplace provider, under which the data marketplace provider undertakes to enable or facilitate 'matchmaking' between the client and other potential parties to data transactions and, in some cases, provide further services facilitating the transaction.**

(2)   **Subject to agreement of the parties and to other principles that take priority under Principle 5, the law should provide that the following terms are included in a data marketplace contract:**

(a)   **Insofar as the data marketplace provider undertakes to facilitate or enable a particular step with regard to a transaction, it must provide reasonable support to the client in complying with any legal duties applicable to that step;**

(b)   **The data marketplace provider must refrain from any use for its own purposes of data, received from its client, that is the subject of the anticipated transaction; and**

(c)   **Upon full performance or termination of the contract, the data marketplace provider must erase any data in its control that is the subject of the anticipated transaction** and that it has received from its client, and any data derived from such data.

(3) In determining which rules and principles to apply by way of analogy, as provided in Principle 5, to data marketplace contracts, consideration should be given in particular to:

(a) whether, and the degree to which, the data marketplace provider gains control of the data concerned; and

(b) whether, and the extent to which, the payment or other performance owed to the data marketplace provider depends on the whether the matchmaking results in a data transaction.

Comment:

a.   Scope. Data marketplaces play an important role in the data economy. They can connect suppliers and recipients of data that, without the help of an intermediary, would not normally be able to find each other and enter into a data transaction without undue burden or expense. The most common transactions facilitated by such intermediaries are contracts for the transfer of data within the meaning of Principle 7, followed by contracts for access to data within the meaning of Principle 8. A 'data marketplace provider' is defined, for the purposes of these Principles, as an intermediary who engages in 'matchmaking' (i.e., acts as an intermediary facilitating transactions between suppliers and recipients of data). Usually, data marketplaces provide a range of further services to the parties, such as providing the infrastructure for transferring the data and any payment, assisting the parties in complying with legal requirements, providing reputational ranking services or services related to complaint handling. There exists a broad variety of types and business models, such as 'one-to-one', 'one-to-many' and 'many-to-many' marketplaces. This Principle can be applied to each of these models. Some marketplaces actually have control of the data supplied, whereas others restrict themselves to the matchmaking between supplier and recipient.

Where data is supplied via a data marketplace, there are usually three contractual relationships involved: the relationship between the supplier and the recipient, the relationship between the supplier and the marketplace, and the relationship between the marketplace and the recipient. Both the relationship between the supplier and the marketplace and between the recipient and the marketplace are marketplace contracts within the meaning of Principle 15.

Illustration:

80. Truck fleet operator T wants to minimize the amount of time lost to required rest breaks and meal breaks taken by its drivers. Through geolocation devices on T's trucks, T is aware of where its trucks are at all times but does not always know the most efficient routing for those trucks to make sure that they are near appropriate rest and food locations at the best time for breaks. T enters into a contract with intermediary I under which I agrees to find a party that can supply real-time data as to rest and food locations and estimated travel time to them in light of current weather and traffic conditions so that T can use this information to direct its trucks to the most efficient locations for rest and meal breaks.

The contract between T and I is a data marketplace contract.

b.   Default terms. As with other data contracts, Principle 15 provides several default terms for data marketplace contracts. Each of the four supplied default terms imposes a duty on the data marketplace provider. Paragraph (2)(a) obligates the provider to assist the client in complying with legal duties that apply to the transaction facilitated by the data marketplace provider.

Paragraph (2)(b) obligates the data marketplace provider to refrain from processing for its own purposes any data that is the subject of a data transaction that it enables or facilitates.

Paragraph (2)(c) obligates a data marketplace provider who enters into a data marketplace contract to erase any data in its control that is the subject of the anticipated transaction and that it has received from its client, and any data derived from such data, upon full performance or termination of the contract.

Illustration:

81.   Accommodations information provider P runs a website on which users can search for hotels available in a particular location on a particular date and compare accommodations and prices. This service enables P to amass significant data concerning the number of people who are considering travel to those locations on particular dates. P believes that this information would be very valuable to car rental companies that have dynamic pricing models so they can adjust their rates in those locations based on anticipated demand. P does not, however, have the expertise necessary to identify the appropriate officials of car rental companies to propose entering into data transactions with them. Accordingly, P enters into

a contract with data marketplace provider I pursuant to which I performs matchmaking between P and car rental companies to enable P to enter into data transactions with those companies. To enable I to perform its matchmaking most effectively, P supplies some of its data to I. When the contract between P and I has been fully performed by I or has otherwise been terminated, I must erase the data supplied to it by P.

c.   Application of other law by analogy. Contracts with a party that provides matchmaking services are well-known in a number of contexts outside the scope of these Principles. For example, parties wishing to sell real property often contract with matchmakers to find buyers for the real property, and potential buyers will often similarly contract with matchmakers to find appropriate real property within the buyer's budget. Similarly, companies seeking loans often contract with matchmakers that can match them with lenders that make loans to other companies in similar circumstances. To the extent that, in the applicable jurisdiction, default rules and principles have been developed for application to such matchmaking contracts, those rules and principles are appropriate to apply to data marketplace contracts by analogy. In some jurisdictions, those legal rules and principles differ depending on whether the compensation owed to the matchmaker only if the matchmaking services are successful and whether the matchmaker obtains control over the subject matter of the match.

Illustration:

82.   R runs a website containing reviews and rankings of various consumer products. R harvests location data with respect to customers who access reviews and rankings. Data as to the number of such cus-

tomers seeking information about consumer products in a particular location has value to retailers in that location. R enters into a data marketplace contract with intermediary I pursuant to which I will be paid a fee for each successful match between R and a retailer with respect to such data; the fee is an agreed fraction of the amount charged by R to the retailer. Under the data marketplace contract, I receives no compensation except for the fee for successful matches. In determining what legal rules and principles to apply by analogy to the data marketplace contract, reference should be made to rules and principles developed for other similar matchmaking contracts and, in particular, to those in which the matchmaker's compensation is determined by the number and magnitude of successful matches.

UNIFORM ELECTRONIC TRANSACTIONS ACT (UETA)

Table of Contents

---

§ 1. Short Title

This [Act] may be cited as the Uniform Electronic Transactions Act.

§ 2. Definitions

In this [Act]:

(1) "Agreement" means the bargain of the parties in fact, as found in their language or inferred from other circumstances and from rules, regulations, and procedures given the effect of agreements under laws otherwise applicable to a particular transaction.

(2) "Automated transaction" means a transaction conducted or performed, in whole or in part, by electronic means or electronic records, in which the acts or records of one or both parties are not reviewed by an individual in the ordinary course in forming a contract, performing under an existing contract, or fulfilling an obligation required by the transaction.

(3) "Computer program" means a set of statements or instructions to be used directly or indirectly in an information processing system in order to bring about a certain result.

(4) "Contract" means the total legal obligation resulting from the parties' agreement as affected by this [Act] and other applicable law.

(5) "Electronic" means relating to technology having electrical, digital, magnetic, wireless, optical, electromagnetic, or similar capabilities.

(6) "Electronic agent" means a computer program or an electronic or other automated means used independently to initiate an action or respond to electronic records or performances in whole or in part, without review or action by an individual.

(7) "Electronic record" means a record created, generated, sent, communicated, received, or stored by electronic means.

(8) "Electronic signature" means an electronic sound, symbol, or process attached to or logically associated with a record and executed or adopted by a person with the intent to sign the record.

(9) "Governmental agency" means an executive, legislative, or judicial agency, department, board, commission, authority, institution, or instrumentality of the federal government or of a State or of a county, municipality, or other political subdivision of a State.

(10) "Information" means data, text, images, sounds, codes, computer programs, software, databases, or the like.

(11) "Information processing system" means an electronic system for creating, generating, sending, receiving, storing, displaying, or processing information.

(12) "Person" means an individual, corporation, business trust, estate, trust, partnership, limited liability company, association, joint venture, governmental agency, public corporation, or any other legal or commercial entity.

(13) "Record" means information that is inscribed on a tangible medium or that is stored in an electronic or other medium and is retrievable in perceivable form.

(14) "Security procedure" means a procedure employed for the purpose of verifying that an electronic signature, record, or performance is that of a specific person or for detecting changes or errors in the information in an electronic record. The term includes a procedure that requires the use of algorithms or other codes, identifying words or numbers, encryption, or callback or other acknowledgment procedures.

(15) "State" means a State of the United States, the District of Columbia, Puerto Rico, the United States Virgin Islands, or any territory or insular possession subject to the jurisdiction of the United States. The term includes an Indian tribe or band, or Alaskan native village, which is recognized by federal law or formally acknowledged by a State.

(16) "Transaction" means an action or set of actions occurring between two or more persons relating to the conduct of business, commercial, or governmental affairs

§ 3. Scope

(a) Except as otherwise provided in subsection (b), this [Act] applies to electronic records and electronic signatures relating to a transaction.

(b) This [Act] does not apply to a transaction to the extent it is governed by:

(1) a law governing the creation and execution of wills, codicils, or testamentary trusts;

(2) [The Uniform Commercial Code other than Sections 1–107 and 1–206, Article 2, and Article 2A];

(3) [the Uniform Computer Information Transactions Act]; and

(4) [other laws, if any, identified by State].

(c) This [Act] applies to an electronic record or electronic signature otherwise excluded from the application of this [Act] under subsection (b) to the extent it is governed by a law other than those specified in subsection (b).

(d) A transaction subject to this [Act] is also subject to other applicable substantive law.

§ 4. Prospective Application

This [Act] applies to any electronic record or electronic signature created, generated, sent, communicated, received, or stored on or after the effective date of this [Act].

§ 5. Use of Electronic Records and Electronic Signatures; Variation By Agreement

(a) This [Act] does not require a record or signature to be created, generated, sent, communicated, received, stored, or otherwise processed or used by electronic means or in electronic form.

(b) This [Act] applies only to transactions between parties each of which has agreed to conduct transactions by electronic means. Whether the parties agree to conduct a transaction by electronic means is determined from the context and surrounding circumstances, including the parties' conduct.

(c) A party that agrees to conduct a transaction by electronic means may refuse to conduct other transactions by electronic means. The right granted by this subsection may not be waived by agreement.

(d) Except as otherwise provided in this [Act], the effect of any of its provisions may be varied by agreement. The presence in certain provisions of this [Act] of the words "unless otherwise agreed", or words of similar import, does not imply that the effect of other provisions may not be varied by agreement.

(e) Whether an electronic record or electronic signature has legal consequences is determined by this [Act] and other applicable law.

§ 6. Construction and Application

This [Act] must be construed and applied:

(1) to facilitate electronic transactions consistent with other applicable law;

(2) to be consistent with reasonable practices concerning electronic transactions and with the continued expansion of those practices; and

(3) to effectuate its general purpose to make uniform the law with respect to the subject of this [Act] among States enacting it.

§ 7. Legal Recognition of Electronic Records, Electronic Signatures, and Electronic Contracts

(a) A record or signature may not be denied legal effect or enforceability solely because it is in electronic form.

(b) A contract may not be denied legal effect or enforceability solely because an electronic record was used in its formation.

(c) If a law requires a record to be in writing, an electronic record satisfies the law.

(d) If a law requires a signature, an electronic signature satisfies the law.

§ 8. Provision of Information in Writing; Presentation of Records

(a) If parties have agreed to conduct a transaction by electronic means and a law requires a person to provide, send, or deliver information in writing to another person, the requirement is satisfied if the information is provided, sent, or delivered, as the case may be, in an electronic record capable of retention by the recipient at the time of receipt. An electronic record is not capable of retention by the recipient if the sender or its information processing system inhibits the ability of the recipient to print or store the electronic record.

(b) If a law other than this [Act] requires a record (i) to be posted or displayed in a certain manner, (ii) to be sent, communicated, or transmitted by a specified method, or (iii) to contain information that is formatted in a certain manner, the following rules apply:

> (1) The record must be posted or displayed in the manner specified in the other law.

> (2) Except as otherwise provided in subsection (d)(2), the record must be sent, communicated, or transmitted by the method specified in the other law.

> (3) The record must contain the information formatted in the manner specified in the other law.

(c) If a sender inhibits the ability of a recipient to store or print an electronic record, the electronic record is not enforceable against the recipient.

(d) The requirements of this section may not be varied by agreement, but:

> (1) to the extent a law other than this [Act] requires information to be provided, sent, or delivered in writing but permits that requirement to be varied by agreement, the requirement under subsection (a) that the information be in the form of an electronic record capable of retention may also be varied by agreement; and

> (2) a requirement under a law other than this [Act] to send, communicate, or transmit a record by [first-class mail, postage prepaid] [regular United States mail], may be varied by agreement to the extent permitted by the other law.

§ 9. Attribution and Effect of Electronic Record and Electronic Signature

(a) An electronic record or electronic signature is attributable to a person if it was the act of the person. The act of the person may be shown in any manner, including a showing of the efficacy of any security procedure applied to determine the person to which the electronic record or electronic signature was attributable.

(b) The effect of an electronic record or electronic signature attributed to a person under subsection (a) is determined from the context and surrounding circumstances at the time of its creation, execution, or adoption, including the parties' agreement, if any, and otherwise as provided by law.

§ 10. Effect of Change or Error

If a change or error in an electronic record occurs in a transmission between parties to a transaction, the following rules apply:

(1) If the parties have agreed to use a security procedure to detect changes or errors and one party has conformed to the procedure, but the other party has not, and the nonconforming party would have detected the change or error had that party also conformed, the conforming party may avoid the effect of the changed or erroneous electronic record.

(2) In an automated transaction involving an individual, the individual may avoid the effect of an electronic record that resulted from an error made by the individual in dealing with the electronic agent of another person if the electronic agent did not provide an opportunity for the prevention or correction of the error and, at the time the individual learns of the error, the individual:

(A) promptly notifies the other person of the error and that the individual did not intend to be bound by the electronic record received by the other person;

(B) takes reasonable steps, including steps that conform to the other person's reasonable instructions, to return to the other person or, if instructed by the other person, to destroy the consideration received, if any, as a result of the erroneous electronic record; and (C) has not used or received any benefit or value from the consideration, if any, received from the other person.

(3) If neither paragraph (1) nor paragraph (2) applies, the change or error has the effect provided by other law, including the law of mistake, and the parties' contract, if any.

(4) Paragraphs (2) and (3) may not be varied by agreement.

§ 11. Notarization and Acknowledgment

If a law requires a signature or record to be notarized, acknowledged, verified, or made under oath, the requirement is satisfied if the electronic signature of the person authorized to perform those acts, together with all other information required to be included by other applicable law, is attached to or logically associated with the signature or record.

§ 12. Retention of Electronic Records; Originals

(a) If a law requires that a record be retained, the requirement is satisfied by retaining an electronic record of the information in the record which:

(1) accurately reflects the information set forth in the record after it was first generated in its final form as an electronic record or otherwise; and

(2) remains accessible for later reference.

(b) A requirement to retain a record in accordance with subsection (a) does not apply to any information the sole purpose of which is to enable the record to be sent, communicated, or received.

(c) A person may satisfy subsection (a) by using the services of another person if the requirements of that subsection are satisfied.

(d) If a law requires a record to be presented or retained in its original form, or provides consequences if the record is not presented or retained in its original form, that law is satisfied by an electronic record retained in accordance with subsection (a).

(e) If a law requires retention of a check, that requirement is satisfied by retention of an electronic record of the information on the front and back of the check in accordance with subsection (a).

(f) A record retained as an electronic record in accordance with subsection (a) satisfies a law requiring a person to retain a record for evidentiary, audit, or like purposes, unless a law enacted after the effective date of this [Act] specifically prohibits the use of an electronic record for the specified purpose.

(g) This section does not preclude a governmental agency of this State from specifying additional requirements for the retention of a record subject to the agency's jurisdiction.

§ 13. Admissibility in Evidence

In a proceeding, evidence of a record or signature may not be excluded solely because it is in electronic form.

§ 14. Automated Transaction

In an automated transaction, the following rules apply:

(1) A contract may be formed by the interaction of electronic agents of the parties, even if no individual was aware of or reviewed the electronic agents' actions or the resulting terms and agreements.

(2) A contract may be formed by the interaction of an electronic agent and an individual, acting on the individual's own behalf or for another person, including by an interaction in which the individual performs actions that the individual is free to refuse to perform and which the in-

dividual knows or has reason to know will cause the electronic agent to complete the transaction or performance.

(3)   The terms of the contract are determined by the substantive law applicable to it.

§ 15.   Time and Place of Sending and Receipt

(a)   Unless otherwise agreed between the sender and the recipient, an electronic record is sent when it:

(1)   is addressed properly or otherwise directed properly to an information processing system that the recipient has designated or uses for the purpose of receiving electronic records or information of the type sent and from which the recipient is able to retrieve the electronic record;

(2)   is in a form capable of being processed by that system; and

(3)   enters an information processing system outside the control of the sender or of a person that sent the electronic record on behalf of the sender or enters a region of the information processing system designated or used by the recipient which is under the control of the recipient.

(b)   Unless otherwise agreed between a sender and the recipient, an electronic record is received when:

(1)   it enters an information processing system that the recipient has designated or uses for the purpose of receiving electronic records or information of the type sent and from which the recipient is able to retrieve the electronic record; and

(2)   it is in a form capable of being processed by that system.

(c)   Subsection (b) applies even if the place the information processing system is located is different from the place the electronic record is deemed to be received under subsection (d).

(d)   Unless otherwise expressly provided in the electronic record or agreed between the sender and the recipient, an electronic record is deemed to be sent from the sender's place of business and to be received at the recipient's place of business. For purposes of this subsection, the following rules apply:

(1)   If the sender or recipient has more than one place of business, the place of business of that person is the place having the closest relationship to the underlying transaction.

(2)   If the sender or the recipient does not have a place of business, the place of business is the sender's or recipient's residence, as the case may be.

(e)   An electronic record is received under subsection (b) even if no individual is aware of its receipt.

(f) Receipt of an electronic acknowledgment from an information processing system described in subsection (b) establishes that a record was received but, by itself, does not establish that the content sent corresponds to the content received.

(g) If a person is aware that an electronic record purportedly sent under subsection (a), or purportedly received under subsection (b), was not actually sent or received, the legal effect of the sending or receipt is determined by other applicable law. Except to the extent permitted by the other law, the requirements of this subsection may not be varied by agreement.

§ 16.   Transferable Records

(a) In this section, "transferable record" means an electronic record that:

(1)   would be a note under [Article 3 of the Uniform Commercial Code] or a document under [Article 7 of the Uniform Commercial Code] if the electronic record were in writing; and

(2)   the issuer of the electronic record expressly has agreed is a transferable record.

(b) A person has control of a transferable record if a system employed for evidencing the transfer of interests in the transferable record reliably establishes that person as the person to which the transferable record was issued or transferred.

(c) A system satisfies subsection (b), and a person is deemed to have control of a transferable record, if the transferable record is created, stored, and assigned in such a manner that:

(1)   a single authoritative copy of the transferable record exists which is unique, identifiable, and, except as otherwise provided in paragraphs (4), (5), and (6), unalterable;

(2)   the authoritative copy identifies the person asserting control as:

(A)   the person to which the transferable record was issued; or

(B)   if the authoritative copy indicates that the transferable record has been transferred, the person to which the transferable record was most recently transferred;

(3)   the authoritative copy is communicated to and maintained by the person asserting control or its designated custodian;

(4)   copies or revisions that add or change an identified assignee of the authoritative copy can be made only with the consent of the person asserting control;

(5)   each copy of the authoritative copy and any copy of a copy is readily identifiable as a copy that is not the authoritative copy; and

(6)   any revision of the authoritative copy is readily identifiable as authorized or unauthorized.

(d)   Except as otherwise agreed, a person having control of a transferable record is the holder, as defined in [Section 1–201(20) of the Uniform Commercial Code], of the transferable record and has the same rights and defenses as a holder of an equivalent record or writing under [the Uniform Commercial Code], including, if the applicable statutory requirements under [Section 3–302(a), 7–501, or 9–308 of the Uniform Commercial Code] are satisfied, the rights and defenses of a holder in due course, a holder to which a negotiable document of title has been duly negotiated, or a purchaser, respectively. Delivery, possession, and indorsement are not required to obtain or exercise any of the rights under this subsection.

(e)   Except as otherwise agreed, an obligor under a transferable record has the same rights and defenses as an equivalent obligor under equivalent records or writings under [the Uniform Commercial Code].

(f)   If requested by a person against which enforcement is sought, the person seeking to enforce the transferable record shall provide reasonable proof that the person is in control of the transferable record. Proof may include access to the authoritative copy of the transferable record and related business records sufficient to review the terms of the transferable record and to establish the identity of the person having control of the transferable record.

[§ 17.   Creation and Retention of Electronic Records and Conversion of Written Records By Governmental Agencies[1]

[Each governmental agency] [The designated state officer] of this State shall determine whether, and the extent to which, [it] [a governmental agency] will create and retain electronic records and convert written records to electronic records.]

[§ 18.   Acceptance and Distribution of Electronic Records By Governmental Agencies

(a)   Except as otherwise provided in Section 12(f), [each governmental agency] [the [designated state officer]] of this State shall determine whether, and the extent to which, [it] [a governmental agency] will send and accept electronic records and electronic signatures to and from other persons and otherwise create, generate, communicate, store, process, use, and rely upon electronic records and electronic signatures.

(b)   To the extent that a governmental agency uses electronic records and electronic signatures under subsection (a), the [governmental agen-

---

[1] Sections 17–19 are optional sections for consideration by individual legislatures for adoption, and have been bracketed to make this clear.

cy] [designated state officer], giving due consideration to security, may specify:

(1) the manner and format in which the electronic records must be created, generated, sent, communicated, received, and stored and the systems established for those purposes;

(2) if electronic records must be signed by electronic means, the type of electronic signature required, the manner and format in which the electronic signature must be affixed to the electronic record, and the identity of, or criteria that must be met by, any third party used by a person filing a document to facilitate the process;

(3) control processes and procedures as appropriate to ensure adequate preservation, disposition, integrity, security, confidentiality, and auditability of electronic records; and

(4) any other required attributes for electronic records which are specified for corresponding nonelectronic records or reasonably necessary under the circumstances.

(c) Except as otherwise provided in Section 12(f), this [Act] does not require a governmental agency of this State to use or permit the use of electronic records or electronic signatures.]

[§ 19. Interoperability

The [governmental agency] [designated officer] of this State which adopts standards pursuant to Section 18 may encourage and promote consistency and interoperability with similar requirements adopted by other governmental agencies of this and other States and the federal government and nongovernmental persons interacting with governmental agencies of this State. If appropriate, those standards may specify differing levels of standards from which governmental agencies of this State may choose in implementing the most appropriate standard for a particular application.]

§ 20. Severability Clause

If any provision of this [Act] or its application to any person or circumstance is held invalid, the invalidity does not affect other provisions or applications of this [Act] which can be given effect without the invalid provision or application, and to this end the provisions of this [Act] are severable.

§ 21. Effective Date

This [Act] takes effect _____

ELECTRONIC SIGNATURES IN GLOBAL AND NATIONAL COMMERCE ACT (E-SIGN)

(SELECTED SECTIONS)

§ 1. (15 U.S.C.A. § 7001 Note). Short Title.

This Act may be cited as the "Electronic Signatures in Global and National Commerce Act".

TITLE I

ELECTRONIC RECORDS AND SIGNATURES IN COMMERCE

§ 101. (15 U.S.C.A. § 7001). General Rule of Validity.

(a) IN GENERAL.—Notwithstanding any statute, regulation, or other rule of law (other than this title and title II), with respect to any transaction in or affecting interstate or foreign commerce—

(1) a signature, contract, or other record relating to such transaction may not be denied legal effect, validity, or enforceability solely because it is in electronic form; and

(2) a contract relating to such transaction may not be denied legal effect, validity, or enforceability solely because an electronic signature or electronic record was used in its formation.

(b) PRESERVATION OF RIGHTS AND OBLIGATIONS.—This title does not—

(1) limit, alter, or otherwise affect any requirement imposed by a statute, regulation, or rule of law relating to the rights and obligations of persons under such statute, regulation, or rule of law other than a requirement that contracts or other records be written, signed, or in nonelectronic form; or

(2) require any person to agree to use or accept electronic records or electronic signatures, other than a governmental agency with respect to a record other than a contract to which it is a party.

(c) CONSUMER DISCLOSURES.—

(1) CONSENT TO ELECTRONIC RECORDS.—Notwithstanding subsection (a), if a statute, regulation, or other rule of law requires that information relating to a transaction or transactions in or affecting interstate or foreign commerce be provided or made available to

a consumer in writing, the use of an electronic record to provide or make available (whichever is required) such information satisfies the requirement that such information be in writing if—

(A) the consumer has affirmatively consented to such use and has not withdrawn such consent;

(B) the consumer, prior to consenting, is provided with a clear and conspicuous statement—

(i) informing the consumer of (I) any right or option of the consumer to have the record provided or made available on paper or in nonelectronic form, and (II) the right of the consumer to withdraw the consent to have the record provided or made available in an electronic form and of any conditions, consequences (which may include termination of the parties' relationship), or fees in the event of such withdrawal;

(ii) informing the consumer of whether the consent applies (I) only to the particular transaction which gave rise to the obligation to provide the record, or (II) to identified categories of records that may be provided or made available during the course of the parties' relationship;

(iii) describing the procedures the consumer must use to withdraw consent as provided in clause (i) and to update information needed to contact the consumer electronically; and

(iv) informing the consumer (I) how, after the consent, the consumer may, upon request, obtain a paper copy of an electronic record, and (II) whether any fee will be charged for such copy;

(C) the consumer—

(i) prior to consenting, is provided with a statement of the hardware and software requirements for access to and retention of the electronic records; and

(ii) consents electronically, or confirms his or her consent electronically, in a manner that reasonably demonstrates that the consumer can access information in the electronic form that will be used to provide the information that is the subject of the consent; and

(D) after the consent of a consumer in accordance with subparagraph (A), if a change in the hardware or software requirements needed to access or retain electronic records creates a material risk that the consumer will not be able to access or retain a subsequent electronic record that was the subject of the consent, the person providing the electronic record—

(i) provides the consumer with a statement of (I) the revised hardware and software requirements for access to and retention of the electronic records, and (II) the right to withdraw consent without the imposition of any fees for such withdrawal and without the imposition of any condition or consequence that was not disclosed under subparagraph (B)(i); and

(ii) again complies with subparagraph (C).

(2)   OTHER RIGHTS.—

(A)   PRESERVATION OF CONSUMER PROTECTIONS.— Nothing in this title affects the content or timing of any disclosure or other record required to be provided or made available to any consumer under any statute, regulation, or other rule of law.

(B)   VERIFICATION OR ACKNOWLEDGMENT.—If a law that was enacted prior to this Act expressly requires a record to be provided or made available by a specified method that requires verification or acknowledgment of receipt, the record may be provided or made available electronically only if the method used provides verification or acknowledgment of receipt (whichever is required).

(3)   EFFECT OF FAILURE TO OBTAIN ELECTRONIC CONSENT OR CONFIRMATION OF CONSENT.—The legal effectiveness, validity, or enforceability of any contract executed by a consumer shall not be denied solely because of the failure to obtain electronic consent or confirmation of consent by that consumer in accordance with paragraph (1)(C)(ii).

(4)   PROSPECTIVE EFFECT.—Withdrawal of consent by a consumer shall not affect the legal effectiveness, validity, or enforceability of electronic records provided or made available to that consumer in accordance with paragraph (1) prior to implementation of the consumer's withdrawal of consent. A consumer's withdrawal of consent shall be effective within a reasonable period of time after receipt of the withdrawal by the provider of the record. Failure to comply with paragraph (1)(D) may, at the election of the consumer, be treated as a withdrawal of consent for purposes of this paragraph.

(5)   PRIOR CONSENT.—This subsection does not apply to any records that are provided or made available to a consumer who has consented prior to the effective date of this title to receive such records in electronic form as permitted by any statute, regulation, or other rule of law.

(6)   ORAL COMMUNICATIONS.—An oral communication or a recording of an oral communication shall not qualify as an electronic record for purposes of this subsection except as otherwise provided under applicable law.

(d)   RETENTION OF CONTRACTS AND RECORDS.—

(1)   ACCURACY AND ACCESSIBILITY.—If a statute, regulation, or other rule of law requires that a contract or other record relat-

ing to a transaction in or affecting interstate or foreign commerce be retained, that requirement is met by retaining an electronic record of the information in the contract or other record that—

    (A) accurately reflects the information set forth in the contract or other record; and

    (B) remains accessible to all persons who are entitled to access by statute, regulation, or rule of law, for the period required by such statute, regulation, or rule of law, in a form that is capable of being accurately reproduced for later reference, whether by transmission, printing, or otherwise.

    (2) EXCEPTION.—A requirement to retain a contract or other record in accordance with paragraph (1) does not apply to any information whose sole purpose is to enable the contract or other record to be sent, communicated, or received.

    (3) ORIGINALS.—If a statute, regulation, or other rule of law requires a contract or other record relating to a transaction in or affecting interstate or foreign commerce to be provided, available, or retained in its original form, or provides consequences if the contract or other record is not provided, available, or retained in its original form, that statute, regulation, or rule of law is satisfied by an electronic record that complies with paragraph (1).

    (4) CHECKS.—If a statute, regulation, or other rule of law requires the retention of a check, that requirement is satisfied by retention of an electronic record of the information on the front and back of the check in accordance with paragraph (1).

  (e) ACCURACY AND ABILITY TO RETAIN CONTRACTS AND OTHER RECORDS.—Notwithstanding subsection (a), if a statute, regulation, or other rule of law requires that a contract or other record relating to a transaction in or affecting interstate or foreign commerce be in writing, the legal effect, validity, or enforceability of an electronic record of such contract or other record may be denied if such electronic record is not in a form that is capable of being retained and accurately reproduced for later reference by all parties or persons who are entitled to retain the contract or other record.

  (f) PROXIMITY.—Nothing in this title affects the proximity required by any statute, regulation, or other rule of law with respect to any warning, notice, disclosure, or other record required to be posted, displayed, or publicly affixed.

  (g) NOTARIZATION AND ACKNOWLEDGMENT.—If a statute, regulation, or other rule of law requires a signature or record relating to a transaction in or affecting interstate or foreign commerce to be notarized, acknowledged, verified, or made under oath, that requirement is satisfied if the electronic signature of the person authorized to perform those acts, together with all other information required to be included by other applicable statute, regulation, or rule of law, is attached to or logically associated with the signature or record.

(h)   ELECTRONIC AGENTS.—A contract or other record relating to a transaction in or affecting interstate or foreign commerce may not be denied legal effect, validity, or enforceability solely because its formation, creation, or delivery involved the action of one or more electronic agents so long as the action of any such electronic agent is legally attributable to the person to be bound.

(i)   INSURANCE.—It is the specific intent of the Congress that this title and title II apply to the business of insurance.

(j)   INSURANCE AGENTS AND BROKERS.—An insurance agent or broker acting under the direction of a party that enters into a contract by means of an electronic record or electronic signature may not be held liable for any deficiency in the electronic procedures agreed to by the parties under that contract if—

(1)   the agent or broker has not engaged in negligent, reckless, or intentional tortious conduct;

(2)   the agent or broker was not involved in the development or establishment of such electronic procedures; and

(3)   the agent or broker did not deviate from such procedures.

§ 102.   (15 U.S.C.A. § 7002). Exemption to Preemption.

(a)   IN GENERAL.—A State statute, regulation, or other rule of law may modify, limit, or supersede the provisions of section 101 with respect to State law only if such statute, regulation, or rule of law—

(1)   constitutes an enactment or adoption of the Uniform Electronic Transactions Act as approved and recommended for enactment in all the States by the National Conference of Commissioners on Uniform State Laws in 1999, except that any exception to the scope of such Act enacted by a State under section 3(b)(4) of such Act shall be preempted to the extent such exception is inconsistent with this title or title II, or would not be permitted under paragraph (2)(A)(ii) of this subsection; or

(2)(A)   specifies the alternative procedures or requirements for the use or acceptance (or both) of electronic records or electronic signatures to establish the legal effect, validity, or enforceability of contracts or other records, if—

(i)   such alternative procedures or requirements are consistent with this title and title II; and

(ii)   such alternative procedures or requirements do not require, or accord greater legal status or effect to, the implementation or application of a specific technology or technical specification for performing the functions of creating, storing, generating, receiving, communicating, or authenticating electronic records or electronic signatures; and

(B)   if enacted or adopted after the date of the enactment of this Act, makes specific reference to this Act.

(b)   EXCEPTIONS FOR ACTIONS BY STATES AS MARKET PAR-TICIPANTS.—Subsection (a)(2)(A)(ii) shall not apply to the statutes, regulations, or other rules of law governing procurement by any State, or any agency or instrumentality thereof.

(c)   PREVENTION OF CIRCUMVENTION.—Subsection (a) does not permit a State to circumvent this title or title II through the imposition of nonelectronic delivery methods under section 8(b)(2) of the Uniform Electronic Transactions Act.

§ 103.   (15 U.S.C.A. § 7003). Specific Exceptions.

(a)   EXCEPTED REQUIREMENTS.—The provisions of section 101 shall not apply to a contract or other record to the extent it is governed by—

(1)   a statute, regulation, or other rule of law governing the creation and execution of wills, codicils, or testamentary trusts;

(2)   a State statute, regulation, or other rule of law governing adoption, divorce, or other matters of family law; or

(3)   the Uniform Commercial Code, as in effect in any State, other than sections 1–107 and 1–206 and Articles 2 and 2A.

(b)   ADDITIONAL EXCEPTIONS.—The provisions of section 101 shall not apply to—

(1)   court orders or notices, or official court documents (including briefs, pleadings, and other writings) required to be executed in connection with court proceedings;

(2)   any notice of—

(A)   the cancellation or termination of utility services (including water, heat, and power);

(B)   default, acceleration, repossession, foreclosure, or eviction, or the right to cure, under a credit agreement secured by, or a rental agreement for, a primary residence of an individual;

(C)   the cancellation or termination of health insurance or benefits or life insurance benefits (excluding annuities); or

(D)   recall of a product, or material failure of a product, that risks endangering health or safety; or

(3)   any document required to accompany any transportation or handling of hazardous materials, pesticides, or other toxic or dangerous materials.

(c) REVIEW OF EXCEPTIONS.—

(1) EVALUATION REQUIRED.—The Secretary of Commerce, acting through the Assistant Secretary for Communications and Information, shall review the operation of the exceptions in subsections (a) and (b) to evaluate, over a period of 3 years, whether such exceptions continue to be necessary for the protection of consumers. Within 3 years after the date of enactment of this Act, the Assistant Secretary shall submit a report to the Congress on the results of such evaluation.

(2) DETERMINATIONS.—If a Federal regulatory agency, with respect to matter within its jurisdiction, determines after notice and an opportunity for public comment, and publishes a finding, that one or more such exceptions are no longer necessary for the protection of consumers and eliminating such exceptions will not increase the material risk of harm to consumers, such agency may extend the application of section 101 to the exceptions identified in such finding.

§ 106. (15 U.S.C.A. § 7006). Definitions.

For purposes of this title:

(1) CONSUMER.—The term "consumer" means an individual who obtains, through a transaction, products or services which are used primarily for personal, family, or household purposes, and also means the legal representative of such an individual.

(2) ELECTRONIC.—The term "electronic" means relating to technology having electrical, digital, magnetic, wireless, optical, electromagnetic, or similar capabilities.

(3) ELECTRONIC AGENT.—The term "electronic agent" means a computer program or an electronic or other automated means used independently to initiate an action or respond to electronic records or performances in whole or in part without review or action by an individual at the time of the action or response.

(4) ELECTRONIC RECORD.—The term "electronic record" means a contract or other record created, generated, sent, communicated, received, or stored by electronic means.

(5) ELECTRONIC SIGNATURE.—The term "electronic signature" means an electronic sound, symbol, or process, attached to or logically associated with a contract or other record and executed or adopted by a person with the intent to sign the record.

(6) FEDERAL REGULATORY AGENCY.—The term "Federal regulatory agency" means an agency, as that term is defined in section 552(f) of title 5, United States Code.

(7) INFORMATION.—The term "information" means data, text, images, sounds, codes, computer programs, software, databases, or the like.

(8)   PERSON.—The term "person" means an individual, corporation, business trust, estate, trust, partnership, limited liability company, association, joint venture, governmental agency, public corporation, or any other legal or commercial entity.

(9)   RECORD.—The term "record" means information that is inscribed on a tangible medium or that is stored in an electronic or other medium and is retrievable in perceivable form.

(10)   REQUIREMENT.—The term "requirement" includes a prohibition.

(11)   SELF-REGULATORY ORGANIZATION.—The term "self-regulatory organization" means an organization or entity that is not a Federal regulatory agency or a State, but that is under the supervision of a Federal regulatory agency and is authorized under Federal law to adopt and administer rules applicable to its members that are enforced by such organization or entity, by a Federal regulatory agency, or by another self-regulatory organization.

(12)   STATE.—The term "State" includes the District of Columbia and the territories and possessions of the United States.

(13)   TRANSACTION.—The term "transaction" means an action or set of actions relating to the conduct of business, consumer, or commercial affairs between two or more persons, including any of the following types of conduct—

    (A)   the sale, lease, exchange, licensing, or other disposition of (i) personal property, including goods and intangibles, (ii) services, and (iii) any combination thereof; and

    (B)   the sale, lease, exchange, or other disposition of any interest in real property, or any combination thereof.

§ 201.   (15 U.S.C.A. § 7021). Transferable Records.

(a)   DEFINITIONS.—For purposes of this section:

(1)   TRANSFERABLE RECORD.—The term "transferable record" means an electronic record that—

    (A)   would be a note under Article 3 of the Uniform Commercial Code if the electronic record were in writing;

    (B)   the issuer of the electronic record expressly has agreed is a transferable record; and

    (C)   relates to a loan secured by real property.

A transferable record may be executed using an electronic signature.

(2)   OTHER DEFINITIONS.—The terms "electronic record", "electronic signature", and "person" have the same meanings provided in section 106 of this Act.

(b)   CONTROL.—A person has control of a transferable record if a system employed for evidencing the transfer of interests in the transferable record reliably establishes that person as the person to which the transferable record was issued or transferred.

(c)   CONDITIONS.—A system satisfies subsection (b), and a person is deemed to have control of a transferable record, if the transferable record is created, stored, and assigned in such a manner that—

   (1)   a single authoritative copy of the transferable record exists which is unique, identifiable, and, except as otherwise provided in paragraphs (4), (5), and (6), unalterable;

   (2)   the authoritative copy identifies the person asserting control as—

      (A)   the person to which the transferable record was issued; or

      (B)   if the authoritative copy indicates that the transferable record has been transferred, the person to which the transferable record was most recently transferred;

   (3)   the authoritative copy is communicated to and maintained by the person asserting control or its designated custodian;

   (4)   copies or revisions that add or change an identified assignee of the authoritative copy can be made only with the consent of the person asserting control;

   (5)   each copy of the authoritative copy and any copy of a copy is readily identifiable as a copy that is not the authoritative copy; and

   (6)   any revision of the authoritative copy is readily identifiable as authorized or unauthorized.

(d)   STATUS AS HOLDER.—Except as otherwise agreed, a person having control of a transferable record is the holder, as defined in section 1–201(20) of the Uniform Commercial Code, of the transferable record and has the same rights and defenses as a holder of an equivalent record or writing under the Uniform Commercial Code, including, if the applicable statutory requirements under section 3–302(a), 9–308, or revised section 9–330 of the Uniform Commercial Code are satisfied, the rights and defenses of a holder in due course or a purchaser, respectively. Delivery, possession, and endorsement are not required to obtain or exercise any of the rights under this subsection.

(e)   OBLIGOR RIGHTS.—Except as otherwise agreed, an obligor under a transferable record has the same rights and defenses as an equivalent obligor under equivalent records or writings under the Uniform Commercial Code.

(f)   PROOF OF CONTROL.—If requested by a person against which enforcement is sought, the person seeking to enforce the transferable record shall provide reasonable proof that the person is in control of the transferable record. Proof may include access to the authoritative copy of the transferable record and related business records sufficient to review the terms of the transferable record and to establish the identity of the person having control of the transferable record.

(g) UCC REFERENCES.—For purposes of this subsection, all references to the Uniform Commercial Code are to the Uniform Commercial Code as in effect in the jurisdiction the law of which governs the transferable record.

UNITED NATIONS CONVENTION ON CONTRACTS FOR THE INTERNATIONAL SALE OF GOODS

COMPILERS' NOTE

Since January 1, 1988 American exporters and importers have been subject to the Convention on Contracts for the International Sale of Goods (CISG). With respect to transactions within its scope, it displaces much of Article 2, Sales, of the Uniform Commercial Code—including, for example, the requirements of the statute of frauds (CISG 11).[1]

The Convention "applies to contracts for the sale of goods between parties whose places of business are in different States . . . when the States are Contracting States" (CISG 1).[2] The Convention preserves the autonomy of the parties by allowing them to "exclude the application of this Convention or . . . derogate from or vary the effect of any of its provisions" (CISG 6). The Convention does not displace rules of national law that relate to "the validity of the contract or of any of its provisions or of any usages." (CISG 4(a)).[3]

Work on the Convention began in the 1930s when the International Institute for the Unification of Private Law in Rome, then under the auspices of the League of Nations, set up a drafting committee of European scholars to work on a uniform law for international sales. By the outbreak of the Second World War, the committee had prepared a first draft, solicited comments from governments, and prepared a revised draft taking account of these comments.

After the War the Dutch Government appointed a commission to do further work, solicited comments from governments and, in 1964, convened a diplomatic conference at The Hague. The conference approved a uniform law on the international sale of goods (ULIS) and a shorter companion uniform law on the formation of contracts for the international sale of goods.

---

[1] The United States did not make the declaration described in CISG 12.

[2] In this context "States" means nations and "Contracting" means adopting. The United States did not accept CISG 1(b), which would have given the Convention a broader application.

[3] For a definitive treatment of the Convention, see J. Honnold, Uniform Law for International Sales under the 1980 U.N. Convention (4th ed. 2009). See also C. Bianca, M. Bonell et al., Commentary on the International Sales Law: The 1980 Vienna Convention (1987); P. Schlechtriem et al., Commentary on the UN Convention on the International Sale of Goods (CISG) (2d English ed. 2005).

Although the United States had quickly put together a delegation to The Hague to consider a draft prepared by a group of exclusively European scholars, that delegation's influence was not pervasive enough to produce a final text that justified United States ratification.[4] Nevertheless, ULIS did receive eight adoptions by other countries, enough for it to take effect.

Even before ULIS had taken effect, however, efforts were afoot under United Nations auspices to produce a revised international sales law that would be more widely acceptable. In 1966, the United Nations General Assembly established the United Nations Commission on International Trade Law (UNCITRAL). The Commission has "for its object the promotion of the progressive harmonization and unification of the law of international trade." Its members include common law as well as civil law countries, developing as well as industrialized countries, and countries with centrally planned economics as well as those with free-market economies.

In 1969, UNCITRAL appointed a fourteen-member Working Group on Sales to consider what changes in ULIS would make it more acceptable to countries of varied legal, social, and economic systems. The United States was an active member of this Working Group from its inception. In 1977 UNCITRAL revised and approved a text of CISG prepared by the Working Group on Sales, and in 1978 it integrated into CISG additional provisions on formation and interpretation. In 1980, the United Nations held in Vienna a diplomatic conference to propose a final text of CISG. After five weeks of intensive effort by the sixty-two countries represented, CISG—often referred to as "the Vienna Convention"—was adopted.

The final product of this half-century of work consists of eighty-eight substantive articles (what we in the United States would call "sections") plus thirteen more articles on effective date, reservations, and the like. Only the eighty-eight substantive articles are set out below. CISG took effect following adoption by ten countries. It has now been adopted by 89 countries (as of April 25, 2018), including the United States.

---

[4] The traditional scheme for international unification results in a multilateral treaty, put in final form at a diplomatic conference and then adopted by ratification or accession. One important difference between this scheme and that used for unification within the United States is that a country ratifying or acceding to a treaty cannot make changes in its text, except for a few variations that the diplomatic conference has allowed countries to make by means of reservations.

CONVENTION ON CONTRACTS FOR THE INTERNATIONAL SALE OF GOODS

THE STATES PARTIES TO THIS CONVENTION,

Bearing in mind the broad objectives in the resolutions adopted by the sixth special session of the General Assembly of the United Nations on the establishment of a New International Economic Order,

Considering that the development of international trade on the basis of equality and mutual benefit is an important element in promoting friendly relations among States,

Being of the opinion that the adoption of uniform rules which govern contracts for the international sale of goods and take into account the different social, economic and legal systems would contribute to the removal of legal barriers in international trade and promote the development of international trade,

Have agreed as follows:

Part I. Sphere of application and general provisions

CHAPTER I. SPHERE OF APPLICATION

Article 1

(1)   This Convention applies to contracts of sale of goods between parties whose places of business are in different States:

(a)   when the States are Contracting States; or

(b)   when the rules of private international law lead to the application of the law of a Contracting State.

(2)   The fact that the parties have their places of business in different States is to be disregarded whenever this fact does not appear either from the contract or from any dealings between, or from information disclosed by, the parties at any time before or at the conclusion of the contract.

(3)   Neither the nationality of the parties nor the civil or commercial character of the parties or of the contract is to be taken into consideration in determining the application of this Convention.

CONVENTION ON CONTRACTS FOR THE INTERNATIONAL SALE OF GOODS

Article 2

This Convention does not apply to sales:

- (a) of goods bought for personal, family or household use, unless the seller, at any time before or at the conclusion of the contract, neither knew nor ought to have known that the goods were bought for any such use;

- (b) by auction;

- (c) on execution or otherwise by authority of law;

- (d) of stocks, shares, investment securities, negotiable instruments or money;

- (e) of ships, vessels, hovercraft or aircraft;

- (f) of electricity.

Article 3

(1) Contracts for the supply of goods to be manufactured or produced are to be considered sales unless the party who order the goods undertakes to supply a substantial part of the materials necessary for such manufacture or production.

(2) This Convention does not apply to contracts in which the preponderant part of the obligations of the party who furnishes the goods consists in the supply of labour or other services.

Article 4

This Convention governs only the formation of the contract of sale and the rights and obligations of the seller and the buyer arising from such a contract. In particular, except as otherwise expressly provided in this Convention, it is not concerned with:

- (a) the validity of the contract or of any of its provisions or of any usage;

- (b) the effect which the contract may have on the property in the goods sold.

Article 5

This Convention does not apply to the liability of the seller for death or personal injury caused by the goods to any person.

Article 6

The parties may exclude the application of this Convention or, subject to article 12, derogate from or vary the effect of any of its provisions.

CHAPTER II.   GENERAL PROVISIONS

Article 7

(1)   In the interpretation of this Convention, regard is to be had to its international character and to the need to promote uniformity in its application and the observance of good faith in international trade.

(2)   Questions concerning matters governed by this Convention which are not expressly settled in it are to be settled in conformity with the general principles on which it is based or, in the absence of such principles, in conformity with the law applicable by virtue of the rules of private international law.

Article 8

(1)   For the purposes of this Convention statements made by and other conduct of a party are to be interpreted according to his intent where the other party knew or could not have been unaware what that intent was.

(2)   If the preceding paragraph is not applicable, statements made by and other conduct of a party are to be interpreted according to the understanding that a reasonable person of the same kind as the other party would have had in the same circumstances.

(3)   In determining the intent of a party or the understanding a reasonable person would have had, due consideration is to be given to all relevant circumstances of the case including the negotiations, any practices which the parties have established between themselves, usages and any subsequent conduct of the parties.

Article 9

(1)   The parties are bound by any usages to which they have agreed and by any practices which they have established between themselves.

(2)   The parties are considered, unless otherwise agreed, to have impliedly made applicable to their contract or its formation a usage of which the parties knew or ought to have known and which in international trade is widely known to, and regularly observed by, parties to contracts of the type involved in the particular trade concerned.

Article 10

For the purposes of this Convention:

  (a)   if a party has more than one place of business, the place of business is that which has the closest relationship to the contract and its performance, having regard to the circumstances known to or contemplated by the parties at any time before or at the conclusion of the contract;

(b)   if a party does not have a place of business, reference is to be made to his habitual residence.

Article 11

A Contract of sale need not be concluded in or evidenced by writing and is not subject to any other requirement as to form. It may be proved by any means, including witnesses.

Article 12

Any provision of article 11, article 29 or Part II of this Convention that allows a contract of sale or its modification or termination by agreement or any offer, acceptance or other indication of intention to be made in any form other than in writing does not apply where any party has his place of business in a Contracting State which has made a declaration under article 96 of this Convention. The parties may not derogate from or vary the effect of this article.

Article 13

For the purposes of this Convention "writing" includes telegram and telex.

Part II.   Formation of the contract

Article 14

(1)   A proposal for concluding a contract addressed to one or more specific persons constitutes an offer if it is sufficiently definite and indicates the intention of the offeror to be bound in case of acceptance. A proposal is sufficiently definite if it indicates the goods and expressly or implicitly fixes or makes provision for determining the quantity and the price.

(2)   A proposal other than one addressed to one or more specific persons is to be considered merely as an invitation to make offers, unless the contrary is clearly indicated by the person making the proposal.

Article 15

(1)   An offer becomes effective when it reaches the offeree.

(2)   An offer, even if it is irrevocable, may be withdrawn if the withdrawal reaches the offeree before or at the same time as the offer.

Article 16

(1)   Until a contract is concluded an offer may be revoked if the revocation reaches the offeree before he has dispatched an acceptance.

(2)   However, an offer cannot be revoked:

(a)   if it indicates, whether by stating a fixed time for acceptance or otherwise, that it is irrevocable; or

(b) if it was reasonable for the offeree to rely on the offer as being irrevocable and the offeree has acted in reliance on the offer.

Article 17

An offer, even if it is irrevocable, is terminated when a rejection reaches the offeror.

Article 18

(1) A statement made by or other conduct of the offeree indicating assent to an offer is an acceptance. Silence or inactivity does not in itself amount to acceptance.

(2) An acceptance of an offer becomes effective at the moment the indication of assent reaches the offeror. An acceptance is not effective if the indication of assent does not reach the offeror within the time he has fixed or, if no time is fixed, within a reasonable time, due account being taken of the circumstances of the transaction, including the rapidity of the means of communication employed by the offeror. An oral offer must be accepted immediately unless the circumstances indicate otherwise.

(3) However, if, by virtue of the offer or as a result of practices which the parties have established between themselves or of usage, the offeree may indicate assent by performing an act, such as one relating to the dispatch of the goods or payment of the price, without notice to the offeror, the acceptance is effective at the moment the act is performed, provided that the act is performed within the period of time laid down in the preceding paragraph.

Article 19

(1) A reply to an offer which purports to be an acceptance but contains additions, limitations or other modifications is a rejection of the offer and constitutes a counter-offer.

(2) However, a reply to an offer which purports to be an acceptance but contains additional or different terms which do not materially alter the terms of the offer constitutes an acceptance, unless the offeror, without undue delay, objects orally to the discrepancy or dispatches a notice to that effect. If he does not so object, the terms of the contract are the terms of the offer with the modifications contained in the acceptance.

(3) Additional or different terms relating, among other things, to the price, payment, quality and quantity of the goods, place and time of delivery, extent of one party's liability to the other or the settlement of disputes are considered to alter the terms of the offer materially.

Article 20

(1) A period of time for acceptance fixed by the offeror in a telegram or a letter begins to run from the moment the telegram is handed in for

dispatch or from the date shown on the letter or, if no such date is shown, from the date shown on the envelope. A period of time for acceptance fixed by the offeror by telephone, telex or other means of instantaneous communication, begins to run from the moment that the offer reaches the offeree.

(2) Official holidays or non-business days occurring during the period for acceptance are included in calculating the period. However, if a notice of acceptance cannot be delivered at the address of the offeror on the last day of the period because that day falls on an official holiday or a non-business day at the place of business of the offeror, the period is extended until the first business day which follows.

Article 21

(1) A late acceptance is nevertheless effective as an acceptance if without delay the offeror orally so informs the offeree or dispatches a notice to that effect.

(2) If a letter or other writing containing a late acceptance shows that it has been sent in such circumstances that if its transmission had been normal it would have reached the offeror in due time, the late acceptance is effective as an acceptance unless, without delay, the offeror orally informs the offeree that he considers his offer as having lapsed or dispatches a notice to that effect.

Article 22

An acceptance may be withdrawn if the withdrawal reaches the offeror before or at the same time as the acceptance would have become effective.

Article 23

A contract is concluded at the moment when an acceptance of an offer becomes effective in accordance with the provisions of this Convention.

Article 24

For the purposes of this Part of the Convention, an offer, declaration of acceptance or any other indication of intention "reaches" the addressee when it is made orally to him or delivered by any other means to him personally, to his place of business or mailing address or, if he does not have a place of business or mailing address, to his habitual residence.

Part III. Sale of goods

CHAPTER I. GENERAL PROVISIONS

Article 25

A breach of contract committed by one of the parties is fundamental if it results in such detriment to the other party as substantially to deprive him of what he is entitled to expect under the contract, unless the party in breach did not foresee, and a reasonable person of the same kind in the same circumstances would not have foreseen, such a result.

Article 26

A declaration of avoidance of the contract is effective only if made by notice to the other party.

Article 27

Unless otherwise expressly provided in this Part of the Convention, if any notice, request or other communication is given or made by a party in accordance with this Part, and by means appropriate in the circumstances, a delay or error in the transmission of the communication or its failure to arrive does not deprive that party of the right to rely on the communication.

Article 28

If, in accordance with the provisions of this Convention, one party is entitled to require performance of any obligation by the other party, a court is not bound to enter a judgment for specific performance unless the court would do so under its own law in respect of similar contracts of sale not governed by this Convention.

Article 29

(1) A contract may be modified or terminated by the mere agreement of the parties.

(2) A contract in writing which contains a provision requiring any modification or termination by agreement to be in writing may not be otherwise modified or terminated by agreement. However, a party may be precluded by his conduct from asserting such a provision to the extent that the other party has relied on that conduct.

CHAPTER II.   OBLIGATIONS OF THE SELLER

Article 30

The seller must deliver the goods, hand over any documents relating to them and transfer the property in the goods, as required by the contract and this Convention.

Section I.   Delivery of the goods and handing over of documents

Article 31

If the seller is not bound to deliver the goods at any other particular place, his obligation to deliver consists:

(a) if the contract of sale involves carriage of the goods—in handing the goods over to the first carrier for transmission to the buyer;

(b) if, in cases not within the preceding subparagraph, the contract relates to specific goods, or unidentified goods to be drawn from a specific stock or to be manufactured or produced, and at the time of the conclusion of the contract the parties knew that the goods were at, or were to be manufactured or produced at, a particular place—in placing the goods at the buyer's disposal at that place;

(c) in other cases—in placing the goods at the buyer's disposal at the place where the seller had his place of business at the time of the conclusion of the contract.

Article 32

(1) If the seller, in accordance with the contract or this Convention, hands the goods over to a carrier and if the goods are not clearly identified to the contract by markings on the goods, by shipping documents or otherwise, the seller must give the buyer notice of the consignment specifying the goods.

(2) If the seller is bound to arrange for carriage of the goods, he must make such contracts as are necessary for carriage to the place fixed by means of transportation appropriate in the circumstances and according to the usual terms for such transportation.

(3) If the seller is not bound to effect insurance in respect of the carriage of the goods, he must, at the buyer's request, provide him with all available information necessary to enable him to effect such insurance.

Article 33

The seller must deliver the goods:

(a) if a date is fixed by or determinable from the contract, on that date;

(b) if a period of time is fixed by or determinable from the contract, at any time within that period unless circumstances indicate that the buyer is to choose a date; or

(c) in any other case, within a reasonable time after the conclusion of the contract.

Article 34

If the seller is bound to hand over documents relating to the goods, he must hand them over at the time and place and in the form required by the contract. If the seller has handed over documents before that time, he may, up to that time, cure any lack of conformity in the documents, if the exercise of this right does not cause the buyer unreasonable inconvenience or unreasonable expense. However, the buyer retains any right to claim damages as provided for in this Convention.

Section II.   Conformity of the goods and third party claims

Article 35

(1)   The seller must deliver goods which are of the quantity, quality and description required by the contract and which are contained or packaged in the manner required by the contract.

(2)   Except where the parties have agreed otherwise, the goods do not conform with the contract unless they:

    (a)   are fit for the purposes for which goods of the same description would ordinarily be used;

    (b)   are fit for any particular purpose expressly or impliedly made known to the seller at the time of the conclusion of the contract, except where the circumstances show that the buyer did not rely, or that it was unreasonable for him to rely, on the seller's skill and judgment;

    (c)   possess the qualities of goods which the seller has held out to the buyer as a sample or model;

    (d)   are contained or packaged in the manner usual for such goods or, where there is no such manner, in a manner adequate to preserve and protect the goods.

(3)   The seller is not liable under subparagraphs (a) to (d) of the preceding paragraph for any lack of conformity of the goods if at the time of the conclusion of the contract the buyer knew or could not have been unaware of such lack of conformity.

Article 36

(1)   The seller is liable in accordance with the contract and this Convention for any lack of conformity which exists at the time when the risk passes to the buyer, even though the lack of conformity becomes apparent only after that time.

(2)   The seller is also liable for any lack of conformity which occurs after the time indicated in the preceding paragraph and which is due to a breach of any of his obligations, including a breach of any guarantee that for a period of time the goods will remain fit for their ordinary purpose or for some particular purpose or will retain specified qualities or characteristics.

Article 37

If the seller has delivered goods before the date for delivery, he may, up to that date, deliver any missing part or make up any deficiency in the quantity of the goods delivered, or deliver goods in replacement of any nonconforming goods delivered or remedy any lack of conformity in the goods delivered, provided that the exercise of this right does not cause the buyer unreasonable inconvenience or unreasonable expense. However, the buyer retains any right to claim damages as provided for in this Convention.

Article 38

(1) The buyer must examine the goods, or cause them to be examined, within as short a period as is practicable in the circumstances.

(2) If the contract involves carriage of the goods, examination may be deferred until after the goods have arrived at their destination.

(3) If the goods are redirected in transit or redispatched by the buyer without a reasonable opportunity for examination by him and at the time of the conclusion of the contract the seller knew or ought to have known of the possibility of such redirection or redispatch, examination may be deferred until after the goods have arrived at the new destination.

Article 39

(1) The buyer loses the right to rely on a lack of conformity of the goods if he does not give notice to the seller specifying the nature of the lack of conformity within a reasonable time after he has discovered it or ought to have discovered it.

(2) In any event, the buyer loses the right to rely on a lack of conformity of the goods if he does not give the seller notice thereof at the latest within a period of two years from the date on which the goods were actually handed over to the buyer, unless this time-limit is inconsistent with a contractual period of guarantee.

Article 40

The seller is not entitled to rely on the provisions of articles 38 and 39 if the lack of conformity relates to facts of which he knew or could not have been unaware and which he did not disclose to the buyer.

Article 41

The seller must deliver goods which are free from any right or claim of a third party, unless the buyer agreed to take the goods subject to that right or claim. However, if such right or claim is based on industrial property or other intellectual property, the seller's obligation is governed by article 42.

Article 42

(1) The seller must deliver goods which are free from any right or claim of a third party based on industrial property or other intellectual property, of which at the time of the conclusion of the contract the seller

knew or could not have been unaware, provided that the right or claim is based on industrial property or other intellectual property:

    (a)   under the law of the State where the goods will be resold or otherwise used, if it was contemplated by the parties at the time of the conclusion of the contract that the goods would be resold or otherwise used in that State; or

    (b)   in any other case, under the law of the State where the buyer has his place of business.

(2)   The obligation of the seller under the preceding paragraph does not extend to cases where:

    (a)   at the time of the conclusion of the contract the buyer knew or could not have been unaware of the right or claim; or

    (b)   the right or claim results from the seller's compliance with technical drawings, designs, formulae or other such specifications furnished by the buyer.

Article 43

(1)   The buyer loses the right to rely on the provisions of article 41 or article 42 if he does not give notice to the seller specifying the nature of the right or claim of the third party within a reasonable time after he has become aware or ought to have become aware of the right or claim.

(2)   The seller is not entitled to rely on the provisions of the preceding paragraph if he knew of the right or claim of the third party and the nature of it.

Article 44

Notwithstanding the provisions of paragraph (1) of article 39 and paragraph (1) of article 43, the buyer may reduce the price in accordance with article 50 or claim damages, except for loss of profit, if he has a reasonable excuse for his failure to give the required notice.

Section III.   Remedies for breach of contract by the seller

Article 45

(1)   If the seller fails to perform any of his obligations under the contract or this Convention, the buyer may:

    (a)   exercise the rights provided in articles 46 to 52;

    (b)   claim damages as provided in articles 74 to 77.

(2)   The buyer is not deprived of any right he may have to claim damages by exercising his right to other remedies.

(3)   No period of grace may be granted to the seller by a court or arbitral tribunal when the buyer resorts to a remedy for breach of contract.

Article 46

(1)   The buyer may require performance by the seller of his obligations unless the buyer has resorted to a remedy which is inconsistent with this requirement.

(2)   If the goods do not conform with the contract, the buyer may require delivery of substitute goods only if the lack of conformity constitutes a fundamental breach of contract and a request for substitute goods is made either in conjunction with notice given under article 39 or within a reasonable time thereafter.

(3)   If the goods do not conform with the contract, the buyer may require the seller to remedy the lack of conformity by repair, unless this is unreasonable having regard to all the circumstances. A request for repair must be made either in conjunction with notice given under article 39 or within a reasonable time thereafter.

Article 47

(1)   The buyer may fix an additional period of time of reasonable length for performance by the seller of his obligations.

(2)   Unless the buyer has received notice from the seller that he will not perform within the period so fixed, the buyer may not, during that period, resort to any remedy for breach of contract. However, the buyer is not deprived thereby of any right he may have to claim damages for delay in performance.

Article 48

(1)   Subject to article 49, the seller may, even after the date for delivery, remedy at his own expense any failure to perform his obligations, if he can do so without unreasonable delay and without causing the buyer unreasonable inconvenience or uncertainty of reimbursement by the seller of expenses advanced by the buyer. However, the buyer retains any right to claim damages as provided for in this Convention.

(2)   If the seller requests the buyer to make known whether he will accept performance and the buyer does not comply with the request within a reasonable time, the seller may perform within the time indicated in his request. The buyer may not, during that period of time, resort to any remedy which is inconsistent with performance by the seller.

(3)   A notice by the seller that he will perform within a specified period of time is assumed to include a request, under the preceding paragraph, that the buyer make known his decision.

(4)   A request or notice by the seller under paragraph (2) or (3) of this article is not effective unless received by the buyer.

Article 49

(1) The buyer may declare the contract avoided:

(a) if the failure by the seller to perform any of his obligations under the contract or this Convention amounts to a fundamental breach of contract; or

(b) in case of non-delivery, if the seller does not deliver the goods within the additional period of time fixed by the buyer in accordance with paragraph (1) of article 47 or declares that he will not deliver within the period so fixed.

(2) However, in cases where the seller has delivered the goods, the buyer loses the right to declare the contract avoided unless he does so:

(a) in respect of late delivery, within a reasonable time after he has become aware that delivery has been made;

(b) in respect of any breach other than late delivery, within a reasonable time:

(i) after he knew or ought to have known of the breach;

(ii) after the expiration of any additional period of time fixed by the buyer in accordance with paragraph (1) of article 47, or after the seller has declared that he will not perform his obligations within such an additional period; or

(iii) after the expiration of any additional period of time indicated by the seller in accordance with paragraph (2) of article 48, or after the buyer has declared that he will not accept performance.

Article 50

If the goods do not conform with the contract and whether or not the price has already been paid, the buyer may reduce the price in the same proportion as the value that the goods actually delivered had at the time of the delivery bears to the value that conforming goods would have had at that time. However, if the seller remedies any failure to perform his obligations in accordance with article 37 or article 48 or if the buyer refuses to accept performance by the seller in accordance with those articles, the buyer may not reduce the price.

Article 51

(1) If the seller delivers only a part of the goods or if only a part of the goods delivered is in conformity with the contract, articles 46 to 50 apply in respect of the part which is missing or which does not conform.

(2) The buyer may declare the contract avoided in its entirety only if the failure to make delivery completely or in conformity with the contract amounts to a fundamental breach of the contract.

Article 52

(1)   If the seller delivers the goods before the date fixed, the buyer may take delivery or refuse to take delivery.

(2)   If the seller delivers a quantity of goods greater than that provided for in the contract, the buyer may take delivery or refuse to take delivery of the excess quantity. If the buyer takes delivery of all or part of the excess quantity, he must pay for it at the contract rate.

CHAPTER III.   OBLIGATIONS OF THE BUYER

Article 53

The buyer must pay the price for the goods and take delivery of them as required by the contract and this Convention.

Section I.   Payment of the price

Article 54

The buyer's obligation to pay the price includes taking such steps and complying with such formalities as may be required under the contract or any laws and regulations to enable payment to be made.

Article 55

Where a contract has been validly concluded but does not expressly or implicitly fix or make provision for determining the price, the parties are considered, in the absence of any indication to the contrary, to have impliedly made reference to the price generally charged at the time of the conclusion of the contract for such goods sold under comparable circumstances in the trade concerned.

Article 56

If the price is fixed according to the weight of the goods, in case of doubt it is to be determined by the net weight.

Article 57

(1)   If the buyer is not bound to pay the price at any other particular place, he must pay it to the seller:

   (a)   at the seller's place of business; or

   (b)   if the payment is to be made against the handing over of the goods or of documents, at the place where the handing over takes place.

(2)   The seller must bear any increase in the expenses incidental to payment which is caused by a change in his place of business subsequent to the conclusion of the contract.

Article 58

(1)   If the buyer is not bound to pay the price at any other specific time, he must pay it when the seller places either the goods or documents controlling their disposition at the buyer's disposal in accordance with the contract and this Convention. The seller may make such payment a condition for handing over the goods or documents.

(2)   If the contract involves carriage of the goods, the seller may dispatch the goods on terms whereby the goods, or documents controlling their disposition, will not be handed over to the buyer except against payment of the price.

(3)   The buyer is not bound to pay the price until he has had an opportunity to examine the goods, unless the procedures for delivery or payment agreed upon by the parties are inconsistent with his having such an opportunity.

Article 59

The buyer must pay the price on the date fixed by or determinable from the contract and this Convention without the need for any request or compliance with any formality on the part of the seller.

Section II.   Taking delivery

Article 60

The buyer's obligation to take delivery consists:

(a)   in doing all the acts which could reasonably be expected of him in order to enable the seller to make delivery; and

(b)   in taking over the goods.

Section III.   Remedies for breach of contract by the buyer

Article 61

(1)   If the buyer fails to perform any of his obligations under the contract or this Convention, the seller may:

(a)   exercise the rights provided in articles 62 to 65;

(b)   claim damages as provided in articles 74 to 77.

(2)   The seller is not deprived of any right he may have to claim damages by exercising his right to other remedies.

(3)   No period of grace may be granted to the buyer by a court or arbitral tribunal when the seller resorts to a remedy for breach of contract.

Article 62

The seller may require the buyer to pay the price, take delivery or perform his other obligations, unless the seller has resorted to a remedy which is inconsistent with this requirement.

Article 63

(1) The seller may fix an additional period of time of reasonable length for performance by the buyer of his obligations.

(2) Unless the seller has received notice from the buyer that he will not perform within the period so fixed, the seller may not, during that period, resort to any remedy for breach of contract. However, the seller is not deprived thereby of any right he may have to claim damages for delay in performance.

Article 64

(1) The seller may declare the contract avoided:

(a) if the failure by the buyer to perform any of his obligations under the contract or this Convention amounts to a fundamental breach of contract; or

(b) if the buyer does not, within the additional period of time fixed by the seller in accordance with paragraph (1) of article 63, perform his obligation to pay the price or take delivery of the goods, or declares that he will not do so within the period so fixed.

(2) However, in cases where the buyer has paid the price, the seller loses the right to declare the contract avoided unless he does so:

(a) in respect of late performance by the buyer, before the seller has become aware that performance has been rendered; or

(b) in respect of any breach other than late performance by the buyer, within a reasonable time:

(i) after the seller knew or ought to have known of the breach; or

(ii) after the expiration of any additional period of time fixed by the seller in accordance with paragraph (1) of article 63, or after the buyer has declared that he will not perform his obligations within such an additional period.

Article 65

(1) If under the contract the buyer is to specify the form, measurement or other features of the goods and he fails to make such specification either on the date agreed upon or within a reasonable time after receipt of a request from the seller, the seller may, without prejudice to any other

rights he may have, make the specification himself in accordance with the requirements of the buyer that may be known to him.

(2)   If the seller makes the specification himself, he must inform the buyer of the details thereof and must fix a reasonable time within which the buyer may make a different specification. If, after receipt of such a communication, the buyer fails to do so within the time so fixed, the specification made by the seller is binding.

CHAPTER IV.   PASSING OF RISK

Article 66

Loss of or damage to the goods after the risk has passed to the buyer does not discharge him from his obligation to pay the price, unless the loss or damage is due to an act or omission of the seller.

Article 67

(1)   If the contract of sale involves carriage of the goods and the seller is not bound to hand them over at a particular place, the risk passes to the buyer when the goods are handed over to the first carrier for transmission to the buyer in accordance with the contract of sale. If the seller is bound to hand the goods over to a carrier at a particular place, the risk does not pass to the buyer until the goods are handed over to the carrier at that place. The fact that the seller is authorized to retain documents controlling the disposition of the goods does not affect the passage of the risk.

(2)   Nevertheless, the risk does not pass to the buyer until the goods are clearly identified to the contract, whether by markings on the goods, by shipping documents, by notice given to the buyer or otherwise.

Article 68

The risk in respect of goods sold in transit passes to the buyer from the time of the conclusion of the contract. However, if the circumstances so indicate, the risk is assumed by the buyer from the time the goods were handed over to the carrier who issued the documents embodying the contract of carriage. Nevertheless, if at the time of the conclusion of the contract of sale the seller knew or ought to have known that the goods had been lost or damaged and did not disclose this to the buyer, the loss or damage is at the risk of the seller.

Article 69

(1)   In cases not within articles 67 and 68, the risk passes to the buyer when he takes over the goods or, if he does not do so in due time, from the time when the goods are placed at his disposal he commits a breach of contract by failing to take delivery.

(2)   However, if the buyer is bound to take over the goods at a place other than a place of business of the seller, the risk passes when delivery is due and the buyer is aware of the fact that the goods are placed at his disposal at that place.

(3)   If the contract relates to goods not then identified, the goods are considered not to be placed at the disposal of the buyer until they are clearly identified to the contract.

Article 70

If the seller has committed a fundamental breach of contract, articles 67, 68, and 69 do not impair the remedies available to the buyer on account of the breach.

CHAPTER V.   PROVISIONS COMMON TO THE OBLIGATIONS OF THE SELLER AND OF THE BUYER

Section I.   Anticipatory breach and installment contracts

Article 71

(1)   A party may suspend the performance of his obligations if, after the conclusion of the contract, it becomes apparent that the other party will not perform a substantial part of his obligations as a result of:

  (a)   a serious deficiency in his ability to perform or in his credit-worthiness; or

  (b)   his conduct in preparing to perform or in performing the contract.

(2)   If the seller has already dispatched the goods before the grounds described in the preceding paragraph become evident, he may prevent the handing over of the goods to the buyer even though the buyer holds a document which entitles him to obtain them. The present paragraph relates only to the rights in the goods as between the buyer and the seller.

(3)   A party suspending performance, whether before or after dispatch of the goods, must immediately give notice of the suspension to the other party and must continue with performance if the other party provides adequate assurance of his performance.

Article 72

(1)   If prior to the date for performance of the contract it is clear that one of the parties will commit a fundamental breach of contract, the other party may declare the contract avoided.

(2)   If time allows, the party intending to declare the contract avoided must give reasonable notice to the other party in order to permit him to provide adequate assurance of his performance.

(3)   The requirements of the preceding paragraph do not apply if the other party has declared that he will not perform his obligations.

Article 73

(1)   In the case of a contract for delivery of goods by instalments, if the failure of one party to perform any of his obligations in respect of any instalment constitutes a fundamental breach of contract with respect to that instalment, the other party may declare the contract avoided with respect to that instalment.

(2)   If one party's failure to perform any of his obligations in respect of any instalment gives the other party good grounds to conclude that a fundamental breach of contract will occur with respect to future instalments, he may declare the contract avoided for the future, provided that he does so within a reasonable time.

(3)   A buyer who declares the contract avoided in respect of any delivery may, at the same time, declare it avoided in respect of deliveries already made or of future deliveries if, by reason of their interdependence, those deliveries could not be used for the purpose contemplated by the parties at the time of the conclusion of the contract.

Section II.   Damages

Article 74

Damages for breach of contract by one party consist of a sum equal to the loss, including loss of profit, suffered by the other party as a consequence of the breach. Such damages may not exceed the loss which the party in breach foresaw or ought to have foreseen at the time of the conclusion of the contract, in the light of the facts and matters of which he then knew or ought to have known, as a possible consequence of the breach of contract.

Article 75

If the contract is avoided and if, in a reasonable manner and within a reasonable time after avoidance, the buyer has bought goods in replacement or the seller has resold the goods, the party claiming damages may recover the difference between the contract price and the price in the substitute transaction as well as any further damages recoverable under article 74.

Article 76

(1)   If the contract is avoided and there is a current price for the goods, the party claiming damages may, if he has not made a purchase

or resale under article 75, recover the difference between the price fixed by the contract and the current price at the time of avoidance as well as any further damages recoverable under article 74. If, however, the party claiming damages has avoided the contract after taking over the goods, the current price at the time of such taking over shall be applied instead of the current price at the time of avoidance.

(2) For the purposes of the preceding paragraph, the current price is the price prevailing at the place where delivery of the goods should have been made or, if there is no current price at that place, the price at such other place as serves as a reasonable substitute, making due allowance for differences in the cost of transporting the goods.

Article 77

A party who relies on a breach of contract must take such measures as are reasonable in the circumstances to mitigate the loss, including loss of profit, resulting from the breach. If he fails to take such measures, the party in breach may claim a reduction in the damages in the amount by which the loss should have been mitigated.

Section III. Interest

Article 78

If a party fails to pay the price or any other sum that is in arrears, the other party is entitled to interest on it, without prejudice to any claim for damages recoverable under article 74.

Section IV. Exemptions

Article 79

(1) A party is not liable for a failure to perform any of his obligations if he proves that the failure was due to an impediment beyond his control and that he could not reasonably be expected to have taken the impediment into account at the time of the conclusion of the contract or to have avoided or overcome it or its consequences.

(2) If the party's failure is due to the failure by a third person whom he has engaged to perform the whole or a party of the contract, that party is exempt from liability only if:

(a) he is exempt under the preceding paragraph; and

(b) the person whom he has so engaged would be so exempt if the provisions of that paragraph were applied to him.

(3) The exemption provided by this article has effect for the period during which the impediment exists.

(4) The party who fails to perform must give notice to the other party of the impediment and its effect on his ability to perform. If the notice is

not received by the other party within a reasonable time after the party who fails to perform knew or ought to have known of the impediment, he is liable for damages resulting from such non-receipt.

(5)   Nothing in this article prevents either party from exercising any right other than to claim damages under this Convention.

Article 80

A party may not rely on a failure of the other party to perform, to the extent that such failure was caused by the first party's act or omission.

Section V.   Effects of avoidance

Article 81

(1)   Avoidance of the contract releases both parties from their obligations under it, subject to any damages which may be due. Avoidance does not affect any provision of the contract for the settlement of disputes or any other provision of the contract governing the rights and obligations of the parties consequent upon the avoidance of the contract.

(2)   A party who has performed the contract either wholly or in part may claim restitution from the other party of whatever the first party has supplied or paid under the contract. If both parties are bound to make restitution, they must do so concurrently.

Article 82

(1)   The buyer loses the right to declare the contract avoided or to require the seller to deliver substitute goods if it is impossible for him to make restitution of the goods substantially in the condition in which he received them.

(2)   The preceding paragraph does not apply:

  (a)   if the impossibility of making restitution of the goods or of making restitution of the goods substantially in the condition in which the buyer received them is not due to his act or omission;

  (b)   if the goods or part of the goods have perished or deteriorated as a result of the examination provided for in article 38; or

  (c)   if the goods or part of the goods have been sold in the normal course of business or have been consumed or transformed by the buyer in the course of normal use before he discovered or ought to have discovered the lack of conformity.

Article 83

A buyer who has lost the right to declare the contract avoided or to require the seller to deliver substitute goods in accordance with article 82 retains all other remedies under the contract and this Convention.

Article 84

(1)   If the seller is bound to refund the price, he must also pay interest on it, from the date on which the price was paid.

(2)   The buyer must account to the seller for all benefits which he has derived from the goods or part of them:

(a)   if he must make restitution of the goods or part of them; or

(b)   if it is impossible for him to make restitution of all or part of the goods or to make restitution of all or part of the goods substantially in the condition in which he received them, but he has nevertheless declared the contract avoided or required the seller to deliver substitute goods.

Section VI.   Preservation of the goods

Article 85

If the buyer is in delay in taking delivery of the goods or, where payment of the price and delivery of the goods are to be made concurrently, if he fails to pay the price, and the seller is either in possession of the goods or otherwise able to control their disposition, the seller must take such steps as are reasonable in the circumstances to preserve them. He is entitled to retain them until he has been reimbursed his reasonable expenses by the buyer.

Article 86

(1)   If the buyer has received the goods and intends to exercise any right under the contract or this Convention to reject them, he must take such steps to preserve them as are reasonable in the circumstances. He is entitled to retain them until he has been reimbursed his reasonable expenses by the seller.

(2)   If goods dispatched to the buyer have been placed at his disposal at their destination and he exercises the right to reject them, he must take possession of them on behalf of the seller, provided that this can be done without payment of the price and without unreasonable inconvenience or unreasonable expense. This provision does not apply if the seller or a person authorized to take charge of the goods on his behalf is present at the destination. If the buyer takes possession of the goods under this paragraph, his rights and obligations are governed by the preceding paragraph.

Article 87

A party who is bound to take steps to preserve the goods may deposit them in a warehouse of a third person at the expense of the other party provided that the expense incurred is not unreasonable.

Article 88

(1) A party who is bound to preserve the goods in accordance with article 85 or 86 may sell them by any appropriate means if there has been an unreasonable delay by the other party in taking possession of the goods or in taking them back or in paying the price or the cost of preservation, provided that reasonable notice of the intention to sell has been given to the other party.

(2) If the goods are subject to rapid deterioration or their preservation would involve unreasonable expense, a party who is bound to preserve the goods in accordance with article 85 or 86 must take reasonable measures to sell them. To the extent possible he must give notice to the other party of this intention to sell.

(3) A party selling the goods has the right to retain out of the proceeds of sale an amount equal to the reasonable expenses of preserving the goods and of selling them. He must account to the other party for the balance.

UNIDROIT PRINCIPLES OF INTERNATIONAL COMMERCIAL CONTRACTS

COMPILERS' NOTE[1]

In 1994, an important body of rules for international contracts, the UNIDROIT Principles of International Commercial Contracts, was promulgated.[2] Like the Restatements, the Principles are not designed for legislative enactment. What is the source of these Principles? "For the most part," their Introduction explains, they "reflect concepts to be found in many, if not all, legal systems," though "they also embody what are perceived to be the best solutions, even if still not yet generally adopted." These concepts are drawn from a variety of sources such as the United Nations Convention on Contracts for the International Sale of Goods (CISG), generally recognized principles of civil law systems, and generally recognized principles of common law systems—including the Uniform Commercial Code and the Restatement (Second) of Contracts.

Since the Principles have not been enacted by a legislature, parties that want them to apply should incorporate them, either by name or generally. According to their Preamble, they "set forth general rules for international commercial contracts" to be applied "when the parties have agreed that their contract be governed by [them or by] 'general principles of law,' the 'lex mercatoria' or the like." It is likely that their impact will be largely in international arbitration, and their Preamble suggests that arbitrators apply them if "it proves impossible to establish the relevant rule of the applicable law." This might be the case if it is uncertain what law is applicable or if, though this is certain, that law lacks a clear rule. Because CISG covers international sales of goods, it is likely that the Principles will be significant in disputes arising under other types of contracts, notably contracts for services.

The Principles are the product of the same organization that began the work on the unification of the law of international sales, the International Institute for the Unification of Private Law (UNIDROIT) in Rome.

---

[1] Copyright by E. Farnsworth. This Note is adapted from Farnsworth on Contracts § 1.8a (3d ed. 2004) and is used with permission.

[2] For discussion by the chair of the working group that drafted the Principles, see M. Bonell, An International Restatement of Contract Law: The UNIDROIT Principles of International Commercial Contracts (2d ed.1997) (includes bibliography and the text in eight languages). See generally Perillo, UNIDROIT Principles of International Commercial Contracts: The Black Letter Text and a Review, 63 Fordham L.Rev. 281 (1994); Zimmermann, The Present State of European Private Law, 57 Am.J.Comp.L. 479 (2009); Symposium, 69 Tul.L.Rev. 1121 (1995); Symposium, 3 Tul.J.Intl. & Comp.L. 45 (1995); Symposium, 40 Am.J.Comp.L. 541 (1992).

Founded in 1926 under the auspices of the League of Nations, it has continued as an independent governmental organization of which the United States is a member. The idea of drafting the Principles dates back to 1971, when the topic was put on the Institute's work program, but it was not until 1980 that the Institute set up a working group, which the United States joined toward the end of that decade. After more than a decade of semiannual meetings of the working group, the Institute's Governing Council approved publication of the Principles in 1994. Like the Restatement and the Uniform Commercial Code, they are accompanied by comments, illustrations, and section captions. Their initial success was such that the set of Principles has been expanded twice—in 2004 and 2011. A similar effort, under different auspices, has prepared a set of Principles of European Contract Law.[3]

The Principles contain some 211 articles and deal with such matters as contract formation, performance, excuse from performance, and remedies. As to many of these matters they track the provisions of CISG. On some matters, however, the Principles break fresh ground. These include precontractual liability, hardship as an excuse for nonperformance, specific performance, and stipulated damages.

The Principles also break fresh ground by stating a number of general principles. One is freedom of contract: "parties are free to enter into a contract and to determine its contents"[4] and "may exclude the application of these Principles . . . or vary [their] effect."[5] A second is *pacta sunt servanda* (agreements are to be observed): if "performance becomes more onerous for one of the parties, that party is nevertheless bound to perform its obligations."[6] A third is fairness: a party may avoid a contract or term "if, at the time of the conclusion of the contract, the contract or term unjustifiably gave the other party an excessive advantage,"[7] and a term "contained in standard terms" that "is of such a character that the other party could not reasonably have expected it" is not effective unless expressly accepted by that party.[8] A fourth is good faith and fair dealing: a "party must act in accordance with good faith and fair dealing in international trade."[9]

The Principles raise troublesome questions concerning mandatory rules—rules that the parties are not free to change by agreement. Given that the Principles are generally applicable only as a result of agreement of the parties, one might make two assumptions as to mandatory rules. The first is that the parties would be completely free to exclude or modify the Principles, an assumption that seems to be confirmed by the principle of freedom of contract mentioned above. The second is that the parties

---

[3] Principles of European Contract Law (Parts I & II) (2000) (includes comments, illustrations, and citations to largely European national sources).

[4] Art. 1.1 ("Freedom of contract").

[5] Art. 1.5 ("Exclusion or modification by the parties").

[6] Art. 6.2.1 ("Contract to be observed").

[7] Art. 3.10 ("Gross disparity").

[8] Art. 2.20 ("Surprising terms").

[9] Art. 1.7 ("Good faith and fair dealing").

could not themselves exclude or modify mandatory rules of the applicable law, an assumption that seems to be confirmed by a provision that the Principles do not "restrict the application of mandatory rules . . . which are applicable in accordance with the relevant rules of private international law."[10]

Perhaps surprisingly, the Principles qualify both assumptions. As to the first assumption, despite the general principle of freedom of contract, the Principles subject their declaration that they may be excluded or varied by the parties to an exception where "otherwise provided in the Principles."[11] These exceptions include the rules on good faith and fair dealing[12] and on gross disparity.[13] It is, to be sure, unlikely that parties would include in their contracts explicit provisions derogating from either of these rules, but if they were to do so it might be difficult to explain why such provisions should not be given effect. As to the second assumption, despite the statement that the Principles cannot affect mandatory rules, the Principles seem to contemplate exceptions as to the requirement of a writing, the requirement for modification of an agreement, the availability of specific performance, and the enforceability of a provision for stipulated damages. As to all of these, the Principles state rules that change common law rules that the parties cannot change by agreement—common law mandatory rules.

At its 83rd session in 2004 the Governing Council of UNIDROIT adopted a second edition of the UNIDROIT Principles. As compared to the 1994 edition, the new edition contained 5 additional chapters as well as an expanded Preamble and new provisions on Inconsistent Behaviour and on Release by Agreement. In addition, wherever appropriate the 1994 edition of the Principles were adapted to meet the needs of electronic contracting.

At its 90th session the Governing Council of UNIDROIT adopted the third edition of the UNIDROIT Principles of International Commercial Contracts ("UNIDROIT principles 2010"). The UNIDROIT Principles 2010 contain new provisions on restitution in case of failed contracts, illegality, conditions, and plurality of obligors and obligees, while with respect to the text of the 2004 edition the only significant changes made relate to the Comments to Article 1.4.

The third edition of the UNIDROIT Principles consists of 211 Articles (as opposed to the 120 Articles of the 1994 edition and the 185 Articles of the 2004 edition) structured as follows: Preamble (*unchanged*); Chapter 1: General provisions (*unchanged*); Chapter 2, Section 1: Formation (*unchanged*); Section 2: Authority of agents (*unchanged*); Chapter 3, Section 1: General provisions (*containing former Articles 3.1 (amended), 3.2, 3.3*

---

[10] Art. 1.4 ("Mandatory rules").
[11] Art. 1.5.

[12] Art. 1.7.
[13] Art. 3.10.

and 3.19 (*amended*)), Section 2: Ground for avoidance (*containing former Articles 3.4 to 3.16, 3.17 (amended), 3.18 and 3.20, and a new Article 3.2.15*), Section 3: Illegality (*new*); Chapter 4: Interpretation (*unchanged*); Chapter 5, Section 1: Content (*unchanged*); Section 2: Third Party Rights (*unchanged*); Section 3: Conditions (*new*); Chapter 6, Section 1: Performance in general (*unchanged*), Section 2: Hardship (*unchanged*); Chapter 7, Section 1: Non-performance in general (*unchanged*); Section 2: Right to performance (*unchanged*); Section 3: Termination (*containing former Articles 7.3.1 to 7.3.5, 7.3.6 (amended) and a new Article 7.3.7*), Section 4: Damages (*unchanged*); Chapter 8: Set-off (*unchanged*); Chapter 9, Section 1: Assignment of rights (*unchanged*); Section 2: Transfer of obligations (*unchanged*); Section 3: Assignment of contracts (*unchanged*); Chapter 10: Limitation periods (*unchanged*); Chapter 11, Section 1: Plurality of obligors (*new*), Section 2: Plurality of obligees (*new*).

In 2016, a fourth edition of the UNIDROIT Principles was adopted. The main objective of the fourth edition of the UNIDROIT Principles is to take better into account the special needs of long-term contracts. To do so, the content of the 2010 edition has been altered only marginally: only six provisions have been amended, i.e. the Preamble and Articles 1.11, 2.1.14, 5.1.7, 5.1.8, and 7.3.7. Indeed, the majority of alterations were made to the Comments, in particular on the Preamble (amendments to Comment 2) and Articles 1.11 (addition of a new Comment 3), 2.1.14 (amendments to Comments 1–3 and addition of a new Comment 4), 2.1.15 (amendments to Comment 2 and addition of a new Comment 3), 4.3 (amendments to Comment 3 (which has become Comment 4) and addition of a new Comment 3), 4.8 (amendments to Comments 1–3), 5.1.3 (amendments to the Comment (which has become Comment 1) and addition of a new Comment 2), 5.1.4 (addition of a new Comment 3), 5.1.7 (amendments to Comments 2–3), 5.1.8 (amendments to the Comment (which has become Comment 1) and addition of a new Comment 2), 7.1.7 (addition of a new Comment 5), 7.3.5 (amendments to Comment 3 and addition of a new Comment 4), 7.3.6 (amendments to Comment 1), and 7.3.7 (amendments to Comments 1–2).

UNIDROIT PRINCIPLES OF INTERNATIONAL COMMERCIAL CONTRACTS 2016[1]

Table of Contents

PREAMBLE

(Purpose of the Principles)

CHAPTER 1.   GENERAL PROVISIONS

CHAPTER 2.   FORMATION AND AUTHORITY OF AGENTS

Section 1.   Formation

---

[1] Reproduced by kind permission of the International Institute for the Unification of Private Law (UNIDROIT). Readers are reminded that the complete text of the UNIDROIT Principles of International Commercial Contracts 2016 is composed of both black-letter rules and accompanying Comments. The full text is available in book form directly from UNIDROIT and is also available in PDF on the UNIDROIT website at https://www.unidroit.org/instruments/commercial-contracts/unidroit-principles-2016. For select case law and a bibliography relating to the Principles, see www.unilex.info.

Section 2.   Transfer of Obligations

Section 3.   Assignment of Contracts

CHAPTER 10.   LIMITATION PERIODS

CHAPTER 11. PLURALITY OF OBLIGORS AND OF OBLIGEES

Section 1. Plurality of Obligors

Section 2. Plurality of Obligees

PREAMBLE

(Purpose of the Principles)

These Principles set forth general rules for international commercial contracts.

They shall be applied when the parties have agreed that their contract be governed by them.[*]

They may be applied when the parties have agreed that their contract be governed by general principles of law, the *lex mercatoria* or the like.

They may be applied when the parties have not chosen any law to govern their contract.

They may be used to interpret or supplement international uniform law instruments.

They may be used to interpret or supplement domestic law.

They may serve as a model for national and international legislators.

---

[*] Parties wishing to provide that their agreement be governed by the Principles might use one of the *Model Clauses for the use of the UNIDROIT Principles of International Commercial Contracts* (see http://www.unidroit.org/instruments/commercial-contracts/upicc-model-clauses).

CHAPTER 1—GENERAL PROVISIONS

Article 1.1

(Freedom of contract)

The parties are free to enter into a contract and to determine its content.

Article 1.2

(No form required)

Nothing in these Principles requires a contract, statement or any other act to be made in or evidenced by a particular form. It may be proved by any means, including witnesses.

Article 1.3

(Binding character of contract)

A contract validly entered into is binding upon the parties. It can only be modified or terminated in accordance with its terms or by agreement or as otherwise provided in these Principles.

Article 1.4

(Mandatory rules)

Nothing in these Principles shall restrict the application of mandatory rules, whether of national, international or supranational origin, which are applicable in accordance with the relevant rules of private international law.

Article 1.5

(Exclusion or modification by the parties)

The parties may exclude the application of these Principles or derogate from or vary the effect of any of their provisions, except as otherwise provided in the Principles.

Article 1.6

(Interpretation and supplementation of the Principles)

(1)   In the interpretation of these Principles, regard is to be had to their international character and to their purposes including the need to promote uniformity in their application.

(2)   Issues within the scope of these Principles but not expressly settled by them are as far as possible to be settled in accordance with their underlying general principles.

Article 1.7

(Good faith and fair dealing)

(1)   Each party must act in accordance with good faith and fair dealing in international trade.

(2)   The parties may not exclude or limit this duty.

Article 1.8

(Inconsistent behaviour)

A party cannot act inconsistently with an understanding it has caused the other party to have and upon which that other party reasonably has acted in reliance to its detriment.

Article 1.9

(Usages and practices)

(1)   The parties are bound by any usage to which they have agreed and by any practices which they have established between themselves.

(2)   The parties are bound by a usage that is widely known to and regularly observed in international trade by parties in the particular trade concerned except where the application of such a usage would be unreasonable.

Article 1.10

(Notice)

(1)   Where notice is required it may be given by any means appropriate to the circumstances.

(2)   A notice is effective when it reaches the person to whom it is given.

(3)   For the purpose of paragraph (2) a notice "reaches" a person when given to that person orally or delivered at that person's place of business or mailing address.

(4)   For the purpose of this Article "notice" includes a declaration, demand, request or any other communication of intention.

Article 1.11

(Definitions)

In these Principles

—   "court" includes an arbitral tribunal;

—   where a party has more than one place of business the relevant "place of business" is that which has the closest relationship to the contract and its performance, having regard to the circumstances known to or contemplated by the parties at any time before or at the conclusion of the contract;

— "long-term contract" refers to a contract which is to be performed over a period of time and which normally involves, to a varying degree, complexity of the transaction and an ongoing relationship between the parties;

— "obligor" refers to the party who is to perform an obligation and "obligee" refers to the party who is entitled to performance of that obligation;

— "writing" means any mode of communication that preserves a record of the information contained therein and is capable of being reproduced in tangible form.

Article 1.12

(Computation of time set by parties)

(1) Official holidays or non-business days occurring during a period set by parties for an act to be performed are included in calculating the period.

(2) However, if the last day of the period is an official holiday or a non-business day at the place of business of the party to perform the act, the period is extended until the first business day which follows, unless the circumstances indicate otherwise.

(3) The relevant time zone is that of the place of business of the party setting the time, unless the circumstances indicate otherwise.

CHAPTER 2—FORMATION AND AUTHORITY OF AGENTS

SECTION 1: FORMATION

Article 2.1.1

(Manner of formation)

A contract may be concluded either by the acceptance of an offer or by conduct of the parties that is sufficient to show agreement.

Article 2.1.2

(Definition of offer)

A proposal for concluding a contract constitutes an offer if it is sufficiently definite and indicates the intention of the offeror to be bound in case of acceptance.

Article 2.1.3

(Withdrawal of offer)

(1)   An offer becomes effective when it reaches the offeree.

(2)   An offer, even if it is irrevocable, may be withdrawn if the withdrawal reaches the offeree before or at the same time as the offer.

Article 2.1.4

(Revocation of offer)

(1)   Until a contract is concluded an offer may be revoked if the revocation reaches the offeree before it has dispatched an acceptance.

(2)   However, an offer cannot be revoked

   (a)   if it indicates, whether by stating a fixed time for acceptance or otherwise, that it is irrevocable; or

   (b)   if it was reasonable for the offeree to rely on the offer as being irrevocable and the offeree has acted in reliance on the offer.

Article 2.1.5

(Rejection of offer)

An offer is terminated when a rejection reaches the offeror.

Article 2.1.6

(Mode of acceptance)

(1)   A statement made by or other conduct of the offeree indicating assent to an offer is an acceptance. Silence or inactivity does not in itself amount to acceptance.

(2)   An acceptance of an offer becomes effective when the indication of assent reaches the offeror.

(3)   However, if, by virtue of the offer or as a result of practices which the parties have established between themselves or of usage, the offeree may indicate assent by performing an act without notice to the offeror, the acceptance is effective when the act is performed.

Article 2.1.7

(Time of acceptance)

An offer must be accepted within the time the offeror has fixed or, if no time is fixed, within a reasonable time having regard to the circumstances, including the rapidity of the means of communication employed by the offeror. An oral offer must be accepted immediately unless the circumstances indicate otherwise.

Article 2.1.8

(Acceptance within a fixed period of time)

A period of acceptance fixed by the offeror begins to run from the time that the offer is dispatched. A time indicated in the offer is deemed to be the time of dispatch unless the circumstances indicate otherwise.

Article 2.1.9

(Late acceptance. Delay in transmission)

(1)   A late acceptance is nevertheless effective as an acceptance if without undue delay the offeror so informs the offeree or gives notice to that effect.

(2)   If a communication containing a late acceptance shows that it has been sent in such circumstances that if its transmission had been normal it would have reached the offeror in due time, the late acceptance is effective as an acceptance unless, without undue delay, the offeror informs the offeree that it considers the offer as having lapsed.

Article 2.1.10

(Withdrawal of acceptance)

An acceptance may be withdrawn if the withdrawal reaches the offeror before or at the same time as the acceptance would have become effective.

Article 2.1.11

(Modified acceptance)

(1)   A reply to an offer which purports to be an acceptance but contains additions, limitations or other modifications is a rejection of the offer and constitutes a counter-offer.

(2)   However, a reply to an offer which purports to be an acceptance but contains additional or different terms which do not materially alter the terms of the offer constitutes an acceptance, unless the offeror, without undue delay, objects to the discrepancy. If the offeror does not object, the terms of the contract are the terms of the offer with the modifications contained in the acceptance.

Article 2.1.12

(Writings in confirmation)

If a writing which is sent within a reasonable time after the conclusion of the contract and which purports to be a confirmation of the contract contains additional or different terms, such terms become part of the contract, unless they materially alter the contract or the recipient, without undue delay, objects to the discrepancy.

Article 2.1.13

(Conclusion of contract dependent on agreement on specific matters or in a particular form)

Where in the course of negotiations one of the parties insists that the contract is not concluded until there is agreement on specific matters or in a particular form, no contract is concluded before agreement is reached on those matters or in that form.

Article 2.1.14

(Contract with terms deliberately left open)

(1) If the parties intend to conclude a contract, the fact that they intentionally leave a term to be agreed upon in further negotiations or to be determined by one of the parties or by a third person does not prevent a contract from coming into existence.

(2) The existence of the contract is not affected by the fact that subsequently

    (a) the parties reach no agreement on the term;

    (b) the party who is to determine the term does not do so; or

    (c) the third person does not determine the term,

provided that there is an alternative means of rendering the term definite that is reasonable in the circumstances, having regard to the intention of the parties.

Article 2.1.15

(Negotiations in bad faith)

(1) A party is free to negotiate and is not liable for failure to reach an agreement.

(2) However, a party who negotiates or breaks off negotiations in bad faith is liable for the losses caused to the other party.

(3) It is bad faith, in particular, for a party to enter into or continue negotiations when intending not to reach an agreement with the other party.

Article 2.1.16

(Duty of confidentiality)

Where information is given as confidential by one party in the course of negotiations, the other party is under a duty not to disclose that information or to use it improperly for its own purposes, whether or not a contract is subsequently concluded. Where appropriate, the remedy for breach of that duty may include compensation based on the benefit received by the other party.

Article 2.1.17

(Merger clauses)

A contract in writing which contains a clause indicating that the writing completely embodies the terms on which the parties have agreed cannot be contradicted or supplemented by evidence of prior statements or agreements. However, such statements or agreements may be used to interpret the writing.

Article 2.1.18

(Modification in a particular form)

A contract in writing which contains a clause requiring any modification or termination by agreement to be in a particular form may not be otherwise modified or terminated. However, a party may be precluded by its conduct from asserting such a clause to the extent that the other party has reasonably acted in reliance on that conduct.

Article 2.1.19

(Contracting under standard terms)

(1)   Where one party or both parties use standard terms in concluding a contract, the general rules on formation apply, subject to Articles 2.1.20–2.1.22.

(2)   Standard terms are provisions which are prepared in advance for general and repeated use by one party and which are actually used without negotiation with the other party.

Article 2.1.20

(Surprising terms)

(1)   No term contained in standard terms which is of such a character that the other party could not reasonably have expected it, is effective unless it has been expressly accepted by that party.

(2)   In determining whether a term is of such a character regard shall be had to its content, language and presentation.

Article 2.1.21

(Conflict between standard terms and non-standard terms)

In case of conflict between a standard term and a term which is not a standard term the latter prevails.

Article 2.1.22

(Battle of forms)

Where both parties use standard terms and reach agreement except on those terms, a contract is concluded on the basis of the agreed terms and of any standard terms which are common in substance unless one party clearly indicates in advance, or later and without undue delay informs the other party, that it does not intend to be bound by such a contract.

SECTION 2: AUTHORITY OF AGENTS

Article 2.2.1

(Scope of the Section)

(1)   This Section governs the authority of a person ("the agent") to affect the legal relations of another person ("the principal") by or with respect to a contract with a third party, whether the agent acts in its own name or in that of the principal.

(2)   It governs only the relations between the principal or the agent on the one hand, and the third party on the other.

(3)   It does not govern an agent's authority conferred by law or the authority of an agent appointed by a public or judicial authority.

Article 2.2.2

(Establishment and scope of the authority of the agent)

(1)   The principal's grant of authority to an agent may be express or implied.

(2)   The agent has authority to perform all acts necessary in the circumstances to achieve the purposes for which the authority was granted.

Article 2.2.3

(Agency disclosed)

(1)   Where an agent acts within the scope of its authority and the third party knew or ought to have known that the agent was acting as an agent, the acts of the agent shall directly affect the legal relations between the principal and the third party and no legal relation is created between the agent and the third party.

(2)   However, the acts of the agent shall affect only the relations between the agent and the third party, where the agent with the consent of the principal undertakes to become the party to the contract.

Article 2.2.4

(Agency undisclosed)

(1)   Where an agent acts within the scope of its authority and the third party neither knew nor ought to have known that the agent was acting as an agent, the acts of the agent shall affect only the relations between the agent and the third party.

(2)   However, where such an agent, when contracting with the third party on behalf of a business, represents itself to be the owner of that business, the third party, upon discovery of the real owner of the business, may exercise also against the latter the rights it has against the agent.

Article 2.2.5

(Agent acting without or exceeding its authority)

(1)   Where an agent acts without authority or exceeds its authority, its acts do not affect the legal relations between the principal and the third party.

(2)   However, where the principal causes the third party reasonably to believe that the agent has authority to act on behalf of the principal and that the agent is acting within the scope of that authority, the principal may not invoke against the third party the lack of authority of the agent.

Article 2.2.6

(Liability of agent acting without or exceeding its authority)

(1)   An agent that acts without authority or exceeds its authority is, failing ratification by the principal, liable for damages that will place the third party in the same position as if the agent had acted with authority and not exceeded its authority.

(2)   However, the agent is not liable if the third party knew or ought to have known that the agent had no authority or was exceeding its authority.

Article 2.2.7

(Conflict of interests)

(1)   If a contract concluded by an agent involves the agent in a conflict of interests with the principal of which the third party knew or ought to have known, the principal may avoid the contract. The right to avoid is subject to Articles 3.2.9 and 3.2.11 to 3.2.15.

(2)   However, the principal may not avoid the contract

(a) if the principal had consented to, or knew or ought to have known of, the agent's involvement in the conflict of interests; or

(b) if the agent had disclosed the conflict of interests to the principal and the latter had not objected within a reasonable time.

Article 2.2.8

(Sub-agency)

An agent has implied authority to appoint a sub-agent to perform acts which it is not reasonable to expect the agent to perform itself. The rules of this Section apply to the sub-agency.

Article 2.2.9

(Ratification)

(1) An act by an agent that acts without authority or exceeds its authority may be ratified by the principal. On ratification the act produces the same effects as if it had initially been carried out with authority.

(2) The third party may by notice to the principal specify a reasonable period of time for ratification. If the principal does not ratify within that period of time it can no longer do so.

(3) If, at the time of the agent's act, the third party neither knew nor ought to have known of the lack of authority, it may, at any time before ratification, by notice to the principal indicate its refusal to become bound by a ratification.

Article 2.2.10

(Termination of authority)

(1) Termination of authority is not effective in relation to the third party unless the third party knew or ought to have known of it.

(2) Notwithstanding the termination of its authority, an agent remains authorised to perform the acts that are necessary to prevent harm to the principal's interests.

CHAPTER 3—VALIDITY

SECTION 1: GENERAL PROVISIONS

Article 3.1.1

(Matters not covered)

This Chapter does not deal with lack of capacity.

Article 3.1.2

(Validity of mere agreement)

A contract is concluded, modified or terminated by the mere agreement of the parties, without any further requirement.

Article 3.1.3

(Initial impossibility)

(1)   The mere fact that at the time of the conclusion of the contract the performance of the obligation assumed was impossible does not affect the validity of the contract.

(2)   The mere fact that at the time of the conclusion of the contract a party was not entitled to dispose of the assets to which the contract relates does not affect the validity of the contract.

Article 3.1.4

(Mandatory character of the provisions)

The provisions on fraud, threat, gross disparity and illegality contained in this Chapter are mandatory.

SECTION 2: GROUNDS FOR AVOIDANCE

Article 3.2.1

(Definition of mistake)

Mistake is an erroneous assumption relating to facts or to law existing when the contract was concluded.

Article 3.2.2

(Relevant mistake)

(1)   A party may only avoid the contract for mistake if, when the contract was concluded, the mistake was of such importance that a reasonable person in the same situation as the party in error would only have concluded the contract on materially different terms or would not have concluded it at all if the true state of affairs had been known, and

(a)   the other party made the same mistake, or caused the mistake, or knew or ought to have known of the mistake and it was contrary to reasonable commercial standards of fair dealing to leave the mistaken party in error; or

(b)   the other party had not at the time of avoidance reasonably acted in reliance on the contract.

(2)   However, a party may not avoid the contract if

(a) it was grossly negligent in committing the mistake; or

(b) the mistake relates to a matter in regard to which the risk of mistake was assumed or, having regard to the circumstances, should be borne by the mistaken party.

Article 3.2.3

(Error in expression or transmission)

An error occurring in the expression or transmission of a declaration is considered to be a mistake of the person from whom the declaration emanated.

Article 3.2.4

(Remedies for non-performance)

A party is not entitled to avoid the contract on the ground of mistake if the circumstances on which that party relies afford, or could have afforded, a remedy for non-performance.

Article 3.2.5

(Fraud)

A party may avoid the contract when it has been led to conclude the contract by the other party's fraudulent representation, including language or practices, or fraudulent non-disclosure of circumstances which, according to reasonable commercial standards of fair dealing, the latter party should have disclosed.

Article 3.2.6

(Threat)

A party may avoid the contract when it has been led to conclude the contract by the other party's unjustified threat which, having regard to the circumstances, is so imminent and serious as to leave the first party no reasonable alternative. In particular, a threat is unjustified if the act or omission with which a party has been threatened is wrongful in itself, or it is wrongful to use it as a means to obtain the conclusion of the contract.

Article 3.2.7

(Gross disparity)

(1) A party may avoid the contract or an individual term of it if, at the time of the conclusion of the contract, the contract or term unjustifiably gave the other party an excessive advantage. Regard is to be had, among other factors, to

651

(a) the fact that the other party has taken unfair advantage of the first party's dependence, economic distress or urgent needs, or of its improvidence, ignorance, inexperience or lack of bargaining skill, and

(b) the nature and purpose of the contract.

(2) Upon the request of the party entitled to avoidance, a court may adapt the contract or term in order to make it accord with reasonable commercial standards of fair dealing.

(3) A court may also adapt the contract or term upon the request of the party receiving notice of avoidance, provided that that party informs the other party of its request promptly after receiving such notice and before the other party has reasonably acted in reliance on it. Article 3.2.10(2) applies accordingly.

Article 3.2.8

(Third persons)

(1) Where fraud, threat, gross disparity or a party's mistake is imputable to, or is known or ought to be known by, a third person for whose acts the other party is responsible, the contract may be avoided under the same conditions as if the behaviour or knowledge had been that of the party itself.

(2) Where fraud, threat or gross disparity is imputable to a third person for whose acts the other party is not responsible, the contract may be avoided if that party knew or ought to have known of the fraud, threat or disparity, or has not at the time of avoidance reasonably acted in reliance on the contract.

Article 3.2.9

(Confirmation)

If the party entitled to avoid the contract expressly or impliedly confirms the contract after the period of time for giving notice of avoidance has begun to run, avoidance of the contract is excluded.

Article 3.2.10

(Loss of right to avoid)

(1) If a party is entitled to avoid the contract for mistake but the other party declares itself willing to perform or performs the contract as it was understood by the party entitled to avoidance, the contract is considered to have been concluded as the latter party understood it. The other party must make such a declaration or render such performance promptly after having been informed of the manner in which the party

entitled to avoidance had understood the contract and before that party has reasonably acted in reliance on a notice of avoidance.

(2) After such a declaration or performance the right to avoidance is lost and any earlier notice of avoidance is ineffective.

Article 3.2.11

(Notice of avoidance)

The right of a party to avoid the contract is exercised by notice to the other party.

Article 3.2.12

(Time limits)

(1) Notice of avoidance shall be given within a reasonable time, having regard to the circumstances, after the avoiding party knew or could not have been unaware of the relevant facts or became capable of acting freely.

(2) Where an individual term of the contract may be avoided by a party under Article 3.2.7, the period of time for giving notice of avoidance begins to run when that term is asserted by the other party.

Article 3.2.13

(Partial avoidance)

Where a ground of avoidance affects only individual terms of the contract, the effect of avoidance is limited to those terms unless, having regard to the circumstances, it is unreasonable to uphold the remaining contract.

Article 3.2.14

(Retroactive effect of avoidance)

Avoidance takes effect retroactively.

Article 3.2.15

(Restitution)

(1) On avoidance either party may claim restitution of whatever it has supplied under the contract, or the part of it avoided, provided that the party concurrently makes restitution of whatever it has received under the contract, or the part of it avoided.

(2) If restitution in kind is not possible or appropriate, an allowance has to be made in money whenever reasonable.

(3)   The recipient of the performance does not have to make an allowance in money if the impossibility to make restitution in kind is attributable to the other party.

(4)   Compensation may be claimed for expenses reasonably required to preserve or maintain the performance received.

Article 3.2.16

(Damages)

Irrespective of whether or not the contract has been avoided, the party who knew or ought to have known of the ground for avoidance is liable for damages so as to put the other party in the same position in which it would have been if it had not concluded the contract.

Article 3.2.17

(Unilateral declarations)

The provisions of this Chapter apply with appropriate adaptations to any communication of intention addressed by one party to the other.

SECTION 3: ILLEGALITY

Article 3.3.1

(Contracts infringing mandatory rules)

(1)   Where a contract infringes a mandatory rule, whether of national, international or supranational origin, applicable under Article 1.4 of these Principles, the effects of that infringement upon the contract are the effects, if any, expressly prescribed by that mandatory rule.

(2)   Where the mandatory rule does not expressly prescribe the effects of an infringement upon a contract, the parties have the right to exercise such remedies under the contract as in the circumstances are reasonable.

(3)   In determining what is reasonable regard is to be had in particular to:

    (a)   the purpose of the rule which has been infringed;

    (b)   the category of persons for whose protection the rule exists;

    (c)   any sanction that may be imposed under the rule infringed;

    (d)   the seriousness of the infringement;

    (e)   whether one or both parties knew or ought to have known of the infringement;

    (f)   whether the performance of the contract necessitates the infringement; and

(g)   the parties' reasonable expectations.

Article 3.3.2

(Restitution)

(1)   Where there has been performance under a contract infringing a mandatory rule under Article 3.3.1, restitution may be granted where this would be reasonable in the circumstances.

(2)   In determining what is reasonable, regard is to be had, with the appropriate adaptations, to the criteria referred to in Article 3.3.1(3).

(3)   If restitution is granted, the rules set out in Article 3.2.15 apply with appropriate adaptations.

CHAPTER 4—INTERPRETATION

Article 4.1

(Intention of the parties)

(1)   A contract shall be interpreted according to the common intention of the parties.

(2)   If such an intention cannot be established, the contract shall be interpreted according to the meaning that reasonable persons of the same kind as the parties would give to it in the same circumstances.

Article 4.2

(Interpretation of statements and other conduct)

(1)   The statements and other conduct of a party shall be interpreted according to that party's intention if the other party knew or could not have been unaware of that intention.

(2)   If the preceding paragraph is not applicable, such statements and other conduct shall be interpreted according to the meaning that a reasonable person of the same kind as the other party would give to it in the same circumstances.

Article 4.3

(Relevant circumstances)

In applying Articles 4.1 and 4.2, regard shall be had to all the circumstances, including

(a)   preliminary negotiations between the parties;

(b)   practices which the parties have established between themselves;

(c)   the conduct of the parties subsequent to the conclusion of the contract;

(d) the nature and purpose of the contract;

(e) the meaning commonly given to terms and expressions in the trade concerned;

(f) usages.

Article 4.4

(Reference to contract or statement as a whole)

Terms and expressions shall be interpreted in the light of the whole contract or statement in which they appear.

Article 4.5

(All terms to be given effect)

Contract terms shall be interpreted so as to give effect to all the terms rather than to deprive some of them of effect.

Article 4.6

(Contra proferentem rule)

If contract terms supplied by one party are unclear, an interpretation against that party is preferred.

Article 4.7

(Linguistic discrepancies)

Where a contract is drawn up in two or more language versions which are equally authoritative there is, in case of discrepancy between the versions, a preference for the interpretation according to a version in which the contract was originally drawn up.

Article 4.8

(Supplying an omitted term)

(1) Where the parties to a contract have not agreed with respect to a term which is important for a determination of their rights and duties, a term which is appropriate in the circumstances shall be supplied.

(2) In determining what is an appropriate term regard shall be had, among other factors, to

(a) the intention of the parties;

(b) the nature and purpose of the contract;

(c) good faith and fair dealing;

(d) reasonableness.

CHAPTER 5—CONTENT AND THIRD PARTY RIGHTS

SECTION 1: CONTENT

Article 5.1.1

(Express and implied obligations)

The contractual obligations of the parties may be express or implied.

Article 5.1.2

(Implied obligations)

Implied obligations stem from

    (a)   the nature and purpose of the contract;

    (b)   practices established between the parties and usages;

    (c)   good faith and fair dealing;

    (d)   reasonableness.

Article 5.1.3

(Co-operation between the parties)

Each party shall cooperate with the other party when such co-operation may reasonably be expected for the performance of that party's obligations.

Article 5.1.4

(Duty to achieve a specific result. Duty of best efforts)

(1)   To the extent that an obligation of a party involves a duty to achieve a specific result, that party is bound to achieve that result.

(2)   To the extent that an obligation of a party involves a duty of best efforts in the performance of an activity, that party is bound to make such efforts as would be made by a reasonable person of the same kind in the same circumstances.

Article 5.1.5

(Determination of kind of duty involved)

In determining the extent to which an obligation of a party involves a duty of best efforts in the performance of an activity or a duty to achieve a specific result, regard shall be had, among other factors, to

    (a)   the way in which the obligation is expressed in the contract;

    (b)   the contractual price and other terms of the contract;

    (c)   the degree of risk normally involved in achieving the expected result;

(d)   the ability of the other party to influence the performance of the obligation.

Article 5.1.6

(Determination of quality of performance)

Where the quality of performance is neither fixed by, nor determinable from, the contract a party is bound to render a performance of a quality that is reasonable and not less than average in the circumstances.

Article 5.1.7

(Price determination)

(1)   Where a contract does not fix or make provision for determining the price, the parties are considered, in the absence of any indication to the contrary, to have made reference to the price generally charged at the time of the conclusion of the contract for such performance in comparable circumstances in the trade concerned or, if no such price is available, to a reasonable price.

(2)   Where the price is to be determined by one party and that determination is manifestly unreasonable, a reasonable price shall be substituted notwithstanding any contract term to the contrary.

(3)   Where the price is to be fixed by one party or a third person, and that party or third person does not do so, the price shall be a reasonable price.

(4)   Where the price is to be fixed by reference to factors which do not exist or have ceased to exist or to be accessible, the nearest equivalent factor shall be treated as a substitute.

Article 5.1.8

(Termination of a contract for an indefinite period)

A contract for an indefinite period may be terminated by either party by giving notice a reasonable time in advance. As to the effects of termination in general, and as to restitution, the provisions in Articles 7.3.5 and 7.3.7 apply.

Article 5.1.9

(Release by agreement)

(1)   An obligee may release its right by agreement with the obligor.

(2)   An offer to release a right gratuitously shall be deemed accepted if the obligor does not reject the offer without delay after having become aware of it.

SECTION 2: THIRD PARTY RIGHTS

Article 5.2.1

(Contracts in favour of third parties)

(1)   The parties (the "promisor" and the "promisee") may confer by express or implied agreement a right on a third party (the "beneficiary").

(2)   The existence and content of the beneficiary's right against the promisor are determined by the agreement of the parties and are subject to any conditions or other limitations under the agreement.

Article 5.2.2

(Third party identifiable)

The beneficiary must be identifiable with adequate certainty by the contract but need not be in existence at the time the contract is made.

Article 5.2.3

(Exclusion and limitation clauses)

The conferment of rights in the beneficiary includes the right to invoke a clause in the contract which excludes or limits the liability of the beneficiary.

Article 5.2.4

(Defences)

The promisor may assert against the beneficiary all defences which the promisor could assert against the promisee.

Article 5.2.5

(Revocation)

The parties may modify or revoke the rights conferred by the contract on the beneficiary until the beneficiary has accepted them or reasonably acted in reliance on them.

Article 5.2.6

(Renunciation)

The beneficiary may renounce a right conferred on it.

SECTION 3: CONDITIONS

Article 5.3.1

(Types of condition)

A contract or a contractual obligation may be made conditional upon the occurrence of a future uncertain event, so that the contract or the contractual obligation only takes effect if the event occurs (suspensive condition) or comes to an end if the event occurs (resolutive condition).

Article 5.3.2

(Effect of conditions)

Unless the parties otherwise agree:

   (a)   the relevant contract or contractual obligation takes effect upon fulfilment of a suspensive condition;

   (b)   the relevant contract or contractual obligation comes to an end upon fulfilment of a resolutive condition.

Article 5.3.3

(Interference with conditions)

(1)   If fulfilment of a condition is prevented by a party, contrary to the duty of good faith and fair dealing or the duty of co-operation, that party may not rely on the non-fulfilment of the condition.

(2)   If fulfilment of a condition is brought about by a party, contrary to the duty of good faith and fair dealing or the duty of co-operation, that party may not rely on the fulfilment of the condition.

Article 5.3.4

(Duty to preserve rights)

Pending fulfilment of a condition, a party may not, contrary to the duty to act in accordance with good faith and fair dealing, act so as to prejudice the other party's rights in case of fulfilment of the condition.

Article 5.3.5

(Restitution in case of fulfilment of a resolutive condition)

(1)   On fulfilment of a resolutive condition, the rules on restitution set out in Articles 7.3.6 and 7.3.7 apply with appropriate adaptations.

(2)   If the parties have agreed that the resolutive condition is to operate retroactively, the rules on restitution set out in Article 3.2.15 apply with appropriate adaptations.

CHAPTER 6—PERFORMANCE

SECTION 1: PERFORMANCE IN GENERAL

Article 6.1.1

(Time of performance)

A party must perform its obligations:

(a) if a time is fixed by or determinable from the contract, at that time;

(b) if a period of time is fixed by or determinable from the contract, at any time within that period unless circumstances indicate that the other party is to choose a time;

(c) in any other case, within a reasonable time after the conclusion of the contract.

Article 6.1.2

(Performance at one time or in instalments)

In cases under Article 6.1.1(b) or (c), a party must perform its obligations at one time if that performance can be rendered at one time and the circumstances do not indicate otherwise.

Article 6.1.3

(Partial performance)

(1) The obligee may reject an offer to perform in part at the time performance is due, whether or not such offer is coupled with an assurance as to the balance of the performance, unless the obligee has no legitimate interest in so doing.

(2) Additional expenses caused to the obligee by partial performance are to be borne by the obligor without prejudice to any other remedy.

Article 6.1.4

(Order of performance)

(1) To the extent that the performances of the parties can be rendered simultaneously, the parties are bound to render them simultaneously unless the circumstances indicate otherwise.

(2) To the extent that the performance of only one party requires a period of time, that party is bound to render its performance first, unless the circumstances indicate otherwise.

Article 6.1.5

(Earlier performance)

(1)   The obligee may reject an earlier performance unless it has no legitimate interest in so doing.

(2)   Acceptance by a party of an earlier performance does not affect the time for the performance of its own obligations if that time has been fixed irrespective of the performance of the other party's obligations.

(3)   Additional expenses caused to the obligee by earlier performance are to be borne by the obligor, without prejudice to any other remedy.

Article 6.1.6

(Place of performance)

(1)   If the place of performance is neither fixed by, nor determinable from, the contract, a party is to perform:

(a)   a monetary obligation, at the obligee's place of business;

(b)   any other obligation, at its own place of business.

(2)   A party must bear any increase in the expenses incidental to performance which is caused by a change in its place of business subsequent to the conclusion of the contract.

Article 6.1.7

(Payment by cheque or other instrument)

(1)   Payment may be made in any form used in the ordinary course of business at the place for payment.

(2)   However, an obligee who accepts, either by virtue of paragraph (1) or voluntarily, a cheque, any other order to pay or a promise to pay, is presumed to do so only on condition that it will be honoured.

Article 6.1.8

(Payment by funds transfer)

(1)   Unless the obligee has indicated a particular account, payment may be made by a transfer to any of the financial institutions in which the obligee has made it known that it has an account.

(2)   In case of payment by a transfer the obligation of the obligor is discharged when the transfer to the obligee's financial institution becomes effective.

Article 6.1.9

(Currency of payment)

(1)   If a monetary obligation is expressed in a currency other than that of the place for payment, it may be paid by the obligor in the currency of the place for payment unless

(a)   that currency is not freely convertible; or

(b)   the parties have agreed that payment should be made only in the currency in which the monetary obligation is expressed.

(2)   If it is impossible for the obligor to make payment in the currency in which the monetary obligation is expressed, the obligee may require payment in the currency of the place for payment, even in the case referred to in paragraph (1)(b).

(3)   Payment in the currency of the place for payment is to be made according to the applicable rate of exchange prevailing there when payment is due.

(4)   However, if the obligor has not paid at the time when payment is due, the obligee may require payment according to the applicable rate of exchange prevailing either when payment is due or at the time of actual payment.

Article 6.1.10

(Currency not expressed)

Where a monetary obligation is not expressed in a particular currency, payment must be made in the currency of the place where payment is to be made.

Article 6.1.11

(Costs of performance)

Each party shall bear the costs of performance of its obligations.

Article 6.1.12

(Imputation of payments)

(1)   An obligor owing several monetary obligations to the same obligee may specify at the time of payment the debt to which it intends the payment to be applied. However, the payment discharges first any expenses, then interest due and finally the principal.

(2)   If the obligor makes no such specification, the obligee may, within a reasonable time after payment, declare to the obligor the obligation to which it imputes the payment, provided that the obligation is due and undisputed.

(3)   In the absence of imputation under paragraphs (1) or (2), payment is imputed to that obligation which satisfies one of the following criteria in the order indicated:

(a)   an obligation which is due or which is the first to fall due;

(b)   the obligation for which the obligee has least security;

(c)   the obligation which is the most burdensome for the obligor;

(d)   the obligation which has arisen first.

If none of the preceding criteria applies, payment is imputed to all the obligations proportionally.

Article 6.1.13

(Imputation of non-monetary obligations)

Article 6.1.12 applies with appropriate adaptations to the imputation of performance of non-monetary obligations.

Article 6.1.14

(Application for public permission)

Where the law of a State requires a public permission affecting the validity of the contract or its performance and neither that law nor the circumstances indicate otherwise

(a)   if only one party has its place of business in that State, that party shall take the measures necessary to obtain the permission;

(b)   in any other case the party whose performance requires permission shall take the necessary measures.

Article 6.1.15

(Procedure in applying for permission)

(1)   The party required to take the measures necessary to obtain the permission shall do so without undue delay and shall bear any expenses incurred.

(2)   That party shall whenever appropriate give the other party notice of the grant or refusal of such permission without undue delay.

Article 6.1.16

(Permission neither granted nor refused)

(1)   If, notwithstanding the fact that the party responsible has taken all measures required, permission is neither granted nor refused within an agreed period or, where no period has been agreed, within a reason-

able time from the conclusion of the contract, either party is entitled to terminate the contract.

(2)   Where the permission affects some terms only, paragraph (1) does not apply if, having regard to the circumstances, it is reasonable to uphold the remaining contract even if the permission is refused.

Article 6.1.17

(Permission refused)

(1)   The refusal of a permission affecting the validity of the contract renders the contract void. If the refusal affects the validity of some terms only, only such terms are void if, having regard to the circumstances, it is reasonable to uphold the remaining contract.

(2)   Where the refusal of a permission renders the performance of the contract impossible in whole or in part, the rules on non-performance apply.

SECTION 2: HARDSHIP

Article 6.2.1

(Contract to be observed)

Where the performance of a contract becomes more onerous for one of the parties, that party is nevertheless bound to perform its obligations subject to the following provisions on hardship.

Article 6.2.2

(Definition of hardship)

There is hardship where the occurrence of events fundamentally alters the equilibrium of the contract either because the cost of a party's performance has increased or because the value of the performance a party receives has diminished, and

(a)   the events occur or become known to the disadvantaged party after the conclusion of the contract;

(b)   the events could not reasonably have been taken into account by the disadvantaged party at the time of the conclusion of the contract;

(c)   the events are beyond the control of the disadvantaged party; and

(d)   the risk of the events was not assumed by the disadvantaged party.

Article 6.2.3

(Effects of hardship)

(1)   In case of hardship the disadvantaged party is entitled to request renegotiations. The request shall be made without undue delay and shall indicate the grounds on which it is based.

(2)   The request for renegotiation does not in itself entitle the disadvantaged party to withhold performance.

(3)   Upon failure to reach agreement within a reasonable time either party may resort to the court.

(4)   If the court finds hardship it may, if reasonable,

(a)   terminate the contract at a date and on terms to be fixed, or

(b)   adapt the contract with a view to restoring its equilibrium.

CHAPTER 7—NON-PERFORMANCE

SECTION 1: NON-PERFORMANCE IN GENERAL

Article 7.1.1

(Non-performance defined)

Non-performance is failure by a party to perform any of its obligations under the contract, including defective performance or late performance.

Article 7.1.2

(Interference by the other party)

A party may not rely on the non-performance of the other party to the extent that such non-performance was caused by the first party's act or omission or by another event for which the first party bears the risk.

Article 7.1.3

(Withholding performance)

(1)   Where the parties are to perform simultaneously, either party may withhold performance until the other party tenders its performance.

(2)   Where the parties are to perform consecutively, the party that is to perform later may withhold its performance until the first party has performed.

Article 7.1.4

(Cure by non-performing party)

(1)   The non-performing party may, at its own expense, cure any non-performance, provided that

(a) without undue delay, it gives notice indicating the proposed manner and timing of the cure;

(b) cure is appropriate in the circumstances;

(c) the aggrieved party has no legitimate interest in refusing cure; and

(d) cure is effected promptly.

(2) The right to cure is not precluded by notice of termination.

(3) Upon effective notice of cure, rights of the aggrieved party that are inconsistent with the non-performing party's performance are suspended until the time for cure has expired.

(4) The aggrieved party may withhold performance pending cure.

(5) Notwithstanding cure, the aggrieved party retains the right to claim damages for delay as well as for any harm caused or not prevented by the cure.

Article 7.1.5

(Additional period for performance)

(1) In a case of non-performance the aggrieved party may by notice to the other party allow an additional period of time for performance.

(2) During the additional period the aggrieved party may withhold performance of its own reciprocal obligations and may claim damages but may not resort to any other remedy. If it receives notice from the other party that the latter will not perform within that period, or if upon expiry of that period due performance has not been made, the aggrieved party may resort to any of the reme-dies that may be available under this Chapter.

(3) Where in a case of delay in performance which is not fundamental the aggrieved party has given notice allowing an additional period of time of reasonable length, it may terminate the contract at the end of that period. If the additional period allowed is not of reasonable length it shall be extended to a reasonable length. The aggrieved party may in its notice provide that if the other party fails to perform within the period allowed by the notice the contract shall automatically terminate.

(4) Paragraph (3) does not apply where the obligation which has not been performed is only a minor part of the contractual obligation of the non-performing party.

Article 7.1.6

(Exemption clauses)

A clause which limits or excludes one party's liability for non-performance or which permits one party to render performance substantially different from what the other party reasonably expected may not be invoked if it would be grossly unfair to do so, having regard to the purpose of the contract.

Article 7.1.7

(Force majeure)

(1)   Non-performance by a party is excused if that party proves that the non-performance was due to an impediment beyond its control and that it could not reasonably be expected to have taken the impediment into account at the time of the conclusion of the contract or to have avoided or overcome it or its consequences.

(2)   When the impediment is only temporary, the excuse shall have effect for such period as is reasonable having regard to the effect of the impediment on the performance of the contract.

(3)   The party who fails to perform must give notice to the other party of the impediment and its effect on its ability to perform. If the notice is not received by the other party within a reasonable time after the party who fails to perform knew or ought to have known of the impediment, it is liable for damages resulting from such non-receipt.

(4)   Nothing in this Article prevents a party from exercising a right to terminate the contract or to withhold performance or request interest on money due.

SECTION 2: RIGHT TO PERFORMANCE

Article 7.2.1

(Performance of monetary obligation)

Where a party who is obliged to pay money does not do so, the other party may require payment.

Article 7.2.2

(Performance of non-monetary obligation)

Where a party who owes an obligation other than one to pay money does not perform, the other party may require performance, unless

(a)   performance is impossible in law or in fact;

(b)   performance or, where relevant, enforcement is unreasonably burdensome or expensive;

(c)   the party entitled to performance may reasonably obtain performance from another source;

(d)   performance is of an exclusively personal character; or

(e) the party entitled to performance does not require performance within a reasonable time after it has, or ought to have, become aware of the non-performance.

Article 7.2.3

(Repair and replacement of defective performance)

The right to performance includes in appropriate cases the right to require repair, replacement, or other cure of defective performance. The provisions of Articles 7.2.1 and 7.2.2 apply accordingly.

Article 7.2.4

(Judicial penalty)

(1) Where the court orders a party to perform, it may also direct that this party pay a penalty if it does not comply with the order.

(2) The penalty shall be paid to the aggrieved party unless mandatory provisions of the law of the forum provide otherwise. Payment of the penalty to the aggrieved party does not exclude any claim for damages.

Article 7.2.5

(Change of remedy)

(1) An aggrieved party who has required performance of a non-monetary obligation and who has not received performance within a period fixed or otherwise within a reasonable period of time may invoke any other remedy.

(2) Where the decision of a court for performance of a non-monetary obligation cannot be enforced, the aggrieved party may invoke any other remedy.

SECTION 3: TERMINATION

Article 7.3.1

(Right to terminate the contract)

(1) A party may terminate the contract where the failure of the other party to perform an obligation under the contract amounts to a fundamental non-performance.

(2) In determining whether a failure to perform an obligation amounts to a fundamental non-performance regard shall be had, in particular, to whether

(a) the non-performance substantially deprives the aggrieved party of what it was entitled to expect under the contract unless the other party did not foresee and could not reasonably have foreseen such result;

(b) strict compliance with the obligation which has not been performed is of essence under the contract;

(c) the non-performance is intentional or reckless;

(d) the non-performance gives the aggrieved party reason to believe that it cannot rely on the other party's future performance;

(e) the non-performing party will suffer disproportionate loss as a result of the preparation or performance if the contract is terminated.

(3) In the case of delay the aggrieved party may also terminate the contract if the other party fails to perform before the time allowed it under Article 7.1.5 has expired.

Article 7.3.2

(Notice of termination)

(1) The right of a party to terminate the contract is exercised by notice to the other party.

(2) If performance has been offered late or otherwise does not conform to the contract the aggrieved party will lose its right to terminate the contract unless it gives notice to the other party within a reasonable time after it has or ought to have become aware of the offer or of the nonconforming performance.

Article 7.3.3

(Anticipatory non-performance)

Where prior to the date for performance by one of the parties it is clear that there will be a fundamental non-performance by that party, the other party may terminate the contract.

Article 7.3.4

(Adequate assurance of due performance)

A party who reasonably believes that there will be a fundamental nonperformance by the other party may demand adequate assurance of due performance and may meanwhile withhold its own performance. Where this assurance is not provided within a reasonable time the party demanding it may terminate the contract.

Article 7.3.5

(Effects of termination in general)

(1) Termination of the contract releases both parties from their obligation to effect and to receive future performance.

(2) Termination does not preclude a claim for damages for non-performance.

(3) Termination does not affect any provision in the contract for the settlement of disputes or any other term of the contract which is to operate even after termination.

Article 7.3.6

(Restitution with respect to contracts to be performed at one time)

(1) On termination of a contract to be performed at one time either party may claim restitution of whatever it has supplied under the contract, provided that such party concurrently makes restitution of whatever it has received under the contract.

(2) If restitution in kind is not possible or appropriate, an allowance has to be made in money whenever reasonable.

(3) The recipient of the performance does not have to make an allowance in money if the impossibility to make restitution in kind is attributable to the other party.

(4) Compensation may be claimed for expenses reasonably required to preserve or maintain the performance received.

Article 7.3.7

(Restitution with respect to long-term contracts)

(1) On termination of a long-term contract restitution can only be claimed for the period after termination has taken effect, provided the contract is divisible.

(2) As far as restitution has to be made, the provisions of Article 7.3.6 apply.

SECTION 4: DAMAGES

Article 7.4.1

(Right to damages)

Any non-performance gives the aggrieved party a right to damages either exclusively or in conjunction with any other remedies except where the non-performance is excused under these Principles.

Article 7.4.2

(Full compensation)

(1)   The aggrieved party is entitled to full compensation for harm sustained as a result of the non-performance. Such harm includes both any loss which it suffered and any gain of which it was deprived, taking into account any gain to the aggrieved party resulting from its avoidance of cost or harm.

(2)   Such harm may be non-pecuniary and includes, for instance, physical suffering or emotional distress.

Article 7.4.3

(Certainty of harm)

(1)   Compensation is due only for harm, including future harm, that is established with a reasonable degree of certainty.

(2)   Compensation may be due for the loss of a chance in proportion to the probability of its occurrence.

(3)   Where the amount of damages cannot be established with a sufficient degree of certainty, the assessment is at the discretion of the court.

Article 7.4.4

(Foreseeability of harm)

The non-performing party is liable only for harm which it foresaw or could reasonably have foreseen at the time of the conclusion of the contract as being likely to result from its non-performance.

Article 7.4.5

(Proof of harm in case of replacement transaction)

Where the aggrieved party has terminated the contract and has made a replacement transaction within a reasonable time and in a reasonable manner it may recover the difference between the contract price and the price of the replacement transaction as well as damages for any further harm.

Article 7.4.6

(Proof of harm by current price)

(1)   Where the aggrieved party has terminated the contract and has not made a replacement transaction but there is a current price for the performance contracted for, it may recover the difference between the contract price and the price current at the time the contract is terminated as well as damages for any further harm.

(2)   Current price is the price generally charged for goods delivered or services rendered in comparable circumstances at the place where the contract should have been performed or, if there is no current price at that place, the current price at such other place that appears reasonable to take as a reference.

Article 7.4.7

(Harm due in part to aggrieved party)

Where the harm is due in part to an act or omission of the aggrieved party or to another event for which that party bears the risk, the amount of damages shall be reduced to the extent that these factors have contributed to the harm, having regard to the conduct of each of the parties.

Article 7.4.8

(Mitigation of harm)

(1)   The non-performing party is not liable for harm suffered by the aggrieved party to the extent that the harm could have been reduced by the latter party's taking reasonable steps.

(2)   The aggrieved party is entitled to recover any expenses reasonably incurred in attempting to reduce the harm.

Article 7.4.9

(Interest for failure to pay money)

(1)   If a party does not pay a sum of money when it falls due the aggrieved party is entitled to interest upon that sum from the time when payment is due to the time of payment whether or not the non-payment is excused.

(2)   The rate of interest shall be the average bank short-term lending rate to prime borrowers prevailing for the currency of payment at the place for payment, or where no such rate exists at that place, then the same rate in the State of the currency of payment. In the absence of such a rate at either place the rate of interest shall be the appropriate rate fixed by the law of the State of the currency of payment.

(3)   The aggrieved party is entitled to additional damages if the non-payment caused it a greater harm.

Article 7.4.10

(Interest on damages)

Unless otherwise agreed, interest on damages for non-performance of non-monetary obligations accrues as from the time of non-performance.

Article 7.4.11

(Manner of monetary redress)

(1)   Damages are to be paid in a lump sum. However, they may be payable in instalments where the nature of the harm makes this appropriate.

(2)   Damages to be paid in instalments may be indexed.

Article 7.4.12

(Currency in which to assess damages)

Damages are to be assessed either in the currency in which the monetary obligation was expressed or in the currency in which the harm was suffered, whichever is more appropriate.

Article 7.4.13

(Agreed payment for non-performance)

(1)   Where the contract provides that a party who does not perform is to pay a specified sum to the aggrieved party for such non-performance, the aggrieved party is entitled to that sum irrespective of its actual harm.

(2)   However, notwithstanding any agreement to the contrary the specified sum may be reduced to a reasonable amount where it is grossly excessive in relation to the harm resulting from the non-performance and to the other circumstances.

CHAPTER 8—SET-OFF

Article 8.1

(Conditions of set-off)

(1)   Where two parties owe each other money or other performances of the same kind, either of them ("the first party") may set off its obligation against that of its obligee ("the other party") if at the time of set-off,

(a)   the first party is entitled to perform its obligation;

(b)   the other party's obligation is ascertained as to its existence and amount and performance is due.

(2)   If the obligations of both parties arise from the same contract, the first party may also set off its obligation against an obligation of the other party which is not ascertained as to its existence or to its amount.

Article 8.2

(Foreign currency set-off)

Where the obligations are to pay money in different currencies, the right of set-off may be exercised, provided that both currencies are freely convertible and the parties have not agreed that the first party shall pay only in a specified currency.

Article 8.3

(Set-off by notice)

The right of set-off is exercised by notice to the other party.

Article 8.4

(Content of notice)

(1)   The notice must specify the obligations to which it relates.

(2)   If the notice does not specify the obligation against which set-off is exercised, the other party may, within a reasonable time, declare to the first party the obligation to which set-off relates. If no such declaration is made, the set-off will relate to all the obligations proportionally.

Article 8.5

(Effect of set-off)

(1)   Set-off discharges the obligations.

(2)   If obligations differ in amount, set-off discharges the obligations up to the amount of the lesser obligation.

(3)   Set-off takes effect as from the time of notice.

CHAPTER 9—ASSIGNMENT OF RIGHTS, TRANSFER OF OBLIGATIONS, ASSIGNMENT OF CONTRACTS

SECTION 1: ASSIGNMENT OF RIGHTS

Article 9.1.1

(Definitions)

"Assignment of a right" means the transfer by agreement from one person (the "assignor") to another person (the "assignee"), including transfer by way of security, of the assignor's right to payment of a monetary sum or other performance from a third person ("the obligor").

Article 9.1.2

(Exclusions)

This Section does not apply to transfers made under the special rules governing the transfers:

(a)   of instruments such as negotiable instruments, documents of title or financial instruments, or

(b)   of rights in the course of transferring a business.

Article 9.1.3

(Assignability of non-monetary rights)

A right to non-monetary performance may be assigned only if the assignment does not render the obligation significantly more burdensome.

Article 9.1.4

(Partial assignment)

(1) A right to the payment of a monetary sum may be assigned partially.

(2) A right to other performance may be assigned partially only if it is divisible, and the assignment does not render the obligation significantly more burdensome.

Article 9.1.5

(Future rights)

A future right is deemed to be transferred at the time of the agreement, provided the right, when it comes into existence, can be identified as the right to which the assignment relates.

Article 9.1.6

(Rights assigned without individual specification)

A number of rights may be assigned without individual specification, provided such rights can be identified as rights to which the assignment relates at the time of the assignment or when they come into existence.

Article 9.1.7

(Agreement between assignor and assignee sufficient)

(1) A right is assigned by mere agreement between the assignor and the assignee, without notice to the obligor.

(2) The consent of the obligor is not required unless the obligation in the circumstances is of an essentially personal character.

Article 9.1.8

(Obligor's additional costs)

The obligor has a right to be compensated by the assignor or the assignee for any additional costs caused by the assignment.

Article 9.1.9

(Non-assignment clauses)

(1)   The assignment of a right to the payment of a monetary sum is effective notwithstanding an agreement between the assignor and the obligor limiting or prohibiting such an assignment. However, the assignor may be liable to the obligor for breach of contract.

(2)   The assignment of a right to other performance is ineffective if it is contrary to an agreement between the assignor and the obligor limiting or prohibiting the assignment. Nevertheless, the assignment is effective if the assignee, at the time of the assignment, neither knew nor ought to have known of the agreement. The assignor may then be liable to the obligor for breach of contract.

Article 9.1.10

(Notice to the obligor)

(1)   Until the obligor receives a notice of the assignment from either the assignor or the assignee, it is discharged by paying the assignor.

(2)   After the obligor receives such a notice, it is discharged only by paying the assignee.

Article 9.1.11

(Successive assignments)

If the same right has been assigned by the same assignor to two or more successive assignees, the obligor is discharged by paying according to the order in which the notices were received.

Article 9.1.12

(Adequate proof of assignment)

(1)   If notice of the assignment is given by the assignee, the obligor may request the assignee to provide within a reasonable time adequate proof that the assignment has been made.

(2)   Until adequate proof is provided, the obligor may withhold payment.

(3)   Unless adequate proof is provided, notice is not effective.

(4)   Adequate proof includes, but is not limited to, any writing emanating from the assignor and indicating that the assignment has taken place.

Article 9.1.13

(Defences and rights of set-off)

(1) The obligor may assert against the assignee all defences that the obligor could assert against the assignor.

(2) The obligor may exercise against the assignee any right of set-off available to the obligor against the assignor up to the time notice of assignment was received.

Article 9.1.14

(Rights related to the right assigned)

The assignment of a right transfers to the assignee:

> (a)   all the assignor's rights to payment or other performance under the contract in respect of the right assigned, and
>
> (b)   all rights securing performance of the right assigned.

Article 9.1.15

(Undertakings of the assignor)

The assignor undertakes towards the assignee, except as otherwise disclosed to the assignee, that:

> (a)   the assigned right exists at the time of the assignment, unless the right is a future right;
>
> (b)   the assignor is entitled to assign the right;
>
> (c)   the right has not been previously assigned to another assignee, and it is free from any right or claim from a third party;
>
> (d)   the obligor does not have any defences;
>
> (e)   neither the obligor nor the assignor has given notice of set-off concerning the assigned right and will not give any such notice;
>
> (f)   the assignor will reimburse the assignee for any payment received from the obligor before notice of the assignment was given.

SECTION 2: TRANSFER OF OBLIGATIONS

Article 9.2.1

(Modes of transfer)

An obligation to pay money or render other performance may be transferred from one person (the "original obligor") to another person (the "new obligor") either

> (a) by an agreement between the original obligor and the new obligor subject to Article 9.2.3, or
>
> (b) by an agreement between the obligee and the new obligor, by which the new obligor assumes the obligation.

Article 9.2.2

(Exclusion)

This Section does not apply to transfers of obligations made under the special rules governing transfers of obligations in the course of transferring a business.

Article 9.2.3

(Requirement of obligee's consent to transfer)

The transfer of an obligation by an agreement between the original obligor and the new obligor requires the consent of the obligee.

Article 9.2.4

(Advance consent of obligee)

(1) The obligee may give its consent in advance.

(2) If the obligee has given its consent in advance, the transfer of the obligation becomes effective when a notice of the transfer is given to the obligee or when the obligee acknowledges it.

Article 9.2.5

(Discharge of original obligor)

(1) The obligee may discharge the original obligor.

(2) The obligee may also retain the original obligor as an obligor in case the new obligor does not perform properly.

(3) Otherwise the original obligor and the new obligor are jointly and severally liable.

Article 9.2.6

(Third party performance)

(1) Without the obligee's consent, the obligor may contract with another person that this person will perform the obligation in place of the obligor, unless the obligation in the circumstances has an essentially personal character.

(2) The obligee retains its claim against the obligor.

Article 9.2.7

(Defences and rights of set-off)

(1)   The new obligor may assert against the obligee all defences which the original obligor could assert against the obligee.

(2)   The new obligor may not exercise against the obligee any right of set-off available to the original obligor against the obligee.

Article 9.2.8

(Rights related to the obligation transferred)

(1)   The obligee may assert against the new obligor all its rights to payment or other performance under the contract in respect of the obligation transferred.

(2)   If the original obligor is discharged under Article 9.2.5(1), a security granted by any person other than the new obligor for the performance of the obligation is discharged, unless that other person agrees that it should continue to be available to the obligee.

(3)   Discharge of the original obligor also extends to any security of the original obligor given to the obligee for the performance of the obligation, unless the security is over an asset which is transferred as part of a transaction between the original obligor and the new obligor.

SECTION 3: ASSIGNMENT OF CONTRACTS

Article 9.3.1

(Definitions)

"Assignment of a contract" means the transfer by agreement from one person (the "assignor") to another person (the "assignee") of the assignor's rights and obligations arising out of a contract with another person (the "other party").

Article 9.3.2

(Exclusion)

This Section does not apply to the assignment of contracts made under the special rules governing transfers of contracts in the course of transferring a business.

Article 9.3.3

(Requirement of consent of the other party)

The assignment of a contract requires the consent of the other party.

Article 9.3.4

(Advance consent of the other party)

(1)   The other party may give its consent in advance.

(2)   If the other party has given its consent in advance, the assignment of the contract becomes effective when a notice of the assignment is given to the other party or when the other party acknowledges it.

Article 9.3.5

(Discharge of the assignor)

(1)   The other party may discharge the assignor.

(2)   The other party may also retain the assignor as an obligor in case the assignee does not perform properly.

(3)   Otherwise the assignor and the assignee are jointly and severally liable.

Article 9.3.6

(Defences and rights of set-off)

(1)   To the extent that the assignment of a contract involves an assignment of rights, Article 9.1.13 applies accordingly.

(2)   To the extent that the assignment of a contract involves a transfer of obligations, Article 9.2.7 applies accordingly.

Article 9.3.7

(Rights transferred with the contract)

(1)   To the extent that the assignment of a contract involves an assignment of rights, Article 9.1.14 applies accordingly.

(2)   To the extent that the assignment of a contract involves a transfer of obligations, Article 9.2.8 applies accordingly.

CHAPTER 10—LIMITATION PERIODS

Article 10.1

(Scope of the Chapter)

(1)   The exercise of rights governed by the Principles is barred by the expiration of a period of time, referred to as "limitation period", according to the rules of this Chapter.

(2)   This Chapter does not govern the time within which one party is required under the Principles, as a condition for the acquisition or exercise of its right, to give notice to the other party or to perform any act other than the institution of legal proceedings.

Article 10.2

(Limitation periods)

(1)   The general limitation period is three years beginning on the day after the day the obligee knows or ought to know the facts as a result of which the obligee's right can be exercised.

(2)   In any event, the maximum limitation period is ten years beginning on the day after the day the right can be exercised.

Article 10.3

(Modification of limitation periods by the parties)

(1)   The parties may modify the limitation periods.

(2)   However they may not

(a)   shorten the general limitation period to less than one year;

(b)   shorten the maximum limitation period to less than four years;

(c)   extend the maximum limitation period to more than fifteen years.

Article 10.4

(New limitation period by acknowledgement)

(1)   Where the obligor before the expiration of the general limitation period acknowledges the right of the obligee, a new general limitation period begins on the day after the day of the acknowledgement.

(2)   The maximum limitation period does not begin to run again, but may be exceeded by the beginning of a new general limitation period under Article 10.2(1).

Article 10.5

(Suspension by judicial proceedings)

(1)   The running of the limitation period is suspended

(a)   when the obligee performs any act, by commencing judicial proceedings or in judicial proceedings already instituted, that is recognised by the law of the court as asserting the obligee's right against the obligor;

(b)   in the case of the obligor's insolvency when the obligee has asserted its rights in the insolvency proceedings; or

(c)   in the case of proceedings for dissolution of the entity which is the obligor when the obligee has asserted its rights in the dissolution proceedings.

(2)   Suspension lasts until a final decision has been issued or until the proceedings have been otherwise terminated.

Article 10.6

(Suspension by arbitral proceedings)

(1)   The running of the limitation period is suspended when the obligee performs any act, by commencing arbitral proceedings or in arbitral proceedings already instituted, that is recognised by the law of the arbitral tribunal as asserting the obligee's right against the obligor. In the absence of regulations for arbitral proceedings or provisions determining the exact date of the commencement of arbitral proceedings, the proceedings are deemed to commence on the date on which a request that the right in dispute should be adjudicated reaches the obligor.

(2)   Suspension lasts until a binding decision has been issued or until the proceedings have been otherwise terminated.

Article 10.7

(Alternative dispute resolution)

The provisions of Articles 10.5 and 10.6 apply with appropriate modifications to other proceedings whereby the parties request a third person to assist them in their attempt to reach an amicable settlement of their dispute.

Article 10.8

(Suspension in case of force majeure, death or incapacity)

(1)   Where the obligee has been prevented by an impediment that is beyond its control and that it could neither avoid nor overcome, from causing a limitation period to cease to run under the preceding Articles, the general limitation period is suspended so as not to expire before one year after the relevant impediment has ceased to exist.

(2)   Where the impediment consists of the incapacity or death of the obligee or obligor, suspension ceases when a representative for the incapacitated or deceased party or its estate has been appointed or a successor has inherited the respective party's position. The additional one-year period under paragraph (1) applies accordingly.

Article 10.9

(Effects of expiration of limitation period)

(1)   The expiration of the limitation period does not extinguish the right.

(2)   For the expiration of the limitation period to have effect, the obligor must assert it as a defence.

(3)   A right may still be relied on as a defence even though the expiration of the limitation period for that right has been asserted.

Article 10.10

(Right of set-off)

The obligee may exercise the right of set-off until the obligor has asserted the expiration of the limitation period.

Article 10.11

(Restitution)

Where there has been performance in order to discharge an obligation, there is no right of restitution merely because the limitation period has expired.

CHAPTER 11—PLURALITY OF OBLIGORS AND OF OBLIGEES

SECTION 1: PLURALITY OF OBLIGORS

Article 11.1.1

(Definitions)

When several obligors are bound by the same obligation towards an obligee:

    (a)   the obligations are joint and several when each obligor is bound for the whole obligation;

    (b)   the obligations are separate when each obligor is bound only for its share.

Article 11.1.2

(Presumption of joint and several obligations)

When several obligors are bound by the same obligation towards an obligee, they are presumed to be jointly and severally bound, unless the circumstances indicate otherwise.

Article 11.1.3

(Obligee's rights against joint and several obligors)

When obligors are jointly and severally bound, the obligee may require performance from any one of them, until full performance has been received.

Article 11.1.4

(Availability of defences and rights of set-off)

A joint and several obligor against whom a claim is made by the obligee may assert all the defences and rights of set-off that are personal to it or that are common to all the co-obligors, but may not assert defences or rights of set-off that are personal to one or several of the other co-obligors.

Article 11.1.5

(Effect of performance or set-off)

Performance or set-off by a joint and several obligor or set-off by the obligee against one joint and several obligor discharges the other obligors in relation to the obligee to the extent of the performance or set-off.

Article 11.1.6

(Effect of release or settlement)

(1) Release of one joint and several obligor, or settlement with one joint and several obligor, discharges all the other obligors for the share of the released or settling obligor, unless the circumstances indicate otherwise.

(2) When the other obligors are discharged for the share of the released obligor, they no longer have a contributory claim against the released obligor under Article 11.1.10.

Article 11.1.7

(Effect of expiration or suspension of limitation period)

(1) Expiration of the limitation period of the obligee's rights against one joint and several obligor does not affect:

   (a)   the obligations to the obligee of the other joint and several obligors; or

   (b)   the rights of recourse between the joint and several obligors under Article 11.1.10.

(2) If the obligee initiates proceedings under Articles 10.5, 10.6 or 10.7 against one joint and several obligor, the running of the limitation period is also suspended against the other joint and several obligors.

Article 11.1.8

(Effect of judgment)

(1) A decision by a court as to the liability to the obligee of one joint and several obligor does not affect:

(a) the obligations to the obligee of the other joint and several obligors; or

(b) the rights of recourse between the joint and several obligors under Article 11.1.10.

(2) However, the other joint and several obligors may rely on such a decision, except if it was based on grounds personal to the obligor concerned. In such a case, the rights of recourse between the joint and several obligors under Article 11.1.10 are affected accordingly.

Article 11.1.9

(Apportionment among joint and several obligors)

As among themselves, joint and several obligors are bound in equal shares, unless the circumstances indicate otherwise.

Article 11.1.10

(Extent of contributory claim)

A joint and several obligor who has performed more than its share may claim the excess from any of the other obligors to the extent of each obligor's unperformed share.

Article 11.1.11

(Rights of the obligee)

(1) A joint and several obligor to whom Article 11.1.10 applies may also exercise the rights of the obligee, including all rights securing their performance, to recover the excess from all or any of the other obligors to the extent of each obligor's unperformed share.

(2) An obligee who has not received full performance retains its rights against the co-obligors to the extent of the unperformed part, with precedence over co-obligors exercising contributory claims.

Article 11.1.12

(Defences in contributory claims)

A joint and several obligor against whom a claim is made by the co-obligor who has performed the obligation:

(a) may raise any common defences and rights of set-off that were available to be asserted by the co-obligor against the obligee;

(b) may assert defences which are personal to itself;

(c) may not assert defences and rights of set-off which are personal to one or several of the other co-obligors.

Article 11.1.13

(Inability to recover)

If a joint and several obligor who has performed more than that obligor's share is unable, despite all reasonable efforts, to recover contribution from another joint and several obligor, the share of the others, including the one who has performed, is increased proportionally.

SECTION 2: PLURALITY OF OBLIGEES

Article 11.2.1

(Definitions)

When several obligees can claim performance of the same obligation from an obligor:

- (a) the claims are separate when each obligee can only claim its share;

- (b) the claims are joint and several when each obligee can claim the whole performance;

- (c) the claims are joint when all obligees have to claim performance together.

Article 11.2.2

(Effects of joint and several claims)

Full performance of an obligation in favour of one of the joint and several obligees discharges the obligor towards the other obligees.

Article 11.2.3

(Availability of defences against joint and several obligees)

(1) The obligor may assert against any of the joint and several obligees all the defences and rights of set-off that are personal to its relationship to that obligee or that it can assert against all the co-obligees, but may not assert defences and rights of set-off that are personal to its relationship to one or several of the other co-obligees.

(2) The provisions of Articles 11.1.5, 11.1.6, 11.1.7 and 11.1.8 apply, with appropriate adaptations, to joint and several claims.

Article 11.2.4

(Allocation between joint and several obligees)

(1) As among themselves, joint and several obligees are entitled to equal shares, unless the circumstances indicate otherwise.

(2) An obligee who has received more than its share must transfer the excess to the other obligees to the extent of their respective shares.

SELECTED CONTRACTS

COMPILERS' NOTE

This section offers the complete contracts that underlie the disputes in some well-known cases. The cases, presented in chronological order, are: Wood v. Lucy, Peevyhouse v. Garland Coal & Mining Co., and In the Matter of Baby M.

CONTRACT IN WOOD V. LUCY[*]

"Whereas, the said Lucy, Lady Duff-Gordon, occupies a unique and high position as a creator of fashions in America, England and France,

"And whereas, her personal approval and endorsement over her own name of certain articles and fabrics used not only in the manufacture of dresses, millinery and other adjuncts of fashion, but also divers other articles of use to people of taste has a distinct monetary value to the manufacturers of such articles,

"And whereas, the said Otis F. Wood possesses a business organization adapted to the placing such endorsements as the said Lucy, Lady Duff-Gordon, has approved,

"It is agreed by the said Lucy, Lady Duff-Gordon, that the said Otis F. Wood is hereby granted the exclusive right to place such endorsements on such terms and conditions as may in his judgment, and also in the judgment of the said Lucy, Lady Duff-Gordon, or A. Merritt, her personal business adviser, be most advantageous to the said Lucy, Lady Duff-Gordon, and the said Otis. F. Wood.

"And whereas, the said Lucy, Lady Duff-Gordon's approval and selection of certain articles and fabrics used in the manufacture of her model gowns, millinery and other adjuncts of fashion which she designs, has a distinct monetary value to the manufacturers of such articles used,

"It is agreed, that the said Otis F. Wood shall have the exclusive right to make such terms, under the same conditions as set forth in this agreement, but it is expressly understood and agreed by both parties that no such arrangement can be entered into before such goods have been personally passed upon and approved by the said Lucy, Lady Duff-Gordon, and also that nothing in this limits the right of the said Lucy, Lady Duff-Gordon, to select and use any fabrics or other articles whatsoever in her business, provided the said Lucy, Lady Duff-Gordon, does not allow her endorsement to be used for said goods.

"And whereas, the said Lucy, Lady Duff-Gordon, creates from time to time different articles, such as parasols, belts, handbags, garters, etc., etc., and these also have a distinct monetary value independent of their specific use in her own dress creations sold at her own houses of 'Lucile,'

"It is agreed, that the said Otis F. Wood shall have the exclusive right of placing these articles on sale or licensing the rights to others to manufacture and market of such articles.

---

[*] 18 N.E. 214 (N.Y. 1914). The contract is taken from the Amended Complaint, Read in Support of Motion. Thanks to Victor Goldberg for providing this material. For more on the contract, see Reading Wood v. Lucy, Lady Duff Gordon with Help from the Kewpie Dolls in Professor Goldberg's FRAMING CONTRACT LAW: AN ECONOMIC ANALYSIS (2007), also available at http://papers.ssrn.com/sol3/papers.cfm?abstract_id=870474.

"It is expressly understood and agreed by both parties that nothing in this agreement shall apply to any other executed or pending contract made by the said Lucy, Lady Duff-Gordon, prior to this date, nor does this agreement include any rights to moving pictures, theatrical performances and lectures, the distribution of photographs of her gowns or publication of signed articles by the said Lucy, Lady Duff-Gordon, or any articles or books which may be hereafter written by her, or the sale of portraits of dresses unless said permission be expressly granted by the said Lucy, Lady Duff-Gordon, or by the said A. Merritt, from time to time, as such permission may be asked by the said Otis F. Wood.

"It is agreed, that in the event any arrangement is made with the third party running longer than the time stated in this agreement, that the said Otis F. Wood is to share in the returns from same during his lifetime of such agreement, and the said Otis F. Wood's rights thereunder are not to cease at the expiration of this agreement.

"It is understood, that the Fashion Portfolio Service, suggested by the said Otis F. Wood, is covered under the terms of this agreement.

"It is agreed, that all profits and revenues derived under and contracts made with third persons hereunder are to be paid over and collected by the said Otis F. Wood, and that all said profits and royalties are to be divided equally between the parties hereto, it being expressly understood, however, that the cost of securing such profits and royalties shall be directed toward this half share of Otis F. Wood, the said Lucy, Lady Duff-Gordon, receiving a full half share of all said profits and royalties without any expense whatsoever being directed against it; and it is further expressly understood that the said Otis F. Wood shall account monthly, to wit, on the first day of each month, to the said Lucy, Lady Duff-Gordon, for all such moneys received by him. The said Otis F. Wood agrees to take out and procure such patents, copyrights or trade-marks as may in his judgment be necessary to protect such names, ideas, or articles as are affected hereby and to carry out such actions or proceedings as may, in his judgment, be necessary in order to protect such patents, copyrights or trade-marks. And it is further understood that such patents, copyrights or trade-marks shall be held in the name of the said Lucy, Lady Duff-Gordon, and that the expense of obtaining such patents, copyrights, or trade-marks and of protecting the same from infringement, shall be shared equally by parties hereto. But it is expressly understood and agreed that no such suit or action can be begun by the said Otis F. Wood without the consent of the said Lucy, Lady Duff-Gordon, or of the said A. Merritt.

"It is agreed, that this contract shall cover a period of one year from the signing hereof, and that at the expiration of the said period it shall automatically renew itself for another year, and thereafter from year to year, unless either party shall give notice in writing to the other party of his or her intention to terminate this agreement not less than ninety (90) days preceding the expiration of the said term of one year or the expiration of any succeeding term thereafter."

691

CONTRACT IN PEEVYHOUSE V. GARLAND COAL & MINING CO.*

COAL LEASE

THIS LEASE executed this **23rd** day of **November** 19**54** by and between **Willie Peevyhouse and Lucille Peevyhouse, husband and wife,** hereinafter called Lessors, and **Garland Coal and Mining Company,** hereinafter called Lessee:

WITNESSETH

WHEREAS, the Lessors are the owners of, or have the right to mine and remove the coal underlying and the right to take all or any part of the surface of the following described lands in **Haskell** County, State of **Oklahoma** to-wit:

The Southwest Quarter of the Southwest Quarter of Section 7, Township 8 North and Range 21 East, and, the South Half of the Northeast Quarter of the Southeast Quarter of Section 12, Township 8 North and Range 20 East,

WHEREAS, Lessee desires to mine and remove the coal underlying said premises and Lessors desire to lease the same to Lessee for that purpose:

NOW, THEREFORE, in consideration of the sum of One Dollar ($1.00) cash in hand paid by Lessee to Lessors, receipt whereof is hereby acknowledged, and in consideration of the performance by each party of the conditions hereinafter set forth, Lessors grant and lease to the Lessee the exclusive right to slope, shaft, deep mine or strip and remove coal underlying the above described property, together with the right to use and/or remove any and/all the surface of said lands necessarily incidental thereto, subject to the following terms and conditions:

1.

This lease shall be in full force and effect for a term and period of 5 years from and after the date hereof, unless terminated sooner under its provisions. [illegible struck-through text] the minimum royalty [illegible]

2. The Lessee agrees to commence operations on said land within one year from date hereof or in lieu thereof will pay to the Lessor an advance royalty [illegible struck-through text]

Lessee agrees to pay to the Lessors upon all coal mined, removed and sold from these premises a royalty of **20/15** cents per ton of 2000 pounds, railroad weights to govern if shipped by rail, track scale weights if loaded on trucks, such royalty to be paid not later than the 20th day of each month succeeding the month in which the same be mined, removed and sold, provided that minimum royalty which may have been advanced at the rates per acre herein set forth shall be credited on royalty due for coal mined and sold. And Lessee will furnish to the Lessors on or before said date a statement showing the amount of coal mined and removed and sold during the preceding month; the Lessors shall have the right at reasonable times to inspect Lessee's books for the purpose of verifying the amount of coal so mined and Lessors shall have the right at reasonable times to inspect Lessee's operations.

Lessee shall have the exclusive right to enter upon same and prospect for coal, drill holes and make any necessary excavations and if it determines coal be present in paying quantities, then to dig, mine or strip, remove, sell and dispose of all the mineable and marketable coal that in the opinion of the Lessee can be profitably mined and removed therefrom, together with all incidental mining rights necessary to the success of such operation, and the right of ingress and egress in, to and across said property, [illegible] owned by Lessors for the purpose of entering upon said premises in connection with the production and transportation of coal from said premises on adjacent lands.

After commencement, such operations shall be carried on in a miner-like and workmanlike manner, as usually conducted in similar operations. Lessee may strip the overburden from such coal as shall be profitably mineable and marketable and will pay all taxes arising from the mining operation, and Lessors agree that they will pay and keep paid all taxes upon the premises herein leased. Lessee shall pay for damages caused by Lessee's prospecting operations, to growing crops on said lands.

It is understood that in the mining operations hereunder the surface of said land may be excavated and the Lessors agree to furnish Lessee, in consideration of said royalty, all surface as may be necessary to be used by Lessee in the operation of strip pits, and may be used by Lessee for drainage ditches, haulage roads, spoil banks, tipples, tracks, and any other structures that Lessee finds necessary in the operation of said strip pit or pits or coal mine and the Lessee agrees that all such structures shall be located consistent with good operating practice so as to cause the least damage or inconvenience to the owner or user of such surface; Lessee agrees that he will save Lessors harmless from claims arising out of the actual mining and removing of said coal and Lessors agree that they will save harmless and indemnify the Lessee from any claim or liability arising from any damage to the surface of these lands caused by such operations; it is further recognized the Lessee shall have the right without liability to the Lessor, wherever it may be necessary in conducting such operations, to change the course of any streams or water courses and to erect and maintain such drainage ditches as it shall deem advisable having due regard for the successful operation of said strip pit and damage to the remainder of the property.

It is understood and agreed that in the type of operation contemplated by Lessee it is necessary to procure leases of other property from which coal can be mined or stripped so as to justify the investment to be made by Lessee and in consideration of the royalty herein paid, Lessors grant to the Lessee the right to haul over and across said premises and through said pits coal from adjacent lands free from any charge.

---

* 382 P.2d 109 (Okla.1962). Thanks to Professor Judith L. Maute for unearthing this contract. Prof. Maute describes the lease as "a preprinted form lease containing some handwritten modifications and one typed page defining the remedial and other specific duties." Maute, Peevyhouse v. Garland Coal and Mining Co. Revisited: The Ballad of Willie and Lucille, 89 Northwestern L. Rev. 1341 (1995). We include a copy of the original lease followed by a more legible, retyped version.

- 7a -

Lessors hereby acknowledges receipt of the sum of $2,000.00 as advanced royalty which is to be credited on any royalty due for coal thereafter mined from said lands by said Lessee from the first coal produced.

- 7b -

Lessee agrees to make fills in the pits dug on said premises on the property lines in such manner that fences can be placed thereon and access had to opposite sides of the pits.

- 7c -

Lessee agrees to smooth off the top of the spoils banks on the above premises.

- 7d -

Lessee agrees to leave the creek crossing the above premises in such a condition that it will not interfere with the crossings to be made in pits as set out in 7b.

- 7e -

Lessee agrees to build and maintain a cattle guard in the south fence of SW¼ SW¼ of Section 7 if an access road is made through said fence.

- 7f -

Lessee further agrees to leave no shale or dirt on the high wall of said pits.

- 7g -

It is further agreed between the parties hereto that this lease is not to be assigned, transferred or sub-let without the written permission of the lessors: Provided however, that an assignment of this lease to the Canadian Mining Company shall not require such written permission.

- 7h -

Lessee agrees to have the above described premises surveyed and the boundary lines on said premises established prior to commencement of digging coal.

—8—

The right is hereby conferred upon Lessee to cancel this Lease upon thirty (30) days' written notice when the operation of removal of coal therefrom shall in his judgment become unprofitable and Lessee shall be the sole judge as to when same is unprofitable.

—9—

In case Lessee fails to pay the royalty when due or fails to comply with any one of the other terms of this Lease, the Lessors shall give the Lessee fifteen (15) days' written notice, calling attention to the default by Lessee, specifying wherein the Lessee has failed to comply with the terms of this agreement, and, if at the end of said period, Lessee is still in default, the Lessors shall have the right to take immediate possession of the leased premises without let or hindrance, and the Lessee shall not have the right to remove any of its property, machinery, tools or supplies from the demised premises until all amounts due the Lessors have been paid in full.

In the event this Lease expires by operation of its own terms, or the Lessee elects to cancel the same under the provisions hereinabove set out, the Lessee shall have, provided it is not in default, six (6) months from said termination or cancellation within which to remove all of its property, machinery, tools, supplies or equipment that it might have upon said demised premises. All structures built or erected upon said premises shall be and remain the sole and separate property of the Lessee.

—10—

It is mutually understood and agreed that the right, privileges and obligations herein conferred on the parties shall be binding on the executors, administrators, heirs, successors or assigns of the parties hereto whether so specifically stated herein or not; ~~in the event that the Lessee shall own less than the fee of the premises and coal herein demised Lessee shall pay royalty to them as their respective interests shall appear.~~ If the property is encumbered by a mortgage or other liens, Lessee shall have the right to pay said liens and deduct from royalty due Lessors.

IN WITNESS WHEREOF, the parties have set their hands this ___23rd___ day of ___November___, 19__54__

Willie Peevyhouse

Lucille Peevyhouse

Lessors

Garland Coal & Mining Company

By *Burton Crampton*

Lessee

STATE OF ___Oklahoma___

COUNTY OF ___Haskell___

Before me, the undersigned, a Notary Public, in and for the said County and State, on this ___23rd___ day of ___November___, 19__54__ personally appeared ___Willie Peevyhouse and Lucille Peevyhouse, his wife___ to me known to be the identical persons who executed the within and foregoing instrument and acknowledged to me that they executed the same as their free and voluntary act and deed for the uses and purposes therein set forth.

IN WITNESS WHEREOF, I have hereunto set my hand and official seal the day and year last above written.

J. F. Hudson

Notary Public

My Commission Expires ___9-24-1957___

STATE OF _____

COUNTY OF _____ } ss.

Before me, the undersigned, a Notary Public, in and for the said County and State, on this _____ day of _____, 19___ personally appeared _____ to me known to be the identical person who executed the within and foregoing instrument and acknowledged to me that he executed the same as his free and voluntary act and deed for the uses and purposes therein set forth.

IN WITNESS WHEREOF, I have hereunto set my hand and official seal the day and year last above written.

Notary Public

My Commission Expires _____

State of Oklahoma,

        ss:

County of Haskelll,

    Before me, the undersigned, a Notary Public in and for said State, on this 23rd day of November, 1954, personally appeared Burrow Cumpton, to me known to be the identical person who executed the within and foregoing instrument as attorney in fact of Garland Coal & Mining Company, and acknowledged to me that he executed the same as his free and voluntary act and deed and as the free and voluntary act and deed of Garland Coal and Mining Company, for the uses and purposes therein set forth.

    Witness my hand and official seal the day and year last above written.

                                     Notary Public

My commission expires:

    9-24-1957

CONTRACT IN PEEVYHOUSE V. GARLAND COAL & MINING CO.

(Retyped)

Whereas, Lessee desires to mine and remove the coal underlying said premises and Lessors desire to lease the same to Lessee for that purpose:

Now, therefore, in consideration of the sum of One Dollar ($1.00) cash in hand paid by Lessee to Lessors, receipt whereof is hereby acknowledged and in consideration of the performance by each party of the conditions hereinafter set forth, Lessors grant and lease to the Lessee the exclusive right to slope, shaft, deep mine or strip and remove coal underlying the above described property, together with the right to use and/or remove any and/all the surface of said lands necessarily incidental thereto, subject to the following terms and conditions:

–1–

This lease shall be in full force and effect for a term and period of 3 years from and after the date hereof unless terminated sooner under its provisions. The xxxxxxxxxx xxxxxxxxxx xxxxxxxxxx xxxxxxxxx xxxxxxxxxx to the Lessor xxx xxxxxxxxxx xxxxxxxxxx xxxxxxxxxx lessee for xxxxxxxx xxxxxxxxx xxxxxxxxx xxxxxxxxx xxxxxxxxxx xxxxxxxx xxxxxxxx xxxxxxxx xxxxxxxx the minimum royalty xxxxxxxxx xxxxxxxxx xxxxx.

–2–

The Lessee agrees to common operations on said land within one year from date hereof or in xxxx thereof will pay to the Lessor an advance royalty on any part or portion of within described land Lessee shall determine needed in Lessees operation of any time during the life of this lease the sum of 50 xxxx xxx xxxx the second year 75 xxxx xxx xxxx the third year, and One Dollar ($1.00) per acre the fourth and all subsequent years during the term of this Lease as minimum royalty on coal to be mined from said lands these payments to begin one year from the date hereof and to be credited xx xxx royalty due for coal these after mined from said lands by said Lessee, his heirs, successors, and assigns.

–3–

Lessee agrees to pay the Lessors upon all coal mined, removed and sold from these premises a royalty of 16 XX 20 cents per ton of 2000 pounds, railroad weights to govern if shipped by rail, truck scale weights if loaded on trucks, such royalty to be paid not later that the 20th day of each month succeeding the month in which the same to be mined, removed and sold, provided that minimum royalties which may have been advanced at the rates per acre herein set forth shall be credited on royalty due for coal mined and sold. And Lessee will furnish to the Lessors on or before said date a statement showing the amount of coal mined and removed and sold during the preceding month: the Lessors shall have the right at reasonable times to inspect Lessee's books for the purpose of verifying the amount of coal so mined and Lessors shall have the right at reasonable times to inspect Lessee's operations.

–4–

Lessee shall have the exclusive right to enter upon same and prospect for coal, drill holes and make any necessary excavations and if it determines coal be present in paying quantities, then to dig, mine or strip, remove, sell and dispose of all the mineable and marketable coal that in the opinion of the Lessee can be profitably mined and removed therefrom, together with all incidental mining rights necessary to the success of such operation, and the right of ingress and egress in, to and across said property. Or xxx the property owned by Lessors for the purpose of entering upon said premises in connection with the production and transportation of coal from said premises on adjacent lands.

–5–

After commencement, such operations shall be carried on in a miner-like and workmanlike manner, as usually conducted in similar operations. Lessee may strip the overburden from such coal as shall be profitably mineable and marketable and will pay all taxes arising from the mining operation, and Lessors agree that they will pay and keep paid all said taxes upon the premises herein leased. Lessee shall pay for damages, caused by Lessee's prospecting operations, to growing crops on said lands.

–6–

It is understood that in the mining operations hereunder the surface of said land may be excavated and the Lessors agree to furnish Lessee, in consideration of said royalty, all surface as may be necessary to be used by Lessee in the operation of strip pits, and may be used by Lessee for drainage ditches, haulage roads, spoil banks, tipples, tracks, and any other structures that Lessee finds necessary in the operation of said strip pit or pits or coal mine and the Lessee agrees that all such structures will be located consistent with good operating practice so as to cause the least damage or inconvenience to the owner or user of such surface: Lessee agrees that he will save Lessors harmless from claims arising out of the actual mining and removing of said coal and Lessors agree that they will save harmless and indemnity the Lessee from any claim or liability arising from any damage to the surface of these lands caused by such operations: it is further recognized that the Lessee shall have the right without liability to the Lessor, wherever it may be necessary in conducting such operations, to change the course of any streams or water courses and to erect and maintain such drainage ditches as it shall deem advisable having due regard for the successful operation of said strip pit and damage to the remainder of the property.

–7–

It is understood and agreed that in the type of operation contemplated by the Lessee it is necessary to procure leases of other property from which coal can be mined or stripped so as to justify the investment to be made by the Lessee and in consideration of the royalty herein paid, Lessors grant to the lessee the right to haul over and across said premises and through said pits coal from adjacent lands free from any charge.

–7a–

Lessors hereby acknowledges receipt of the sum of $2,000.00 as advanced royalty which is to be credited on any royalty due for coal thereafter mined from said lands by said Lessee from the first coal produced.

–7b–

Lessee agrees to make fills in the pits dug on said premises on the property lines in such manner that fences can be place thereon and access had to opposite sides of the pits.

–7c–

Lessee agrees to smooth off the top of the spoils banks on the above premises.

–7d–

Lessee agrees to leave the creek crossing the above premises in such a condition that it will not interfere with the crossings to be made in pits as set out in 7b.

–7e–

Lessee agrees to build and maintain a cattle guard in the south fence of SWL SWL of Section 7 if an access road is made through said fence.

–7f–

Lessee further agrees to leave no shale or dirt on the high wall of said pits.

–7g–

It is further agreed between the parties hereto that this lease is not to be assigned, transferred, or sub-let without the written permission of the lessors. Provided however, that an assignment of this lease to the Canadian Mining Company shall not require such written permission.

–7h–

Lessee agrees to have the above described premises surveyed and the boundary lines on said premises established prior to commencement of digging coal.

–8–

The right is hereby conferred upon Lessee to cancel this Lease upon thirty (30) days' written notice when the operation of removal of coal therefrom shall in his judgment become unprofitable and Lessee shall be the sole judge as to when same is unprofitable

–9–

In case Lessee fails to pay the royalty when due or fails to comply with any one of the other terms of this lease, the Lessors shall give the Lessee fifteen (15) days' written notice, calling attention to the default by Lessee, specifying wherein the Lessee has failed to comply with the terms of this agreement, and if at the end of said period, Lessee is still in default, the Lessors shall have the right to take immediate possession of the leased premises without let or hindrance, and the Lessee shall not have the right to remove any of its property, machinery, tools, or supplies from the demised premises until all amounts due the Lessors have been paid in full.

In the event this lease expires by operation of its own terms, or the Lessee elects to cancel the same under the provisions hereinabove set out, the Lessee shall have, provided it is not in default, six (6) months from said termination or cancellation within which to remove all of its property, machinery, tools, supplies, or equipment that it might have upon said demised premises. All structures built or erected upon said premises shall be and remain the sole and separate property of the Lessee.

–10–

It is mutually understood and agreed that the right, privileges and obligations herein conferred on the parties shall be binding on the executors, administrators, heirs, successors, or assigns of the parties hereto whether so specifically stated herein or not: ~~in the event that the Lessors shall own less than the fee of the premises and coal herein xxxxxxx Lessee shall pay royalty to them as their respective interests shall appear.~~ If the property is encumbered by a mortgage or other liens, lessee shall have to the right to pay said liens and deduct from royalty due Lessors.

In witness whereof, the parties have set their hands this <u>23rd</u> day of <u>November</u> 19<u>54</u>.

Willie Peevyhouse (signature)

Lucille Peevyhouse (signature)

SELECTED CONTRACTS

Lessors

Garland Coal and Mining Company

By <u>xxxxxxxx Compton (signature)</u>

CONTRACT IN IN THE MATTER OF BABY M*

SURROGATE PARENTING AGREEMENT

THIS AGREEMENT is made this 6th day of February, 1985, by and between MARY BETH WHITEHEAD, a married woman (herein referred to as "Surrogate"), RICHARD WHITEHEAD, her husband (herein referred to a "Husband"), and WILLIAM STERN, (herein referred to as "Natural Father").

RECITALS

THIS AGREEMENT is made with reference to the following facts:

(1) WILLIAM STERN, Natural Father, is an individual over the age of eighteen (18) years who is desirous of entering into this Agreement.

(2) The sole purpose of this Agreement is to enable WILLIAM STERN and his infertile wife to have a child which is biologically related to WILLIAM STERN.

(3) MARY BETH WHITEHEAD, Surrogate, and RICHARD WHITEHEAD, her husband, are over the age of eighteen (18) years and desirous of entering into this Agreement in consideration of the following:

NOW THEREFORE, in consideration of the mutual promises contained Herein and the intentions of being legally bound hereby, the parties agree as follows:

1. MARY BETH WHITEHEAD, Surrogate, represents that she is capable of conceiving children. MARY BETH WHITEHEAD understands and agrees that in the best interest of the child, she will not form or attempt to form a parent-child relationship with any child or children she may conceive, carry to term and give birth to, pursuant to the provisions of this Agreement, and shall freely surrender custody to WILLIAM STERN, Natural Father, immediately upon birth of the child; and terminate all parental rights to said child pursuant to this Agreement.

2. MARY BETH WHITEHEAD, Surrogate, and RICHARD WHITEHEAD, her husband, have been married since 12/2/73, and RICHARD WHITEHEAD is in agreement with the purposes, intents and provisions of this Agreement and acknowledges that his wife, MARY BETH WHITEHEAD, Surrogate, shall be artificially inseminated pursuant to the provisions of this Agreement. RICHARD WHITEHEAD agrees that in the best interest of the child, he will not form or attempt to form a parent-child relationship with any child or children MARY BETH WHITEHEAD, Surrogate, may conceive by artificial insemination as described herein, and agrees to freely and readily surrender immediate custody of the child to WILLIAM STERN, Natural Father; and terminate his parental rights; RICHARD WHITEHEAD further acknowledges he will do all acts neces-

* Appendix A, 537 A2d 1227, 1265 (N.J.1988).

sary to rebut the presumption of paternity of any offspring conceived and born pursuant to aforementioned agreement as provided by law, including blood testing and/or HLA testing.

3.   WILLIAM STERN, Natural Father, does hereby enter into this written contractual Agreement with MARY BETH WHITEHEAD, Surrogate, where MARY BETH WHITEHEAD shall be artificially inseminated with the semen of WILLIAM STERN by a physician. MARY BETH WHITEHEAD, Surrogate, upon becoming pregnant, acknowledges that she will carry said embryo/fetus(s) until delivery. MARY BETH WHITEHEAD, Surrogate, and RICHARD WHITEHEAD, her husband, agree that they will cooperate with any background investigation into the Surrogate's medical, family and personal history and warrants the information to be accurate to the best of their knowledge. MARY BETH WHITEHEAD, Surrogate, and RICHARD WHITEHEAD, her husband, agree to surrender custody of the child to WILLIAM STERN, Natural Father, immediately upon birth, acknowledging that it is the intent of this Agreement in the best interests of the child to do so; as well as institute and cooperate in proceedings to terminate their respective parental rights to said child, and sign any and all necessary affidavits, documents, and the like, in order to further the intent and purposes of this Agreement. It is understood by MARY BETH WHITEHEAD, and RICHARD WHITEHEAD, that the child to be conceived is being done so for the sole purpose of giving said child to WILLIAM STERN, its natural and biological father. MARY BETH WHITEHEAD and RICHARD WHITEHEAD agree to sign all necessary affidavits prior to and after the birth of the child and voluntarily participate in any paternity proceedings necessary to have WILLIAM STERN'S name entered on said child's birth certificate as the natural or biological father.

4.   That the consideration for this Agreement, which is compensation for services and expenses, and in no way is to be construed as a fee for termination of parental rights or a payment in exchange for a consent to surrender the child for adoption, in addition to other provisions contained herein, shall be as follows:

(A) $10,000 shall be paid to MARY BETH WHITEHEAD, Surrogate, upon surrender of custody to WILLIAM STERN, the natural and biological father of the child born pursuant to the provisions of this Agreement for surrogate services and expenses in carrying out her obligations under this Agreement;

(B) The consideration to be paid to MARY BETH WHITEHEAD, Surrogate, shall be deposited with the Infertility Center of New York (hereinafter ICNY), the representative of WILLIAM STERN, at the time of the signing of this Agreement, and held in escrow until completion of the duties and obligations of MARY BETH WHITEHEAD, Surrogate, (see Exhibit "A" for a copy of the Escrow Agreement), as herein described.

(C) WILLIAM STERN, Natural Father, shall pay the expenses incurred by MARY BETH WHITEHEAD, Surrogate, pursuant to her pregnancy, more specifically defined as follows:

(1) All medical, hospitalization, and pharmaceutical, laboratory and therapy expenses incurred as a result of MARY BETH WHITEHEAD'S pregnancy, not covered or allowed by her present health and major medical insurance, including all extraordinary medical expenses and all reasonable expenses for treatment of any emotional or mental conditions or problems related to said pregnancy, but in no case shall any such expenses be paid or reimbursed after a period of six (6) months have elapsed since the date of the termination of the pregnancy, and this Agreement specifically excludes any expenses for lost wages or other non-itemized incidentals (see Exhibit "B") related to said pregnancy.

(2) WILLIAM STERN, Natural Father, shall not be responsible for any latent medical expenses occurring six (6) weeks subsequent to the birth of the child, unless the medical problem or abnormality incident thereto was known and treated by a physician prior to the expiration of said six (6) week period and in written notice of the same sent to ICNY, as representative of WILLIAM STERN by certified mail, return receipt requested, advising of this treatment.

(3) WILLIAM STERN, Natural Father, shall be responsible for the total costs of all paternity testing. Such paternity testing may, at the option of WILLIAM STERN, Natural Father, be required prior to release of the surrogate fee from escrow. In the event WILLIAM STERN, Natural Father, is conclusively determined not to be the biological father of the child as a result of an HLA test, this Agreement will be deemed breached and MARY BETH WHITEHEAD, Surrogate, shall not be entitled to any fee. WILLIAM STERN, Natural Father, shall be entitled to reimbursement of all medical and related expenses from MARY BETH WHITEHEAD, Surrogate, and RICHARD WHITEHEAD, her husband.

(4) MARY BETH WHITEHEAD'S reasonable travel expenses incurred at the request of WILLIAM STERN, pursuant to this Agreement.

5. MARY BETH WHITEHEAD, Surrogate, and RICHARD WHITEHEAD, her husband, understand and agree to assume all risks, including the risk of death, which are incidental to conception, pregnancy, childbirth, including but not limited to, postpartum complications. A copy of said possible risks and/or complications is attached hereto and made a part hereof (see Exhibit "C").

6. MARY BETH WHITEHEAD, Surrogate, and RICHARD WHITEHEAD, her husband, hereby agree to undergo psychiatric evaluation by JOAN EINWOHNER, a psychiatrist as designated by WILLIAM STERN or an agent thereof. WILLIAM STERN shall pay for the cost of said psychiatric evaluation. MARY BETH WHITEHEAD and RICHARD WHITEHEAD shall sign, prior to their evaluations, a medical release permitting

dissemination of the report prepared as a result of said psychiatric evaluations to ICNY or WILLIAM STERN and his wife.

7. MARY BETH WHITEHEAD, Surrogate, and RICHARD WHITE-HEAD, her husband, hereby agree that it is the exclusive and sole right of WILLIAM STERN, Natural Father, to name said child.

8. "Child" as referred to in this Agreement shall include all children born simultaneously pursuant to the inseminations contemplated herein.

9. In the event of the death of WILLIAM STERN, prior or subsequent to the birth of said child, it is hereby understood and agreed by MARY BETH WHITEHEAD, Surrogate, and RICHARD WHITEHEAD, her husband, that the child will be placed in the custody of WILLIAM STERN'S wife.

10. In the event that the child is miscarried prior to the fifth (5th) month of pregnancy, no compensation, as enumerated in paragraph 4(A), shall be paid to MARY BETH WHITEHEAD, Surrogate. However, the expenses enumerated in paragraph 4(C) shall be paid or reimbursed to MARY BETH WHITEHEAD, Surrogate. In the event the child is miscarried, dies or is stillborn subsequent to the fourth (4th) month of pregnancy and said child does not survive, the Surrogate shall receive $1,000.00 in lieu of the compensation enumerated in paragraph 4(A). In the event of a miscarriage or stillbirth as described above, this Agreement shall terminate and neither MARY BETH WHITEHEAD, Surrogate, nor WILLIAM STERN, Natural Father, shall be under any further obligation under this Agreement.

11. MARY BETH WHITEHEAD, Surrogate, and WILLIAM STERN, Natural Father, shall have undergone complete physical and genetic evaluation, under the direction and supervision of a licensed physician, to determine whether the physical health and well-being of each is satisfactory. Said physical examination shall include testing for venereal diseases, specifically including but not limited to, syphilis, herpes and gonorrhea. Said venereal diseases testing shall be done prior to, but not limited to, each series of inseminations.

12. In the event that pregnancy has not occurred within a reasonable time, in the opinion of WILLIAM STERN, Natural Father, this Agreement shall terminate by written notice to MARY BETH WHITEHEAD, Surrogate, at the residence provided to the ICNY by the Surrogate, from ICNY, as representative of WILLIAM STERN, Natural Father.

13. MARY BETH WHITEHEAD, Surrogate, agrees that she will not abort the children conceived except, if in the professional medical opinion of the inseminating physician, such action is necessary for the physical health of MARY BETH WHITEHEAD or the child has been determined by said physician to be physiologically abnormal. MARY BETH WHITE-HEAD further agrees, upon the request of said physician to undergo amniocentesis (see Exhibit "D") or similar tests to detect genetic and congen-

ital defects. In the event said test reveals that the fetus is genetically or congenitally abnormal, MARY BETH WHITEHEAD, Surrogate, agrees to abort the fetus upon demand of WILLIAM STERN, Natural Father, in which event, the fee paid to the Surrogate will be in accordance to Paragraph 10. If MARY BETH WHITEHEAD refuses to abort the fetus upon demand of WILLIAM STERN, his obligations as stated in this Agreement shall cease forthwith, except as to obligation of paternity imposed by statute.

14.   Despite the provisions of Paragraph 13, WILLIAM STERN, Natural Father, recognizes that some genetic and congenital abnormalities may not be detected by amniocentesis or other tests, and therefore, if proven to be the biological father of the child, assumes the legal responsibility for any child who may possess genetic or congenital abnormalities. (See Exhibits "E" and "F").

15.   MARY BETH WHITEHEAD, Surrogate, further agrees to adhere to all medical instructions given to her by the inseminating physician as well as her independent obstetrician. MARY BETH WHITEHEAD also agrees not to smoke cigarettes, drink alcoholic beverages, use illegal drugs, or take non-prescription medications or prescribed medications without written consent from her physician. MARY BETH WHITEHEAD agrees to follow a prenatal medical examination schedule to consist of no fewer visits then: one visit per month during the first seven (7) months of pregnancy, two visits (each to occur at two-week intervals) during the eighth and ninth month of pregnancy.

16.   MARY BETH WHITEHEAD, Surrogate, agrees to cause RICHARD WHITEHEAD, her husband, to execute a refusal of consent form as annexed hereto as Exhibit "G".

17.   Each party acknowledges that he or she fully understands this Agreement and its legal effect, and that they are signing the same freely and voluntarily and that neither party has any reason to believe that the other(s) did not freely and voluntarily execute said Agreement.

18.   In the event any of the provisions of this Agreement are deemed to be invalid or unenforceable, the same shall be deemed severable from the remainder of this Agreement and shall not cause the invalidity or unenforceability of the remainder of this Agreement. If such provision shall be deemed invalid due to its scope or breadth, then said provision shall be deemed valid to the extent of the scope or breadth permitted by law.

19.   The original of this Agreement, upon execution, shall be retained by the Infertility Center of New York, with photocopies being distributed to MARY BETH WHITEHEAD, Surrogate and WILLIAM STERN, Natural Father, having the same legal effect as the original.

WILLIAM STERN, Natural Father

DATE 2/6/85

STATE OF NEW YORK

SS.:

COUNTY OF NEW YORK

On the 6th day of February, 1985, before me personally came WILLIAM STERN, known to me, and to me known, to be the individual described in the foregoing instrument and he acknowledged to me that he executed the same as his free and voluntary act.

NOTARY PUBLIC

APPENDIX B

We have read the foregoing five pages of this Agreement, and it is our collective intention by affixing our signatures below, to enter into a binding legal obligation.

MARY BETH WHITEHEAD, Surrogate

DATE 1–30–85

RICHARD WHITEHEAD, Surrogate's Husband

DATE 1–30–85

STATE OF NEW YORK

SS.:

COUNTY OF NEW YORK

On the 6th day of February, 1985, before as personally came MARY BETH WHITEHEAD, known to me, and to me known to be the individual described in the foregoing instrument and she acknowledged to me that she executed the same as her free and voluntary act.

NOTARY PUBLIC

STATE OF NEW YORK

SS.:

COUNTY OF NEW YORK

On the 6th day of February, 1985, before as personally came RICHARD WHITEHEAD, known to me, and to me known to be the individual described in the foregoing instrument and he acknowledged to me that he executed the same me his free and voluntary act.

NOTARY PUBLIC